CERTIFIED PARALEGAL REVIEW MANUAL

REVIEW MANUAL

Fourth Edition

CERTIFIED PARALEGAL REVIEW MANUAL

Fourth Edition

A Practical Guide to CP® Exam Preparation

Prepared by
Virginia Koerselman Newman, J.D.
VKN Law Publications
Hemingway, South Carolina

In cooperation with
The National Association of Legal Assistants, Inc.
Tulsa, Oklahoma

CENGAGE
Learning®

Australia • Brazil • Mexico • Singapore • United Kingdom • United States

CENGAGE
Learning·

**Certified Paralegal Review Manual:
A Practical Guide to CP® Exam
Preparation, Fourth Edition**
Virginia Koerselman Newman

Vice President and General Manager-Skills
and Planning: Dawn Gerrain

Senior Director, Development-Skills and
Planning: Marah Bellegarde

Senior Product Development Manager:
Larry Main

Senior Content Developer: Melissa Riveglia

Product Assistant: Diane E. Chrysler

Market Development Manager: Jonathan
Sheehan

Marketing Manager: Scott Chrysler

Senior Production Director: Wendy Troeger

Production Manager: Mark Bernard

Senior Content Project Manager:
James Zayicek

Art Director: Heather Marshall, PMG

Software Development Manager: Joe Pliss

Media Developer: Deborah Bordeaux

Cover image(s): ©mg1408/shutterstock

For product information and technology assistance, contact us at
Cengage Learning Customer & Sales Support, 1-800-354-9706

For permission to use material from this text or product,
submit all requests online at **www.cengage.com/permissions.**
Further permissions questions can be e-mailed to
permissionrequest@cengage.com

Library of Congress Control Number: 2013941867

ISBN-13: 978-1-285-16258-4

Cengage Learning
200 First Stamford Place, 4th Floor
Stamford, CT 06902
USA

Cengage Learning is a leading provider of customized learning solutions
with office locations around the globe, including Singapore, the United
Kingdom, Australia, Mexico, Brazil, and Japan. Locate your local office at:
www.cengage.com/global

Cengage Learning products are represented in Canada by
Nelson Education, Ltd.

To learn more about Cengage Learning, visit **www.cengage.com**

Purchase any of our products at your local college store or at our
preferred online store **www.cengagebrain.com**

Notice to the Reader
Publisher does not warrant or guarantee any of the products described herein or perform any independent analysis in connection with any of the product information
contained herein. Publisher does not assume, and expressly disclaims, any obligation to obtain and include information other than that provided to it by the manufacturer.
The reader is expressly warned to consider and adopt all safety precautions that might be indicated by the activities described herein and to avoid all potential hazards. By
following the instructions contained herein, the reader willingly assumes all risks in connection with such instructions. The reader is notified that this text is an educational
tool, not a practice book. Since the law is in constant change, no rule or statement of law in this book should be relied upon for any service to the client. The reader should
always refer to standard legal sources for the current rule or law. If legal advice or other expert assistance is required, the services of the appropriate professional should be
sought. The publisher makes no representations or warranties of any kind, including but not limited to, the warranties of fitness for particular purpose or merchantability, nor
are any such representations implied with respect to the material set forth herein, and the publisher takes no responsibility with respect to such material. The publisher shall
not be liable for any special, consequential, or exemplary damages resulting, in whole or part, from the readers' use of, or reliance upon, this material.

Printed in the United States of America
4 5 6 7 17 16

BRIEF CONTENTS

CONTENTS

CONTENTS

DEDICATION

This edition of the CP® Review Manual is dedicated to the memory of my son, Ken Koerselman II, whose days on earth were far too few and passed much too quickly. He bedeviled us in his childhood, he pushed us to our outer limits in his youth, and he amazed and delighted us by becoming the man we always had prayed for him to be. Then he was gone. We could not have survived his loss without the grace of God.

When I took the CLA/CP® certification examination in 1977, it occurred to me that someone ought to compile a comprehensive study manual to help people like me who were struggling to prepare for the exam. Law school and many years intervened, during which both NALA and I matured and grew larger; but there still was no national study manual for the CLA/CP® examination.

At NALA's request and with its assistance, the *CP® Review Manual* first became a reality in 1992. Several editions later, we hope it still provides some degree of focus and direction for the study efforts of applicants everywhere, although it is not designed to "teach the test" and should not be used as an applicant's sole reference source.

The *CP® Review Manual* includes basic background information, general administrative policies, and an expanded outline for each section of the examination as they existed at the time of publication. Any administrative policy, any examination section, or the examination as a whole is subject to change at any time at the discretion of the NALA Certifying Board. Although every reasonable effort is made to keep this *Review Manual* current, there always will be some lag between the time of an examination or policy change and the ability to incorporate it into a publication of this type. Always check with NALA Headquarters to determine whether any changes have occurred.

The *CP® Review Manual* contains tips for studying and for taking examinations in general. It also includes distilled and condensed topic coverage for each section and subsection of the examination as well as frequent examples, tables, and charts to aid the study effort. A self-test is provided at the end of each chapter.

We commend all those who undertake certification as a professional goal. To the extent that this *Review Manual* helps them to achieve that goal, we shall have achieved ours.

Student Companion Site

A free companion website includes updates to the book. To access these materials, visit www.cengage.brain.com and search for the title or ISBN of this book.

ACKNOWLEDGEMENTS

The author gratefully acknowledges the contributions of the following individuals, each of whom provided invaluable assistance in compiling the *CP® Review Manual:*

Robert W. Baker, M.B.A.
Omaha, Nebraska

Kirk Brumbaugh, J.D.
Omaha, Nebraska

Robert Francis Cryne, J.D.
Omaha, Nebraska

Karen Douglas, J.D.
Omaha, Nebraska

Marge Dover, CAE
Tulsa, Oklahoma

Karen M. Dunn, ACP
Vail, Colorado

Marie Greninger
Tulsa, Oklahoma

Elizabeth Hannan
Minneapolis, Minnesota

Kim Hawekotte, J.D.
Omaha, Nebraska

Patricia Holt, M.S.
Omaha, Nebraska

Connie Kretchmer, ACP
Omaha, Nebraska

Vicki Kunz, ACP
Bismarck, North Dakota

Karen Sanders-West, J.D., ACP
Wichita, Kansas

Melissa Vander Weide, ACP
Orlando, Florida

She thanks the many students who have passed through her classroom over the years, leaving her significantly richer for the experience. She also thanks the following paralegal educators who reviewed the manuscript and provided suggestions:

Janet Kazmier
Tulane University

Anita Whitby
Park University

Paula Montlary
Florida Community College

ABOUT THE AUTHOR

Virginia Koerselman Newman, Attorney at Law, practiced for many years in banking and commercial litigation in Omaha, Nebraska, before she relocated to South Carolina. Ms. Koerselman Newman is a graduate of the Creighton University School of Law. She was a professor and the director of the Paralegal Program at Metropolitan Community College, Omaha, from 1987 to 2008. A frequent speaker at seminars and workshops, Virginia has authored, co-authored, and edited many paralegal texts, study guides, and instructor manuals. She developed the content and is principal author for NALA Campus courses. Recipient of NALA's Founder's Award in 1998, Virginia is a regular columnist for *Facts & Findings*, is a former member of the NALA Certifying Board, and currently serves as consultant to the Advanced Paralegal Certifying Board. She was a long-time faculty member for the CLA/CP® Short Course, is a recurrent instructor on NALA Campus LIVE as well as the Essential Skills Institute, and continues to teach and to write about paralegal topics in varied forums.

INTRODUCTION

Even if you're on the right track, you'll get run over if you just sit there.

—Will Rogers

CLA/CP® Certification
A Professional Goal

Certification bestows a measure of professional recognition to those who achieve significant competence in the field.

This opportunity for the legal assistant profession is provided by the National Association of Legal Assistants, Inc. (NALA), through its national certification program. The CLA/CP® Certification Program consists of successful completion of a comprehensive five-part examination. Thereafter, evidence of continuing legal education must be submitted periodically to maintain the certification. The program is administered by NALA through its Certifying Board, legal assistants who have attained the Advanced Certified Paralegal designation, attorneys, and paralegal educators. In 2012, the number of Certified Legal Assistants and Certified Paralegals throughout the nation exceeded 16,000. To date, paralegals and legal assistants in 48 states, the District of Columbia, the Virgin Islands, Canada, France, Belgium, Japan, and Taiwan have been certified by NALA.

Although the goal of becoming a Certified Legal Assistant (or a Certified Paralegal) is a voluntary commitment, the NALA certification is recognized in the legal field as denoting high standards of professionalism and excellence. The legal community recognizes that the experience and knowledge of a CLA or a CP are not restricted to a few limited areas but, rather, encompass a general knowledge and understanding of the entire profession and capabilities far exceeding minimal requirements.

The CLA/CP® Certification Program involves successful completion of a computer-based examination administered in testing windows during the months of January, May, and September. Details concerning specific testing sites are provided by NALA with the CLA/CP® application forms. For additional information, contact:

NALA Headquarters
1516 South Boston Avenue, Suite 200
Tulsa, OK 74119
918-587-6828
www.nala.org
nalanet@nala.org

The body of knowledge required to attain the Certified Paralegal (also called Certified Legal Assistant) designation is large. Although the NALA Certifying Board recognizes the expertise required of a legal assistant cannot be reduced to a formula, certain skills common to the profession are measurable: written communication skills, judgment, and analytical abilities; and an understanding of ethics, human relations, interviewing techniques, legal terminology, and legal research. The examination covers these areas as well as substantive knowledge of law and procedures. The substantive law section requires each candidate to complete a section on the American legal system (general law), business organizations, contract law, and litigation. As a standardized national examination, all sections focus on the national level—no specific state laws or procedures are tested.

As with all NALA programs, the purpose of the examination program is to help the legal assistant profession by serving as a means of distinguishing and recognizing excellence among legal assistants and by serving as a stabilizing force and directional tool in the growth of the profession. The Certified Legal Assistant Program is not rigid; its foundation allows methodical and thoughtful change. It helps by attesting to the competency of certified legal assistants and by serving as a guideline for colleges and schools offering paralegal and legal assistant programs. As the profession advances, its members also must advance. Paralegals and legal assistants are an integral part of the legal services team and must strive to improve the profession. NALA's voluntary certification program is one answer to those needs.

Because the terms "legal assistant" and "paralegal" have become interchangeable in much the same way as the terms "lawyer" and "attorney," NALA has registered the certification marks "CP" and "CLA."

CP® is a certification mark registered with the U.S. Patent and Trademark Office (No. 78213275). Any unauthorized use is strictly forbidden.

CLA® is a certification mark registered for many years with the U.S. Patent and Trademark Office (No. 1131999). Any unauthorized use is strictly forbidden.

The Certified Legal Assistant Examination
Summary Outline

Each section of the examination (except Judgment and Analytical Ability) contains objective questions that include multiple choice, true/false, and matching. The Judgment and Analytical Ability section consists of a single essay question. The exact testing schedule is available from NALA Headquarters upon request.

In 2001, the Certifying Board consolidated the section Human Relations and Interviewing Techniques with the Communications and Ethics sections. The section Legal Terminology was consolidated with the Substantive Law section. Although human relations, interviewing, and terminology no longer exist as separate sections of the exam, these subjects continue as substantial components of the examination as well as this *Review Manual*.

Communications

This section of the CLA/CP® examination covers the following areas of communications:

- Word usage, punctuation, capitalization, grammar
- Correspondence, concise writing, vocabulary
- Rules of composition
- Nonverbal communications
- Skills encompassing professional and social contacts with employers, clients, office visitors, coworkers, and the public

Interviewing techniques are integrated into the communications section, including basic principles of interviewing and the following specifics:

- Interviewing situations (courtesy, empathy, physical setting, and body language)
- Initial roadblocks to interviewing (lapse of time, prejudice, and the like)
- Manner of questions
- Use of checklists
- Special situations (the elderly, the very young, and so forth)
- Interviewing clients and witnesses; initial and subsequent interviews

Strunk & White, *The Elements of Style*, has been adopted by the NALA Certifying Board as the authority for the Communications section.

Examination Time: 1.5 hours

Ethics

This section deals with:
- Ethical responsibilities centering on performance of delegated work including confidentiality, unauthorized practice of law, legal advice, conflict of interest, billing, and client communications
- Client/public contact including identification as a nonlawyer, advertising, and initial client contact
- Professional integrity and competence including knowledge of paralegal codes of ethics
- Relationships with coworkers and support staff
- Attorney codes and discipline.

Knowledge of the American Bar Association's *Model Rules of Professional Conduct* and the NALA *Code of Ethics and Professional Responsibility* is required by this examination.

Examination Time: 1 hour

Judgment and Analytical Ability

This section includes:
- Comprehension of data—identifying and understanding a problem

•Application of analytical techniques—ability to link facts and to develop legal issues from other sources to the problem at hand, recognizing similarities and differences
•Evaluating and categorizing data
•Organizing data and findings in a written document

This section consists of one essay question that requires analysis of a research request, finding applicable law, and writing a responsive memo.

Examinees will be graded on the ability to
•identify which facts are relevant and state them concisely and accurately;
•identify the threshold (or entry) issue as well as the main issue(s);
•identify the relevant legal authority and apply it to the facts; and
•draw persuasive, logical conclusions with explanation of the rationale.

Examination Time: 2.0 hours

Legal Research

It is important for the paralegal to be able to use the most important tool of the legal profession—the law library. The purpose of the Legal Research section of the CLA/CP® Certifying Examination is to test the applicant's knowledge of

•sources of law including primary authority, secondary authority, and understanding how law is recorded; and
•research skills including finding the law, updating the law, and procedural rules of citation.

A Uniform System of Citation, Harvard Law Review Association, has been adopted by the NALA Certifying Board as the authority for the Legal Research section.

The amount of study and practice that an applicant will need to pass this section of the examination will depend on his or her current knowledge and experience with legal research. One can gain excellent practice by researching various topics on one's own.

Examination Time: 1.5 hours

Substantive Law

The Substantive Law section of the exam is divided into four parts:

- American Legal System (including general law principles)
- Business Organizations
- Contract Law
- Litigation

The skills required by these tests involve recall of facts and principles that form the basis of the selected specialty practice areas, including the procedures related to each of the selected specialty practice areas.

Those who plan to take the examination, but who have not had formal law courses, will benefit from a study of one or more current textbooks in the area. A great deal of the material covered in this section of the examination is acquired through work experience in the legal field. The substantive law section of the examination is designed to test the paralegal's general knowledge of those fields of law most commonly used by them.

Examination Time: 2.0 hours total

Grading and Retake Policy

A passing score of 73 percent is required for each of the examination sections. The substantive law section is graded as a whole. In other words, the applicant must achieve a 73 percent average, regardless of how the points are distributed among the four subparts. Results are announced by the Certifying Board in writing to all applicants, generally five to seven weeks after the close of each testing window. Results are not available by any other method.

Applicants who take at least one section of the examination are in retake status. Applicants in retake status may attend a maximum of five testing windows within a two-year period. Applicants in retake status will be allowed to choose which sections will be retaken during any testing window. Again, an applicant can take part in no more than five testing windows within a two-year period. The examination must be completed successfully within two years. Otherwise, credit for all passed sections is forfeited, and the applicant then must reapply for the full examination.

Eligibility Requirements

To be eligible for the examination, a paralegal must meet one of the following requirements:

Category 1

Graduation from a legal assistant program that is:

a. approved by the American Bar Association, or
b. an associate degree program, or
c. a post-baccalaureate certificate program in legal assistant studies, or
d. a bachelor's degree program in legal assistant studies, or
e. a legal assistant program that consists of a minimum of 60 semester (or equivalent quarter)* hours, of which at least 15 semester hours (or equivalent quarter hours)** are substantive law courses.

900 clock hours of a legal assistant program is equivalent to 60 semester hours. 90 quarter hours of a legal assistant program is equivalent to 60 semester hours.

**225 clock hours of substantive law courses is equivalent to 15 semester hours. 22½ quarter hours of substantive law courses is equivalent to 15 semester hours.*

NOTE: Under Category 1(e), an applicant may combine college hours from more than one institution. The applicant must have graduated from a legal assistant program consisting of a minimum of 15 semester hours (or 225 clock hours or 22½ quarter hours). Evidence of the minimum hours required under Category 1(e) must be provided with the application form.

Category 2

A bachelor's degree in any field plus one (1) year's experience as a legal assistant.*
Successful completion of at least 15 semester hours (or 22½ quarter hours or 225 clock hours) of substantive paralegal courses is equivalent to one year's experience as a legal assistant.

Category 3

A high school diploma or equivalent plus seven years' experience as a legal assistant under the direct supervision of a member of the Bar plus evidence of a minimum of 20 hours of continuing legal education credit to have been completed within the two-year period immediately preceding the application date. In connection with an application under this category, evidence of continuing education credit is documented by the attorney/employer attestation that must be signed to complete the application form. No further documentation is required.

Individuals currently incarcerated for any offense or on probation, parole, or other court-imposed supervision for a felony offense are ineligible to sit for the CLA/CP® examination.

Additional forms will be required of all candidates who file applications prior to meeting the eligibility requirements. Contact NALA Headquarters for further information.

Application forms and information concerning testing sites for the Certified Legal Assistant/Certified Paralegal examination are available from:

National Association of Legal Assistants, Inc.
1516 South Boston Avenue, Suite 200
Tulsa, OK 74119
(918) 587-6828
www.nala.org
nalanet@nala.org

Maintaining the CLA/CP® Designation

In recognition of the continuing change in laws and procedures that have a direct impact on the quality of work performed by legal assistants, Certified Legal Assistants and Certified Paralegals are required to maintain their certified status by submitting proof of continuing legal education. The Certified Legal Assistant and Certified Paralegal designations are conferred for a period of five years. If the Certified Legal Assistant or Certified Paralegal submits to the Certifying Board proof of continuing legal education in accordance with the requirements of the Certifying Board, the designation is renewed for an additional five-year period. The continuing legal education requirement begins anew with each renewal period of the CLA/CP® designation. Lifetime certification is not available.

The Certified Legal Assistant or Certified Paralegal designation *may be revoked* for any one of the following reasons:

1. Falsification of information on the application form.
2. Subsequent conviction of the unauthorized practice of law.
3. Failure to meet continuing legal education requirements as required by the Certifying Board.
4. Divulging the contents of any examination questions.
5. Subsequent conviction of a felony.
6. Violation of the NALA Code of Ethics and Professional Responsibility.
7. Violation of the terms and conditions of testing.

Preparation for the Examination

There is no simple or precise formula for success on the CLA/CP® certification examination. The minimum requirements for success are embodied in the eligibility requirements themselves. However, nearly all applicants require additional, intensive study to prepare themselves adequately for the examination.

The form, method, and amount of study will vary from individual to individual. It is not possible to divulge the contents of the CLA/CP® examination. Neither is it possible to disclose the precise format of the examination. There are, however, study methods that have proved successful for large numbers of applicants. Those are described here. In addition, this chapter contains suggestions on how to get the most from your study efforts, whether you study individually or as part of a study group, and how to approach the examination itself.

Individual Study

A major advantage of individual study is that it can be adapted very easily to suit your own needs in preparing for the exam. In fact, many applicants use individual study as the sole method of preparation.

There is no substitute for individual study, even though it requires substantial commitment and discipline. No one is equally good at everything. Each of us has an area where our skills are not used as much and are therefore not as sharp as we would like them to be; some of us have more than one such area. Individual study allows each applicant to assess what those weak points are and then to devote more study time to them, with less time spent on more familiar areas. The key to successful individual study is to give yourself enough time to prepare adequately, but not so much time that you tarry too long on the threshold of the study project.

What to Study   As with any major project, study for the CLA/CP® examination requires planning. The first step is to inventory your current skills in relation to the requirements of the examination. You may have a good deal of experience with interviewing and drafting, with very little exposure to legal research. Or you may use your research and writing skills every day, with little or no exposure to clients. Everyone's situation is different, and you are the only one who can assess yours accurately.

Statistically, those parts of the examination that cause the most difficulty for most applicants are: (1) Judgment and Analytical Ability, (2) Substantive Law, (3) Communications, and (4) Legal Research.

Self-Assessment   Make a list of the sections of the examination that you must take, including the four substantive law subsections that you have selected. Privately and realistically, evaluate yourself against each section, one at a time. Review the topic coverage of the section and gauge how you might do if you were to be rigorously tested right now. A checklist is provided to assist you.

Self-Assessment Checklist

_____

(name of section)

	Have you taken a formal course in this subject matter? Yes = 5 No = 0
	If you have taken a formal course, how long ago did you take it? Less than 1 yr = 20 1–2 yrs = 16 2–3 yrs = 12 4–5 yrs = 8 5+ yrs = 4
	Rate your test-taking ability: Easier than for others = 20 About the same = 10 Harder than for others = 0
	% of monthly, billable hours spent using skills tested by this section: 61–80% = 40 41–60% = 32 21–40% = 24 11–20% = 16 10% or less = 8
	How familiar are you with the *details* of this section in the *Review Manual*? Extremely = 20 Very = 16 Moderately = 12 Somewhat = 8 Vaguely = 4
	Total Self-Assessment Points
	If there is more than a 20-point variance between the Self-Assessment and the Self-Test Scores, use the average of the two scores (add both scores and divide by two).

90–100%	Thorough review of this *Review Manual* may be sufficient
70–90%	Study of law summaries (Nutshell, Gilbert's, or Emanuel) + *Manual*
50–70%	Textbook study (see Bibliography) + law summary study + *Manual*
0–50%	Formal course may be advisable

Nutshell Series	Emanuel Law Outlines	Gilbert Law Summaries
store.westlaw.com	info@wolterskluwer	store.westlaw.com

Give yourself an overall, pencil score for the section, using a percentile scale. Continue the process for each section, making the same type of evaluation and giving yourself a pencil score for each one. Even though the substantive law subsections (American legal system, business organizations, contract law, and litigation) are averaged together for examination purposes, consider each subsection separately in formulating your study plan.

This represents a conservative approach to gauge where you are now in relation to where you need to be by the time you sit for the examination.

When to Study

As is true of nearly everything connected with preparing for the CLA/CP® examination, decisions about study schedules and when they should begin must be based upon individual needs. The self-assessment checklist may be helpful in gauging how much preparation is required. Unless formal course work is needed, three to six months of relatively intensive study is suggested. This assumes a paralegal who is working full time and who has been away from a classroom for three to five years. It also assumes that this hypothetical paralegal schedules two or three study periods of each week, with each study period lasting from two to four hours. During the four weeks immediately preceding the examination, study periods would increase to four each week, with each period lasting two to four hours. These are guidelines only. Each applicant must establish a realistic schedule based upon his or her own needs.

The only inflexible rule about establishing a study schedule is this: Do it. Every other decision can be based upon convenience or need. It is helpful, though, to schedule study periods on the same days and at the same times each week, such as Tuesday, Thursday, and Sunday evenings from 6:00 to 9:00 p.m. Changing the days and times of study periods from one week to the next invites ultimate abandonment of the schedule.

Once a study schedule has been established, it must be followed religiously. Otherwise, there is little point in having a schedule. Mark each study period on the calendar, just like any other planned event; then stick to it. Professional certification is a vital step in your career as a paralegal. If it were not, you would not have purchased this *Review Manual* to help you prepare for it. You give vast amounts of time and energy to your employer, to your family, to volunteer organizations, and often to your community. Give this study time to yourself and be firm about it.

Those who have been away from a classroom for a time may have difficulty getting started, at least during the first few sessions. This is normal. The way to overcome such an obstacle is to persevere. Make yourself use the full time allotted for the study period, even if it does not seem to be especially productive. This circumstance makes it doubly important that no scheduled study period is missed. Studying is a skill like any other skill. The more you do it, the easier it gets.

Along with perseverance, developing good study skills requires the efficient use of the scheduled study period. There are a number of ways to maximize the productivity of your study time.

How to Study

Ultimately, everyone develops study methods that work best for him or her. If you have developed study methods that have proven themselves successful for you, use them. If not, the following suggestions are offered as methods that have worked for others, including this author. Use the ones that work for you; feel free to modify them to suit your particular situation and needs.

The Study Environment   The environment in which a person studies is critical in maximizing the study effort. Whether you live in a large house or in an efficiency apartment, you must have one special place for quiet study. It doesn't matter whether that special place is a den of your own or the kitchen table, as long as it is relatively quiet. Once you have selected a location, use it for every study session. Keep the following considerations in mind as well.

- ▶ Use good lighting to avoid eyestrain.

- ▶ Sit in a straight-back chair and work at a desk or a table. Do not sit on a sofa and try to write on the coffee table; do not lie on the floor or on a bed.

- ▶ Reduce the room temperature if possible. Cool (but not frigid) temperatures boost energy and improve concentration.

▶ Avoid distractions. Turn the television and music off. Do not take telephone calls; offer to call back later.

▶ Avoid unnecessary interruptions by keeping reference books and supplies near at hand.

The most important part of your study environment is you. To obtain maximum benefit from each study session, it is imperative that you be in good condition. Avoid unnecessary stress in every way that you can. This is not the time to go on a diet, to stop smoking, to move, to change jobs, or to undergo elective surgery. No less than a law student studying for the bar, you must be able, physically and mentally, to assume an increasingly rigorous study schedule as the examination date draws near. There are positive steps that you can take to assure your best performance at each study session.

▶ Wear loose, comfortable clothing when you study.

▶ Take a short break (five to ten minutes) once each hour. Leave the study area, do stretching exercises, move about, get a drink of water or a snack, and then get back to work.

▶ If you snack, keep it light. Fresh vegetables, fresh fruit, or carbohydrates (without toppings) are best. Lightly salted, plain popcorn seems to be a favorite among students. Do not eat candy or snacks generally classified as junk food; they provide a very short burst of energy, followed by sleepiness.

▶ Unless there is a medical reason to avoid exercise, plan to exercise at least 20 minutes at a time, three times a week, throughout the three to six months of the study schedule. Regular aerobic exercise—walking, swimming, jogging, and so forth—releases tension; it also improves stamina and concentration. If you try it for a full three weeks and then skip a week, you will see a marked decline in your ability to study effectively. Exercise regularly.

▶ Record your progress as you move through the study schedule that you have established, and give yourself small rewards when you reach prescribed milestones. Have dinner with a supportive friend, see a good comedy show, or treat yourself to a massage.

As silly as some of these suggestions may seem at first glance, be assured that they are sound investments in your physical and mental well-being throughout the preparation and examination process. They work.

Study Aids   Once you have estimated the depth of preparation needed for each section and subsection of the examination, you will need access to a suitable library of reference books and study aids. Refer to the section on self-assessment, *supra*, to determine whether you need a textbook, a law summary or outline, or some other study aid.

A list of reference books recommended by NALA's Certifying Board is shown in the Bibliography section of this *Review Manual*. This list, of course, is not intended to be exhaustive; neither is it intended as a limitation of the reference books that may be used. For instance, if you do not have access to any of the legal research texts shown in the bibliography, but do have a legal research text that is both thorough and current, use your text.

If you can borrow up-to-date textbooks and study aids from the library or from lawyers or from CLAs or CPs whom you know, this will reduce the expense of textbook acquisition substantially. You will want to avoid acquisition of materials in a way that violates copyright laws, such as photocopying. Aside from being against the law, photocopied material tends to be less legible and less durable than the original; more difficult to store; and almost as expensive as purchasing the reference yourself.

Whether you acquire reference materials by loan or by purchase, however, use discrimination in your selections. Don't try to obtain every textbook and study aid recommended to you. Notwithstanding the exorbitant cost of such an approach, it would be unreasonable to try to study all of them. The better course is to talk with several people who have passed the CLA/CP® examination, compare their recommendations, and then select the study aids best suited to your needs. Regardless of the materials selected, assure yourself that they are up to date.

This *CLA / CP*® *Review Manual* has been published specifically to provide a condensed, overall foundation for study. It is to a textbook or to a horn book what *Readers Digest* is to a novel. The *NALA Manual for Legal Assistants,* Fifth Edition, addresses many of the subjects covered in the nonsubstantive sections of the examination and contains an excellent glossary of legal terms, which can be used as part of the preparation for the Legal Terminology section. The Certifying Board has adopted Strunk & White, *The Elements of Style,* most recent edition, as its primary composition and style reference and *A Uniform System of Citation*, by the Harvard Law Review

Association, as the authority for the Legal Research section. Every applicant will be wise to obtain these texts.

Having obtained the reference books and study aids of your choice, you are ready to begin the study process.

Effective Study Methods   Study methods for the CLA/CP® examination, like study methods in general, are as varied as the people who use them. While there is no single study method to ensure success, certain techniques emerge repeatedly when one analyzes the study patterns of successful students in general and of successful CLA/CP® applicants in particular.

- Use only up-to-date textbooks and reference materials.

- Limit your study to the national level. Because this is a national examination, no state-specific questions will be asked. General legal rules that are common among states will be covered, however.

- Don't try to cram. Unless you have a photographic memory, cramming doesn't work; and it breeds unnecessary panic. Organize your study plan so that you have enough time to cover all of the topic areas, giving more time to those areas with which you are least familiar.

- When you encounter difficult or complex principles in your studies, read them aloud to improve clarity or to fix them more firmly in your mind.

- Obtain a large three-ring binder and make dividers for each section of the examination. Keep all of your outlines and notes in it for easy reference.

- Prepare basic outlines of the material to be tested in each section of the examination.

- After the basic outlines are completed, prepare detailed, annotated outlines for each section, using one or more of the reference books in your possession. State all important rules fully, together with any exceptions to those rules, and give examples of how the rules are applied. Include the source and page number from which the information was taken so that you can find it later if you need or want to do so.

- Create time lines or flow charts for technical areas. This method works especially well for substantive law areas. Use the flow chart or time line to track a case from beginning to end, showing each of the steps involved along with any underlying statutory or procedural rules. *(See the Litigation chapter for a sample flow chart.)*

- Prepare and use flash cards (standard index cards work fine). This study method works especially well for legal terminology and is quite effective in studying legal research and substantive law areas.

   In legal research, for example, use flash cards to learn the specific characteristics of a particular case reporter: identity of the publisher; features (official or unofficial, type of cases reported, whether it reports all cases or only selected cases, contains a table of cases or a descriptive word index, and the like); how it is supplemented; and so forth. Prepare similar flash cards for each legal research reference tool.

- Do not use outlines, flash cards, or study aids created by others except for comparative reference. The act of creating your own is a critical part of the learning process. If you read the material **and** write it down, your chances of remembering it are doubled.

- Where feasible, create acronyms or mnemonics to help you remember especially troublesome phrases or lists. For instance, if you were trying to remember the elements needed to form a valid contract, you might create the acronym OACA:

      O—Offer
      A—Acceptance
      C—Consideration
      A—Absence of defenses

   Similarly, use a mnemonic to remember the common law felonies. Murder, rape, manslaughter, robbery, sodomy, larceny, arson, mayhem, and burglary become MR & MRS LAMB.

Used sparingly, this technique can be very helpful. If too many acronyms are created, however, remembering all of the acronyms can become a bigger problem than remembering what they were intended to signify in the first place.

- Take as many mock exams as you can find. The self-test portions of this *Review Manual* are good starting points. NALA offers the *CLA/CP® Mock Examination and Study Guide*, Fourth Edition. Mock exams are also available from NALA Affiliate Associations in a few states. For more information, contact:

> ***National Association of Legal Assistants, Inc.***
> ***1516 South Boston Avenue, Suite 200***
> ***Tulsa, OK 74119***
> ***918-587-6828***
> ***www.nala.org***
> ***nalanet@nala.org***

- Without referring to your outlines, practice writing brief essays that require you to discuss or to compare the principles involved in any particular examination section. Mock exams or old tests from an instructor or a student of a paralegal program are excellent sources. Otherwise, test yourself. One way is to put questions on slips of paper immediately after you have prepared a particular outline (or have someone do this for you), fold the question slips and put them into an envelope marked with the name of the section, and put the envelope away until you are ready to review.

At review time, have someone select a question slip from each envelope or simply cover your eyes and select the question yourself. Write the essays without checking your outlines. When you have finished, compare them with the outlines to see whether you covered all points, covered them accurately, said too much, and so forth. Make the necessary corrections. This will reinforce the details you need to know for any given section.

- If possible, have someone else read your essays to be sure they make sense. The reviewer does not need a legal background to perform this function (no legal background may be even better). Otherwise, leave them for a day or so and read them again very critically—as if they were drafted by someone whom you do not like. Are the words precise? Are the thoughts concise? Are they stated as simply as possible? Are they crystal clear? Edit them until they meet these criteria.

These are suggestions only, designed to aid the working paralegal who plans to study alone and who has been away from the classroom for some time. While they are known to produce the desired results, they require a substantial investment of time, effort, discipline, and commitment. Others have done it before you, and you can do it too. Visualize your name with the CLA or the CP designation following it; that should keep you going. Nothing worthwhile is ever easy.

For the successful CLA/CP® applicant, there is no way to avoid the rigors of individual study altogether. However, if suffering alone is not your cup of tea, organizing a study group may be a viable option.

Group Study

Group study has been used successfully by a number of CLA/CP® applicants. It can be an excellent addition to the study schedules of most applicants, as long as its purposes, benefits, and limitations are understood.

A study group may be able to share some of the stresses associated with preparation for the examination; to provide a supportive, motivational network for study group members; or to reinforce the discipline needed to adhere to the study schedule. Using the theory that two heads are better than one, it may even serve as a filter or as a forum to refine members' understanding—or to expose misunderstanding—of principles likely to be covered on the examination. A study group cannot, however, serve as a substitute for individual study. Neither will it reduce the preparation effort of any individual. If anything, it is likely that a study group will increase the workload of its members.

So why join a study group if it means extra time and extra work? Because it is a good insurance policy. When applicants join a study group, it's because they believe that the extra work is a small price to pay for a support network, a sounding board, enforced discipline (albeit through guilt), and a cheering section—all rolled into one. The common goal of the group makes it easier for some applicants to persevere. Left to themselves, they may falter and then get too far behind. As a team member, however, they will be able to overcome almost any obstacle to fulfill their obligations to the team. This is neither good nor bad; it is simply a fact of human nature.

Since the NALA Certifying Board does not give extra points to those who do it the hard way, do whatever makes it easiest for you to be successful.

How to Organize a Study Group

If you choose to study with a group in addition to your individual study, let the experiences of others guide you. Many state and local NALA affiliates have first-hand experience in organizing study groups and are happy to share their wealth of information and suggestions. To find the NALA affiliate closest to you, contact:

National Association of Legal Assistants, Inc.
1516 South Boston Avenue, Suite 200
Tulsa, OK 74119
918-587-6828
www.nala.org
nalanet@nala.org

Keep these considerations in mind as you contemplate organizing a study group. They may provide a basis for discussion when you contact the NALA affiliate, together with any specific questions that you may have.

- Poll the participants to determine the substantive law sections for which each has registered. If no one has registered to take the bankruptcy section, for instance, there is no need to cover bankruptcy as part of the study group schedule.

- Select a group leader. Co-leaders are preferred by many, assuming that two qualified people are available. The CLAs or CPs in your geographic area may provide an excellent resource pool; they even may be able to obtain CLE credits for recertification (check with NALA Headquarters for details). The CLA/CP® group leader may not, however, divulge the contents or the specific format of exam questions.

- If no CLAs or CPs are available, locate other experts who can assist you—an English teacher or an attorney with superior writing skills for Communications, one or more attorneys for the substantive areas, and so forth.

- Establish a study schedule. Generally, the study group will meet once a week, leaving an additional week or two for individual review before the examination is taken.

- Take a mock exam prepared by one of the group members (possibly with the assistance of a group leader) at the beginning of each group session. This is generally a good way to get the discussion started. In fact, have group members prepare as much of the material as possible (coordinate with the group leader, of course). It's a good way to study and it takes some of the burden from the group leader.

- Decide how the expense of materials will be shared among the group members.

Taking the Examination

The ultimate goal of nearly everyone who may read this *Review Manual* is to pass the CLA/CP® examination. That being so, and assuming that you have already qualified to take the examination, a few important observations should be made.

Based upon personal experience with both the CLA/CP® exam and with the state bar exam, be assured that the CLA/CP® exam was every bit as difficult within its realm of expertise as the bar exam was. The two examinations were comparable in other ways, the most prominent of which was the ever-mounting levels of stress associated with preparation for the exams and then with taking the exams themselves. By preparing for the stress, you will be in a much better position to manage it.

Some stress is good; it heightens performance. It is only when stress gets out of control and turns into panic that it becomes destructive. For stress management before the examination, refer to the suggestions on preparing for the examination. During the examination itself, there are some things that you can do to ease the stress and to ensure your best performance in an examination of this kind.

Prepare Yourself

- If possible, visit the testing site the day before the examination is to be taken. Determine the best route to take and estimate the time needed to arrive there. Allow for morning rush-hour traffic and plan to arrive 20 to 30 minutes ahead of time. Determine where you will park and how much it will cost. Familiarize yourself with the location of the testing room and of the other facilities located in the building, such as the restroom(s); snack bar or coffee shop, if any; and so forth.

- On the evening before the examination, review your outlines and notes one last time for the sections to be administered the next day. Then put them away.

- Get a good night's rest. You will need all of your energy when the test begins. Don't squander it by sitting up half the night, worrying about what will happen tomorrow or trying to cram. Cramming now will do nothing but cause confusion and panic. Don't do it.

- Relax. Immediately before the exam begins, panic can immobilize you unless you stay in control. Before entering the examination room, walk around and stretch your neck, shoulders, arms, hands, and legs. Don't just pace.

- Breathe deeply—breathe in through the nose, bring the air all the way down to the knees, and hold it for a count of five; then breathe out through the mouth s-l-o-w-l-y until all of the air is released. Continue this exercise until the air comes out slowly and smoothly.

- If you begin to panic (evidenced by the inability to think clearly: you see the words, but they don't register in your head) while taking the exam, stop and quietly perform the breathing exercise. As you breathe in, imagine yourself going down an elevator all the way to the lower sub-basement. Stay at that level for a count of five and then slowly breathe out as you return to ground level. Do it again. Then go back to work. This 30-second exercise is well worth the time invested.

Test Questions in General

- All test questions are designed within a national framework. Do not rely on the rules of a specific state when answering any of the questions.

- Answer all questions, even if you have to guess. Because there is no additional penalty for a wrong answer, guessing may result in a few extra points here and there. An unanswered question, however, never can be correct.

- Read the instructions for each question *very carefully*. Be absolutely certain that you know what you are being asked to do before you begin.

- Be sure that you understand each question before you attempt to answer it. Read it twice if necessary. Fine-line distinctions commonly are drawn in examinations like this one. If you read a question too quickly, important words will be overlooked.

- Read the question as it is, not as you expected it to be. Don't try to help the question-writer by qualifying your answer. The question means exactly what it says.

- Pace yourself in relation to the length of the examination section. Answer the questions you know first. Write the question number of the others on your scratch paper or noteboard and come back to them later. Don't spend too much time on any one question.

- Do not change your answers unless you are positive that you selected the wrong answer the first time. If you read the question carefully, your first impulse is almost always right. If you second-guess yourself, the second guess likely will be wrong.

- If you happen to finish the section before the allotted time has expired, stop. Do not go back through the questions, because second-guessing problems will arise (*see above*).

- Use the break between each testing period effectively. Walk, stretch, relax, and mentally prepare yourself for the upcoming testing period. Do not squander this valuable time by dwelling on the section that you just finished. It is over. Move on.

- Resist the temptation to compare your answers with those of other applicants while on break, during lunch, or at the end of the day. Do not even listen to this type of discussion while sections remain to be taken. Politely excuse yourself if anyone else talks about specific answers. If any of their answers were different from yours (and some of them will be different), it will create unnecessary anxiety, which, in turn, will have a negative effect on your performance during the next testing period.

True–False Questions

- Be wary of true–false questions that contain the word "always" or "never." While there are occasional exceptions, few things in the law are "always true" or "never true."

- If any part of the statement is inaccurate or is incorrect, the entire statement is incorrect, in which case the answer is "false."

- The word "generally" or "may" in a true–false question often indicates that the answer is true. Once again, this is only a general rule; there are exceptions.

Multiple Choice Questions

- Read the questions carefully. Multiple choice questions generally will ask you to select the most correct answer or the best answer, but some will ask you to select the least correct answer or the worst answer. Watch for these.

- Beware of "none of the above" and "all of the above" selections. Certainly there are some questions for which "none" or "all" is the correct answer. More often, however, "none" or "all" is incorrect.

- If a question or a set of answers sounds totally foreign, leave that question and go on to those you can answer. If you return to the question and still do not know the answer, guess. There is no penalty for wrong answers, so there is no benefit in leaving any question unanswered.

- Make an educated guess or use a process of elimination. Eliminate as many of the wrong selections as you can and then pick from the remaining selections. If your instincts point to one of them, choose it and move on to another question.

- If you cannot make even an educated guess about the correct answer and if you have not already eliminated the "c" selection as being wrong, "c" is the best guess (based upon generic testing statistics). Although the "a" selection is sometimes the correct answer for a particular question, it is the worst guess statistically. Comparing statistics and educated guesses, your educated guess is always the better choice.

Matching Questions

- Read the instructions to determine whether items from either list can be used more than once. If not, the items can be matched through a process of elimination. Match those that you know are correct and select the others by eliminating those that you know are wrong.

- Matching questions tend to take more time than either true–false or multiple choice questions. Budget your time with this in mind.

Essay Questions

- Quickly skim the instructions and the question to get a feel for the material. Then read them again, very carefully this time. With this reading, note any important points or items together with their location in the question. This makes it easier to find things later, which saves time.

- Be absolutely sure you understand what it is that you are to do (whether it is to summarize, to compare, to discuss, to analyze, and so forth).

- If you are asked to summarize material, condense it to the bare bones facts. Do not editorialize; do not change facts or add facts that are not clearly stated in the original material. In general, a summary should be no longer than one-fourth the length of the original material. Double-check to be certain that the names, places, times, and so forth in your summary coincide with the original material.

- If you are asked to compare one thing with another, limit the essay to comparison and contrast (similarities and differences). Don't engage in extraneous dissertations. For instance, do not explain how a particular concept or principle evolved historically when the question asks simply that you compare it with another specified concept or principle.

- When asked to explain or to discuss an issue, concept, term, or the like, do precisely that. At a minimum, the discussion must provide a concise definition. It may also include usage: when, how, and why it is used. Do not compare it with something else unless that is the only way to explain it, which seldom is the case.

- Do not define terms by using those terms as part of the definition. In other words, do not say, "Criminal law is the law that defines criminal conduct." This is a circular statement. It defines nothing, and no points could be given for it.

- Do not ask rhetorical questions in an essay answer. For example, do not ask, "Why have the rule if it is not enforced?" Rephrase the thought into a declarative statement, such as: "The rule means nothing if it is not enforced."

- Plan to spend at least as much time thinking about and planning your answer as you spend writing it.

- Use the scratch paper or noteboard provided to you to plan your answer completely before typing *anything* on the computer screen. Do not merely begin to type, believing (or hoping) that you can clarify your thoughts as you progress. It almost never works.

- Get to the point. In planning your answer, write down the three or four (three is better) most important points to be made. Then put them in complete sentences; be sure they convey complete thoughts and make sense. Use abbreviations and brief forms of words to speed the process. Once you have done this, number them in the logical order in which they should be presented or discussed. Decide whether there are any sub-points that *must* be included for clarity. If so, jot a word or a phrase under the main point as a reminder. Unless the sub-point is absolutely necessary, leave it out.

- Formulate a brief, introductory sentence and draft the final answer. Stick to your planned outline. To the extent that you digress, your answer will appear disjointed and disorganized.

- Say what you need to say in as few words as possible and then stop. Refer to the Communications section of this *Review Manual* for more information.

- Double-check spelling, punctuation, grammar, and word usage. Make corrections as needed, recognizing that spell check and grammar check features will be disabled on your computer during this exam. Errors will result in lost points.

- Do not attempt to divert the grader's attention by bluffing or by discussing peripheral issues at length. This technique does not work and can backfire in such a way that the resulting essay score is less than it would have been if the applicant had stopped at those things that were known and were relevant to the question.

- Do not try to be humorous; it generates no points. Likewise, do not include explanatory or apologetic notes to the grader. It's unprofessional.

After the Examination

Once the examination is finished, give yourself as much time as possible to unwind before you attempt to resume your normal schedule. If you plan to drive yourself to the testing site, do not plan to drive back home immediately. If your home is more than 30 or 40 miles away, it may be wise to drive home the following day. The CLA/CP® designation will have significantly less value to you if it must be awarded posthumously.

Nearly everyone experiences some degree of shell shock after the last testing period is concluded. Be prepared for the wide range of feelings that you will have if you are like most other applicants.

Stage One: Cessation of all discernable brain function (or so it will seem).

Stage Two: Relief that it is over, followed quickly by mild depression, followed by feelings of hopelessness. By now, you will have convinced yourself that you could not possibly have passed any section of the examination. This is not true, of course; but no one will be able to convince you otherwise.

Stage Three: Hope, fear, and dread, sometimes experienced all at once. First, you will hope that the notification letter arrives soon. Within a few weeks, you will feel a little better and will begin to hope that you passed *all* of the sections that you took during the testing window, because you don't want to take *any* of the sections again. At the same time, you will fear that you passed none of the sections; and for this reason, you will begin to experience both eagerness and dread about receiving the notification letter. Waiting will become torturous. Your patience will register on a minus scale, and everyone who is not at least as miserable as you are will irritate you.

All of these feelings are normal, but most of them are unfounded. They can be minimized by keeping the entire experience in perspective and by focusing on those parts of it that are important.

1.   Certification is a voluntary, professional goal. The fact that you have undertaken it says who you really are; attaining it is merely a question of docket control.

2.   All information about your application and your exam results is strictly confidential. No one will know that you are taking the exam (other than limited Headquarters staff) unless you elect to share this information. Not even the graders on the Certifying Board know whose examination is being graded.

3.   The worst that can happen is that you may fail *this time.* If you do, it will be either (1) because of inadequate preparation or (2) because of panic. You have the power to eliminate both obstacles; and once you become certified, no one will care how many times you—or anyone else—may have taken a particular section to pass it. Failure is not a reason for self-denigration; giving up is.

4.   Only those who are willing to risk failure ever succeed; only those who are satisfied with mediocrity never fail.

Expect the best, prepare for the worst, and capitalize on whatever happens. If you prepared and if you did not panic, you will pass the examination. In the meantime, save your outlines and notes and use those time periods previously reserved for study to pursue a favorite hobby while you wait for the results.

COMMUNICATIONS

Only a mediocre writer is always at his best.
                              —Somerset Maugham

This section of the Certified Legal Assistant examination covers the following areas of communication:

Word Usage	Rules of Composition
Punctuation	Concise Writing
Capitalization	Vocabulary
Grammar	Correspondence
Human Relations	Nonverbal Communication
Interviewing	

Knowledge of these topics is tested with true–false, multiple choice, matching, and essay questions. Human relations and interviewing techniques and skills are covered in a separate chapter immediately following this one in the *CLA/CP® Review Manual*, although both chapters are included in the Communications section of the exam.

Historically, the Communications section of the CLA/CP® examination has caused great difficulty to applicants. This may lie in the fact that many paralegals assume they know communication rules reasonably well.

Consequently, they may allot less preparation time to this section than to some of the others. Do not fall into the trap created by this complacent view.

Recall, too, that the NALA Certifying Board has adopted Strunk and White, *The Elements of Style,* as its primary reference on the subject. It can be purchased in most retail bookstores. When Strunk and White covers a particular topic, its rules control. Use the other texts listed in the bibliography as supplemental references only.

The communication rules stated in Strunk and White are incorporated throughout this *Review Manual*. When Strunk and White is silent about a particular rule, however, this *Review Manual* uses the following references: Fowler and Aaron, *The Little, Brown Handbook*; *Texas Law Review Manual on Style* (Texas Law Review Publications, Inc.), which is based upon both the Fowler and the Strunk and White texts; and Hollis Hurd, *Writing for Lawyers* (Journal Broadcasting & Communications).

Word Usage

The Word Usage portion of the Communications section tests the applicant's knowledge of how words are used in a particular context. These include words that are often confused, as well as words and phrases that are misused by inexperienced writers.

In general, and in particular for examination purposes, avoid slang expressions and colloquialisms. The formal, concise expression of thought is preferred over the informal in legal writing. There may be the occasional situation when a lawyer or legal assistant purposely uses a slang expression or a colloquialism for a specific effect, perhaps in the preparation of a brief. However, this should happen rarely and certainly should not be taken as authority for poor writing generally.

Slang

Slang expressions are words or phrases that have been coined, usually by younger people, for use in a way that is inconsistent with their standard definitions. Slang is often regional and short-lived. While a legal assistant should be familiar with slang expressions in use at a particular time in his or her region, slang has no place in good writing. A few slang words and expressions to avoid are shown below. This list is not intended to include all of the slang words that exist.

bag, bag lady	drag	payoff
bananas	flake off, flaky	peel out
bomb, bomb out	flunk, flunked	right on
bonkers	foxy lady	rip off
bread	gizmo	slick
burned	gross, gross out	space cadet
bug off	hang-up	space off
bummed, bummer	hooked	space out
chill, chill out	hooker	split
cold	jacked up	stuff
clobber	junk	turn off, turn on
cool, cool it	make out	up tight
cop, cops	out of sight	

Colloquialisms

A colloquialism is a word or expression used in an informal, conversational setting. The term also may be used to indicate an expression of regional dialect. Colloquialisms are inappropriate in professional conversation. Their use is incorrect in legal writing as well as in all other types of formal writing.

The italicized words and phrases in the following sentences are representative of the types of colloquialisms that should be avoided. A more appropriate expression is shown in bold.

I was ill but I am *alright* now.
I was ill but I am **all right** now.   OR   I was ill but I am **well** now.

I have *around* eight books in my library.
I have **approximately** eight books in my library.

She is regarded *as being* the best lawyer in the state.
She is regarded **as** the best lawyer in the state.

Let me know *as to whether* you plan to attend.
Let me know **whether** you plan to attend.

The judge has not arrived *as yet*.
The judge has not arrived **yet**.

I am *awfully* tired.
I am **extremely** tired.   OR   I am tired.

Joe *claimed* he saw the entire incident.
Joe **stated** he saw the entire incident.

I simply could not *cope*.
I simply could not **cope with the situation**.

We are no *different than* other people.
We are no **different from** other people.

There is no *doubt but* that you are a valued employee.
There is no **doubt** that you are a valued employee.

Jack was *enthused* about the wedding plans.
Jack was **enthusiastic** about the wedding plans.

I could not *help but notice* that the defendant was late.
I could not **help noticing** that the defendant was late.

Irregardless of anything else, I am determined to pass this test.
Regardless of anything else, I am determined to pass this test.

He *got sick* as soon as he retired.
He **became ill** as soon as he retired.

This part of the country is *kind of* pretty.
This part of the country is *sort of* pretty.
This part of the country is **rather** pretty.

It looks *like* it might snow.
It looks **as if** it might snow.

The cake tasted good, *like* homemade cake should.
The cake tasted good, **as** homemade cake should.

Lots of people have nightmares about public speaking.
Many people have nightmares about public speaking.

My raise was *nowhere near* as large as it should have been.
My raise was **not** as large as it should have been.

We were *plenty* worried.
We were **quite** worried.   OR   We were worried.

Your essay was *real* good.
Your essay was **very** good.

Do you *reckon* we can win?
Do you **think** we can win?

She *sure* is brilliant.
She is **surely** brilliant.   OR   She is **certainly** brilliant.

Be *sure and* edit your work.
Be **sure to** edit your work.

I am *terribly* worried about arriving on time.
I am worried about arriving on time.

Try and come home on time.
Try to come home on time.

The attorney *put across* her idea very well.
The attorney **expressed** her idea very well.

I *put in* many hours on the project.
I **spent** many hours on the project.

We *should of* spent more time researching the issues.
We **should have** spent more time researching the issues.

Words Confused and Misused

Write it right. As this statement demonstrates, some words (called homonyms) sound alike but have totally different meanings. Other words with similar meanings (called synonyms) sometimes are used as if they were interchangeable when the context of a sentence indicates that one is more accurate than the other. The CLA/CP applicant is expected to recognize the most appropriate word to use in a given context.

Still other words are used incorrectly because the writer does not know their meaning and does not take the time to consult a dictionary. A complete list of confusing words is not feasible in a manual like this one. It may not be feasible in any kind of book other than a dictionary or a thesaurus. However, a list of those words most often confused (and therefore misused) has been included, along with definitions and examples for comparison.

accede (verb): *to agree, to accept*
exceed (verb): *to go beyond*

The supervisor acceded to all of our recommendations.
We must use care not to exceed the authority given to us.

accept (verb): *to receive willingly*
except (preposition): *other than*

> I cannot accept gifts from clients.
> Everyone was there except the host.

access (noun): *admission*
excess (adjective): *surplus*

> How can we gain access to the rest of the information?
> The firm can contract the excess work to smaller companies.

adapt (verb): *to adjust*
adept, used as *adept at* (adjective): *skillful*
adopt (verb): *to choose as one's own*

> You can adapt to the new management structure.
> Connie is adept at handling public relations problems.
> If I cannot have a child of my own, I would like to adopt one.
> I hope the Board of Directors will adopt my proposal.

advice (noun): *suggestion, recommendation*
advise (verb): *to suggest, to recommend*

> Legal assistants cannot give direct legal advice.
> Legal assistants may not advise clients by giving legal opinions.
> I advise you to heed my advice.

affect (verb): *to produce an effect, to influence*
effect (noun): *result, outcome*

> How will the new law affect you?
> What effect will the new law have on others?
> The new law may affect others, but it will have no effect on me.

aggravate (verb): *to make a bad situation worse*
irritate (verb): *to annoy, to vex*

> The neighbors' feud was aggravated by their children's fights.
> Pompous people irritate everyone.

all ready (adjective): *fully prepared*
already (adverb): *previously*

The applicants were all ready to begin the examination.
I tried to call but you already had left the office.

all right (adjective): *satisfactory, well*
all right (adverb): *well enough, very well*
alright: ***incorrect*** — use "all right" instead

They were ill but they are all right now.
She may not be a scholar, but she does all right in school.
All right, let's go.

all together: ***incorrect*** — use "together" instead
altogether (adverb): *completely, wholly*

We want everyone to work together.
The proposal was altogether unsatisfactory.

allude (verb): *to hint, to mention indirectly* ***(not synonymous with refer)***
elude (verb): *to evade, to escape* ***(compare "illusion," infra)***

Is it permissible to allude to the answers if we do not disclose them?
No matter how hard I try, athletic skills elude me.

among (preposition): *used to indicate three or more*
between (preposition): *used to indicate two*

It is difficult to choose among so many qualified candidates.
This dispute is between John and me.

amount (noun): *designates a quantity that is the whole*
number (noun): *designates a quantity divisible into units*

Judge Benson has an incredible amount of energy.
A number of members have expressed their dissatisfaction.

anxious (adjective): *apprehensive, uneasy*
eager (adjective): *marked by enthusiasm or impatience*

Nearly all students are anxious about their final grades.
I am eager to go on vacation this year.

any way (noun): *a possible way to do something*
anyway (adverb): *in any case, in any event*

> Is there any way to resolve this situation?
> I didn't want to be an actor anyway.

adverse (adjective): *unfavorable, opposite, hostile*
averse, used as averse to (adjective): *feeling of repugnance,*
abhorrence

> Adverse winds prevent us from sailing today.
> We were disappointed with the adverse verdict.
> I am averse to strenuous exercise only when it is my own.

bad (adjective): *unfavorable, severe, spoiled, disobedient*
badly (adverb): *poorly, disagreeably*

> The applicant made a bad impression.
> Alice has a bad cold.
> The restaurant is known for its bad food.
> There is no such thing as a bad child.
> All children behave badly from time to time.
> I felt bad because my head hurt too badly to attend the meeting.

born (verb): *to be brought into existence by birth*
borne (verb): *past participle of to bear*

> I was born in St. Louis, Missouri.
> The cost of title insurance will be borne by the seller.

capital (noun): *assets calculated to produce income*
capitol (noun): *place where a legislative body meets*

> Starting a business without enough capital is the formula for failure.
> The capitol of Illinois is in Springfield.

cite (verb): *to quote as authority, to name*
sight (noun): *vision*
site (noun): *location*

> Remember to cite only those statutes that apply directly to the case.
> Alice was cited for bravery during the Iraq War.
> We watched the plane until it was no longer in sight.
> Union leaders decided to picket the construction site.

composed [of] (participle adjective): *made up of*
divided [into] (participle adjective): *separated*

> An orange is composed of skin, fruit, and seeds.
> When peeled, an orange can be divided into sections.

comprise (verb): *to include*
constitute (verb): *to establish, to make (create)*

> A family comprises parents and one or more children.
> Parents and children constitute a family.

conscience (noun): *internal distinction between right and wrong*
conscious (adjective): *alert, aware*

> Your conscience would bother you if you were to lie.
> After the surgery, he was barely conscious.

council (noun): *an official group*
counsel (verb): *to advise*
counsel (noun): *advice or advisor, attorney*

> The town council meets on the first Monday of each month.
> How shall we counsel her?
> The elderly lawyer gave me sound counsel.
> I cannot discuss this matter on advice of counsel.

credible (adjective): *believable, trustworthy*
creditable (adjective): *worthy of praise*
credulous (adjective): *willing to take at face value, gullible*

> Our client's version of the facts was more credible than the plaintiff's.
> The litigation team's performance was creditable.
> The monitor was so credulous that he believed my excuse.

currently (adverb): *at this time*
presently (adverb): *in the very near future*

> The temperature is currently 87°.
BETTER > The temperature is 87°.

> The dinner guests will arrive presently.
BETTER > The dinner guests will arrive soon.

delusion (noun): *false belief about the self or about other people or things*
illusion (noun): *misleading image*

Insecure people often have delusions of grandeur.
Samuel appears self-confident, but this is an illusion.

device (noun): *object, vehicle*
devise (verb): *to give, as in a will or other testamentary document*

A toaster is an electrical device.
Upon my death, I devise all of my property to my bulldog.

disinterested (adjective): *impartial, unbiased*
uninterested (adjective): *lack of curiosity, not interested*

A judge must be disinterested in the outcome of the case.
I should learn more about cars but I am uninterested in grime.

eminent (adjective): *prominent in reference to a person*
imminent (adjective): *about to occur, threatening*

Oliver Wendell Holmes was an eminent legal scholar.
The black sky indicates that a storm is imminent.

expect (verb): *to look forward to*
suspect (verb): *to think probable or likely*

I expect to pass the certification examination next April.
I suspect that I will have to study hard between now and then.

farther (adverb): *distance*
further (adverb): *time, quantity*

I can hit the ball farther than anyone on the team.
We must investigate further before we reach any conclusions.

fewer (adjective): *reduced number*
less (adjective): *reduced extent or degree*

There are fewer students enrolled this year.
Anything less than full participation is unacceptable.

foreword (noun): *prefatory comments to a book, not by the author*
forward (adverb): *progressively toward the front, ahead*

> In the foreword of the text, the editor reviewed the author's research.
> We can accomplish nothing by standing still; we must move forward.

good (adjective): *suitable, satisfactory*
well (adjective): *healthy, desirable*
well (adverb): *suitably, satisfactorily*

> This steak tastes good.
> We believe our client has good title to the land.
> I am very well, thank you.
> It may be well for you to leave now.
> Alice did well on the examination.
> Ms. West spoke well of you.

imply (verb): *to suggest, to hint*
infer (verb): *to deduce, to draw a conclusion*

> The instructor implied that I was doing well in class.
> Based upon the instructor's words, I inferred that I would get an A.
> Though I may imply that I am tired, do not infer that I need to sleep.

incredible (adjective): *unbelievable*
incredulous (adjective): *unwilling to take at face value, skeptical*

> It seemed obvious that the defendant had told some incredible lies.
> I am somewhat incredulous about being able to pass without study.

it's (contraction): *it is*
its (possessive pronoun): *belonging to it (a place or thing)*

> It's dangerous to jog when it's hot outdoors.
> A court must preserve its dignity.
> When problems arise, society must look to its members for solutions.

later (adverb): *at a subsequent time*
latter (adjective): *near the end, the last mentioned of the two*

> The Model Rules were adopted later than was the Model Code.
> I did not become tired until the latter part of the exercise.
> Given the choice of prestige or fulfillment, I would choose the latter.

lay, laying, laid, laid (verb): *to place a person or an object – this verb requires a direct object*
lie, lying, lay, lain (verb): *to be in or to take a reclining position – this verb does not use a direct object*

Please lay your glasses on the table.
Laying cement is hard work.
Yesterday, I laid the baby in his crib.
I have laid my rings on the windowsill every day of my adult life.
I love to lie in the grass.
My glasses are lying on the table.
Yesterday, I lay in the grass for nearly an hour.
My children have lain in the grass with me on a number of occasions.

lend (verb): *to relinquish temporarily*
loan (noun): *a thing given for the borrower's temporary use*

Please lend me your textbook until tomorrow.
If I ever buy a car, I will need to obtain a loan.

liable (adjective): *responsible or legally bound*
libel (noun): *defamatory statement in written form*

You may be liable for damages if you cause an accident.
It is sometimes easier to prove libel than it is to prove slander.

may be (verb phrase): *might come to pass*
maybe *(adverb): perhaps, possibly*

If we find better cases, we may be able to overturn the decision.
If we don't find better cases, we may be in deep trouble.
Maybe we should search for more favorable cases.

nauseated (adjective): *affected by nausea (stomach distress)*
nauseous (adjective): *causing nausea*

I became nauseated by the smell.
I was nauseated.
The smell was nauseous.

To say, "I was nauseous," is **incorrect** *in formal writing, unless one intends to say, "I caused someone else to experience nausea."*

passed (verb): *past participle of "to pass"*
past (noun or preposition): *previous time, beyond*

> I passed the examination.
> It is not good to live in the past.
> Cars flew past me as if I were standing still.

percent (noun): *use with a specific number*
percentage (noun): *use when no specific number is stated*

> Only 65 percent of the students complete the program of study.
> A large percentage of our case load involves commercial litigation.

precede (verb): *to be, go, or come ahead or in front of*
proceed (verb): *to go forward, to continue*

> Thunder generally precedes a rainstorm.
> If negotiations fail, we can proceed with litigation.

principal (adjective or noun): *primary, leader of*
principle (noun): *rule*

> Professional recognition is a principal reason for certification.
> A corporate president is usually a principal in the business operation.
> A child's worst fear is to be sent to the principal's office.
> Karen believes in the principle of tradition.

sit (verb): *to rest on the posterior; to be situated—this verb does not use a direct object*
set (verb): *to place in a position; to arrange—this verb requires a direct object*

> Please sit with me.
> I left my briefcase sitting on the elevator.
> Please set your books on the shelf.
> Our grandchildren like setting the table for family dinners.

suppose (verb): *to assume, to conjecture*
supposed (adjective): *alleged, expected*

> I suppose that I can handle this matter, but I am not certain.
> When did the supposed masked man appear?
> Are you supposed to be here?

than (conjunction): *used in making a comparison*
then (adverb): *specifies when, used in describing time*

> Pat is much brighter than I.
> What did you do then?

that, who (pronoun): *introduces restrictive (essential) description*
which, who (pronoun): *introduces nonrestrictive (nonessential) description*

> The book that I want for Christmas is *Poor Richard's Almanac*.
> The person who works hard likely will succeed.
> My bicycle, which is broken, is in the attic.
> Stevie Wonder, who is blind, is an outstanding musician.

their (possessive pronoun): *belonging to them*
there (adverb): *specifies where, used in describing a place*
they're (contraction): *they are*

> People in London usually take their umbrellas to work.
> Please put your book there.
> They're certain to miss the game if they don't get there soon.

to (preposition): *used as part of infinitives, connector in various idioms*
too (adverb): *also, in an excessive amount*

> I find it difficult to think when I am tired.
> To know me is to love me.
> Jack will be there, and Jill may be there too.
> Both of us were too tired to study.

use (verb): *to employ, to implement, to consume*
use (noun): *function, purpose, utility*
used (adjective): *not new, accustomed*

> Lawyers and paralegals alike must know how to use a computer.
> Perhaps you can find a use for these old textbooks.
> I like used books better than new ones.
> Paralegals are used to hard work.

Punctuation

Punctuation is the use of standardized marks or signs in written material to clarify meaning and to separate structural units. Paralegals must be able to punctuate their own work correctly and must be able to recognize incorrect punctuation when it is presented to them. Common punctuation marks include the apostrophe, the hyphen, the dash, the comma, the semicolon, the colon, the period, the question mark, the exclamation point, quotation marks, ellipses, parentheses, and brackets.

It has been said that no matter what the rules are concerning punctuation, they will change about every five years. That statement is not correct, at least not as it applies to formal writing. If legal writing is anything, it is formal. As they are used in legal writing, accepted rules of punctuation and grammar have changed very little through the years. Notice, for instance, that the rules from Strunk and White's *Elements of Style*, which is the primary reference of the NALA Certifying Board and of numerous law reviews around the country, have not changed. In fact, the copyright on the original book has expired, and this book can be downloaded from the Internet without cost. It is incumbent upon lawyers and paralegals to learn and to use punctuation rules correctly.

The proper use of punctuation marks will be tested in the objective portion of the exam, sometimes in very complicated sentence structures. For all essay questions (and for all writing in general), strive for simplicity in both writing style and punctuation.

The Apostrophe

The apostrophe is used to create possessive forms of some nouns, indefinite pronouns, abbreviations, and acronyms. It is also used to form contractions and to indicate a quotation within a quotation.

Singular Possessives

The possessive form of singular nouns, abbreviations, and acronyms is achieved by adding **'s**.

a child's toys	a witch's broomstick
the boy's book	a month's notice
a dollar's worth	a year's accumulation
the group's decision	my mother-in-law's garden
Bill Jones's farm	one country's wealth
Alan Smith Jr.'s home	Susan's graduation
YWCA's charter	CEO's parking space
CPA's resume	CLA's or CP's certificate
Tess's son	witness's statement

Plural Possessives

Forming the possessive of plural nouns, abbreviations, and acronyms is a two-step process: (1) correctly show the plural form of the word and (2) add **'s** unless the plural form already ends in s or the s sound. If the plural form of the word ends in s or the s sound, add only the apostrophe.

children's toys	witches' broomsticks
the boys' book	two months' notice
ten dollars' worth	five years' accumulation
the groups' decisions	all mothers-in-law's gardens
Bill and Mary Joneses' farm	many countries' wealth
The Alan Smith Jrs.' home	Susan and Shiela's graduation
YWCAs' charters	CEOs' parking spaces
CPAs' resumes	CLAs' or CPs' certificates
Tesses' sons	witnesses' statements

Possessive Form of Some Indefinite Pronouns

Personal pronouns and the relative pronoun *who* have possessive forms (*see section on Pronouns*) that eliminate the use of the apostrophe. Some indefinite pronouns, however, have possessive forms that require the use of **'s**.

another's ideas
everybody's nightmare
one's rights
someone else's problem

Contractions

A contraction is a shortened word group, formed by omitting a letter or sound. The omission is indicated by an apostrophe.

I would	I'd
I would not	I wouldn't
could not	couldn't
we are	we're
he is	he's
of the clock	o'clock
cannot*	can't

*Note that **cannot** is written as one word, not two words.

The Hyphen

The hyphen is used to signal some, but not all, compound words. A compound word is a combination of words that are joined to express a single thought. While the rules that control compound words are almost as varied as the compound words themselves, some general patterns do emerge; and those rule patterns are stated below. When in doubt about a particular combination of words, consult a good dictionary.

Numbers   When writing numbers in words, use a hyphen to join the numbers *one* through *nine* to the base number (twenty, thirty, forty, and so forth).

> fifty-five
> nine hundred sixty-seven
> one thousand three hundred eighty-six dollars and seventy-nine cents

When a compound is created by combining a number and a noun, and when that compound appears before the noun that it modifies, the number is always singular and the compound is hyphenated.

> four-way stop   second-class citizen
> one-horse town   five-drawer desk

Fractions   Use a hyphen to separate the numerator and the denominator of a fraction unless one of them already contains a hyphen.

> one-half
> four-fifths
> one and three-fourths

BUT

> forty-five hundredths
> eighteen thirty-thirds
> thirty-seven forty-fifths

Dual Job Titles   When a person holds more than one job at the same time, a title may be formed by joining the two job titles with a hyphen.

> secretary-treasurer
> producer-director

Familial Relationships   Compound words that begin with the prefix *great* are hyphenated. Compound words that begin with the prefix *grand* are not hyphenated.

> great-grandson   great-grandfather
> great-niece   great-aunt

BUT

> granddaughter   grandmother
> grandnephew   granduncle

Compound words describing in-laws are hyphenated.

mother-in-law	father-in-law
brother-in-law	sister-in-law

All, Ex, Self, Quasi, and Well Prefixes

Compound words created with the prefixes *all*, *ex*, *self*, *quasi*, and *well* are compound adjectives and are hyphenated when they precede the noun they modify.

all-American team	all-inclusive
ex-officio member	ex-husband
self-esteem	self-indulgent
quasi-contract	quasi-judicial
well-known fact	well-established rule

BUT

That fact is well known. *(no hyphen)*
The rule has been well established. *(no hyphen)*

Cross and Counter Prefixes

The prefixes *cross* and *counter* are hyphenated or not hyphenated, depending on the specific word compound. Since there is no rule pattern that emerges for these words, writers simply must memorize the words that require a hyphen and the words that do not.

cross-petition	cross-claim
cross-examine	cross-referenced

BUT

crossroads

counterclaim	counteroffer
counterpart	counterattack

BUT

counter-petition	counter-clockwise

Prefixes That Are Not Hyphenated

The prefixes *anti, co, de, inter, intra, multi, non, para, post, pre, pro, re, semi, super,* and *un* are not hyphenated unless the second part of the word is capitalized, hyphenated, or a number, or unless a hyphen is needed for clarity.

antidepressant	codefendant
devalue	interoffice memorandum
intracompany newsletter	multipurpose room
nonlawyer	paramedic
postoperative	preexistence
proactive	reconstruct

semimonthly	superimpose
unnecessary	

BUT

anti-American	non-Dutch
pre-1776	post-Revolutionary War
re-create*	de-emphasize

With the hyphen, this word means "to create again"; without the hyphen, it means "to engage in recreation."

Compound Adjectives

In general, a hyphen is used to join two or more words that function as a single adjective preceding a noun.

holier-than-thou attitude	cloak-and-dagger tactics
half-baked idea	tax-free earnings
seat-of-the-pants solution	soft-spoken judge
all-or-nothing proposal	part-time employee

BUT

Joe's idea was half baked.

Earnings on municipal bonds are usually tax free.

It may help to remember that in general, compounds used as adjectives (modifying nouns, words used as nouns, pronouns, or other adjectives) are hyphenated, while compounds used as adverbs (modifying verbs or adjectives) are not hyphenated.

The Dash

Use a dash, sometimes known as the em dash, to set off a sudden break or interruption in thought. A dash also may be used to signal a summary of the idea that precedes it or to signal a long appositive. An appositive, which is a parenthetical or explanatory expression, also may be signaled by parentheses or by commas. Use a dash only when a more common punctuation mark, such as a comma or parentheses, is too weak to convey the writer's meaning.

We must condemn—we do condemn—the cruelties of war.

Life, liberty, and the pursuit of happiness—all constitutional goals—are the birthright of every American.

The halcyon days of youth—their challenges, their joys, their innocence—will be remembered for the rest of our lives.

POOR   My suspicions proved true—it was not me she liked—it was
            my vast library.

BETTER   My suspicions proved true. It was not me she liked; it was
            my vast library.

The Comma

The comma is the most overused, and therefore misused, punctuation mark in the English language. The purpose of the comma is to signal a slight pause to the reader, not to signal each pause or hesitation of the writer. Gradually longer pauses are signaled by semicolons and colons, respectively. A full stop is signaled by a period. Once writers understand the purpose of each of these punctuation marks, choosing among them in a given situation becomes simpler.

Of all the rules concerning commas in formal writing, the most important one is this: **When in doubt, leave it out**.

In a Series   According to Professor Strunk, use a comma after each item—whether a word, phrase, or clause—except the last in a series of three or more items when those items are joined by a single conjunction.

>   coat, hat, and gloves
>   He opened the mail, read it, and tossed it aside.
>   I ordered wine, cheese, crackers, and so forth.

Semicolons are used in place of commas to separate a series of phrases or clauses in which commas (a series within a series) occur.

>   The examination covered excise, income, and property
>   taxes; personal, corporate, and private property law; and
>   employment and labor relations law.

To see the logic of this rule, read the example with semicolons and then again with commas substituted for the semicolons. With semicolons, the reader is signaled to pause slightly longer after each group than after each item within the group. With all commas, the reader is signaled to pause equally after each item and each group. Such a reading is not only exhausting, it is also confusing.

With Parenthetic Expressions   Use a comma to enclose parenthetic expressions. A parenthetic expression is one that amplifies, explains, repeats in another way, or digresses from the passage into which it is inserted. As a part of speech, a parenthetic expression may be a nonrestrictive, nonessential phrase, which is always set off by commas. A nonrestrictive phrase or clause is one that does not identify or define the preceding noun and could be omitted entirely without detracting from the meaning of the rest of the sentence. ***Hint:*** Nonrestrictive clauses often are introduced by the word *which, who, when,* or *where.*

> Alice, however, was not interested in going to the opera.
> Marsha paid $175,000.00, her entire savings, for the house.
> St. Louis, which is my birthplace, has many tourist attractions.
> Synonyms, words with similar meanings, are covered on the test.
> Antique books, none of them mine, will be sold at the auction.

Restrictive (essential) phrases and clauses, on the other hand, are not parenthetic and are not set off by commas. Such phrases and clauses cannot be eliminated without affecting the meaning of the rest of the sentence. ***Hint:*** Restrictive clauses often are introduced by the word *who* or *that.*

> People who have poor vision should wear glasses.
> The car that hit me was a red convertible.
> My brother Fred drives a motorcycle to work.
> *(I have two brothers, making Fred's name essential for identity.)*

BUT

> My husband, who is retired, is on the golf course every weekend.
> Fred, my brother, drives a motorcycle to work.
> My father, Fred, retired last year.
> *(I have only one father; his name is not essential for identity.)*

Dashes and parentheses sometimes can be used to signal a parenthetic expression. In deciding whether to use parentheses, commas, or dashes, it may help to remember that parentheses whisper the expression, commas state the expression in a normal tone, and dashes emphasize the expression.

> Marsha paid $175,000.00 (her entire savings) for the house.
> St. Louis (which is my birthplace) has many tourist attractions.
> Synonyms—words with similar meanings—are covered on the test.
> Antique books—none of them mine—will be sold at the auction.

If the interruption created by the parenthetic expression is slight, however, the commas can be omitted.

> Jack was exhausted and therefore was irritable.

A noun of address is parenthetic and must be enclosed within commas unless it appears at the beginning or at the end of the sentence.

> Wherever you go, Mary, your reputation goes with you.
> Jack, please bring me the correspondence file.
> I cannot find anything in this box of papers, Neal.

Dates generally contain parenthetic words or numbers and require commas.

> Tuesday, January 5, 2010
> April 19, 2007

BUT

> 19 April 2007

Use a comma to separate unrelated numbers.

> In 2009, 328 paralegal attended the refresher course.

Degrees and titles that follow a name are parenthetic and require commas.

> Mary Fulbright, Ph.D., was elected to the Board.
> The Reverend Nelson Kelly, S.J.
> Woodard Collins III, J.D.
> William C. Ramsey, Attorney at Law

Although *Junior* and *Senior*, together with their respective abbreviations Jr. and Sr., have been regarded by some as parenthetic, logic dictates that both are restrictive (essential for identity), used to distinguish one person from the other. Used as restrictive parts of a name, they are not parenthetic and do not need a comma.

> Fred Gerberding Jr.
> Fred Gerberding Sr.

Before Conjunctions and Transitional Words

Use a comma before a conjunction that joins two independent clauses. A comma is not required when both independent clauses are very short and are closely connected in thought.

> I have to be in court in an hour, and the tire on my car is flat.
> The hour was late, and the judge became increasingly irritated.
> The hour is late and I want to go home.

Similarly, use a comma before the second clause in a compound sentence when the second clause is introduced by any of these transitional words: *because, as* (meaning *because*), *for* (meaning *because*), *or, nor, since,* or *while* (meaning *at the same time*). Once again, it is permissible to omit the comma when the two clauses are very short and are closely connected in thought.

We will not add web cams to our system, because we do not need them.
Printers will be purchased, as they are essential to the system.
Use care, for there is danger at every street corner.
Either do it right, or we shall need to find someone who can.
Neither of us could find the theater, nor could we find the restaurant.

I could not help her, nor did I try.
Jack prepared our dinner, while I went to the bakery.

BUT

Either you do it or she will.
I climbed the mountain because it was there.

When a sentence has a single subject with two verbs that are joined by the conjunction *but*, a comma may be used before the conjunction. On the other hand, when a sentence has a single subject with two verbs that are joined by the conjunction *and*, no comma is used. Given that Strunk and White does not *require* a comma, however, it may be easier simply to omit the comma in both situations.

I wanted dessert, but could not eat another bite.
ALSO CORRECT   I wanted dessert but could not eat another bite.

We listened to his story, but were still unconvinced.
ALSO CORRECT   We listened to his story but were still unconvinced.

BUT

We listened to his story and were still unconvinced.

Do not join independent clauses with a comma; use a semicolon instead.

I don't want ham and eggs; I prefer doughnuts.

After Introductory Expressions   When any one of the following types of introductory expressions is used, it must be followed by a comma:

(1) Introductory infinitive or participial phrase

To become more knowledgeable, I took a course in the subject.
Having lost my glasses, I was unable to see the street signs.

(2) Introductory dependent clause

As I turned the corner, I saw my supervisor seated in my office.

(3) Introductory prepositional phrase

Until discovery is finished, we cannot discuss the case with anyone.

Note: Very short prepositional phrases do not require a comma.

> In 2008 the decision was reversed.
> After work I went directly home.

(4) Transitional expressions, such as those listed below

accordingly	besides
consequently	finally
first	for example
furthermore	however
meanwhile	moreover
namely	nevertheless
second	that is
therefore	

> Meanwhile, the band continued to play.
> Nevertheless, work proceeded on schedule.
> Therefore, we had no reason to continue with the deposition.

BUT

> We had no reason, therefore, to continue with the deposition.
> My family went, namely, my husband, my daughter, and my son.

(5) Introductory mild interjection

> Well, that must have been how it happened.
> Oh, go ahead and buy it.

Between Consecutive Adjectives   Use a comma to separate consecutive, coordinated adjectives that precede the noun they modify, but only when each adjective modifies the noun. When the first adjective modifies the second adjective (rather than the noun), no comma is required. *Hint:* One way to tell whether adjectives are coordinated is to substitute *and* for the comma. If the sentence still makes sense, the adjectives are coordinated and a comma is required. Another way is to reverse the order of the adjectives; if they still make sense, a comma is required to separate them.

> She had a quiet, regal air. (She had a quiet and regal air. She had a regal, quiet air.)
> It was a dark, dreary day. (It was a dark and dreary day. It was a dreary, dark day.)
> She wore a mint green coat. (*Mint* modifies *green*, not coat.)
> He made a weak legal argument. (*Weak* modifies *legal,* not argument.)

With Informal Quotations   Use a comma to introduce or to conclude an informal, direct quotation.

> Uncle Harry always says, "Children are to be seen and not heard."
> "I wonder what time we shall eat," Mary asked.

Formal quotations are introduced by a colon (see section on colons), while indirect quotations are paraphrased and do not use any specific punctuation mark.

> Thoreau said that civil disobedience is sometimes a good thing.

The Semicolon

The semicolon is used to signal a break that is stronger than the comma but is not as strong as the colon within a phrase, independent clause, or sentence. The rules for use of semicolons are fewer than the rules for commas, because the semicolon is used much less often. As is true of all punctuation marks, do not use the semicolon unless there is a specific rule requiring it to be used.

In a Series   Use a semicolon to separate a series of phrases or clauses in which commas (signaling a series within a series) already occur.

> The examination covered excise, income, and property taxes; personal, corporate, and private property law; and employment and labor relations law.

To see the logic of this rule, read the example with semicolons and again with commas substituted for the semicolons. With semicolons, the reader is signaled to pause slightly longer after each group than after each item within the group. With only commas, the reader is signaled to pause equally after each item and each group. Such a reading is both exhausting and confusing.

Between Independent Clauses without Conjunction   Use a semicolon to join two or more grammatically complete clauses that are not joined by a conjunction or connective word.

> We always vacation in New England; it's cooler there in July.
> The jury was sequestered for many hours; awaiting its decision was torturous.

When a conjunction or connective word is inserted, the proper punctuation mark is always a comma.

> We always vacation in New England, for it's cooler there in July.
> The jury was sequestered for many hours, and awaiting its decision was torturous.

Notice that each of the sentences in the first example group could have been written correctly as two separate sentences.

> We always vacation in New England. It's cooler there in July.
> The jury was sequestered for many hours. Awaiting its decision was torturous.

Between Independent Clauses with Conjunction   Use a semicolon to join two or more grammatically complete clauses that are joined by a conjunction when any one of the clauses contains a comma. Compare this rule with the rule stated immediately above. When neither of the independent clauses already contains a comma, however, the correct punctuation mark is a comma.

> No matter how I tried to follow the directions, I rarely hit the ball; and that angered me.
>
> As the day wore on without any end to the negotiations in sight, I became more and more tired; and all I wanted was to go home.

BUT

> I rarely hit the ball, and that angered me.
>
> I became more and more tired, and all I wanted was to go home.

The logic of this rule is similar to the logic of the rule requiring semicolons to separate a series in which commas already occur. The pause between the independent clauses (signaled by a semicolon) should be longer than the pause after the introductory phrase (signaled by a comma). If each of the example sentences were punctuated with a second comma in place of the semicolon, the reader would pause equally at both commas, making the reader's job more difficult.

The Colon

The colon signals a pause that is longer than the pause required by either a comma or a semicolon. In formal writing, the colon is used most commonly to introduce a formal quotation or rule, a question, an antithesis, or a list.

A colon should precede a list only when formal words of introduction—for example, *as follows* or *the following*—are used. Notice that when words of introduction are used, the first word following the colon is capitalized; otherwise, it is not.

> As we waited for the verdict, I was reminded of the words of Samuel Goldwyn: "A verbal contract isn't worth the paper it's written on."

> In reversing the decision, the Court said: "The case of *Roe v. Wade* involved the protection of privacy rights."

> Of all the rules concerning punctuation, the most important one is this: When in doubt, leave it out.

> There is just one thing that I want to know: How long have you had this information?

> Someone wins: another loses. (*A semicolon is also proper.*)

> To ensure success, legal assistants need the following characteristics: High intelligence, unflinching tenacity, and a great sense of humor.

Other Uses   The colon has a number of other uses, all of them related to separating different levels of the same item. The colon is used to separate:

- The title and subtitle of a literary work

  Certification: A Professional Goal

- The page and line numbers in depositions and briefs

  C. Kretchmer deposition, page 137, line 22   C. Kretchmer 137:22

- Chapter and verse numbers in Biblical references

  chapter 23, verse 4 of the Book of Psalms   Psalms 23:4

- The differential in ratios or proportions

  20 to 1   20:1

•Hour and minutes in expression of time

> fifteen minutes before six a.m.   5:45 a.m.

•The salutation from the body of a formal business letter

> Dear Mr. Smith:

The Period

The period is most frequently used to signal a complete stop at the end of a sentence. In addition, this punctuation mark is used to create abbreviations, decimals, outlines, and lists. Sentence termination and abbreviations are covered in this *Review Manual*.

At the End of a Sentence   The period is used at the end of a sentence to signal the reader to come to a complete stop. A sentence may be the simple, declarative kind (with both the subject and the verb shown) or it may be elliptical (one in which words are omitted but are understood).

> Amy arrived before Connie did.
> (you) Put the memorandum on the desk.
> (you) Stop that.
> (my answer is) No.

Never use a period when a comma is the required punctuation mark.

INCORRECT   I met him on an airplane many years ago. Coming home from San Francisco.

CORRECT   I met him on an airplane many years ago, coming home from San Francisco.

INCORRECT   He was fascinating. A person who had traveled the world and who told hilarious stories.

CORRECT   He was fascinating, a person who had traveled the world and who told hilarious stories.

With Abbreviations   Abbreviations should be used sparingly in formal writing or, for that matter, in any writing or conversation unless the abbreviation is defined for the reader or the listener first or unless the abbreviation is so common that no confusion can result from its use. The same is true of acronyms. Although it may be permissible to abbreviate common nouns in the business world, common nouns—account (acct.), amount (amt.), each (ea.), and so forth— are not abbreviated in formal writing.

Some abbreviations use periods; others do not. Learning the difference between the two is simply a matter of memorization and practice. Many abbreviations are already familiar to the experienced paralegal.

Jane Terhune, ACP	Bill Campbell, CPA	Dr. Jane Doe
Dale McHenry, Ph.D.	Oscar Wilde Jr.	St. Paul, MN
Mr. Alex Jones	Mrs. Ruth Ann Newman	Ms. Karen Dunn
1015 B.C.	1992 A.D.	12:40 a.m. EST
IBM	AT&T	U.S.A. or USA
USDA	SEC	IRS
Co.	Corp.	Inc.

The primary difference between an abbreviation and an acronym is pronunciation. Both are formed by using only the first letter(s) of each word comprising the abbreviation (*see above*), or the acronym (*see below*). Abbreviations are pronounced by saying each letter of the resulting combination of letters, while acronyms are pronounced phonetically. Acronyms are **not** punctuated with periods.

Mothers Against Drunk Drivers	MADD
National Association of Legal Assistants, Inc.	NALA
National Organization of Wranglers	NOW
North Atlantic Treaty Organization	NATO
Zone Improvement Plan	ZIP
light amplification by stimulated emission of radiation	laser

Periods are placed inside quotation marks but are placed outside single quotation marks. When a quoted sentence appears within another independent sentence, use a comma instead of a period to punctuate the internal quotation.

> Erin reported, "I have completed the deposition summaries."
> The class was asked to define the term "common law."
> The instructor said, "Please define the term 'common law'."
> Mary said, "I cannot do this anymore," as she left the office.

When parentheses or brackets are used to enclose or to set off an independent sentence, the period is placed inside the final parenthesis or bracket. However, when parentheses or brackets are used to enclose other words, phrases, or clauses within an independent sentence, the period is placed outside the final parenthesis or bracket.

> The client searched everywhere for the invoice. (It was never found.)
> "I cannot find the document [it was never found] or the transmittal letter."
> He could not find them (the document or the transmittal letter).
> Heed this warning (if it applies to you).

When an abbreviation requiring a period appears at the end of the sentence (also requiring a period), only one period is used.

> Send these interrogatories to our client at Acme & Co.
> He works in the Legal Department of Thunderbird Enterprises, Inc.

The Question Mark

The question mark is used to indicate an independent inquiry (question) or an interrogative element (question) within a sentence. A sentence that is declarative in structure may become a question by substituting a question mark for the period.

> How can we finish everything on time?
> The form indicates that he was born in 1999 (?) and was married in 1924.
> They reimbursed you?

Conversely, a command that is structured as a question should be punctuated with a period, not with a question mark. Indirect questions are punctuated with periods as well.

> Please join me in welcoming our guest.
> Will you take these documents to the courthouse.
> The client wanted to know what he should do.
> How to reconcile the two cases was the question before the court.

The question mark should be placed inside quotations, parentheses, or brackets only when it is part of the quoted or parenthetical material.

> Allison inquired, "Where are the deposition summaries?"
> When I found the client's file (where is it now?), I gave it to Richard.

BUT

> Was she upset when she said, "I cannot condone this behavior"?
> Why did you wait so long to call me (a whole week)?

The Exclamation Point

The exclamation point is used to signal strong emotion, such as surprise, disbelief, or enthusiasm. To preserve its effectiveness, the exclamation point should be used sparingly in all writing and even more sparingly in legal writing.

> Oh, no!
> How can you say that!

Like the question mark, the exclamation point should be placed inside quotation marks, parentheses, or brackets only when it is part of the quoted or parenthetical material. Otherwise, it should be placed outside.

> "The boat is sinking!" he shouted.
> Our young son told the cashier (we were so embarrassed!)
> that we starved him.

The Quotation Mark

Quotation marks are used to signal exact words that have been either spoken or written.

> On appeal the court held: "Where there is a right, there is a remedy."
> Jack said, "I can't hear the witness."

When a quotation appears within another quotation already enclosed between quotation marks, the inner quotation is enclosed between two apostrophes. Apostrophes used in this way are called single quotation marks.

> Harry said, "The article 'Contract as Right' is a favorite among lawyers."

When a quotation is 50 words or more in length, it is signaled by indenting it from both the left and right margins rather than by using quotation marks. When an inner quotation appears within an indented quotation, the inner quotation is signaled by quotation marks. Lengthy excerpts from court opinions demonstrate this method of quotation, such as this footnote from *Missouri v. Jenkins*, 109 S. Ct. 1463 (1989):

> Of course, purely clerical or secretarial tasks should not be billed at
> a paralegal rate, regardless of who performs them. What the court
> in *Johnson v. Georgia Highway Express, Inc.,* 488 F.2d 714, 717

(CA5 1974), said in regard to the work of attorneys is applicable by analogy to paralegals: "It is appropriate to distinguish between legal work in the strict sense, and investigation, clerical work, compilation of facts and statistics and other work which can often be accomplished by non-lawyers but which a lawyer may do because he has no other help available. Such non-legal work may command a lesser rate. Its dollar value is not enhanced just because a lawyer does it."

Amicus National Association of Legal Assistants reports that 77 percent of 1,800 legal assistants responding to a survey of the association's membership stated that their law firms charged clients for paralegal work on an hourly billing basis. Brief for National Association of Legal Assistants as *Amicus Curiae* 11.

If the passage in the second paragraph were short enough to be shown between quotation marks, rather than indented, the inner quotation would appear between single quotation marks (apostrophes).

Quotation marks are used to enclose any material introduced by these words and expressions: **endorsed, entitled, marked, signed, the term,** or **the word**.

The class was asked to define the term "common law."
The document marked "Exhibit A" was illegible.

When used with quotation marks, the comma and period are placed inside the quotation marks. Other punctuation marks are placed outside the quotation marks unless they are part of the quotation.

We were asked to define the term "common law."
We were asked to define the term "common law," but I could not do it.
We were asked to define the term "common law"; I could not do it.

The Ellipsis

Ellipses (also called ellipsis points) are punctuation marks consisting of three spaced periods (. . .), which are used to indicate an omission within quoted material. When the omission occurs at the end of a quoted sentence, use the ellipses and then the period from the quoted sentence. When the omission occurs at the beginning of a quoted sentence (so that the first quoted word begins with a lower case letter in the original work), signal the omission with the ellipses and enclose the first letter of the next quoted word in brackets.

"Plaintiff's claim involved lost wages . . . medical expenses, and property damage.

"Viewed in such a way, this is a case of first impression . . . ."

". . . [W]e affirm the superior court's ruling."

Parentheses

Parentheses are used to enclose material that explains, amplifies, or digresses from another element in the sentence; thus, the term "parenthetical expression." Remember that commas or dashes may be used to enclose parenthetical expressions as well. (*See the comma section, supra, for examples of each.*)

The National Association of Legal Assistants (NALA) offers the CLA/CP exam.
The black Cadillac (it's a convertible) is mine.
I bought it as a repossession (at the wholesale price) from a client.

Parentheses may be used to enclose numbers or letters identifying separate elements of a list that is shown as part of a sentence.

Parenthetical expressions may be signaled by (1) parentheses, (2) commas, or (3) hyphens.

When the parenthetical material is either a question or an exclamation, show the question mark or the exclamation mark before the final parenthesis. The period is not shown inside the parentheses unless the parenthetical material is a stand-alone, parenthetical sentence.

Patricia Holt (do you know her?) is the software expert at our office.
Our young son told the cashier (we were so embarrassed!) that we starved him.
The black Cadillac (it's a convertible) is mine.
The black Cadillac is mine. (It's a convertible.)
(This is a parenthetic sentence.)

Other, internal punctuation marks are shown outside the parentheses unless they are part of the parenthetical material.

By waiting so long to call (a whole week), your case has been weakened.
Decide what you want to do (press charges, sue, or settle); then call me.

The Bracket

Brackets are used to enclose editorial comments, corrections, or explanations within quoted material. They are also used to signal a parenthetic expression contained within another parenthetic expression.

> "Despite the damaging evidence [it was discovered by Sherlock Holmes], the defendant maintained his innocence."

> "The practice of lew [sic] by nonlawyers is prohibited."

> While young men, James and his brother (Andrew Ellis, who later discovered a new glue process [ustickum]) were demolition derby champions.

Capitalization

Capitalization is the practice established for the use of uppercase (capital) letters to identify or to emphasize. Capitalization of a word signals the reader to give more attention to it, signifying that it is more important than the words surrounding it. This *Review Manual* covers only the more common rules of capitalization, grouped according to the general categories to which they apply. Applicants will be wise to consult other references suggested in the bibliography for detailed capitalization rules.

The First Word

Always capitalize the first word of a sentence. Capitalize the first word of a quoted sentence unless it flows into the underlying sentence structure.

> Simple sentences are best.
> The instructor said, "Simple sentences are best."
> The instructor said that "[s]imple sentences are best," and I believe him.

Capitalize the first word following a colon only if words of formal introduction are used, that is, if the words preceding the colon create an expectation that additional material will follow the colon.

> The most important punctuation rule is this one: When in doubt, leave it out.
> To pass the test, one must do the following: Prepare, prepare, and prepare.

BUT

> Excellence in all that we do: that was the organization's motto.

Capitalize the first word of each item in a formal list, as well as the first word of each entry in an outline.

1. Dark shoes
2. Brown coat
3. Black tie

I. First words
   A. In a sentence
   B. In a quotation
   C. In a list

Personal Names

Capitalize names and initials of specific persons, as well as nicknames and fictitious names. Capitalize a foreign name according to the conventions of the language from which it derives.

R. W. Williams	JFK	Suzy Q
John Doe	Charles de Gaulle	de Gaulle

Derivatives of Proper Names

Coined nouns and adjectives derived from personal or geographic names are capitalized unless they have become so commonly used (generic) that the capital letter is dropped. The names of nationalities and languages are always capitalized.

French	Spanish	English
American know-how	Native American history	Germans
Parkinson's disease	Canadian bacon	French cooking

BUT

india ink	manila envelope	french fries

Titles and Offices

When used as part of narrative text, capitalize titles when they precede a personal name, as part of the name. Do not capitalize titles when they are used as an appositive following the name or when no specific name is stated. When used to refer to the President of the United States, however, the title *President* may—but need not—be capitalized.

President Lincoln	Abraham Lincoln, president of the United States	the president
President Lincoln	Abraham Lincoln, President of the United States	the President
Senator DeMint	Jim DeMint, senator of the state of South Carolina	the senator
Chairman Benson	Robert Benson, chairman of the Finance Committee	the chairman
Dr. Ruth Ames	Ruth Ames, doctor of internal medicine	the doctor
Judge A. Richards	Ann Richards, judge of the Utah Supreme Court	the judge

When titles are shown following names in a formal list or as part of either the inside address or the signature block of business correspondence, the titles are capitalized. (*See the section on correspondence.*)

A title used alone, in place of a personal name, is capitalized in the context of a toast or an introduction. Likewise, titles used in place of names of direct address are capitalized.

> Ladies and gentlemen, the Governor of New York.
> Thank you, Mr. Chairman.
> I would have objected, Your Honor; but I could not hear the question.

BUT

> Can you tell me, sir, where the law library is located?

A title of kinship begins with a lowercase letter when a modifier precedes it. When used before a proper name or when used alone, in place of the name, it is usually capitalized.

> My father lives in Illinois.
> The Williams sisters joined us for dinner.
> Alice's brother is older than she.

BUT

> My Uncle Ed cut a wide swath when he was young.
> Let me go with you, Dad.
> I remember that Mother always wore a hat to church.

Education and Academic Degrees   Academic degrees are capitalized following a personal name whether abbreviated or written in full. Academic degrees are not capitalized when they are not connected with a specific name.

> Nadine B. Trew, Juris Doctor
> Nadine B. Trew, J.D.
> One must have a juris doctor degree before taking most state bar exams.

The name of a specific course is capitalized; otherwise, courses are not capitalized unless they are required to be capitalized under some other rule (such as English, French, Spanish, and the like).

> I want to take more courses in accounting and in English composition.
> I have registered for Accounting 212 and English Composition 300 this term.

Geographic (Place) Names

Certain nouns and adjectives designating parts of the world or regions of a continent or country are generally (but not always) capitalized.

the Arctic Circle	the Arctic	arctic climate
the Eastern Seaboard	the East	east, eastern (direction or locality)
the Wild West	the Western world	western states

> *Note: Compass points (north, south, east, and west) and their derivatives (northerly, southerly, and so forth) are never capitalized when they are used merely to indicate direction.*

Topographic Names   Names of specific mountains, rivers, oceans, and so forth are capitalized, including the generic terms *mountain, river,* or *ocean* when used as part of the specific names.

Pacific Ocean	Mississippi River	Black Forest

Do not capitalize the generic terms when they are used descriptively, rather than as part of the specific name.

the coast of South Carolina	BUT	the East Coast (referring to region)
the Arizona desert	BUT	the Painted Desert
the Kansas prairie	BUT	the Prairie State

Buildings and Public Places   Names of specific buildings, monuments, and thoroughfares are capitalized. Generic terms like *avenue, boulevard, bridge, building, street,* and so forth are capitalized when they are part of the formal name. When they stand alone, they are not capitalized.

Fifth Avenue	BUT	the avenue where I live
Brooklyn Bridge	BUT	a bridge over the river

Government

Words designating political divisions or governmental units (country, state, city, and so forth) are capitalized when they follow the name and are an accepted part of it.

New York City	BUT	the city of New York
Harrison County	BUT	the county of Harrison
Washington State	BUT	the state of Washington

the state (referring to a government generally)

Governmental Bodies   When the full name or the abbreviation of a legislative body or an administrative body is used, it is generally capitalized. When the name of the governmental body is paraphrased or when no specific governmental unit is named, do not capitalize. (See examples of exceptions below.)

> General Assembly of Ohio
> Ohio legislature
> state legislature
> state senate
>
> St. Louis City Council
> city council
> council
>
> Federal Bureau of Investigation (FBI)
> the Bureau
>
> Bureau of the Census
> Census Bureau
> the bureau

Although the following terms are governmental references, they generally are not capitalized:

> federal government
> national government
> state government
> church and state
> the state

Courts, Documents, and Parties   Both the formal name and the paraphrased name of a specific court are capitalized. Standing alone, the word court is not capitalized unless it refers to the United States Supreme Court or unless it is used as a noun of address for a particular court.

> United States Supreme Court
> the Supreme Court
> the Court

Colorado Supreme Court
State Supreme Court (referring to a specific state supreme court)
state supreme court (generally)
the supreme court
the court

the Juvenile Court of Wade County
Wade County Juvenile Court
juvenile court

The Court convenes on the first Tuesday in October. *(U.S. Supreme Court)*
All state statutes are subject to review by that state's supreme court.
COMES NOW the defendant and requests this Court to enter an order . . .
The witness appeared under court order.
The lower court found for the plaintiff in this case.

Do not capitalize terms referring to documents or pleadings unless they are included as part of the exact title of a document in existence. This is a common error among lawyers and legal assistants. Do not capitalize the word *appellant, appellee, defendant, movant, petitioner, plaintiff, respondent,* or the like unless it must be capitalized under another rule (such as the first word of a sentence or part of a document title or a pleading caption).

Due process applies to states via the Fourteenth Amendment to the Constitution.
Please refer to page 12 of the Brief for Petitioner Harris.
The brief of the petitioner covered all salient points.
The motion of plaintiff Collins was filed only yesterday.
The purchase agreement was executed by Johnson Brothers, Ltd., the seller.

The term *state* is capitalized when it is used as a proper noun or as a proper adjective referring to a specific state or to "the State" as a party to litigation. Otherwise, it is treated as a generic term and is not capitalized.

Applications must be filed with the State Department of Health.
The state legislature adopted a new gun law during its last session.
Nebraska is the only state with a unicameral legislature.
Under Michigan state law, most contracts of minors are voidable.
All witnesses for the State were sequestered during trial.
The separation of church and state is a fiction of the Court, because it is in no founding document.

Political Organizations   The names of national and international organizations and alliances are generally capitalized, as are members of a specific political party.

the Democratic Party	a Democrat	a democratic view	democracy
the Republican Party	a Republican	a republican view	republic
the Socialist Party	a Socialist	a socialistic philosophy	socialism

Other Names

Other nouns and adjectives may require capitalization, based upon their source or based upon the way in which they are used. As with all capitalization, the underlying rule is not to capitalize any word unless a specific rule requires its capitalization.

Associations, Companies, and Institutions   The full names of associations, companies, and institutions are capitalized, together with their departments and divisions. However, the words *association, company, society,* and the like are not capitalized when used alone.

National Association of Football Coaches	NAFC	the association
General Foods Corporation	General Foods	the corporation
Creighton University School of Law	Creighton Law School	the law school
Boy Scouts of America	a Boy Scout	a scout
New York Yankees	the Yankees	the team
Union of Electrical Workers of America	U.E.W.	the union

Historical Documents, Events, and Periods   The names of specific documents, events, and historical periods are capitalized.

| the Magna Carta | the Boston Tea Party | the Roaring Twenties |
| the Constitution (U.S.) | the Vietnam War | the Middle Ages |

BUT

| the nineteenth century | the eighteen hundreds |
| the twenties | the 1920s |

Calendar and Time Designations   Names of the 12 months of the year are capitalized, as are the names of the days of the week. The names of specific holidays are also capitalized.

| January | June | Thursday |
| Lent | Independence Day | Halloween |

BUT

| election day | inauguration day | graduation day |

A season of the year is not capitalized unless the term is personified (as in poetry) or is part of the title of either a literary work or a special event.

winter	summer solstice	spring break
O, Spring, how welcome!	the NALA Fall Seminar	The Winter of Our Discontent

Time zones are not capitalized when designated in words; however, time zone abbreviations are capitalized.

eastern standard time	EST
eastern daylight savings time	EDST

For further discussion of abbreviations and acronyms, see the section on punctuation.

Titles of Works   All words in the titles and subtitles of specific articles, books, periodicals, and newspapers are capitalized except (1) articles (a, an, the) unless the article is the first word of the title; (2) coordinating conjunctions (and, for, or, nor); and (3) prepositions, regardless of length, unless they are the first or last words of the title or subtitle.

The Winter of Our Discontent	Talk of the Town
the Wall Street Journal	A Man for All Seasons
A Miracle on Thirty-fourth Street	The French-American Connection
The Truth about a Cat in a Hat	Passages from a Stargazer's Notebook

Note: *The titles of complete works are underlined (or italicized), while articles and serial parts of an entire program or work are enclosed in quotation marks.*

Grammar

Questions within this category of the CLA/CP® examination require the applicant to demonstrate knowledge of various parts of speech by recognizing their correct (or incorrect) use within the sentence structure. The words (parts of speech) used to construct a sentence generally can be categorized as nouns, pronouns, adjectives, verbs, adverbs, prepositions, conjunctions, articles, or interjections, with variations for each of these.

Every part of speech has a specific function within a sentence, each with rules that must be observed to assure cohesiveness of the idea being conveyed. Constructing a sentence is much like constructing a house. Large or small, fancy or plain, every good house must have a framework that matches on all sides; and the connecting points must be perfectly aligned. Without this precision, the house would be fairly drafty—if it could stand at all. Constructing a sentence is much the same. Long or short, elaborate or simple, its subject and all modifiers must match its verb (predicate) and all modifiers; and its mood, voice, and tense must be perfectly aligned. Without this balance and alignment, even the most eloquent collection of words will fall apart; and the idea will be buried in a heap of unintelligible terms.

Words are the essential stock in trade of lawyers and paralegals, to be assembled into cohesive sentences. A mastery of the parts of speech and of the rules of sentence construction is critical to those who aspire to the CLA/CP® designation.

Parts of Speech Defined

Every word in the English language can be categorized as a part of speech (noun, pronoun, verb, and so forth). Many words can fit into more than one category, defined by the way in which they are used, or can fit into more than one category by changing the form slightly. These words are classified according to their form and function within a particular sentence.

Noun   A noun is the name of a person, a place, a thing, a concept, or a quality. Nouns are classified as common nouns *(child, river, book, patriotism, happiness)* or proper nouns *(Mariah, Mississippi River, Bible, World War II)*. Used as the subject of a sentence or clause, a noun answers the question: Who or what? Used as the direct object or indirect object of a sentence (or as the object of a phrase), a noun answers the question: What or whom? Nouns are the identifiers of actors and topics within a sentence.

Pronoun   A pronoun is a word that substitutes for a noun *(I, me, you, he, she, it, him, her, they, them, themselves, everyone, myself, this, that, those, who, which,* and so forth). Pronouns are used in place of nouns and perform the same functions as nouns within a sentence.

Verb   A verb can be either a word indicating action *(see, do, run, read, walk)* or a word of being *(am, is, are, was, were)*. The verb is the heart of every sentence. It sets the tone of the entire sentence by its tense (present, past, future); voice (active or passive); and mood (indicative, imperative, or subjunctive).

Helping verbs *(can, could, did, do, does, has, have, may, might, must, shall, should, will, would)*, sometimes called auxiliary verbs, often combine with verbs to form a verb phrase. This verb phrase, together with its modifiers, is known as a predicate.

A verb preceded by the word "to" creates an infinitive. Infinitives function as nouns within a sentence.

Adjective   Adjectives are words that describe or modify nouns or pronouns *(tender, harmful, one, some, all)*. Adjectives answer the question: Which, what kind of, or how many within the sentence structure.

Adverb   Adverbs describe or modify verbs, adjectives, other adverbs, or groups of words with these characteristics *(tenderly, simply, harmfully, nearly, almost, always, someday, somewhere, really, there)*. Adverbs answer the question: How, when, where, to what extent, or how often within the sentence structure. Adverbs often (but not always) end in the letters *ly*.

Preposition   Prepositions *(about, around, at, down, for, in, near, of, off, regarding, to, with, without)* are words that link nouns or pronouns to other words in the sentence structure. The applicant who has difficulty with prepositions may find it helpful to think of them as the "doghouse" words. They generally are not part of the main structure of the sentence and can be identified by saying: *around* the doghouse, *for* the doghouse, *regarding* the doghouse, *to* the doghouse, and so on. This method is not foolproof, but it identifies the vast majority of prepositions.

Conjunction   Conjunctions are linking words. They link words, phrases, and clauses within the sentence. Coordinate conjunctions *(and, but, or, either . . . or, neither . . . nor, both . . . and, not only . . . but also)* link words, phrases, and clauses of equal value or importance within the sentence. Subordinate conjunctions *(although, because, if, whenever)* link subordinate clauses to the main sentence.

Article   Articles are easy. There are only three of them: *a, an,* and *the*. They precede nouns as well as words, phrases, and clauses used as nouns within the sentence structure.

Interjection   Interjections *(oh, hey, wow)* are words inserted to express feeling or to command attention. They can be used alone or as part of the sentence. When used alone, they usually are followed by an exclamation point. When used as part of the sentence, they usually are followed by a comma.

Defined by Function   Whether a word is categorized as one part of speech or as another depends upon its function within the sentence structure. The same word can have different functions in different sentences. Accordingly, one must know how a word functions within a particular sentence before it can be categorized as a noun, verb, or so on.

> The victims received medical **aid**. (*Aid* functions as a noun.)
> Physicians **aid** the sick. (*Aid* functions as a verb.)

A General Approach

This *Review Manual* is not intended as a substitute for an English grammar course but, rather, is intended to review common faults in grammar and sentence construction. Most faulty sentences could be avoided if the writer would use the simple exercise learned in elementary school: diagram sentences.

Diagram the sentence, whether mentally or on paper. Either draw or visualize the horizontal and vertical lines to separate the subject from the predicate (verb or verb phrase and its modifiers). If applicable, draw or visualize the backslash line after the predicate and put the direct object there. Show the indirect object if there is one. Then show the modifiers under the subject, predicate, or object to which they belong. Compare the diagram to the sentence. If the sentence is not grouped in the same basic way as the diagram, its construction is faulty; and it must be redrafted. This ritual is performed so often by good writers and becomes so automatic to them that they barely recognize it as diagramming the sentence.

For those who were not cursed with a Miss Tigner in elementary school, the skill of diagramming sentences can be acquired with thoughtful practice. While preparing for the CLA/CP® examination, try this exercise with the sentences in your practice essay answers or with your drafting at the office. Diagram the sentences of others for additional practice.

- Draw a horizontal line and then draw two vertical lines to divide the horizontal line into thirds.

- Place the verb (main verb and any helping verbs) of the sentence inside the middle section of the horizontal line. Remember that the verb is the center of every sentence. No sentence can exist without a verb.

To find the main verb, look for either an action word *(run, grow, bring, give, help)* or a word of being *(be, become, is, was, seem)*.

Include any helping verbs *(can, could, did, do, does, has, have, may, might, must, shall, should, will, would)* that complete the verb phrase.

•Place the subject on the left section of the horizontal line.

To find the subject, use the verb to ask the question: Who or what ran? grew? brought? became? is? was? seemed? Remember that the subject is understood in some sentences but these are few. Remember, too, that the subject is the main actor (the predominant noun) in the sentence.

>   Stop it.   =   (You) stop it.

If there is no stated or understood word to answer the question, look for another verb for which the question: Who or what? can be answered. If there is no other verb, the word group is not a sentence and must be redrafted.

•Place the direct object (if there is one) on the right section of the horizontal line.

To find the direct object, use the subject + the predicate to ask the question: What or whom? In the sample sentence above, for example, ask the question: (You) stop what or whom? The answer is the pronoun *it*. Therefore, the direct object of the sentence is *it*.

That's all there is to it. This simple diagram identifies the basic structure of the sentence. All other words, phrases, or clauses used in the sentence must modify one of the basic sentence parts shown in the main diagram. Modifiers should be placed on diagonal lines under the sentence part which they are intended to modify.

Diagram these examples:

1. The tornado flattened the town.
2. Mary saw Bill running from the murder scene.
3. Joe will be running in the Olympic tryouts.
4. The man who knows too much.

1. There is only one action word (flattened); there is no word of being. The word *flattened* is the main verb. Who or what flattened? The answer is *tornado*. Tornado is the subject of the sentence. Tornado flattened what or whom? The answer is *town*. The word town is the direct object of the sentence.

2. There are two action words (saw and running); there is no word of being. Bill was running, but Bill is not the main actor in the sentence; Mary is. Therefore, the verb *saw* is the main verb and *Mary* is the subject (main actor) of the sentence. Mary saw what or whom? The answer is *Bill*. Bill is the direct object, and the phrase "running from the accident scene" modifies Bill.

3. There is one action word (running); the words of being (will be) are helping verbs in this sentence, used to augment the main verb (running). The question is: Who or what will be running? The answer is *Joe*. Joe is the subject. Joe will be running what or whom? There is no answer; therefore, there is no direct object in this sentence. The phrase "in the Olympics" tells where Joe will be running; therefore, it is a prepositional phrase, used as an adverb to modify the verb phrase *will be running*.

4. There is only one action word (knows); there is no word of being. The question is: Who or what knows? Because of the construction, the answer would have to be *who*, which cannot be correct. *Who* is not the main actor; *man* is. Therefore, this is not a sentence; it must be redrafted. Either of the following constructions solves the problem:

   a. *The man knows too much.* Striking the word *who* eliminates the construction problem.

   b. *The man who knows too much will make a poor juror.* In this sentence, the predicate is *will make*. Who or what will make? The answer is *man*, which is the subject of the sentence. Man will make what or whom? The answer is *juror*, which is the direct object. The word *poor* modifies juror. The phrase *who knows too much* modifies man.

Faulty grammar is nothing more than a failure to observe the rules of sentence construction. Every word of the sentence must have a specific function, and every word must coordinate with the words around it; there can be no words "left over." If the sentence is constructed in this way, correct grammar will follow. The first step, of course, is to identify the basic sentence structure (*see above*). Performing this exercise will eliminate many of the grammar problems that plague applicants on the CLA/CP® examination. Once the basic sentence structure has been identified, the rules of correct grammar become easier to apply.

The Verb

Because the verb is the focal point of every sentence, it seems appropriate to begin the grammar review with the verb. A verb can be either a word indicating action *(see, do, run, read, walk)* or a word of being *(am, is, are, was, were)*. The verb is the heart of the sentence. It sets the tone of the sentence by its voice (active or passive); by its mood (indicative, imperative, subjunctive); and by its tense (present, present perfect, past, past perfect, future, future perfect).

The applicant must be able to recognize when any of these verb characteristics is used incorrectly within the context of a particular sentence and must be able to use verbs correctly in all essay answers.

<u>**Active or Passive Voice**</u>   If the subject of the sentence performs the action of the sentence, that is, directs the action toward an object, the active voice of the verb is used.

> Jane summarized the depositions.
> The jury deliberated for many hours.
> Dick mailed the notices of hearing to all parties.
>
> *Jane, the jury, and Dick performed the action indicated by their respective verbs.*

If, on the other hand, the subject of the sentence is acted upon, the passive voice of the verb is used.

> The depositions were summarized by Jane.
> The verdict was deliberated for many hours by the jury.
> The notices of hearing were mailed to all parties by Dick.

> *The depositions, the verdict, and the notices received the action indicated by the respective verbs.*

Nearly all authorities agree that the active voice is preferred over the passive voice. The active voice is the stronger, more interesting, and more persuasive of the two. Use the passive voice when the actor is unknown or when the intent is to minimize the actor's participation. Government agencies, for instance, tend to use the passive voice when discussing their actions, which leaves the impression that they are not directly responsible. Beyond these limited circumstances, use the active voice in all writing.

> The murder appears to have been committed by an intruder.
> The regulation was adopted by the IRS to prevent fraud by taxpayers.

Mood   A verb's mood indicates the attitude of the writer or of the speaker, as expressed by the verb. The verbal mood can be indicative, imperative, or subjunctive.

The indicative mood states a fact, expresses an opinion, or asks a question.

> The textbook was published in 2008. *(fact)*
> The text is an excellent reference tool. *(opinion)*
> Have you used this text? *(question)*

The imperative mood makes a request, states a command, or gives direction.

> Please call me after you have read the reports. *(request)*
> Review the discovery file right away. *(command)*
> Return all copies to me when you have finished. *(direction)*

The subjunctive mood states a suggestion or a requirement; expresses a desire or wish; or asserts conditions that are improbable, doubtful, or contrary to fact. Notice that the subjunctive mood uses distinctive verb forms.

> Dale should be told of your plans. *(suggestion)*
> Dale must be told of your plans. *(requirement)*

I wish you would tell Dale of your plans. *(desire)*
If I were you *(but I am not you)*, I would tell Dale.
If you had your degree *(but you do not)*, you could apply for the job.
George acted as if he were in charge. *(but he was not in charge)*

BUT

If Max was in Boston all week, he did not receive my letter. *(fact—indicative mood)*

Tense   The tense of the verb shows the time of the action or event. Based upon the time of the action or event, the correct verb tense is shown in the table below.

Table of Verb Tense Forms
Regular Verbs

	Past	**Past Perfect**	**Present**	**Present Perfect**	**Future**	**Future Perfect**
Time	started in the past and finished in the past	started and finished in the past, prior to some other past action	happening now	started in the past and continuing now	will happen in the future	will be finished in the future
Form	add *d* or *ed* to base verb	*had* + past participle	base verb (add *s* to third person singular)	*has* or *have* + past participle	*shall* (first person) or *will* (all others) + base verb	*shall* or *will* + *have* + past participle
Samples	I helped you helped she helped he helped it helped we helped you helped they helped	I had helped you had helped she had helped he had helped it had helped we had helped you had helped they had helped	I help you help he helps she helps it helps we help you help they help	I have helped you have helped she has helped he has helped it has helped we have helped you have helped they have helped	I shall help you will help she will help he will help it will help we shall help you shall help they shall help	I shall have helped you will have helped she will have helped he will have helped it will have helped we shall have helped you will have helped they will have helped

I **helped** Gary with his homework. *(past)*
I **had read** many books by the time I **graduated**. *(both past, one before the other)*
Mother **helps** a great deal when she **visits** me. *(present)*
We **have helped** each other for many years. *(past, continuing now)*
She **will help** me with Gene's graduation party next month. *(future)*
I **shall have helped** many people by the time I leave. *(to be completed in the future)*

Irregular verbs vary their tense forms for present, past, future, and past participle forms. Consult a dictionary for tense formation of irregular verbs. If the verb's tenses are not shown, it is a regular verb and follows the conventions shown in the above table. Some of the more common irregular verbs are shown below, together with their past and past participle forms.

Common Irregular Verbs

Present	Past	Past Participle
am, are, is	was, were	been
become	became	become
begin	began	begun
bring	brought	brought
choose	chose	chosen
come	came	come
do	did	done
get	got	gotten
give	gave	given
go	went	gone
know	knew	known
lay	laid	laid (to put or place)
lie	lay	lain (to rest or recline)
make	made	made
run	ran	run
see	saw	seen
take	took	taken
write	wrote	written

Helping Verbs   Helping verbs *(can, could, did, do, does, has, have, may, might, must, shall, should, will, would)*, sometimes called auxiliary verbs, often combine with verbs to "help" indicate voice or tense. The tense indicated by a helping verb shows whether something was happening (past progressive), had happened (past perfect), had been happening (past perfect progressive), is happening (present progressive), has happened (present perfect), has been happening (present perfect progressive), will have happened (future perfect), or will have been happening (future perfect progressive).

Agreement of Subject and Verb   The subject and verb of the sentence must agree in number. The number of the subject determines the number of the verb (whether singular or plural). A singular subject requires a singular verb, and a plural subject requires a plural verb.

It **is** fascinating to wander through old courthouses.
Old courthouses **are** fascinating.
Bob Gronstal's name **was** mentioned among the acknowledgments.
The Andersons' names **were** included on the guest list.

A verb with more than one subject (compound subject) is almost always plural. The exception is the compound subject, often a cliché, that is considered as a single unit.

Bob and Judy Baker **have** a new granddaughter.
A fool and his money **are** soon parted.
Ian Jones and the woman who jogged across America, Jan Clark, **were** invited.

BUT

Give and take **is** critical to a lasting relationship.
Bread and butter **was** all that I could find to eat.

Use a singular verb when the subject is *anybody, anyone, each, each one, either, everybody, everyone, neither,* or *nobody* or when the subject is qualified by any of these words. ***Hint:*** When the subject of the sentence is *none* (meaning *no one* or *not one*), the verb is singular most of the time.

Anyone who knows melons **knows** that this one is too ripe.
Nobody **is** responsible.
Each one of the applicants **was** prepared for the examination.
Either of the candidates **is** qualified for the job.
None of our children **was** permitted to chew tobacco.
None of the paralegals in our firm **is** ever late.

BUT

None **are** so blind as those who refuse to see.

When the word *all* is used as a subject, a plural verb is almost always required.

All **were** tested but only a few were qualified.
All but one **have** the measles.
All of the funds **were** spent on publicity.

BUT

All of the money **was** spent on publicity.

Plural words that intervene between a singular subject and its verb do not change the singular number of the subject.

Helen Dail, who has chaired many committees and workshops, **believes** this one is her best.

A singular subject remains singular even when other nouns are connected to it by words such as with, as well as, in addition to, except, together, and no less than.

> Her grammar as well as her spelling **was** poor.
> Scott, with all of his fine qualities, **is** not my first choice.
> Our neighbor as well as his cars **irritates** everyone on our block.

When compound subjects are joined by the words *either . . . or, neither . . . nor,* or *not only . . . but also,* the verb must agree in number with the subject closest to it.

> Neither the legal assistants nor their supervisor **was** ready to leave by 5:00 p.m.
> Either the attorney or her legal assistants **are** doing a creditable job.

Some nouns appear to be plural but are often treated as singular; these require a singular verb.

> Gymnastics **is** one sport that I will never master.
> NALA Headquarters **is** located in Tulsa, Oklahoma.
> Communications **causes** problems for most applicants.

BUT

> Calisthenics **are** good for sore muscles.
> My studies **require** more time than I had allotted.
> Communications **were** strained between us.

Group nouns (sometimes called collective nouns) require a singular verb when the members of the group act as one unit but require a plural verb when the members of the group act independently.

> The legal department **is** preparing to move to its new offices.
> The group **is** growing restless.

BUT

> The fish **were** swimming furiously upstream.
> The group **are** writing letters, calling volunteers, and drafting proposals.

The Pronoun

Pronouns cause more difficulty than any other single part of speech. Sometimes the difficulty stems from a simple failure to **keep pronouns logistically close to their antecedents**. This failure creates confusion about the antecedent to which the pronoun refers.

INCORRECT   When *she* arrived at the office, Roger gave the letter to Joan; and Joan gave it to Ms. Wallace, the supervisor. (*Does **she** refer to Joan or to Ms. Wallace?*)

Roger gave the letter to **Joan** when **she** arrived at the office; and Joan gave it to Ms. Wallace, the supervisor.

EITHER MAY
BE CORRECT   Roger gave the letter to Joan; and Joan gave it to **Ms. Wallace**, the supervisor, when **she** arrived at the office.

Person, Number, and Gender   Pronouns and their antecedents—the words to which they refer—must agree in person (whether first, second, or third); in number (whether singular or plural); and in gender (whether masculine, feminine, or neuter). A common fault with **person agreement** of pronouns derives from the incorrect use of the pronoun *we*.

How are *we* feeling today? (*This is incorrect when the speaker means: How are **you** feeling?*)

I think that *we* shall have just a salad, thank you. (*This is incorrect when the speaker means: **I** shall have just a salad. As written, the sentence indicates that two or more people intend to share one salad.*)

INCORRECT   Congress gave *their* approval of the tax increase.
CORRECT   Congress gave **its** approval of the tax increase.

A **pronoun's number** depends upon the singular or plural status of its antecedent, using the same rules stated for agreement of subject and verb (see above). Separate but similar problems arise in **gender agreement** of pronouns with their antecedents. Nevertheless, the same rule applies: Refer to the number and gender of the antecedent to determine the number and gender of the pronoun.

A civilized society resolves **its** disputes in courtrooms.
Civilized societies resolve **their** disputes in courtrooms.
The federation decided to disband **itself**.
The jazz trio planned a special concert in honor of **its** reunion.
BUT
The audience arose from **their** seats to cheer the actors.
The old gang have gone **their** separate ways.

Notice, too, the distinctions in the following examples.

INCORRECT	The National Association of Legal Assistants (NALA) is a leader in the paralegal profession. *Their* work with the American Bar Association has brought many positive changes to the field.

CORRECT	The National Association of Legal Assistants (NALA) is a leader in the legal assistant profession. **Its** work with the American Bar Association has brought many positive changes to the field. *(stressing the organization as a whole rather than its individual members)*

INCORRECT	Everyone in the car feared for *their* lives.

CORRECT	Everyone in the car feared for **his or her** life.

BETTER	All passengers in the car feared for **their** lives.

Pronoun Case   Misuse of **pronoun case** accounts for many errors on examinations. Because of this fact, pronoun case deserves careful attention in the applicant's review process. Pronoun case refers to how the pronoun functions within a sentence (whether subjective [nominative], objective, or possessive). The chart following the examples may be helpful in distinguishing among the three functions of pronouns.

INCORRECT	Come with *I* to the clerk's office.
CORRECT	Come with **me** to the clerk's office. *(used as object)*

INCORRECT	Bill and *me* want you to come with us.
CORRECT	Bill and **I** want you to come with us. *(used as subject)*

INCORRECT	This is *her* speaking.
CORRECT	This is **she** speaking. *(used as subject complement)*

INCORRECT	We can't hear anything above *him* talking.
CORRECT	We can't hear anything above **his** talking. *(used as possessive adjective)*

INCORRECT	I do not want to go with *he*.
CORRECT	I do not want to go with **him**. *(used as object of preposition)*

INCORRECT	*Us* Americans are independent people.
CORRECT	**We** Americans are independent people. *(used with the subject)*

INCORRECT	Give the job to *we* paralegals.
CORRECT	Give the job to **us** paralegals. *(used with object of preposition)*

PRONOUN CASE FORMS

Personal Pronouns	Subjective	Objective	Possessive
(Singular)			
First Person	I	me	my, mine
Second Person	you	you	your, yours
Third Person	he, she, it	him, her, it	his, her, hers, its
(Plural)			
First Person	we	us	our, ours
Second Person	you	you	your, yours
Third Person	they	them	their, theirs
Relative and Interrogative Pronouns			
	who	whom	whose
	whoever	whomever	—
	which that	which that	—

A pronoun must be used according to its case (function) in the sentence. Use the **subjective case** when the pronoun functions as one of the following:

•*Subject of a sentence (independent clause)*

> **He and I** are first cousins.
> **They** ran to the courthouse in pouring rain.

•*Subject of a subordinate clause*

> Welfare laws often ignore the people **who** need their benefits most.
> The plaintiff offered all of the evidence that **he** had.
> Give the deposition project to **whoever** can finish it by tomorrow.

•*Subject of an understood verb*

> You have more tenacity than **they** (have).
> William is not as sophisticated as **she** (is).

•*Subject complement*

> It is **I**.
> Yes, this is **she**.
> The most pleasant guests were **she and he**.

•*Appositive identifying the subject of a sentence*

> Only two lawyers, **she and he**, have been with the firm longer than I.
> They are always together, **she and he**.

Use the **objective case** when the pronoun functions as one of the following:

•*Direct or indirect object of a verb*

> Edgar left with **whom?**
> We don't care **whom** the president selected for the post.

•*Object of a preposition*

> For **whom** shall we ask?
> Most of **us** were too busy to notice.

•*Object of a gerund, infinitive, or participle*

> Why not try singing **them** to sleep? *(gerund)*
> The chairperson tried to shout **her and me** into silence. *(infinitive)*
> Having seen **them**, Jane turned and raced across the street. *(participle)*

•*Appositive identifying the object of a clause or sentence.*

> The Board appointed two chairpersons, **her and him**.

Choosing between the pronouns *we* and *us* continues to perplex many applicants when the pronoun precedes a noun. Simply eliminate the noun and see which pronoun makes more sense. For the rule-minded, *we* is used with a noun subject; *us* is used with a noun object.

We legal assistants want no part of this proposal. *(**We** want no part . . . .)*

Just between **us** CLAs, the preparation was worth the time that it took. *(Just between **us**, the preparation was . . . .)*

The judge told **us** lawyers to try to settle the case. *(The judge told **us** to try . . . .)*

Regardless of what **we** quilters may think, it is not true that the person who dies with the most fabric wins. *(Regardless of what **we** may think, ...)*

A gerund usually is preceded by the **possessive case** of the noun or pronoun that modifies it.

> The **judge's** singing startled all of us.
> The judge disapproved of **our** singing with him.
> **Their** singing was louder than ours.
> **My** singing was the best of all.

Relative and Interrogative Pronouns

Relative and interrogative pronouns are sources of difficulty in both objective and essay questions. **Relative pronouns** (see chart above) are used to **relate** a subordinate clause to the main clause of the sentence. **Interrogative pronouns** are used to **ask questions** (interrogate).

(Interrogative: singular)
Who shall I say is calling? (I shall say **she** is calling.)
To **whom** is the letter addressed? (The letter is addressed to **her**.)

(Interrogative: plural)
Who were the three bullfighters? (**They** were the three bullfighters.)
To **whom** are the letters addressed? (The letters are addressed to **them**.)

(Relative: singular)
Lee was the one **who** read the novel. (**She** read the novel.)
Terry, **whom** I know well, does good work. (I know **her**.)

(Relative: plural)
Lee and Ann were the ones **who** read the novel. (**They** read the novel.)
Terry and Jo, **whom** I know well, do good work. (I know **them**.)

To tell whether to use the subjective case (who, whoever) or the objective case (whom, whomever), simply rephrase the sentence, substituting the pronouns *she* and *her* (*they* and *them* for plurals) to see which one makes more sense. If the pronoun *she* makes more sense, then use *who* or *whoever*; if the pronoun *her* makes more sense, then use *whom* or *whomever*.

> **Who is the president-elect?** *(**She** is the president-elect.)*
> Cora is the one **who** we think will do the job. *(We think Cora [**she**] will do the job.)*
> She is the one **whom** we should elect. *(We should elect **her**.)*
> Sarah is the one **who** everyone says will win. *(**She** will win.)*
> Berniece is the one **whom** we respect. *(We respect **her**.)*
> **Whoever** arrives first will get the job. *(**She** arrives first.)*
> You may call upon **whomever** to assist you. *(You may call upon **them**.)*
> Please give this to **whomever**. *(Please give this to **her**.)*

BUT

> Please give this to **whoever** is in charge.

> *Here, the subjective case (whoever) must be used even though it is the object of the preposition "to." This is because the entire clause "whoever is in charge" is the object of the preposition, with "whoever" used as the subject of that clause.*

When *than* and *as* are used to make comparisons, the clauses they introduce are sometimes incomplete. The subject and verb are understood in this type of sentence construction. In the first sentence below, the meaning is clear: Alice likes cola better than (she likes) coffee. The second sentence, however, can have one of two meanings.

> Alice likes cola better than coffee.
> Jack likes Jill more than Arthur.

As written, the second sentence may mean that Jack likes Jill more than (he likes) Arthur. It also may mean that Jack likes Jill more than Arthur (likes Jill). When a pronoun is used in place of a noun, a specific meaning attaches to the pronoun, depending upon whether it is stated in the subjective case or in the objective case. Applicants must be familiar with the meaning implicit in using one case or the other; otherwise, the meaning intended may not be the same as the meaning conveyed.

> Jack likes Jill more than **she**. *(more than she likes Jill)*
> Jack likes Jill more than **her**. *(more than Jack likes her)*
>
> Alice admires Doris more than **we**. *(more than we admire Doris)*
> Alice admires Doris more than **us**. *(more than Alice admires us)*
>
> Andrew cares for ice cream as much as **I**. *(as much as I care for ice cream)*
> Andrew cares for ice cream as much as **me**. *(as much as Andrew cares for me)*

One way to eliminate the entire issue, at least for essay questions, is to state specifically what is meant. Do not omit words to be understood; instead, write all of the words that are needed to avoid misunderstanding.

> Alice admires Doris more than we do.
> Andrew cares for ice cream more than he cares for me.

The relative pronouns *who, which,* and *that* cause problems for nearly everyone. Even seasoned grammarians have to think about which one is proper in certain situations. Because each of these relative pronouns connects (relates) a subordinate clause to the main sentence, many writers solve the dilemma by using this simplified, general formula:

who *for all clauses related to people, whether restrictive or nonrestrictive*

which *for all nonrestrictive clauses related to non-people*

that *for all restrictive clauses related to non-people*

> The man **who** helped us with directions was kind. *(restrictive)*
> Connie's mother, **who** sat next to you, is a physicist. *(nonrestrictive)*
> The art book, **which** I cannot find, belongs to Dr. McHenry. *(nonrestrictive)*
> The book **that** I borrowed from Dr. McHenry has been misplaced. *(restrictive)*

This formula works for essay answers, where applicants may select the pronouns that they will use. It even may work for some of the objective questions, but it is not sufficiently precise to work for all of them. The precise rule is:

who *for clauses related to an individual or group of individuals, whether restrictive or nonrestrictive*

which *for clauses related to places, objects, and animals, whether restrictive or nonrestrictive, and to introduce a nonrestrictive clause*

that *for clauses related to a class, species, or type of person or group; for clauses related to objects or animals; or to introduce a restrictive clause*

The Gerund

A gerund is a verb form ending in **-ing** that functions as a noun. Gerunds may be used as subjects or as objects within the sentence structure.

> **Playing** the harmonica is Richard's favorite pastime. *(subject)*
> Ann went to the laundromat to do her **washing**. *(object of infinitive "to do")*
> The mayor disapproved of **picketing** after sunset. *(object of preposition)*

Do not confuse gerunds and present participles, both of which have the **-ing** ending. The gerund functions as either a subject or an object, while the present participle functions as an adjective. (*See the section on participles below*.)

> Your **snoring** was too loud to ignore. *(gerund)*
> The entire congregation heard you **snoring**. *(participle)*
> **Teaching** is demanding work. *(gerund)*
> Joy hopes to earn a **teaching** degree. *(participle)*

The Infinitive

An infinitive is formed when a verb (usually first person singular) is preceded by the word *to*. Infinitives may function as nouns, adjectives, or adverbs.

> Martin loves **to shop**. *(used as a noun, the object of this sentence)*
> Richard is a sight **to see**. *(used as an adjective, modifying "sight")*
> Canoeing is difficult **to do**. *(used as an adverb, modifying the adjective "difficult")*

Avoid "split infinitives" (an adverb inserted between *to* and the verb). For clarity, the adverb should be placed either before or after the infinitive.

INCORRECT   We need *to* carefully *proofread* the brief.
CORRECT   We need **to proofread** the brief carefully.

The **tense** of the infinitive is determined by the tense of the verb in the predicate. The **present infinitive** indicates action at the same time as or later than that of the verb.

> I hope **to see** you soon. *(seeing will occur after the hope)*
> I would have liked **to meet** you long ago. *(liking and meeting at the same past time)*

The (past) **perfect infinitive** indicates action earlier than that of the verb and is formed by combining the words *to have* with the past participle of the verb.

> I would like **to have attended** Harvard. *(attended occurs before like)*
> We believe the vote **to have been** secret. *(vote occurs before belief)*

Modifiers

A modifier is a word or group of words used to explain, limit, or qualify the meaning of another word or group of words. Modifiers include adjectives and adverbs as well as those words, phrases, and clauses that function as adjectives or adverbs.

<u>**Adjectives**</u>   Adjectives are words that describe or modify nouns or pronouns. Adjectives answer the question: Which?, what kind of?, or how many? within the sentence structure.

> The **downtown** office handles all of the computer equipment. *(which office)*
> **Loose** screws will ruin a car. *(what kind of screws)*
> **All** students hope to earn an A in the course. *(how many students)*

A group of words—a phrase or a subordinate clause—may function as an adjective within the sentence.

> The man **in the yellow cap** came toward us. *(adjective phrase modifying man)*
> Applicants **who plan for success** will have it. *(adjective clause modifying applicants)*

<u>**Adverbs**</u>   Adverbs are words that describe or modify verbs, adjectives, other adverbs, or groups of words that function as verbs, adjectives, or adverbs. Adverbs answer the question: How?, when?, where?, to what extent?, or how often? within the sentence structure. Adverbs often (but not always) end with the letters *ly*.

> The test was **extremely** long. *(how)*
> Maurice will be here **tomorrow**. *(when)*
> Please put the book **here**. *(where)*
> I **nearly** lost my watch. *(to what extent)*
> Ron **frequently** drives to Las Vegas. *(how often)*

A group of words—a phrase or a subordinate clause—may function as an adverb within the sentence.

> **At dawn** the city comes to life. *(adverb phrase)*
> The seminar was not as successful **as we had hoped**. *(adverb clause)*

<u>**Adjectives and Adverbs for Comparison**</u>   Adjectives and adverbs can be used to compare one person or thing to other people or things. The **comparative degree** is used to compare two people or things; the **superlative degree** is used to make comparisons among three or more people or things.

Who is **older**, Brit Hume or Juan Williams? *(comparative)*
Garnets are **less** expensive than rubies. *(comparative)*
The laser printer is **more** expensive than the ink jet. *(comparative)*

Who is the **oldest** living reporter? *(superlative)*
Crystals are the **least** expensive of all gemstones. *(superlative)*
The laser is the **most** expensive printer. *(superlative)*

Participles   Every verb has two participle forms: present and past. The **present participle** is formed by adding *-ing* to the present tense verb form (working, helping, knowing). The **past participle** is formed by adding -d or -ed to the present tense of regular verbs (worked, helped). Irregular verbs use their own past participle form (known). Both present and past participles function as adjectives to modify nouns and pronouns.

Working mothers are busy people. *(present participle, modifies mothers)*
Everyone needs a **helping** hand. *(present participle, modifies hand)*
Karen gave us a **knowing** smile. *(present participle, modifies smile)*

Having **worked** hard, Jill was promoted first. *(past participle, modifies hard)*
Ben's story is **helped** by his sincerity. *(past participle, modifies story)*
Known to be fair, Robert will make a good judge. *(past participle, modifies Robert)*

Nouns and Pronouns   Nouns can function as modifiers of other nouns in limited circumstances. Pronouns frequently are used as adjectives to modify nouns.

office building   **sweat** shop   **slave** labor

Her scores were higher than **his** scores.
This paper has many errors.

Misplaced Modifiers   A misplaced modifier is one that seems to modify the wrong part of the sentence or that creates confusion about which part of the sentence it modifies. Misplaced modifiers can produce humorous results on occasion; more times than not, however, they are simply awkward and confusing. Nearly all problems with misplaced modifiers can be eliminated by following the rule stated at the beginning of the grammar section: diagram the sentence to determine its basic structure. Then keep related words and word groups together.

INCORRECT   He barely died a month ago. *(Is he barely dead as a result?)*
CORRECT   He died barely a month ago.

| INCORRECT | Adam served drinks to his guests in glasses. *(Those not wearing glasses went thirsty?)* |
| CORRECT | Adam served drinks in glasses to his guests. |

| INCORRECT | I knew that a crime had been committed by the smell of marijuana. *(Did the smell commit a crime?)* |
| CORRECT | I knew by the smell of marijuana that a crime had been committed. |

When a participial phrase is placed at the beginning of a sentence, it must refer to the grammatical subject of the sentence. In fact, this rule applies to most introductory phrases.

> Speeding down the street, we noticed two men in a red car.
> In need of body work, Joe bought a car for a good price.
> Just having had kittens, I was unable to coax Tabby from under the bed.

As written, the first sentence above indicates that *we* were speeding down the street. If the writer intends to say that the men were speeding down the street, the sentence must be rewritten. In the second sentence, it seems likely that the car needed body work—not Joe; the sentence must be rewritten. In the third sentence, surely it was Tabby who had kittens and not the writer; it, too, must be rewritten.

> We noticed two men speeding down the street in a red car.
> Joe bought a car in need of body work for a good price.
> I was unable to coax Tabby, just having had kittens, from under the bed.

By keeping the basic parts of a sentence close to their modifiers, the vast majority of misplaced modifier problems can be avoided.

Dangling Modifiers   A dangling modifier is a misplaced modifier carried to its ultimate extreme; a dangling modifier does not modify anything in the sentence. Dangling modifiers often produce ludicrous sentences.

| INCORRECT | Uncertain of what to do next, the doorbell rang. |
| CORRECT | Sam was uncertain of what to do next when the doorbell rang. |

| INCORRECT | While in grammar school, my mother earned a college degree. |
| CORRECT | While I was in grammar school, my mother earned a college degree. |

| INCORRECT | At three years of age, both of Bill's parents died. |
| CORRECT | When Bill was three years old, both of his parents died. |

To locate dangling modifiers, verify that the modifier describes the subject of the sentence. If it does not, it may be a dangling modifier. To avoid dangling modifiers, either rewrite the modifier and give it a subject of its own or change the sentence so that the modifier describes the right subject.

Conjunctions

A conjunction is a word that connects words, phrases, and clauses to form a cohesive sentence. Conjunctions may be coordinate, correlative, or subordinate. Applicants must be able to use conjunctions appropriately and to recognize their incorrect use within a given sentence.

Coordinate Conjunctions   A coordinate conjunction is one that connects words or groups of words that have equal grammatical value or rank. For instance, a coordinate conjunction may connect two nouns or may connect two independent clauses. The words *and, but, or, nor,* and *yet* are examples of coordinate conjunctions.

The conjunction *and* is used to connect words or groups of words to be given equal emphasis or to be considered as a single unit. The conjunctions *but* and *yet*, on the other hand, indicate contrast between two words or between two units. The conjunctions *or* and *nor* indicate that the connected words or groups of words should be considered individually, sometimes as a choice between the two. Use care to select the appropriate conjunction within the context of a particular sentence.

> It was the land of milk **and** honey.
> I had always longed to see it, **and** I am glad that we came.
> It has been a wonderful trip, **but** it's time to go home.
> Shall we travel by plane **or** by car?

Correlative Conjunctions   Correlative conjunctions are pairs of words used to connect words or word groups of equal grammatical rank. The most common correlative conjunctions are *either . . . or, neither . . . nor,* and *not only . . . but also.*

> I had hoped that **either** my parents **or** my sister would offer to house-sit.
> **Neither** my father **nor** my mother took the hint, however.
> Hiring a professional will be **not only** expensive, **but also** inconvenient.

Subordinate Conjunctions A subordinate conjunction is a word used to connect a subordinate word or group of words to the main sentence. Examples of subordinate conjunctions include the words *after, although, as, because, if, though, when, whether,* and *while.* Subordinate conjunctions occasionally may be combined *(as if, as though)*, but this should be done sparingly.

> I plan to return to work **after** I finish my dinner.
> It must be done, **although** I would prefer to watch television.
> I am working as quickly **as** I can.
> This task is important **because** it is the first step.
> I must hurry **if** I am to finish by Wednesday.
> There are corrections needed, **though** they are small.
> I hope to take a vacation **when** this project is finished.
> First, I need to see **whether** I can afford a vacation.
> Someone must care for our dog **while** we are away.
> Our dog acts **as if** he were in charge of our household.

Ambiguous and Misused Conjunctions Most conjunctions indicate specific relationships between the words that they connect. For instance, the conjunction *because* signals that a cause or reason follows it. A few subordinate conjunctions, however, seem to create substantial confusion concerning their proper use. Among these, the words *as, while*, and *like* are the primary offenders.

The subordinate conjunction ***as*** properly may be used to signal either time or comparison relationships to the main sentence.

> We arrived at the theater **as** the movie was beginning. *(time)*
> I am working as quickly **as** I can. *(comparison)*

When ***as*** is used as a conjunction to indicate reason or cause, it may cause confusion. The best solution is to use a more accurate conjunction as the connector.

UNCLEAR *As* I was at the courthouse, I ordered the Smith land records. *(time or reason?)*

CLEAR **Because** I was at the courthouse, I ordered the Smith land records. *(reason)*
CLEAR **When** I was at the courthouse, I ordered the Smith land records. *(time)*

The subordinate conjunction ***while*** may be used to signal either time or concession. Unless this conjunction is used in such a way that its meaning is absolutely clear, choose a more precise conjunction as the connector.

UNCLEAR	*While* we were in trial, we did not see the witness enter. *(time or concession?)*

CLEAR	**When** we were in trial, we did not see the witness enter. *(time)*
CLEAR	**Although** we were in trial, we did not see the witness enter. *(concession)*

CLEAR	**While** I was working, Jim watched every movement that I made. *(time)*
CLEAR	**While** I do not agree with you, I understand your position. *(concession)*

Sometimes the subordinate conjunction **_while_** is used as if it were a coordinate conjunction. Notwithstanding the confusion to the reader, it is simply wrong.

INCORRECT	I want to go to Myrtle Beach, *while* Mary wants to go to San Diego.
CORRECT	I want to go to Myrtle Beach, **but** Mary wants to go to San Diego.

INCORRECT	Jack is studying medicine, *while* Ruth is studying law.
CORRECT	Jack is studying medicine, **and** Ruth is studying law.

Because the word **_like_** is misused so often as a subordinate conjunction, it warrants special mention. This word is a preposition that is generally used to indicate comparison. It should never be used as a subordinate conjunction. The rule is simple: Never use **_like_** to connect a phrase or clause to the main sentence.

INCORRECT	This pie crust tastes *like* it was made from clay.
CORRECT	This pie crust tastes **as if** it were made from clay.
CORRECT	This pie crust tastes **like** clay.
CORRECT	This pie crust tastes **like** unseasoned clay.

INCORRECT	Jammo works *like* a caulking gun should.
CORRECT	Jammo works **as** a caulking gun should.

INCORRECT	It seems *like* I will never finish my work.
CORRECT	It seems **as though** I will never finish my work.

INCORRECT	It looks *like* it could rain any minute.
CORRECT	It looks **as if** it could rain any minute.

Rules of Composition

Once the basic grammar rules have been substantially mastered, composition rules become infinitely easier to understand and to use. Grammar rules deal with selection of the correct words or word groups for sentence construction; composition rules deal with the construction process itself. Using composition rules, the writer may construct sentences, paragraphs, sections, chapters, and entire books. Taken together, grammar rules and composition rules comprise writing style.

Writing is critical to the function of every lawyer and every legal assistant. The professional success enjoyed by these individuals often is tied directly to writing style. Although much has been written about writing style, certain truths or rules emerge consistently.

Rule 1: **Good writers read good writing.** Newspapers seldom fit the bill. Instead, periodically read and re-read the essays of Thoreau and Emerson; the poems of the Brownings and Poe; and the novels of Faulkner, Hemingway, and Mitchner. Aside from their aesthetic value, notice how these writers construct their sentences and paragraphs (or their prose). Diagram a few of them. This periodic exposure will improve writing skills—not by copying, but by unconscious emulation that approaches osmosis.

Rule 2: **Be precise, concise, simple, and clear.** Continually monitor the written product to ensure that these four principles are met. For the most part, writing is a slow process. It requires the writer to edit again and again until the product meets these four requirements. This process can be accelerated somewhat if the writer is willing to seek constructive criticism from more experienced writers. Accept their comments with an open mind and a positive attitude.

Rule 3: **Practice, practice, practice.** The writing done in the work environment is not enough. Keep a daily journal, offer to write articles for publication by associations to which you belong (or practice writing them as if you intend to offer them for publication), practice writing essay answers, and so forth. Write as much as you can, paying attention to grammar and composition rules. As is true of any skill, the effort, discipline, and frequency of practice have a direct bearing upon the ability to perform well.

Rule 4: **The best writing style is no style at all.** In other words, writing style is at its best when the reader doesn't notice it. The style stays in the background, as the foundation and facilitator of the thoughts being conveyed. If writers observe the basic rules of grammar and composition, their styles surface naturally.

A General Approach

Rules of composition are rules of construction, regardless of whether it is a simple sentence, a paragraph, an essay, a brief, or a book that is to be produced. All construction must start with a plan, whether it is a blueprint for building construction or an outline for composition.

An outline for composition is essential to achieve the intended result. The first step, then, is to determine what the result is to be. What is the goal of the finished product? To survey all known positions on the subject? To discuss and analyze known positions, reaching a conclusion as to those that are best or worst? To persuade the reader to adopt a particular conclusion? Fuzzy writing generally is the product of fuzzy thinking at the outline stage. Take the time to develop the specific outline (plan) for the composition by deciding its intended goal and then listing the points that are essential in achieving this result. An outline can be modified if necessary; and it can be modified many times if necessary to reach the intended result.

After the intended result is determined and the outline has been prepared, the composition process can begin. Nearly every composition, regardless of its length, has three essential parts: the **introduction**, the **body**, and the **conclusion**. In a one-paragraph product, these parts are presented in the form of paragraph sentences. If the finished product is to be an essay or a longer work, the introduction, body, and conclusion generally are presented in the form of paragraphs, with transitional sentences used to shift the reader from one paragraph to another.

The Paragraph

The **paragraph is the primary unit** of composition. It may have a transitional sentence at its beginning or at its end or both, but it must be centered around a topic sentence. The **topic sentence** is that sentence which tells the reader what the paragraph's subject is, that is, why this particular paragraph is part of the composition. The topic sentence generally should be placed at the beginning or near the beginning of the paragraph, as a guidepost to tell the reader where the paragraph is headed. While it is possible to place the topic sentence at the end of the paragraph, this requires still greater attention to the remaining composition rules if the effect of its changed position is to be achieved.

Other sentences within the paragraph may amplify, limit, explain, argue, or question the subject raised by the topic sentence. Keep the reader in mind as these sentences are added, to be sure that they form a coherent, cohesive paragraph unit. If the reader must stop to wonder how a particular sentence (or a particular word) fits into the paragraph, the writer's objective is destroyed; and the paragraph should be revised. There are specific methods and techniques used by writers to ensure sound paragraph construction. The result of following these rules is strong, forceful writing that is a pleasure to read. This is, after all, the ultimate goal of every writer. The most common of these techniques and rules are discussed in the sections that follow.

Forceful Writing

Forceful writing combines the rules of grammar and composition in the sound construction of sentences and paragraphs. In this sense, forceful writing does not mean argumentative writing, though a particular composition may be argumentative by design. It means writing that is **unified, cohesive, clear, and concise**. It means writing that **flows smoothly**, with no stumbling blocks to distract the reader's attention from the thought being conveyed.

<u>**Use Verbs**</u>   Writing that uses active verbs is always more forceful and more interesting to read. Compare the following examples.

made a decision	decided
is binding upon	binds
have knowledge of	know
make a payment	pay

<u>**Split Verbs**</u>   Splitting verb phrases (verbs and their helping words) interrupts the flow of the sentence and should be avoided. Similarly, avoid splitting subjects and their verbs with clauses and phrases that can be placed elsewhere.

POOR
:   The *plaintiff had*, at great expense to himself, *amassed* volumes of reference materials.

BETTER
:   At great expense to himself, the **plaintiff had amassed** volumes of reference materials.

POOR
:   The *lawyers*, who were preparing for trial, *had*, by working through the night, *completed* the trial brief.

BETTER
:   In preparing for trial, the **lawyers had completed** the trial brief by working through the night.

BETTER
:   The **lawyers worked** through the night to complete the trial brief.

Refer to the grammar rules concerning misplaced and dangling modifiers. Acquire the habit of keeping related words and word groups together and placing modifiers as close as possible to the words they modify.

Active Voice   As a general rule, use the active voice, rather than the passive voice. Recall that there are some justifiable exceptions to this rule (see prior discussion of active-passive voice in the Grammar section).

POOR   A more favorable climate *was hoped* to be created with the new rules.
BETTER   The agency **hoped** to create a more favorable climate with the new rules.

POOR   The question that *is proposed to be discussed* is compensation.
BETTER   We **shall discuss** compensation.

POOR   The decision *was attempted* to be appealed to a higher court.
BETTER   The plaintiff **tried** to appeal the decision to a higher court.

Positive Statements   State facts, propositions, and the like in a positive way rather than in a negative way.

did not remember	forgot
did not give consideration to	ignored
not important	trivial, minor
not very often	seldom

POOR   This provision *does not apply* to owners who do not live on their land.
BETTER   This provision **applies** only to owners who live on their land.

When writing about conduct of an opposing party, however, it may be more effective to say, for example, "the defendant did not remember" than to say simply "the defendant forgot." In this context, the writer may intend to cast the conduct in a negative light.

Parallel Construction   Construct similar parts of a sentence in a similar way, so that they parallel each other. This signals the reader that they belong together in thought. Use parallel construction when items are part of a series or a group to be considered as one, when items are compared or contrasted with each other, and when items are arranged in a list. When listing a series, such as in the first example below, place the most important word at the end for emphasis.

POOR   The defendant was convicted of robbery, murdering his victim, and rape.
BETTER   The defendant was convicted of robbery, murder, and rape.
BETTER   The defendant was convicted of robbery, rape, and murder.

POOR   American workers are disturbed about their prospects and economic plight.

BETTER   American workers are disturbed <u>about their prospects</u> and <u>about their economic plight.</u>

POOR   Not only does the act violate the commerce clause but also the due process clause.

BETTER   The act violates not only the commerce clause but also the due process clause.

BETTER   The act not only violates the commerce clause; it also violates the due process clause.

POOR   Legal assistants are capable of interviewing clients, performing research, and can implement discovery plans.

BETTER   Legal assistants are capable of interviewing clients, of performing research, and of implementing discovery plans.

In the same vein, cohesiveness of the paragraph is damaged by inappropriate shifts in person, number, and tense within the same sentence or from one sentence to another in the paragraph. Although a shift may be required because of meaning, it should be done judiciously and in a way that is consistent with the rest of the structure.

POOR   *This is a relatively new profession; they who enter it are blazing a trail for the ones who follow them. They must possess an insatiable curiosity, and you must have an eye for detail. The person who will be a good legal assistant could also be a good lawyer.*

BETTER   The legal assistant profession is relatively new; those who enter it are the trail blazers for all who follow. Legal assistants must have an insatiable curiosity and an eye for detail. Those who are good legal assistants possess the qualities to be good lawyers as well.

POOR   *Law is not the field for everyone. It requires agility and patience at the same time. You must be able to speak in public and think of answers on their feet in all kinds of settings. They must be tenacious but patient, for the wheels of the legal system can be slow yet exasperating.*

BETTER   Law is not for everyone. It requires both agility and patience. Its members must be able to speak in public and to think on their feet in all kinds of settings. They must be both tenacious and patient, for the wheels of the legal system can be both exasperating and slow.

<u>Precision</u>   Precision in writing means **choosing the right word or expression** to convey the thought intended. Mark Twain once said that the difference between the right word and the almost right word is the difference between lightning and the lightning bug.

Because legal writing is exposed to the scrutiny of opposing counsel and others so often, imprecise or ambiguous language can spring like a trap upon the unwary. Lawyers and legal assistants, more than others, must be able to say exactly what they mean. Their vocabularies must be extensive to select the precisely correct word from among all those words that could be used. The dictionary and the thesaurus are as much staples to them as statute books are. Though both words in the following sentence mean approximately the same thing, notice the different impressions that they convey.

> Law *requires* both agility and patience.
> Law *demands* both agility and patience.

The first rule of precision is: ***Never use a word unless you know exactly what it means***. When in doubt, look it up. If a dictionary is unavailable (such as during examinations), don't use the questioned word. Select another one instead or the results could be disastrous. For instance, this phrase appeared in one student's factual summary: *the fence circumventing the premises* . . . No instructor would be favorably impressed. Notice the precision problems in the following sentences as well.

INCORRECT	Traffic laws should be one *aura* of certainty from state to state.
CORRECT	Traffic laws should be one **area** of certainty from state to state.

INCORRECT	Your testimony is critical; without it, our case is extremely *tenable*.
CORRECT	Your testimony is critical; without it, our case is extremely **tenuous**.

The next rule of precision is: ***It's okay to repeat the right word once you have found it***. It gives continuity to the writing. Trying to find a new word for the sake of variety can produce unintended results, such as this statement from a news article.

> Two of the Democratic candidates are women; all of the Republican candidates are ladies.
> *(Does this mean the Democrats are not ladies?)*

Switching to a different word in legal writing creates the presumption that a different meaning is intended for each of the two words—a dangerous practice in legal documents. This is the stuff that lawsuits are made of.

When writing is precise, it generally is clear. Take the time to ensure that the writing says precisely what was intended. This means reading each sentence critically, trying to find words or expressions that may be misunderstood by others. If it can be misunderstood, rest assured that it will be. Redraft as many times as are necessary to remove all ambiguity. (*See section on misplaced modifiers.*)

> The deceased consented to surgery. *(How could a corpse consent to anything?)*

> The defendant stabbed the deceased when he thought he was about to shoot him. *(Does this mean the defendant stabbed a corpse in self-defense? Or does it mean that the defendant decided that it was better to stab the corpse than to shoot it?)*

> The game warden filed a complaint, alleging illegal hunting in the Wade County Court. *(Does this mean that some hunting is legal at the courthouse?)*

> Millions of children do not go to school in South America. *(Certainly, that includes all of the children who do not live there.)*

> We arranged a meeting for small business people. *(Does this mean short business people or people who own small businesses?)*

Weasel Words   For all that has been said about precision in writing, legal writing sometimes must be seasoned lightly with ambiguity for the sake of accuracy. This is done with weasel words.

According to Hurd, *Writing for Lawyers* (1982), weasel words allow the writer to "weasel out" of a hard-line statement by using terms like *appears, would appear to be, could reasonably be viewed as, could argue that, may be that,* and so forth. Legal writing, unlike other writing, sometimes requires qualifiers like these because the law itself is packed with qualifiers. We may argue that a rule should be interpreted this way or that, but we know that law is inherently imprecise. No one can predict results with 100 percent accuracy, so we qualify some of what we say with weasel words.

Used in moderation, weasel words perform a necessary function in legal writing. They allow lawyers to take a defensive position without appearing to be defensive. They keep options open so that a position can be altered if the character of a case changes midstream. They provide maneuvering room when absolutes would have to be filled with exceptions or when accurate generalizations would be too vague to be helpful. Weasel words have their place; the trick is to keep them in it.

Simplicity   The best writing is simple writing. **Never use a long word when a short one will do**. Never use a convoluted expression when a direct one says the same thing. Simple writing does not equate to simple ideas. Nor does it require the writer to patronize, as if the reader were someone of lower intelligence. The reader who finds it difficult to understand complicated legal jargon and 10-syllable words is not necessarily moronic. Most people can grasp even complex concepts if they are explained in simple English. If a writer does not understand an idea well enough to explain it in simple English, the writer does not understand it well enough.

The following passage, delivered by Franklin D. Roosevelt, is written in simple English. No word contains more than three syllables. Notice the parallelism, repetition, and rhythm of words. Other examples could be given, but this one says it all.

> I have seen war. I have seen war on land and sea. I have seen blood running from the wounded. I have seen men coughing out their gassed lungs. I have seen the dead in the mud. I have seen cities destroyed. I have seen two hundred limping, exhausted men come out of line—the survivors of a regiment of one thousand that went forward forty-eight hours before. I have seen children starving. I have seen the agony of mothers and wives. I hate war.

A Writer's Eye   Everyone who creates must acquire an eye for the aesthetic presentation of the final product. Actors use props and a stage, for instance. Artists use color and texture. No less than these, writers must have an eye for presentation. The final product must *look* interesting to read, first of all. Vary the length of paragraphs; occasionally use a single-sentence paragraph to make an important point; and never, ever create a paragraph longer than half a page. If the layout of the page looks interesting, readers will be more eager to read it.

Make the paragraphs themselves more interesting by varying length of sentences to pique the reader's interest and to maintain the reader's attention. Vary the structure, so that some sentences begin with transitional expressions and others do not. Occasionally, invert the order of subject, verb, and object to make important ideas stand out, but never at the cost of rules of grammar and composition.

Concise Writing

Special emphasis is given to concise writing on the CLA/CP® examination, perhaps because those connected with the law are prone to the disease of verbosity. The cure: **Never use two words when one word will do.** Brevity is the key.

Unnecessary words water down the necessary words. They clutter sentences and obscure ideas. The most important rules of composition are: Omit needless words; then omit more needless words.

After the first draft has been written, go back and do precisely that: omit needless words. Eliminate empty words and expressions such as these:

all things considered	—
as far as I am concerned	—
at the present time	now
at this point in time	now
by means of	by
by virtue of the fact that	because
due to the fact that	because
for all intents and purposes	—
for the purpose of	for
for the reason that	because
in my opinion	—
in the event that	if
in the nature of	like
until such time as	until

POOR   In my opinion, due to the fact that ongoing discrimination continues to exist in the field of law, women have not yet reached equality with men.

BETTER   Because of continuing discrimination in law, women have not yet reached equality with men.

POOR   I came to this college because of many factors, but most of all because of the fact that I want to be a paralegal.

BETTER   I came to this college mainly because I want to be a paralegal.

Redundant Words   In the editing process, check for redundant words and phrases. They add nothing to the meaning of the sentence, and they weaken the words that are important. Eliminate them.

basic essentials
circle *around*
consensus *of opinion*

continue *to remain*
cooperate *together*
definite decisions
few *in number*
final completion
frank *and honest* discussion
invisible *to the eye*
most unique
repeat *again*
return *again*
revert *back*
square *in shape*
surrounding circumstances
terribly important
true and correct
true facts
unexpected surprise
usual habits

POOR	He successfully resisted the temptation to have dessert.
BETTER	He resisted the temptation to have dessert.

POOR	The intention of the parties is found by looking to the contract to determine what was intended.
BETTER	The parties' intent is found in the terms of the contract.

The last rule of composition is to redraft as many times as are necessary. The ideal is to wait a day or two before editing. No one writes so well that he or she cannot find ways to write better. When we read our own writing critically, we usually can find ways to improve it. Perhaps the structure of a particular sentence needs to be changed. Perhaps there is a better word that could be used. Perhaps there is a more concise way to express an idea.

History tells us that Plato redrafted the first paragraph of *The Republic* about 12 times before he was satisfied with it. The Founding Fathers spent the better part of a summer redrafting the Constitution before they were satisfied with it. If those documents had to be rewritten again and again, surely ours could benefit from redrafting as well.

Vocabulary

Because writing is such a vital part of a legal assistant's job, every CLA/CP is expected to have a strong vocabulary at his or her command. The best way to acquire vocabulary skills (plus the type of broad, general knowledge that every successful legal assistant must have) is to read—frequently and with an inquisitive mind. Read everything that you can find: newspapers, magazines, novels, and poems by good authors, or legal opinions. If a word is unfamiliar, look it up in a dictionary right away. Write the meaning on paper or on a card and then draft a sentence or two of your own, using the new word. Dictionaries often include sample phrases that use the defined word. These will get you started. Look for ways to incorporate the new word into your spoken and written vocabulary. This helps to cement it into your mind.

An extensive vocabulary is acquired over a long period of time. There are no tricks to make the process easier or shorter. When you look up a word in the dictionary, notice its root word and the origin of the root word. More than half of the words in the English language come from Latin or Greek. Try to think of other words from the same root word. Keep your own mini dictionary of the words you look up, noting their root words; and you will see that there is similarity among many of the words we use.

Root Word	Source	Meaning	English Derivatives
aster, astr	Greek	star	astrology, astronomy
audi	Latin	hear	audible, audience
bene	Latin	good, well	benefit, benevolent
bio	Greek	life	biology, biography
cir	Latin	around	circle, circumference
dict	Latin	speak	dictator, dictionary
fer	Latin	carry	refer, transfer
fin	Latin	end	finale, finite
fix	Latin	fasten	fix, prefix, suffix
geo	Greek	earth	geology, geography
graph	Greek	write	autograph, photograph
jur, jus	Latin	law	jury, justice
litera	Latin	letter	illiterate, literal
log, logue	Greek	word, speech	biology, catalog
luc	Latin	light	lucid, translucent
manu	Latin	hand	manual, manuscript
meter, metre	Greek	measure	barometer, metric
op, oper	Latin	work	operate, optimum
path	Greek	feeling	pathetic, sympathy
ped	Greek	child	pediatrics, pedophile
phil	Greek	love	philosophy, philander
phys	Greek	body, nature	physics, physician
scrib, script	Latin	write	scribble, transcript
tele	Greek	far off	telegraph, television
ter, terr	Latin	earth	terra cotta, territory

vac	Latin	empty	vacant, vacuum
verb	Latin	word	verbiage, verbose
vid, vis	Latin	to see	video, vision

See how many other root words and examples of English derivatives you can add to this list.

When you encounter a new word, whether on an examination or in your reading, try to guess its meaning by the context within which it is used. Sometimes the other words in the sentence will give clues about its meaning. Then look it up in the dictionary to see if you are correct. (This won't work on examinations, of course, until after the fact.) The study of words, their variations of form, and their uses can be fascinating, especially for those who work with words as much as paralegals do.

> The *audiogram* showed that Bill could benefit from a hearing aid.
> Rejecting a *vacuous* lifestyle, the rich widow devoted herself to helping others.
> Jack does not own any *mundane* ties, preferring bright colors and unusual patterns.

The following list provides examples of the type of words included on the exam but is not intended to be all-inclusive. Neither does it imply that any of the words on the list will be on the exam. It should be used as a starting point from which to build a more complete list.

aberrant	- deviant, abnormal	catharsis	- purging, venting
abrogate	- annul, revoke	cerulean	- as blue as the sky
abysmal	- endless, immense	convivial	- festive, merry
accretion	- addition, expansion	copious	- voluminous, abundant
acolyte	- admirer, fan	denigrate	- defame, slander
acrimonious	- caustic, sarcastic	deprecate	- condemn, criticize
adroit	- skillful, clever	desecrate	- dishonor, contaminate
aeon	- infinitely long time	desuetude	- period of disuse
allegory	- symbolic story, parable	diffident	- reserved, insecure
amulet	- charm, ornament	dilatory	- causing delay
aperture	- opening, hole	doltish	- moronic
arcane	- esoteric, obscure	draconian	- cruel, harsh
assay	- analyze	ebullient	- effervescent, sparkling
aver	- allege, claim	edifice	- building, structure
baleful	- evil, sinister	efface	- annul, erase
banal	- ordinary, trite	eleemosynary	- charitable
berceuse	- lullaby, tranquil music	empirical	- pragmatic
capacious	- spacious, vast	encomium	- praise, tribute
capricious	- flighty, impulsive	enervate	- to tire, to debilitate
cataclysm	- catastrophe	epicurean	- connoisseur, gourmet

epithet	- a disparaging term	panoply	- ceremonial array
erudite	- learned, scholarly	paradox	- contradiction
esoteric	- confidential, obscure	pejorative	- belittle, make worse
exacerbate	- worsen, intensify	percipient	- discerning
expiate	- make amends, repent	peremptory	- unchallengeable
expository	- explanatory	perspicuous	- clear
fastuous	- arrogant, ostentatious	perfunctory	- superficial, routine
fatuous	- foolish, silly	pique	- arouse, provoke
ferret (out)	- to hunt (search) for	platitude	- cliché
flagellate	- to punish by whipping	plebeian	- common, crude
fortuitous	- by luck, accidental	plenary	- full, complete
gambol	- cavort, play	pleonastic	- redundant
garrulous	- talkative	precipitous	- headlong, impulsive
halcyon	- golden, happy	proclivity	- inclination
harbinger	- forerunner, herald	profligate	- spendthrift
heterogeneous	- diverse, varied	prognosticate	- predict
iconoclastic	- dissident	propitious	- favorable
ignominious	- degrading, shameful	promulgate	- announce
imbue	- to endow, to infuse	pugnacious	- antagonistic
impugn	- attack	punctilious	- careful, by the rules
indolent	- lazy	rapacious	- fierce, savage
ineffable	- indescribable	raze	- demolish
inertia	- failure to move	rectitude	- righteousness
innocuous	- harmless	refraction	- deflection of light
insipid	- dull, empty	relume	- rekindle
integral	- essential	remittent	- recurring
intrinsic	- inherent	remunerate	- compensate
irascible	- cantankerous, ornery	reparation	- indemnification
lascivious	- lecherous, lustful	replicate	- duplicate
loquacious	- talkative, verbose	requite	- repay
lyceum	- hall for public lectures	reticulation	- network
magnanimous	- generous	rudimentary	- elementary, basic
malapropism	- misuse of a word	riparian	- natural waterway
mendacity	- lies (falsehoods)	rhetoric	- discourse, oratory
mendicant	- a parasite, moocher	ruminate	- ponder, reflect
metamorphosis	- transformation	salubrious	- promoting health
metaphor	- symbol	sardonic	- mocking, sarcastic
morass	- quagmire	sedulous	- diligent
myopic	- lacking foresight	senescent	- aging, becoming old
neolithic	- outmoded	servile	- subservient
nemesis	- downfall, ruin	similitude	- counterpart
nescience	- ignorance	stellar	- star-like, outstanding
nettle	- irritate	temerity	- audacity
numinous	- mysterious, spiritual	tenacious	- persistent, dogged
obdurate	- stubborn	tenets	- principles
officious	- nosey, obtrusive	timorous	- mousy
omniscient	- all-knowing	umbrage	- shadows, hint
ossify	- to become rigid	vapid	- boring, dull
ostensible	- apparent	veracity	- truthfulness
panacea	- cure-all	vicissitude	- changing fortunes

venal	- mercenary
venerate	- revere
vicinal	- local
vilify	- defame
virulent	- deadly, toxic
visceral	- from deep within
vitiate	- to make faulty, debase
vituperate	- berate
vociferous	- boisterous
volatile	- explosive
voluble	- talkative
voracious	- insatiable

The vocabulary portion of the CLA/CP® examination tests the mettle of the best wordsmiths. Approach it with the knowledge that it is only one small part of a larger communications section and do the best you can.

Correspondence

Correspondence refers to business correspondence in the form of business letters and interoffice memoranda. Legal assistants should be sufficiently familiar with the essential parts of a business letter that they can replicate them, whether in an office setting or on an examination.

Business Letter Styles

The most widely used business letter styles are full block, modified block, and simplified.

Full Block: All lines begin at the left margin. This is the preferred style in most private law firms across the country.

Modified Block with Block Paragraphs: All lines begin at the left margin except the date, complimentary close, and signature lines, all of which begin at the center of the page.

Modified Block with Indented Paragraphs: This style is identical to the modified block, except that the first word of each paragraph within the body of the letter is indented five to ten spaces. Additionally, the subject line may be either centered or indented five to ten spaces to match the paragraphs.

Simplified: All lines begin at the left margin. To *simplify* the keyboarding of this letter: the inside address is keyed in all capital letters; the salutation is omitted and is replaced by a subject line keyed in all caps; the complimentary close is omitted; and the writer's name and title are both keyed in all caps.

Business Letter Punctuation

Two punctuation styles are used in office correspondence:

Mixed Punctuation: This is the most widely used punctuation style. It requires a colon after the salutation and a comma after the complimentary close.

Open Punctuation: No punctuation is used after the salutation or the complimentary close.

Parts of a Business Letter

All business letters have certain basic elements. Other elements may or may not be included, depending upon the letter's requirements.

Required Business Letter Parts:

- Letterhead or return address of the writer
- Date
- Inside address
- Salutation (not used in simplified style)
- Body
- Complimentary close (not used in simplified style)
- Signature block (writer's name)
- Reference initials (writer and typist or typist only)

Optional Letter Parts:

- Mailing or special notations (air mail, confidential)
- Attention line
- Subject line
- Typed firm name
- Title of writer
- Enclosure notation
- Copy notation(s)
- Postscript

Full Block Style with Mixed Punctuation

Bilkum & Billum
123 Park Place
Timbuktu, Anywhere 00000
444-000-0000

July 15, 2013

PERSONAL

Mary Client, M.D.
466 North Forrest Drive
Anytown AN 00000

Re: Client Deposition

Dear Dr. Client:

We have received a notice to take your deposition on Monday, August 31, 2013, at 11:00 a.m. The deposition is scheduled to be taken in Randy Popp's office, which is located in the Second National Bank Building downtown.

Please check your schedule to see if this date and time are convenient for you and then let me know. If you cannot have your deposition taken at that time, please provide me with three alternative dates when you could be deposed. We anticipate that the deposition will take approximately two hours.

Mr. Popp has not requested that you bring anything with you to the deposition, which should make things go much more smoothly. We will need to visit with you prior to the deposition, so that Ms. Bilkum can review the deposition coverage with you. We can arrange that time as well when you call.

I look forward to hearing from you within the next few days.

Sincerely,

Jane Doe, Legal Assistant

JD:mb

When drafting business letters, keep the reader in mind. Be concise. When a letter is longer than one page, the reader's attention diminishes by the time he or she reaches the second page. Avoid legalese as much as possible when writing to clients and to other nonlawyers. In addition, avoid archaic, meaningless expressions that are found too often in the business letters of lawyers and nonlawyers alike.

POOR   Enclosed please find our check in the amount (or in the sum) of $3,000.00.
BETTER   Enclosed is our check for $3,000.00.
BETTER   Our check for $3,000.00 is enclosed.

POOR   Please allow me to hear from you at your earliest convenience.
BETTER   I look forward to hearing from you within the next week.

POOR   Thanking you in advance for your kind consideration in this matter, I remain
BETTER   Thank you.

A letter is written to a specific person and should be written in such a way that it focuses on that person. In a one-on-one conversation, we would not say, for example, "In reply to your letter, . . ."; "we are in receipt of . . ."; or—the worst of all— "This is to acknowledge your letter of recent date, the contents of which have been duly received." That being the case, we should not use such archaic expressions in letters. There are better ways for letters to begin, all of which get directly to the point and focus on the reader.

> The court has scheduled a trial date in your case . . .
> We have received interrogatories from the defendant's attorneys . . .
> The information that came with your letter . . .
> How soon will you be able to . . .
> Please send me . . .
> Please provide me with . . .
> Your concern about . . . is understandable.
> You are correct that . . .
> You will be glad to know that . . .

Use personal, rather than impersonal, language when writing letters, especially letters to clients or to those who are allies in the case.

POOR   A mortgage holder has the right to assign . . .
BETTER   You have the right to assign . . .

POOR   It will be observed from a reading of the first paragraph thereof . . .
BETTER   You will see by reading the first paragraph of the contract . . .

Nonverbal Communication

Nonverbal communication refers to the way in which we communicate, over and above the words we use. It is the image that we portray. Nonverbal communication includes office environment, physical appearance, and body language. A lawyer generally attempts to convey an image of trustworthiness, stability, and conservatism through the office environment, including furnishings and decor. Regardless of how lavish or how Spartan an office may be, however, the nonverbal communication skills of the lawyer and his or her legal assistant are critical to their effectiveness.

Nonverbal communication, sometimes called body language or demeanor, speaks as loudly as our voices. Time and time again, studies show that the things we do and the way in which we do them send messages that are just as powerful as the words we use. In fact, when the message is a negative one, it is more powerful than words. Keep the following points in mind to ensure that your verbal messages are consistent with your nonverbal messages.

- Be courteous. Regardless of the situation, courtesy costs nothing and pays dividends that will come back to you in all kinds of ways throughout your professional career.

- Use a conservative, understated manner of dress and appearance. This sends messages of professionalism, stability, and trustworthiness, which are critical to the work that legal assistants do.

- Crossing the arms sends mixed messages. It may mean that the person is closed to or disapproving of whatever is happening or it may signal a defensive position.

- When seated, crossed legs send mixed messages, neither of which is suitable in the office environment. Practice sitting with the ankles and knees aligned, since this indicates that the person is open or receptive.

- Stand and sit in an erect position; these make a person appear to be alert and interested. Slouching or leaning on objects indicates lack of energy, carelessness, and lack of interest.

- Maintain a reasonable distance between yourself and the person with whom you are speaking. Many people become uncomfortable when their personal space is invaded. Touching is usually taboo as well. Placing a hand on someone's shoulder outside a social setting may signal a superior-inferior relationship between the individuals—a message that the legal assistant does not want to send. Never touch a person with a pointed finger; this is a signal of attempted dominance and is certain to evoke a defensive, retaliatory reaction.

•Be careful of hand gestures. People who "talk with their hands," for instance, can be distracting in a one-on-one situation, so that the hand movements command more attention than the words.

•Maintain good eye contact during conversation. It indicates sincerity and interest. Conversely, no eye contact can indicate subservience or untruthfulness.

•Use facial expressions that indicate a positive attitude, interest, and professional concentration. Never display shock, disbelief, disapproval, or similar, negative expressions that are signaled by excessive frowning, raised brows, pursed lips, and the like.

As a corollary, the way we say things is just as important as what we say. Use correct pronunciation and good diction to ensure that words are clearly understood. Be mindful of voice tone and modulation to provide the right measure of calm reassurance that is so necessary for legal assistants. Voice inflection plays a significant role as well. Use care to ensure that the inflection is one that demonstrates a pleasant or at least a neutral attitude. This requires the ability to "shift into neutral" in stressful situations, so that impatience, disapproval, or other negative attitudes do not become apparent to others during a conversation.

This chapter, together with the self-test given below, should provide a basic review of the communication principles that may be encountered on the CLA/CP® certifying examination. If the applicant is unfamiliar with any of the material covered, he or she is advised to consider close study of a relevant textbook or other study aid. *See the bibliography for additional study references.*

Communications Self-Test

Allow an uninterrupted 30-minute period to answer all questions. At the end of 30 minutes, check your answers against those in the Answer Key Section of this manual. Deduct two points each for each incorrect answer (100 total possible points). Unanswered questions are counted as incorrect answers. Follow directions carefully and observe the time limit precisely to provide an accurate self-assessment.

Choose the more correct word by circling it.

1.   Please (lend) (loan) me a pen to finish the examination.

2.   An association should screen (their) (its) membership applicants.

3.   If Sophie (was) (were) ill, she did not have time to complete the research.

4.   Rosa is (adverse) (averse) to air travel.

5.   Theo felt (bad) (badly) about missing the party.

6.   Invention is (borne) (born) of adversity.

7.   None of the computers (are) (is) working today.

8.   Marcus acts as if he (was) (were) infallible.

9.   We were (nauseated) (nauseous) by the time we left the restaurant.

10.   (Regardless) (Irregardless) of the outcome, you did a superb job.

11.   We can do nothing without (him) (his) knowing about it.

12.   There are (less) (fewer) applicants for scholarships this year than ever before.

13.   A law library (comprises) (constitutes) books and periodicals.

In the following sentences, mark the underlined portions with "C" for Correct or "I" for Incorrect.

14.   Thomas knows that we cannot win unless we work <u>altogether.</u>

15.   When I am in town, I always visit Ami; and she always visits me in Springfield.

16.   <u>Us</u> legal assistants are a hearty breed.

17.   Rod is the one <u>who</u> we selected for the job.

18.   All in the group <u>was</u> prepared for the examination.

19.   <u>Between </u>the three of us, we should be able to think of one good idea.

20.   <u>Mothers-in-law's </u>advice is received poorly by its beneficiaries throughout the world.

21.   It is <u>presently</u> 37° outdoors.

22.   I cannot say that it was a complete fabrication, but it was the worst case of <u>acclaim</u> that I have encountered recently.

23.   I had studied the definition for the word "didactic"<u>,</u> but I could not remember it.

Choose the best answer for each of the following questions.

24.   Neither the teacher nor the children were ready to leave the playground.

    a.   The sentence contains faulty punctuation.
    b.   The sentence contains faulty grammar.
    c.   The sentence is verbose.
    d.   The sentence is correct.

25.   Thank you for your letter of January 7, the contents of which have been duly recorded.

    a.   The sentence contains faulty punctuation.
    b.   The sentence contains faulty grammar.
    c.   The sentence is verbose.
    d.   The sentence is correct.

26.   To _____ success, we must set goals for ourselves.

    a.   ensure
    b.   insure
    c.   either is correct
    d.   neither is correct

27.   I recall my mother sewing every evening after dinner.

    a.   The sentence contains faulty punctuation.
    b.   The sentence contains faulty grammar.
    c.   The sentence is verbose.
    d.   The sentence is correct.

28.   It is difficult to choose _____ the options available to us.

    a.   between
    b.   among
    c.   either is correct
    d.   neither is correct

29.   This file has been _____ on your desk for more than a week.

    a.   laying
    b.   lying
    c.   either is correct
    d.   neither is correct

30.   The examination covered federal and state criminal law; contract, tort, and equitable remedies; and punctuation, grammar, and spelling.

    a.   The sentence contains faulty punctuation.
    b.   The sentence contains faulty grammar.
    c.   The sentence is verbose.
    d.   The sentence is correct.

31.   Cheryl is the one _____ we believe will be elected.

    a.   that
    b.   which
    c.   who
    d.   whom

32.   We must eliminate the _____ that impede us before we can revitalize this organization.

    a.   falsehoods
    b.   principles
    c.   tenets
    d.   paradigms

33.   Either of these could be _____.

    a.   Charleses' paper.
    b.   Charles' paper.
    c.   Charles's paper.
    d.   the paper of Charles.

34.   My knees hurt too bad to play tennis every week.

    a.   The sentence contains faulty punctuation.
    b.   The sentence contains faulty grammar.
    c.   The sentence is verbose.
    d.   The sentence is correct.

35.   As far as I am concerned, Tort Law was the most interesting class that I took due to the fact that it was taught by an experienced personal injury lawyer who had a tremendous sense of humor.

    a.   The sentence contains faulty punctuation.
    b.   The sentence contains faulty grammar.
    c.   The sentence is verbose.
    d.   The sentence is correct.

36.   This painting is the most unique piece of art that I have seen.

    a.   The sentence contains faulty punctuation.
    b.   The sentence contains faulty grammar.
    c.   The sentence is verbose.
    d.   The sentence is correct.

37.   It seems as if we still have so much to do.

    a.   The sentence contains faulty punctuation.
    b.   The sentence contains faulty grammar.
    c.   The sentence is verbose.
    d.   The sentence is correct.

38.   Two legal assistants were appointed to the committee: _____.

    a.   he and I
    b.   him and me
    c.   he and me
    d.   him and I

39.   The consensus of opinion is that grammar, punctuation, and spelling are the basic essentials for a successful legal assistant.

    a.   The sentence contains faulty punctuation.
    b.   The sentence contains faulty grammar.
    c.   The sentence is verbose.
    d.   The sentence is correct.

40.   Once she finished the brief, Ms. Schaffer congratulated Marie; and she passed it on to her legal assistant.

    a.   The sentence contains faulty punctuation.
    b.   The sentence contains faulty grammar.
    c.   The sentence is verbose.
    d.   The sentence is correct.

41.   Stephanie ran quickly across the wet street and jumped clumsily into the rear seat of the moving car.

    a.   The sentence contains faulty punctuation.
    b.   The sentence contains faulty grammar.
    c.   The sentence is verbose.
    d.   The sentence is correct.

42.   To make matters worse, the instructor asked me to recite the first verse of "Desiderata"; and I was unable to recall any of it.

    a.   The sentence contains faulty punctuation.
    b.   The sentence contains faulty grammar.
    c.   The sentence is verbose.
    d.   The sentence is correct.

43.   I wish I was a better writer.

    a.   The sentence contains faulty punctuation.
    b.   The sentence contains faulty grammar.
    c.   The sentence is verbose.
    d.   The sentence is correct.

44. _____ arguments are unlikely to convince a court to modify existing rules.

    a.   Arcane
    b.   Erudite
    c.   Adroit
    d.   Eleemosynary

Match each word in the left column with the most correct definition from the right column.

45. _____ timorous   a.   mousy

46. _____ vicissitude   b.   trite

47. _____ obdurate   c.   demolish

48. _____ banal   d.   audacity

49. _____ temerity   e.   inclination

50. _____ raze   f.   stubborn

                                        g.   preachy

                                        h.   changing fortunes

HUMAN RELATIONS AND INTERVIEWING TECHNIQUES

If you aren't fired with enthusiasm, you will be fired with enthusiasm.

—Vince Lombardi

Now combined with the Communications section of the CLA/CP® examination, human relations encompass professional contacts with employers, clients, and other office visitors; co-workers and subordinates; and persons outside the law office. For this reason, the legal assistant should be familiar with unauthorized practice of law prohibitions, ethics rules, practice rules, delegation of authority, consequences of delegation, and confidentiality.

The interviewing techniques portion of the examination section covers basic interviewing procedures, as agreed upon by most authors on the subject; definitions of terms and basic principles; and handling of specialized interviews. Subject areas included in this portion are as follows:

- General considerations for the interview situation: courtesy, empathy, physical setting, and body language

- Initial roadblocks: lapse of time, prejudice, and so forth

- Form and manner of questions

• Use of checklists for specific matters

• Situations involving the very young, the elderly, and other persons who may require special handling.

Both initial and subsequent interviews are covered, as are interviews involving clients and other witnesses.

Human Relations

Human relations involve a wide range of associations between individuals, both positive and negative. Legal assistants must deal with all types of people in all types of situations, which demands superior human relations skills. The successful legal assistant is one who (1) has mastered the technical skills of his craft and (2) can relate to and work well with people from all walks of life.

Human relations skills are measured by the legal assistant's ability to deal with others in a positive way. Those who possess this ability have several things in common: They genuinely like themselves, like what they are doing, and like people in general. They are interested in the well-being of others; they are compassionate without gushing. They practice courtesy and common sense in their professional relationships.

The successful legal assistant is the one who observes ethics rules and office policies enthusiastically, who can be firm without being overly aggressive, and who is flexible enough to compromise or to try new approaches when situations warrant them. He strives to be a team player in relation to his employer and co-workers. He always is courteous in contacts with persons outside the office, realizing that he is an emissary for his employer. He protects client confidences and willingly assumes additional responsibilities connected with his position. He respects the contributions of others on the legal services team (lawyers, legal secretaries, law clerks, and messengers) and does not view himself as the most important contributor. A sincere interest in others, and the ability to generate empathetic understanding from them, are key ingredients in building the trust and confidence which engender positive human relations.

Contacts Outside the Office

The legal assistant frequently comes into contact with individuals outside the office in person, by letter, or by telephone as part of her responsibilities. These situations provide opportunities to foster long-term relationships based upon honesty, mutual respect, and professional cooperation. The legal assistant should strive to be congenial without being too familiar.

When requests are made of others, provide sufficient lead time for them to comply. No one likes to be pushed with last-minute requests for information. When little lead time is possible, however, the clerk, court reporter, or other person is more likely to comply with a rush request when it is the exception rather than the rule. Convey appropriate thanks for a job well done. Better still, express appreciation to the person's immediate supervisor or employer.

From time to time, every lawyer and legal assistant encounters a public official who is uncooperative or difficult in general (a court clerk, for example). Rather than further alienate such a person by demanding that he do his job, the experienced lawyer or legal assistant strives to gain his support. Ask how he prefers to have documents submitted or what is the best way to go about a certain task, even if you already know. Thank him for his time and for his help. Acknowledge him in the courthouse hall. Ask about his family and take the time to remember his wife's name if you happen to know it. It may take several months, but even the most surly court clerk can be converted to an ally over time. Having an ally in a position such as this can be an invaluable asset.

When the legal assistant must contact a legal assistant, attorney, or other person aligned with the opposing party, she should avoid power games or tricks of one-upmanship. In the long run, these tactics are counterproductive and can result in retaliatory actions which cause additional harm or expense to this client or to a future one. When power tactics are used by the opposing side, the best advice is to sidestep and ignore them as much as possible without harm to the client—as difficult as this is to do at times. Power games are a ploy of insecure people, and nothing is more frustrating to an insecure person than to be ignored.

Office Politics

The only way to avoid office politics is not to work in an office. Office politics exist wherever there are two or more people working together in an office setting. Although office politics often carry a negative connotation, they provide the vehicle for beneficial changes as well.

When a legal assistant is new to any law office, he is wise to form no firm alliances until he has had time to assess the "lay of the land" by determining where the power centers are. The power centers may or may not correspond with the firm's official hierarchy. For instance, if the senior partner's legal secretary carries great influence with the senior partner, the legal secretary (rather than the senior partner) may be a power center. An assistant to the administrator (rather than the administrator) may be the true power center in allocating assignments and general workloads. By the same token, an alliance formed too soon may be difficult to overcome.

> Bill is a new legal assistant at Samson & Woodward and knows no one except Jane Mitchell, the attorney who hired him. Another legal assistant in the firm, Betsy Barnes, invites Bill to join her for lunch on his first day. He accepts and also accepts two other invitations later in the same week. After about a month, Bill discovers that Betsy is regarded by nearly everyone in the firm as a gossip and a general troublemaker.

Bill may have difficulty extricating himself from the perceived alliance with Betsy, which can create unnecessary obstacles for a person without a proven track record of his own.

Knowledge of the political structure of a particular law office is necessary to effect change when change is either necessary or desirable. (*See Chapter 4 on judgment.*)

Although office politics certainly have a role in developing and maintaining rapport within the law office, one seldom can go wrong by being a courteous, cooperative, and competent member of the legal services team.

Personal Recognition

Everyone needs recognition for his or her contributions. This may come as part of a formal evaluation process, by informal evaluation, or through feedback from the supervising attorney on a specific project.

The first step in receiving recognition for a job well done is to do a good job, no matter how menial or insignificant that job may seem. As a general rule, one who can do a superior job of photocopying and marking voluminous exhibits will be given more challenging tasks in the natural scheme of things. If that does not happen within a reasonable time and if the legal assistant is certain that past and current tasks have been performed well and on time, she can ask to assist with a specific project which she knows is pending. Alternately, she might try her hand at drafting interrogatories or answers to interrogatories based upon information already in the file and then take the draft to the attorney for review. Most lawyers recognize the value of a self-motivated individual and, if the drafting job is done reasonably well, are quite willing to delegate other tasks to such a person.

The legal assistant should keep track of major projects that he has completed and should review those prior to formal, scheduled performance evaluations. An appointment diary or calendar can be used for this purpose. Unless the project is recorded, it may be forgotten or overlooked—especially if it was completed early in the evaluation period.

If formal evaluations are not performed regularly (which may be true in a very small law office), the legal assistant can visit informally with the supervising attorney concerning job performance and future goals. The exact approach may vary from one attorney to another, but most are willing to discuss these matters if the legal assistant asks to talk about them and specifically schedules a time to do so. Try to select a time that is likely to be more quiet than other times—if there is such a thing—based upon the lawyer's usual court and appointment schedules. Although it is a good idea to ask for the lawyer's advice or input concerning increased responsibilities, the legal assistant must have specific goals in mind as well. The attorney's needs and the legal assistant's goals generally can be combined in a way that benefits both of them.

One of the best ways to receive deserved recognition is to give recognition when and where it is due. The person who is willing to share the limelight often finds it is reciprocated by others. Do not overlook legal secretaries and other key support staff members. Mutual respect, support, and goodwill between a legal assistant and a legal secretary can be invaluable in the success of future projects.

A thorough analysis of all aspects of human relations skills required of legal assistants is beyond the scope of this *Review Manual*. The CLA applicant will be well served, however, by reviewing the materials from other chapters as they relate to ethics, judgment, and communications and by reviewing the human relations perspectives of the interviewing materials discussed immediately below.

Interviewing

Legal interviewing involves the exchange of information between individuals, the objective of which is to elicit relevant facts based on personal knowledge, leads to other witnesses who may possess relevant facts, and corroboration of facts.

Interviews typically are conducted either in person or by telephone. The interviewer controls the process, assisted by checklists to facilitate collection of information and to keep the dialogue focused. A question-and-answer approach is used to obtain maximum details from the person interviewed, to separate facts from beliefs, and to provide clues to other sources that can be used to corroborate the facts supplied by the client or by the witness.

Although checklists and forms can expedite the interview, no two legal interviews are exactly the same. Throughout the interview process, the interviewer must be sensitive and responsive to the reactions, attitude, and emotions of the client or the witness. This frequently puts the interviewer's best human relations skills to the test.

The interview process requires preparation and flexibility from the interviewer. The facts and information obtained during the interview are collected and summarized in a memorandum or witness statement, which is essential in the lawyer's legal analysis of the case.

Types of Interviews

As a general rule, an interview is conducted with either a client or a non-client witness and may be conducted either in person or by telephone. Each situation presents different considerations and requires different techniques for interview management, although common themes do emerge.

Client Interviews   The client usually is the lawyer's first source of information, and the initial client interview should be conducted in person if at all possible. Because one interview may not provide the depth of information needed, subsequent interviews—either in person or by telephone—may be required before the attorney can complete a full analysis of the facts and legal issues of a particular case.

The details of ascertainable facts must be complete, their accuracy must be verified, and resulting inconsistencies must be reported to the attorney. Probing the factual details of sensitive matters requires tact and diplomacy. An intense, confrontational interrogation is certain to escalate the client's discomfort. Depending on the sensitivity of the client and the subject matter, an interviewer can damage the attorney-client relationship irreparably. Should this occur, the fact that the interviewer obtained a complete factual account is of little value.

The lawyer or legal assistant should explain the investigative process to the client as well as how each step lays the foundation for the next. The client needs to know that the legal assistant will interview others to corroborate the client's facts and to obtain additional facts. Not explaining the importance of corroborating evidence can strain the attorney-client relationship. If a client does not understand the process, she may infer that other people are being interviewed because the lawyer or the legal assistant did not believe her.

Witness Interviews   In addition to the corroboration provided through documentary evidence (reports, contracts, leases, invoices, and so forth), personal interviews of witnesses often are used to verify factual details and to corroborate the client's allegations. A witness can be anyone with personal knowledge of facts related to the case. Witnesses generally are classified according to their relationship to the client or to matters involved in the client's case.

A.   The Neutral Witness   The neutral witness is one who has personal knowledge of facts relevant to the case but who has no relationship with either the client or the opposing party. Neutral witnesses with favorable facts are the most desirable, of course. Neutral witnesses might include a disinterested bystander to an assault or a driver who witnessed an accident while she was stopped nearby.

B.   The Friendly Witness   This witness generally shares the same perspective, business interests, or career as that of the client. He may be a social acquaintance of the client. The friendly witness often is willing to speak freely but may offer a slightly different perspective than the client. This witness, however, generally corroborates the client's claims; and his statement is used for comparison with statements made by the opposing party's witnesses.

C.   The Official Witness   A person is an official witness because of employment or because of a position held through election or affiliation with an organization. For instance, a police officer, a tax assessor, a city planning director, and a court clerk are official witnesses. In theory, official witnesses are impartial to both sides of a controversy. They generally provide factual background which neither advances nor restricts either side's legal theories in any dramatic way.

D.   The Expert Witness   An expert witness may be either friendly or hostile. As a practical matter, this may be influenced—at least in part—by which party retains the expert's services. An expert witness should be interviewed at length to determine his depth of expertise, his presentation skills, and his preparation abilities. An expert witness must have the ability to cope calmly with attacks on his general credibility and on the thoroughness of his conclusions. Examples of expert witnesses include real estate appraisers, architects, engineers, doctors, and other individuals with substantial training and experience in a technical area.

E.   The Hostile Witness   A hostile witness is not necessarily one who exhibits hostility. Rather, it is one who is unwilling to divulge information. A hostile witness may have knowledge of facts that support either side of the case but is reluctant to volunteer the information. Thus, an individual can be a hostile witness even though she supports the client's position in the case. Such a person technically is an objectively hostile witness, although the term *hostile witness* is used more commonly.

As the term ordinarily is used, a hostile witness may be reluctant to provide information because of inconvenience to herself or because of uncooperativeness in general—not because of a personality clash between the witness and the client or between the witness and the interviewer.

Less frequently, the term *hostile witness* is used to describe a witness who displays personal distaste for the client or for the interviewer. If the interviewer believes the hostility is directed toward him (rather than toward the client) and if adjustments in the interviewer's approach prove ineffective, someone else should interview the witness. Acknowledging a personality conflict early in the interview can save time and effort. Having another interviewer conclude the interview is not a failure of the initial interviewer; rather, it indicates maturity and strength in having recognized the incompatibility.

All interviewers encounter personal hostility from a witness on occasion. If this situation occurs more frequently, however, the interviewer must re-evaluate his interviewing style thoroughly and thoughtfully and must make constructive changes.

Personal Interviews   Personal interviews are those conducted face to face between the interviewer and the client or the witness. The law office generally is the most conducive location for personal interviews, because the environment is more easily controlled by the interviewer. Client interviews, especially initial client interviews, generally are conducted in the law office; witness interviews, however, frequently are conducted at the witness's place of employment or home. These types of interviews are called *field interviews*.

When the legal assistant or the attorney must travel to the witness to conduct a personal interview (field interview), adapting to the witness's environment is critical in establishing rapport. This is where the flexibility of the interviewer pays its greatest dividends. Because the environment is foreign to the interviewer, using a prepared outline and planning the questions to ask create a measure of confidence that will benefit both the interviewer and the witness.

The primary advantage of a personal interview is that it facilitates more personal interaction than a telephone interview does. The relationship of trust and confidence between the attorney and her client is fostered by personal contact. A personal interview allows the legal assistant or attorney to use all of her senses to evaluate the client (or the witness) and the facts related by him. Unusual physical characteristics, body language, and physical mannerisms are important in assessing credibility and the way in which the client or witness likely will be perceived by a jury. None of these things can be determined in a telephone interview.

Telephone Interviews   When a personal interview cannot be arranged, a telephone interview may be the next best option. At the beginning of every telephone interview of a witness, state the purpose of the interview and obtain permission to conduct the interview. In addition, clarify who the parties are in the case and who it is that the law firm represents.

The legal assistant's telephone skills are tested regularly when dealing with individuals who are reluctant to divulge information. Making a simple inquiry such as "Can you help me?", followed with an explanation of what information is needed, often opens the conversation. People usually want to help, and they certainly like to be asked.

Although a telephone interview may not be the most desirable interview method, it is efficient and economical. Many individuals and agencies can be contacted by telephone in a short time, without great expense to the client. Those who have personal knowledge about the case can be scheduled for personal interviews. Even if an individual has little or no personal knowledge about the matter, she may provide leads to others who do have helpful information. Also, contacting a witness early in the case—even by telephone—may generate a psychological alignment of that witness with the client rather than with the opposing party.

A major disadvantage of the telephone interview is the inability to see the witness. Being unable to observe the reaction and body language of the witness is an obstacle for the interviewer. The witness's reaction to questions can be revealing in evaluating the information provided by him. Nervousness, fidgeting, twitching, lack of eye contact, or similar conduct may indicate a problem with credibility; however, these exhibitions cannot be detected in a telephone interview.

The decision to record or not to record a telephone interview is left to the supervising attorney. If the attorney approves the use of a recording device, the legal assistant must seek permission of the witness to record before any recording takes place. If permission is given, the legal assistant must follow the same rules that apply when recording a personal interview (*see below*).

The Interviewer's Role

Creating rapport and building trust throughout the interview are the responsibility of the interviewer, whether the interviewer is the legal assistant or the lawyer. Treating clients and witnesses with respect goes far in establishing and maintaining the requisite level of trust.

Attitude   The legal assistant often has significant contact with the client and with witnesses during the investigation period of a case. Thus, the legal assistant is a public relations representative for the firm; she has great impact on these important people. Courtesy, truthfulness, and discretion throughout this process are critical to the credibility of the legal assistant and of the firm. *The legal assistant **never** expresses personal opinions, **never** patronizes a client or a witness, and **never** is condescending.*

On very rare occasions, one encounters a legal assistant or a lawyer who assumes an attitude of superiority, particularly when dealing with a client or witness with less education or with a lower economic position. This approach assumes that education or money equate to intelligence. Frequently, the exact opposite is true; and the fact that an educated person ever could make such an assumption proves the assumption wrong. The interviewer who views herself as superior to a client or witness cannot possibly hope to be successful in eliciting full cooperation from that person; her attitude will come across in a negative way no matter how much she tries to hide it. These types of interviewers seldom are found in private law offices for the simple reason that they cannot sustain themselves as effective members of the legal services team for very long.

Concern   For a client more than for a witness, a visit to the law office frequently is triggered by some traumatic event. Divorce, personal injury, death, rape, criminal charges, or business failure can produce intense stress. Although the situation may be minor, routine, or "old hat" to the interviewer, the client's perception is quite different. His problem is unique and traumatic for him, making it essential for the interviewer to exercise patience, understanding, and sensitivity to the client's plight. Generating a feeling of empathy shows concern for the client.

Sensitivity to the client's situation provides countless benefits in establishing a solid attorney-client relationship. Studies indicate that it is not the lawyer's win-loss ratio that retains clients or that prompts them to refer others to a particular lawyer. Rather, it is the respect and genuine concern shown by the lawyer and the lawyer's staff. Despite all of the marketing techniques now available to lawyers, repeat and referral business ultimately make the difference between a lawyer who is successful and one who is not.

Courtesy   Courtesy always is a correct approach to dealing with people, no matter what the situation is. Extending small courtesies to a client or to a witness pays huge dividends. An open, communicative environment begins with common courtesy. For example, greet the client in the reception area and personally escort him to the conference room or to your office; this is a simple but essential client development technique. Remember and mention significant occasions previously referred to by the client (an anniversary, a birthday); this demonstrates personal interest. When the interview is over, escort the client back to the reception area as a common courtesy. It can be both embarrassing and awkward for the client to try to find his way out of the office unescorted. Every client wants to be assured that he is important to the law firm, and personal attention from the lawyer and from the legal assistant symbolizes a client's importance.

During the interview and throughout the progress of the case, a simple way to demonstrate genuine interest in the client is to listen closely to what he has to say, whether in person or by telephone. People generally like to talk if they have an audience and will reveal information readily to a courteous, interested listener. This approach allows the legal assistant to hear what the client says, to relate the information to data gathered previously, and to formulate relevant questions at the appropriate time. The courtesy of listening is a powerful tool for building the attorney-client relationship.

Return the client's telephone calls promptly. Although information may not be the positive news hoped for, the client expects and deserves to know all information related to her case. Delaying calls sends a negative message about the lawyer, which can extend to the legal assistant as well.

Send courtesy copies of correspondence and periodic status reports to the client. These simple communications keep clients informed and happy. Lack of communication is the most frequent criticism of lawyers and sends a negative message. Inundating the client with relevant information is essential for maintaining a positive professional relationship.

Avoid Legal Jargon   Avoid technical legal terms as much as possible during an interview. Using a foreign vocabulary of legal jargon will not impress any client. More likely than not, it will be a source of genuine frustration, which can shatter all previous efforts to establish rapport with that client. Asking questions in plain English generally is one of the things that legal assistants do best; the interview process allows them to capitalize on this asset.

If, on the other hand, the client uses technical terms connected with his expertise or profession, the legal assistant should seek precise definitions for those terms to ensure that she uses them in the same context as the client uses them. It is helpful for the legal assistant to adapt to the jargon of the client, but is unrealistic to expect the client to adapt to the jargon of the law office. To understand the technical terminology of a case better, the legal assistant should review available documents or materials as well as the attorney's notes prior to the interview. This will provide some familiarity with the terminology and will prepare the legal assistant to ask appropriate questions for clarification during the interview.

Personal Opinions   The legal assistant never expresses his personal opinions or personal judgments about the case, the opposing party, the opposing party's lawyer, or anyone else connected with the client's case—not even if his opinions concur with those expressed by the client and not even if his motive is to show support for the client. Find some other way to show support.

Limiting personal opinion during the fact-gathering process does not mean the legal assistant is not allowed to express personal feelings about any topic. It is appropriate to identify with a client's joy or frustration, as the case may be, as long as the legal assistant does not lose his objectivity. It would be insensitive, for example, not to show pleasure if the client relates that she has won a $30,000 lottery.

False Expectations   Never should the lawyer or the legal assistant give the impression that a client's case is a sure winner. Letting the client know that the law firm will work diligently on the client's behalf is the best message.

Keep the Client Involved   Describing the legal process and explaining the steps involved are basic to the client's understanding of her legal matter. The lawyer also should give the client a realistic explanation of the range of anticipated results, and the client should be involved in any decisions affecting the outcome of the case. When the lawyer shares authority with the client, the end result often is more positive for both.

Whenever possible, involve the client in the fact-gathering process. In some situations, only the client can obtain privileged records. If the client is cost conscious (who is not these days?), she will feel she is contributing to the cost containment of her case. Keeping her involved by asking her to obtain some of the records and documents needed for the case produces a cooperative spirit between the client, on the one hand, and the lawyer and her staff, on the other.

Ethical Limitations   The lawyer should explain the legal assistant's function and role in the overall case management. If the lawyer has not explained the legal assistant's role, the legal assistant must explain her status to the client and the purpose of her involvement. The client must be informed, for example, that the legal assistant is not a lawyer and cannot offer legal advice, represent the client in court, or discuss fees. With these limitations, the legal assistant will be involved in all phases of the case and will work closely with the lawyer throughout the case.

Any information conveyed to the legal assistant by the client is confidential, just the same as if the information had been conveyed directly to the lawyer. The legal assistant has a responsibility to furnish all information she obtains to the lawyer, even if the client requests that specific information be withheld. Everything must be shared with the lawyer. If a client asks the legal assistant not to tell the lawyer about a particular fact or situation, she should try to stop the client before he divulges the information and should remind the client of her ethical obligation to deliver all information to the lawyer. The client then can decide whether to provide the information or not. If the client elects not to discuss the matter, the legal assistant also has an obligation to inform the lawyer of the client's reluctance to share specific information.

The Interview Environment

The setting of the interview should be conducive to the fact-gathering process. Ideally, this means a private interview in a controlled environment. Interviews conducted in the law office usually meet this criterion; field interviews seldom do.

Office Interviews   The interview should be conducted in a location which is completely private, orderly, and conservatively furnished. A private conference room is ideal if one is available. To avoid potential distractions, remove all other files and materials not associated with the client's case from the room. Anticipate any needs that the client or witness may have (beverages, tissues, and so forth) and bring those items to the conference room.

If a conference room is unavailable, the legal assistant may conduct the interview in his office as long as his desk is clear and the office is neat. All files and loose papers other than those related to the client should be removed from sight. Nothing other than the client's materials and a notepad should be on the desk. This conveys the message that the client's case is the most important thing on the legal assistant's agenda.

If the legal assistant's office is used for interviewing, the decor should be as understated as possible; any artwork, conservative; and the color scheme, muted. Male interviewers may find it helpful to incorporate a few plants or photographs of children into the decor; this indicates his nurturing side. Female interviewers should avoid having more than one plant in the office for the same but opposite reason. Females may benefit from a decor which incorporates a framed Bill of Rights, Gettysburg address, or similar items. Hopefully, sexual stereotyping is on its way to becoming an archaic social blunder. In the meantime, however, the legal assistant cannot ignore its impact—particularly when dealing with older people who are not ready for radical social changes.

A.   Privacy   Privacy is the most important environmental characteristic of a successful interview. When clients are interviewed, privacy underscores client confidentiality, which is critical to free exchange of information between the client and the legal assistant.

Let the receptionist know when an interview begins and arrange for the telephone to be answered during the interview conference. Making these arrangements emphasizes to the client that her case is important and is taken seriously by the interviewer. As a practical matter, the information from the client will flow more easily if distractions and interruptions are held to a minimum.

B.   Image   First impressions count and frequently are difficult to displace. Just as the office setting creates a first impression, the appearance of the legal assistant leaves a distinct and lasting impression on the client.

Clients and witnesses expect lawyers and those associated with lawyers to look professional; they should not be disappointed. Conservative, tailored business attire creates a favorable impression. Simple jewelry (no excessive number of rings, no gaudy tie tacks), conservative hairstyles, and only the most subtle perfumes or colognes (if any at all) likewise should advance the client's first impression of a conservative professional.

C.   Seating Arrangements   The seating arrangement is important to the interview process. For example, a particularly gregarious client or witness may need to be kept at a distance (such as across the desk) as an unspoken reminder that the legal assistant is in charge.

In interviewing a shy client, it may be better for the interviewer to move her chair to the side of the desk (to minimize the authority symbol of the desk) to promote the client's sense that she and the legal assistant are much the same. Using an excuse of poor hearing or some other pretext, the interviewer even may move to a chair located on the same side of the desk as the client's chair, using care not to move so close as to invade the client's personal space—especially during a first interview.

Many lawyers use a small, round table; a small sofa; or overstuffed chairs located away from the desk area, sometimes in the corner of the office, to create an impression of intimacy that is similar to a home environment. This frequently puts people at ease and helps to build trust and confidence with the client or witness. The more comfortable a person feels, the more information the interviewer will obtain.

Field Interviews   The environment in which a field interview is conducted is difficult for the interviewer to control. The interview may be conducted at a construction site, in a manufacturing plant, or at the home or office of the witness. Each of these locations is approached differently by the interviewer.

It may be necessary, for example, to interview a witness at a construction site with heavy equipment operating in the background or at a manufacturing plant with assembly-line noise. The interviewer's ability to adapt calmly to these types of environments helps to establish trust and confidence with the witness.

The legal assistant may be required to wear protective clothing, a helmet, or goggles in some field settings. At a construction site, a male legal assistant may elect to loosen or to remove his tie or to roll up his sleeves to bridge the identity gap with the witness more quickly. A female legal assistant in the same setting may want to wear flat shoes and a simple, open-collared blouse—perhaps with slacks or a denim skirt—that day. It will be easier for a witness to identify with an interviewer whose appearance in the field is somewhat similar to his own. The more information the interviewer can glean from the witness and from observing applicable procedures or processes at the field site, the better prepared the case will be for settlement or trial.

If manufacturing procedures or processes are not an issue in the case, the field interview should be conducted in a private location, preferably one that is quiet enough to permit normal conversation. Avoid high-traffic areas, such as a lunchroom or a loading dock, where the curiosity of other workers may be aroused. More information will be obtained if the witness is comfortable that he will not be overheard by others. If no other quiet place is available to conduct the interview, an automobile may provide some privacy. Another option may be to invite the witness to lunch at a nearby restaurant or diner. Field interviews often test the interviewer's creativity as well as the soundness of her interviewing skills.

Preparing for the Interview

A well-executed interview cannot occur without thoughtful preparation. In addition to planning the interview's general direction ahead of time, the legal assistant must gather all necessary files, paperwork, and equipment for the interview. This may include authorization or release forms, checklists, business cards, notepads, and recording devices (if appropriate). If copies of documents will be distributed during the interview, extra sets of these documents should be available. The organization and efficiency of the interviewer create a favorable impression in any interview setting.

Review Relevant Data   Well before the scheduled interview, the legal assistant should review carefully any information about the case and the client or the witness that may be available. This should include at least a brief conference with the supervising attorney to obtain her preliminary evaluation, analysis, and instructions.

When it is possible to do so, initial interviews with clients should be preceded by a review of any applicable statutes and case law. This helps to define the legal issues as well as the elements of proof required in a particular type of case, which, in turn, helps to focus the direction of the interview.

Checklists   Select the appropriate checklists and related forms prior to the interview. Use checklists to help stay on track and to obtain the information needed but do not be a slave to them. Recognize that every interview flows differently because the person being interviewed is different; the checklist should facilitate—not obstruct—the interview process.

Each practice area typically generates its own checklist, which should be revised frequently to hone the procedures and the interview style of the interviewer. Used appropriately, a checklist improves the interviewer's efficiency and effectiveness. It allows the interviewer to concentrate on what the client is saying rather than on the next item of information that the interviewer needs to obtain.

Forms   Determine whether any preprinted forms may be needed in connection with the client's matter and gather all such forms prior to the interview.

If the interview relates to a personal injury claim, for example, authorizations or releases usually are required to investigate the claim. Several authorization or release forms should be signed during the interview. The signed forms then are presented to doctors, hospitals, insurance companies, and others to obtain privileged information.

Each area of the law typically requires its own standardized forms for authorization or release of pertinent information. For instance, estate planning or probate administration requires releases to obtain financial information from various institutions; labor law requires signed forms to acquire personnel records; and real estate mortgage companies require releases from individuals before financial information is relinquished. Anticipating what forms may be necessary will save contacting the client again merely to sign forms.

Notepad   Use a notepad to record the client's or the witness's comments during the interview process. The legal assistant never should allow note-taking to impede the flow of the interview. Notes must be sufficient to allow the legal assistant to prepare a detailed memorandum or witness statement of the facts related to him. At the same time, however, the interviewer must be attentive to the client (or to the witness) by using frequent eye contact and other active listening techniques. This reassures the client that the legal assistant is listening and is interested.

Over time, most interviewers develop their own codes to record notes efficiently during the interview. Studies indicate that significant rapport is lost when answers are recorded by the longhand method while the client or witness sits quietly, waiting for the next question. Using a shorthand or speed writing method to take notes maintains spontaneity and rapport. Immediately after the interview, the legal assistant should dictate or otherwise prepare the memorandum—while the notes still are fresh (*see below*).

A notepad also comes in handy if a field witness is willing to sign a written statement. When the witness agrees to sign a written statement during the interview, it is best to obtain his signature before returning to the office. In this situation, the statement ordinarily is written in longhand. After the interview is over, witnesses sometimes decline to sign statements. The lapse of time occasionally causes people to question their involvement or to be influenced negatively by the opinions of others. Some interviewers make it a practice to use the signed, handwritten statement to prepare a typewritten statement, which then is delivered to the witness for signature. This may seem less threatening, because the witness already will have signed one statement (the handwritten one) and can compare the two statements to be certain that nothing has been changed. *Additional information on witness statements is covered later in the chapter.*

Recording Devices   Lawyers differ in their views about recording interviews. Some lawyers believe that recording inhibits the client or witness, making her more concerned about how sentences are structured than about telling what she knows. Some witnesses feel uncomfortable about being involved if their every word is recorded at the first interview. (Recorded interviews of witnesses can be a disadvantage if the information is more beneficial to the opposing party than it is to the client.)

Other lawyers believe that the benefits of a recording outweigh the disadvantages. A recording keeps the witness honest by providing an irrefutable record of the facts and events related by the witness; the witness becomes committed to that version of the facts contained in the recording; and subsequent, contradictory statements are minimized. A recorded interview occasionally is so convincing that it can be used as leverage to negotiate a favorable settlement for a client. Another advantage of a recorded witness statement is that it accurately reflects voice inflection and mood, which notes cannot do.

If recording occurs, certain formalities must be observed.

- The interviewer states his name, date, and the purpose and site of the interview.

- The witness is introduced and is asked for permission to record the interview, and a statement is made or acknowledged by the witness that the interview is given voluntarily.

- All persons in the room are identified, together with their connection to the litigation and their reason for appearance.

- Any interruption is identified by time, date, and reason for the interruption. When recording recommences, the time, date, and those present are announced once again.

- Some jurisdictions require that the witness receive a copy of the transcribed statement or of the taped interview.

- The conclusion of the recording includes a statement that the recorded interview was given freely and that the witness was given the opportunity to make any changes.

An indirect benefit of recording an interview is that it allows the interviewer to assess his own performance. This is particularly helpful for an apprentice interviewer. Allowing him to evaluate his interviewing style and verbal skills provides a means to improve his interviewing technique.

Photocopy Equipment   Photocopy equipment should be accessible at the interview site. If a witness brings useful information to the interview and is willing to share it, copies of everything should be made immediately. After the interview is concluded, the witness may misplace the information or may not feel as cooperative as he did during the interview.

Before a field interview takes place, determine where the nearest photocopy machine is located. Timely access to valuable information through photocopies can affect the strategy of the case. Until a comprehensive analysis of the facts and legal issues is performed, all information potentially is relevant.

Preparation for Field Interviews   The preparation for a field interview proceeds in much the same way as preparation for an interview in the law office. One additional consideration in a field interview is transporting the interview items (file, forms, documents, tapes, recording devices, and business cards) to the interview site. A good leather briefcase is a status symbol in the corporate world and serves the legal assistant well, particularly in conducting field interviews. It enhances the legal assistant's professional image and solves the problem of transporting equipment and supplies.

A business card identifies the interviewer to unfamiliar witnesses in the field. If a letter was mailed to the witness to arrange the field interview, show a copy of the letter to the witness to establish further identification. Provide as much information as is necessary to make the witness comfortable with the legal assistant's identity.

Conducting the Interview

A successful interview requires planning, effective use of equipment and resources, and superior human relations skills of the interviewer. The ultimate purpose of an interview is to obtain the facts within the personal knowledge of the client or the witness. The way in which facts are gathered sets the climate and the tone of the interview; it directly affects the quality and quantity of facts that a client or witness may be willing to share. A successful interview depends on

- the interviewer's demeanor or "bedside manner";
- the client's (or witness') impression of the interviewer;
- the interviewer's method of seeking information;

- the interviewer's comprehension of the facts related by the client;
- the client's expectations of the outcome of the case; and
- the interviewer's ability to address the client's (or witness') apprehensions.

Interviewing skills are used in both litigation and nonlitigation matters. Preparing for litigation requires considerable client and witness interviewing. With proper discovery work and thorough investigation of facts before and during litigation, a case often can be settled without trial. This saves time and effort for the lawyer and saves money for the client.

In addition, client interviewing is used extensively in (i) the corporate area to create new businesses, for mergers, consolidations, and acquisitions; (ii) the estate administration area to create estate plans and administer probates; (iii) the labor relations area to investigate discrimination matters and union/management disputes; (iv) the bankruptcy area to gather financial data and to investigate financial records; and (v) the real estate area in relation to closings and other transactions.

Once the lawyer determines that she may be interested in accepting the case, the fact-gathering process begins.

The time of the interview must be convenient for the client or the witness. Allocating sufficient time is essential to the interview's success, although planning around the schedules of professional people can be challenging. The interviewer's sensitivity to schedule demands will gain the cooperation of these busy people. To be effective, interviews should not be sandwiched too tightly between other appointments for either the interviewer or the client. Otherwise, needless time pressures and stress can result.

Introductions   Proper introductions are essential to establish the credibility and the roles of all those involved in the interview process. Especially in connection with an initial client interview, the lawyer should introduce the legal assistant formally to the client—either during or immediately following the lawyer's preliminary conference with the client. The lawyer should use the introduction as an opportunity to explain the involvement of the legal assistant to reassure the client of the legal assistant's competence and expertise.

For example, the lawyer might call the legal assistant into her office and say, *"This is Chris Baker, my legal assistant, who works closely with me on several of my cases. I have asked him to assist me with your case as well. Feel free to discuss anything with Chris that you would discuss with me. If ever you need to reach me and if I am not available, do not hesitate to get in touch with Chris. He usually can locate me within a very short time and will be able to answer many of the questions that you might have. Since Chris is not a lawyer, your overall attorney fees will be reduced if we use him. Chris is extremely capable; and, fortunately, he has some time to help me with your case."*

If the legal assistant is not introduced at the initial conference but meets with the client alone at a later time, he must describe his role clearly and must explain that he is not a lawyer. At any subsequent meeting with the client, the legal assistant should be aware of how the client refers to him. Any confusion concerning the legal assistant's status should be corrected immediately. The client must understand that the legal assistant *cannot*

- *offer direct legal advice or interpret the law;*
- *accept a case;*
- *represent individuals before a court; or*
- *set or adjust fees.*

Any inquiries concerning these subjects must be referred to the lawyer for response.

Getting Started   In the ideal situation, the lawyer will have introduced the legal assistant to the client (*see above*). After introductions are made, the legal assistant should escort the client to the location where the interview will take place, whether in a conference room or in the legal assistant's office.

Offer to do something personal for the client (or the witness), such as getting a cup of coffee or a cold beverage. The interviewer should not ask someone else to do this but, rather, should do it himself. This small gesture often puts a nervous client more at ease, particularly when the client is a private person rather than a large corporation being interviewed through an officer or other representative. Even if the client is not nervous, everyone likes to receive special, personal attention. The process of building rapport begins the moment the legal assistant meets the client or the witness, and personal courtesies extended by the legal assistant will speed the process.

On the way to the interview site, make small talk about whether the client was able to find the office easily, parking, the weather, travel conditions, or a newsworthy event of the day. This exchange allows the legal assistant to begin her assessment of the client's attitude and communication style. It also allows the client to size up the legal assistant and to become comfortable with the law office atmosphere (if that is the interview site).

Explain the Process   Early in the interview, explain the interview process to the client, including the fact that notes will be taken to record the information which the client provides. Also explain that questions will be asked to clarify facts. This type of explanation prepares the client or witness for those events when they occur.

Because a lawsuit generates a winner and a loser, the environment of the client's interview can become strained when the legal assistant begins to probe for specific details. Questioning must be used to establish the factual basis for the client's claims or defenses. Nevertheless, an unintentional confrontation can arise if the client has not been properly prepared for extensive inquiries. Without a full explanation of the process and proper handling by the legal assistant, a client may regard extensive questioning as an affront to her integrity or to her powers of recollection. If the client knows what is going to happen, she will be more at ease during the interview.

Framing the Questions   The question-and-answer segment may begin with routine matters such as personal background information about the client. Background information is necessary for a complete factual picture, and this type of questioning allows both the client and the legal assistant to ease into the more substantive—and possibly more difficult—questioning that lies ahead. Background information generally includes the client's full name, address, telephone number, date of birth, social security number, place of employment, length of employment, job title, marital status, and so forth.

Once the client's personal background information is recorded, the interview can move to the substantive facts related to the client's case. Ideally, varied questioning techniques are employed by the legal assistant during the interview, with most of the following types of questions being used:

- ***Open Questions***   An open question is one designed to elicit a narrative response. This type of question is particularly effective at the beginning of an interview but may be used at any time that a narrative description or explanation is sought. Examples of open questions include the following:

  ▸*Starting from the beginning, what do you remember about the accident?*

  ▸*Tell me something about _____ (your business, your marriage, your son's problems at school, the way you want your property divided after your death).*

  ▸*How did you happen to be in Cincinnati that weekend?*

- ***Closed Questions***   A closed question is one which seeks a specific, narrow answer. Closed questions generally are used in combination with open questions—and much more sparingly—to obtain specific details or to verify details previously provided by the client. Examples of closed questions include the following:

    ►*What color was the traffic light when you first noticed it?*

    ►*Have you and your wife ever seen a marriage counselor?*

    ►*Were you in Cincinnati on business?*

- ***Leading Questions***   A leading question is one which either (1) suggests the answer desired by the questioner or (2) suggests a fact not stated previously by the client. Leading questions may be used to good effect during cross-examination of a witness at a deposition or at a trial. However, their utility is limited in a client or witness interview, where the objective is to elicit facts and information. Examples of leading questions include the following:

    ►*Of course, you were wearing your seat belt at the time of the accident, weren't you?*

    ►*Surely you don't believe that your wife is having an affair, do you?*

    ►*Where did you and your girlfriend stay while you were in Cincinnati? (The client did not say that he had a girlfriend or that anyone accompanied him to Cincinnati.)*

- ***Silent Questions***   A silent question is not a question at all; rather, it is a questioning technique by which the interviewer maintains an extended, expectant silence after an answer is given. The implication is that the interviewer is waiting for the rest of the answer. Faced with this situation, a client or a witness often will supply further details or explanation without being asked a specific question. This technique can be extremely effective in the right circumstance; however, because it creates some anxiety, it should be used judiciously.

Of all the questioning techniques described, open questions generally are the best method to obtain the most details about the facts known to the client.

A.   Flexibility   A successful interviewer adapts to the communication style of the client or witness as much as possible. The sensory terms used by the client during conversation reveal his communication style. For example, if he uses the phrase "I see what you mean," he probably is a visual communicator. The most effective questions for this type of individual are those phrased in terms of vision, such as *"When you recall the accident, describe what you see."* If a person uses a phrase such as "I hear what you say," the interviewer should try to ask questions in auditory terms whenever possible, for example, *"Did you hear anything unusual in the way he spoke?"* **or** *"What sounds did the pump make before it stopped operating?"* Imitating the communication style of the client or witness minimizes misunderstanding of both the questions asked and the answers provided. A person is more comfortable and open with an interviewer when they both use the same communication style.

Flexibility also includes the recognition that the words of a question can mean different things to different people. The legal assistant must be able to tailor questions to the background, cultural circumstances, and vocabulary of the client or of the witness. For example, a witness may not have *perceived* anything, even though he saw the entire incident. He may have no *acquaintances*; however, he may know many people.

The questions should be phrased simply and clearly. Avoid multiple-part questions and limit those questions that which can be answered by a "yes" or "no" or by a single word. Above all, beware of using leading questions.

Leading questions can turn a credible, honest person into an untrustworthy witness. Questions such as *"You did see John Blackhart deliberately crash into the department store window, didn't you?"* or *"You saw John's pals looting merchandise from the store, right?"* create an obligation to agree with the questioner rather than to provide an answer based on personal knowledge. Leading questions such as these plant ideas in the client's mind and put words into his mouth. The end result is that the interviewer supplies the facts, and the client merely agrees. The better practice is to use open questions as much as possible to obtain facts during the interview.

Open questions produce narrative answers, which include fact details known by the client. The more details that are obtained, the more successful the interview and the easier it is to secure corroboration from other witnesses and sources.

Finally, prepare for the unexpected. Although ultimate control of the interview rests with the legal assistant, she should allow the interview to take a natural course. This flexibility sometimes produces unanticipated, revealing information with tremendous impact on the case.

B.   Seeking Sensitive Information   As valuable as tact is to an interviewer, legal assistants and lawyers alike sometimes take this attribute too far when dealing with topics such as death, suicide, or sexual activities. Taken to its most extreme level, tact becomes evasion. An evasive question indicates the interviewer is uncomfortable with the subject matter or that the topic cannot be discussed candidly. Moreover, the most typical response to an evasive question is an evasive answer, which does nothing to advance the purpose of the interview.

To illustrate, it is more direct to ask, *"How do you want your assets distributed at your death?"* than it is to ask, *"If you should pass on, how should your property be distributed?"* It is apparent that everyone will die one day. The client would not visit an attorney to discuss his estate plan unless he knew this to be true. The more direct question reinforces the client's perceived need for legal services and paves the way for a frank discussion of his specific situation.

Direct questions are most effective when they are combined with the interviewer's sensitivity to a particular client's emotional state. The topic of death, for example, evokes a very different emotional reaction when a client discusses his own death in relation to an estate plan than it does when he discusses the situation which led to the death of his child. The death of a child is a traumatic experience. When a person has difficulty describing a traumatic experience, acknowledge the difficulty and move to a more neutral topic until the person regains enough composure to return to the difficult—but necessary—topic of the interview. It may be necessary to take one or more breaks during an interview related to a traumatic experience or to conduct the full interview in more than one session. The best way to gauge a particular client's emotional state during the interview process is to let the client talk.

C.   Let the Client Talk   Every individual has her own chain of beliefs concerning facts and events as well as her own, unique way of describing them. Allowing a client to describe a sequence of events freely and without interruption is an efficient way to measure her testimony in terms of both substance and style of presentation.

It also permits a client to tell her story, very possibly for the first time, to someone who she is reasonably certain will be on her side. Many people are reluctant to discuss their most personal affairs or their financial situations even with close friends for fear of criticism, ridicule, or rejection. This may be especially true if they believe that they may be at fault in some way or if they believe that they have an obligation to protect someone close to them.

While the client tells her story, listen for and note those facts that require further clarification or verification. Encourage the client or witness to continue her narrative with active listening techniques (*see below*), with additional open questions, and with supportive comments such as, "*Please go on,*" "*That must have been difficult for you,*" or "*Anyone would have been worried at that point.*"

A narrative allows the legal assistant to evaluate the client and her testimony style in a way that cannot be done with a series of closed questions. The legal assistant should assess the client's familiarity with details and her level of articulation: logical or rambling, composed or nervous, self-assured or shy, and so forth.

Note any extraordinary physical characteristics (stuttering, a noticeable birthmark, a limp, extremely long hair on a man) or mannerisms (popping of knuckles, tugging at an ear, fidgeting) that may distract a juror from the client's testimony during a trial or that may create unfavorable bias or prejudice in a juror. These types of features generally are noticed when the lawyer or legal assistant first meets a client but are overlooked and quickly forgotten after a very short time. Noting them tactfully in the interview memorandum (*discussed below*) ensures that whoever prepares the case for trial will be reminded to address them during jury selection or during the opening statement.

Long hair can be cut; but if the client stutters, for example, a jury is certain to notice it at trial—just as the legal assistant notices it during the initial interview. Some jurors may be so distracted by it that they will not hear the substance of her testimony. To avoid this result, a trial attorney might say during jury selection, "*My client, Mary Jones, is very embarrassed about this—and she probably will be a little upset with me for mentioning it—but Mary sometimes stutters when she gets nervous. I just want Mary to be reassured that you could render a fair verdict without being affected by her stuttering if it happens. Do you think her stuttering would affect your final verdict in the case?*" Of course, no one will answer "yes"; but the real advantage is that the jurors will expect Mary to stutter, will not be distracted by it, and may be even more supportive of her as a result of the explanation. If her stutter is not included as part of the original interview memorandum, it might be overlooked in the trial preparation.

D.   Who, What, When, Where, How, and Why   Encourage the client or witness to supply details through supportive questioning. After the initial story is told fully, questions are phrased to authenticate the details of the narrative. Brusque, interrogation-type questioning likely will result in brusque answers. Even if a witness is aligned with the opposing party, there is no justification to alienate the witness further by terse questions or by an argumentative style. Tactful, carefully phrased questions will produce more information and a more cooperative spirit. After a case has been concluded, adverse witnesses—and sometimes adverse parties—have been known to seek assistance from the lawyer's office where they were treated well as adversaries rather than return to the lawyer who represented them originally.

Questions phrased in terms of who, what, when, where, how, and why are more likely to produce detailed, narrative answers. This type of question encourages a storytelling atmosphere: *"Who delivered the box to the Trade Center?"; "What was the messenger wearing when the box was delivered?"; "When did you first meet your wife?"; "Where were you when you first noticed the messenger?"; "How would you describe the messenger?"; or "Why were you at the Trade Center that day?"* This form of question also may be used to ask follow-up questions to verify some previous answer.

If statements seem to conflict, ask the client's help in resolving the misunderstanding. The client or witness never should have the sense that the legal assistant believes he is lying. Asking for clarification because of the legal assistant's (not the client's) confusion likely will produce the needed information. If the client senses that his integrity is being questioned, an opposite result can occur: he may recoil quietly or he may become obstinate and refuse to answer further questions.

Use Checklists to Stay on Track   Checklists should be designed and used to facilitate, not inhibit, the interview process. Used correctly, they serve as a map to a specific destination, allowing frequent side trips along the way. The legal assistant should be flexible enough to ask pertinent questions not listed on the checklist as the dialogue progresses. If the client or the witness wanders too far from the subject, however, the checklist provides focus to put the interview back on track.

Forms or questionnaires completed by the client sometimes provide an efficient method to gather facts. They work best, however, after the working relationship already has been established between the lawyer and the client. A prospective client who has no previous working relationship with the law office may be offended understandably by forms or questionnaires sent to her for completion before the initial client interview. In this situation, the prospective client justifiably may conclude that she will be just another form in a vast sea of forms located somewhere in the lawyer's office. Each client prefers to believe her case is the most interesting one that the lawyer has, and she expects the lawyer and the legal assistant to feel the same way. A pre-interview questionnaire makes this belief difficult to maintain.

If a follow-up form or questionnaire is given or sent to a client for completion after the client relationship has been established, it should be client friendly. It should be constructed simply, with ample "white space" to provide answers. Questions should be phrased in a clear and concise way and should be couched in terms which demonstrate sensitivity to the typical situation addressed by the form. A bankruptcy questionnaire, for example, might include the following:

POOR   List the name and address of each creditor holding a disputed, contingent, or nonliquidated claim against the debtor's estate:

BETTER   Give the name and address of anyone who claims you owe money if you think the claim is wrong (1) because you do not owe the money or (2) because you do not owe as much as the creditor says you owe (do not include claims that are part of a past or present lawsuit):

POOR   List all debts for which you have defaulted in payments:

BETTER   List each of the bills for which payments are not current:

The second question in each group is better, because it states the instruction in simple English and because it avoids words that imply the client is to blame for his situation.

Corroboration of Facts   All relevant facts obtained during a client or witness interview must be corroborated. Corroboration is the process used to substantiate or to verify the accuracy of a particular fact. It assures the attorney of the client's (or witness') credibility; it also provides supporting evidence which can be used during trial to assure the jury of the credibility of a particular witness or of the justness of the overall claim or defense raised by the client.

After any interview, the legal assistant must verify the information gathered, distinguishing facts of personal knowledge from conjecture, opinion, or gossip. Clients and witnesses frequently are confused or mistaken about dates, times, events, distances, and other specific details (unless they are among those rare individuals who record everything that happens during the course of a day). Investigate outside sources for corroborating evidence to substantiate the client's recollection of facts and the lawyer's legal theory. Corroboration is essential for every factual statement made during the interview.

A.   Identity of People   Obtaining the complete name, address, telephone number, and place of employment of any person mentioned during a client or witness interview is important to the investigative process. For example, if a client relates that her neighbor was present when the defendant threatened her, the legal assistant must obtain as much identifying information about the neighbor as possible. After the interview, the neighbor is contacted to corroborate the client's story.

A witness interview may reveal that a particular witness has little or no firsthand knowledge about the case. Although a witness may not offer the strong statement hoped for, she may be able to provide leads to others who have relevant information.

Every lead must be checked. The person thought least likely to have relevant information may become the star witness in a case. In conducting the investigation, the legal assistant should determine why a particular person was in the area at the time of the event or incident, whether he frequented the area, how he may know the client, the person's relationship (if any) to the client or any witness, and whether he has given this or similar information to others. If a person seems to have useful information, a background check should be conducted to assure his credibility and reliability. Careful scrutiny of witnesses eliminates surprises at trial.

B.   Identity of Documents   The client generally is the first source of documents connected with a case, which he often brings with him to the initial interview. If there are other documents which may be relevant to the case but which the client does not have, the legal assistant must obtain as many details as possible about those documents from the client, including their location and the identity of the person who has them.

If geography, weather conditions, technical structure, or similar conditions are relevant to an issue in the case, the legal assistant may need to obtain plat drawings from the city or county engineers, weather maps from the weather service, evaluation reports from technical engineers, or other documentation from appropriate specialists. If there is a charge for any of the information, authorization must be obtained from the supervising attorney.

Keep documents produced by the opposing party separate from those supplied by the client. Compare documents in the two groups to determine if there is a "smoking gun" among the documents which may be detrimental to the client's case.

Listen   The legal assistant or lawyer must listen actively throughout the interview, which means more than simply hearing and recording the facts. Gathering facts is only one small part of active listening.

Active listening requires the legal assistant to visualize the situation as the client relates it. This means being quiet and letting the client speak; it also means being actively engaged with the storyteller. An active listener places himself into the story and imagines being there as the events are described. This sometimes is called imaginative listening or *empathy*. An active listener feels what the client feels, and he is able to express those feelings in objective terms.

The way to understand the meaning of words and the feeling behind them is to listen closely to the client. The client's story is central to the fact-gathering process. It delineates the experiences and expectations of the client. By allowing the client to talk freely, the legal assistant is able to see the situation or the problem from the client's vantage point.

Equally important to active listening is the client's nonverbal communication (body language). The way she presents herself (relaxed or nervous, pleasant or angry) frequently communicates messages much more loudly than her words. If the client appears wary, distrustful, or guarded, the legal assistant needs to work harder at gaining the trust necessary for a good working relationship. Recognizing the client's unwillingness to talk or unwillingness to talk about a particular subject requires the legal assistant to be flexible enough to discuss more neutral topics until the client is ready to move back to the issues at hand.

Active listening results in signals from the interviewer to indicate that she hears and understands what the client or witness is saying and that she wants to hear more. The signals include an attentive posture, the proper amount of eye contact, approving nods, and supportive comments such as *"please go on,"* *"I see,"* *"of course,"* *"it must have been very hard for you,"* and so forth.

A.   Is That a Fact?   As part of the interview process, the legal assistant records information, sorting it into broad categories according to whether it is a fact or not. Clients frequently inject opinions, speculation, conjecture, or assumptions as they relate facts. Without interrupting the natural flow of the narrative, the legal assistant segregates the facts and obtains as many details as possible about those facts during subsequent questioning.

A *fact* is a situation, event, or occurrence which is within the personal knowledge of the client or witness. With the exception of an expert witness, clients and most other witnesses are permitted to testify about only those things they know personally; they cannot testify about their opinions, impressions, or assumptions. This distinguishes fact witnesses from expert witnesses. For example, a fact witness could not testify at trial that a particular thing tasted like dirt without first establishing that he had tasted dirt. Likewise, a fact witness generally could not testify that the defendant was intoxicated, because few fact witnesses are experts in the area of intoxication. The witness could testify about only what he saw, heard, smelled, and the like. He could testify that the defendant was unsteady on his feet (the witness could see this), that the defendant's speech was slurred (the witness could hear this), or that the defendant reeked of alcohol (the witness could smell this). Although it may be profitable to pursue a client's opinion statements during an interview to determine their factual basis, the legal assistant's ultimate objective is to obtain as many facts and details about facts as possible from the interview.

A more complete discussion of segregation of facts is contained in Chapter 4 on judgment and analytical ability in this *Review Manual*.

B.   Does It Make Sense?   Active listening means listening critically to what the client or witness says to determine if it makes sense. Sometimes people simply make errors or misstate the facts when they relate them (*see below*). Frequently, however, people determine ahead of time what it is that they think the interviewer needs to know; and that is the narrative they give. Generally speaking, facts obtained through this type of filtering must be explored by the legal assistant to ensure that all facts are exposed and to evaluate credibility of the facts provided based on principles of logic.

Understanding the client's communication style is helpful in recognizing her pattern of logic. During an interview, answers fall into a pattern which tends to reveal more than their factual content. If the client talks in circles, the message may be that she is reluctant to face the issue. For example, a driver who hits a child pedestrian may have difficulty describing the sequence of events because of guilt feelings, even though the accident was not his fault. A battered woman who explains in detail how she acquired bruises through her clumsiness may not even mention her abusive husband's behavior toward her. The facts must be pieced together carefully to re-create an accurate chain of events. This is particularly important for jury trials, where the jury must be able to relate to a logical sequence of events. Showing how the pieces fit together is the lawyer's job, with the help of the client and the witnesses.

Every interviewer has an obligation to practice active listening techniques. Devoting less than full attention to the dialogue is a disservice to the client. Attentive listening exposes not only the facts, but also groundless beliefs, false interpretations, misconceptions, and fears. When several people are interviewed about the same incident, their stories may contain inconsistencies even though all of them point to the same ultimate conclusion. All inconsistencies must be investigated to determine the true details and sequence of events.

Contradictory Statements   Stories filled with contradictions or inconsistencies present challenges to the legal assistant. The legal assistant must (1) recognize the inconsistency and (2) analyze the motive of the client or witness who is telling the story. Some inconsistencies may be simple misunderstandings or misperceptions; others may be deliberate deceptions.

    A.   Error   Clients and witnesses frequently become confused about specific details of facts and events unless they can identify the event with a special occurrence. The confusion leads to errors or to misstatements of fact. For example, a client may be certain of the date of an accident because it happened on his birthday; his recollection that the day was a Wednesday may be wrong, however. The interviewer always should ask if there is anything special about the date that causes the client to remember it. If there is no special reason to remember it, be skeptical about details related to dates, times, and so forth. Most people cannot remember what they had for lunch last Wednesday unless there is a special reason to remember. They become confused and then convince themselves that it must have happened on a particular day or in a particular way.

    Interviews conducted soon after an incident provide the most accurate information. Memories fail after a period of time—the longer the time between the incident and the interview, the weaker the recollection of the witness. If the witness cannot remember the facts surrounding an incident, or if he knew only part (but not all) of the facts in the first place, he may engage in presumption and conjecture about what he thinks must have happened rather than report only what he knows to be the fact. It is more difficult for the legal assistant to separate fact from conjecture when statements are taken long after the incident because by then, the witness will have convinced himself that all of it is fact.

    A corollary to this problem is the witness who knows only a few facts and fills in the gaps with information that he thinks the interviewer wants to hear or that he thinks make his story more believable. This sometimes is called ***confabulation***. Faced with a thorough and tactful interviewer, this witness may be able to back away from the fictional parts of his statement without losing face. This type of witness generally is somewhat easier to deal with than one who has become convinced that his conjecture is fact (*see above*).

B.   Misperception   Misperception and differences in perception sometimes occur because people perceive things differently. The differences in what two different people perceive may stem from the fact that each was located at a different vantage point when the incident occurred. If two different witnesses were standing on opposite corners of an intersection, for example, a comparison of their statements likely would show inconsistencies or contradictions. What each witness saw genuinely could be different, because each saw a different side of the accident scene.

Even if both witnesses were standing on the same street corner, they may give different accounts of the accident. A classic illustration of how this phenomenon works is used in evidence classes across the country. Shortly after the class begins, an unidentified person darts into the room, grabs something from the professor's podium or desk, and darts out again. Everyone is startled except the professor, who arranged for the incident to occur. The professor asks the students to write a description of the thief. None of the students has any reason to misrepresent the facts (who would not want to get a good grade?); yet, if there are 15 students in the class, there will be 15 different descriptions of the thief. He might be described variously as wearing a blue jacket, a black jacket, a navy blue jacket, or no jacket at all. The balance of the thief's description will be just as diverse as the information reported about his jacket. When the "thief" returns to the classroom for inspection, students generally are astounded to see for themselves how inaccurate most of their descriptions are.

This type of inconsistency or contradiction occurs all the time, particularly in connection with a startling event. It has nothing to do with lying; different people simply perceive things in different ways.

C.   Deception   Occasionally, a legal assistant encounters a witness who misrepresents facts and events intentionally. The best efforts to establish rapport with a witness may not prevent her from telling distortions and lies. Probing with diplomatic questions will not accomplish much if the witness is intent on concealing the truth. The motive for such behavior may never be known, but this witness should not be dismissed lightly. An unscrupulous witness may align himself with the opposing party and can create havoc, at least for a short time. When such a witness is discovered in the investigation of a case, a second interview may be warranted—preferably conducted by the attorney and conducted with recording equipment.

If it becomes clear during an initial interview that a client or witness deliberately is lying, the legal assistant should excuse himself tactfully and advise the lawyer immediately. If the lawyer is not available, the alternative is to end the interview on some pretext and to advise the lawyer when she returns.

<u>**Verify Accuracy**</u>   Factual contradictions and inconsistencies can arise through error, misperception, or deception. Because of this, every factual account must be verified. Those factual accounts provided by clients must, in addition, be corroborated through written documentation and the testimony of witnesses.

A.   During the Interview   During the interview and after the client has concluded her initial narrative, the legal assistant asks questions designed to verify what the client said and to fill the factual gaps left by the narrative. Empathetic questioning, rather than showmanship, reaps the greatest rewards in this process. For example, a question that begins, *"Isn't it true that . . .?"* is the worst way to obtain additional information. This type of leading question may be appropriate in a cross-examination during trial, but it serves no beneficial purpose in the interview process. If it is asked during an interview, the client or witness may become defensive and refuse to provide helpful information or may refuse to provide further information of any kind.

Instead, phrase the question as a request for help or clarification. For example, questions that begin with *"Let me see if I understand . . ."* or *"I am confused about . . ."* are less intimidating and are more likely to be answered freely. Questioning has two purposes: (1) to obtain specific information and (2) to guide the discussion to meaningful details concerning that information. The client or witness usually is more willing to cooperate by helping if the interviewer is confused than if the interviewer seems to think that he (the client or witness) is confused or—even worse—that he is lying.

The process of verifying facts and details with the client or the witness during the interview is sometimes called ***internal verification***. In addition to probing gently for further facts to verify details previously supplied, the legal assistant may misstate a detail purposely. This gives the client an opportunity to correct the error, which tells the legal assistant how certain the client is about the facts. This technique is quite effective if it is used in moderation. Overused, the client may infer that the legal assistant was not paying attention at all while he was relating his problem.

B.   After the Interview   Once the interview is concluded, the legal assistant prepares a list of potential documents to acquire as well as a list of agencies, companies, and other witnesses to contact for supplemental information and documentation. In addition, ***external verification*** is used to check outside sources to verify the facts obtained from the client or witness.

Accounts reported by newspapers and other media may verify or corroborate the client's claims. Other sources might include hospital records, photographs, police reports, employment records, business records, school records, military records, driving records, court records, and vital statistics records. If a case involves a personal injury claim related to employment, investigation of the employment background of the claimant may reveal a history of job-related personal injury claims. Investigation of the claimant's medical records for similar injuries previously sustained also may be useful. Even if these sources are not accessible early in the case because the claimant is the opposing party, anyone can check the records of those courts where prior cases would have been filed. If this type of information exists, the lawyer certainly will want to have it as early in the case as possible, without regard to which side she represents.

The public also has access to weather maps, geography maps, demographics of a city, census information, engineer plats and surveys, real estate records, and similar types of official records. Depending on the issues involved in a particular case, this type of documentation can be helpful.

Obtaining official records from a government agency or from a private organization can test the patience and perseverance of the most experienced legal assistant. Writing or telephoning the agency and asking for the record is the most direct approach. However, because some records are privileged, it may be necessary to obtain signed authorizations or releases from the client. Even with the client's written authorization, some information may not be available to the law office. Certain government agencies will release documents and information to the client only. One such agency is the Social Security Administration.

Obtaining public and private records has its price. Agencies normally charge a fee for information. Always check with the supervising attorney first to determine if the record's benefit to the case justifies its cost. Clients generally are not happy about being charged to stockpile useless documents.

Any individual named by the client or the witness should be contacted to learn what information this person has. Each lead needs to be thoroughly checked because the next lead could produce a key witness in the case. Some leads will be dead ends; a few will be worthwhile pursuing.

The legal assistant searches for verification (whether internal or external) of every factual detail related to him. Gentle probing of the client or witness is necessary to seek additional information or to raise the client's awareness to remember other details and other witnesses. During the questioning and at the conclusion of the interview, the issues raised by the client or the witness are separated between personal knowledge and conjecture. The legal assistant has the responsibility to confirm (corroborate) those items of personal knowledge through witnesses and documentation.

Complete All Required Forms   Before the client leaves an interview, the legal assistant should have any appropriate forms available for the client's signature. Bringing anticipated forms to the initial interview reflects the organization, efficiency, and professionalism of the lawyer and her staff. These forms might include medical authorization forms, powers of attorney for tax information, or releases to obtain financial information from banking institutions. If the required forms are signed right away, work on the client's case can begin more quickly.

Conclude the Interview   The legal assistant should end the interview cordially, outlining any responsibility that either she or the client has to furnish supplemental data. An agreed deadline is set so that each knows the time frame, and the date is recorded on the calendar. If the client is to bring or to send additional documents to the law office, list them on a separate sheet of paper so the client can take the list with her when she leaves the office.

If a deadline cannot be met, the legal assistant should inform the lawyer as soon as that fact is known. An explanation also may be necessary to the client if she is involved. Keeping the client informed and involved throughout the case is important in maintaining a positive attorney-client relationship.

When the interview is over, accompany the client or witness back to the reception area of the law office. Abandoning visitors in the hallway is a poor practice (*see above*).

Documenting the Interview

Immediately following the interview, the legal assistant must summarize the interview and record the facts obtained, based on her interview notes. The less time that elapses between the conclusion of the interview and its documentation, the more accurate the documentation will be. All relevant information (whether it is helpful or is damaging) is included in a written memorandum, which is provided to the lawyer, with a copy placed in the client file.

Notes and Memorandum   In addition to a neatly typed file memorandum to summarize the interview, all handwritten notes are preserved in the client file. The file memorandum should follow a standardized format established by office policy, which typically includes heading, personal data, stated assignment, chronology of facts, and conclusion. A sample memorandum is shown on the following page.

MEMORANDUM

TO:	Virginia Koerselman, Staff Attorney
FROM:	Susan Lewis, CLA, Legal Assistant
DATE:	July 3, 2013
RE:	Clyde Client v. ABC Corporation File 06-345, Personal Injury
WITNESS:	I.C. Awl (witness at scene of accident)
INTERVIEW DATE:	July 3, 2013

****

<u>Personal Data</u>

Name and Address:	I.C. Awl 1234 Main Street Anywhere, D.C. 12345
Telephone:	101-555-3333 (Home) 101-555-0000 (Work)
Marital Status	Single
Employer	Wacky Widgets, Inc. 333 LaSalle Street Anywhere, D.C. 12347

****

<u>Assignment</u>

Interview I.C. Awl, witness to a personal injury accident on January 1, 2013, to obtain information about the accident scene, to identify who was at the scene and location of vehicles before and after the accident, weather conditions, and other relevant details.

<u>Chronology of Facts</u>

On January 1, 2013, I.C. Awl was driving to a friend's house located at 100 Murphy Drive, Nowhere, D.C. to attend a New Year's Day football party. On his way to the party, I.C. Awl witnessed an accident involving our client, Clyde Client.

The remainder of the chronology section lists the sequence of events and the details reported by the witness. Every relevant detail is included in logical, chronological order for further investigation. The chronology is presented in a narrative paragraph format, similar to that of a story.

<u>Conclusion</u>

Summarize the major points of the chronology, together with the interviewer's evaluation of the witness, his knowledge of the facts, and his believability. These are important considerations to the lawyer in the management of the case. In addition, the conclusion may include a list of additional investigative steps to be taken by the legal assistant or a list of documents or other items to be produced by the witness.

Recorded Interviews Whether to record an interview is a decision made by the attorney (*see above*). If the attorney elects to record an interview, the recording is transcribed and the original recording is preserved. The transcription should reflect exactly what was recorded, grammatical errors and all.

It is not uncommon after the initial interview of a witness that a second interview is necessary to clarify inconsistent statements or details of events. When this occurs, a recorded interview may be advisable, not only to provide clarity but also to determine the basis or motivation for the inconsistent or contradictory facts provided. A witness usually is eager to correct the record, particularly if he knows the information will be used in a court proceeding.

Witness Statements Witness statements may take various forms:

- Handwritten statement

- Typewritten statement

- Questionnaire completed by the witness

- Tape-recorded statement in a question-answer format

- Statement recorded and transcribed by a court reporter in a question–answer format.

The purpose of a witness statement is to memorialize the exact events recalled by a witness in a form which may be used in court, without violating evidence rules related to hearsay and privilege. A witness statement is a different document than the interview memorandum prepared by the legal assistant. Both types of documentation can result from a single witness interview.

A witness statement should identify the witness, the date and place of the interview, and the interviewer. Additional information may include the address of the witness, her place of employment, or any other identifying information.

The interviewer may guide the witness to present the events in sequential order and to give the statement focus and organization. However, the words should be those of the witness. At its end, a witness statement should contain specific language to show that the witness made the statement voluntarily.

A handwritten statement may be prepared either by the interviewer or by the witness. The important factors are to record the information accurately as the witness stated it to be and to have the witness review and sign the handwritten statement. If the interviewer handwrites the statement, he may make an intentional error of fact so that when the witness reviews the statement, the error is discovered, corrected, and initialed by the witness. The initials and correction in the handwriting of the witness show that the witness reviewed the statement.

In a typewritten statement, everything is transcribed exactly as the witness stated. An impartial investigator (someone other than the legal assistant) may seek some insignificant information so the witness has an opportunity to make unfavorable statements about the client. This reinforces the investigator's objectivity.

At the conclusion of a typewritten statement, a sentence similar to the following should be included: *I have read ___ pages of this statement, and the information recorded is correct to the best of my knowledge.* Asking the witness to initial each page provides further evidence that she had the opportunity to review the entire document and that no pages were substituted. The witness signs the statement and is provided with a signed copy.

Taking witness statements soon after an incident is the best practice. Recollection of events is clearer and usually is more accurate at that time. During trial, properly recorded witness statements may be used as a source for refreshing the memory of the witness.

Special Interview Challenges

Because each interview is unique, it can present a unique set of challenges to the interview process. Among the challenges encountered by legal assistants with some frequency are clients or witnesses with special communication needs. Interviewing persons who do not speak fluent English, persons with disabilities, very young children, or persons of advanced age requires special accommodation and consideration.

Foreign-Born Persons   A client or a witness who does not speak English (or who does not speak English as her first language) may require an interpreter to translate information during the interview. A friend or family member may not be the best choice if the case involves an estate plan, a proposed guardianship, relinquishment of parental rights, or similar matter. If an independent interpreter is arranged, use care to ensure that his or her reputation for reliability is above reproach. If the firm has not used an independent interpreter in the past, an immigration lawyer in the community may be able to provide possible sources.

If the person speaks enough English to communicate in an interview setting, special care must be taken to ensure that she understands fully the questions asked of her and that the legal assistant understands the answers given. An interview with this type of individual usually requires more time and planning than the typical client interview.

Disabled Persons   The client (or witness) with a physical or mental disability affecting her sight, speech, hearing, or level of comprehension presents a special set of challenges. This individual may require a sign interpreter, a Braille expert, or special equipment to communicate. The legal assistant must make arrangements prior to the interview to accommodate the person's special communication needs.

The legal assistant must be especially sensitive to this person's situation in planning and in conducting the interview.

Young Children   When a child is interviewed, the permission of at least one parent is required to conduct the interview.

The best situation is to interview the child without a parent in the room if he is old enough to engage in an interview on that basis. With or without a parent, additional time generally is required to gain a child's trust before the substantive portion of the interview begins—how much time depends on the age of the child and the interviewer's expertise in working with children. Because a young child's attention span is extremely short, it may be necessary to schedule more than one session to complete the interview.

If the child is too young to be interviewed effectively without his parent, arrange the seating so that the parent is nearby but the child cannot see the parent during the interview (perhaps by seating the parent in a chair next to the child's chair but placed slightly back). If the child cannot see his parent's reaction to the questions, he is more likely to give his own account of the events. Otherwise, he may rely on the parent's facial expression to respond in whatever way he thinks will please the parent.

Elderly Persons   Clients and witnesses of advanced age may present an entirely different set of challenges. As much as possible, the legal assistant should determine this client's general physical and mental condition well before the interview. It may be that no special accommodation is required. If that is not the case, however, the interview should be planned in whatever way best accommodates the client or witness.

As a general rule, an elderly person tires more easily; his attention span is relatively brief; and his powers of concentration are not as sharp as those of a younger individual. Interviews scheduled in the middle of the morning are more successful than those scheduled in the late afternoon or evening. These factors must be taken into account in planning an interview with an elderly client.

If the client is hospitalized or if he resides in a nursing home, a field interview may be the only type of interview that is possible. Even if an elderly client is ambulatory, a field interview nevertheless may be advisable. Traveling to the law office can be an exhausting endeavor, which reduces the amount of energy left for the interview itself.

A client who is hospitalized (whether aged or not) frequently is taking some type of prescribed medication. If it is a type which substantially impairs mental clarity, the interview should be postponed if that can be done effectively.

Even in the very best of circumstances, interviewing is an inherently imperfect art which has many styles. The objective of each interview is to find the truth. The legal assistant who enjoys people, challenges, and changes will find interviewing gratifying. *See the bibliography for additional study references.*

Human Relations and Interviewing Techniques Self-Test

Allow an uninterrupted 30-minute period to answer all questions. At the end of 30 minutes, check your answers against those in the Answer Key Section of this Manual. Deduct two points for each incorrect answer (100 total possible points). Unanswered questions are counted as incorrect answers. Follow directions carefully and observe the time limit precisely to provide an accurate self-assessment.

Choose the most correct answer to the following questions unless a specific question instructs you to do otherwise.

1.   True or False.   Part of the interview summary should relate to the interviewer's observations concerning the apparent credibility of the witness and the information upon which the interviewer's conclusions are based.

2.   True or False.   When large numbers of witnesses must be interviewed, the legal assistant should endeavor to schedule group interviews of three or more witnesses each to save time.

3.   True or False.   Generally speaking, the interviewer may rely on a witness's recollection of details related to times and dates.

4.   True or False.   A legal assistant should not take photographs of accident scenes or of visible injuries of victims, because the legal assistant's position prevents him or her from providing the foundation testimony needed to admit the photographs at trial.

5.   True or False.   If the legal assistant suspects that a client would prefer to be interviewed by a lawyer, it is acceptable to resolve the issue by simply asking the client.

6.   Which of the following witness statements requires corroboration?

   a.   I was furious.
   b.   Amy punched me in the stomach.
   c.   I cannot remember.
   d.   None requires corroboration.

7.   The capacity of a witness to manufacture details to make known facts more believable is called:

   a.   confabulation
   b.   corroboration
   c.   configuration
   d.   fabrication

8.   The ideal client interview is one in which:

   a.   The client controls the interview process.
   b.   The checklist controls the interview process.
   c.   The legal assistant controls the interview process.
   d.   The process moves forward in its own direction and at its own pace.

9.   Which of the following statements requires corroboration of some type?

   a.   I hated to sell the house.
   b.   David was severely depressed for nearly a year.
   c.   Maggie is incapable of such a cruel act.
   d.   None requires corroboration.

10. Which of the following witness statements requires documentary verification?

    a. We sold our house on June 1.
    b. David was severely depressed after he lost his job.
    c. Maggie is incapable of harming anyone.
    d. None requires documentary verification.

11. True or False.   Because witnesses want to be believed, they generally relate facts in such a way that they can be reasonably certain of accomplishing this result.

12. True or False.   Listening is the most passive part of the interview process.

13. True or False.   To conduct an effective interview, the legal assistant must control the pace, purpose, and direction of the dialogue.

14. True or False.   When a legal assistant prepares a statement for the signature of the witness who provided the facts for the statement, the legal assistant must take special care to ensure an error-free document before it is submitted to the witness for review and signature.

15. True or False.   Witnesses tend to be inhibited by the use of checklists and by note taking of the interviewer during the interview process.

16. A witness who is known to oppose the client's position is a(n):

    a. opposing party
    b. negative witness
    c. negative party
    d. hostile witness

17. Ideally, interviews with very small children should be conducted:

    a. with a parent present, who should be seated beside the interviewer.
    b. with a parent present, who should be seated bedside the child.
    c. with a parent present, who is seated slightly behind the child.
    d. without a parent present.

18.   Which of the following interview questions is most likely to elicit further narrative explanation from a witness?

     a.   Please state your complete name and address.
     b.   How long have you been employed by the defendant?
     c.   How did you happen to get into this line of work?
     d.   Where were you at 3:00 p.m. on the day of the murder?

19.   When a witness uses a slang word that the legal assistant does not understand during an interview, the legal assistant should:

     a.   stop the witness and seek an explanation of the word.
     b.   ask the witness about the word later in the interview.
     c.   make note of the word and ask the attorney after the interview.
     d.   None of these is satisfactory.

20.   Collaboration occurs when:

     a.   the testimony of a witness is supported by another witness.
     b.   the testimony of a witness is supported by an independent source.
     c.   two or more people work together on a project.
     d.   None of these is correct.

21.   True or False.   Once the legal assistant has been introduced to a new client, he should reiterate his nonlawyer status to the client before the interview begins.

22.   True or False.   Generally speaking, legal assistants should not conduct extensive investigations of background facts; instead, this type of investigation should be done by a private investigator.

23.   True or False.   When a legal assistant interviews a witness who seems uncooperative, the legal assistant should re-evaluate his own conduct and mannerisms and should alter them if necessary to relate better to the witness.

24.   True or False.   The first documentation in a client's file, usually made after the initial interview, is a memorandum.

25.   True or False.   When two different witnesses give two different versions of the facts of an incident, the legal assistant can be reasonably certain that one of them is lying.

26.   Judicious use of silence by the legal assistant during the interview process indicates to the witness:

    a.   That the legal assistant accepts the witness' statements as true.
    b.   That the legal assistant is concentrating on the witness' words.
    c.   That the legal assistant is concerned for the witness' well-being.
    d.   None of these is indicated.

27.   When a witness is reluctant to talk with the legal assistant during a field interview, the legal assistant's best course of action is to:

    a.   Advise the witness that if he does not talk voluntarily, he can be deposed.
    b.   Offer to come back at another time.
    c.   Get the witness to talk about unrelated things, hoping to come back to the reason for the interview.
    d.   See if the witness knows anyone else who might have relevant information.

28.   Which of the following witness statements relates a fact?

    a.   I left the restaurant between 10:00 p.m. and 10:30 p.m.
    b.   I don't know when Tom left.
    c.   Tom was extremely drunk, even before dinner was served.
    d.   He may have been drinking before I arrived.

29.   As a general rule, an interview should be recorded:

    a.   Always.
    b.   Never.
    c.   Only when instructed by the attorney.
    d.   Except when instructed otherwise by the attorney.

30.   Which of the following is (are) closed questions?

    a.   What happened next?
    b.   Where did you go after that happened?
    c.   What leads you to say that?
    d.   How long have you known the plaintiff?
    e.   Two of the above.
    f.   None of the above.

31.   True or False.   When interviewing, the legal assistant should stick closely to the interview checklist to avoid wasting time on extraneous information.

32.   True or False.   With experience, a legal assistant is able to acclimate to witnesses who have attention problems, language barriers, or similar difficulties in the traditional interview setting.

33.   True or False.   When conducting an interview, the legal assistant should not pursue any of the statements made unless they are directly relevant to the issues in the case.

34.   True or False.   When it is apparent that a client is upset with the opposing party in the case, the legal assistant should show agreement with and support for the client by agreeing with her negative statements.

35.   True or False.   The ideal client interview is one in which the client relates events in his or her own words.

36.   Which of the following is the best way to handle a client who has dissolved into uncontrolled tears during the initial interview?

   a.   Take a break.
   b.   Offer tissues, sit quietly, and wait.
   c.   Ask the client not to cry.
   d.   Tell the client to be strong and continue with the interview.

37.   Among the following items, the best corroboration for a client's statement that the other party caused the client's injuries is:

   a.   the other party's admission under oath.
   b.   a favorable police report.
   c.   a favorable eye witness.
   d.   skid marks from the other party's vehicle.

38.   Which of the following witness statements should be verified?

   a.   Before he died, he told me many times when we were alone that I would inherit the farm upon his death.
   b.   It was so foggy that I could not see more than four feet ahead.
   c.   I want to place my child for adoption.
   d.   It was extremely embarrassing for me.

39.   Which of the following represents the type of supportive comment that may be made by a legal assistant during an interview to gain the trust of the witness?

     a.   Don't worry about a thing; (name of lawyer) never loses a case.
     b.   I'm sure it was difficult for you.
     c.   You can rest assured that (name of lawyer) is a tiger in the courtroom.
     d.   Trust me.

40.   True or False.   One acceptable way to verify details during the interview is to misstate them purposely to see if the witness corrects the interviewer.

41.   True or False.   The most successful interviewer is one who can demonstrate surprise, approval, disbelief, and disapproval by facial expression alone during the interview.

42.   True or False.   Witnesses tend to be inhibited by the use of a recording device during the interview process.

43.   True or False.   When conflicts arise in information supplied by a witness, the legal assistant may assume that the witness is either lying or mistaken.

44.   True or False.   A witness who is uncooperative during an interview generally is classified as a hostile witness.

45.   True or False.   An expert witness generally may be classified as an official witness as well.

46.   True or False.   Statements concerning size or distance may be verified by personal examination of the interviewer.

47.   Which of the following witnesses generally are the least reliable?

     a.   expert witnesses
     b.   friendly witnesses
     c.   hostile witnesses
     d.   official witnesses

48.   If the legal assistant has reason to believe that a witness is lying during an interview, the legal assistant should:

    a.   discontinue the interview and notify the supervising attorney.
    b.   point out the inconsistencies to the witness and allow him to offer an explanation if he can.
    c.   continue the interview, noting the inconsistencies as the interview progresses.
    d.   continue the interview to see how far the witness will take the fabrication.

49.   True or False.   When a legal assistant records a telephone interview, he or she first must obtain the consent of the witness and should refer to the recording at several points during the telephone interview.

50.   True or False.   If a witness seems unusually anxious during the interview, the interviewer should ask leading questions about the central facts until the witness relaxes enough to provide narrative information.

ETHICS

If you can dream it, you can do it.

—Walt Disney

This section deals with ethics in contacts with employers, clients, coworkers, and the general public. Unauthorized practice, ethics rules, practice rules, and confidentiality are among the topics tested in this section.

Knowledge of the American Bar Association (ABA) Model Rules of Professional Conduct and the National Association of Legal Assistants and Paralegals, Inc. (NALA) Code of Ethics and Professional Responsibility is required for successful completion of this section. Familiarity with the NALA Model Standards and Guidelines for the Utilization of Paralegals also is helpful.

Ethics Defined

Ethics are those standards by which conduct is measured. Generally speaking, a professional is held to a higher ethical standard than an average person is. Professional ethics usually are governed by a set of written rules (a *code*) that establish the limits of permissible conduct in the professional's contacts with others as well as the manner in which the professional advances his or her practice. Most ethics rules seek to enhance the integrity of a profession by establishing the minimum levels of conduct required of its members.

In a nutshell, the objectives of professional ethics for legal assistants are twofold:

1. *To maintain high levels of competence; and*

2. *To refrain from the unauthorized practice of law.*

Implicit in both of these objectives is that the legal assistant possesses a level of personal integrity which is above reproach. Much like lawyers, legal assistants occupy positions of trust, which require them not only to observe the specific language of ethics rules, but also to embrace the spirit of those rules.

Sources of Ethics Rules

Each state has adopted a set of ethics standards to govern the professional conduct and practices of licensed attorneys. These standards generally are based upon the unauthorized practice of law (UPL) statute of that state plus the Model Rules or the Model Code adopted by the ABA. As an employee of the attorney, the paralegal likewise must be familiar with these ethics rules.

The most recent ethics standards of the ABA are incorporated in the Model Rules of Professional Conduct, which has been adopted in whole or in part by the substantial majority of states. Very few states still follow the older Model Code of Professional Responsibility, also a product of the ABA. *All ethics questions on the CLA/CP® exam are based upon the more recent **ABA Model Rules of Professional Conduct**.*

Incorporating and supplementing the ABA standards, every member of NALA is governed by the NALA Code of Ethics and Professional Responsibility. At the time of application, every Certified Legal Assistant (CLA)/Certified Paralegal (CP) applicant agrees to be bound by the NALA Code of Ethics, whether or not the applicant is a member of NALA.

In addition to the ethics codes, NALA adopted its Model Standards and Guidelines for the Utilization of Legal Assistants and Paralegals, which subsequently have been adopted in substantial part by the ABA and by a growing number of state bar associations. The Model Standards and Guidelines are designed to assist attorneys by delineating the proper uses of the legal assistant's skills.

The CLA/CP® applicant should be knowledgeable about all applicable ethics standards. Accordingly, summaries of selected portions of the ABA Model

Rules of Professional Conduct are presented below. Immediately following the summaries, the NALA Code of Ethics and the NALA Standards and Guidelines are reprinted in their entirety.

Topical Summaries of Selected ABA Model Rules

The ABA Model Rules of Professional Conduct originally were adopted in 1983 and have been modified in part several times since then. The summaries that follow are designed to give applicants an overview of the main topics covered by the Model Rules. They are not all-inclusive. Accordingly, applicants may benefit from independent review of the complete Model Rules and comments.

Competence and Procrastination   Competence means ability, capability, expertise, mastery, proficiency, or skill. Competence in any field requires the acquisition of sufficient knowledge, training, and experience to do the job.

A lawyer must have those skills necessary to practice law, such as the ability to analyze precedent, to evaluate evidence, to advise clients, and to draft legal documents. For special legal problems, the lawyer must conduct legal research and, where needed, seek the help of more experienced lawyers. It would be unethical for a lawyer to have a caseload in which any case cannot be handled competently. It would be unethical for a lawyer to proceed with a case without adequate preparation.

Competence and education go hand in hand. Each is an ongoing process that cannot exist in a stagnant state. As soon as a person stops actively pursuing knowledge through education, his knowledge begins to erode; and with that erosion, his competence is diminished. Highly competent professionals are the first to acknowledge that the more they learn about their fields of practice, the more they realize how much there is left to learn. Only by their perpetual search for more knowledge do they maintain personal levels of high competence.

Because legal assistants also are expected to maintain high levels of competence, they must take advantage of educational opportunities whenever and wherever those opportunities arise. Education can occur in informal settings, such as during a one-on-one exchange between a lawyer and a legal assistant while working on a client's case or by reading professional literature from cover to cover. It also can occur in more formal settings, such as professional meetings, seminars, workshops, and college classrooms. A high level of competence exists only when it is perpetually evolving.

Unreasonable procrastination also is unethical under the Model Rules. Excessive delay must be avoided. Many firms use a case progression or other system similar to those employed by courts to prevent a case from slipping through the cracks.

Advertising   Advertising is permitted in a telephone directory, legal directory, newspaper or other periodical, radio, TV, billboards, the Internet, and other types of public media. Lawyers cannot pay referral fees to private parties, but it is permissible for them to pay the fee ordinarily charged by nonprofit referral services.

Many states impose further restrictions about what information the lawyer can give about herself, and some states prohibit or limit undignified advertising. The Model Rules, however, do not require these types of restriction.

Solicitation   The Model Rules forbid a lawyer to have direct contact in person or by telephone with those known or thought to need legal services and with whom the lawyer has had no prior professional relationship. This has become known as the rule against "ambulance chasing." In other words, a lawyer cannot chase ambulances to the scene of an accident to hand out his business card; cannot loiter in emergency rooms waiting for ambulances to arrive; or cannot call or visit the parties whose names are listed on accident reports.

Lawyers can, however, send a brochure or a letter to the names found on an accident report if the mailing includes the phrase "Advertising Material" on the outside envelope. They also can identify a particular demographic (senior citizens, for example) and send this type of advertising by mail.

The "ambulance chasing" rule is intended to prevent a lawyer from taking advantage of a person who may be overwhelmed by the circumstances for which legal services are needed and may not be able to think clearly when confronted with an attorney soliciting his business, whether in person or on the telephone. The rule permits general mailings or autodial messages to prospective clients unless a particular prospective client has indicated that he does not wish to receive such information. Similarly, if a mailing or autodial message evokes no response from the prospective client, the lawyer may be prohibited from making any further contact.

Nothing in this rule prohibits a lawyer from participating in a prepaid or group legal services plan not owned or directed by the lawyer, even though those who sponsor or manage the plan to solicit memberships use in-person or telephone contacts.

Candor and Honesty by the Lawyer A lawyer cannot make a false statement of material fact or law to a court, cannot knowingly offer false evidence, or cannot knowingly fail to disclose material facts to a court when necessary to prevent a client from committing fraud or some other criminal act.

A lawyer must be zealous in the representation of her client, but this cannot include deception by the lawyer in making false statements or in offering false or perjured testimony. Also, if the lawyer's research has uncovered cases, statutes, or other authority in the jurisdiction that go against her client, the lawyer must tell the court about this authority if it is not raised by the other side.

In addition, lawyers cannot obstruct opposing counsel's access to evidence and cannot destroy, alter, or falsify evidence in any way. Lawyers cannot offer an illegal inducement to a witness in exchange for the witness's testimony. A fact witness generally can be paid a fixed statutory fee and expenses within the boundaries established by law or court rule. However, it is unlawful in most jurisdictions for an expert witness to be paid a contingent fee for his or her testimony.

Communication with Clients A lawyer must keep a client reasonably informed about the status of the client's case, must comply with a client's reasonable requests for information, and must explain things to the client so that the client can make informed decisions.

Studies have shown that one of the most common types of complaint against lawyers is failure to communicate with the client about the status of his or her case.

A client has a right to know about events as they happen in the case. Legal assistants can assist the lawyer in this area by drafting status letters to clients and by helping to develop a system to ensure that all telephone calls and correspondence from clients receive prompt replies.

Communication with Opposing Party A lawyer cannot have any contact with the opposing party about a pending case unless that party's counsel agrees to the contact in advance, which rarely will happen. However, the rule does not prevent a lawyer from communicating with the opposing party about matters unrelated to the pending case when no attorney represents the party in the unrelated matter. Because of his many contacts on a lawyer's behalf, the paralegal should be particularly familiar with this rule, recognizing that it applies to the lawyer and to the paralegal alike.

A person who is not represented by counsel, especially one who is a novice to the legal system, can misunderstand the role of a lawyer to be that of a disinterested authority on the law. A lawyer never should give advice to an unrepresented person beyond the advice to obtain legal counsel.

Confidentiality of Information A lawyer cannot disclose information concerning the representation of a client unless the client consents or unless the disclosure is necessary to carry out the representation.

This rule relates to client confidentiality and applies to paralegals as well as to lawyers. It is intended to encourage clients to disclose all facts to their lawyers without fear that the lawyer may be required to divulge the information to others. It coordinates with the attorney-client privilege permitted by evidence rules, but it is not the same thing. If a lawyer is charged in a disciplinary proceeding for disclosing a client confidence, the charge will be based upon this rule and not upon the evidence rule.

Exceptions are made to the rule to allow a lawyer to disclose limited information to prevent a client from committing a criminal act that is likely to result in death or great bodily harm, to establish a defense for the lawyer against criminal charges, or to establish a defense in a civil action between the lawyer and the client related to the lawyer's representation. A client's perjured testimony which is given without the attorney's prior knowledge also is excepted from the confidentiality protection.

The duty of confidentiality applies during the period of representation and continues after the attorney-client relationship ends. Clearly, it prohibits the lawyer or the paralegal from discussing either the client or the client's case in social settings outside the office. In addition, it prohibits such things as the following:

•Discussing the client or his case with others in the firm who have no specific need to know the information;

•Disclosing to opposing counsel or to others more about the client than is necessary to accomplish the required objective;

•Confirming to third parties that the client is represented by the firm unless that fact clearly is a matter of public record;

•Engaging in telephone conversations where the client's name or any identifiable information about the client or the case is mentioned within the hearing range of third parties (such as another client waiting in the firm's reception area);

•Permitting client files or papers to be in plain view where they can be seen by anyone who happens to pass by, such as on a receptionist's desk where visitors can see them or on any other desk where night cleaning staff or others can see them without so much as opening a file folder; or

•Inadvertently mailing information about a client's case to unintended persons, which can happen if multiple mailings are mishandled.

Where client confidentiality is concerned, the innocent intentions of the attorney or of the paralegal may mitigate the sanctions imposed; but they cannot absolve the offender.

Conflict of Interest   A lawyer cannot represent opposing parties in a legal matter unless (1) the lawyer reasonably believes that the representation will not affect either party adversely and (2) each party consents.

This rule is directed at conflicts of interest. A single law firm cannot, for instance, represent both a debtor and a creditor in the same bankruptcy proceeding without adversely affecting the position of one or both of the parties. The conflict exists even if two different lawyers in the firm are involved. Because of this rule, law firms traditionally maintain an adverse party index that is checked before a new client is accepted by the firm. Similarly, paralegals who freelance by providing services to lawyers on a contract basis, as well as the lawyers for whom they perform these services, must be especially sensitive to potential conflict of interest problems that can arise.

When the interests of two clients are fundamentally antagonistic to each other (husband and wife seeking divorce), dual representation should be avoided. When a lawyer for an organization also sits on its board of directors, a potential conflict of interest exists.

The conflict-of-interest rule also applies to lawyers and to paralegals who leave one firm to become employed by another. If the new firm represents parties adverse to those parties represented by the old firm, a conflict of interest exists. This difficulty may be resolved by isolating the lawyer or the paralegal from all contacts with the conflicting case until it is concluded, sometimes referred to as a **Chinese Wall**. However, in at least one California case, a paralegal was prevented (enjoined) from accepting employment at the new firm based upon this type of conflict of interest.

Lawyers specifically are prohibited from entering into these types of transactions:

▸*Cannot enter into business ownership transactions with a client unless the terms are fair, the client has a chance to seek independent legal advice, and the client consents.*

▸*Cannot negotiate or agree to obtain from a client media or literary rights to a portrayal based upon his or her representation in a case.*

▸*Cannot provide financial assistance to a client in a pending claim, except that court costs and expenses can be advanced in a contingency fee case and except that court costs and expenses can be paid for an indigent client.*

▸*Cannot accept payment of fee from anyone other than the client unless the client consents, the lawyer remains independent of the third party, and client information remains confidential.*

▸*Cannot settle a civil case for multiple clients or plea bargain for multiple criminal defendants unless all clients know all details of all other interests and consent to the multiple representation.*

▸*Cannot require a client to agree prospectively to limit the lawyer's malpractice liability in a case.*

▸*Cannot assume representation when the opposing party is represented by counsel who is related to the lawyer, unless the client knows of the relationship and consents to representation.*

▸*Cannot acquire proprietary interest in litigation being handled for a client except by reasonable contingency fee contract or lawful attorney's lien to secure fees or expenses.*

Fraud or Criminal Conduct by the Client   A lawyer cannot advise or assist a client to engage in conduct that the lawyer knows is fraudulent or criminal. In other words, it is unethical for a lawyer to tell a client how to commit a crime or a fraudulent act, i.e., to cheat on an income tax return, to fabricate evidence, or to destroy evidence that must be preserved.

Fees   A lawyer's fee must be reasonable. To determine if a particular fee is reasonable, courts consider factors such as the time and labor required; the difficulty of the legal issues involved; the time constraints to obtain a result; the results obtained; and the expertise, reputation, and experience of the lawyer(s) performing the service. Lawyers must advise clients right away of the rate that will be charged.

A contingent fee is one that is a percentage of the total amount collected on behalf of a client. Contingent fees are commonly used in personal injury, property damage, and debt collection cases.

Contingent fees cannot be charged in criminal cases.

Contingent fees also are prohibited in cases where a divorce will be granted or where support or property settlement will be awarded. However, when the objective is collection of support previously ordered and now in default because of nonpayment, contingent fees are permitted on much the same terms as any other case involving collection of a debt.

Retainer letters should be provided to all clients in all cases as a matter of good practice. If the fee is to be contingent, however, a retainer letter must be provided to comply with the rules. In addition, clients should be told that paralegals will be used and the rate that will be charged for the paralegal's work on the case.

Fees can be divided between lawyers in different firms only if the division is proportionate to the services provided, or if each lawyer assumes joint responsibility for the representation; the client knows and does not object to the fee division; and the total fee is reasonable.

Fees never can be divided between a lawyer and a paralegal or other nonlawyer. In addition, the rule prevents paying bonuses to nonlawyers based upon the fee earned in a specific case. The rule does not prevent the inclusion of nonlawyer employees in a retirement plan, even though the plan is based in whole or in part on a profit-sharing arrangement. In many jurisdictions, nonlawyer employees likewise may participate in year-end bonuses based upon overall profits for the preceding year or for a portion of the year. These types of bonuses may be paid either to all employees or only to some employees, as long as no part of the bonus is related to any specific case.

All discussions concerning fees are strictly the attorney's responsibility. A lawyer may require advance payment for all or a portion of the services to be performed (called a retainer), but she must return any unearned portion to the client. A lawyer may accept property or ownership interests in a business enterprise in payment of legal services but cannot accept any type of proprietary interest in the outcome of a case. This type of proprietary interest, called ***champerty***, is forbidden.

Frivolous Claims and Frivolous Discovery Requests   A lawyer cannot file a frivolous case. This is a case that advances a claim or defense which is unwarranted under existing law unless a good faith argument can be made for a change in the existing law. In other words, lawyers cannot file lawsuits solely for the purpose of harassing or maliciously injuring another person.

Under both the Model Rules and the Federal Rules of Civil Procedure, a lawyer is forbidden to file a frivolous discovery request. Violation can lead to severe sanctions for the lawyer. Paralegals typically assist with discovery requests, both those transmitted and those received, and can help to assure that this rule is honored.

Gifts from Clients   A lawyer cannot prepare a document for a client, such as a will, in which the client gives the lawyer a substantial gift, unless the lawyer is related to the client. The prohibition also applies if the gift is given to a close relative or spouse of the lawyer.

The most obvious illustration of the need for this rule is the elderly, probably widowed, client whose children live far away or are otherwise estranged. In coming to trust and rely on the lawyer, this client easily can begin to see the lawyer as more deserving of her estate than her faraway children. It is a form of conflict of interest that the lawyer must eschew.

Many firms resolve the entire matter with a rule against all gifts from clients. If a client sends a gift without asking first, the attorney or paralegal is expected to pass it on for donation to a nursing home, to a school, or to some other charity. Regardless of a particular firm's policy, it makes sense for the paralegal who receives such a gift to tell his or her attorney supervisor right away and to follow the supervisor's direction.

Property of the Client   A lawyer must hold property of clients or third parties separate from the lawyer's own property. Money must be held in a separate account located in the same state where the lawyer's office is located, and complete records must be kept. Clients or third parties must be notified immediately when the lawyer receives money or property on their behalf; the money or property must be disbursed promptly; and the lawyer must make a full accounting.

This is the attorney trust account provision. Every law firm is required to maintain a trust account for clients and others in which no money of the lawyers can be commingled. Advance payment of fees from clients must be kept in the trust account until the lawyer performs work to earn the fees. Only that portion of the retainer which has been earned can be transferred to the lawyer's operating account. Paralegals often deal with trust funds in the performance of their duties and must be familiar with the rules of conduct that govern this area.

Money held for a specific client in a lawyer's trust account may be subject to claims of creditors by proper garnishment proceedings or otherwise; however, the lawyer cannot unilaterally presume to serve as arbiter between the client and a creditor.

Irregularities in a lawyer's trust account or in its management can result in extremely severe sanctions to the lawyer. The case law of some states indicates that when problems arise concerning a trust account, the lawyer should plan for disbarment without regard to the severity of, source, or reason for the problem.

Reporting Professional Misconduct

Rules 8.1 through 8.5 deal with a lawyer's responsibilities in maintaining the integrity of the legal profession and cover topics ranging from making false statements on bar admission applications to reporting professional misconduct of other lawyers.

There is no blanket rule that requires a legal assistant to report (or that forbids a legal assistant from reporting) the professional misconduct of a lawyer. In the usual situation, the lawyer and the legal assistant work toward the same ethical goals. As team members, they provide support to each other for nearly all aspects of the case, including ethics. Most lawyers appreciate non-accusatory questions about potential ethics issues that may arise. They provide the basis for a thoughtful review and appraisal of the situation from all perspectives. However, close questions concerning the ethical implications of a particular course of action must be left for ultimate decision by the lawyer.

Withdrawal of a Lawyer from a Case   A lawyer must not represent a client, or must withdraw from representation of a client, if the representation will result in a violation of the rules of professional conduct; if the lawyer's physical or mental condition materially impairs the ability to represent the client; or if the lawyer is discharged.

If a court orders her to do so, the lawyer must continue the representation. If representation ends, the lawyer must give the client reasonable notice so that other counsel can be obtained and must cooperate with substitute counsel to protect the client's interests.

If a client demands that a lawyer engage or assist in conduct that is illegal or that violates any rule of professional conduct, the lawyer should withdraw from the case. If a client makes such a demand of a paralegal, it should be reported to the supervising attorney at once. Learning that a defendant in a criminal case is guilty, however, is not a valid basis for withdrawal from the case. Lawyers have a duty to protect the rights of all clients without regard to guilt or innocence.

If a lawyer is fired by a client, any property owned by the client should be returned except to the extent that the lawyer is permitted to retain papers and the like under existing law.

Unauthorized Practice of Law (UPL)   Defining the UPL is difficult, because there is no single definition for the practice of law. Each state defines the practice of law by statute, and each state's statutes are slightly different. One thing they all have in common, however, is that violation of the UPL statute is a criminal offense.

Each state requires lawyers to be licensed before they can practice in that state. Before a license is issued, the applicant must demonstrate (1) good moral character; (2) graduation from an accredited law school; and (3) minimal competence by passing a state bar examination. California is the only state that does not require law school graduation as a prerequisite to taking the bar. Once issued, a license grants the holder the privilege to practice law—but only in the state where the license is issued.

In broad, general terms, the ***practice of law*** is any act that involves the giving of legal advice or opinions to others or involves representing others in legal matters. Generally speaking, legal assistants cannot

- accept cases,
- set fees,
- give direct legal advice to clients,
- negotiate legal matters on behalf of clients, or
- represent clients in court settings.

because these actions constitute the practice of law. Beyond these specific limitations, legal assistants ethically can perform virtually every other type of legal task imaginable on behalf of clients as long as three criteria are met:

> *1.   The legal assistant's work is properly super-*
> *vised by a licensed attorney.*

2.   *The supervising attorney maintains a direct relationship with the client.*

3.   *The supervising attorney assumes full professional responsibility for the work product.*

Any legal assistant who violates a UPL statute may incur one or more of the following sanctions:

▶   criminal prosecution;

▶   civil liability to any client damaged by the negligence of the legal assistant while engaging in unauthorized acts; and/or

▶   termination of employment.

In addition, the CLA/CP® designation may be revoked permanently for this type of violation.

As serious as these sanctions are, they do not prevent the offender from obtaining other employment as a paralegal—assuming that some other attorney is willing to hire him. The same is not true for the offender's supervising attorney who can (1) incur civil liability to any client damaged by the negligence of the paralegal and/or (2) be disbarred as a result of the misconduct of the paralegal. If disbarment occurs, it is possible that the attorney never may practice law again.

Paralegals are expected to distinguish between permissible and impermissible conduct in the UPL area. A few examples are illustrated by the problems presented below.

> Jane, an experienced and skilled paralegal in the field of domestic relations, is dissatisfied with the fact that lawyers in her community have failed to provide low-cost legal services to the working poor. She believes that many litigants could handle their own uncontested divorces if they were provided with a procedure handbook and the necessary forms. Jane leaves her employment and compiles a procedure handbook with forms, which she sells in bookstores and by mail order for $50.00. Jane has no contact with purchasers. She does not represent herself as an attorney and, in fact, large notices are placed conspicuously and frequently throughout the handbook, urging that all questionable situations should be handled by a licensed attorney. The handbook gives no legal advice.

As presented, this situation does not violate the UPL statutes of most states. Members of the general public may purchase the handbook or not, as they choose; and, of course, a person always may represent himself in court proceedings if he chooses to do so.

> Continuing with the same problem, Jane discovers that purchasers of her handbook occasionally have difficulty in selecting the proper forms for their situations. A few others have encountered problems in putting the correct information in the correct blanks. For this reason, Jane decides to open an office where she can assist with these simple matters for a small, additional charge.

If she pursues this plan, Jane will have stepped over the line of permissible conduct and into the area of UPL. She cannot help people to select forms without advising them, and her advice constitutes the unauthorized practice of law in most states. Telling handbook purchasers what information goes into which blanks of the forms they have selected likewise requires advice, which is illegal.

By judicial decision, similar operations have been held in violation of UPL statutes. Included among them are typing services run by nonlawyers, where the nonlawyers provided advice on how to complete various legal documents; a credit counseling service that counseled in favor of bankruptcy for some clients and then helped them prepare their own bankruptcy petitions; a landlord's eviction service; and similar enterprises. In each case, the nonlawyer went beyond supplying forms.

> Joe is a paralegal whose attorney-employer is away on a trip. Things have been particularly slow. A woman calls the office, saying she needs to see someone right away because her husband has filed for divorce. Joe visits with the woman to obtain details and tells her the office will take her case. Joe knows the attorney can use the business. Joe then calls the opposing counsel, pretending to be his employer, to see where things stand; and, before he realizes what is happening, he and the lawyer are discussing property settlement for the parties.

Based upon these facts, Joe has committed compound UPL violations. He was wrong to accept the case; wrong to impersonate his employer, regardless of the reason; and wrong to participate in negotiations with opposing counsel. Standing alone, any one of these three things may result in criminal charges, civil liability for damages incurred by the client, and termination of employment.

> Chris is a freelance paralegal who contracts her work to lawyers in the community. In addition, she represents clients independently in proceedings before the Social Security Administration. Her clients know that she is not a lawyer, and this is the only type of case that she handles without attorney supervision. When it is necessary to appeal cases beyond the agency level or when her clients require other types of legal services, she refers them to various young lawyers in the community, who are happy to get the work.

Nothing in these facts indicates a violation of UPL statutes. The rules and regulations of a number of federal administrative agencies permit both lawyers and nonlawyers to appear before them on behalf of others. Included among them are the Social Security Administration, the Internal Revenue Service, and the Immigration and Naturalization Service. Because the rules of the agency permit nonlawyer practice and because Chris's independent practice is limited to proceedings before that agency, there is no violation.

In a similar vein, a small number of courts allow a limited motion practice by nonlawyers who are either paralegals or third-year law students. This is accomplished by a court rule, which generally allows the qualified nonlawyer to appear before the court to argue motions, provided the nonlawyer is sponsored by a licensed attorney. Even where this is permitted, the nonlawyer generally cannot sign pleadings alone or try a case alone. Other courts allow a limited motion practice by third-year law students but not by paralegals. Still other courts allow only licensed attorneys to appear.

> Ben is a prison inmate who has become extremely proficient in post-sentencing matters related to his own incarceration. Before long, Ben finds himself devoting almost all of his free time to helping other inmates by doing legal research and by helping them prepare appropriate applications, petitions, and so forth to pursue earlier releases or lighter sentences.

Ben appears to have become what is known as a "jailhouse lawyer"— an inmate who has studied law and legal procedure on his own, usually in the prison library. Jailhouse lawyers are permitted to provide legal services to other inmates so long as (1) the other inmate requests it, (2) no other legal services are reasonably available, and (3) the legal services are related solely to post-sentencing matters. If an inmate commits a new crime while in prison, for example, the jailhouse lawyer cannot assist him for the trial or sentencing in that case. Neither can the jailhouse lawyer represent him in any civil proceeding, such as a divorce or a debt collection, that may arise while the inmate is in prison.

These examples are not intended to be comprehensive. The situations in which UPL issues can arise are as varied as the people governed by the statute. Additional examples are included in the self-test for this chapter.

Miscellaneous Provisions   A lawyer is expected to provide pro bono or reduced-fee legal services to people of limited means, or should provide financial support to organizations that provide legal services to people of limited means.

Responsibility for providing legal services to those who are unable to pay for them, or who are unable to pay the full rate, ultimately rests with the individual lawyer. Every lawyer should devote a certain amount of time to providing legal services for this segment of the community. Similarly, paralegals are encouraged to provide *pro bono* paralegal services to lawyers representing clients of this type.

A lawyer can state that he does or does not practice in a particular field of law but can neither state nor imply that he is a specialist unless he is a patent attorney or is engaged in admiralty practice. This rule prevents lawyers from portraying themselves as specialists in a particular area of legal practice. Although some states may permit communication of specialty practice, the rules of any specific state are not tested on the CLA/CP® exam.

A lawyer cannot use a firm name, letterhead, or other professional designation that conveys false or misleading information. The name of a lawyer holding public office cannot be used in the name of the law firm during any period when the lawyer is not actively and regularly practicing with the firm. A lawyer cannot state or imply a partnership or other form of practice that does not exist.

This rule does not prevent a firm from continuing to use the names of its deceased members as part of the firm name. It does, however, prohibit lawyers who merely share office facilities and personnel from representing themselves as a partnership by using a firm name such as "Jefferson and Davis" or the like.

A paralegal may sign his name on law firm stationery if his nonlawyer status is clear and if the letter does not contain direct legal advice or otherwise violate an ethics rule. The best way to ensure that the author's nonlawyer status is clear is to include the title "Paralegal" or "Paralegal to _____" directly under the legal assistant's name in the signature block.

Under ABA Informal Opinion 89-1527, names of nonlawyer support staff may be printed on law firm stationery so long as the nonlawyer status is clear. Some states allow this practice; others do not.

National Association of Legal Assistants and Paralegals, Inc.
Code of Ethics and Professional Responsibility

Each NALA member agrees to follow the canons of the NALA Code of Ethics and Professional Responsibility Violations of the Code may result in cancellation of membership. First adopted by the NALA membership in May of 1975, the Code of Ethics and Professional Responsibility is the foundation of ethical practices of paralegals in the legal community.

A paralegal must adhere strictly to the accepted standards of legal ethics and to the general principles of proper conduct. The performance of the duties of the paralegal shall be governed by specific canons as defined herein so that justice will be served and goals of the profession attained. (See Model Standards and Guidelines for Utilization of Legal Assistants, Section II.)

The canons of ethics set forth hereafter are adopted by the NALA, as a general guide intended to aid paralegals and attorneys. The enumeration of these rules does not mean there are not others of equal importance although not specifically mentioned. Court rules, agency rules, and statutes must be taken into consideration when interpreting the canons.

Definition
Legal assistants, also known as paralegals, are a distinguishable group of persons who assist attorneys in the delivery of legal services. Through formal education, training and experience, legal assistants have knowledge and expertise regarding the legal system and substantive and procedural law which qualify them to do work of a legal nature under the supervision of an attorney.

In 2001, NALA members also adopted the ABA definition of a legal assistant/paralegal, as follows:

A legal assistant or paralegal is a person qualified by education, training or work experience who is employed or retained by a lawyer, law office, corporation, governmental agency or other entity who performs specifically delegated substantive legal work for which a lawyer is responsible. (Adopted by the ABA in 1997.)

Canon 1.   A paralegal must not perform any of the duties that attorneys only may perform nor take any actions that attorneys may not take.

Canon 2.   A paralegal may perform any task which is properly delegated and supervised by an attorney, as long as the attorney is ultimately responsible to the client, maintains a direct relationship with the client, and assumes professional responsibility for the work product.

Canon 3. A paralegal must not: (a) engage in, encourage, or contribute to any act which could constitute the unauthorized practice of law; (b) establish attorney-client relationships, set fees, give legal opinions or advice or represent a client before a court or agency unless so authorized by that court or agency; and (c) engage in conduct or take any action which would assist or involve the attorney in a violation of professional ethics or give the appearance of professional impropriety.

Canon 4. A paralegal must use discretion and professional judgment commensurate with knowledge and experience but must not render independent legal judgment in place of an attorney. The services of an attorney are essential in the public interest whenever such legal judgment is required.

Canon 5. A paralegal must disclose his or her status as a paralegal at the outset of any professional relationship with a client, attorney, a court or administrative agency or personnel thereof, or a member of the general public. A paralegal must act prudently in determining the extent to which a client may be assisted without the presence of an attorney.

Canon 6. A paralegal must strive to maintain integrity and a high degree of competency through education and training with respect to professional responsibility, local rules and practice, and through continuing education in substantive areas of law to better assist the legal profession in fulfilling its duty to provide legal service.

Canon 7. A paralegal must protect the confidences of a client and must not violate any rule or statute now in effect or hereafter enacted controlling the doctrine of privileged communications between a client and an attorney.

Canon 8. A paralegal must disclose to his or her employer or prospective employer any pre-existing client or personal relationship that may conflict with the interests of the employer or prospective employer and/or their clients.

Canon 9. A paralegal must do all other things incidental, necessary, or expedient for the attainment of the ethics and responsibilities as defined by statute or rule of court.

Canon 10. A paralegal's conduct is guided by bar associations' codes of professional responsibility and rules of professional conduct.

National Association of Legal Assistants and Paralegals, Inc.
Model Standards and Guidelines for Utilization of Legal Assistants and Paralegals

Introduction

The purpose of this annotated version of the NALA Model Standards and Guidelines for the Utilization of Legal Assistants (the "Model," "Standards" and/or the "Guidelines") is to provide references to the existing case law and other authorities where the underlying issues have been considered. The authorities cited will serve as a basis upon which conduct of a legal assistant may be analyzed as proper or improper.

The Guidelines represent a statement of how the legal assistant may function. The Guidelines are not intended to be a comprehensive or exhaustive list of the proper duties of a legal assistant. Rather, they are designed as guides to what may or may not be proper conduct for the legal assistant. In formulating the Guidelines, the reasoning and rules of law in many reported decisions of disciplinary cases and unauthorized practice of law cases have been analyzed and considered. In addition, the provisions of the ABA's Model Rules of Professional Conduct, as well as the ethical promulgations of various state courts and bar associations have been considered in the development of the Guidelines.

These Guidelines form a sound basis for the legal assistant and the supervising attorney to follow. This Model will serve as a comprehensive resource document and as a definitive, well-reasoned guide to those considering voluntary standards and guidelines for legal assistants.

Preamble

Proper utilization of the services of legal assistants contributes to the delivery of cost-effective, high-quality legal services. Legal assistants and the legal profession should be assured that measures exist for identifying legal assistants and their role in assisting attorneys in the delivery of legal services. Therefore, the NALA, hereby adopts these Standards and Guidelines as an educational document for the benefit of legal assistants and the legal profession.

Comment   The three most frequently raised questions concerning legal assistants are (1) How do you define a legal assistant? (2) Who is qualified to be identified as a legal assistant? and (3) What duties may a legal assistant perform? The definition adopted by the NALA answers the first question. The Model sets forth minimum education, training and experience through standards which will assure that an individual utilizing the title "legal assistant" or "paralegal" has the qualifications to be held out to the legal community and the public in that capacity. The Guidelines identify those acts which the reported cases hold to be proscribed and give examples of services which the legal assistant may perform under the supervision of a licensed attorney.

These Guidelines constitute a statement relating to services performed by legal assistants, as defined herein, as approved by court decisions and other sources of authority. The purpose of the Guidelines is not to place limitations or restrictions on the legal assistant profession. Rather, the Guidelines are intended to outline for the legal profession an acceptable course of conduct. Voluntary recognition and utilization of the Standards and Guidelines will benefit the entire legal profession and the public it serves.

History
NALA adopted this Model in 1984. At the same time, the following definition of a legal assistant was adopted:

> Legal assistants, also known as paralegals, are a distinguishable group of persons who assist attorneys in the delivery of legal services. Through formal education, training, and experience, legal assistants have knowledge and expertise regarding the legal system and substantive and procedural law which qualify them to do work of a legal nature under the supervision of an attorney.

Historically, there have been similar definitions adopted by various legal professional organizations. Recognizing the need for one clear definition the NALA membership approved a resolution in July 2001 to adopt the legal assistant definition of the ABA. This definition continues to be utilized today.

Definition
A legal assistant or paralegal is a person qualified by education, training or work experience who is employed or retained by a lawyer, law office, corporation, governmental agency or other entity who performs specifically delegated substantive legal work for which a lawyer is responsible. (Adopted by the ABA in 1997 and by NALA in 2001.)

Comment This definition emphasizes the knowledge and expertise of legal assistants in substantive and procedural law obtained through education and work experience. It further defines the legal assistant or paralegal as a professional working under the supervision of an attorney as distinguished

Source: www.nala.org. This information is subject to updates and edits at any time.

from a non-lawyer who delivers services directly to the public without any intervention or review of work product by an attorney. Such unsupervised services, unless authorized by court or agency rules, constitute the unauthorized practice of law.

Statutes, court rules, case law, and bar association documents are additional sources for legal assistant or paralegal definitions. In applying the Standards and Guidelines, it is important to remember that they were developed to apply to the legal assistant as defined herein. Lawyers should refrain from labeling those as paralegals or legal assistants who do not meet the criteria set forth in this definition and/or the definitions set forth by state rules, guidelines or bar associations. Labeling secretaries and other administrative staff as legal assistants/paralegals is inaccurate.

For billing purposes, the services of a legal secretary are considered part of overhead costs and are not recoverable in fee awards. However, the Court has held that fees for paralegal services are recoverable as long as they are not clerical functions, such as organizing files, copying documents, checking docket, updating files, checking court dates, and delivering papers. As established in *Missouri v. Jenkins*, 491 U.S.274, 109 S.Ct. 2463, 2471, n.10 (1989) tasks performed by legal assistants must be substantive in nature which, absent the legal assistant, the attorney would perform.

There are also case law and Supreme Court Rules addressing the issue of a disbarred attorney serving in the capacity of a legal assistant.

Standards

A legal assistant should meet certain minimum qualifications. The following standards may be used to determine an individual's qualifications as a legal assistant:

1. Successful completion of the Certified Legal Assistant (CLA)/Certified Paralegal (CP) certifying examination of the NALA;

2. Graduation from an ABA-approved program of study for legal assistants;

3. Graduation from a course of study for legal assistants which is institutionally accredited but not ABA approved, and which requires not less than the equivalent of 60 semester hours of classroom study;

4. Graduation from a course of study for legal assistants, other than those set forth in (2) and (3) above, plus not less than six months of in-house training as a legal assistant;

5.   A baccalaureate degree in any field, plus not less than six months in-house training as a legal assistant;

6.   A minimum of three years of law-related experience under the supervision of an attorney, including at least six months of in-house training as a legal assistant; or

7.   Two years of in-house training as a legal assistant.

For purposes of these Standards, "in-house training as a legal assistant" means attorney education of the employee concerning legal assistant duties and these Guidelines. In addition to review and analysis of assignments, the legal assistant should receive a reasonable amount of instruction directly related to the duties and obligations of the legal assistant.

Comment   The Standards set forth suggest minimum qualifications for a legal assistant. These minimum qualifications, as adopted, recognize legal-related work backgrounds and formal education backgrounds, both of which provide the legal assistant with a broad base in exposure to and knowledge of the legal profession. This background is necessary to assure the public and the legal profession that the employee identified as a legal assistant is qualified.

The CLA/CP examination established by NALA in 1976 is a voluntary nationwide certification program for legal assistants. (CLA and CP are federally registered certification marks owned by NALA.) The CLA/CP designation is a statement to the legal profession and the public that the legal assistant has met the high levels of knowledge and professionalism required by NALA's certification program. Continuing education requirements, which all certified legal assistants must meet, assure that high standards are maintained. The CLA/CP designation has been recognized as a means of establishing the qualifications of a legal assistant in supreme court rules, state court and bar association standards and utilization guidelines.

Certification through NALA is available to all legal assistants meeting the educational and experience requirements. Certified Legal Assistants may also pursue advanced certification in specialty practice areas through the APC, Advanced Paralegal Certification, credentialing program. Legal assistants/paralegals may also pursue certification based on state laws and procedures in California, Florida, Louisiana, North Carolina, and Texas.

Guidelines
These Guidelines relating to standards of performance and professional responsibility are intended to aid legal assistants and attorneys. The ultimate

responsibility rests with an attorney who employs legal assistants to educate them with respect to the duties they are assigned and to supervise the manner in which such duties are accomplished.

Comment   In general, a legal assistant is allowed to perform any task which is properly delegated and properly supervised by an attorney, as long as the attorney is ultimately responsible to the client and assumes complete professional responsibility for the work product.

The ABA Model Rules of Professional Conduct at Rule 5.3 tell us that a senior partner of a law firm which employs, retains, or is associated with a nonlawyer must take reasonable steps to ensure that the nonlawyer's conduct is consistent with the professional conduct duties of the partner and of the law firm. The same mandate applies to any lawyer who has supervisory authority over the nonlawyer's conduct.

Moreover, the lawyer bears professional responsibility for nonlawyer misconduct if:

A.   The nonlawyer's actions would violate professional conduct rules if they were performed by a lawyer and if

B.   The lawyer orders or knowingly ratifies the conduct or

C.   The lawyer is a law firm partner or has direct supervision over the non-lawyer and knows of the nonlawyer's conduct when its effects still can be avoided or mitigated but fails to take corrective action.

There are many interesting and complex issues involving the use of legal assistants. In any discussion of the proper role of a legal assistant, attention must be directed to what constitutes the practice of law. Proper delegation to legal assistants is further complicated and confused by the lack of an adequate definition of the practice of law.

Kentucky became the first state to adopt a Paralegal Code by Supreme Court Rule. This Code sets forth certain exclusions to the unauthorized practice of law:

For purposes of this rule, the unauthorized practice of law shall not include any service rendered involving legal knowledge or advice, whether representation, counsel or advocacy, in or out of court, rendered in respect to the acts, duties, obligations, liabilities or business relations of the one requiring services where:

The client understands that the paralegal is not a lawyer;

The lawyer supervises the paralegal in the performance of his or her duties; and

The lawyer remains fully responsible for such representation including all actions taken or not taken in connection therewith by the paralegal to the same extent as if such representation had been furnished entirely by the lawyer and all such actions had been taken or not taken directly by the attorney. Paralegal Code, Ky.S.Ct.R3.700, Sub-Rule 2.

South Dakota Supreme Court Rule 97-25 Utilization Rule a(4) states:

The attorney remains responsible for the services performed by the legal assistant to the same extent as though such services had been furnished entirely by the attorney and such actions were those of the attorney.

Guideline 1   Legal assistants should:

Disclose their status as legal assistants at the outset of any professional relationship with a client, other attorneys, a court or administrative agency or personnel thereof, or members of the general public; Preserve the confidences and secrets of all clients; and Understand the attorney's Rules of Professional Responsibility and these Guidelines in order to avoid any action which would involve the attorney in a violation of the Rules, or give the appearance of professional impropriety.

Comment   Routine early disclosure of the paralegal's status when dealing with persons outside the attorney's office is necessary to assure that there will be no misunderstanding as to the responsibilities and role of the legal assistant. Disclosure may be made in any way that avoids confusion. If the person dealing with the legal assistant already knows of his/her status, further disclosure is unnecessary. If at any time in written or oral communication the legal assistant becomes aware that the other person may believe the legal assistant is an attorney, immediate disclosure should be made as to the legal assistant's status.

The attorney should exercise care that the legal assistant preserves and refrains from using any confidence or secrets of a client, and should instruct the legal assistant not to disclose or use any such confidences or secrets.

The legal assistant must take any and all steps necessary to prevent conflicts of interest and fully disclose such conflicts to the supervising attorney. Failure to do so may jeopardize both the attorney's representation of the client and the case itself.

Guidelines for the Utilization of Legal Assistant Services adopted December 3, 1994 by the Washington State Bar Association Board of Governors states:

> "Guideline 7: A lawyer shall take reasonable measures to prevent conflicts of interest resulting from a legal assistant's other employment or interest insofar as such other employment or interests would present a conflict of interest if it were that of the lawyer."

In Re Complex Asbestos Litigation, 232 Cal. App. 3d 572 (Cal. 1991), addresses the issue wherein a law firm was disqualified due to possession of attorney-client confidences by a legal assistant employee resulting from previous employment by opposing counsel.

In Oklahoma, in an order issued July 12, 2001, in the matter of *Mark A. Hayes, M.D. v. Central States Orthopedic Specialists, Inc.*, a Tulsa County District Court Judge disqualified a law firm from representation of a client on the basis that an ethical screen was an impermissible device to protect from disclosure confidences gained by a nonlawyer employee while employed by another law firm. In applying the same rules that govern attorneys, the court found that the Rules of Professional Conduct pertaining to confidentiality apply to nonlawyers who leave firms with actual knowledge of material, confidential information and a screening device is not an appropriate alternative to the imputed disqualification of an incoming legal assistant who has moved from one firm to another during ongoing litigation and has actual knowledge of material, confidential information. The decision was appealed and the Oklahoma Supreme Court determined that, under certain circumstances, screening is an appropriate management tool for nonlawyer staff.

In 2004 the Nevada Supreme Court also addressed this issue at the urging of the state's paralegals. The Nevada Supreme Court granted a petition to rescind the Court's 1997 ruling in *Ciaffone v. District Court*. In this case, the court clarified the original ruling, stating "mere opportunity to access confidential information does not merit disqualification." The opinion stated instances in which screening may be appropriate, and listed minimum screening requirements. The opinion also set forth guidelines that a district court may use to determine if screening has been or may be effective. These considerations are:

> substantiality of the relationship between the former and current matters;
> the time elapsed between the matters;
> size of the firm;
> number of individuals presumed to have confidential information;
> nature of their involvement in the former matter;
> timing and features of any measures taken to reduce the danger of disclosure;

whether the old firm and the new firm represent adverse parties in the same proceeding rather than in different proceedings.

The ultimate responsibility for compliance with approved standards of professional conduct rests with the supervising attorney. The burden rests upon the attorney who employs a legal assistant to educate the latter with respect to the duties which may be assigned and then to supervise the manner in which the legal assistant carries out such duties. However, this does not relieve the legal assistant from an independent obligation to refrain from illegal conduct. Additionally, and notwithstanding that the Rules are not binding upon nonlawyers, the very nature of a legal assistant's employment imposes an obligation not to engage in conduct which would involve the supervising attorney in a violation of the Rules.

The attorney must make sufficient background investigation of the prior activities and character and integrity of his or her legal assistants.

Further, the attorney must take all measures necessary to avoid and fully disclose conflicts of interest due to other employment or interests. Failure to do so may jeopardize both the attorney's representation of the client and the case itself.

Legal assistant associations strive to maintain the high level of integrity and competence expected of the legal profession and, further, strive to uphold the high standards of ethics.

NALA's Code of Ethics and Professional Responsibility states "A legal assistant's conduct is guided by bar associations' codes of professional responsibility and rules of professional conduct."

Guideline 2　　Legal assistants should not:

Establish attorney-client relationships; set legal fees; give legal opinions or advice; or represent a client before a court, unless authorized to do so by said court; nor engage in, encourage, or contribute to any act which could constitute the unauthorized practice law.

Comment　　Case law, court rules, codes of ethics and professional responsibilities, as well as bar ethics opinions now hold which acts can and cannot be performed by a legal assistant. Generally, the determination of what acts constitute the unauthorized practice of law is made by state supreme courts.

Numerous cases exist relating to the unauthorized practice of law. Courts have gone so far as to prohibit the legal assistant from preparation of divorce kits and assisting in preparation of bankruptcy forms and, more specifically, from providing basic information about procedures and requirements, deciding where information should be placed on forms, and responding to questions from debtors regarding the interpretation or definition of terms.

Cases have identified certain areas in which an attorney has a duty to act, but it is interesting to note that none of these cases state that it is improper for an attorney to have the initial work performed by the legal assistant. This again points out the importance of adequate supervision by the employing attorney.

An attorney can be found to have aided in the unauthorized practice of law when delegating acts which cannot be performed by a legal assistant.

Guideline 3   Legal assistants may perform services for an attorney in the representation of a client, provided:

> The services performed by the legal assistant do not require the exercise of independent professional legal judgment;
> The attorney maintains a direct relationship with the client and maintains control of all client matters;
> The attorney supervises the legal assistant;
> The attorney remains professionally responsible for all work on behalf of the client, including any actions taken or not taken by the legal assistant in connection therewith; and
> The services performed supplement, merge with and become the attorney's work product.

Comment   Paralegals, whether employees or independent contractors, perform services for the attorney in the representation of a client. Attorneys should delegate work to legal assistants commensurate with their knowledge and experience and provide appropriate instruction and supervision concerning the delegated work, as well as ethical acts of their employment. Ultimate responsibility for the work product of a legal assistant rests with the attorney. However, a legal assistant must use discretion and professional judgment and must not render independent legal judgment in place of an attorney.

The work product of a legal assistant is subject to civil rules governing discovery of materials prepared in anticipation of litigation, whether the legal assistant is viewed as an extension of the attorney or as another representative of the party itself. Fed.R.Civ.P. 26 (b) (3) and (5).

Guideline 4 In the supervision of a legal assistant, consideration should be given to

> Designating work assignments that correspond to the legal assistant's abilities, knowledge, training and experience;
>
> Educating and training the legal assistant with respect to professional responsibility, local rules and practices, and firm policies;
>
> Monitoring the work and professional conduct of the legal assistant to ensure that the work is substantively correct and timely performed;
>
> Providing continuing education for the legal assistant in substantive matters through courses, institutes, workshops, seminars and in-house training; and
>
> Encouraging and supporting membership and active participation in professional organizations.

Comment Attorneys are responsible for the actions of their employees in both malpractice and disciplinary proceedings. In the vast majority of cases, the courts have not censured attorneys for a particular act delegated to the legal assistant, but rather, have been critical of and imposed sanctions against attorneys for failure to adequately supervise the legal assistant. The attorney's responsibility for supervision of his or her legal assistant must be more than a willingness to accept responsibility and liability for the legal assistant's work. Supervision of a legal assistant must be offered in both the procedural and substantive legal areas. The attorney must delegate work based upon the education, knowledge and abilities of the legal assistant and must monitor the work product and conduct of the legal assistant to insure that the work performed is substantively correct and competently performed in a professional manner.

Michigan State Board of Commissioners has adopted Guidelines for the Utilization of Legal Assistants (April 23, 1993). These guidelines, in part, encourage employers to support legal assistant participation in continuing education programs to ensure that the legal assistant remains competent in the fields of practice in which the legal assistant is assigned.

The working relationship between the lawyer and the legal assistant should extend to cooperative efforts on public service activities wherever possible. Participation in pro bono activities is encouraged in ABA Guideline 10.

Guideline 5 Except as otherwise provided by statute, court rule or decision, administrative rule or regulation, or the attorney's rules of professional responsibility, and within the preceding parameters and proscriptions, a legal assistant may perform any function delegated by an attorney, including, but not limited to the following:

Conduct client interviews and maintain general contact with the client after the establishment of the attorney-client relationship, so long as the client is aware of the status and function of the legal assistant, and the client contact is under the supervision of the attorney;

Locate and interview witnesses, so long as the witnesses are aware of the status and function of the legal assistant.

Conduct investigations and statistical and documentary research for review by the attorney;

Conduct legal research for review by the attorney;

Draft legal documents for review by the attorney;

Draft correspondence and pleadings for review by and signature of the attorney;

Summarize depositions, interrogatories and testimony for review by the attorney;

Attend executions of wills, real estate closings, depositions, court or administrative hearings and trials with the attorney;

Author and sign letters providing the legal assistant's status is clearly indicated and the correspondence does not contain independent legal opinions or legal advice.

Comment The United States Supreme Court has recognized the variety of tasks being performed by legal assistants and has noted that use of legal assistants encourages cost-effective delivery of legal services, *Missouri v. Jenkins*, 491 U.S.274, 109 S.Ct. 2463, 2471, n.10 (1989). In Jenkins, the court further held that legal assistant time should be included in compensation for attorney fee awards at the market rate of the relevant community to bill legal assistant time. Courts have held that legal assistant fees are not a part of the overall overhead of a law firm. Legal assistant services are billed separately by attorneys, and decrease litigation expenses. Tasks performed by legal assistants must contain substantive legal work under the direction or supervision of an attorney, such that if the legal assistant were not present, the work would be performed by the attorney.

In *Taylor v. Chubb*, 874 P.2d 806 (Okla. 1994), the Court ruled that attorney fees awarded should include fees for services performed by legal assistants and, further, defined tasks which may be performed by the legal assistant under the supervision of an attorney including, among others: interview clients; draft pleadings and other documents; carry on legal research, both conventional and computer aided; research public records; prepare discovery requests and responses; schedule depositions and prepare notices and subpoenas; summarize depositions and other discovery responses; coordinate and manage document production; locate and interview witnesses; organize pleadings, trial exhibits and other documents; prepare witness and exhibit lists; prepare trial notebooks; prepare for the attendance of witnesses at trial; and assist lawyers at trials.

Except for the specific proscription contained in Guideline 1, the reported cases do not limit the duties which may be performed by a legal assistant under the supervision of the attorney.

An attorney may not split legal fees with a legal assistant, nor pay a legal assistant for the referral of legal business. An attorney may compensate a legal assistant based on the quantity and quality of the legal assistant's work and value of that work to a law practice.

Conclusion

These Standards and Guidelines were developed from generally accepted practices. Each supervising attorney must be aware of the specific rules, decisions and statutes applicable to legal assistants within his/her jurisdiction.

Addendum

For further information, the following cases may be helpful to you:

Duties

Taylor v. Chubb, 874 P.2d 806 (Okla. 1994)
McMackin v. McMackin, 651 A.2d 778 (Del.Fam Ct 1993)

Work Product

Fine v. Facet Aerospace Products Co., 133 F.R.D. 439 (S.D.N.Y. 1990)

Unauthorized Practice of Law

Akron Bar Assn. v. Green, 673 N.E.2d 1307 (Ohio 1997)
In Re Hessinger & Associates, 192 B.R. 211 (N.D. Calif. 1996)
In the Matter of Bright, 171 B.R. 799 (Bkrtcy. E.D. Mich)
Louisiana State Bar Assn v. Edwins, 540 So.2d 294 (La. 1989)

Attorney/Client Privilege

In Re Complex Asbestos Litigation, 232 Cal. App. 3d 572 (Calif. 1991)
Makita Corp. v. U.S., 819 F.Supp. 1099 (CIT 1993)

Conflicts

In Re Complex Asbestos Litigation, 232 Cal. App. 3d 572 (Calif. 1991)
Makita Corp. v. U.S., 819 F.Supp. 1099 (CIT 1993)
Phoenix Founders, Inc., v. Marshall, 887 S.W.2d 831 (Tex. 1994)
Smart Industries v. Superior Court, 876 P.2d 1176 (Ariz. App. Div.1 1994)

Supervision

Matter of Martinez, 754 P.2d 842 (N.M. 1988)
State v. Barrett, 483 P.2d 1106 (Kan. 1971)
Hayes v. Central States Orthopedic Specialists, Inc., 2002 OK 30, 51 P.3d 562

Leibowitz v. Eighth Judicial District Court of Nevada Nev Sup Ct., No 39683, November 3, 2003 clarified in part and overrules in part
Ciaffone v. District Court, 113 Nev 1165, 945. P2d 950 (1997)

Fee Awards

In Re Bicoastal Corp., 121 B.R. 653 (Bktrcy.M.D.Fla. 1990)
In Re Carter, 101 B.R. 170 (Bkrtcy.D.S.D. 1989)
Taylor v. Chubb, 874 P.2d 806 (Okla.1994)
Missouri v. Jenkins, 491 U.S. 274, 109 S.Ct. 2463, 105 L.Ed.2d 229 (1989) 11 U.S.C.A.'330
McMackin v. McMackin, Del.Fam.Ct. 651 A.2d 778 (1993)
Miller v. Alamo, 983 F.2d 856 (8th Cir. 1993)
Stewart v. Sullivan, 810 F.Supp. 1102 (D.Hawaii 1993)
In Re Yankton College, 101 B.R. 151 (Bkrtcy. D.S.D. 1989)
Stacey v. Stroud, 845 F.Supp. 1135 (S.D.W.Va. 1993)

Court Appearances

Louisiana State Bar Assn v. Edwins, 540 So.2d 294 (La. 1989)

In addition to the above referenced cases, you may contact your state bar association for information regarding guidelines for the utilization of legal assistants that may have been adopted by the bar, or ethical opinions concerning the utilization of legal assistants.

Model Standards and Guidelines: Copyright 1984; Adopted 1984; Revised 1991, 1997, 2005, 2007. Reprinted with permission of NALA, the Association for Paralegals-Legal Assistants. Inquiries should be directed to NALA, 1516 S. Boston, #200, Tulsa, OK 74119, www.nala.org.

Application of Ethics Rules

Like lawyers, paralegals must be vigilant concerning ethics rules, both their specific terms and their intent. It is inexcusable for a lawyer or a paralegal to run afoul of the rules based upon a lack of familiarity with them. The paralegal should review applicable ethics rules routinely to refresh her memory concerning their specific provisions.

In addition to the rules themselves, informal opinions of bar associations concerning specific rules provide insight into their proper interpretation. Likewise, the body of judicial opinions related to ethics rules provides a practical framework with which to evaluate the conduct governed by the rules. Both of these sources apply rules to specific factual situations. The more factual situations to which a paralegal can relate, the more likely it is that he will be able to recognize potential ethics problems when they arise.

Presented below are a series of ethics questions involving paralegals, each of which is followed by its probable resolution based upon current rules, ethics opinions, and case law. The questions are not intended to be all-inclusive.

When considered with the rules, however, their comments, and the hypothetical situations presented in the self-test section for this chapter, the applicant is provided with a concise overview of the concepts that likely will appear on any ethics examination directed at paralegals.

Are business cards permissible for paralegals employed by a law firm?

Yes, according to a substantial majority of states. Care must be taken, however, to ensure that the nonlawyer status of the cardholder is displayed prominently on the card. This helps to avoid any misunderstanding that the cardholder is an attorney.

May a paralegal's name appear on the law firm's stationery?

In many states, the answer is yes. The name must be set apart from the lawyers' names, and the paralegal's title must be shown clearly. Some firms print lawyers' names on one side of the stationery and print paralegals' names on the other.

May a paralegal sign letters prepared on firm stationery?

Yes, provided (1) the letter contains no direct legal advice or opinions and (2) the paralegal's status is shown clearly. Even if the paralegal's name and title are printed on the letterhead, the best practice is to include the title "Paralegal" or "Paralegal to _____" directly below the typed name in the signature block of the letter.

May a paralegal's name be shown on pleadings and briefs?

A few states permit a nonlawyer's name to appear on pleadings; most do not. More states allow the name of a nonlawyer (paralegal or law clerk) to appear on briefs, provided that the nonlawyer made a significant contribution to its research and drafting. The name generally is shown immediately below the attorney's signature block, using language such as:

Jane Doe, Paralegal
Participating on Briefs.

Even where the paralegal's name may be shown on pleadings or on briefs, the paralegal never signs the pleading or the brief.

> May a paralegal's name be included in a firm's listing in public telephone directories or as part of the listing at a law firm's entrance?

Where these questions have been considered, the answer generally is no. Including paralegals in these listings is more likely to lead the general public to believe that the paralegal must be some type of lawyer.

> May a paralegal use the title "legal specialist," "legal aide," "legal technician," or the like?

These and similar titles may confuse or mislead the public about the paralegal's status. It may lead one to believe that the paralegal is a type of lawyer or that the paralegal is engaging in illegal conduct by offering legal services directly to the public. For that reason, most jurisdictions frown upon their use.

The term "paralegal" has a specific meaning that involves working under the direct supervision of a licensed attorney. Since there is a specific title for this occupational function, it should be used for the sake of simplicity and clarity.

> How often and in what way must a paralegal identify his or her nonlawyer status?

There is no single, correct way to identify the paralegal's status. To keep things simple, just use the title "Paralegal" after the name. Telephone courtesy generally requires the caller to identify him or herself at the beginning of the conversation in any event. It should be a simple matter to add the title "Paralegal" when placing telephone calls. Alternately, one might say, "Hello. This is Jack Samson, Bill Mitchell's paralegal."

Neither is there a magic number of times at which the paralegal must identify his status. It seems prudent to do so at the beginning of all telephone conversations and at the beginning of every initial conference with a client or witness. If it appears that the other party may believe the paralegal to be a lawyer, that impression should be corrected right away. Any questions about the paralegal's function should be answered in such a way that a statement is included to clarify that the paralegal is not a lawyer. The issue is not how often identity must be clarified to comply with the rules; it is how often should identity be clarified to protect the paralegal from charges related to the unauthorized practice of law.

May a paralegal discuss fee ranges with a client on a preliminary basis, leaving the final discussion and decision to the supervising attorney?

All discussions related to fees must be deferred to the attorney. Even when a firm uses an internal fee schedule, it generally serves as a guideline only. It is solely the attorney's responsibility to measure the situation presented by each case and to set the fee.

Uniform fee schedules—the same fee schedule used by all attorneys within a specific regional area—are prohibited by judicial decision.

If a client relates information to a paralegal in confidence, is the paralegal required to keep the information to himself?

The answer is yes, except for the attorney handling the case. Other than the limitations related to giving legal advice and the like, the paralegal is an extension of the attorney and cannot operate independently of the attorney where clients are concerned. The client should be informed that the paralegal cannot withhold information from the attorney, preferably before the client relates the information. If the client then elects not to confide in the paralegal, that fact also must be related to the attorney.

May a paralegal accept gifts from clients?

Lawyers are prohibited from accepting gifts from clients, and the prohibition extends to paralegals as well. A client occasionally may express thanks for a job well done by taking the lawyer or the paralegal to lunch or to dinner or by sending flowers, a pair of theater tickets, or similar token of the client's appreciation. Small gifts such as these probably are permissible when they are infrequent, are not solicited, and are reported to the paralegal's supervising attorney. If the attorney or the firm has a policy against accepting these types of small gifts, the paralegal must adhere to that policy.

> May a paralegal counsel a close friend or a relative about a legal matter when the friend or relative knows that the paralegal is not a lawyer and when the paralegal is not paid for the advice?

Other than suggesting that the friend or relative see a lawyer of his or her own choice, the paralegal cannot give advice or comment in any way that may be taken as a legal opinion. Whether the paralegal is paid or not is irrelevant; legal advice cannot be given by the paralegal under any circumstances.

The problem arises most frequently at family dinners, parties, and other social events. Friends and relatives can create an extremely uncomfortable situation, particularly when the legal matter appears to be a simple one and when the paralegal is reasonably certain of the advice that probably would be given by most attorneys. However, the difficult situations are the ones most likely to backfire in catastrophic proportions.

It may be helpful to realize that responsible attorneys likewise will decline to offer legal opinions or advice in these settings. Rather than risk an erroneous opinion based upon incomplete, misperceived, or distilled facts related by the questioner, the attorney might say, "It sounds as if your situation may involve some fairly complicated legal issues. I think it might be better if you were to call the office tomorrow and make an appointment to explore it fully." *The questioner generally will not be offended by this type of approach—not very much, at least; and the attorney will have saved herself from rendering a shotgun opinion that could come back to haunt her.*

> May a paralegal communicate with an opposing party in an emergency situation, such as when the opposing counsel cannot be reached?

The rule is absolute: A lawyer cannot communicate with an opposing party who is represented by counsel concerning the subject matter of the representation unless the opposing counsel gives his or her prior consent. Opposing counsel rarely will consent. If an act is forbidden for the attorney, whether by this or by any other rule, it is also forbidden for the paralegal. There is no emergency that can justify violation of this rule.

> How much supervision is required under existing ethics rules for work delegated to a paralegal?

The type and amount of supervision must vary according to the experience and capabilities of the paralegal and according to the task(s) delegated to him or her. The attorney is the only person who is equipped to judge the precise level of supervision that is required. Inexperienced paralegals, no matter how bright they are, never should be assigned major projects unless frequent progress checkpoints are also established. This is as much a principle of sound management as it is one of ethics. As the paralegal matures in the position and builds a successful track record, less intensified supervision may be warranted. Refer to the NALA Model Standards and Guidelines for the Utilization of Paralegals, which is reprinted earlier in this chapter.

No matter how much experience or skill a paralegal has, however, the attorney always is required to supervise tasks delegated to him or her. Ethics rules demand this. At a minimum, this means routine spot checks as a project is underway and careful review of the final work product. When an attorney fails to provide the proper level of supervision, she jeopardizes not only her own career but also the career of the paralegal.

Paralegals never should be asked to "cover" or to "fill in" for the lawyer by performing tasks that only a lawyer ethically may perform, such as accepting cases, setting fees, negotiating settlements, executing wills, appearing in court, and the like.

> May a paralegal prepare a procedure manual in a specific area of law that is intended for use by new associates and law clerks?

Clearly, the answer is yes. A procedure manual is no different than any other document drafted under an attorney's supervision, and an experienced paralegal may be the ideal person to undertake such a project. Within this context, "procedure" means the way in which a task is accomplished. It includes review and interpretation of statutes, administrative rules and regulations, court rules, and judicial decisions. All work of the paralegal merges with and becomes the work product of the attorney who supervises the project.

> May a paralegal prepare a discovery plan for a particular litigation case and then implement that plan?

For all of the same reasons mentioned in response to the immediately preceding question, the answer is yes. Once the legal issues have been established by the supervising attorney, a paralegal experienced in litigation is capable of proposing a discovery plan directed at locating and documenting all relevant facts in a usable form from all available sources. When the discovery plan is approved by the supervising attorney, the task of implementing the plan by drafting interrogatories and similar discovery devices; scheduling depositions; monitoring discovery responses; and cataloging discovery results can be delegated to the paralegal. Working under the attorney's supervision and at her direction, the paralegal ethically may initiate nearly all phases of the discovery plan except signing discovery documents on behalf of the firm or asking questions during depositions.

What is meant by "procedure" when it is said that a paralegal ethically may answer client questions about procedural matters?

Within this context, the term "procedure" has the same meaning that is provided above: the way in which a task is done. It involves those matters which are fixed (meaning that they generally do not change according to changes in a client's factual situation) and which have been reviewed and confirmed previously with the supervising attorney. Client questions in this area may cover such things as (1) how long it will take to obtain a trial date or to process an appeal, (2) what must be filed with the Secretary of State to form a new corporation, or (3) how much it costs to obtain an authenticated copy of a court order. The paralegal can be expected to recognize the difference between a certified copy and an authenticated copy, for example, and to provide accurate information to the client at the attorney's direction.

When a client asks a question about which the paralegal is uncertain, she should provide the same answer that most attorneys provide when they find themselves in that situation—that she does not know but will check and then will contact the client with the answer. By the same token, if a particular attorney directs his or her paralegal not to answer these types of client questions, the attorney's instructions must be followed.

Paralegals may not answer client questions about substantive matters, of course. Substantive legal questions require either a legal opinion or legal advice, both of which constitute the practice of law and can be provided only by a licensed attorney. Although they can cover a wide range of topics, a few examples of substantive legal questions include (1) whether the client can sue her landlord for damages under a particular commercial lease, (2) whether the client can remove money from a joint account in view of a temporary restraining order that was just entered, or (3) what risks are involved if a case is appealed.

> May a paralegal's time be billed to clients for things such as organizing and photocopying exhibits for trial?

The answer is yes for organizing the exhibits, but no for photocopying them. The paralegal's time can be billed to a client only when it constitutes the performance of legal services. In other words, it must be the type of service which an attorney would perform if the paralegal were not available.

The same rule applies when the attorney organizes and photocopies exhibits for trial. She can bill the client for organizing the exhibits but not for making photocopies. Photocopying generally is a clerical function. It remains a clerical function, no matter who performs it and, therefore, cannot be billed to the client. The cost of clerical services presumably are built into the hourly fee rate charged for both the attorney's and the paralegal's legal services.

Simple questions permit simple answers. For example, it is clear that a paralegal is permitted to draft pleadings, documents, and instruments of all kinds for review and use by an attorney. It is also clear that a paralegal cannot advise a client concerning rights and obligations in a substantive legal matter. The black-and-white situations are easy to resolve. More difficult are the varying shades of gray—those situations that fit somewhere between the two divergent examples given.

Ethics for paralegals can involve complex circumstances, requiring thorough knowledge of the ABA Model Rules, the NALA Code of Ethics, and the NALA Standards and Guidelines, together with superior judgment and reasoning techniques and highly polished human relations skills. To illustrate, read the following ethics problems and the reasoning process used to resolve each of them.

Problem 1.   True or False. While working on a personal injury case for one of the firm's clients, Paralegal Bob Baker interviews Mary Wishbone. Ms. Wishbone was a witness to the accident and relates facts during the interview which, if they are true, place liability for the accident on the firm's client. After the case is filed, Ms. Wishbone suffers a stroke and dies without making any formal statements to anyone else concerning the accident. Opposing counsel has learned of her statement to Bob and now seeks either a copy of the statement or Bob's testimony concerning the statement. The statement cannot be provided to opposing counsel without violating the client's right to confidentiality.

The answer is *true* only if a client confidence would be violated by providing the statement. The ethics rules governing this issue are Canon 7 of the NALA Code of Ethics and the ABA Model Rule relating to confidentiality of client information, which is intended to encourage clients to tell their attorneys everything without fear of subsequent disclosure to others. To violate this rule, then, the information must have been obtained from the client. However, the information in the Wishbone statement was not obtained from the client; it was obtained from a non-client witness as part of the investigation in the client's case. Since it was not obtained from the client, the statement is not protected by the rule on client confidentiality. Therefore, *the correct answer is false*. (The attorney may try to block opposing counsel from obtaining the statement based upon something other than confidentiality, of course.)

> **Problem 2.**   Approximately two months after the settlement of a lengthy litigation related to a corporate takeover, one of the directors of the corporate client returns to the attorney and confesses that he lied during his deposition testimony concerning key issues related to the case. Since then, his wife has filed for divorce and is blackmailing him concerning the perjured testimony. What should the attorney do?
>
> a.   Disclose the facts to the court.
> b.   Disclose the facts to the authorities.
> c.   Urge the director to make the disclosure.
> d.   Do nothing.

Among the four options, the third one presents the best choice; therefore, *c is the correct answer*. This problem raises a number of issues: the crime of perjury (perjury can occur during a deposition as well as during trial); the ethics rule that excepts perjured testimony from the usual client confidentiality requirement; the attorney's responsibility as an officer of the court; and the attorney's potential conflict of interest if the interest of the director and the interest of the corporate client are different. If the director can be prompted to do the right thing on a voluntary basis, the attorney's dilemma is resolved without further action on her part.

The first option is the next best choice; if the director could not be urged to make the disclosure, the attorney would be well-advised to pursue this course of action. Since litigation was pending before the case was settled, there must have been a judge assigned to the case. If not, the chief judge of the court should be informed of the situation and allowed to participate in its resolution. Because perjured testimony is outside the scope of client confidentiality, and because the attorney is an officer of the court, she has an obligation to disclose the perjury if the director does not do so. The second option also fulfills the attorney's obligation but suggests less sensitivity to the participation of others in resolving the problem (the director and the court). The final option—do nothing—is the worst choice of the four. Once the attorney becomes aware of the facts, she is obliged to do something to preserve the integrity of the legal system. Doing nothing cannot be justified based upon the facts provided.

Problem 3.   You are a freelance paralegal who contracts with the law firm of Billings & Munne to provide paralegal services for a large probate estate. Ms. Munne is the supervising attorney. After the initial probate documents are filed with the court and as you begin the work needed to prepare the inventory, Ms. Munne compliments you on your fine work and states that she could not manage the case without you, since she never has worked in the probate area. Your best course of action is to:

a.   Discontinue work on the case unless Ms. Munne agrees to upgrade her probate knowledge to the point where she can supervise you properly or agrees to affiliate with a probate attorney who can supervise you properly;

b.   Continue with the case because Ms. Munne needs your help more than a probate lawyer would need it.

c.   Continue with the case until you can obtain a ruling from the bar association's disciplinary agency concerning your proper course of action.

d.   Discontinue work on the case and do nothing.

Among the four options, the first one represents the best course of action; therefore, *a is the correct answer*. The issue here is adequate supervision of the paralegal's work by the attorney. The supervision required for freelance paralegals is the same as that required for in-house paralegals.

The second option implies that you could continue working on the case without adequate supervision; clearly, that is wrong, making this the worst option of the four. The third option is problematic for two reasons: (1) It requires you to continue working without adequate supervision until a ruling is made; and (2) it suggests that it is proper for a paralegal to report a lawyer without discussing the underlying problem with the lawyer first. It may be that Ms. Munne's partner is experienced in probate matters or that affiliation with an unrelated probate lawyer can be accomplished without difficulty. Finally, if the first option were not provided, the fourth option would be the best of the remaining three. It is not an ideal solution, however. It appears from the facts that Ms. Munne does not recognize her duty to provide supervision. If you discontinue work on the case and do nothing, she may find a paralegal to do the work who, like Ms. Munne, does not recognize the ethics problem.

The CLA/CP® applicant must be able to recognize a breach of ethics when it is presented, to determine how a breach can be avoided, and to resolve ethics problems in a variety of situations. This chapter, together with the following self-test, is designed to highlight the major ethics principles that paralegals should know. *See the bibliography for additional references.*

Ethics Self-Test

Allow an uninterrupted 30-minute period to answer all questions. At the end of 30 minutes, check your answers against those in the Answer Key Section of this Manual. Deduct two points for each incorrect answer (100 total possible points). Unanswered questions are counted as incorrect answers. Follow directions carefully and observe the time limit precisely to provide an accurate self-assessment.

Choose the most correct answer to the following questions unless a specific question instructs you to do otherwise.

1.   True or False.   The NALA document that provides an outline for the proper use of paralegals by attorneys is known as NALA Code of Ethics and Professional Responsibility.

2.   True or False.   In an effort to resolve the situation without a hearing and at the instruction of the supervising attorney, it is permissible for a paralegal to review with opposing counsel preliminary objections to answers to interrogatories submitted by that attorney's client.

3.   True or False.   It is permissible for a busy attorney to undertake representation of a client if she knows that she will not be able to do anything with the case for another nine months, so long as she discloses this fact to the client and so long as the client consents.

4.   True or False.   It is unethical for a lawyer knowingly to offer evidence that is prejudicial.

5.   True or False.   A paralegal cannot give a presentation of social security law at a senior citizens' center if any portion of the presentation will be devoted to answering specific questions from the audience.

6.   True or False.   Sharon is a paralegal for Adam Williams and is also a notary public. One morning Adam brings an affidavit to Sharon, which already has been signed by Adam's client, Javier Garcia, and asks Sharon to notarize the affidavit. Sharon should not notarize the signature unless Mr. Garcia calls her and confirms that it is his signature.

7.   True or False.   It is permissible for a paralegal to propose and to implement a discovery plan in a personal injury case.

8.   True or False.   If the rules of an administrative agency permit nonlawyer practice, an attorney ethically may not restrict the right of a paralegal employed by her to appear before that agency on behalf of the lawyer's clients.

9.   True or False.   While interviewing a witness in a personal injury case, the witness relays facts to the paralegal which indicate that our client may have been the cause of the collision. If the paralegal were deposed about this interview, she could refuse to answer questions based upon attorney-client privilege.

10.   True or False.   Under existing ethics rules, all contingent fee arrangements must be in writing.

11.   True or False.   It is never permissible for a lawyer to represent adverse parties in a case.

12.   Which of the following represent(s) unethical conduct by a paralegal?

     a.   Drafting correspondence to a client to be signed by the paralegal.
     b.   Arranging a deposition with opposing counsel.
     c.   Performing legal research.
     d.   Two of the above.
     e.   All of the above.
     f.   None of the above.

13.   Donna is a licensed financial planner in her state. As part of her services to clients, she reviews their financial situations and recommends that combination of savings accounts, life insurance, and property ownership that she believes will best suit their needs. When they need a will or a trust, she refers them to a local law firm. Lawyers have been quite receptive to her referrals; as a result, several of them have provided her with a series of standardized will and trust forms to use in advising her clients. Which of the following is most correct?

     a.   Donna may not recommend or select forms for her clients.
     b.   Donna may select and complete a form based upon its standard use.
     c.   Donna may select the form so long as the client completes it himself.
     d.   Donna may recommend a form but the client must complete it.

14.   Marty is a paralegal for Michelle Michaels. While Ms. Michaels is in Europe, Marty receives a notice that a probate hearing is scheduled at the end of next week. Ms. Michaels is not scheduled to return to the office until after that time. Marty knows that a motion for continuance is needed to postpone the hearing. Which of the following is the worst course of action for Marty to take in this situation?

    a.   Mail the unsigned motion to the court for filing.

    b.   Arrange to have the client sign the motion and file it with the court.

    c.   Sign his name to the motion and show his paralegal title.

    d.   Sign Ms. Michael's name to the motion and place his initials under the signature.

15.   Which of the following represents ethical conduct by a paralegal?

    a.   Telling a prospective client that hers is the type of case the firm likes to handle.

    b.   Drafting and signing status letters to clients where the nonlawyer status is shown clearly.

    c.   Confirming that the firm once represented a particular client.

    d.   Two are ethical.

    e.   All are ethical.

    f.   None are ethical.

16.   It is permissible for paralegals to perform work that otherwise would be performed by an attorney if:

    a.   the attorney supervises the delegated work.

    b.   the attorney maintains a direct relationship with the client.

    c.   the attorney assumes full professional responsibility for the work product.

    d.   Two of the above.

    e.   All of the above.

    f.   None of the above.

17.   Brian is a paralegal employed by Richard Tyler. Brian's deposition is being taken concerning his investigation of an auto accident two years ago in which Mr. Tyler represented one of the parties. When a particular question is asked, Mr. Tyler objects on the basis of attorney work product and instructs Brian not to answer the question. The deposing attorney notes the objection for the record and demands that

Brian answer the question. Under these circumstances, Brian's worst option is to:

a. comply because the answer will not be admissible anyway.
b. not answer the question based upon Mr. Tyler's instructions.
c. request a recess to discuss the situation with Mr. Tyler.
d. comply only if the answer can be given off the record.

18. Of the following tasks, which ethically may not be performed by paralegals under existing rules?

a. Prepare answers to interrogatories.
b. Prepare questions for a deposition.
c. Assist a client in executing her will.
d. Two of the above.
e. All of the above.
f. None of the above.

19. While at a professional meeting, Brenda (who is a paralegal with the Davis & Lucas Law Firm) becomes involved in a conversation with Bruce and Wade, both of whom are paralegals in another law firm in the city. Wade, an obnoxious boor by anyone's standards, begins to relate courthouse rumors about Jake Thompson's recent arrest and the pending criminal charges. Brenda knows at least part of what Wade is saying to be untrue because her firm represents Jake. Brenda should:

a. correct Wade concerning those parts that she knows to be untrue.
b. inform Wade that he is incorrect but that she cannot discuss details because of client confidentiality.
c. report Wade to the district attorney for his breach of ethics.
d. say nothing.

20. A friend who is a paralegal in another law firm calls you to ask if your firm has handled any recent litigation in federal court. There have been major changes in the rules of procedure in that court within the past six months, and your friend is uncertain about filing pleadings under the new rules. Your firm has just completed its first case under the new rules. What is your best course of action?

a. Decline to answer his questions because it would constitute the unauthorized practice of law.
b. Decline to answer his questions because he should figure it out for himself.

c. Answer any of the questions that you know concerning procedure.
d. Answer any of the questions that you know, provided that your friend promises not to divulge where he got the information.

21. Guy is a paralegal, newly hired to go to work for another law firm. Before starting the new job, the legal administrator at the new law firm tells Guy she wants to review the names of the files with which Guy has worked to avoid any potential conflict of interest in his new position. It is permissible for Guy to:

a. reveal the names of the files.
b. reveal the names of the files as well as the status of each file.
c. refuse to reveal any information about clients from the other law firm on the grounds of confidentiality.
d. None of the above.

22. True or False.   It is unethical for a law firm to advise a client's creditors of a settlement made in a case so that the creditor may attach the settlement.

23. True or False.   Lawyers are required to segregate client funds from operating funds because of ethics rules.

24. True or False.   Under current ethics rules, a lawyer who is also a licensed insurance broker may join both business activities in the same office.

25. True or False.   Stacey is a paralegal at Mason & Frey. After working on a complex real estate case for nearly three years, the case is concluded successfully on behalf of Riverton Realty. Benjamin Riverton arranges to have Super Bowl tickets sent to Stacey's father to show his appreciation for Stacey's fine work on the case. Stacey, upon learning about the tickets, which are nearly impossible to obtain and are quite expensive, should call Mr. Riverton to inform him that her father's acceptance of the tickets will create ethical problems for her and for her attorney supervisor.

26. True or False.   Different ethics rules apply to paralegals who offer their services only to licensed attorneys than to paralegals who are employed full-time by licensed attorneys.

27. True or False.   A paralegal who discusses a client's case while at a friend's wedding violates the client's special right to privacy, which is called confidentiality.

28.   True or False.   If the supervising attorney instructs him to do so, a paralegal ethically may contact opposing counsel and try to determine the possible range of settlement figures that the opposing party might be willing to accept, so long as the paralegal identifies himself and so long as no specific amount is offered in settlement.

29.   After an initial client interview, the client asks you what the normal fee would be for the will. What is the best reply?

    a.   Paralegals cannot quote fees.
    b.   The standard charge for a will is $100.
    c.   The charge probably will be between $50 and $200.
    d.   Attorney Johnson must determine the charge, which can vary widely depending on the amount of time needed to draft the will.

30.   Three months after the entry of the decree, a client in a divorce case returns to the attorney and confesses that he concealed assets while the divorce case was pending. Now his business partner is trying to blackmail him. What should the attorney do?

    a.   Disclose the facts to the court.
    b.   Disclose the facts to the authorities.
    c.   Urge the client to disclose the facts.
    d.   Do nothing.

31.   Michael is a paralegal and at the law firm McEvoy & Skelton he works with Robin, one of the lawyers at the firm. Michael and Robin want to form a partnership. Under what circumstances might this be possible?

    a.   Michael and Robin form a company where, under the supervision of Robin, Michael creates legal forms to sell to the public.
    b.   Michael and Robin form an asset management company to purchase and manage apartment buildings.
    c.   Both a and b.
    d.   Neither a nor b; paralegals and lawyers cannot form partnerships.

32.   It is permissible for a paralegal to give legal advice as part of his pro bono activities, as long as:

    a.   the recipient does not pay for the advice.
    b.   the paralegal makes his or her nonlawyer status clear.
    c.   Both a and b.
    d.   Neither a nor b.

33. A retainer for legal services must be:

   a. agreed upon in advance.
   b. reasonable.
   c. deposited in a lawyer's trust account.
   d. All of the above.
   e. Two of the above.
   f. None of the above.

34. It is permissible to discuss a case with an opposing party who is represented by counsel, so long as:

   a. the opposing counsel does not know about the meeting.
   b. the opposing party consents.
   c. the opposing counsel consents.
   d. None of the above.

35. Tim is a paralegal for Robert Shale, a licensed attorney. Robert and two of his law school classmates (Megan Finnin and Barry Tobin) decide to join forces by sharing the cost of a suite of offices, equipment, and personnel. Robert asks Tim to arrange to have a bronze plate bearing the name "Shale, Finnin, and Tobin" placed on the office door. Which of the following is least correct?

   a. The lawyers can use this name only if they are a partnership.
   b. Tim may incur joint civil liability if he works for the lawyers.
   c. The lawyers may incur joint civil liability if they use this name.
   d. The lawyers cannot use the name unless all of them consent in advance.

36. It would be unethical for a paralegal to:

   a. review a complaint and draft an answer to it.
   b. explain appeal procedures to a client.
   c. attend a deposition.
   d. Two of the above.
   e. All of the above.
   f. None of the above.

37.   Which of the following represent(s) ethical conduct by a paralegal?

    a.   Negotiating settlements within dollar limits established by the attorney.
    b.   Obtaining a personal computer at 50% discount from a client who is a computer retailer.
    c.   Performing ministerial acts at a real estate closing.
    d.   Two of the above.
    e.   All of the above.
    f.   None of the above.

38.   True or False.   When statements are sent to clients, the paralegal's time may be billed at the same rate as the supervising attorney's, as long as the profit (the difference between the paralegal's billing rate and the lawyer's billing rate) is donated to the client loss fund of the state bar association.

39.   Tammy is a paralegal for Frank Turner, a sole practitioner. While Frank is away from the office on April 15, Tammy is contacted by one of Frank's divorce clients, who insists that he needs to know whether he can remove a portion of the funds from a joint savings account to pay federal income tax. In reviewing the temporary order entered by the court, it seems clear that the savings account can be used for joint obligations. In this case, Tammy should:

    a.   relay this information to the client.
    b.   tell the client he needs to wait until Frank returns so that Frank can advise him about the account.
    c.   tell the client that he should use his own discretion in deciding whether to access the account.
    d.   None of the above.

40.   True or False.   If Tammy is uncertain about what to do in the immediately preceding question or in a similar situation, she should do nothing until she talks with Frank.

41.   True or False.   A law firm may not be paid by a trust company to draft wills in which the trust company is named as trustee.

42.   True or False.   If the rules of an administrative agency permit nonlawyer practice, a paralegal may establish an independent practice which consists exclusively of representing clients before that administrative agency.

43.   True or False.   When an attorney knows that her client has committed the criminal offense as charged, she should withdraw from the case because she cannot zealously defend someone who is guilty.

44.   True or False.   In Kenny's capacity as a paralegal over the last 20 years, he has seen innumerable people simply plead guilty or no contest to minor criminal charges because they earned too much to have appointed counsel but did not earn enough to hire a lawyer. Quite troubled by this situation, Kenny prepares a brochure that outlines the steps of basic criminal procedure as well as the various options that a defendant may request when he appears in court. Kenny wants to have the brochure distributed on the sidewalk outside the courthouse. There will be no charge for the brochure, and he plans to use volunteers for distribution. If Kenny distributes the brochure as planned, he will be in violation of most states' UPL statutes.

45.   True or False.   Laura is a paralegal with the O&I Law Firm. Her supervisor has asked her to draft a type of document that she has never drafted before and that is not contained in the firm's form files. While searching some older files, she finds a document published and copyrighted by a real estate company which is exactly what she needs. Because the document comes from an old client file found in the law office, it is permissible for Laura to copy it as her own work product.

46.   True or False.   A grateful client sends a diamond-studded pen holder to a paralegal, as a way to say thanks for a job well done. It is permissible for the paralegal to accept the pen holder.

47.   True or False.   Under current ethics rules, sanctions may be imposed upon the supervising attorney when his or her paralegal drafts a frivolous discovery request.

48.   Kendall is a paralegal employed by Cori Lansing, a sole practitioner. Cori's practice has become much busier over the last few months, and she is considering the addition of another attorney. In the meantime, however, it is very difficult for her to be in all of the places where she needs to be at the same time. Cori suggests to Kendall that since nothing ever happens at pretrial hearings in county court except to set a trial date, perhaps Kendall can cover these hearings until another lawyer is hired. Which of the following is correct?

     a.   Kendall's appearance would be unethical without a court rule that permits him to appear.

     b.   Kendall's appearance would be ethical as long as he handles procedural matters only.

     c.   Kendall's appearance would be ethical as long as the attorney and the client consent.

     d.   None of these is correct.

49.   Assume that Russ is a paralegal and that he misappropriates client money from a trust account. What sanctions may be imposed on Russ?

     a.   Termination of employment.

     b.   Civil liability to the client.

     c.   Criminal conviction.

     d.   All of the above.

     e.   None of the above.

50.   In the immediately preceding situation, what course of action may be imposed against Russ's employer as a result of Russ's conduct?

     a.   Criminal charges.

     b.   Civil suit by the client.

     c.   Disciplinary proceedings.

     d.   Two of the above.

     e.   All of the above.

JUDGMENT AND ANALYTICAL ABILITY

The mind, stretched to a new idea, never goes back to its original dimension.

—Oliver Wendell Holmes

This section of the CLA/CP® examination relates to (1) comprehend data to identify a problem; (2) identify relevant facts and state them concisely and accurately; (3) apply analytical techniques to link facts and legal rules to develop legal issues; (4) recognize similarities and differences; (5) paralegal's relationship with the lawyer, the legal secretary, the client, the courts, and other law firms; and (6) draw persuasive, logical conclusions with explanation of the reasoning used to reach them.

Judgment and analytical ability go hand in hand. As a practical matter, they are so closely tied to each other that it sometimes is hard to tell where one begins and the other one ends.

<u>Judgment Defined</u> By definition, ***judgment*** is the process used to reach a decision or a conclusion. A particular judgment is good or bad, depending on its consequences. To exercise good judgment, one must

- have a thorough understanding of the parameters of the task assigned;

- use available resources (rules of law, applicable documents, and instructions from the supervising attorney) to complete the assignment;

•have a thorough understanding of the relevant facts;

•exercise sound analytical techniques (*see below*); and

•be sensitive to ethical obligations.

The person who develops a reputation for good judgment is the person who consistently takes the time to cultivate the skills outlined above. Acquiring good judgment skills is an evolutionary process that combines technical knowledge with experience. As a result, the paralegal—like the lawyer—finds that challenging assignments increase in direct proportion to his or her demonstrated exercise of good judgment.

Analytical Ability Defined   *Analytical ability* is the process of sorting facts and related information into categories, separating that which is relevant from that which is not. To analyze is to break the whole into its parts and to determine the relationship of the parts (1) to each other and (2) to the whole, using logical reasoning techniques and the rules that govern the specific situation under analysis. *Assume nothing*.

In its practical application within the legal environment, analytical ability requires some creativity and imagination. More important, however, it requires a disciplined, thorough, methodical, and painstakingly detailed approach to the project—whatever the project may be. Paralegals must be able to understand, propose, and implement systems to manage factual analyses, including testimony and source information.

Effect of Ethics Rules   Ethical considerations, including both the spirit of ethics rules and the rules themselves, are so interwoven into judgment and analytical ability that it is impossible to discuss either without taking ethics into account. For instance, if logical reasoning techniques suggest options that are (or may be) unethical or that exceed the bounds of responsible conduct, those options must be eliminated. Similarly, if the range of possible judgments includes acts or omissions that are (or may be) unethical, those judgments cannot be implemented.

The type of success that sustains a professional career over an entire lifetime cannot be achieved by cutting ethical corners or by rationalizing ethics away. To believe otherwise simply is bad judgment.

Practical Judgment and Analysis by Paralegals

Analytical processes are used to reach conclusions (judgments) about everything from organizing for a special project to avoiding conduct that may be interpreted as the unauthorized practice of law. The first step in any analysis is thorough comprehension of the data to be analyzed.

Comprehension of Data   All analysis begins with the review of instructions, applicable rules, basic facts, and other preliminary data. Implicit in the concept of review is the reviewer's ability to comprehend the data under review. Comprehension means understanding; it begins with a knowledge of what words mean, both literally and by reasonable inference.

To illustrate, read the following passage and circle the correct answers to the questions that follow it. Then place a check mark in front of those questions whose answers are implied by the passage but are not stated directly.

Adults engage in sexual stereotyping when they encourage children to behave in ways that traditionally have been considered appropriate for males and females. For instance, when parents encourage a son to wrestle but discourage a daughter from wrestling, they set the pattern for all sexual stereotyping that follows.

_____

1.   Parents engage in sexual stereotyping when they
       a.   encourage traditional behaviors.
       b.   write pornographic literature.
       c.   teach daughters to type.
       d.   discourage sons from wrestling.

2.   Parents engage in sexual stereotyping when they encourage
       a.   a girl to ride a bike.
       b.   a boy to care for a cat.
       c.   a girl to clean a house.
       d.   a boy to cook meals.

3.   Sexual stereotyping can be done by
       a.   relatives.
       b.   teachers.
       c.   ministers.
       d.   all of the above.

4.   Which of the following is not an example of sexual stereotyping?
       a.   telling a boy not to cry
       b.   teaching a girl to fight back
       c.   teaching a girl to be sweet
       d.   teaching a boy to fight back

You should have placed check marks in front of the second, third, and fourth questions. The answers are not stated in the passage; they are implied. Explanations of the correct answers follow.

1. The answer, *a*, is stated in the first sentence; the answers to all other questions are not directly stated in the passage.

2. The *c* answer is implied; you should have checked this question. Cleaning house and cooking traditionally have been considered more appropriate for females than for males. Riding bikes and caring for pets are not considered more appropriate for one sex than for the other; these activities usually are gender neutral.

3. The *d* answer is implied; you should have checked this question. Sexual stereotyping can be done by any adult who influences a child's behavior, including parents, grandparents, aunts, uncles, teachers, and ministers.

4. The *b* answer is implied; you should have checked this question. Fighting back traditionally has been considered more appropriate for males than for females. Boys traditionally have been encouraged not to cry, and girls traditionally have been encouraged to be sweet.

The distinction between a reasonable inference and an unreasonable assumption can be obscure at times. The paralegal is expected to recognize that point at which obscurity begins and to exercise caution to stay within the bounds of reasonable inference.

For the paralegal, a superior command of the English language and of specific legal terms is essential. If a paralegal were assigned to help finalize existing drafts of a proposed contract between a wobblewonk manufacturing company and its widget supplier, for instance, the paralegal could do very little without knowing the precise definitions of the terms *wobblewonk* and *widget*. Although terminology certainly is an appropriate starting point, comprehension involves much more than merely knowing textbook definitions.

The review of a series of corporate operating statements and balance sheets, for example, requires more than being able to recite dictionary definitions of the words found in those documents. The reviewer must be able to translate the terms and numbers from financial gobbledegook into plain English. This requires knowledge of how corporations work, knowledge of how corporations use operating statements and balance sheets in general (and how this corporation uses them in particular), and an understanding of generally accepted accounting principles and practices. Without this background, the reviewer cannot expect to comprehend the information contained in the operating statements.

Analysis of Facts   Thorough analysis demands a good memory and the ability to link specific facts to the legal issues or requirements of the case. As a corollary, conflicts and gaps in factual data must be noted and resolved.

Armed with the legal rules to be applied, the paralegal analyzes facts and sorts them into categories according to their source and degree of relevance as they are gathered from available resources, including public records; private documents; witness statements; and interviews in various forms. The analytical methods used most generally are deductive reasoning and analogical reasoning, which often are used in combination with each other.

Deductive reasoning is an analytical process that uses a major premise and a minor premise to deduce a logical conclusion, also known as a syllogism.

MAJOR PREMISE:	All men have beards.
MINOR PREMISE:	Sam is a man.
CONCLUSION:	Sam has a beard.

MAJOR PREMISE:	Most men have beards.
MINOR PREMISE:	Sam is a man.
CONCLUSION:	Sam has a beard.

The conclusion is valid (logical) in the first example. If *all* men have beards and if Sam is a man, he is included in the same category as all other men. Therefore, logic dictates that Sam has a beard. The conclusion in the second example is not valid, however, because there is no way to know whether Sam is included in the same category as *most* men. He may be among the minority of men who do not have beards.

The conclusion reached through deductive reasoning is valid only if the major premise and the minor premise are themselves valid and only if they relate to similar things.

MAJOR PREMISE:	A foot is 12 inches long.
MINOR PREMISE:	William has two feet.
CONCLUSION:	William's feet total 24 inches in length.

Although each premise in the example is valid standing alone, neither is valid in context with the other. The term *foot* in the major premises implies a linear foot, while the term *feet* in the minor premise implies body parts. Therefore, the conclusion is invalid.

The analytical method that uses similarities and differences to categorize is called ***analogical reasoning***. The ability to recognize similarities and differences by analogy is found in many aptitude tests, including law school aptitude tests, using problems such as these:

1.   Horse is to animal as _____ is to _____.
     a.   cow; milk
     b.   farm; pig
     c.   tree; branch
     d.   oak; wood

2.   Thermometer is to temperature as _____ is to _____.
     a.   telescope; astronomy
     b.   clock; minutes
     c.   scale; weight
     d.   microscope; biologist

To solve the first problem, one would reason: "Horse is to animal as *blank* is to *blank*. A horse is an animal; it is a type or species of animal. Comparing cow and milk, a cow is not a type of milk; it produces milk. Comparing farm and pig, a farm is not a type of pig. Comparing tree and branch, a tree is not a type of branch; it contains branches. Comparing oak and wood, oak is a type of wood; this forms an analogy to the first pair of terms in the question. So the correct answer is *d, oak and wood*."

To solve the second problem, one might reason: "Thermometer is to temperature as *blank* is to *blank*. A thermometer measures temperature. Comparing telescope and astronomy, a telescope does not measure astronomy. Eliminate this answer. Comparing clock and minutes, a clock measures minutes. This could be the answer. Comparing scale and weight, a scale measures weight. This could be the answer also. Comparing microscope and biologist, a microscope does not measure a biologist. Eliminate this answer. So, a thermometer measures temperature, a clock measures minutes, and a scale measures weight; but the word *minutes* is different from either *temperature* or *weight*. A clock measures time, not just minutes; minutes are units of time—just as degrees are units of temperature and pounds are units of weight. So the best answer is *c, scale; weight*. Temperature and weight are complete dimensions in themselves. A thermometer measures the dimension *temperature*, and a scale measures the dimension *weight*."

Analogical reasoning is the principal method used in *stare decisis*, which requires cases with like facts to be decided alike and cases with different facts to be decided differently—if the differences are important.

If legal research discloses a case reciting facts A, B, and C, *stare decisis* (analogical reasoning) requires all subsequent cases with facts A, B, and C to be decided in the same way as the first case. If a subsequent case contains facts

A and B—but not fact C—the importance of fact C to the outcome of the original case must be analyzed. Similarly, if a subsequent case contains facts A, B, C, and D, the addition of fact D must be analyzed in light of the original case: Does it seem likely that the additional fact would have changed the outcome of the original case? If not, the original case retains its value as precedent and must be followed in the subsequent case. To illustrate:

CASE NO. 1   Fact A: Joe owns a prize bulldog.
              Fact B: Susan steals the bulldog and sells it to Ken.
              Fact C: Ken does not know the bulldog is stolen.
              Result: *Joe wins against Ken, because Ken acquires no better title than the thief.*

CASE NO. 2   Fact A: Joe owns a prize bulldog.
              Fact B: Susan buys the dog with an insufficient funds check.
              Result: *Joe wins against Susan, who has committed fraud.*

CASE NO. 3   Fact A: Joe owns prize a bulldog.
              Fact B: Susan buys the dog with a bad check and sells it to Ken.
              Fact C: Ken does not know about the bad check.
              Fact D: Ken has heard gossip that Susan "pulled a fast one" on Joe.
              Result: *Joe wins against Ken, because Ken knew something was amiss even though he did not know specifically what it was.*

Regardless of the analytical method used, analysis of facts requires the paralegal to read (or to listen to) facts critically to detect factual gaps and factual conflicts. **Factual gaps** occur when certain facts are missing or are unknown. Where possible, factual gaps must be supplied by other witnesses or other sources. **Factual conflicts** occur when the facts obtained from a single source are inconsistent with each other (*internal conflict*) or when they are inconsistent with those facts obtained from other sources (*external conflict*). Internal conflict may be more problematic, especially if the internal conflict occurs within a client's statement of the facts. This may indicate that the client does not know what happened or is not telling the truth about what happened. Either way, factual conflicts must be brought to the attorney's attention and must be resolved through other sources.

Segregation of Relevant Data   Along with their many other duties, paralegals are information managers. In working with a particular case file, the paralegal comes into contact with vast amounts of information or data. Some of it is relevant; some of it is not.

An important part of an attorney's expectation of the paralegal involves the ability to separate relevant from irrelevant information. Using applicable statutes or rules—or legal theories supplied by the attorney—as the measuring stick, the paralegal sifts through all of the facts to segregate those that are relevant and then categorizes them according to the issue or the element of an issue to which they relate. This applies both to facts that tend to support the client's claim and to facts that tend to refute it. The paralegal who can perform this important task in a consistent and reliable manner, streamlining relevant facts and avoiding factual surprises, is invaluable to a busy attorney. To illustrate, the following exercise is provided.

Assume the following transcribed statement is handed to you by your supervising attorney after her initial conference with a potential client. The attorney tells you that the case involves a two-vehicle collision on an icy street and that no passengers were in either vehicle. She indicates that liability likely will be the major issue in the case and instructs you to start a new case file, to review the statement, and then to schedule a follow-up interview with the client.

My name is Nadine Kelly. I am a widow and have lived alone for 10 years. I was on my way home late one night when this terrible accident happened. Let's see, I think it was January 12. That would be this year. Yes, this year; I am certain of that.

Anyway, it was pretty late. I'd say it was between 9:30 and 10:00 p.m. I was driving my truck west on Ames Avenue. I had just passed the stoplight at 52nd Street and was headed uphill on Ames when, all of a sudden, this yellow bus (maybe it was a yellow van) was in my lane and was headed straight for me.

I don't know how fast the guy was going, but it was too fast for me to get out of his way. I had just left the stoplight, so I couldn't have been driving very fast—maybe 10 or 15 m.p.h. Anyhow, when I saw that he was coming right for me, I tried to get out of his way. I hit the gas and headed for the curb, but I wasn't fast enough. He hit me almost head on. It broke out my headlight and smashed my fender into the tire on one side of the car, so that I couldn't drive it home. It had to be towed.

He got out of his car and started yelling that I was a crazy old bat, why didn't I watch where I was going, and stuff like that. I was real upset. It was pretty bad to be hit; but when he started yelling, that really upset me.

I don't remember a whole lot after that except that I think he must have been drunk—the way he was yelling and all. He was none too steady on his feet, either. He said his name was Earl or Darrell something-or-other. I have it written down on a piece of paper at home. I forgot to bring it with me.

A guy from the gas station came over to where we were. We all went back to the gas station to call the police, but they couldn't come because there were too many accidents that night. It was real icy and everything. The police said for us to give each other our names and the names of our insurance companies and then to file a police report the next day.

I guess I should have stayed at Pearl's house. She begged me to stay, but the roads didn't seem that bad then. The gas station guy towed my car and drove me home. I was still upset, but he was real nice about it.

Among the following statements, which are statements of fact? Indicate by writing the word "fact" in front of each such statement. Of the factual statements selected, which are relevant to the issue identified by the attorney? Indicate by placing a check mark in front of them.

1.   Mrs. Kelly is a widow.

2.   Her husband died 10 years ago.

3.   The accident happened on January 12 this year.

4.   Mrs. Kelly was driving in a westerly direction.

5.   The accident happened at the intersection of 52nd Street and Ames Avenue.

6.   The other vehicle was driving in an easterly direction.

7.   The roads were icy.

8.   The other vehicle was speeding.

9.   The other driver was drunk.

10.   A gas station attendant witnessed the accident.

<u>Answers</u>

1.   *Fact—irrelevant to the issue of liability, however.*
2.   *Assumption: Not all widows live alone; children or others may have lived with her.*
3.   *Assumption: She only thinks the accident occurred on January 12.*
4.   *Fact—relevant to the issue of liability.*
5.   *Misstatement: She states she already had passed the intersection.*
6.   *Fact—relevant to the issue of liability.*
7.   *Fact—relevant to the issue of liability.*
8.   *Conclusion of client; it may or may not be true.*
9.   *Conclusion of client; it may or may not be true.*
10.   *Assumption: No inference can be drawn about witnesses to the accident.*

Although substantially oversimplified, this exercise illustrates the type of filtering process that paralegals use to segregate facts and to assess their relevancy. Where they may be relevant, the conclusions and assumptions suggested by the statement would be investigated and verified. In addition, the many factual gaps within the statement would be addressed in the paralegal's investigation. Once gathered and verified, these facts likewise must be separated for relevancy and then must be categorized according to the issues to which they apply. A single fact may relate to more than one issue in the case.

Summarize Relevant Data   Once relevant facts and data have been segregated and placed within appropriate categories, summaries (or abstracts) generally are prepared. The form of the summary depends on the purpose for which it will be used. The summary of a particular witness's statement may be in a brief, narrative form for the attorney's working file or it may be summarized in a bullet format for the witness section of a trial notebook, similar to many of the lists used throughout this *Review Manual*. The same witness statement generally will be abstracted still further for purposes of indexing and cross-referencing evidence in preparation for trial.

Unless the attorney specifies a particular format, the paralegal must know the purpose of the summary to determine which format will be most useful. Sound judgments must be made at the beginning of the case about indexing and retrieval systems to be used, as well as their formats. If the format (or the system) becomes unworkable, the financial costs to change the system can be substantial. The credibility cost to the paralegal, however, is much greater. Working closely with the attorney, the paralegal must make initial judgments about information management systems and the forms they should take. The system and system format selected should be the simplest ones available for the job.

Upon selection of an appropriate information management system, the paralegal is responsible for summarizing all of the data that comprises it: witness statements, answers to interrogatories, depositions, answers to requests for admission, public records, relevant documents, legal memoranda, and so forth.

In preparing summaries, a good rule of thumb is to concentrate on subjects and verbs from an original witness statement, adding other information only if it is essential for clarity. Ordinarily, this is easier to accomplish with a bullet format than it is with a narrative. When a narrative is required, such as for the statement of a particular witness, it should be no longer than approximately one-fourth of the original (as a general rule). If it can be shortened further without sacrificing substance, do so. When summarizing depositions, the general rule of thumb is seven to ten pages of deposition testimony for each page of summary.

Interpretation of Procedural Matters

Paralegals routinely interpret matters of procedure within the parameters established by law, ethics rules, and office policy. Within these parameters, the degree of procedural authority granted to a particular paralegal is based upon his or her experience and the level of confidence engendered with the supervising attorney as that attorney's "good right arm." This type of confidence does not come quickly or easily; it is earned over a long period of time and is based upon a demonstrable history of good judgments by the paralegal. As the attorney's confidence in a particular paralegal grows, so does the delegation of procedural authority to that paralegal.

Everything done by the paralegal ultimately must be approved by the attorney, either expressly or tacitly, and incorporated into the attorney's final work product. Within this structure, however, paralegals can and do make decisions about procedural matters related to client services, rule compliance, and case progression.

Experienced paralegals routinely answer client questions regarding procedure: How much notice must be given to creditors? How long is the statutory waiting period for a particular type of case? They prepare and calculate inheritance tax, estate tax, and income tax returns. They prepare preliminary schedules and forms for probate, bankruptcy, and family law cases. They organize and maintain litigation files, including the trial notebook. They prepare preliminary drafts of pleadings, motions, notices, wills, trusts, and legal memoranda based upon legal research performed by them or by others. They conduct initial reviews of title binders and closing statements, draft deeds and related documents, and perform other ministerial tasks in real estate matters. At the attorney's direction, they communicate directly with clients (by letter, in person, and on the telephone) about the status of clients' cases.

Using guidelines set by the supervising attorney, paralegals review statutes and court rules on a preliminary basis to determine procedural requirements; establish compliance checklists; and implement systems to comply with those requirements. They calculate deadlines (for example, hearings which must be set not sooner than 60 days and not later than 120 days after an occurrence; three-day notice requirement for hearing notices; and so forth), which requires them to know such things as whether a three-day notice includes the day of service; whether three days means three calendar days or three working days; and whether additional time is granted by a court when its deadline falls on a weekend or legal holiday. Paralegals monitor all discovery, including that which is sent and that which is received, to assure compliance with applicable rules.

Paralegals streamline case progression by implementing various forms of record searches and investigation at the instruction of the supervising attorney; by implementing and monitoring the discovery process in litigation matters; and by working closely with the attorney to ensure that cases move forward in an expeditious manner. Paralegals play a vital role in elevating the attorney's efficiency by providing higher quality legal service to clients at a lower cost.

In addition to their work on specific cases, paralegals often provide assistance in administrative areas. Their superior organizational skills frequently are used in establishing systems of all kinds: training new personnel; library maintenance and acquisitions; general office procedures; filing systems; timekeeping systems; and billing systems. This systems list is not intended to be exhaustive, because the skills of a paralegal can be used in any area where organization, attention to detail, and good judgment are required.

Good judgment in administrative areas demands a thorough familiarity with the system or project assigned, including its history; sensitivity to the office hierarchy; diplomacy in working with the personalities to be affected by any change that may be implemented; enough flexibility and self-confidence to be receptive to constructive criticism; and perseverance to see the project to successful completion.

Establish Priorities   Paralegals with proven capabilities in matters requiring good judgment are blessed—and cursed—with ever-increasing responsibilities in the areas of case management and office administration. Since they do not receive ever-increasing amounts of time within which to accomplish these responsibilities, paralegals must become adept at establishing and maintaining priorities.

Simply stated, establishing priorities means recognizing the difference between those things that can wait and those things that cannot (or should not) wait. The situation that involves being called away from a long-range project to complete an emergency assignment requested by the senior partner is an easy judgment call. If the project is one that must be completed before trial begins tomorrow morning, however, the judgment becomes more complex; and announcing it may require the most skilled judgment of all.

To establish reasonable priorities, the paralegal must be able to distinguish between internal and external deadlines; must make an accurate assessment of the time required for any given project; must be willing to delegate responsibility wherever possible; and must take the priorities of others into account.

An internal deadline is one which is self-imposed or is imposed from within the law office, such as restructuring the trial brief file maintained by most litigation firms or drafting a modification to the personnel policy manual.

An external deadline is one which is imposed by an outside source, such as the deadline to file an appellate brief with the court; a board of directors meeting scheduled by a corporate client; or a license renewal deadline for a client governed by an administrative agency.

As a general rule, external deadlines take priority over internal deadlines. The deadline for an appellate brief, for example, typically takes precedence over assignments connected with modifying a policy manual—even when the policy manual assignment comes from a senior partner. Missing a brief deadline may result in a malpractice claim; delaying the modification of an internal policy manual rarely does. In this situation, the paralegal's good judgment should prompt him to enlist the aid of his immediate supervisor in gaining the senior firm member's support for the shift in priorities. Establishing priorities among conflicting external deadlines (two different appellate briefs due within a day or two of each other, for example) requires the full panoply of good judgment skills.

To ensure that all external deadlines are met, a paralegal must assess accurately the time requirements for each project, recognizing that the tendency is to underestimate the time needed to do a thorough job. Most rush projects are needed yesterday. Since that deadline cannot be met in any event, the paralegal must use care to make reasonable estimates of the time needed for completion. Otherwise, credibility with superiors is jeopardized when the deadline is not met. The delay wastes valuable time that could be used to obtain assistance from others or, if that is not possible, to obtain an extension of the deadline without the additional difficulty and stress associated with a last-minute request.

One generally knows ahead of time that there may be problems in meeting a deadline. As soon as that possibility appears, the experienced paralegal prepares to address it. This can be done in one of two ways: (1) Obtain the necessary help from others to meet the deadline; or (2) Delegate unrelated assignments to others if that will allow sufficient time to meet the deadline. Frequently, other paralegals, associates, or law clerks can be reassigned to provide assistance until the priority project is completed. The inexperienced paralegal sometimes tries to be superhuman and to do it all. The results of this type of judgment can be disastrous for the project and for the paralegal.

Establishing priorities requires that the priorities of others be accommodated in every reasonable way. Assume, for example, that a case is unexpectedly moved forward on the court's trial docket. In what order should the paralegal perform the following tasks: (1) Confer with his supervising attorney about final preparation for trial, as requested; (2) Call to cancel his dental appointment for the first morning of trial; and (3) Call to find out when the court reporter will have the final deposition transcribed so that it can be summarized and indexed?

First, call the court reporter. Until the paralegal knows the reporter's transcription schedule, he does not have all necessary information to engage in a meaningful discussion with the attorney about final trial preparations. Moreover, the reporter's schedule may need to be rearranged to accommodate the earlier trial date. If so, the reporter should be informed as quickly as possible. **Second**, armed with all relevant information (including the date when the deposition will be completed), confer with the attorney as requested about final preparations for trial. If additional priority tasks emerge from this discussion which require the assistance of others, contact those individuals before attending to personal matters. Any unnecessary delay at this point seldom can be justified. **Third**, although it may take less than 60 seconds to call the dentist's office, this is the least important task and, therefore, the last one that should be undertaken. Imagine, for instance, the justifiable reaction of the trial lawyer who may enter the paralegal's office as the dental call is being made. The better judgment, therefore, is to cancel the dental appointment later in the day, after trial preparations are underway.

Reaction to Specific Situations   There is no single rule to handle the wide array of situations encountered by a paralegal. Rather, the paralegal must draw upon his or her experience in handling a variety of procedural matters, in working with people in general and with clients in particular, and in working with a specific attorney.

The ideal professional relationship of the paralegal and the attorney is one grounded in loyalty, trust, and mutual respect developed over a long period of time. To attain this ideal, the attorney must be willing to delegate tasks to the paralegal in permissible areas and to serve as a professional mentor in developing the paralegal's analytical and decision-making skills. The paralegal must be willing and able to accept the responsibilities delegated to him or her in a reliable, professional way.

In any situation, the paralegal should determine the objective to be reached within the parameters of office policy and sound ethics. Once the objective is known, the paralegal's cautious common sense, analytical abilities, and diplomacy will go far in consistently exercising good judgment. A thorough understanding of office policy (both written and unwritten) and of legal ethics will assist the paralegal in successfully managing situations such as these:

- Client questions about the merits of a case or about the course of action that he or she should take in the attorney's absence.

- The client who attempts to enlist the paralegal's help—or silence—in providing inaccurate or incomplete information.

- Irate clients encountered in person and on the telephone, whether or not the supervising attorney may be a source of their irritation.

- The attorney who procrastinates about getting things done or who is inconsistent about returning telephone calls to clients and to others.

- The attorney who is lax in reviewing the paralegal's work before incorporating it into his or her final work product.

- The attorney who works in spurts, making it virtually impossible to maintain an orderly work schedule.

- The attorney who shifts to the paralegal blame which clearly rests with the attorney alone.

- The coworker who always needs help to meet deadlines.

- The coworker or the supervisor who persists in conduct that is unprofessional or that may be unethical.

- The supervisor who makes unreasonable demands or who finds some reason to criticize, no matter how quickly or how well a project is done.

- The supervisor who gives incomplete instructions.

- The supervisor who avoids using the paralegal's skills to their full potential.

Approach to Essay Questions

There is one essay question for this section of the CLA/CP® examination. It requires the applicant to demonstrate superior written communication skills, together with his or her analytical abilities and good judgment. For this section of the examination, more than for the others, practical experience is the applicant's most valuable asset. Those who are relatively new to the profession can substitute a rational and considered approach for practical experience.

In examinations of this type, questions dealing with analytical abilities may require a stated situation to be broken down, separating relevant from irrelevant data, with the relevant data to be accurately categorized or summarized or both. Questions dealing with judgment are designed to test the applicant's decision-making skills in specific situations that are outlined in the question. The applicant who possesses these skills will be able to demonstrate them to their best advantage by using the following approach:

- Quickly skim the question to get a feel for its general subject matter.

- Determine specifically what the question seeks: an analysis and recommendation; a listing or summary of relevant data; a survey of permissible options; a proposed plan of action; or other, stated objective.

- Reread the question, carefully this time, noting words and phrases that may be important, given the subject matter of the question and the objective that it seeks.

- Prepare an outline of the proposed answer first and use the outline to prepare the final answer.

- Review the suggestions for taking tests in general, which are found in the introduction to this *Review Manual*.

A sample essay question is included as part of the self-test for this chapter; a sample answer for that question is shown in the Self-Test Answer Key.

Judgment and Analytical Ability Self-Test

Allow 30 minutes to answer all objective questions and 40 minutes to answer the essay question (70 minutes total). At the end of the time period, check your answers to the questions against those in the Answer Key Section of this Manual. Deduct two points each for incorrect answer (60 total possible points for objective questions). Unanswered questions are counted as incorrect answers. Add this score to the score from the essay question to determine the overall score for this section. Follow directions carefully and observe the time limit precisely to provide an accurate self-assessment.

Choose the most correct answer to the following questions unless you are instructed to do otherwise.

1.   True or False.   When a paralegal hears office rumors concerning his supervising attorney, he should report them to his supervising attorney as soon as he is reasonably able to do so.

2.   True or False.   When a client relates information about her case to a paralegal in confidence, the paralegal nevertheless should report the information to the supervising attorney.

3.   True or False.   A paralegal assigned to reorganize the preprinted form files may assume that he has authority to charge the necessary supplies to complete the project.

4.   True or False.   Errors in judgment are to be expected of a paralegal who is beginning a new job with a new law firm.

5.   True or False.   A paralegal is permitted to exercise independent judgment in procedural matters.

6.   Fur is to bear as _____ is to _____.

    a.   coat; man
    b.   warmth; animal
    c.   rug; floor
    d.   wool; sheep

7.   _____ is to cave as car is to _____.

    a.   stone; steel
    b.   primitive; modern
    c.   apartment house; horse
    d.   modern; primitive

8.   Tar is to _____ as coal is to _____.

    a.   roofing; shovel
    b.   derived; heating
    c.   construction; heating
    d.   black; heating

9.   _____ is to liquid as ice is to _____.

     a.   flowing; solid
     b.   warm; cold
     c.   milk; cream
     d.   water; solid

10.   _____ is to dollar as year is to _____.

     a.   money; calendar
     b.   dime; month
     c.   penny; century
     d.   savings; century

11.   A statute requires that a special meeting of shareholders cannot be held without three days notice. If a notice of special meeting is mailed to all shareholders on Monday, November 30, the meeting should not be scheduled before:

     a.   December 2
     b.   December 3
     c.   December 4
     d.   December 5

Questions 12 and 13 are based on the following facts:
Tony was stopped on the street by a man in dark glasses. The man offered to sell Tony an Apex watch, which normally sells for $750, for only $50. Tony agreed and gave the man $50. Later that day, Tony learned that the watch was an Ampax, which normally retails for $19.95.

12.   Which of the following is not an appropriate criticism of Tony's action?

     a.   You must look before you leap.
     b.   A fool and his money are soon parted.
     c.   There is a sucker born every minute.
     d.   The man who wants something for nothing is an easy mark.
     e.   Nothing ventured, nothing gained.

13.   Which of the following could Tony best use in an effort to justify his action?

     a.   You cannot judge a book by its cover.
     b.   You must strike while the iron is hot.
     c.   Beware of Greeks bearing gifts.

d. A bird in the hand is worth two in the bush.
e. The guilty fleeth when no man pursueth.

14. Isn't it true that you and your wife had a bitter argument just before she was killed? The form and emphasis of this question is most closely paralleled by which of the following?

a. Did you leave the theater just before the fire broke out?
b. Were you aware that he had been siphoning funds for his own use?
c. Did you not, in fact, recognize the robber as your own brother?
d. Was your husband aware of the fact that you had decided to leave him?
e. Was your wife aware of the fact that you had decided to leave her?

15. Dennis Taylor is a paralegal with Mannon & Wise. Kate Karcher also is a paralegal with the firm. Kate has acquired the habit of coming to Dennis with questions and problems when they arise. Dennis does not mind; he is glad to help. Recently, however, Kate has started to bring her personal problems to Dennis as well. He now believes that he may have made a mistake in trying to help Kate with any of her difficulties, professional or personal. Which of the following is the least effective alternative for Dennis to choose?

a. Invite Kate to a place away from the office and explain that he feels uncomfortable about becoming so involved in her personal life.
b. Meet with Kate at the office and explain that he feels uncomfortable about becoming so involved in her personal life.
c. Wait until the next time Kate asks him about a personal problem and tell her that he feels uncomfortable about getting involved.
d. Wait until the next time Kate asks him about a personal problem and feign puzzlement about what she should do.

16. Kim Wang has worked for attorney Mark Thomas for several years. More and more, Kim finds herself covering for him with clients and others when he fails to return telephone calls. Kim has come to resent being put in this position and wants it to end. What is the best thing for her to do at this point?

a. Speak with other paralegals in the office about Mark and get their advice.
b. Visit with Mark and ask him if there is anything she can do to help him with returning calls more promptly.

c.   Look for another job because Mark is unlikely to change old habits for very long if Kim is there to cover for him.

d.   Seek intervention from the senior attorney to whom Mark reports.

17.   Carol's supervising attorney recently undertook a very messy divorce case involving a prominent public official. One of the associate attorneys came into Carol's office while she was working on the file, asked what she was doing, and said, "Hey, let me see that. I bet there are things in there that would curl your hair." Carol's best course of action is:

a.   Remind him that all client information is confidential and decline to show him the file.

b.   Let him see the file because he is an attorney.

c.   Let him see the file only if he insists, but inform her supervising attorney about the incident.

d.   Tell him she can't show him the file because she needs it to finish her project, and the supervising attorney wants it back right away.

18.   As part of the investigation in a dog bite case, Sophie's supervising attorney asked her to go to the address of the defendant and to take photographs of the dog in question if he happened to be in the yard. The address was in a bad neighborhood. When Sophie arrived, she parked across the street; and as she was crossing the street to reach the defendant's yard, a huge dog raced across the yard in her direction and began jumping ferociously at the chain-link fence. Startled by the dog and fumbling to focus the camera, she then noticed a small, wiry man emerge from the house. The man shouted at her to get off his property (she was on the city street) and began moving in her direction. Sophie became completely unnerved, quickly got into her car, and drove away. When she related the incident to the attorney, he was visibly annoyed and said, "Well, if you hadn't given up so easily, you probably could have gotten at least one or two photos before you left." In retrospect, Sophie should have:

a.   Remained calm and tried to snap at least one photograph before she left.

b.   Done nothing different.

c.   Described the man as being more threatening than he was.

d.   Returned at a different time to take the photos before giving up.

19.   Democracy is the great leveler. The sentiment expressed in this statement is most closely paralleled by which of the following?

a.   Birds of a feather flock together.
b.   A bird in the hand is worth two in the bush.
c.   The grazing herd eats the choicest stalks first.
d.   Mediocrity tends toward gregariousness.

20.   An old man walked into a police station and confessed to having just killed his wife. The desk sergeant excused himself and left the room. When he returned, he explained to the old man: "We have no record of your wife's ever having been born. So, if she has not been born yet, she could not have died yet. Therefore, you have committed no crime." Which of the following best embodies the sergeant's way of thinking?

a.   My mind is made up; don't confuse me with the facts.
b.   Don't believe everything you read.
c.   If it's not official, it doesn't exist.
d.   The quality of mercy is not strained.
e.   If all else fails, read the directions.

21.   Everyone who is patriotic will vote in the presidential election. Betty is patriotic. If both of these statements is true, it is correct to conclude that:

a.   Betty will vote in the presidential election.
b.   Betty may vote in the presidential election.
c.   Betty will not vote in the presidential election.
d.   No conclusions can be made.

22.   Every taxicab that I have seen in Chicago is painted yellow; therefore, there must be a law that says cabs must be yellow. The logic of this statement is most similar to the logic contained in which of the following statements?

a.   Every time I have dropped a rock, it has fallen to the ground; therefore, there must be a law of gravity.
b.   Every dog I have seen in New York is on a leash; therefore, there must be a law that requires dogs to be on leashes.
c.   There is a law that requires all children under age 16 to be in school, which explains why I see no children on the street during school hours.
d.   Every drunk I have seen in New York has been micturating in the subway; therefore, there must be no law against it.
e.   Every time I pass over the toll bridge, I pay the toll; therefore, there must be a law requiring it.

Questions 23–25 are based on the following facts:
Alcohol has been labeled by safety experts as the number one medical factor in traffic accidents. A national medical panel funded by a government grant over the past two years finds alcohol to be a significant factor in a majority of personal injury cases related to driving. The panel recommended a sharp reduction in the amount of drinking tolerated in many states where a blood-alcohol blood level of 0.15 percent must be reached to be accepted as evidence of intoxication while driving. The panel reported that blood levels of 0.05 percent alcohol constitute medical impairment of a person's driving ability, and blood levels of 0.10 alcohol indicate intoxication. Doctors on the panel declined to interpret these findings in terms of how many drinks a person could consume before exceeding these different blood-alcohol levels. They said there are too many variables, including the weight of the drinker, the length of time over which the alcohol is consumed, and the potency of each drink consumed.

23. Of the following statements concerning the preceding passage, which is most correct?

    a. Football players generally can tolerate more alcohol than marathon runners can tolerate.
    b. Doctors say it is not alcohol but the weight of the drinker and other such variables that determine whether a person should drive after drinking.
    c. A short, thin person will reach a 0.15 blood-alcohol level faster than will a tall, heavy person.
    d. Thin people are less likely to be affected by alcohol consumption.

24. Of the following statements concerning the preceding passage, which is least correct?

    a. Alcohol is a significant factor in traffic-related injuries.
    b. A 0.15 blood-alcohol level is legal intoxication in most states.
    c. Tolerable blood-alcohol levels vary from individual to individual.
    d. Doctors believe that blood-alcohol levels above 0.10 should not be tolerated.

25. Based upon the preceding passage, which of the following conclusions is most valid?

    a. Doctors will not be happy until all states adopt a 0.05 blood-alcohol level as evidence of intoxication for purposes of driving.
    b. The findings of the panel are suspect, because the panel was funded by a government grant.

c. Laws should be adopted to prohibit drivers from drinking.

d. Alcohol is the most significant factor in accidents on streets and highways.

26. Bo White works for Karen Hall, a sole practitioner. Keith Martin, one of the attorney's best clients, called Bo one afternoon in a state of panic. Mr. Martin stated that he had to catch a plane to Boston in two hours and needed a trust deed to take with him to complete a real estate transaction there. At the attorney's direction, Bo has prepared a number of trust deeds for Mr. Martin, who deals extensively in real estate matters all over the country. Bo told Mr. Martin that Karen was expected to be in court for the rest of the day. The client became extremely agitated and said, "All I want is a simple form, and I need it right now. I can't wait all afternoon. If you don't give it to me, I will see that you are fired the first thing tomorrow morning; and don't think that I won't do it." Which of the following is Bo's best course of action?

a. Offer to give the client a blank trust deed if the client agrees to absolve Bo of any liability if the attorney would have wanted the form changed in any way.

b. Offer to give the client the bailiff's telephone number at the court-house so that he can contact Karen himself.

c. Offer to call the bailiff to ask her to send a message in to Karen to contact the office right away.

d. Offer to prepare the deed, have it approved by Karen when she returns, and fax it to Boston first thing in the morning.

27. Some snakes are amphibians. Some amphibians are intelligent. Some intelligent creatures are not snakes. Based upon these propositions, which of the following could be true?

a. No amphibians are intelligent.

b. Some snakes are intelligent.

c. No intelligent creatures are amphibians.

d. All amphibians are snakes.

e. All snakes are intelligent.

28. Which is the most logical sequence of the following statements?

I. Under such a view, there is but one alternative to majority rule: minority rule.

II. As the great statesman Fromte once observed: "Democracy is not a very good form of government, but it is the best we have."

III.   Ultimately, democracy rests upon the simple proposition that every person has an equal right to make choices and that no single choice is right for all.

IV.   The danger of minority rule is obvious; for if humans are capable of incorrect choices, is not that danger magnified if the choice is that of the few?

V.   If everyone has an equal right to choose, then majority rule is the only way to take account of conflicting choices.

a.   I, V, II, III, IV
b.   V, I, IV, II, III
c.   III, I, V, II, IV
d.   III, I, V, IV, II
e.   III, V, I, IV, II

29.   A Supreme Court Justice once observed: "We are not the last word because we are infallible; we are infallible because we are the last word." Which of the following most closely parallels the logic of this statement?

a.   Congressman: "Although I may make some mistakes, I always will use my best judgment to protect the interests of my constituents."

b.   Doctor: "Doctors can ill afford to make errors when human lives are at stake, because they are the judges of life and death in our society."

c.   Teacher: "I am the highest authority in the classroom because I am the teacher, not because I always know the right answer."

d.   Lawyer: "I cannot assure my client of victory, because I cannot predict with certainty what it is that any court may do at any time."

Allow 40 minutes to answer the following essay question. Follow the directions in the memorandum, analyzing the facts presented and using your judgment skills. Do not rely on any other authority or on your knowledge of the law. Use only the material presented with the question. Your answer should be in the form of a memorandum to the attorney, which will include the following: Facts, Issue(s), Discussion, and Conclusion. The memorandum must be well organized and concise.

At the end of 40 minutes, check your essay answer against the sample found at the end of the Answer Key Section of this Review Manual. Allocate 20 points to style and 20 points to content. Allow 30 minutes to answer all objective questions and 40 minutes to answer the essay question (70 minutes total). At the end of the time period, check your answers to the questions against those in the Answer Key Section of this Manual. Deduct two points each for incorrect answer (60 total possible points for objective questions). Unanswered questions are counted as incorrect answers. Add this score to the score from the essay question to determine the overall score for this section. Follow directions carefully and observe the time limit precisely to provide an accurate self-assessment.

Memorandum

TO: Michael Parkins, Paralegal

FROM: Virginia Koerselman Newman, Staff Attorney

DATE:

RE: Landon Gray Employment Termination

Our client Landon Gray has been employed by the District Attorney's Office for the State of Anywhere for the last 22 years. He recently was fired for the unlawful sale of junk food at his workplace, and he visited with me this morning about his termination.

Landon is married and has three children, two of them in college. His wife is the nutritionist for Pinefield Public Schools. His youngest daughter, Chloe, is in middle school; Chloe sold nearly 400 boxes of Girl Scout cookies this year, some of them to people in Landon's office. To help his daughter, Landon delivered boxes of Girl Scout cookies to coworkers from the trunk of his car over the lunch hour. His car was parked in the employee parking lot.

When James Oliver, Chief Deputy District Attorney, heard about the delivery of contraband cookies, he called Landon to his office immediately. Following a heated discussion, James fired Landon and ordered him to leave that very day. Mary Littleton helped Landon put his personal belongings into a small file box, and he left.

Earlier this year and in response to a World Health Organization study showing that one in every five Utopian workers is obese, the federal congress passed a number of statutes designed to limit workers' access to junk food while at work. The rationale was that obese people are less productive at work, miss work more often, and place a greater burden on the health care system. The congress then declared the workplace a "Sugar-and-Fat-Free Zone" and encouraged employers to establish zero tolerance policies for noncompliance.

Landon Gray is a very physically fit man who works out three or four times a week. None of the coworkers involved in this incident is obese, although several may be close to it.

Attached are the statutes that I want you to consider in reviewing this matter. Using these statutes, prepare a memorandum to me that evaluates the probable result of a legal proceeding on behalf of Mr. Gray. The memorandum should include facts, issues, discussion, and conclusion sections.

Selected Statutes

---

§ 15-245. The government of the United Utopian States is granted the power to assemble a military to protect its borders and its citizens; to coin money; to operate a post office system; to protect interstate commerce; to ensure the right of citizens to pass freely from one state to another; and to enact legislation in furtherance of these enumerated powers. All other powers are reserved specifically to the states and to the people.

§ 24-109 Classification of Crimes. The range of punishment that may be set for particular classification of crimes is:

Class I felony	10–50 years	or	$20,000–$100,000 fine	or both;
Class II felony	5–20 years	or	$5,000–$50,000 fine	or both;
Class III felony	1–20 years	or	$1,000–$25,000 fine	or both;
Class IV felony	1–10 years	or	$100–$10,000 fine	or both;
Class I misdemeanor	6–12 months	or	$100–$5,000 fine	or both;
Class II misdemeanor	3–9 months	or	$50–$2,000 fine	or both;
Class III misdemeanor	60–180 days	or	$50–$1,500 fine	or both;
Class IV misdemeanor	30–90 days	or	$25–$1,000 fine	or both.

§ 52-115. A food product, food ingredient, or food additive exceeds statutory limitation (a) if its sugar content is greater than 10 grams or (b) if its fat content is greater than 3 grams. Any food item described herein or any food item generally known for its high sugar content or for its high fat content shall be known as junk food and thereby prohibited under the provisions of this Act.

§ 52-714. It shall be a Class IV felony to sell, purchase, exchange, ingest, or consume any high-sugar or high-fat food or food ingredient to, with, or by any employee within the jurisdictional boundaries of the United Utopian States or its territories. Such foods likewise are banned from cafeterias, lunch rooms, meeting rooms, kitchens, vending machines, or stores located in or within 150 feet of any building that contains businesses with employees.

§ 52-723. It shall be a Class III misdemeanor to accept, possess, procure, or solicit any high-sugar or high-fat food or food ingredient to, with, or by any employee within the jurisdictional boundaries of the United Utopian States or its territories.

§ 67-4224. No federal statute or regulation shall impinge unnecessarily or limit unreasonably the personal liberty or freedom of any citizen unless the government can show a compelling state interest that cannot be accomplished by any other means and the statute or regulation is narrowly tailored to satisfy the compelling state interest.

Chapter

5

LEGAL RESEARCH

Every accomplishment starts with the decision to try.
—Anonymous

The paralegal or legal assistant must be able to use the most important tool of the legal profession—the law library. The purpose of the Legal Research section of the CLA/CP® Certifying Examination is to test the applicant's knowledge of the state and federal codes, statutes, digests, case reports, various legal encyclopedias, Shepardizing, and research procedures.

The amount of study and practice that an applicant will need to pass this section of the examination will depend on his or her current knowledge and experience with legal research. One can gain excellent practice by researching various topics on one's own.

Reference to West Publishing Co. and to Lawyers Cooperative Publishing Co. in this text is intended to include the predecessor(s) as well as the successor(s) of each. Classification as a West resource or as a Lawyers Co-op resource remains relevant because of the types of research tools unique to each.

The Objective of Legal Research

The objective of legal research is to find specific authorities (legal rules) that govern a specific factual question. Like a seasoned traveler, the experienced researcher knows his or her ultimate destination and the quickest, simplest route to reach it. If a driver wanted to go to Timbuktu, Texas, she would not get into the car and simply start driving. Instead, she would use a map to plan the best route. That route likely would include some combination of federal or interstate expressways, state highways, and local streets or roads.

Similarly, to locate the specific legal authorities that govern a specific factual issue, one must plan ahead to determine

> •the type of system in which the factual issue arises (whether federal, state, or local);

> •the type of substantive law involved (whether constitutional, statutory [civil or criminal], administrative, or case law [judicial decisions]); and

> •the type of procedural law (which combination of statutes, rules of procedure [civil, criminal, or administrative], rules of evidence, and court rules) that must be followed to accomplish the desired result.

Until the researcher has determined which legal system and which type(s) of law may apply to a known set of facts, no legal research can be done.

The two major types of legal authorities are (1) those that are ***primary*** (mandatory) and (2) those that are ***secondary*** (persuasive).

Sources of Primary Law

Within the context of legal research, all legal authorities are categorized by system and type. Primary law includes—listed in the order of its general rank—constitutions, statutes, case law, rules of procedure, rules of evidence, administrative rules, court rules, executive orders, and so forth.

Primary law is ***mandatory***, which refers to amount of weight that it must be given in the decision-making process. Primary law carries the most weight; it must be followed within the legal system to which it applies. Whether federal, state, or local, each legal system has its own primary laws.

<u>Types of Legal Systems</u>   Ours is a nation of many legal systems. In addition to the federal system, there are 50 state systems and an indeterminate number of local systems. *(See the chapter on American legal systems for a more complete review of the summaries provided here.)*

Each system has its own areas of exclusive authority (jurisdiction) within its geographic boundary lines. For example, the federal government has exclusive authority to regulate interstate commerce; each state government has exclusive authority to regulate marriage and divorce, probate of estates, and intrastate commerce; and each local government has exclusive authority to regulate traffic laws within its boundaries.

In addition, areas of concurrent jurisdiction can and do exist. For example, both federal and state laws have been enacted to prohibit certain types of employment discrimination. Federal and state courts have equal authority to hear and to decide employment discrimination cases.

Each legal system (whether federal or state) is separated into a legislative, an executive, and a judicial branch (***separation of powers***). Within each system, the legislative branch authorizes certain administrative agencies to exist and delegates limited powers to them. For these specified, limited areas only, agencies can adopt rules and regulations (quasi-legislative power) and can render decisions (quasi-judicial power).

The primary laws of each legal system are categorized according to their type, often determined by the branch of government from which they are issued. Then they are recorded and published so that citizens have notice of what the rules are. Legal research is the process of finding these rules.

Sometimes the rules are published by the issuing legislature, court, or agency; these are official publications. In addition, private companies often publish their own collections of statutes and case law that include additional aids and features to assist the legal researcher. The primary legal publishers in the United States are West Publishing Company and Lawyers Cooperative Publishing Company (formerly Bancroft-Whitney Publishing Company). Wherever these publishers appear in this chapter, they are intended to include their successors.

Types of Law (Substantive)   Substantive law establishes and defines the basic rights and duties that govern a society. Within American legal systems, it consists of constitutions, legislative enactments, judicial opinions at the federal level, common law at the state level (which includes judicial opinions and stare decisis principles), and certain executive actions.

A.   Constitutional Law   A constitution exists for the federal system as well as for each state system. A constitution embodies the government's authority to exist and serves as an outline for the exercise of governmental powers. At the local level, this authorizing document is called a charter. Within any legal system, constitutional rules carry the most weight and always prevail when they conflict with other rules issued within that system.

B.   **Statutory Law**   A legislative enactment is called a *statute* at the federal and state levels; an *ordinance* at the local level. Statutes do not carry as much weight as a constitutional provision, but they carry more weight than an administrative rule or a prior judicial opinion. Administrative rules and regulations adopted in the proper exercise of an administrative agency's quasi-legislative power carry slightly less weight than a statute or an ordinance but are given more weight in its limited area of expertise than a prior judicial decision on the same subject.

C.   **Case Law or Common Law**   When identifying the categories of primary law, the terms *case law* and *common law* are used in their most narrow sense to mean judicial opinions (as opposed to statutory law or constitutional law). In addition to articulating common law principles at the state level, judicial opinions (both state and federal) are used to explain and to clarify existing constitutional and statutory law. This is called judicial interpretation. Case law carries less weight than statutory law as a general principle; however, a particular judicial opinion can overrule a specific statute on constitutional grounds.

Case law (judicial opinions) at the state level articulates common law principles as they evolve. In this sense, the term *common law* has a much more expansive meaning based upon the way in which case law is used under the doctrine of *stare decisis*. **Stare decisis** is the process used to synthesize legal principles from all prior cases with similar facts and similar issues of law (called precedent) to arrive at a decision in a specific case. When a court has formulated a principle of law in a case, it then follows that principle by applying it to future cases where the facts and the legal issues are substantially the same. Common law exists only at the state level; however, both state and federal courts use concepts of precedent.

A prior case is **precedent** within a particular jurisdiction if (1) its facts and legal issues were substantially similar to the facts of the case before the court, sometimes called the *instant case*; (2) it was decided by majority decision of a higher court of that jurisdiction; and (3) the case was reported (published). Thus, a case published by a particular federal court of appeals is precedent for all federal trial courts of that circuit. It is not precedent, however, for other federal courts of appeals. A case published by the United States Supreme Court is precedent for all state and federal courts. Although *stare decisis* and *precedent* often are used as if they were synonymous, they have different meanings. There is no federal common law.

In exercising its quasi-judicial powers to decide whether its rules and regulations have been violated and the sanctions to be imposed for the violation, an administrative agency may decide administrative cases and publish administrative decisions affecting the party (or parties) brought before it. These decisions are precedent within that particular agency but have no precedential value outside the agency.

D.   Executive Action   Some types of executive action taken by the President (or by the governor of a state) have the force of law. Typical among these are the following:

> 1.   An *executive order* issued by the President under special authority granted by Congress. An executive order might direct the Justice Department to place emphasis on the enforcement of specific civil rights laws. An executive order is different from a Presidential Proclamation, which might be issued by the President to declare "National Paralegals Day" on November 14 of a given year;

> 2.   A *treaty* (agreement made between the United States and one or more of the other sovereign nations of the world); and

> 3.   An *interstate compact* (agreement made by two or more states) concerning such things as disposal of radioactive waste or use of a common waterway.

Types of Law (Procedural)   Procedural law, sometimes called *adjective law*, prescribes the manner in which substantive laws must be enforced. The gist of most procedural rules is to assure parties of a fair and uniform adversary process, culminating in a fair hearing. Procedural rules can vary widely from jurisdiction to jurisdiction and can vary from court to court within a particular jurisdiction.

A.   Federal Procedural Law   Several distinct sets of procedural rules operate within trial courts of the federal jurisdiction. They are as follows:

> 1.   The **Federal Rules of Criminal Procedure** govern the way in which a defendant is charged, tried, and sentenced for a federal crime.

> 2.   The **Federal Rules of Civil Procedure** govern how civil actions are handled, including rules that cover the complaint, summons, answer, discovery process, trial, and post-trial procedures.

> 3.   The **Federal Rules of Appellate Procedure** govern the form and procedure for appeals from the

U.S. District Court to the Court of Appeals within the federal system.

4.   The **Federal Rules of Evidence** govern the types of evidence that are admissible in criminal and civil trials and, in some situations, the manner in which the evidence can be presented during trial.

5.   **Local Court Rules** In addition to the sets of procedural rules listed above, which govern all federal trial courts, each court typically adopts its own rules to govern things not covered by other procedural rules, such as management of the trial docket, how hearings are scheduled, and so forth. For example, the Federal Rules of Civil Procedure state that the first pleading to be filed in a case shall be called a complaint. Local court rules cannot change that rule by requiring the first pleading to be called a petition or an application, but a local court rule can require that all complaints be filed electronically.

B.   **State Procedural Rules**   Many states have adopted procedural rules similar to those used at the federal level. They may be included as part of a state's statutory code or may be included as part of the court rules of a state's supreme court. Local court rules of state courts perform the same function as local court rules of federal courts. They augment—fill the gaps that may have been left by—a state statute or other procedural rule, but they cannot change the statutes or procedural rules adopted by the state.

How Primary Law Is Recorded

At both the federal and state levels, primary law is recorded predominantly in constitutions, statutes, administrative rules and regulations, and court cases. The researcher must be familiar with how the recording process works as well as with the forms that primary law takes as it evolves within that process.

Constitutions   Because the U.S. Constitution is the organizing document of the federal legal system, it does not undergo frequent change. It can be found at the front of the United States Code. An index of its articles and amendments has been included with the index to the United States Code.

Similarly, the constitution of each state generally is included with that state's statutory code and statutory index; a local government's charter may or may not be included with its ordinances.

Statutes   When a statute is adopted by a legislature, it is recorded in different forms at different stages of the legislative process. These differences are important when conducting a legislative history.

A *bill* is a proposed legislative measure. Until it is enacted by the legislature, it is not law. Once the bill is enacted, it becomes a *slip law*, meaning that it is printed singly rather than as a part of a group of laws.

At the close of each legislative session, all slip laws enacted during that session are arranged in chronological order according to date of enactment and are published as *session laws*. Because they are arranged chronologically, session laws can be difficult to use unless the researcher knows the exact date when the statute was enacted together with the dates of any later modifications that may have been adopted. As a result, statutes generally are *codified* (collected into a statutory code) as well. The code arranges the statutes and their amendments by topic (subject matter). This arrangement makes statutes much easier to find.

A.   Federal   Federal session laws are published in the **Statutes at Large (Stat.)**. They also are codified and published in the **United States Code (U.S.C.)**. Because the codification of federal statutes is selective (not every statute is included), the Statutes at Large is the only complete collection of federal statutory law.

When an official body (Congress in this case) authorizes and directs the collection and publication of law, it is an *official* publication. An *unofficial* publication is one that is not specifically authorized or sanctioned by an official body but, rather, is compiled by a private publisher. Its status as an unofficial publication relates only to the source of the publication and not to its accuracy. Both the Stat. and the U.S.C. are official publications.

In addition to the official publications for federal statutes, West Publishing Company (West) and Lawyers Cooperative Publishing Company (Lawyers Co-op) offer unofficial publications as well:

United States Code Annotated (U.S.C.A.) published by West; and
United States Code Service (U.S.C.S.) published by Lawyers Co-op.

The advantage of these unofficial publications is that each offers additional resources for the researcher in the form of explanatory notes, cases, and other helpful information relating to each code section.

U.S.C.A., like all West publications, uses the ***key number system*** to aid the researcher. Every topic and subtopic is assigned its own key number (a number displayed on the head of the familiar West key). The same key numbers are reserved to the same topics throughout all West publications, so that the researcher does not have to search for the topic alphabetically more than once. From that point forward, the researcher can use the key number so long as he or she is using a West publication.

U.S.C.S. contains the same distinguishing feature for which all Lawyers Co-op publications are known: extensive use of annotations. An ***annotation*** is an explanatory note. It may contain references to cases, but case references usually are more limited than in the West publications; the emphasis of the annotation is the explanatory material.

B.   State and Local   State legislatures typically publish their session laws at the close of each legislative session. In addition, most states publish either a codified version or rely upon a private company to publish the codified version. Some states have both, such as New Jersey Revised Statutes (official) and New Jersey Statutes Annotated (unofficial, published by West).

Local legislatures publish their ordinances, but the form of publication is much less consistent than it is for state statutes. Ordinances of larger cities sometimes are codified in a municipal code, but the practice varies from city to city.

Administrative Rules and Regulations   Within the federal system, the rules and regulations of administrative agencies are published chronologically in the **Federal Register (Fed. Reg.)** at the time of their adoption. In addition, they are codified (arranged by subject matter) in the **Code of Federal Regulations (C.F.R.)**. A complete set of rules and regulations for a particular agency generally can be obtained from the agency as well.

The rules and regulations of state administrative agencies often are codified; however, the rules and regulations of local administrative agencies seldom are codified.

Case Law   From the standpoint of volume alone, case law (sometimes called law reports, common law, court opinions, or court decisions) represents the bulk of recorded primary law. It consists of the opinions of reported cases, usually from appellate courts, of a particular jurisdiction. A reported case is one which is published. Reported cases are collected and published in case reporters, which may be either official or unofficial. Some jurisdictions have both.

Before reviewing specific case reporters, a brief summary of case law terminology is provided, followed by a table showing the elements typically found in a reported case. Even experienced researchers sometimes use the terms *court decision* and *court opinion* as if they were synonymous; they are not:

court decision	the court's ruling or disposition of the case (whether affirmed, reversed, remanded, or dismissed).
court opinion	the court's explanatory comments, which include the holding, the rationale for the holding, and dicta.

A court's opinion may be one or more of the following types:

majority opinion	opinion issued by the majority of judges of the appellate court; the holding of this opinion may be cited as precedent if all other criteria are met (discussed supra). There is only one majority opinion in a case.
concurring opinion	opinion issued by one or more judges of the appellate court that agrees with the result reached by the majority but disagrees with the reasoning of the majority opinion. There can be more than one concurring opinion.
dissenting opinion	opinion issued by one or more judges of the appellate court that disagrees with both the result and the reasoning of the majority opinion. There can be more than one dissenting opinion.
per curiam opinion	opinion of the entire court (all judges who heard the case), as opposed to an opinion written by a specific judge.
en banc	the entire court participates rather than the permissible quorum. This does not mean that the entire court agrees on the outcome, however.
memorandum opinion	a very brief opinion; a cursory opinion; an opinion so abbreviated that it is hardly an opinion at all.

A single opinion may be a memorandum, *per curiam* opinion, reached by a court sitting *en banc*. This describes a very brief opinion written unanimously by the entire appellate court.

The review process used by an appellate court is determined by the form of appeal authorized for a particular type of case. The form of appeal changes according to the amount of deference the appellate court gives to the factual findings determined in the trial court:

de novo	anew, from the beginning; the case is tried in the appellate court as if it had not been tried previously, and witnesses are allowed to testify. The initial appeal from a small claims court to a district court or to a superior court, for instance, might be tried de novo.
de novo on the record	anew on the record; the appellate court must base its decision on the record (no new testimony can be received) but may reach an independent factual finding if the facts from the trial court are "clearly erroneous" based on the record as a whole. Appellate courts never defer to trial courts concerning issues of law.
on the record	the appellate court reviews the record for prejudicial legal errors committed in the trial court but gives great deference to the findings of fact; factual findings generally are reversed only when they are "arbitrary or capricious" (little or no factual basis). Appellate courts never defer to trial courts concerning issues of law. Appeals from administrative decisions are typical among those appealed on the record.

The *record* consists of the pleadings from the court file of the trial court (together with any motions or orders that may be part of the errors claimed on appeal) and the recorded transcript of the trial proceedings, including the exhibits offered during trial.

Elements of a Reported Case

CAPTION	Identifies the court issuing the opinion, the parties, and the docket number assigned to the case.
DATE OF DECISION	The date on which the decision was rendered.
PARALLEL CITATION(S)	If the same case is published in another case reporter, the volume and page number of that reporter is shown.
HEADNOTE OR SYLLABUS	Brief summary of a legal rule discussed in the opinion; headnotes are numbered. Key numbers are used in West publications.
STATEMENT OF FACTS	Brief summary of facts of case, including its procedural posture.
OPINION	Court's explanation; includes the holding, rationale, and dicta.
HOLDING	Rule of law for which the case is cited as precedent; it is the legal effect of the facts of the case.

RATIONALE	*Ratio decidendi*—court's reasoning or basis for its holding and decision.
DICTA	*Obiter dictum*—comments of the court about minor issues or concerns other than the specific holding, rationale, and decision. Dicta is never cited as precedent.
DECISION	Result or disposition of the case.

Federal Case Reporters   Within the federal system, cases are reported from the U.S. Supreme Court, the U.S. Courts of Appeals, and the U.S. District Courts.

When a federal court first decides a case, a ***slip opinion*** is issued. This is a single opinion of the court issued without headnotes and without indexing. Periodically, the slip opinions are collected and published in a softbound or loose-leaf format called ***advance sheets*** (in advance of the next bound volume of the case reporter series). The page numbering used in advance sheets generally is the same as the page numbering that will appear in the case reporter volume when it is published in bound form.

In addition to the texts of reported cases, each case reporter volume usually includes a table of the cases contained in the volume, a table of statutes interpreted by the cases contained in that volume, a subject index or digest of the reported cases, and judicial definition of words and phrases used in the reported cases. Within a particular case reporter series, separate volumes may be devoted to the tables of cases, descriptive word index, or words and phrases contained in the entire reporter series or set.

Case reporters may cover a specific jurisdiction (United States Supreme Court), a specific geographical area (Arizona), or a specific subject (Bankruptcy Reporter). Cases within a particular reporter are arranged chronologically by the date of decision.

A.   United States Supreme Court   While the Court is in session, slip opinions are issued as cases are decided. These are collected periodically and published in two different sets of advance sheets: United States Law Week (U.S.L.W.) published by the Bureau of National Affairs and the United States Supreme Court Bulletin published by Commerce Clearing House. There are three case reporters for U.S. Supreme Court cases:

1.   United States Reports, *cited* U.S.
2.   Supreme Court Reporter, *cited* S. Ct.
3.   United States Supreme Court Reports, Lawyers' Edition, *cited* L. Ed. or L. Ed. 2d

United States Reports is the official case reporter for the U.S. Supreme Court. The first 90 volumes of United States Reports originally were compiled by seven successive, private reporters (Dallas, Cranch, Wheaton, Peters, Howard, Black, and Wallace), which were cited, for example, 1 Dall. 233. The Court began using official reporters and its current numbering system in 1817. The original 90 volumes were reprinted later; but because the pagination was different in the reprinted versions, ***star paging*** was used to show where each new page number began in the original volume. Star paging is a star, asterisk, or insertion in the text of the opinion, followed by the page number.

Supreme Court Reporter is an unofficial case reporter published by West. It does not contain decisions prior to 1882 but does contain star paging to the official reporter, U.S. Reports. This allows a researcher to cite to the precise page of U.S. Reports even if he does not have access to U.S. Reports. Because it is a West publication, the Supreme Court Reporter incorporates the key numbering system.

Supreme Court Reporter Lawyers Edition, another unofficial case reporter, is published by Lawyers Co-op. It likewise contains star paging to U.S. Reports. In addition, it includes a summary of each case (located before the headnotes). It is the only Supreme Court case reporter to include summaries of the briefs of counsel. Annotations, the distinctive feature of all Lawyers Co-op publications, are included for all cases beginning with volume 92 of the Lawyers Edition and for all cases in the Lawyers Edition Second Series.

B.   United States Courts of Appeals   The only case reporter for the federal courts of appeals (formerly circuit courts of appeals) is unofficial and is published by West. There is no official case reporter for these courts.

Federal Reporter, Third Series, *cited* F.3d	(1993–present)
Federal Reporter, Second Series, *cited* F.2d	(1924–1993)
Federal Reporter, *cited* F.	(1880–1924)
Federal Cases, *cited* F. Cas.	(1789–1880)

C.   United States District Courts   Like the federal courts of appeals, the only case reporter for the federal district courts is unofficial and is published by West. There is no official case reporter. Reporting for federal trial courts is selective; not all cases are included.

Federal Supplement, *cited* F. Supp.	(1932–present)
Federal Reporter, Second Series, *cited* F.2d	(1924–1932)

Federal Reporter, *cited* F.   (1880–1924)
Federal Cases, *cited* F. Cas.   (1789–1880)

Cases decided by the U.S. Court of International Trade (formerly U.S. Customs Court) are also reported selectively in the Federal Supplement.

D.   Federal Specialty Courts and Case Law   Areas of specialized federal law may be collected and reported in separate case reporters. For instance, cases related to federal rules of civil and criminal procedure are collected in the case reporter series called **Federal Rules Decisions,** *cited* F.R.D. Decisions of federal bankruptcy courts from 1979 forward are reported in the **Bankruptcy Reporter,** *cited* B.R.

Some federal specialty courts, such as the Tax Court, the Claims Court (formerly Court of Claims), and the Court of Military Appeals, publish their own opinions. The Court of International Trade was created in 1980 (formerly U.S. Customs Court) and has published its own decisions since that time; its decisions continue to be published selectively in the Federal Supplement.

A complete list of federal specialty courts and their case reporters can be found in the ***Uniform System of Citation*** (USOC), which is published by the Harvard Law Review Association, Gannett House, 1511 Massachusetts Avenue, Cambridge, MA 02138.

State Case Reporters   At the state level, cases are reported for a state's highest appellate court and intermediate appellate courts only. The exceptions are New York and California, which report lower court cases as well.

Like federal case reporters, state case reporters are preceded by slip opinions and then advance sheets. The page numbers of the advance sheets correspond to the page numbers that will appear in the bound volume of the case reporter.

A particular state may or may not publish an official case reporter; many states have abandoned the publication of an official reporter in favor of the unofficial reporter available through the National Reporter System.

The ***National Reporter System*** is the product of West Publishing Company. In addition to its federal case reporters *(see above)*, it divides the United States into seven geographical regions and reports the decisions of the highest appellate court of each state within that region. Some intermediate appellate court decisions are also reported. Because of the regional divisions, case reporters sometimes are referred to as ***regional reporters***.

Atlantic Reporter, *cited* A. or A.2d	Connecticut, Delaware, District of Columbia (Court of Appeals), Maine, Maryland, New Hampshire, New Jersey, Pennsylvania, Rhode Island, and Vermont
North Eastern Reporter, *cited* N.E. or N.E.2d	Illinois, Indiana, Massachusetts, New York, and Ohio
North Western Reporter, *cited* N.W. or N.W.2d	Iowa, Michigan, Minnesota, Nebraska, North Dakota, South Dakota, and Wisconsin
Pacific Reporter, *cited* P. or P.2d	Alaska, Arizona, California, Colorado, Hawaii, Idaho, Kansas, Montana, Nevada, New Mexico, Oklahoma, Oregon, Utah, Washington, and Wyoming
South Eastern Reporter, *cited* S.E. or S.E.2d	Georgia, North Carolina, South Carolina, Virginia, and West Virginia
South Western Reporter, *cited* S.W. or S.W.2d	Arkansas, Kentucky, Missouri, Tennessee, Texas, and Indian Territories
Southern Reporter, *cited* So. or So.2d	Alabama, Florida, Louisiana, and Mississippi

Sources of Secondary Law

Secondary law consists of legal authorities that are persuasive but are not mandatory (binding) within a particular jurisdiction. Secondary law carries less weight than primary law but may be used effectively, depending upon its source, when primary law is not available or when a change in existing primary law is sought.

Law from Other Jurisdictions   When an issue has not been decided previously within a particular jurisdiction (a case of first impression), case law from other jurisdictions may persuade or influence the court in reaching its decision. When one of the litigants seeks a change in existing law, case law from other jurisdictions may persuade a court to make the requested change.

Generally speaking, case law from neighboring jurisdictions is more persuasive to a court than is case law from distant jurisdictions.

Legal Encyclopedias   Legal encyclopedias are arranged alphabetically by subject matter and contain narrative, expository information on a variety of legal topics. They provide extensive background material in areas unfamiliar to the researcher, with footnotes to cases and other legal authorities on point. Like general encyclopedias, legal encyclopedias consist of a series of volumes. Legal encyclopedias are published both by West and by Lawyers Co-op.

West publishes **Corpus Juris Secundum**, *cited* C.J.S., which is tied to the key number system and is very heavily footnoted with legal authorities. It is so heavily footnoted, in fact, that it is common to find only one line of narrative text on a page and the rest of the page filled with footnotes. This, together with its use of key numbers, attracts many researchers to it.

Lawyers Co-op publishes **American Jurisprudence, Second Series**, *cited* Am. Jur. 2d, which contains more narrative and not as many footnotes. Many researchers prefer it when they want simply to obtain background information, because its uninterrupted text is easier to read. It also cites directly to Annotated Law Reports, another Lawyers Co-op research tool favored by many researchers.

Both sets of legal encyclopedias are kept current with periodic pocket parts inserted at the back of each volume of these multiple-volume collections.

American Law Reports   American Law Reports is the leading annotated law reporter. This secondary legal authority is published by Lawyers Co-op. It does not attempt to report every case or even to report most cases. Rather, it selects and publishes only those state appellate court cases which are significant. A case is significant to Lawyers Co-op editors if it indicates a change in the law or a new trend in legal thinking.

The distinguishing feature of this reporter is not the cases that it reports but, rather, the extensive editorial commentary (annotations) that follows each reported case. The annotations examine all sides of the issue; present general legal principles gleaned from the reported case and from other cases on the subject; and provide exceptions, distinctions, and qualifications of those legal principles. Cross-references to other, related annotations are also provided. To find annotations on a particular topic, one uses the *A.L.R. Quick*

Index volumes that cover A.L.R.3d and A.L.R.4th. The A.L.R. series come in five parts:

> A.L.R. (sometimes called A.L.R. First), supplemented by the *A.L.R. Blue Book of Supplemental Decisions*, which is kept current with a semi-annual supplement pamphlet;

> A.L.R.2d, supplemented by the *A.L.R.2d Later Case Service*, which is kept current with a semi-annual supplement pamphlet;

> A.L.R.3d–A.L.R.5th, supplemented by individual, cumulative pocket parts found at the back of each volume in the series;

> A.L.R. Fed., which reports only federal cases and is supplemented by an individual, cumulative pocket found at the back of each volume.

Whether an A.L.R. series annotation has been superseded (replaced by another annotation) can be determined by checking the Historical Table at the back of the *A.L.R. Quick Index*.

Restatements of Law   Restatements of law have been published by the American Law Institute (A.L.I.) since 1923 on major legal topics (agency, conflict of laws, contracts, foreign relations, judgments, property, restitution, security, torts, and trusts). Restatements are persuasive legal authorities because they are compiled by committees of prominent legal scholars, all experts in the topic area of the restatement.

A restatement collects and distills the primary, general rules in a given legal topic area—what the rules are and sometimes what the committee believes they ought to be. It also provides explanations of the rules and gives examples of how they apply, using brief, hypothetical cases. Because legal rules are continually changing, however, a number of the restatements have been rewritten as a Restatement Second.

Each restatement has its own index. The second editions also contain cross-references to the key number digest system (West) and to the A.L.R. series (Lawyers Co-op).

Dictionaries   Dictionaries, both legal and nonlegal, provide definitions of words and often provide illustrations of how they are used. Legal dictionaries frequently provide the case citation upon which the definition is based. Black's Law Dictionary and Ballentine's Law Dictionary are two of the law dictionaries available.

A nonlegal dictionary, such as *Webster's Collegiate Dictionary*, may be helpful when, for example, a contract term or some other word is the subject of dispute. Absent some specific, technical meaning for the word, it generally will be given its "ordinary meaning."

Treatises　　　Sometimes called a hornbook, a treatise is a single-volume text written by a legal scholar in a given topic area. A treatise usually provides more explanation than a legal encyclopedia but may be less critical than law review articles and other periodicals. *Prosser on Torts* and *Corbin on Contracts* are examples of treatises.

Periodicals　　　Periodicals, both legal and nonlegal, may provide persuasive authority in a given case and should not be overlooked as a research source. Law review articles, in particular, are very detailed and generally provide a critical analysis of the principles involved. The *Index to Legal Periodicals* can be used to access law review articles and other law publications in a specific topic area.

The Technical Skills of Legal Research

Legal research requires two different types of skills: technical and substantive. The researcher must be able to use research tools to find the most current legal authorities on a given point and must be able to cite the authorities correctly; these are technical skills. In addition, the researcher must be able to prepare case briefs and legal memoranda that summarize the legal authorities once they are found; these are substantive skills. This section covers technical skills, which include finding, updating, and citing legal authorities.

Finding the Law　　　After the relevant facts of a client's case are segregated and the legal issues are defined—at least tentatively—the researcher must find legal authorities that relate to the facts and issues (authorities on point). Finding the law means finding all applicable statutes and lines of cases, both favorable and unfavorable, together with any secondary authorities that apply. One cannot wear blinders by collecting only those authorities that seem favorable to a client's position. The attorney must be provided with a complete and accurate picture to evaluate the case properly.

The most difficult part of legal research for the inexperienced researcher is getting started or, more precisely, knowing where to start. There are several effective ways to begin.

A.   Topic Method   When the researcher knows the topic area, this can provide the basis to locate primary and secondary authorities.

Case law, which represents the bulk of recorded law, can be located topically by using a digest. A ***digest*** is a finding tool, usually compiled by the publisher of the case reporter to which it relates. It reprints the headnote summaries of points of law found in reported cases and classifies them by subject, using pre-defined categories established by the publisher. A list of the categories that the publisher uses is located at the beginning of each digest volume.

There is a separate, multi-volume digest to accompany virtually every set of case reporters in existence, with a few notable exceptions. West uses a combined digest to access all federal courts, which is now in its fourth edition series (West's Federal Practice Digest 4th). There are two separate digests that access U.S. Supreme Court cases only: United States Supreme Court Digest (West) and United States Supreme Court Digest, Lawyers' Edition (Lawyers Co-op).

For state courts, West publishes separate digests for nearly every state plus the District of Columbia, as well as digests tied to five of its seven regional case reporters.

In addition, West publishes the American Digest System, a continuing digest series that collects headnote summaries from all federal and state courts (combined) during consecutive 10-year periods. The digest for each 10-year period is called a Decennial (sometimes, a Decennial Digest) except the digest for the current period, which is called the General Digest. At the end of each 10-year period, the General Digest accumulated to that point is published as a Decennial; and the General Digest continues for cases in the then current period.

Century Digest	1658–1896
First Decennial	1897–1906
Second Decennial	1906–1916
Third Decennial	1916–1926
Fourth Decennial	1926–1936
Fifth Decennial	1936–1946
Sixth Decennial	1946–1956

Seventh Decennial	1956–1966
Eighth Decennial	1966–1976
Ninth Decennial	1976–1986
Tenth Decennial Digest	1986–1996
Eleventh Decennial	1996–2004
General Digest	2004–

All headnotes from reported state and federal cases are catalogued in the American Digest System, using West's key number system. This digest series is helpful when the researcher does not want to focus narrowly on one jurisdiction for applicable case law or when the researcher wants to compare the case law of various states as well as federal case law, on a particular topic.

When a case has several different headnotes, each headnote is catalogued. This results in the case's appearance in several different places within the digest. Headnotes in the American Digest System are catalogued under topics and subtopics assigned to key numbers, using the TARP method:

T   *Thing* or subject matter involved in the case, such as theater or bicycle;

A   *Action* (cause of action) or ground for defense to an action, such as negligence or mandamus;

R   *Relief* sought, such as restitution or damages; or

P   *Parties*, meaning the legal relationship of parties, such as invitee or guardian.

In addition to headnote summaries, digests typically contain a *table of cases* listed by both plaintiff and defendant name and a *descriptive word index* to help the researcher find the correct topic area. Some digests contain a section called "Words and Phrases," which refers the researcher to those cases in the digest that interpret specific words and terms. In addition, West publishes a separate set of reference books called *Words and Phrases*, which is a finding tool devoted exclusively to the headnotes of court cases interpreting specific words and terms.

As helpful as digests are, one cannot rely upon their headnote summaries to state the exact principles contained in the case. They are guides only. Headnote summaries may miss a nuance or an element with significant impact on the facts being researched. A digest is a finding tool only. *Never cite a digest as legal authority for any purpose.*

Statutory law and constitutional law can be located by using the ***general index*** included in one or more volumes accompanying each statutory code, whether federal or state. For instance, there is a general index for U.S.C., for U.S.C.A., and for U.S.C.S. Statutory indexes are arranged alphabetically by topic or subject matter. Indexes, like digests, are finding tools; they are not legal authority for any purpose.

Similar to U.S.C.A. or U.S.C.S., many state statutory codes are annotated, which means that they contain notes and references to cases that have interpreted a particular statutory provision. Fortunately for all of us, A.L.R. materials also are available online as e-annotations.

B.   Case Method   There are occasions when the researcher has a case name or a complete case citation from which to begin the search for other authorities. When that occurs, the case method may be more efficient than the topical method.

With only the case name, a researcher can locate the entire citation. Each Decennial of the American Digest System contains an alphabetical table of cases by plaintiff. Each case listed gives the full citation, together with the topics and key numbers under which the case has been digested.

When only the popular name of the case is known, such as the "Dred Scott case," the best sources for finding the full citation are as follows:

- *Shepard's Acts and Cases by Popular Name: Federal and State*

- The Sixth Decennial of the American Digest System contains a cumulative *List of Popular Name Titles*. This feature was discontinued in the Seventh Decennial.

- Most special digests contain a *Table of Cases by Popular Name*.

Once the researcher has the full citation for the case, he may use the appropriate set of *Shepard's Citations* to locate other cases and authorities that have mentioned the cited case, which indicates that the other cases and authorities pertain to the same topic area.

Shepard's Citations   The most comprehensive collection of legal citators is *Shepard's Citations*, originally published by Shepard's/McGraw-Hill. These citators are available in printed volumes and digitally through Westlaw and Lexis *(discussed below)*. They list every published case in every state and federal case reporter, citation by citation, and show every subsequent case that has cited the case in question, as well as the treatment of the cited case by the subsequent case (whether affirmed, reversed, overruled, or modified in some other way). *Shepard's* also shows parallel citations for the cited case, if any, and its prior history, if any.

In addition to later case and treatment citations, *Shepard's* lists A.L.R. annotations, attorney general opinions, restatements, and other authorities where the case is mentioned. These special features of *Shepard's Citations* make it useful for finding case law, as well as for updating the status of a particular case.

A separate set of *Shepard's Citations* is available for U.S. Supreme Court reporters, for federal court reporters, and for state and regional reporters. In addition, *Shepard's Citations* is available for federal and state constitutions and statutes, as well as for some court rules. *Shepard's* also publishes specialized citators, including *Shepard's Federal Law Citations in Selected Law Reviews* and *Shepard's Acts and Cases by Popular Name: Federal and State*.

Each set of *Shepard's Citations* includes one or two bound volumes. These are updated annually with a bright yellow paperback volume and approximately monthly with smaller, red paperback advance sheets. As a matter of practice, the researcher checks the red advance sheets first, since they are the most recent; then the yellow paperback; and finally, the bound volume(s).

Using a *Shepard's* citator is somewhat confusing for everyone at first; however, introductory pages in each citator volume explain its scope, format, and abbreviations. *Shepard's* publishes a teaching booklet entitled *How to Use Shepard's Citations*, which is available in most law libraries or directly from Shepard's/McGraw-Hill at a nominal cost. The best and quickest way to learn how to use *Shepard's Citations* is to have a knowledgeable researcher demonstrate its features, followed by practice and more practice.

<u>Loose-leaf Services</u>   A loose-leaf service consists of one or more loose-leaf binders devoted to a specific topic of law. Pages can be removed and added with relative ease. As a result, changes in the law can be incorporated more quickly than in many other topical sources. Loose-leaf services provide an excellent means to stay abreast of the newest developments in a specialty field.

Loose-leaf services compile all relevant primary authority, regardless of its original source. When the researcher knows the general topic area, a loose-leaf service can save substantial time in locating relevant federal and state statutes, federal and state cases, and federal and state administrative rules and decisions about the topic. Each loose-leaf service contains its own topical index.

There is not a loose-leaf service for every topic of law; rather, loose-leaf services cover only selected topics. Examples of loose-leaf services include *The United States Law Week, Criminal Law Reporter, Family Law Reporter,* and *Securities Regulation & Law Report.* Each of the named services is published by the Bureau of National Affairs (BNA). Another well-known loose-leaf service publisher is Commerce Clearing House (CCH), whose publications include the *Congressional Index, Federal Securities Law Reporter, Standard Federal Tax Reports,* and *Trade Regulation Reporter.*

Computerized Search Tools   Online databases are available to locate statutes and cases, as well as to locate any modifications that may have been made to those statutes and cases. The two predominant legal databases are:

Westlaw, provided by West Publishing Company; and
Lexis, provided by Mead Data Corporation.

A.   Benefits   Although Westlaw and Lexis use different terminology, each database provides relatively quick access to federal and state cases and statutes on a specific topic by using appropriate search words, called search parameters. Access can be achieved by using a case citation as well. The database allows the researcher to view the first page of a case (where headnotes are located) to see if the case applies to the assigned topic area, to view the entire text of a case, or simply to list citations for cases that may be related to the topic.

The digital database can limit the search in almost any way that a researcher needs or wants. For instance, the search can be limited to court opinions written by a specific judge or to court opinions issued during a specific year, either of which would take substantial time to compile manually.

Both Westlaw and Lexis provide online access to *Shepard's Citations* (*discussed above*), which allows the researcher to check for later treatment of cases and statutes without leaving the database. Both systems provide services to verify the accuracy of citations: *InstaCite* for Westlaw and *AutoCite* for Lexis.

Each system also provides software that performs various cite-checking functions on all of the citations located in a brief or other document drafted by the law office: *WestCheck* for Westlaw and *CheckCite* for Lexis. The software checks the form of all citations that it finds in the document, accesses the appropriate system, obtains the needed services, and either downloads or prints a report for the researcher to review.

B.   Drawbacks   The availability of digital databases to aid the legal researcher is not a panacea. Cost is the most significant drawback of computerized systems. Westlaw and Lexis users pay a monthly service charge, plus an additional fee for each minute of online use. Therefore, it makes little economic sense to view an entire case online when a bound set of case reporters is available. Although rates are not as expensive as they once were, they remain prohibitive for many small law firms and for most solo practitioners.

Another drawback is that the researcher who does not use the database frequently may have difficulty in narrowing the search enough to make it effective. For example, even if the researcher wants only a list of cases on a topic—intending to read the cases in the bound case reporters—the search parameter cannot be a term as general as "court." It would take literally reams of paper to print all of the citations to cases in which that word is used. The researcher who uses a digital database, then, must think ahead to determine sufficiently narrow search parameters, along with alternative parameters in case the first ones do not produce the desired results. If the researcher does not use the precise combination of words that are used in a particular court case, for instance, the system may not retrieve that case. If the case is an important one, the results can be devastating to the overall research project.

In addition, researchers (particularly those who had free access to a computerized system during law school) may come to rely too heavily on the system. As is true of digests, the database does not recognize nuances critical to a legal issue. A computer database cannot determine which cases are most important; neither can it distinguish between the holding and dicta.

As helpful as computer databases are, they should be used with these cautions in mind:

> •*Digital databases should not be used by researchers until they are thoroughly familiar with and experienced in manual research methods. It's confusing, expensive, and risky.*

> •*Databases are designed to be used as case-finding tools, not as reporters. They should be used only to locate, skim, and obtain citations and should represent only a part of the overall research plan.*

> •*No citation obtained from the database ever should be used without reading the case thoroughly to ensure that it applies to the facts at hand. In the usual situation, cost constraints require that it be read from a bound case reporter.*

Computerized search tools can save substantial time for the researcher when they are used in their intended manner.

Updating the Law   Once relevant statutes and cases are found in the legal research process, the researcher must assure herself that the statute or case is still good law.

For statutes, updating means determining whether it has been (1) stricken as unconstitutional; (2) repealed; or (3) modified by amendment. All statutory codes are updated by ***statutory supplements***. Some are published as separate, softbound volumes; others, as individual pocket parts for each volume in the code. If the statutory provision or section appears in the supplement, cite the supplement as the most recent version of the statute. If the section does not appear in the supplement, cite the bound volume. When a statute is stricken as unconstitutional by court decision, that fact may not appear in the statutory code. Use *Shepard's Citations for Statutes* to determine whether a statute was reviewed by a court and the result.

For cases, updating means determining whether the case has been (1) reversed or modified on appeal or (2) overruled by a subsequent and different case. If the case has been reversed or overruled, it is not good law and cannot be cited at all. If the case has been diminished by a later modification, it may not be advisable to cite the case. The method used to determine whether a case still is good law is to check the citation in the appropriate set of *Shepard's Citations* (*discussed above*). This process is known as *Shepardizing*.

The procedure to locate statutes and constitutions is different from the procedure to locate cases. A summary of those procedures follows.

Statutes & Constitutions	Cases
• Use index to find statute section • Read the statutory section • Check supplements for status	• Use digest to find case references • Read the case in the reporter • Shepardize to determine status

Citing the Law

A ***citation*** is a reference to a legal authority, such as a constitution, statute, case, administrative rule, or other authority. Citations are included in briefs and legal memoranda to show the reader (often a judge or a supervising attorney) where the statute, case, or other authority can be found. In that sense, citations serve as road maps to a destination—the cited legal authority. Nothing can be worse than giving the wrong directions to reach the legal authority (wrong volume number, wrong page number of the reporter, or wrong statute section).

Precision in citation form is critical for a well-drafted presentation of legal principles or arguments. If the form of a citation is not correct, it sends a nonverbal message that the drafter is not careful. Taking that message to its logical conclusion, if the drafter is not careful about citation form, he probably is not careful about the substance of his research either. Proper citation form does not validate the substance of the research, of course; but it goes far in establishing preliminary credibility for the researcher.

The universally accepted authority on legal citations is *A Uniform System of Citation* (USOC, also known as the Blue Book), which is published jointly by the law reviews of Columbia, Harvard, the University of Pennsylvania, and Yale Law Schools. The Blue Book provides many, many technical rules about citation form as they apply in legal memoranda and briefs and in law review articles. However, this *Review Manual* limits its coverage to a summary of only those rules that relate to the Constitution, statutes, administrative rules, cases, procedural rules, legal encyclopedias, and law reviews as those rules apply to legal memoranda and briefs.

> ***Caveat:*** *The most recent edition of USOC is essential to prepare for the CLA/CP® examination. It can be ordered through bookstores or can be ordered by mail directly from:*

Harvard Law Review Association
Gannett House
Harvard Law School
Cambridge, MA 02138

U.S. Constitution   The U.S. Constitution consists of articles and various amendments. The citation form for an article and for an amendment follow.

U.S. Const. art. IV, § 2, cl. 3.

U.S. Const. amend. XIV, § 1.

Statutes   Federal statutes are cited to the official publications, either the United States Code, cited as U.S.C. (which is the preferred citation reference), or to the Statutes at Large, cited as Stat. The popular name of the statute may, but need not be, included with the citation when citing to the U.S.C.; it is required when citing to the Stat.

•*The components of a <u>United States Code</u> citation are:*

①number of the Code title (title in the Code is analogous to chapter in state statutes);
②abbreviation for United States Code (U.S.C.);
③section symbol, followed by the number of the Code section; and
④date of the Code volume (date of supplement if applicable) in which the most recent version of the section can be found.

①   ②   ③   ④
15 U.S.C. § 7 (1988).

(optional)   ① ②   ③   ④
Robinson-Patman Act, 15 U.S.C. §§ 4-6 (1988).

•*The components of a <u>Statutes at Large</u> citation are:*

①name of the act (required);
②abbreviation for "Public Law" (Pub. L.) and the public law number;
③volume number of the Statutes at Large;
④abbreviation for Statutes at Large (Stat.);
⑤page number where the statute begins; and
⑥the year when the statute was passed as law.

①   ②   ③ ④ ⑤ ⑥
Health Care Act, Pub. L. 92-117, 83 Stat. 624 (1987).

Procedural Rules   The citation forms for various federal rules of procedure are shown below. Notice that each type of procedural rule follows the same citation format.

Fed. R. App. P. 2.	Rule 2 of the Federal Rules of Appellate Procedure
Fed. R. Civ. P. 12	Rule 12 of the Federal Rules of Civil Procedure
Fed. R. Crim. P. 42	Rule 42 of the Federal Rules of Criminal Procedure
Fed. R. Evid. 401	Rule 401 of the Federal Rules of Evidence

Cases   Federal and state case citations use similar citation form, regardless of which court issues the opinion.

Every case citation begins with the case name, identified by the names of the parties. Surnames are used for individual parties (<u>Watson v. Jones</u>). Omit initials in business names unless the initial is part of the widely recognized name (B.J. Hollis Corp. becomes Hollis Corp., but initials are retained for J.C. Penney Co.). Omit *Ltd., Inc.,* and similar terms if the party's name also contains *R.R., Co., Bros., Corp., Assn.,* or other, similar term to indicate clearly that the party is a business rather than an individual.

When the federal government is a party, it is identified as "United States" in the case name (do not abbreviate as U.S. or as U.S.A.). When a state government is a party, such as the plaintiff in a criminal case, it is identified in the case name simply as "State" (<u>State v. Jones</u>), because the identity of the state is apparent from the balance of the citation. When the Internal Revenue Service is a party, the term *Commissioner* is used to identify it (meaning Commissioner of the Internal Revenue Service); never use the abbreviation IRS. For all other administrative agencies, the abbreviation for the agency typically is used in the case name (FCC, SEC, and so forth).

The ***subsequent history*** of a cited case ***must be shown*** as part of the case citation. Prior history is shown only in the extraordinary situation where the prior history is necessary to explain the point for which the case is cited.

Parallel citations should not be used when citing U.S. Supreme Court cases; cite to U.S. Reports only. A ***parallel citation*** is the same case published in more than one case reporter. For instance, citations to the same case published in U.S. Reports, Supreme Court Reporter, and U.S. Supreme Court Reports, Lawyers' Edition are parallel citations. Parallel citations for state cases must be cited if they exist *(discussed below)*.

Case names in legal memoranda and briefs must be either (1) underlined or (2) shown in italics. Both methods are shown in the examples.

•*The components of a standard case citation are:*

    ①case name (identified by names of parties);
    ②case reporter in which the case is published (include volume number,
          abbreviation of case reporter, and page where case begins);
    ③identity of court issuing the opinion unless the issuing court is apparent from
       the reporter abbreviation;
    ④year in which the decision was issued; and
    ⑤subsequent history, if any.

① ② ④
Avery v. Exxon Co., 397 U.S. 812 (1991).

① ② ③ ④
Smith v. Jones, 502 F.2d 233 (3d Cir. 1992).

① ② ③ ④
United States v. Central R.R., 436 F. Supp. 739 (N.D. Ill. 1990).

① ② ③ ④
Commissioner v. J.C. Penney Co., 429 F. Supp. 57 (Neb. 1991),
aff'd, 509 F.2d 318 (8th Cir. 1992), *cert. denied* 417 U.S. 622 (1993).
⑤ ⑤

The final example shows a subsequent case history. If all of the opinions in this example had been decided in the same year, the year would have been shown only once (at the end of the entire citation).

When citing information contained on a specific page of the opinion, rather than to the entire opinion, show the page as follows:

Safeco Ins. Co. of America v. Burr, 551 U.S. 47, 56 (2007) (Stevens, J. dissenting).

This citation directs the reader to page 639 of the dissenting opinion in the case, rather than to the majority opinion; thus, the parenthetic reference at the end of the citation.

Once cited in full, any of the following short forms of the citation may be used when the case is subsequently cited in the memorandum or in the brief:

Safeco, 551 U.S. at 49.
551 U.S. at 49.
Id. at 49.

The short form ***supra*** may not be used to refer to constitutions, statutes, or cases previously cited in full in legal memoranda and briefs; however, it may be so used in general text, in books like this one, and in law review articles. *Supra* may be used in legal memoranda and briefs only when referring to authorities other than constitutions, statutes, or cases (such as an A.L.R. annotation or a legal encyclopedia).

The researcher may use the short form ***infra*** to indicate that the full citation appears later in the memorandum, brief, or other work. This short form is not limited in the same way as the short form *supra*. The short form **id**. is used to indicate that the full citation appears immediately above, meaning that no other citations intervene between the full citation and the short form *id.*

Unlike the rule limiting the use of parallel citations for U.S. Supreme Court cases, the parallel citation for a state case cited in the state where the case was decided *must* be shown if a parallel citation exists. Parallel citations for out-of-state cases need not be cited; instead, cite only to the regional reporter. A citation to the same case appearing in both official and unofficial reporters is an example of a parallel citation.

<u>Sanders v. Keaton, Inc.</u>, 238 Kan. 376, 457 P.2d 609 (1992).
as cited in Kansas

<u>Sanders v. Keaton, Inc.</u>, 457 P.2d 609 (Kan. 1992).
as cited everywhere except Kansas

<u>State v. Bryant</u>, 388 Minn. 271, 439 N.W.2d 811 (1991).
as cited in Minnesota

<u>Chapin v. Brewster</u>, 357 N.E.2d 154 (Ind. 1992).
as cited in Indiana and elsewhere

Notice that no state identification is shown as parenthetic information at the end of the first and third citations, because the identity of the state is apparent in each of them. The second example is a Kansas case cited somewhere other than Kansas. The last example comes from a state that stopped publishing an official case reporter in 1981; therefore, the state must be identified as parenthetic information at the end of the citation regardless of where the case is cited (whether in Indiana or elsewhere).

Administrative Law   The rules and regulations of federal administrative agencies are cited either to the Code of Federal Regulations (arranged by topic and cited as C.F.R.) or to the Federal Register (arranged chronologically and cited as Fed. Reg.). The name of the regulation may be included but is not required.

•*The components of a Code of Federal Regulations citation are:*

①the title (chapter) number;
②abbreviation for Code of Federal Regulations (C.F.R.);

③section number symbol and the section number; and
③year of publication.

①   ②   ③   ④
22 C.F.R. § 145.6 (1992).

•*The components of a <u>Federal Register</u> citation are:*

①volume number of Fed. Reg. (volume number changes each calendar year);
②abbreviation for Federal Register (Fed. Reg.);
③page number where administrative rule begins; and
④year of publication.

①   ②   ③   ④
48 Fed. Reg. 37,315 (1983).

<u>Secondary Authorities</u>   Law review articles, annotations, legal encyclopedias, and dictionaries are cited as secondary authorities.

•*The components of a law review citation are:*

①full name of author;
②designation of type of article (required only if written by a student);
③title of article (underscored or in italics);
④volume number of law review;
⑤abbreviated name of law review (refer to USOC for complete list);
⑥page number where article begins; and
⑦year of publication unless it appears elsewhere in the citation.

    ①   ②   ③   ④

Virginia Koerselman, Comment, *Workmen's Compensation*, 15 Creighton L. Rev. 415 (1981).

⑤   ⑥   ⑦

 ①   ③   ④ ⑤   ⑥

William Benton, *Creation of Fetal Rights*, 29 Geo. L. J. 356 (1985).

Notice that the first example is a student article (it contains element no. 2); the second example is not.

•*The components of an A.L.R. citation are:*

①full name of author;
②the word "Annotation";
③title of annotation (underscored or in italics);

④volume number of A.L.R. series;
⑤abbreviation for Annotated Law Reports (A.L.R.) collection;
⑥page number where the annotation begins; and
⑦year of publication.

①　　　②　　　　　　③
John Willis, Annotation, <u>Industrial Noise: Promoting
an Unsafe Work Environment</u>, 76 A.L.R. Fed. 489
(1986).　　　　　　　　④　　⑤　　　⑥
　　　⑦

•*The components of a legal encyclopedia citation are:*

①volume number of encyclopedia;
②abbreviated name of encyclopedia (either Am. Jur. 2d or C.J.S.);
③title of article (underscored or in italics);
④section symbol and section number within the article;
⑤specific page within section (no page if citing to entire section); and
⑥year of publication.

①　②　③　④　　⑥
88 C.J.S. <u>Trial</u> § 107 (1980).

①　　②　　　　③　　　　　④　⑤　⑥
46 Am. Jur. 2d *Husband and Wife* § 118, 121 (1986).

•*The components of a legal dictionary citation are:*

①full name of dictionary (do not abbreviate; no underscoring or italics);
②page where the term is defined; and
③edition of dictionary and year of publication.

①　　　　　②　　　③
Black's Law Dictionary 411 (9th ed. 1992).

①　　　　　　②　　　③
Ballentine's Legal Dictionary 1078 (3d ed. 1994).

<u>Citation Signals</u>　　　Citations related to propositions made by the writer
of a memorandum or brief are introduced by signals. Signals indicate how the
writer of the memorandum (or brief) wants the reader to view the citation in
relation to the proposition to which the citation relates.

For example, the writer uses different signals to indicate that the cited authority either supports or contradicts the writer's proposition in the memorandum. If no signal is used, the writer's position is that the cited authority clearly states the same proposition as that stated by the writer.

Commonly used signals appear below. A full list of signals, together with their meanings and uses, appears at USOC Rule 1.2.

See generally	The cited authority presents helpful background information about the proposition.
See, e.g.,	The cited authority directly supports the proposition; other authorities also could have been cited but were not cited to avoid duplication.
Cf.	The cited authority states a proposition that is different from the proposition stated by the writer, but the proposition stated in the cited authority is sufficiently similar to lend support to the writer's proposition.
Contra	The cited authority contradicts the proposition stated in the memorandum.

Sequence of Citations within Each Signal   When two or more citations follow a particular signal in a memorandum or brief, there is a prescribed sequence in which the citations should be listed. The sequence compares roughly to the weight or rank of the authority. For example, primary authorities are listed before secondary authorities; U.S. Supreme Court cases are listed before any other cases; and so on.

The sequence begins anew with each introductory signal. No signal is a signal for the purpose of sequential listing as well. In other words, if no signal is given to introduce an authority, the absence of a signal indicates that the writer believes the cited authority is directly on point.

If all of the authorities reviewed in this section on citation form were listed within one signal, they would be listed in the following order:

1.   U.S. Constitutional provisions and amendments.
2.   Federal statutes (most recent listed first).
3.   Federal procedural rules.
4.   Federal cases (U.S., F.3d, then F. Supp.).
5.   State cases (official reporter first, then regional reporter).

6.   Federal administrative rules and regulations.
7.   Law review articles.
8.   Annotations.
9.   Legal encyclopedias.
10.   Law dictionaries.

If there were two or more of the same type of authority (such as two U.S. Supreme Court cases), the most recent one would be listed first.

The Substantive Skills of Legal Research

The skillful legal researcher is one who has exercised patience and practice over a long period of time to acquire techniques that work for him or her in locating applicable legal rules. There is no right or wrong way to research, just as there is no right or wrong way to travel to Chicago. There are, however, processes generally used by experienced legal researchers to maximize their time:

- Obtain as much background information as needed.
- Identify the relevant facts.
- Frame the legal issues involved.
- Find legal authorities that apply to the facts and issues.
- Update the law through statutory supplements and *Shepard's* citators.
- Brief statutes and cases that are on point.
- Analogize the facts of the case with the statutes and cases found.
- Document the results in a memorandum to the supervising attorney.

Background Information   No one knows all of the law. Therefore, no judge, lawyer, paralegal, or legal assistant exists who never needs to review background sources for information before tackling a research project. The fact is that the more knowledgeable a person is about the law, the more she recognizes how much more remains to be learned.

After evaluating the facts to determine the general legal topic involved (search and seizure, breach of an insurance contract, corporate director liability, or the like), the experienced researcher routinely reviews legal encyclopedias, A.L.R. indexes and annotations, treatises, and legal dictionaries to "brush up" on less familiar legal topic areas. Even if the researcher works with the subject matter every day, he nevertheless will conduct at least a scan to remind himself of each of the elements needed to prove—or to disprove—a legal theory or to remind himself to consider the peripheral legal issues that do not present themselves every day. This exercise helps in keeping the researcher's mind open to other theories and options during the balance of the research project.

Where pattern jury instructions exist for a particular state, they often provide an excellent starting point from which to create a checklist of elements that must be proved to support a particular legal theory. The table of contents of a legal encyclopedia may serve the same function.

Identify Relevant Facts   Using background sources and any legal theories supplied by the attorney, the researcher must evaluate all of the known facts in the case, separating those that are legally relevant from those that are not. For example:

> Mayor Roscoe Wiley slipped and fell on an icy sidewalk in front of BJ's Bingo Hall last Sunday, breaking his right arm and collarbone. He was hospitalized for 10 days. Mayor Wiley and B. J. Hollis, the proprietor, have been political enemies for many years.

The fact that Wiley is a mayor may be relevant to the senior management of the firm, but it has no legal relevance. There are no legal rules for mayors who slip and fall that are different from the legal rules for other people who slip and fall. Likewise, the fact that Wiley and Hollis are political enemies has no legal relevance to the issue of liability. The remaining facts stated in the problem are (or may be) relevant to the researcher.

Frame the Legal Issues   All law is based upon classifications. Once the relevant facts are known, they are classified according to the legal rules that most accurately apply to them. These classifications are used as the basis to frame (phrase) the legal issues in relation to the facts of the case.

Framing legal issues and segregating relevant facts typically evolve at the same time, since one cannot frame all legal issues until the relevant facts are segregated. Yet, one cannot segregate all of the relevant facts until the legal issues are framed. The two functions generally are interdependent.

Based upon the abbreviated facts stated in the above example, one might frame the following legal issue: *Is a business proprietor liable to a plaintiff who slips and falls on an icy sidewalk in front of the proprietor's business location?* If background research indicates that liability may not be the same when the business is open as it is when the business is closed and if the researcher knows that bingo halls cannot operate on Sundays, the legal issue might be framed: *Is a business proprietor liable to a plaintiff who slips and falls on an icy sidewalk in front of the proprietor's business location during nonbusiness hours?* In other words, the issue is framed according to the legal classifications that can be drawn from the relevant facts.

Find and Update the Law   Using the facts of the case and the legal issues or legal theories suggested by those facts, the researcher must locate the legal rules that apply. She will use the finding tools (indexes for statutes, digests for cases) and the techniques (topic method, case method) described previously to accomplish this task. All major authorities should be searched—both favorable and unfavorable—and the results reported to the attorney.

Before the memorandum to the supervising attorney is prepared, the researcher must update those legal rules which are on point to determine (1) that the applicable statutes have not been stricken, repealed, or amended and (2) that the applicable cases have not been overruled, reversed, or modified. Statutory supplements and *Shepard's* citators are used for this purpose, both of which were described earlier in this chapter. Only the most recent version of the law can be used as legal authority.

Brief the Law   When the researcher locates relevant authorities (typically statutes and cases), briefing them is an efficient way to preserve their important points for later use. A brief is an abbreviated summary of the case (or statute), generally one page or less in length.

Statutes often contain lists of elements or requirements. When the statutory list is long or complex or both, its important parts usually can be pared down to a shorter or simpler list through the briefing process. To illustrate, an extract from the venue statute for the federal district court, cited as 28 U.S.C. § 1391 (2002), is shown immediately below and is followed by an example of one way in which the extract might be briefed.

> (a)   A civil action wherein jurisdiction is founded only on diversity of citizenship may, except as otherwise provided by law, be brought only in (1) a judicial district where any defendant resides, if all defendants reside in the same state, (2) a judicial district in which a substantial part of the events or omissions giving rise to the claim occurred, or a substantial part of property that is subject to the action is situated, or (3) a judicial district in which the defendants are subject to personal jurisdiction at the time the action is commenced.

> (b)   A civil action wherein jurisdiction is not founded solely on diversity of citizenship may, except as otherwise provided by law, be brought only in (1) a judicial district where any defendant resides, if all defendants reside in the same state, (2) a judicial district in which a substantial part of the

events or omissions giving rise to the claim occurred, or a substantial part of property that is subject to the action is situated, or (3) a judicial district in which any defendant may be found, if there is no district in which the action may otherwise be brought.

(c)   For purposes of venue under this chapter, a defendant that is a corporation shall be deemed to reside in any judicial district in which it is subject to personal jurisdiction at the time the action is commenced. In a State which has more than one judicial district and in which a defendant that is a corporation is subject to personal jurisdiction at the time an action is commenced, such corporation shall be deemed to reside in any district in that State within which its contacts would be sufficient to subject it to personal jurisdiction if that district were a separate State, and, if there is no such district, the corporation shall be deemed to reside in the district within which it has the most significant contacts. . . .

VENUE FOR FEDERAL CIVIL ACTIONS:

(a) Actions based solely upon diversity of citizenship can be filed in district:

(1) Where any defendant resides if all defendants reside in the same state; or
(2) Where a substantial part of the claim arose or subject property is located; or
(3) Where personal jurisdiction exists over all defendants when the action is commenced.

(b) Actions based upon federal questions and other cases can be filed in district:

(1) Where any defendant resides if all defendants reside in the same state; or
(2) Where a substantial part of the claim arose or subject property is located; or
(3) Where any defendant may be found if no other district has venue.

(c) For purposes of venue, a defendant corporation is deemed to reside in any district with personal jurisdiction over such defendant when the action is commenced.

•When a state has more than one district, the corporation is deemed to reside in that district which would have personal jurisdiction based upon minimum contacts if that district were a separate state; and

•If there is no such district, the corporation is deemed to reside in that district where it has the most significant contacts.

When the relevant statutes are few or when they are short, it may be more efficient simply to photocopy them and, using a colored pen, to highlight the key terms or the elements of the statute that apply to the facts of the client's case.

Court opinions, on the other hand, tend to be lengthy, making it impractical to photocopy every relevant case for the research file. Notwithstanding the time and expense, uncondensed photocopies of many cases are virtually useless when the time comes to organize and draft the memorandum of law. Briefing cases is awkward and confusing at first; but, as is true of all skills, it becomes easier with practice.

The components of a full case brief are as follows:

- *Case Name and Citation.*   Include the full name of the case and its complete citation, including parallel citations; they can be omitted in the memorandum if necessary.

- *Identity of Court* issuing the opinion, if it is not apparent from the citation.

- *Judicial History or Procedural Posture.*   Knowing how the case arrived at the appellate court is helpful in understanding its facts and in evaluating the court's decision. For example: Where did the case originate and which other appellate courts, if any, have reviewed it? Was the original decision made at the pretrial stage (dismissal or summary judgment) or was it made after a full trial on the merits? Was it an interlocutory appeal, such as one based upon a disputed order to compel discovery? Many researchers prefer to include the procedural posture with the facts section of the case brief when that can be done reasonably.

- *Facts.*   The researcher condenses the facts reported in the case, focusing on those which are directly relevant to the issue and stating them as succinctly as possible. Researchers often find it necessary to edit this section several times to strike the right balance between utility and brevity.

- *Issue.*   This is the question decided by the court. The parties may present a number of questions for the court to decide; however, the appellate court selects the one (sometimes two) necessary to dispose of the case. This question is the issue. When a number of questions are raised by the parties, it sometimes is difficult to determine which one is the issue—even for an experienced researcher. When this happens, find the holding because it often suggests the issue.

■*Decision*.   This is the disposition or result reached in the case (affirmed, reversed, remanded, or the like).

■*Holding*.   The holding is the rule of law stated by the court which leads to or which supports the decision. The holding becomes precedent for all future cases with similar facts and similar issues that are decided by lower courts of the jurisdiction. It is the rule of law for which the case is cited. The holding is easy to locate when there is only one question presented for decision or when the court states, "This court holds that . . ." or "We hold that . . ." Otherwise, the researcher may need to read the opinion several times to locate the holding. Use the court's language for the holding; do not paraphrase it.

■*Rationale*.   The rationale represents the court's reasoning to support its holding in the case. As a general rule, the rationale is somewhere between one and three sentences in length. (It may be longer.) Use as much of the court's language as needed to retain the thrust of its reasoning.

All other statements in the opinion are dicta (comments unnecessary to the decision). Although dictum never can be cited as precedent, it may be helpful to the attorney in forming analogies and drafting arguments as part of the preparation for trial.

Not every case brief sets out each of the components separately. If an opinion is neither lengthy nor complex, the researcher properly may elect to combine two or more of the components into one or may elect to omit the issue component if it mirrors the holding precisely. To illustrate, read the following extracted case; then review the abbreviated case brief which follows it. Notice that each of the components is present, even though some of them are combined with others.

Just for practice, the applicant may want to prepare his or her own case brief before reviewing the sample case brief that has been supplied. If so, take particular care with the statement of facts to ensure that it is phrased as concisely as possible. Edit it several times if necessary and then compare it with the statement of facts in the sample brief.

E.I. Du Pont de Nemours & Co.
v. Christopher
431 F.2d 1012 (5th Cir. 1970)

Goldberg, Justice

This is a case of industrial espionage in which an airplane is the cloak and a camera the dagger. The defendants-appellants, Rolfe and Gary Christopher, are photographers in Beaumont, Texas. The Christophers were hired by an unknown third party to take aerial photographs of new construction at the Beaumont plant of E.I. Du Pont de Nemours & Company, Inc. Sixteen photographs of the Du Pont facility were taken from the air on March 19, 1969, and these photographs were later developed and delivered to the third party.

Du Pont employees apparently noticed the airplane on March 19 and immediately began an investigation to determine why the craft was circling over the plant. By that afternoon the investigation had disclosed that the craft was involved in a photographic expedition and that the Christophers were the photographers. Du Pont contacted the Christophers that same afternoon and asked them to reveal the name of the person or corporation requesting the photographs. The Christophers refused to disclose this information, giving as their reason the client's desire to remain anonymous.

Having reached a dead end in the investigation, Du Pont subsequently filed suit against the Christophers, alleging that the Christophers had wrongfully obtained photographs revealing Du Pont's trade secrets which they then sold to the undisclosed third party. Du Pont contended that it had developed a highly secret but unpatented process for producing methanol, a process that gave Du Pont a competitive advantage over other producers. This process, Du Pont alleged, was a trade secret developed after much expensive and time-consuming research, and a secret that the company had taken special precautions to safeguard. The area photographed by the Christophers was the plant designed to produce methanol by this secret process, and because the plant was still under construction parts of the process were exposed to view from directly above the construction area. Photographs of that area, Du Pont alleged, would enable a skilled person to deduce the secret process for making methanol. Du Pont thus contended that the Christophers had wrongfully appropriated Du Pont trade secrets by taking the photographs and delivering them to the undisclosed third party. In its suit Du Pont asked for damages to cover the loss it had already sustained as a result of the wrongful disclosure of the trade secret and sought temporary and permanent injunctions prohibiting any further circulation of the photographs already taken and prohibiting any additional photographing of the methanol plant.

The Christophers answered with . . . [Rule 12(b) motions] to dismiss for lack of jurisdiction and failure to state a claim upon which relief could be granted. Depositions were taken during which the Christophers again refused to disclose the name of the person to whom they had delivered the photographs. Du Pont then filed a motion to compel an answer to the question and to all related questions.

On June 5, 1969, the trial court held a hearing on the pending motions . . . [and] granted Du Pont's motion to compel the Christophers to divulge the name of their client. . . . Agreeing with the trial court's determination that Du Pont had stated a valid claim, we affirm the decision of that court.

This is a case of first impression, for the Texas courts have not faced this precise factual issue, and sitting as a diversity court we must sensitize our *Erie* antennae to decide what Texas courts would do if such a situation were presented to them. The only question involved in this interlocutory appeal is whether Du Pont has asserted a claim upon which relief can be granted. The Christophers argued both at trial and before this court that they committed no "actionable wrong" in photographing the Du Pont facility and passing these photographs on to their client because they conducted all of their activities in public airspace, violated no government aviation standard, did not breach any confidential relation, and did not engage in any fraudulent or illegal conduct. In short, the Christophers argue that for an appropriation of trade secrets to be wrong there must be a trespass, other illegal conduct, or breach of a confidential relationship. We disagree.

It is true, as the Christophers assert, that the previous trade secret cases have contained one or more of these elements. However, we do not think that the Texas courts would limit the trade secret protection exclusively to these elements. On the contrary, in *Hyde Corporation v. Huffines*, 1958, 314 S.W.2d 763, the Texas Supreme Court specifically adopted the rule found in the Restatement of Torts which provides:

> One who discloses or uses another's trade secret, without privilege to do so, is liable to the other if
>
> a. he discovered the secret by improper means, or
>
> b. his disclosure or use constitutes breach of confidence reposed in him by the other in disclosing the secret to him . . . .

Thus, although the previous cases have dealt with a breach of a confidential relationship, a trespass, or other illegal conduct, the rule is much broader than the cases heretofore encountered. Not limiting itself to specific wrongs, Texas adopted subsection (a) of the Restatement which recognizes a cause of action for the discovery of a trade secret by an "improper" means. . . .

The question remaining, therefore, is whether aerial photography of plant construction is an improper means of obtaining another's trade secret. We conclude that it is and that the Texas courts would so hold. The Supreme Court of that state had declared that "the undoubted tendency of the law has been to recognize and enforce higher standards of commercial morality in the business world." *Hyde Corporation v. Huffines, at 773.* That court has quoted with approval articles indicating that the proper means of gaining possession of a competitor's secret process is "through inspection and analysis" of the product in order to create a duplicate. Later another Texas court explained:

> The means by which the discovery is made may be obvious, and the experimentation leading from known factors to presently unknown results may be simple and lying in the public domain. But these facts to not destroy the value of the discovery and will not advantage a competitor who by unfair means obtains the knowledge without paying the price expended by the discoverer. (Brown v. Fowler, 316 S.W.2d 111.)

We think, therefore, that the Texas rule is clear. One may use his competitor's secret process if he discovers the process by reverse engineering applied to the finished product; one may use a competitor's process if he discovers it by his own independent research; but one may not avoid these labors by taking the process from the discoverer without his permission at a time when he is taking reasonable precautions to maintain its secrecy. To obtain knowledge of a process without spending the time and money to discover it independently is improper unless the holder voluntarily discloses it or fails to take reasonable precautions to ensure its secrecy.

In the instant case the Christophers deliberately flew over the Du Pont plant to get pictures of a process which Du Pont had attempted to keep secret. The Christophers delivered their pictures to a third party who was certainly aware of the means by which they had been acquired and who may be planning to use the information contained therein to manufacture methanol by the Du Pont process. The third party has a right to use this process only if he obtains this knowledge through his own research efforts; but thus far all information indicates that the third party has gained this knowledge solely by taking it from Du Pont at a time when Du Pont was making reasonable efforts to preserve its secrecy. In such a situation Du Pont has a valid cause of action to prohibit the Christophers from improperly discovering its trade secret and to prohibit the undisclosed third party from using the improperly obtained information. . .

In taking this position, we realize that industrial espionage of the sort here perpetrated has become a popular sport in some segments of our industrial community. However, our devotion to freewheeling industrial competition must not force us into accepting the law of the jungle as the standard of morality expected in our commercial relations. Our tolerance of the espionage game must cease when the protections required to prevent another's spying cost so much that the spirit of inventiveness is dampened. Commercial privacy must be protected from espionage that could not have been reasonably anticipated or prevented. We do not mean to imply, however, that everything not in plain view is within the protected vale, nor that all information obtained through every extra-optical extension is forbidden. Indeed, for our industrial competition to remain healthy there must be breathing room for observing a competing industrialist. A competitor can and must shop his competition for pricing and examine his products for quality, components, and methods of manufacture. Perhaps ordinary fences and roofs must be built to shut out incursive eyes; but we need not require the discoverer of a trade secret to guard against the unanticipated, the undetectable, or the unpreventable methods of espionage now available.

In the instant case Du Pont was in the midst of constructing a plant. Although after construction the finished plant would have protected much of the process from view, during the period of construction the trade secret was exposed to view from the air. To require Du Pont to put a roof over the unfinished plant to guard its secret would impose an enormous expense to prevent nothing more than a schoolboy's trick. We introduce here no new

or radical ethic, since our ethos has never given moral sanction to piracy. The marketplace must not deviate far from our mores. We should not require a person or a corporation to take unreasonable precautions to prevent another from doing that which he ought not to do in the first place. Reasonable precautions against predatory eyes we may require; but an impenetrable fortress is an unreasonable requirement, and we are not disposed to burden industrial inventors with such a duty in order to protect the fruits of their efforts. "Improper" will always be a word of many nuances, determined by time, place, and circumstances. We therefore need not proclaim a catalog of commercial improprieties. Clearly, however, one of its commandments does say, "Thou shalt not appropriate a trade secret through deviousness under circumstances in which countervailing defenses are not reasonably available."

Having concluded that aerial photography, from whatever altitude, is an improper method of discovering the trade secrets exposed during construction of the Du Pont plant, we need not worry about whether the flight pattern chosen by the Christophers violated any federal aviation regulations. Regardless of whether the flight was legal or illegal in that sense, the espionage was an improper means of discovering Du Pont's trade secret.

The decision of the trial court is affirmed and the case remanded to that court for further proceedings on the merits.

———————

SAMPLE CASE BRIEF

<u>Du Pont & Co. v. Christopher</u>, 431 F.2d 1012 (5th Cir. 1970)

<u>Facts:</u>   In this Texas case, Du Pont developed an unpatented process (trade secret) to manufacture methanol. While Du Pont's methanol plant was under construction, the Christopher brothers took 16 pictures of the manufacturing process from an airplane circling over the construction site. The Christophers refused to identify their client, and Du Pont sued for an injunction and damages. During discovery, the trial court ordered the Christophers to identify who hired them; they refused and filed an interlocutory appeal of the trial court's order.

<u>Issue:</u>   Is aerial photography of a plant's construction site an improper means of obtaining another's trade secret?

<u>Holding:</u>   Aerial photography of a construction site is an improper means of obtaining trade secrets.

<u>Rationale:</u>   A trade secret properly may be obtained by reverse engineering or by discovering it through independent research, but one may not avoid these labors by taking it from the discoverer.

To obtain knowledge of a process without spending the time and money to discover it independently is improper unless the holder voluntarily discloses it or fails to take reasonable precautions to ensure its secrecy.

The researcher may vary the case brief format in any way that makes it a more useful tool for whoever will use it to draft the memorandum or the trial brief.

Analogize the Facts   A critical step in the research process is the comparison of the client's facts with the legal rules (usually statutes and cases) that the researcher finds. In this way, the researcher is able to evaluate whether the legal rule is on point (applies) or is not on point (does not apply). When the objective is a memorandum of law for the attorney's review and use, the researcher must use care to present all sides as objectively as possible.

In comparing a statutory list of what is required (or what is prohibited), the researcher evaluates the list, item by item, with the client's facts. For example, if a statute requires items A, B, and C, the researcher compares the client's facts to determine whether each item exists. If any item is missing or if its existence is questionable, one of two avenues may be pursued.

If A + B + C = benefit to client, try to supply the missing item, if possible; otherwise, argue that it exists in the form of the questionable item. In this way, the statute properly applies; and the client may receive the benefit of the statute.

If A + B + C = burden to client, argue that the statute does not apply unless all items exist; and since an item is missing, the client should be free of the statute's burden. If the legislature had intended to impose a burden for something less than A + B + C, it could have said so. Cases interpreting the statute or its legislative intent are helpful to the researcher in determining whether either of these arguments is likely to succeed.

The researcher evaluates case law by comparing the facts and issues of the case with the client's facts for similarities and differences. The more similarities that exist, the more likely it is that the case is on point and will apply to the client's facts. Conversely, the more differences that exist, the more likely it is that the case is not on point.

For example, a researcher working on Mayor Wiley's slip and fall case *(see sample problem above)* is unlikely to find many other cases where the plaintiff had slipped and fallen on an icy sidewalk in front of a bingo hall. In fact, there may be no cases found with these precise facts. The researcher, then, looks for cases with similar facts: Is an icy sidewalk in front of a bookstore sufficiently similar? A grocery store? A courthouse? An apartment complex? A private residence? Is a case related to a snow-covered sidewalk sufficiently similar? A wet sidewalk with large cracks? A dry sidewalk under construction? *A more complete discussion of analogical reasoning is provided with examples in the Judgment and Analytical Ability chapter of this Review Manual.*

Occasionally, a researcher locates a case "on all fours," which literally means that if the client's case were placed over the researched case, they would match on all four corners because the facts and issues are identical—or nearly identical—to each other. If a case is on point or is on all fours, it likely will be precedent in determining the outcome of the client's case.

<u>Acknowledge Ambiguity</u>   If legal research could produce clear answers in every case, there would be no reason for courts or trial attorneys to exist. Although research may provide definite answers to some questions, it is unlikely to provide definite answers to all of the questions raised by a particular client's facts. The more common situation is that statutes and case law merely narrow the legal issues that will be left for a judge to decide.

In researching statutes, ambiguity can occur when a legislature adopts a law that includes lists to deal with a specific type of problem. If the client's case is the same type as those addressed by the statute, but is not included in the statutory list, does this mean (1) that the legislature intended to exclude it or (2) that the legislature would have included it in the list if anyone had thought of it at the time? Statutory ambiguity also can occur when new technologies or new situations arise that were not, and could not have been, anticipated by the legislature (such as privacy rights attached to e-mail or tort liability relating to AIDS exposure). Whether a particular statute is ambiguous is, of course, left to a court to decide.

Memoranda to Attorneys   Once the researcher is reasonably certain that he has located all of the major authorities dealing with the research assignment, he must organize and summarize them in a memorandum of law for the supervising attorney.

The first step is to know the purpose for which the memorandum will be used, whether to determine the procedure required to amend a corporation's bylaws, to draft a civil complaint, to draft an appellate brief, or for some other purpose. The intended use determines the focus of the memorandum, as well as how much technical detail to provide.

The format of the memorandum varies according to office policy and the preference of the supervising attorney. If no standard form is required by office policy, check the files for other memoranda prepared for or by the supervising attorney. Memoranda generally include (1) the heading, (2) date, (3) name of the attorney for whom the memorandum is written, (4) name of the writer, (5) client name or case name, (6) statement of facts, (7) question presented, (8) brief answer or brief summary of the conclusion, (9) discussion, and (10) conclusion. A researcher might prepare a memorandum of law for the attorney in the form shown on the following page.

MEMORANDUM

TO: Name of Attorney

DATE: Today's Date

FROM: Name of Writer

RE: Name of Client or Client File

<u>Statement of Facts</u>:   Recite the relevant facts of the case or problem as you understand them to be. Be as concise as possible. A chronological presentation usually is best, although any form may be used if it is better suited.

<u>Question Presented</u>:   State the issue or subject of the research assignment in question form (see section on framing the issue, discussed earlier in this chapter).

<u>Brief Answer</u>:   Provide the short answer to the question, whether *yes*, *no*, or an abbreviated form of the conclusion.

<u>Discussion</u>:   This section often begins with a statement of the general rule or principle that governs the subject matter, such as "The general rule is. . . or "The law of North Carolina and the general rule throughout the country is. . .

        Relate applicable legal authority, both favorable and unfavorable (including citations), in a logical, narrative form. Exceptions to any general or specific rules are included as well. If more than one alternative or option is possible, each should be discussed.

        Use a detailed outline to stay focused on the overall purpose of the research and redraft as many times as necessary to achieve the desired result.

<u>Conclusion</u>:   The conclusion summarizes the major points of the discussion in one or two concise paragraphs (one is better). If the legal rules are unclear on a point, say so. It is correct to use words and phrases such as "appears," "seems to require," or "may be" if they are more appropriate than absolute statements.

It always makes sense to review the progress of the memorandum with the supervising attorney as it is being drafted. When the outline is completed, in particular, the attorney should review it to ensure that the project is on the right track. Before the memorandum is submitted as a final product, the researcher should review it with these questions in mind:

•*Could the memorandum be understood by someone who knows little or nothing about the case?*

•*Does the question presented in the memorandum focus accurately on the central issue? Could it be stated more precisely?*

•*Are the facts of cited cases given in enough detail to show their relevance?*

•*Do the cited authorities adequately support the conclusion(s) stated?*

•*Does the memorandum provide enough information to allow the attorney to take the next required step without asking further questions and without performing additional research?*

Legal research can be challenging and rewarding to the researcher who takes the time to master its technical and substantive skills. A skilled researcher provides an invaluable service to the attorney and to the profession in the delivery of quality legal services at a reasonable cost. The materials in this chapter, together with the following self-test, are designed to highlight the major principles of legal research. *See the bibliography for additional references.*

Legal Research Self-Test

Allow an uninterrupted 30-minute period to answer all questions. At the end of 30 minutes, check your answers against those in the Answer Key Section of this Review Manual. Deduct two points for each incorrect answer (100 total possible points). Unanswered questions are counted as incorrect answers. Follow directions carefully and observe the time limit precisely to provide an accurate self-assessment.

Choose the most correct answer to the following questions unless a specific question directs you to do otherwise.

1. _____ contain a general commentary on or explanation of the subject.

   a.   Primary authorities
   b.   Secondary authorities
   c.   Case reporters
   d.   Digests

2. If a researcher knows the date when a federal statute was enacted, which of the following will provide the most direct access to the text of that statute?

   a.   Code of Federal Regulations
   b.   Congressional Record
   c.   United States Code
   d.   Federal Rules Decisions

3. To update the status of a particular case, what research tool is used?

   a.   Federal Digest
   b.   Supplement volumes or pocket part supplements
   c.   *Shepard's Citations*
   d.   None of these is correct.

4. In a petition for writ of certiorari to the United States Supreme Court, the _____ appears first in the case caption, regardless of how the caption may have been shown in lower courts.

   a.   case number
   b.   name of the appellate court
   c.   name of the trial court
   d.   name of the appellant

5.   When a researcher is unfamiliar with the subject matter to be researched, what tool may be consulted to provide background information?

    a.   United States Code
    b.   Case digests
    c.   Legal encyclopedias
    d.   Federal Reporter

6.   Which of these legal publishers is noted for its extensive use of annotations?

    a.   West Publishing Co.
    b.   Lawyers-Cooperative Publishing Co.
    c.   Bureau of National Affairs
    d.   Commerce Clearing House

7.   Compilations of cases and historical matters dealing with various aspects of a code or statute, which contain short summaries of other cases, both for and against, are called:

    a.   annotations
    b.   restatements
    c.   encyclopedias
    d.   digests

8.   The principles stated in opinions of judges, to be followed in future cases, are called:

    a.   res judicata
    b.   precedent
    c.   case law
    d.   jurisprudence

9.   True or False.   The United States Supreme Court Reports, Lawyers' Edition contains summaries of the briefs of counsel.

10.   True or False.   Parallel citations for an appellate court opinion may include citations to the trial court reporter series where the trial court opinion is published.

11.   True or False.   Federal statutes are arranged topically in the Statutes at Large.

12.   True or False.   The case summaries found in digests may be cited as primary authority.

13.   True or False.   Star paging is used in all volumes of all official and unofficial Supreme Court reporters.

14.   True or False.   The signal *infra* is used in legal memoranda and briefs to indicate the full citation for the case follows at a later point in the memorandum or brief.

15.   True or False.   Federal Supporter is the reporter in which recent federal trial court opinions are contained.

16.   Which is the correct citation for an article entitled *Nocturnal Crimes*, written by Professor Willard Weitz and published in the 20th volume of the Brooklyn Law Review in 1992. The article appears at page 180.

   a.   W. Weitz, *Nocturnal Crimes*, 20 Brooklyn L. Rev. 180 (1992).
   b.   W. Weitz, *Nocturnal Crimes*, Brooklyn L. Rev. 20-180 (1992).
   c.   W. Weitz, *Nocturnal Crimes*, 20 Brooklyn L. Rev. 180 (1992).
   d.   Willard Weitz, *Nocturnal Crimes*, 20 Brooklyn L. Rev. 180 (1992).

17.   Which of the following is most correct?

   a.   Freedom of Information Act, 46 U.S.C. § 89 (1976).
   b.   Freedom of Information Act, 46 U.S.C.A. § 89 (1976).
   c.   Freedom of Information Act, 197 Stat. 230 (1976).
   d.   46 U.S.C. § 89 (1976).

18.   Digests summarize:

   a.   Judicial decisions
   b.   Statute topics
   c.   Both a and b
   d.   Neither a nor b

19.   Which of the following statements best describes the term *star paging*?

   a.   Signal used to indicate page numbers in another reporter.
   b.   Signal used to indicate original pagination when a reporter is reprinted.

(see next page)

c. Signal used to indicate page where the court's holding is found.
d. None of these is correct.

20. Cases decided by the U.S. Court of International Trade (formerly the U.S. Customs Court) are reported selectively in the:

a. Federal Digest
b. Federal Supplement
c. United States Reporter
d. None of these is correct.

21. What is the primary difference between the Statutes at Large and the United States Code?

a. The Statutes at Large are compiled by topic; the Code, chronologically.
b. The Statutes at Large contains state statutes; the Code, federal.
c. The Statutes at Large contains federal statutes; the Code, state.
d. The Statutes at Large are compiled chronologically; the Code, by topic.

22. True or False.   When a state's highest court elects to publish an official reporter, it must publish all cases decided by that court.

23. True or False.   The American Digest System indexes and classifies all case law, both state and federal.

24. True or False.   When researching a particular federal statute, the United States Code is the most useful source because it is an official publication.

25. True or False.   The American Digest System is sometimes called the Decennial Digest and uses the key number system.

26. True or False.   The typical case reporter contains either a separate section or a separate volume devoted to a table of cases and a descriptive word index.

27. True or False.   Indexing is the accepted process for checking the status of specific cases, while Shepardizing is used for checking the status of statutes.

28.   True or False.   The signal *supra* is used in legal memoranda and briefs to refer to a case that has been cited in full previously.

29.   True or False.   Each state has both an official and an unofficial reporter series for the opinions of its highest state court.

30.   True or False.   American Jurisprudence Second and Corpus Juris Secundum are the two most legal encyclopedias in existence today.

31.   True or False.   A memorandum opinion is an opinion of the entire court, rather than an opinion written by a specific judge.

32.   If one reporter citation of a case is known, its parallel citation(s) can be determined by using:

    a.   *Shepard's Citations*
    b.   Table of Cases
    c.   West's National Reporter Blue Book
    d.   Any one of the above

33.   Which is the correct citation for a case in which Thomas Langdon Jr. is the plaintiff and Yun-lan Sing is the defendant, decided by the federal trial court in the eastern district of Pennsylvania on October 15, 1991 and published in the appropriate reporter series at volume 658, page 139 on October 28, 1991?

    a.   Langdon Jr. v. Sing, 658 F. Supp. 139 (E.D.Pa. 1991).
    b.   Langdon v. Sing, 658 F. Supp. 139 (E.D. Pa. 1991).
    c.   Langdon v. Yun-lan Sing, 658 F. Supp. 139 (E.D. Pa. 1991).
    d.   Langdon v. Yun-lan Sing, 658 F.2d 139 (E.D. Pa. 1991).

34.   Which is the correct citation for a petition for certiorari by the defendant in the preceding question to the United States Supreme Court, where the petition was denied on December 28, 1992 and reported at volume 636 of the United States Reports on page 322, which was published on January 7, 1993?

    a.   *Yun-lan Sing v. Langdon*, 636 U.S. 322 (1993).
    b.   *Sing v. Langdon Jr.*, 636 U. S. 322 (1993).
    c.   *Yun-lan Sing v. Langdon*, 636 U.S. 322 (1-7-93).
    d.   *Yun-lan Sing v. Langdon*, 636 U.S. 322 (1992).

35.   Which is the correct citation for an appeal by the defendant in the preceding question to the Court of Appeals for the Third Circuit, decided on August 28, 1992 and published in the appropriate reporter series at volume 597, page 843 on September 12, 1992?

    a.   <u>Langdon v. Yun-lan Sing</u>, 597 F.2d 843 (3d Cir. 1992).
    b.   <u>Langdon v. Yun-lan Sing</u>, 597 F.2d 843 (3rd Cir. 1992).
    c.   <u>Langdon v. Sing, 597 F</u>. Supp. 843 (3d Cir. 1992).
    d.   <u>Langdon Jr. v. Sing</u>, 597 F.2d 843 (3rd Cir. 1992).

36.   To update the status of a particular statute, what research tool should be used?

    a.   Federal Digest
    b.   Supplement volumes or pocket part supplements
    c.   American Law Reports
    d.   None of these is correct.

37.   True or False.   Digests are compilations of case law for a particular reporter or a particular group of reporters.

38.   True or False.   Parallel citations generally are not provided for federal cases, but they are required for home state cases when parallel citations exist.

39.   True or False.   Within the *Shepard's* Citator volumes, the citations appearing in parentheses indicate other cases that have overruled the case being researched.

40.   The subsequent history of a cited case must be included in the citation when the case has been:

    a.   Affirmed
    b.   Reversed
    c.   Modified on appeal
    d.   All of these are correct.

41.   A type of secondary authority that is not the law itself but is, rather, a persuasive presentation by legal scholars of what the law is or what it should be in a particular topic area, is called:

    a.   Encyclopedia
    b.   Restatement

(*see next page*)

  c. Treatise

  d. None of these is correct.

42. Which of the following case names is correctly cited?

  a. <u>State of Colorado v. Michael O'Brien</u>

  b. <u>Colorado v. O'Brien</u>

  c. <u>State v. O'Brien</u>

  d. <u>In Re State v. O'Brien</u>

43. Which of the following case names is correctly cited?

  a. *Internal Revenue Service v. Lucas*

  b. *IRS v. Lucas*

  c. *Commissioner v. Lucas*

  d. *IRS Commissioner v. Lucas*

44. Which of the following case names is correctly cited?

  a. <u>Jay Turner Company v. Hellman Industries, Ltd.</u>

  b. <u>Jay Turner Co. v. Hellman Industries, Ltd.</u>

  c. <u>Jay Turner Co. v. Hellman Industries</u>

  d. <u>Turner Co. v. Hellman Industries, Ltd.</u>

45. True or False. The signal *supra* is used in law review articles and other textual material (but not in legal memoranda and not in briefs) to indicate that the full citation for the case was given previously.

46. True or False. The case summaries found in digests may be cited as secondary authority.

47. True or False. The United States Code contains all federal statutory law enacted by Congress.

48. True or False. When an appellate judge disagrees with the result and with the reasoning of the majority opinion, but disagrees with the reasoning of the dissenting opinion as well, she may write an abstaining opinion.

49.   Which of the following is the most correct citation form?

a.   <u>Montana v. United States</u>, 440 U.S. 147 (1979).
b.   <u>Montana v. United States</u>, 440 U.S. 147, 99 S. Ct. 970 (1979).
c.   <u>Montana v. United States</u>, 440 U.S. 147, 59 L. Ed. 2d 210, 99 S. Ct. 970 (1979).
d.   <u>Montana v. United States,</u> 440 U.S. 147, 99 S. Ct. 970, 59 L. Ed. 2d 210 (1979).

50.   Which of the following represents the correct citation to a term found at the 15th line of column 1, page 41 of the Third Edition of Ballentine's Law Dictionary, which was published in 1969?

a.   Ballentine 41 (3rd ed. 1969).
b.   Ballentine's Law Dictionary 41 (3rd ed. 1969).
c.   Ballentine's Law Dictionary 41 (3d ed. 1969).
d.   Ballentine at 41-1-15 (3d ed. 1969).

Chapter

6

LEGAL TERMINOLOGY

Diplomacy is the art of saying "Nice Doggie" until you can find a rock.

—Will Rogers

Legal terminology includes (1) Latin phrases, (2) legal phrases and terms in general, and (3) understanding and proper usage of common legal terms. Each applicant must take the General Law section plus four substantive law sections that the applicant chooses. Legal terminology of all types is tested in those substantive sections; however, many applicants may find it helpful to have a special chapter devoted to terminology. The legal terminology and procedures found here are those that one might find in a general practice.

Preparation

The legal terms and procedures used in a general law practice typically are much more varied than they are in a legal specialty practice. A general practitioner does a little bit of everything.

Of those study suggestions found in the Introduction to the *CLA/CP® Review Manual*, flash cards are particularly effective in learning and reinforcing terminology. Terminology flash cards can be purchased in many law school bookstores; however, customized flash cards are the ideal. A customized flash card is one that is prepared by hand (by you) on a 3 × 5 index card. Flash cards fit easily into a pocket, purse, or briefcase and can be reviewed during odd moments of free time in addition to the regularly scheduled study periods.

Latin words and phrases are the most difficult for the greatest number of people, generally because they are used less frequently than are general legal terms. Spend extra time with Latin terms. There is no easy way to learn terminology, whether legal or Latin. It takes discipline, effort, and frequent review.

Latin Terms

a fortiori	with stronger reason
a priori	from what goes before; from the cause to the effect
ab initio	from the beginning
actiones in personam	personal actions
ad curiam	before the court, to the court
ad damnum clause	to the damage, clause of complaint that states plaintiff's monetary loss
ad faciendum	to do
ad hoc	for this purpose, for this occasion
ad litem	for the suit; for the litigation (a guardian *ad litem*, for example)
ad rem	to the thing at hand
ad valorem	according to the value (an *ad valorem* tax, for example)
adversus	against (defendant *adv.* plaintiff)

aggregatio mentium	meeting of minds (relates to formation of contracts)
alias dictus	otherwise called, also known as (as in an assumed name)
alibi	in another place, elsewhere
aliunde	from another place, from without (as in evidence outside the document); see parol evidence under Legal Terms below
alter ego	the other self
amicus curiae	friend of the court (as an *amicus curiae* brief filed with an appellate court)
animo	with intention, disposition, design, will
animus	mind, intention
ante litem motam	before suit brought, before litigation is filed
arguendo	in the course of the argument, for the sake of argument
assumpsit	he undertook, he promised
bona fide	good faith
capias	take, arrest
capita	persons, heads
causa mortis	by reason of death
caveat	beware, a warning
caveat emptor	let the buyer beware

certiorari	send the pleadings up (from an inferior court to a superior court; U.S. Supreme Court uses writ of *certiorari* to review most cases)
cestui	beneficiaries (pronounced "setty")
cestui que trust	beneficiaries of the trust
circa	in the area of, about, concerning
compos mentis	of sound mind
consortium	union of lots or chances; conjugal fellowship of husband and wife
contra	against
coram nobis	before us ourselves
corpus	body
corpus delicti	body of the offense; essence of the crime
cum testamento annexo	with the will annexed
datum (pl., *data*)	1. a thing given; information; 2. a date
de facto	in fact, in deed, actually
de jure	of right, lawful
de novo	anew, afresh
de son tort	of his own wrong
dies non	not a day
duces tecum	bring with you (as in subpoena *duces tecum*, whereby subpoenaed person must appear and bring records)

dum bene se gesserit	while he shall conduct himself, during good behavior
e converso	conversely, on the other hand
en banc	in the bench, all judges present (a three-judge panel sits individually or *en banc*)
eo instanti	upon the instant
erratum (pl., *errata*)	error
et alii	and others (as in <u>Smith *et al*. v. Jones</u>)
et sequentia	and as follows (*et seq.*)
et ux	and wife
et vir	and husband
ex delicto	(arising) from a tort
ex gratia	as a matter of favor
ex officio	from office, by virtue of his office
ex parte	one side only, by or for one party only
ex post facto	after the fact
facto	in fact, in or by the law
felonice	feloniously
fiat	let it be done, a short order that a thing be done
fieri	to be made up, to become
fieri facias	cause to be made (a writ [order] directing the sheriff to reduce a judgment debtor's

	property to money [sell it] for the amount of the judgment, for example)
flagrante delicto	in the very act of committing the crime
forum non conveniens	discretionary power of a court to decline jurisdiction over a case when the court believes it should be tried elsewhere for convenience of parties and witnesses
gravis	serious, of importance
habeas corpus	you have the body (a writ directed to the custodian of a person, commanding the custodian to produce such person)
habendum clause	that part of a deed that begins "to have and to hold"; defines extent of ownership
honorarium	honorary fee or gift; compensation from gratitude
idem	the same as above (*id.*)
idem sonans	having the same sound (as names sounding alike but spelled differently)
in curia	in court
in esse	in being, existence
in forma pauperis	permission given to a poor person to sue without liability for court costs
infra	beneath; below
in limine	at the beginning; threshold
in loco parentis	in place of a parent, one charged with a parent's rights and obligations
in pari delicto	in equal fault

in personam	personally, against the person
in praesenti	at once; now
in re	in the matter
in rem	proceedings against a thing (a bank account or real estate) distinguished from those against a person
in specie	in the same or in similar form
instanter	immediately
inter alia, inter alios	among other things, between other persons
inter se	among themselves
inter vivos	between the living, from one person to another
in toto	in the whole, completely
in transitu	in transit
intra	within, inside
ipse dixit	he himself said (it), as an assertion made but not proved
ipso facto	by the fact itself
ita est	so it is
jura personarum	right of a person, rights of persons
jura rerum	rights of things
jure divino	by divine right
jure uxoris	in his wife's right

jus (pl. *jura*)	law; right; laws collectively
jus ad rem	a right to a thing
jus commune	the common law, the common right
jus gentium	the law of nations, international law
just habendi	the right to have a thing
jus tertii	the right of a third party; the rights of another person
levari facias	cause to be levied, a writ of execution
lex	law
lex loci	law of the place where the cause of action arose
lis pendens	litigation pending, as in a *lis pendens* filed with real estate records to notify the world that the real estate is involved in litigation
locus delicti	the place of the crime or of the tort
locus sigilli (L.S.)	the place for the seal
mala	bad
mala fides	bad faith
mala in se	wrong in itself, an act that is morally wrong
mala praxis	malpractice
mala prohibita	act declared criminal by statute (failure to file a report, for example), though not wrong in itself (as in murder)

malo animo	with evil intent
mandamus	we command, a writ used to compel an official to perform an act that she is required to perform
manu forti	with a strong hand, forcible entry
mens rea	guilty mind (most crimes require the element of intent [*mens rea*])
nihil dicit	he says nothing (as in a default judgment against a defendant who does not raise a defense in the action)
nil	nothing; of no account
nil debet	he owes nothing
nisi prius	unless before (used to distinguish the court where trial was held from the appellate court)
nolle prosequi	unwilling to prosecute (a crime); prosecutor's discretion not to file charges in a particular case
nolo contendere	I will not contest it
non	not
non assumpsit	plea in defense; that he did not promise
non compos mentis	not of sound mind
non est factum	it is not his deed
non obstante	notwithstanding
non sequitur	it does not follow
nota bene (N.B.)	note well; take notice

nudum pactum	nude pact, a bare agreement that lacks the consideration to form a valid contract
nul tort	no wrong done
nulla bona	no goods (wording used on the return of a writ *fieri facias*)
nunc pro tunc	now for then (as in an order *nunc pro tunc* to correct clerical error in a previous order)
obiter dictum	remark that is not central to the main issue
onus probandi	the burden of proof
opus (pl., *opera*)	work, labor
ore tenus	by word of mouth, orally (as in a motion *ore tenus*)
pari delicto	in equal guilt
pari passu	by equal progress, ratably, equitably, without preference
pater familias	father of the family
peculium	private property
pendens	pending
pendente lite	pending the suit, during litigation
per annum	annual, by the year
per capita	by the head, equally shared
per contra	in opposition
per curiam	by the court

per diem	by the day
per se	by itself, taken alone
per stirpes	by representation, by the roots or stocks for purposes of inheritance
post	after, later
post-factum	after the fact, after the event
post-obit	to take effect after death
praecipe	writ commanding a person to do some act or to appear and show cause why she should not do so; order to clerk of court to issue a summons or execution on judgment already rendered
prima facie	at first sight, on the face of it
pro bono	free of charge, without cost
pro forma	as a matter of form
pro hac vice	for this occasion
pro rata	according to the rate or proportion
pro se	appearing for oneself; personally
pro tanto	for so much, to that extent
pro tempore	for the time being, temporarily
prochein ami	next friend
publici juris	of public right
pur autre vie	for or during the life of another
quaere	question, doubt

quantum	how much, the amount
quare	wherefore
quare clausum fregit	breaking the close, trespass
quasi	as if, as if it were
quid pro quo	what for what, something for something (as in consideration for a contract)
quo warranto	by what right or authority
res	thing, object, subject matter
res gestae	things done, excited utterance
res ipsa loquitur	the thing speaks for itself
res judicata	a thing (matter) adjudged
respondeat superior	let the master answer
scienter	knowledge, awareness
scilicet	to wit, that is to say, namely (SS or ss)
scintilla	a spark, the least particle
scire facias	cause to know, give notice (writ used to revive a judgment that has expired [dormant])
secundum	according to
se defendendo	in self-defense
semper	always
seriatim	severally, separately

sic	thus, so, in such manner (used to indicate an error in original, quoted material)
sigillum	a seal
sine	without
sine die	without a day, without a specific day assigned for a future meeting
sine qua non	that without which a thing cannot occur; indispensable condition or part
stare decisis	to abide by decided cases
status quo	state in which, present state
sua sponte	voluntarily, of his own will and motion
sub nomine	under the name of, in the name of, under the title of
sub silentio	under silence, without any notice being taken
sui generis	of its own kind or class, the only one of a kind, unique
sui juris	of his own right, having legal capacity to act for himself
supersedeas	superseding (as in the bond that accompanies a writ commanding a stay of proceedings pending appeal)
supra	above, cited in full above
tenere	to hold, to keep
terminus a quo	the starting point
ultra	beyond, in excess of, outside of

ultra vires	without power, beyond the powers of
venire facias	that you cause to come, a type of summons
versus	against (plaintiff v. defendant)
videlicet (viz.)	it is easy to see, that is to say, namely
vi et armis	by force and arms
vis-à-vis	one who (that which) is face to face with another
vivos	living
voir dire	to speak the truth, the process used to select jurors

Legal Terms

abatement	reduction, termination
abrogation	annulment of a former law by act of a legislative body, by constitutional authority, or by usage
acceptance	in contract law, consent to abide by the terms of an offer; taking or receiving a thing in good faith with the intention of retaining it
accession	that which increases the size or value of property

accommodation	arrangement made as a favor to another rather than for consideration received
acknowledgement	an admission, affirmation, or declaration
acquittal	release or discharge of an obligation or liability; in criminal law, a finding of not guilty
ademption	satisfaction of a legacy by gift prior to testator's death
adhesion contract	standardized contract form in which a party with little or no bargaining power is forced to accept its terms
adjudication	judgment or decision of a court
administrative law	body of rules and regulations having the force of law and promulgated by an administrative body created by Congress or a state legislature
adverse possession	acquiring title to real estate by hostile possession rather than by purchase
affiant	one who makes or swears to the truth of an affidavit
affidavit	sworn statement in writing taken before a notary public or other authorized officer
affirmative defense	allegation of a responsive pleading that, if it can be proved, negates the allegations of the complaint
agent	person authorized by another to act for him, one entrusted with another's business
agreement	meeting of the minds, preliminary to contract formation

allegation	assertion made but not proved
amortization	gradual extinction of a monetary obligation by periodic payments that usually includes interest
amnesty	sovereign forgetfulness of past acts, usually available for a limited time
ancillary	auxiliary, supplemental, subordinate
annotation	remark, note, or commentary intended to illustrate or explain
annul	cancel, make void, destroy
answer	written pleading by which a defendant responds to the plaintiff's complaint
antitrust laws	federal and state laws to prevent restraint of trade, price-fixing, price discrimination, monopolies, or other conduct detrimental to free commerce
appeal	review by a higher court
appellant	party who files an appeal
appellee	party who defends an appeal
appraisal	valuation or estimate of property value, made by qualified expert
arbitration	investigation and determination of dispute by neutral decision-maker; decision is binding on parties
arraignment	in criminal law, hearing at which accused pleads guilty or not guilty
assault	in tort, threat of imminent bodily harm accompanied by apparent ability to carry

	out the threat; in criminal law, often defined as the tort equivalent of battery
asset	real or personal property owned by an individual, estate, business corporation, or other entity
assignment	transfer of any right, title, or interest to another
assumption of risk	doctrine under which a person cannot obtain recovery for injuries received from a dangerous activity to which she voluntarily exposed herself
attachment	prejudgment seizure of property based upon court order
attest	certify or affirm to be true or genuine
attestation	act of witnessing the signing (execution) of a document
attorney-in-fact	one appointed by another to act in specific matters described in a power of attorney or in a letter of attorney
aver	assert, allege, claim
bailment	delivery of personal property to another to be held for a particular person and then returned
beneficiary	one who benefits from the act of another
bequest	gift of personal property by will
breach	failure (without legal justification) to perform when performance is due

brief	written argument of counsel concerning one or more legal issues in a case, sometimes called a memorandum of law
capacity	having legal authority or mental ability; being of sound mind
caption	that part of a pleading that states the name of the court, the name of the parties, the case number assigned, and the name of the pleading
cause of action	fact(s) giving rise to a legal remedy
chattel	personal property
choate	perfected; complete
chose in action	a personal right not yet reduced to judgment
civil code	collection of laws or statutes relating to private rights or remedies
civil law	laws that relate to private rights and remedies, distinguished from criminal law
CLA	abbreviation for Certified Legal Assistant, a professional designation earned through and awarded by the National Association of Legal Assistants (NALA) to those legal assistants who successfully complete an extensive written examination of their general skills and their specific knowledge of substantive legal rules and procedure (use either CLA or CP as prescribed by NALA)
Code Civil	law of the State of Louisiana consisting of a collection of statutes and based upon the Napoleonic Code, distinguished from common law
code	collection of laws or statutes

codicil

an addition or change to an original will

common law

law based upon custom, usage, and judicial decision, distinguished from statutory law

community property

property owned in common by husband and wife, each owning an undivided one-half interest as a result of their marital status

commutation

substitution of a lesser punishment for a greater one

condemnation

the process of taking private property for public use under a government's right of eminent domain

consideration

the lawful price, motive, cause, impelling influence, or inducement for a contract

contract

agreement between competent parties, supported by consideration, to do or to refrain from doing some lawful act

conversion

wrongful taking of personal property with intent to deprive its owner of it permanently

copyright

a right to reap the financial benefits of literary property as this term is defined under federal copyright laws

covenant

agreement or promise, often restricting the use of real estate

CP

abbreviation for Certified Paralegal, a professional designation earned through and awarded by the National Association of Legal Assistants to those legal assistants who successfully complete an extensive written examination of their general skills and their specific knowledge of substantive legal rules and procedure (use either CLA or CP as prescribed by NALA)

creditor

one to whom a debt or obligation is owed

criminal law

laws that control standards of conduct and that prescribe the punishments for disobedience

debenture

bond given as evidence of corporate debt

decree

the final order of an equity court

defamation

that which holds one up to contempt or ridicule; that which injures one's reputation

deponent

one who gives a deposition

deposition

sworn testimony given by question and answer in a non-courtroom setting, which is recorded and transcribed by a court reporter

devise

gift of real property by will

discharge

to release, liberate, annul, disencumber, dismiss

duress

unlawful constraint exercised upon a person, forcing her to do an act that she would not have done otherwise

enjoin

to prevent or forbid by injunction

equity

justice administered by principles of fairness, distinguished from strict rules of law

escheat

reversion of property to the state when there are no heirs to inherit the property at a person's death

estop	to stop, bar, prevent
estoppel	doctrine under which a person's acts or failure to act prevents her from seeking legal relief, although she would have been entitled to relief otherwise
eviction	to recover real estate (from a tenant) by legal process; to force out or remove from real property
evidentiary	constituting evidence or proof, having the quality of evidence
exemptions	immunity from a general burden, tax, or charge; in bankruptcy or in judgment executions, that portion of the debtor's property that cannot be liquidated and applied to her debts
felony	a crime for which the maximum possible punishment is death or imprisonment for one year or more in a penitentiary
fraud	any artifice used by one person to deceive another
general denial	a pleading in the form of an answer, which denies allegations made by the opposing party but which contains no affirmative defenses
grantee	one to whom real estate is conveyed; the buyer of real estate
grantor	one who conveys real estate; the seller of real estate
guarantor	one who agrees to undertake the (financial) obligation of another
guaranty	agreement to undertake the (financial) obligation of another

guardian	one charged with responsibility to manage the personal matters of another who is incompetent because of age, understanding, or lack of self-control
guardian ad litem	person appointed by a court to look after the interests of a child or incompetent during the pendency of a litigation
inchoate	unfinished, incomplete
indemnify	to secure against loss or damage
indictment	written accusation issued by a grand jury against a defendant in criminal law
indorsement	act of a payee, drawee, accommodation indorser, or holder of a bill, note, check, or other negotiable instrument, in writing his or her name upon the back of the instrument to assign or transfer the negotiable instrument to another
infant	one who has not reached the age of majority; a minor
information	written accusation issued by a prosecutor against a defendant in criminal law
injunction	an order issued by a court of equity, requiring a person to do or not to do a specific act
insolvent	condition of a person or entity that exists when total liabilities exceed total assets
interlocutory	provisional, interim, not final
interrogatories	series of formal, written questions addressed to a party for discovery purposes

intestate	without a will, one who dies without a will
judgment	final order of a court of law, based upon a jury verdict or upon findings of fact by the court
jurat	clause of a notary public or authorized officer attesting that a statement or document was sworn to by a specific person on a specific date
jurisdiction	power conferred on a court to hear a particular case and to render a final decision on the merits
jurisprudence	science of law; system of law
laches	a doctrine by which equitable relief is denied to one who has waited too long to seek relief
legal assistant	a distinguishable group of persons who assist attorneys in delivering legal services (within this occupational category, some individuals are known as paralegals); through formal education, training, and experience, legal assistants have knowledge and expertise regarding the legal system and substantive and procedural law that qualify them to do work of a legal nature under the supervision of an attorney
lessee	one who possesses or uses the property of another; tenant
lessor	a title holder of property who contracts for its possession or use by another; landlord
liable	legally responsible
libel	written defamation

lien	a charge, security, or encumbrance on property
liquidated	property or claim that has been converted to its cash equivalent
litigation	contest in a court of law for the purpose of enforcing a right or seeking a remedy
magistrate	court officer with limited judicial authority; a public officer
malfeasance	evil doing; performance of an act with bad intent
malpractice	professional negligence or misconduct
mediation	arrangement to attempt settlement of a dispute by using a neutral party as the referee; unlike an arbitrator, a mediator does not issue a binding decision
memorandum of law	brief of law submitted to a court by the attorney for a party
memorandum opinion	very short opinion of a court
merger	absorption of one thing or right into another
metes and bounds	a method of describing real estate, using boundary lines with terminal points and angles
minor	person who is not an adult; child
misdemeanor	a criminal offense for which the maximum possible punishment is a fine or incarceration for a period less than one year
misfeasance	improper performance of an otherwise lawful act

mitigation	duty of parties to minimize damages after an injury is sustained or a breach occurs
mortgage	conditional conveyance of an interest in real estate, usually as security for a debt
mortgagee	one who receives a mortgage, usually a lender
mortgagor	an owner of real estate who gives a mortgage
motion	application (not a pleading) or request made to a court to obtain an interim ruling or order
motion in limine	application requesting a court to rule in advance that specific, unfairly prejudicial information will not be mentioned during trial
negligence	failure to use the care that a reasonable and prudent person would use in similar circumstances
notary public	public officer who administers oaths, attests and certifies documents, and takes acknowledgments
novation	substitution of a new contract, debt, or obligation for an existing one between the same or different parties
nuncupative	oral; not written
oath	solemn pledge attesting to the truth of a statement
offer	a promise; a commitment to do or to refrain from doing some specific act
offeree	one to whom an offer is made

offeror	one who makes an offer
option	a right supported by consideration to purchase property at an agreed price within a specified time
order	mandate, command, or direction authoritatively given; mandate of a court
ordinance	legislative enactment (law enacted) by a local government such as a county or a city
parol evidence	oral proof of contract terms that are not contained within the written contract document
parole	release from imprisonment upon specific conditions related to conduct or good behavior
patent	inventor's right to exclude others from making, using, or selling the invention for 17 years
paternity	relationship of a father to a child
payee	one to whom payment is made
payor	one who makes payment
pecuniary	monetary; relating to money
perjury	false testimony given under oath
pleading	in federal court, complaint, answer to complaint, and reply to cross-claim (no other pleadings are allowed)
power of attorney	an instrument authorizing one to act as agent or attorney-in-fact for another as to those matters listed in the instrument

precedent	holding of a case which guides the decisions in future cases involving similar facts and similar legal issues
privileged communications	statements made by persons within specific, protected relationships for evidentiary purposes (husband–wife, attorney–client, priest–parishioner, and so forth)
probable cause	justification to believe that a crime was committed and that the accused is the person who committed it
probation	a sentence that releases a convicted person into the community under the supervision of a probation officer
promissory estoppel	a doctrine which prevents a party to a contract from denying that consideration was given for the contract
promissory note	a written promise to pay a specific sum of money at a future time
proximate cause	the last (negligent) act that leads to injury; legal cause
proxy	an instrument authorizing one to cast the votes of another at a corporate meeting
punitive damages	damages awarded over and above the amount of losses, which are awarded as punishment of the wrongdoer
quash	suppress, stop, cease, abate
quiet title action	action to determine clear title to real estate
quitclaim deed	deed without warranty, which passes only that title that the grantor has

recidivist	repeat offender
release	discharge of one party's obligation to another
replevin	action to recover possession of personal property
rescission	an equitable remedy which invalidates a contract on the basis of mutual mistake, fraud, impossibility, and so forth
restitution	restoration of a thing to its rightful owner; a measure of damages according to the defendant's gains rather than the plaintiff's losses
service of process	delivery of a writ, summons, subpoena to the person named therein
settlor	one who creates a trust, trustor
slander	spoken defamation
specific performance	equitable remedy in contract law that requires the breaching party to perform according to the specific terms of the contract
statute	legislative enactment (law enacted) by Congress or a state legislature
statute of limitations	statute that limits the time within which a cause of action may be filed
stipulation	agreement between parties to a lawsuit concerning matters related to the trial
subpoena	a writ commanding the named person to appear at a specific time and place
subpoena duces tecum	a writ commanding the named person to appear at a specific time and place and

	to bring specific records or documents with her
summons	document served upon a defendant to notify her that suit has been filed against her and directing her to answer or to otherwise appear in the case by a specific date
survey	process by which a tract of land is measured and its contents determined, with a map to scale created for it
temporary restraining order	an emergency injunctive remedy (order) of short duration to require or to forbid an act until a hearing can be held
testator, testatrix	man who creates and executes a will; woman who creates and executes a will
testimonium clause	the clause of an instrument that begins "In witness whereof, . . ."
tickler system	reminder system used in law offices to supplement diaries and calendars in the overall docket control system
tort	a civil wrong such as negligence or trespass, as distinguished from a criminal offense (the same conduct may result in both tort liability and criminal liability)
trust account	account where client funds are kept separate from attorney funds
unconscionable	grossly unfair, unscrupulous, terms or conduct that shocks the conscience
usury	the excess over the lawful interest rate
vendee	the purchaser or buyer of property

vendor	the seller of property
venue	the location where an action is tried
verdict	finding(s) of fact by a jury in a civil or criminal trial
verification	confirmation of accuracy; sworn oath by an authorized person that certain statements are true to the best of his or her knowledge and belief
void	having no legal force or effect
voidable	that which is capable of being declared void but which is valid until such declaration is made
warranty	a promise to defend the truth of a fact
warranty deed	a deed conveying land which guarantees that the title is free of defects to marketability
with prejudice	a declaration (usually in connection with an order of dismissal) that ends the right to further relief; it prevents either party from filing future complaints based on the same claim or cause of action
without prejudice	a declaration (usually in connection with an order of dismissal) which preserves any rights or privileges that a party may have to file a future complaint based upon the same claim or cause of action
witness	one who has personal knowledge about facts related to a case; one who can testify about what she has seen, heard, or otherwise observed
writ of execution	order of a court after judgment commanding a court officer to seize property in satisfaction of the judgment

Legal Terminology Self-Test

Allow an uninterrupted 30-minute period to answer all questions. At the end of 30 minutes, check your answers against those in the Answer Key Section at the back of this Review Manual. Deduct two points for each incorrect answer (100 total possible points). Unanswered questions are counted as incorrect answers. Follow directions carefully and observe the time limit precisely to provide an accurate self-assessment.

Choose the most correct answer to the following questions unless you are instructed to do otherwise.

1.   True or False.   Conversion refers to the wrongful taking of personal property with the intent to deprive its owner of it permanently.

2.   True or False.   That which increases the size or value of property is called an accession.

3.   True or False.   *Res gestae* refers to a child in gestation for purposes of applying the Rule Against Perpetuities.

4.   True or False.   A verification is a sworn statement of the truth of the facts stated in an instrument, document, or pleading.

For the next group of questions, match each term in the first column with the word or phrase in the second column that most accurately defines it.

5.   _____ *secundum*   a.   converted to cash

6.   _____ liquidated   b.   a legal fiction

7.   _____ *corpus juris*   c.   second series

8.   _____ *jus ad rem*   d.   termination before completion

9.   _____ laches   e.   according to

10. _____ constructive trust   f.   unreasonable delay in
                                          asserting a right

11.	_____ rescission	g.	trustor
12.	_____ settlor	h.	body of law
13.	_____ ancillary	i.	jurisdiction over a thing
14.	_____ *respondeat superior*	j.	the right to a thing
		k.	auxiliary, in aid of
		l.	employer's liability for employee

15. That portion of a pleading which requests relief against the opposing party or parties is called the:

    a. *habendum* clause
    b. *ad litem* clause
    c. *ad damnum* clause
    d. *ad respondendum* clause

16. One with authority to act for another is a(n):

    a. agency
    b. attorney in fact
    c. principal
    d. all of the above
    e. none of the above

17. When a person dies without surviving heirs and without a will, the state may become the owner of the estate property by:

    a. reversion
    b. intestacy
    c. escheat
    d. none of the above

18. Disparaging statements that are published in *The New York Times* about another person may constitute:

    a. defamation
    b. slander
    c. liable
    d. libel

19.   An order entered by a court without a hearing and with only one party represented is:

   a.   *ex parte*
   b.   *ex officio*
   c.   *ex delicto*
   d.   *ex necessutate legus*

20.   True or False.   A supplemental provision for a will may be annexed by an addendum.

21.   True or False.   Acts performed outside the scope of authority of a public official are *ultra jure*.

22.   True or False.   Mediation is a type of non-judicial dispute resolution that is binding upon the parties.

23.   True or False.   If a court enters an order *sua sponte*, this indicates that the motion of counsel is granted immediately after it is made during a hearing or a trial.

24.   An attorney involved in a case *ab initio* is one who was involved:

   a.   at the beginning of the case but is not involved now.
   b.   from the beginning of the case and continues now.
   c.   at that point in the case when litigation was initiated.
   d.   none of the above.

25.   Knowledge, sometimes known as "guilty knowledge," is:

   a.   carnal knowledge
   b.   *mens rea*
   c.   scienter
   d.   none of the above

26.   A contract that is cancelled, as if it had never occurred, is said to have been:

   a.   vacated
   b.   rescinded
   c.   lapsed
   d.   abandoned

27. Once a claim between parties has been decided on its merits, it may not be re-litigated between the same parties because of the doctrine of:

    a. *res gestae*
    b. *res ipsa loquitur*
    c. *res litigium*
    d. *res judicata*

28. A court order directed to a public official, commanding her to do that which her office requires her to do, is called a(n):

    a. *fiat*
    b. *mandamus*
    c. *quo warranto*
    d. any one of the above
    e. none of the above

29. An order commanding a person to appear and to testify in a legal action:

    a. *subpoena*
    b. *subpoena duces tecum*
    c. *subpoena sub testimonium*
    d. summons

30. True or False.   *Nudum pactum* is a promise enforceable by law.

31. True or False.   An oral contract to purchase real estate is an example of a contract that is voidable.

32. True or False.   *Pendente lite* refers to the jurisdiction acquired by a court over property involved in an action until a final judgment is entered.

33. True or False.   *Ad valorem* refers to a type of tax.

For the next group of questions, match each term in the first column with the word or phrase in the second column which most accurately defines it.

34. _____ *et vir*   a.   and husband

35. _____ *non obstante verdicto*   b.   for the sake of argument

36. _____ *a fortiori*   c.   with stronger reason

37. _____ *jus tertii*   d.   notwithstanding the verdict

38. _____ *a priori*   e.   the right of a third party

                                  f.   and wife

                                  g.   from the cause to the effect

39. The temporary relinquishment of control over one's property to another is called a(n):

   a.   assignment
   b.   bailment
   c.   accession
   d.   none of the above

40. When a testatrix includes a provision in her will to give $1,000 to each of her nieces and nephews and then pays $1,000 to each of them before she dies, this act is called an:

   a.   abatement
   b.   ademption
   c.   accrual
   d.   accretion

For the following group of questions, supply the most precise word or phrase for each of the definitions listed.

41. _____   bond/note given as evidence of corporate debt

42. _____   performed without charge

43. _____   tending to prove or disprove a fact in issue

44. _____   bond accompanying an order of stay

45. _____   testamentary conveyance of real property

46. _____   a collection of legislative enactments

47. _____   a transfer of legal rights to another

48. _____   internal rules adopted by a corporation

49. _____   averment

50. _____   habitual criminal

AMERICAN LEGAL SYSTEM (GENERAL LAW)

Our capacity for justice makes democracy possible; it is our inclination to injustice that makes democracy necessary.

—Reinhold Niebuhr

All applicants are required to take the General Law subsection of the CLA/CP® certifying examination. This chapter highlights and summarizes general legal history, sources, structure, terminology, principles, and concepts, with special emphasis on the American legal system.

Every legal assistant must be able to articulate the American legal structure and the general legal principles that have evolved, and that continue to evolve, within it. The concepts reviewed in this chapter—and those tested on the certifying examination—provide the foundation for every legal practice area that exists, no matter how specialized it is. Advocating the importance of these concepts to legal assistants who are preparing for the CLA/CP® examination may be similar to preaching to the choir; nevertheless, it is difficult to imagine that their importance could be overstated.

Law Defined

There are many definitions of the word *law* within the context of the practice of law, not to mention the system that is served by law practitioners. *Black's Law Dictionary* devotes an entire page to defining the word. Each definition provides a slightly different perspective or nuance, but all of them seem to boil down to this:

> *Law is a system of enforceable rules adopted by a controlling body to govern the conduct of a society.*

Every society or group of people—from the smallest family unit to the largest nation—lives by rules. Because an ordered society cannot exist (not yet, at least) if everyone in the society makes his or her own rules, the rules or laws must emanate from a controlling body. The controlling body might include the parents in a family unit or a dictator of nation. Finally, to ensure their enforceability, rules generally impose sanctions upon those who disobey, which can range from denial of a privilege to capital punishment.

The above definition can be applied to any economic, social, or political unit in the world, including the United States. The characteristic of American law, which distinguishes it from the law of other nations, is the structure of its controlling body—a government of the people, by the people, and for the people. The structure of our democratic republic was unique at its inception, as was the legal system fashioned to meet its needs.

One could devote a lifetime to memorizing the multitude of legal rules that have evolved within the American legal system. It is a poor member of that legal community, however, who acquires only a technical knowledge of the rules. Both technical knowledge and historical understanding are crucial to comprehend the framework of the legal system.

Historical Background

To understand how and why the American legal system has developed the way that has (and is structured the way that it is), we have to look further back in history than the adoption of the U.S. Constitution and even further back than the Revolutionary War. We have to look back to the colonists who settled in America, to the legal systems from which they came, and to the legal philosophies they brought with them.

The English Influence   Although North American colonists came from several different European countries, the vast majority of them came from England at a time when the king and the Church of England had comprised the controlling body of English law for centuries. England's court system reflected these two controlling forces.

Only specific types of legal actions were authorized to resolve disputes among English commoners. They were heard by the king's court, which became known as the ***king's court of common pleas*** or, stated more generally, the law court. The forms of action depended on the issuance of writs and were very technical. Litigants frequently lost cases because of noncompliance with a technical rule. The rigidity of law court actions and their perceived unfairness eventually prompted the king to establish an additional court, the ***Court of Chancery***. This court handled cases for which the law court could not provide relief, that is, when the equities of the case indicated that some type of relief should be granted. Staffed by high-ranking clergy, the idea was that the Court of Chancery could decide cases based on principles of fairness rather than on technical rules.

Parliament had been established as an advisory body to the king, but it had no power to make laws. (The shift of power from the king to Parliament did not occur until long after the Revolutionary War.) The ranks of the king's army and navy were maintained in high numbers through a hated conscription (compulsory draft), which allowed Great Britain to establish colonies in many parts of the world, including in America.

America was not a land of milk and honey in its earliest days. Survival was grueling, and many colonists died. Once colonies initially were founded, only the most adventurous or the most desperate came voluntarily. The rest, primarily political radicals and social misfits, arrived at the point of a sword. Whether they came through banishment or through flight, early colonists considered themselves British subjects; and many dreamed of going home one day.

Although the king generally ignored them, the colonies endured. Because of the problems that caused them to leave England in the first place, colonists persisted in their mistrust of military force. They relied instead on voluntary militia for protection. They mistrusted lawyers and judges even more than they mistrusted the military. The laws they established were of English common law origin, but did not follow English law precisely. The colonists retained those parts of England's common law that suited their needs, modified other parts as they believed necessary (or as they could remember them), and ignored the rest. They retained both the law court and the equity court (originally the Court of Chancery). A law library, if it existed at all, consisted only of *Blackstone's Commentaries* brought from England. This four-volume set fit easily into a lawyer's saddlebags as he traveled from town to town. More often, there was no *Blackstone's*; and even if a set had been available, few would have been able to read it.

The state of American law continued in this way as the colonies began to flourish. The British-Americans cultivated more land, grew more crops, and prospered. Some even were able to educate their sons in England, and the king finally took notice. The writings of John Locke on natural law (and other legal philosophers) were read and debated by the educated, while the king looked more and more to the colonies for commodities (such as lumber) and tax revenues.

Having begun as radicals and misfits and having become self-sufficient in their years of relative isolation, it should have come as no surprise when the British-Americans requested—and then demanded—to be represented in Parliament, the king's advisory body. Their demands were dismissed summarily. The hated British army appeared in increasing numbers, colonists were required to board the soldiers in their homes, taxes continued to escalate, and the Revolutionary War erupted.

From the end of the Revolutionary War until the Constitutional Convention in 1787, the American government operated under the ***Articles of Confederation***. Each state elected delegates to Congress, who, in turn, elected a president from their own ranks. This system was ineffective. There was no enforcement power for any of Congress's decisions, and there was no money to support an army or to provide the needs of government. The U.S. Constitution subsequently replaced the Articles of Confederation.

Both the Declaration of Independence and the U.S. Constitution were influenced strongly by John Locke's natural rights theories. Americans were accustomed to tinkering with the law to make it fit their situation, so it was natural that they would debate and modify Locke's theories as they thought necessary "to form a more perfect government."

The American System   The framers of the Constitution were divided concerning how much power should be given to a federal government, but they finally agreed that each state should retain its sovereign status even if a federal government were established. They did not want any single part of the federal government to hold too much power, so they divided it into three branches (legislative, executive, and judicial) to provide a system of checks and balances. Congress was created with two houses to ensure fair representation of the states.

The system created by the Constitution was unique. It had never been tried before anywhere in the world, and many believed it could not work. When it became clear that some states were reluctant to ratify the Constitution's draft, a group of 10 amendments (the Bill of Rights) was added to list specifically what an individual's rights were. Thomas Jefferson was the most vocal of those who thought it was unnecessary to write individual rights into the Constitution. He and others believed these rights to be so obvious that surely they never could be questioned by anyone. Nevertheless, by adding the Bill of Rights—as redundant as it was thought to be—the Constitution was ratified. It is ironic that the Bill of Rights, which was only an afterthought, has become the soul of constitutional law in protecting individual freedoms.

Understanding legal history gives life and fire to the Constitution. Legal history helps to understand why the Boston Tea Party happened, why the South believed in the justness of its secession from the Union, why we accept civil disobedience as a valid form of protest, and why generation after generation grows up committed to Locke's belief that each of us has basic rights given by God that no one can take away. Legal history also helps to understand why lawyers and judges always have been mistrusted by the public in general; but when a specific individual's rights are threatened, a lawyer is the first person he contacts.

Philosophies of American Law   A legal philosophy is a school of thought (method of reasoning) concerning the purpose of law and how it should operate. Several different legal philosophies are intertwined in the American legal system. Although they evolved at various points in history, they continue to impact the way in which our laws operate. The most prominent legal philosophies are summarized here.

Natural law, sometimes called the natural rights theory, is a philosophy that emphasizes the individual's right to make personal choices as long as those choices do not interfere with another's right to make personal choices. The freedom of choice is a birthright; it is not conferred by anyone and it cannot be taken away by anyone—not even if everyone else in the world believes the choice is stupid. Thomas Jefferson stated the principles of natural law in the Declaration of Independence: *We hold these truths to be self-evident, that all men are created equal; that they are endowed by their creator with certain inalienable rights; that among these are life, liberty, and the pursuit of happiness.*

Legal positivism is a philosophy that emphasizes the institutional rule of law and that distinguishes law from morality. If the process used to adopt a particular rule is just (fair) and if no other rule exists to carve out an exception to that rule, the legal positivist adheres to the rule—even if it leads to a questionable result in a particular case. Legal positivism is reflected in the maxim: *Hard cases make bad law.*

Sociological jurisprudence is a philosophy that promotes society's values as the measuring stick for right and wrong; it evaluates a legal rule by looking at its social effect. If the effect is bad, the legal sociologist favors getting rid of the rule, changing it, or simply ignoring it this time. Law is seen as a tool for *social engineering*. A drawback of sociological jurisprudence—recognized even by its supporters—is that the legal system moves too slowly to respond to needed social change. Roscoe Pound was a strong advocate of sociological jurisprudence.

Legal realism is a philosophy that determines what reasonable people would do in a given situation and then sanctions that conduct. Legal realists treat legal rules as little more than rebuttable presumptions. They look at the underlying policy of the rule and measure conduct according to the policy. This philosophy often gives great weight to economic analysis (a "Brandeis brief," for example) in showing the effect of a legal rule. In short, legal realism took social engineering one step farther, resulting in the doctrine of *economic waste* and similar concepts. Oliver Wendell Holmes and Karl Llewellyn led the cause for legal realism.

Different methods of legal reasoning can (but do not always) lead to different results. Therefore, we look not only at the controlling rule of law stated in a judicial opinion (the holding), but also at the reasoning (rationale) used to support the stated rule. Strains of each of the above philosophies are evident in current judicial opinions, although other philosophies seem to be operating as well.

Legal history, legal structure, and legal philosophies are the dynamics that have brought the American legal system to its present state. Against that background, increasingly complex legal rules have evolved to serve an increasingly complex society.

Classifications of Law

All legal rules can be grouped into broad categories according to their type (classification). A rule's classification tells us the situations to which it applies and how it applies in relation to other rules. For example, all law is classified as either criminal or civil.

This section defines the basic classifications of law and reviews their relationship to each other. The following chart may help to visualize where the classifications fit in relation to each other.

CLASSIFICATIONS OF LAW

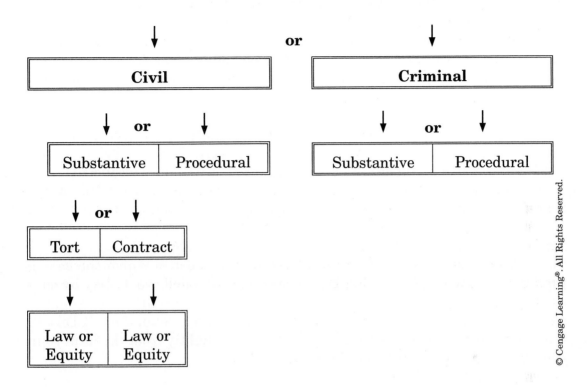

Substantive or Procedural Law   All law is either substantive or procedural. A substantive law is a legal rule that creates or defines rights and duties. For every right, there is a corresponding duty. For example, if Bob owns land, he has a right to its exclusive possession. Bob's right imposes a duty on the rest of the world not to enter the land without his permission.

Examples of substantive law are the constitutional provision establishing Congress, an administrative regulation requiring the registration of publicly traded securities, a state statute limiting the speed of vehicles, or a court opinion interpreting the terms of a contract or further refining common law rules of negligence.

Every substantive law can be classified as either public or private, either criminal or civil (*discussed below*).

Procedural law, sometimes called ***adjective law***, complements substantive law by providing the mechanisms to enforce substantive rights and duties. As it relates to courts and administrative agencies, procedural law typically includes the method for initiating an action, serving summons, making motions, conducting discovery and trial, and appealing the final judgment. As it relates to a legislative body, procedural law includes the steps required to enact a law or a rule (notice, hearing, quorum, majority vote) and the way in which those steps must be performed. Every rule of substantive law can be associated with one or more groups of procedural rules to provide a way of enforcement.

Examples of procedural law are the Federal Rules of Civil Procedure, the Federal Rules of Criminal Procedure, the Federal Rules of Evidence, and the Federal Rules of Appellate Procedure, together with any local court rules adopted for use in connection with them. States also adopt rules of procedure that are similar to the federal rules, sometimes in a separate set of rules and sometimes incorporated with that state's statutes.

A local court rule is a rule adopted by the court in which the case is pending; it supplements the procedural rules mentioned above. It may be more easily conceptualized as a forum court rule. Every federal court and every state court has its own set of local court rules. The local court rules of the U.S. District Court for the Southern District of Iowa may vary slightly from the local court rules of the Northern District of Iowa, for example.

The purpose of local court rules is to augment or to fill the gaps left by the procedural rules mentioned in the preceding paragraph. For example, the Federal Rules of Civil Procedure state that every case is commenced by filing a complaint. Local court rules cannot change the rule of procedure by requiring that cases be commenced by filing an application (instead of a complaint), but local court rules can require that all complaints be filed with specific margins, be filed on letter-size paper, be double-spaced, and so forth.

A.   Public or Private Law   All substantive law is either public or private. Public law consists of rules that involve the relationship of government to society as a whole. Constitutional law, administrative law, and criminal law are examples of public law.

Private law consists of rules that involve the relationship of private individuals to each other. Most civil law is private law, including tort law, contract law, and most property law.

Criminal Law   All substantive law is either criminal or civil. Criminal law consists of rules designed to protect society by providing minimum standards of conduct that must be observed by each of its members. Penal sanctions (punishments) are imposed on those who fail to observe the minimum standards. Crimes generally are defined by statute (federal or state) or by ordinance (local), although common law crimes are still recognized in the District of Columbia. Crimes are classified further as treason, felonies, or misdemeanors.

Treason is an attempt to overthrow the government as defined by Article III, § 3 of the U.S. Constitution.

A *felony* is a crime for which the maximum *possible* punishment is either death or imprisonment for one year or more. The classification focuses on the maximum punishment that *could* be imposed, not on the punishment that is actually imposed.

A *misdemeanor* is a crime for which the maximum *possible* punishment is either a fine or imprisonment for less than one year. A court may impose a lesser punishment in a particular situation.

Civil Law   Civil law consists of those legal rules that focus on the rights and duties of individuals in relation to each other. In contrast to criminal law, which imposes penal sanctions, civil law sanctions are remedial; they grant a remedy (provide relief) to enforce a right.

American civil law is based upon common law principles and traditionally is classified according to (1) the basis of the right or duty to be enforced, whether in tort or in contract; and (2) the type of remedy sought, whether legal or equitable.

A *tort* is a wrongful act (other than breach of a contract) for which the law provides a remedy, typically in the form of monetary damages. Torts are based upon rules of conduct to which each member of society is expected to conform. Examples of torts include assault, battery, conversion, false imprisonment, negligence, and trespass. A tort may be *intentional* (assault, battery, conversion, trespass); *unintentional* (negligence); or based upon *strict liability* (defective product sold to public).

Conduct that creates civil liability in tort may also create criminal liability, depending on the criminal statutes of a particular location. For instance, if Jane punches Ruth in the nose, Ruth could file a civil action against her for the tort of battery. The standard of proof would be *a preponderance of the evidence* (more likely than not that Jane committed the act). Based on the same incident, the state could prosecute Jane for the crime of assault. The standard of proof would be *beyond a reasonable doubt* (very nearly certain that Jane committed the act).

In this situation, the result in the criminal case has no effect whatsoever on the result in the civil case. Neither does the result in the civil case have any effect on the result in the criminal case. They are completely separate. Jane could be found guilty in the criminal case, even though she is held not liable in the civil case.

A ***contract*** is an enforceable agreement between two or more parties (comprised of an offer, an acceptance, and consideration that are not subject to any defenses). The contract is the agreement, not the paper on which the agreement is written. When any party does not perform as agreed, a breach occurs; and the nonbreaching party is entitled to the benefit of her bargain. Her remedy may take the form of damages or equitable relief that can include specific performance if the proper circumstances exist.

A contract can be oral or written; it can be express (specifically stated) or implied in fact or in law from conduct of the parties. *Refer to the chapter on Contracts (Chapter 9) for a more thorough review.*

The remedies available in a civil suit are either legal or equitable. A ***remedy at law*** typically seeks damages (money). If money cannot compensate the plaintiff adequately for her losses, she may be able to obtain equitable relief. A ***remedy in equity*** typically requests some specific act, such as an injunction or the rescission, reformation, or specific performance of a contract. *(Legal and equitable remedies are discussed in greater detail below.)*

Institutional Sources of Law

Under a democratic form of government, the people are the sovereign. They are the source of all power, including the power to establish law, which they exercise through elected representatives.

There are at least 51 legal systems operating simultaneously in the United States: the federal legal system and the legal systems of 50 sovereign states. Within this setting, the institutional sources of substantive law are constitutions, statutes enacted by legislative bodies, rules and regulations adopted by administrative agencies, and the common law.

Constitution   A constitution is a written document that provides the fundamental source of law within a particular geographic region. It establishes the basic principles and the structure under which a government must operate.

The U.S. Constitution is the written agreement that unites the states as one cohesive nation. It incorporates the doctrine of ***separation of powers*** by dividing all governmental power among three branches (legislative, executive, and judicial), which allows each branch to serve as a check and balance on the other two.

Each state has its own constitution, generally with provisions similar to those of the federal Constitution.

Statutes   The second institutional source of substantive law is statutory law. A statute is a written law enacted either by Congress or by a state legislature. Both federal and state statutes must comply with the federal Constitution. In addition, the statutes of each state must comply with that state's constitution. Both state and federal statutes are subject to review and interpretation by courts.

Since the federal government is one of limited powers, federal statutes may be enacted only in those areas specifically delegated to Congress in the U.S. Constitution. State statutes, on the other hand, may be enacted in nearly any area except those that are prohibited to states by the U.S. Constitution (*see below*).

Statutes are collected and published in a code. Federal statutes are published selectively in the United States Code. Each state has its own code of state statutes.

A.   Administrative Rules and Regulations   Legislatures create administrative agencies, boards, and commissions to assist them when the legislature lacks expertise in an area that requires (1) special knowledge and (2) more supervision than the legislature can provide directly. An agency of this type is created by an ***enabling act,*** which authorizes the agency to exist and which lists the specific areas to be administered by it.

Administrative agencies have become so pervasive that they often are referred to as the *fourth branch of government*. Examples of administrative agencies are the Internal Revenue Service (IRS), the Immigration and Naturalization Service (INS), the Social Security Administration (SSA), the Securities and Exchange Commission (SEC), the Federal Communications Commission (FCC), the Equal Employment Opportunity Commission (EEOC), the Food and Drug Administration (FDA), and the Environmental Protection Agency (EPA). There are many, many others.

Subject to some limitations, a legislature may delegate a special form of legislative authority to the agency, which permits the agency to make rules and regulations to clarify or explain statutes within its authorized area of expertise.

This *rulemaking power* is an exercise of the agency's ***quasi-legislative*** function. Although they are not quite on the same level as statutes, administrative rules and regulations carry the same force of law as statutes.

In addition, an administrative agency has authority to investigate, to enforce, and to interpret its own rules and regulations. An administrative law judge or a hearing officer (neither of whom is required to be a lawyer by many administrative agencies) presides over hearings that are similar to trials. This is permitted as part of the agency's ***quasi-judicial*** function. If a violation is found to have occurred, the agency may impose civil sanctions. *No one can be incarcerated by an administrative agency.* When criminal action is warranted, the case is referred to the Justice Department (federal) or to the appropriate state attorney general or equivalent for prosecution.

All federal agencies must comply with the Administrative Procedure Act (APA) when exercising their rulemaking and decision-making functions. Both (1) the rules and regulations and (2) the decisions of an administrative agency are subject to review and interpretation by courts. Before judicial review is granted, however, the appellant or petitioner must demonstrate that he has exhausted all of his administrative remedies. This means that he must have utilized all of the procedures and remedies at the administrative level before he can seek judicial relief.

In general, judicial review of the acts of an administrative agency boils down to two questions: (1) Does the agency have the power to do what it did (based upon its enabling act)? and if it does, (2) Did the agency use the power fairly (due process)?

B. Uniform State Laws and Model Acts   Because each state has inherent power to enact statutes as it thinks appropriate, the statutes on a single topic can vary widely from state to state. If the topic is one of local interest only, the variations make little difference outside a particular state. With ever-increasing interstate activities by businesses and by citizens, however, inconsistent state laws became a significant obstacle by the turn of the century.

The ***National Conference of Commissioners on Uniform State Laws*** was organized in 1915 to resolve this problem. Each state, the District of Columbia, and Puerto Rico appoint at least one commissioner to this organization. The commissioners consider those areas of law requiring uniformity and draft model legislation in the form of *uniform codes, uniform acts*, or *uniform laws*; and they encourage their adoption by each of the states.

Each state legislature considers the uniform code or act in the same way that it considers any other proposed legislation. The legislature may adopt it, adopt it with modifications, adopt only part of it, or adopt none of it—as the legislature chooses. (If substantial changes are made, however, the purpose of a uniform law is destroyed.) If the uniform code or act is adopted, it becomes a part of the state's other statutes and is incorporated into the state code.

The National Conference of Commissioners has drafted more than 250 acts, including the Uniform Commercial Code, the Uniform Partnership Act, the Uniform Limited Partnership Act, the Uniform Fraudulent Conveyance Act, the Uniform Probate Code, and the Uniform Reciprocal Support Enforcement Act.

Other organizations also draft model acts, though not in the same volume as the National Conference. For example, the American Law Institute is responsible for the Model Penal Code. The American Bar Association drafted both the Model Business Corporation Act and the Revised Model Business Corporation Act.

Common Law   The third institutional source of substantive law is common law. In its most narrow sense, common law means the rule of law announced as the holding in a judicial opinion. (Judicial opinions sometimes are called ***case law***.)

In a broader sense, common law means the collection of legal rules extracted from judicial opinions in a particular area of law. For instance, there are common law rules of contract, common law rules of employment relationships, common law rules of negligence, and so forth. To the extent that the common law rules have not been replaced by statutes—which often restate the common law rules in statutory form—the common law rules still are used either alone or to supplement existing statutes. As the term is used in this sense, however, it applies to state law only. Federal law comes only from the federal Constitution, federal statutes, and rules and regulations of federal administrative agencies. The rule is well established since the ***Erie* doctrine** was announced: *There is no federal common law.*

In its broadest sense, common law refers to the judicial decision-making process, which is the foundation of the American legal system. Common law is based on the doctrine of *stare decisis*. ***Stare decisis*** is the *process* used by state court judges to analyze past cases to determine if any exist that had similar facts and similar legal issues as the present case (the one being decided now). If one or more such cases are found, the holding of the past case is ***precedent*** in the present case, which means that the present case must be decided in the same way.

Following precedent in judicial decision-making gives stability and certainty to the law. It allows people to predict the outcome of specific conduct or events, which, in turn, makes them better able to plan their lives. It provides order to a society.

Common law principles do not require judges to follow precedent slavishly or to wear blinders when they decide cases, however. Implicit in the concept of common law is its ability to reflect the mores of society as they exist at any given time. For instance, extramarital relationships are almost universally more acceptable in today's society than they were, say, 50 years ago. The common law should reflect that fact.

Judges are reluctant to overturn past decisions, because it injects an element of instability into the system. However, as technological developments and society's needs change over a long period of time, past decisions must be overruled occasionally. At the turn of the century, for example, industrial development was encouraged; and the courts generally took a *laissez-faire* approach to working conditions and disposal of industrial waste. This is not so today. Although many of the changes have resulted from legislation, a review of judicial opinions shows a stop-and-start change in judicial attitude, which resulted in some past cases being overruled.

Judicial application of common law principles is covered in the section on judicial decision making (*see below*).

Having reviewed the legal system and the institutional sources of law in general, the remaining sections provide a more detailed review of those areas of special concern to legal assistants, including principles of constitutional law and due process, court systems, judicial decision making, and alternative dispute resolution.

Constitutional Law

By its own declaration in Article VI, the U.S. Constitution is the supreme law of the land. The Constitution consists of seven articles and 27 amendments, and it serves three important functions in the legal system:

1. It limits the powers of the states.

2. It enumerates the powers granted to the federal government by the states.

3. It guarantees certain fundamental rights to the people of the United States.

Limitation of State Powers   Because each state is a sovereign, it
has inherent power to enact its own laws. The federal Constitution restricts
that power, however, by making state law subordinate to federal law under
the Supremacy Clause of Article VI. This means that when a state law directly
conflicts with a federal law on the same subject, federal law controls. This is
known as the doctrine of *federalism*.

In addition to the Supremacy Clause, other provisions of the Constitution
restrict state powers in specific areas. For example, states cannot form treaties
with foreign nations, cannot tax imports or exports, cannot coin money, and
cannot impair contractual obligations. If the federal government preempts a
field, such as post offices, no state or private person may enter the same field.
This means that a private person could establish an express parcel service, but
she could not establish a post office because of the *preemption* doctrine.

Aside from those areas covered by the doctrines of federalism and
preemption, a state has inherent and nearly unfettered power to regulate people and
activities within its borders. If a power has not been given specifically to the federal
government, that power is held by the state. For example, Congress has been granted
the specific power to regulate interstate commerce; but if the commerce is purely
*intra*state (wholly within state boundaries), Congress has no power to regulate it.

Each state holds a general *police power*, which allows it to regulate
in any area affecting the *general health, safety, and welfare* of its citizens. The
federal government has no similar power. A state can regulate such things as
marriage, divorce, abortion, probate, and most crimes as long as it does not
violate any constitutional provision in doing so. When a state law violates a
provision of the Constitution, the law may be stricken by the U.S. Supreme
Court in an appropriate appeal.

Enumerated Federal Powers   Unlike the states, the federal
government is one of limited powers. It has no inherent powers; it possesses
only those that have been delegated to it by the states. All other powers are
reserved to the states.

Article I of the Constitution establishes Congress (consisting of
the House of Representatives and the Senate) as the legislative branch of
government and lists the powers of Congress. For example, Congress is given the
power to impose taxes, to borrow money, to regulate interstate commerce and
commerce with foreign countries, to control bankruptcy laws, to issue currency,
to appropriate money, to punish the counterfeiting of money, to establish post
offices, to control patents and copyrights, to create inferior federal courts
(inferior to the Supreme Court), to declare war, to provide for national defense,

to serve as the legislature for District of Columbia, and to make all laws that are necessary and proper to carry out the powers of Congress. Congress exercises its powers by enacting federal statutes.

Article I forbids Congress from suspending the writ of *habeas corpus* except during rebellion or invasion. A ***writ of habeas corpus*** is an order to "deliver the body" of one held in custody; it typically is used to secure the release of a prisoner who is wrongfully held by authorities. Article I further prohibits Congress from passing any bill of attainder or any *ex post facto* law. A ***bill of attainder*** is a law directed against a specific person or against a specific group. An ***ex post facto law*** is one that defines conduct as a crime after the fact (after the act had been committed).

> A law which provides that no lawyer may serve as a member of Congress is a bill of attainder. It is directed at a specific group and is unconstitutional.
>
> A law passed on March 1 provides that any person who gains ten pounds or more between January 1 and March 1 of (the same year) shall be subject to a fine of not less than $100. This is an *ex post facto* law; to be subject to the fine, the weight gain must already have occurred by the time the law is passed. The law is unconstitutional.

As a check on the executive and judicial branches, Congress controls the purse strings of the nation. In addition, the House of Representatives has the power to impeach judicial and executive officers, and the Senate has the power to try all impeachments.

Article II vests executive power in the president, who appoints executive officers, including a cabinet, to assist with executive duties. In addition to enforcing federal laws, the president serves as commander-in-chief of the armed forces. The president has the power, with the advice and consent of the Senate, to make treaties with foreign nations; to appoint ambassadors; and to appoint judges to the Supreme Court. As a check on the legislative branch, the president has the power to veto acts of Congress. Congress, in turn, may override the veto by a two-thirds vote of both houses.

Article III grants judicial power to the U.S. Supreme Court and to such other, inferior federal courts as Congress may establish. Federal courts can hear only limited types of cases (*discussed below*).

The framers of the Constitution viewed the judiciary as the "least dangerous branch" of the three. The Supreme Court was given original jurisdiction in certain cases (*see below*) and was also given the power to review acts of the legislative and executive branches to ensure their compliance with the Constitution. Those acts that do not comply with the Constitution are invalidated by the Supreme Court.

In the landmark case of *Marbury v. Madison*, 5 U.S. 137 (1805), Chief Justice Marshall asserted the doctrine of ***judicial review*** in a situation in which the Court could have exercised original, concurrent jurisdiction. This decision permanently established the Supreme Court as the court of final review. Thus evolved the expression, "The Supreme Court is not the last because it is always right; it is always right because it is the last."

<u>Guarantee of Individual Rights</u>   In addition to limiting the power of states and enumerating the powers of the federal government, those fundamental rights that are guaranteed to the people are listed in the first 10 amendments to the Constitution, called the ***Bill of Rights***. In capsule form, these rights include the following:

1. Freedom of religion, speech, and press; the right to assemble; and the right to petition the government

2. Right to bear arms

3. No soldiers quartered in private homes in time of peace

4. No unreasonable searches or seizures

5. No double jeopardy or self-incrimination in criminal cases; due process of law; just compensation when private property is taken

6. Right of accused to speedy trial and to assistance of counsel

7. Right to a jury trial in civil cases over $20

8. No excessive bail or fines; no cruel or unusual punishment

9. Constitutional powers do not diminish rights retained by the people

10. States retain powers not delegated under the Constitution and not prohibited by it to the States.

The ***Fourteenth Amendment*** prohibits states from making or enforcing any laws that diminish the privileges and immunities of any citizen of the United States. It further requires states to provide ***due process*** of law and the ***equal protection*** of laws to all people within their respective jurisdictions. This Amendment is sometimes called the *Equal Protection Clause.*

In addition to these protections, the Supreme Court has declared a fundamental ***right of privacy***, which is guaranteed to all people. Privacy is not mentioned specifically in the Constitution or in the Bill of Rights; rather, the Supreme Court found it in the *penumbras* of the Constitution, as part of the Necessary and Proper Clause of Article I, § 8(18).

When faced with competing claims to fundamental rights (freedom of the press and privacy, for example), the Supreme Court balances (weighs) the rights and attempts to give effect to each.

Due Process

The due process clause of the Fifth Amendment provides that "no person shall be deprived of life, liberty, or property without due process of law" by the federal government. The Fourteenth Amendment provides: "nor shall any state deprive a person of life, liberty, or property without due process of law."

Due process of law means ***fundamental fairness***. The concept of fundamental fairness, however, can vary according to the type of right involved as well as according to the language and effect of a particular statute or rule. As a result, courts review due process claims on a case-by-case basis. Case law produces some common themes, which are discussed here.

Due process is not an issue unless state action is present. In this context, ***state action*** includes acts of either the federal or state government or any of its agents. If the government is not involved, there is no state action. When a statute or rule is adopted, state action clearly is present. When a sole proprietor of a private business adopts a rule, no state action is present unless the business has some governmental tie—a government contract or some type of governmental grant or subsidy, for example—which permits a court to find that state involvement, and therefore state action, exists.

Once state action is found, due process is classified as either substantive due process or procedural due process.

Substantive Due Process   Substantive due process requires fundamental fairness in the content of the statute or rule.

The content is fundamentally unfair if it *shocks the conscience* or if it is *unreasonable,* **arbitrary,** *or capricious.* For example, a statute limiting the number of children that any one woman could bear would be unconstitutional on substantive due process grounds.

The content of a statute is fundamentally unfair when it is overly broad. When faced with this type of statute, courts frequently quip that *"it paints with too broad a brush."* **Overbreadth** is a form of arbitrariness that occurs when the state has a legitimate purpose for the legislation, but the language of the statute is not sufficiently tailored to the purpose.

Suppose, for example, that a legislature has determined through investigative hearings that males are significantly more likely than females to drive after drinking. If, in response to the overwhelming statistics, the legislature were to pass a law granting driving privileges only to women, the statute would be overly broad and, therefore, unconstitutional on substantive due process grounds. The statute is overly broad because it restricts males who do not drink and drive as well as those who do. At the same time, it fails to restrict those females who drink and drive, which leaves a gap between the purpose and the means.

Finally, the content of a statute is fundamentally unfair when it is too vague. A vague statute leads to arbitrary enforcement and is objectionable on that basis. **Vagueness** occurs when a person of normal intelligence cannot tell from the statute's language what conduct is prohibited (or is required). For instance, if a legislature were to pass a statute prohibiting "undesirable elements" from seeking political office, the statute would be too vague and would be unconstitutional on substantive due process grounds. Similarly, a high school disciplinary rule would be too vague if it were to provide that "any student may be expelled if he or she is found to be a bad influence on fellow students." In either example, a person of ordinary intelligence could not tell what conduct causes one to be an undesirable element or a bad influence. The prohibited conduct could be anything that an enforcement official wants it to be.

Vagrancy ordinances of many cities have been repealed by legislative bodies or have been stricken by courts on vagueness grounds. The following language was typical among those that levied criminal penalties on persons who fit into any of its statutory categories:

rogues and vagabonds, or dissolute persons who go about begging, common gamblers, persons who use juggling or unlawful games or plays, common drunkards, common night walkers, thieves, pilferers, or pickpockets, traders in stolen property, lewd, wanton and lascivious persons, keepers of gambling places, common railers and brawlers, persons wandering or strolling from place to place without any lawful purpose, disorderly persons, persons neglecting all lawful business and habitually spending their time by frequenting houses of ill fame, gaming houses, or places where alcoholic beverages are sold or served, or persons able to work but habitually living upon the earnings of their wives or minor children.

Procedural Due Process

Procedural due process requires fundamental fairness in terms of (1) notice and (2) an opportunity to be heard.

Notice is fundamentally fair if a person is informed of the nature of the charges or claims against her. The *Miranda* warnings in criminal cases are based on procedural due process requirements. In certain situations, notice may also require that she be informed of the general factual basis for the charges and the time limit for defensive action. For example, a notice of criminal prosecution is insufficient if the charges are for "felonious criminal activity." Similarly, a notice of civil suit is insufficient if the complaint alleges "damages for tortious acts."

An opportunity to be heard generally means that a hearing of some type must be held so that the accused can defend herself if she wishes to do so. The fundamental fairness of the hearing varies according to the circumstances. For example, someone who is charged with murder or homicide is entitled to every procedural safeguard available, including assistance of counsel, trial by jury, and formal rules of evidence. One who is charged with jaywalking, by contrast, is entitled to a trial of some type, but generally is not entitled a full-blown jury trial or to the assistance of a public defender unless a conviction could result in incarceration.

Military personnel and students usually receive less in the way of a hearing than those who are charged for similar conduct in other arenas. However, this general rule can vary with the gravity of the offense. If a student were suspended from school for three days, for example, she may not be entitled to anything more than an informal hearing in the school principal's office; formal rules of evidence will not apply; and the hearing even may be held after the three-day suspension period has ended. If the same student were expelled for the balance of the school term, however, the hearing would have to be held either before expulsion takes effect or very shortly afterward. Otherwise, her right to an education could be impaired unfairly if, for example, the hearing did not occur for 30 days and if the basis for the expulsion were shown to be insufficient.

Regardless of the type of hearing required in a given situation, the hearing process must be fair. A hearing is not fair if the judge or hearing officer asks, "Do you have any more witnesses to present before I find you guilty?"

The rules of procedure, whatever they are, must treat both sides evenly. For example, an administrative rule is unconstitutional on its face if it permits the agency to cross-examine witnesses but does not permit the defendant or respondent to do the same.

Equally unfair is a rule that is applied unfairly. Assume that a rule states: "No motor vehicle operator's license may be suspended without a prior hearing." The rule itself may be fair; but if the practice is for the arresting officer to impound the license until the hearing date, the rule is unfair as applied.

The Judicial System

Although the legal assistant must be familiar with all aspects of the American legal system, the practice of law typically revolves around the judicial branch. The function of the judicial branch is to apply law to facts in resolving disputes between adversaries, which is accomplished through the trial and appellate processes.

Each legal system (federal and state) has its own judicial branch, which operates through a system of courts. A court is classified by the system in which it operates (either federal or state) and by the types of cases that it is authorized to hear. These classifications are part of a court's jurisdiction. ***Jurisdiction*** *is the power or authority of a court to hear a specific case.* Both subject matter jurisdiction and personal jurisdiction must exist before a court can decide the merits of a particular case.

Subject Matter Jurisdiction

Within the federal system, the U.S. Supreme Court is created by Article III of the Constitution. All other federal courts are created by federal statute. The highest court of a state system usually is created by state constitution, and all other state courts typically are created by state statute. Whether it is constitutional or statutory, the law that creates a court is the same law that defines its subject matter jurisdiction. ***Subject matter jurisdiction*** *relates to the type of case that a court is authorized to hear.*

If a court does not have subject matter jurisdiction, it lacks the power to decide the merits of the case. In that situation, any action taken by it is void; it has no effect whatsoever. Because it relates to a court's power to act, *subject matter jurisdiction never can be waived*. Moreover, it can be raised by anyone (including the judge) at any point in the litigation process, including the appeal.

Constitutions and statutes use special terms to confer jurisdiction. For example, a provision may state that a court has concurrent, original jurisdiction of certain types of cases and also has appellate jurisdiction of other types of cases. The terms help to understand how subject matter jurisdiction works.

Every court is either a court of limited jurisdiction or a court of general jurisdiction. No court can be both. ***Limited jurisdiction*** means that the court cannot hear every type of case presented to it; it can hear only those types of cases that are listed in its creating constitutional provision or statute. Because the federal government is one of limited powers, every federal court (including the U.S. Supreme Court) is a court of limited jurisdiction.

By contrast, ***general jurisdiction*** means that the court can hear any type of case presented to it unless exclusive jurisdiction has been granted to some other court for a particular type of case (*see below*). Every state has at least one court of general jurisdiction, sometimes called a district court or a superior court.

Every court is either a court of original jurisdiction or a court of appellate jurisdiction, but some courts are both. ***Original jurisdiction*** means that actions are commenced in this court for particular types of cases. A court of original jurisdiction is the trial court for those types of cases specified in its creating constitutional provision or statute.

Appellate jurisdiction means that the court is authorized to review decisions of an inferior court (either a trial court or a lower appellate court) in certain types of cases. A single court, however, may have original jurisdiction in one type of case and appellate jurisdiction in another type of case. Such a court wears two hats: it is a superior court when it exercises its appellate jurisdiction in one type of case, and it is an inferior court when it exercises its original jurisdiction in another type of case.

In relation to a particular type of case, a court is granted either exclusive jurisdiction or concurrent jurisdiction. ***Exclusive jurisdiction*** means that no other court has the power to hear this type of case—not even a court of general jurisdiction. For example, the federal courts have exclusive jurisdiction of all bankruptcy cases. In a state court system, exclusive, original jurisdiction of all probate cases typically is given to one court.

Concurrent jurisdiction means that more than one court is authorized to hear a specific type of case. This allows a plaintiff to choose between (or among) those courts having concurrent jurisdiction of the subject matter of her case. For example, a small claims court typically has concurrent, original jurisdiction of civil cases under a certain dollar amount, say, $1,500. A plaintiff with a civil claim of $1,000 has the option to file it in the small claims court or in any other state court having jurisdiction. At a minimum, her other options will include that state's court of general jurisdiction, which can hear any type of case except those for which exclusive jurisdiction has been granted to another court.

Personal Jurisdiction

A court must have both subject matter jurisdiction and personal jurisdiction (sometimes called *in personam* jurisdiction) before it can hear and decide the merits of a particular case. *Personal jurisdiction refers to the court's power or authority over the parties to the litigation.*

A court acquires personal jurisdiction over a plaintiff when he files his complaint or petition. Personal jurisdiction over a defendant usually can be acquired in one of several ways:

- Defendant's consent;
- Defendant's domicile in the same state where the action is filed; or
- Long-arm statutes (for out-of-state defendants).

To satisfy constitutional requirements, an out-of-state defendant must have *minimum contacts* with the forum state before any court of that state can exercise jurisdiction over him. Minimum contacts exist if the defendant has engaged in some voluntary act in relation to the forum state. Examples of voluntary acts are doing business there, soliciting business, or visiting it. At least one court has found that flying over the forum state may be sufficient to establish minimum contacts.

If a defendant is subject to a state's long-arm statute, he generally has performed acts sufficient to satisfy the minimum contacts requirement. A *long-arm statute* allows a court to reach outside its state boundary lines to reach a defendant and to require him to defend himself in the forum state. Long-arm statutes are designed to reach out-of-state defendants who have caused injury within the forum state. *(A more detailed review of personal jurisdiction is included in the chapter on Litigation (Chapter 10).)*

In Rem Jurisdiction   *In rem* literally means "in relation to the thing." A court has *in rem* jurisdiction when the subject matter of the suit relates directly to property located within the court's geographic boundary lines. The property, or thing, is the **res**.

A court always has jurisdiction of property located within its geographic boundaries. When any claim arises concerning such property, the court with subject matter jurisdiction in that location has *in rem* jurisdiction, without regard to whether it has personal jurisdiction over the defendant or not.

> Benson lives in Brazil and owns real estate in Marshall County, Iowa. Thomas, who lives in Oregon, lends money to Benson and receives a mortgage on the Iowa land as security for the loan. Benson defaults in his payments and Thomas wants to foreclose the mortgage.

Unless Benson consents, no American court can acquire personal jurisdiction over him while he remains in Brazil—not even with a long-arm statute. Because of *in rem* jurisdiction, however, Thomas can file his foreclosure action in the court having subject matter jurisdiction of mortgage foreclosures in Marshall County, Iowa. That court has the power to deal with the property with or without personal jurisdiction over Benson.

The result would be the same even if Benson and Thomas both lived in Oregon. It would be pointless for Thomas to file his mortgage foreclosure action in Oregon, because no Oregon court would foreclose a mortgage against Iowa real estate.

Quasi In Rem Jurisdiction   *Quasi in rem* jurisdiction arises when the subject matter of the suit does not relate to property in the court's jurisdiction, but the defendant has property in the court's jurisdiction that may be used to satisfy the judgment. Again, the court's jurisdiction exists whether or not it has personal jurisdiction over the defendant.

> Same facts as above, except that Benson gives Thomas a promissory note (no mortgage on the Iowa land).

Thomas still can file suit in Iowa. The Iowa court does not have *in rem* jurisdiction, because the subject of the suit does not relate to any Iowa property.

However, since Benson owns property in Iowa, *quasi in rem* jurisdiction operates "as if" the Iowa property were the subject of the suit.

In the second example, Thomas also may elect to file suit in an Oregon court on the promissory note; obtain a judgment; and register the Oregon judgment as a foreign judgment in the Iowa court where the property is located. After the foreign judgment is registered in Iowa, he can enforce it against Benson's Iowa property. This is possible because of the Full Faith and Credit Clause of the Constitution (*discussed below*).

Venue   Venue refers to the place of trial or, more specifically, to the location within a particular jurisdiction where trial should take place.

Venue for a criminal trial generally is the place where the crime was committed. A defendant may be able to request a change of venue if pretrial publicity or public sentiment about the case will make it impossible to obtain a fair and impartial jury where the crime was committed.

Venue for a civil trial generally is the place where the claim arose (or property is located); where the defendant resides; or where the defendant has either a place or business or an agent. In federal civil trials, the forum court may decline to hear the case if *forum non conveniens* is found to exist (the court is inconvenient for witnesses, for obtaining evidence, and so forth). *A more thorough review of venue is contained in the chapter on Litigation (Chapter 10).*

Federal Courts

The federal court system includes the U.S. Supreme Court, a court of appeals divided into 13 regions (one for each circuit); a district court divided into more than 90 federal district trial courts (one for each district, and a series of specialty courts (Tax Court, Court of Claims, Court of International Trade, and so forth).

All federal courts are courts of limited jurisdiction. They have authority to hear only those types of cases specifically authorized by constitutional provision (for the U.S. Supreme Court) or by federal statute (for all other federal courts).

Article III of the Constitution establishes the U.S. Supreme Court and authorizes Congress to establish lower federal courts, which Congress has done (U.S. District Court and U.S. Court of Appeals). These are constitutional courts, and their judges serve life terms subject to good behavior. The salaries of judges of constitutional courts cannot be decreased.

Legislative courts are established by Congress under Article I of the Constitution. Their judges have fixed terms. Legislative courts are the specialty courts (Tax Court, Court of Claims, and so forth).

U.S. Supreme Court   The U.S. Supreme Court is the court of last resort in the American legal system. It is the highest-ranking appellate court in the federal court system. The Supreme Court is comprised of nine justices (one chief justice and eight associate justices), who function as the final authority on—and protectors of—the Constitution.

Of all federal courts, the Supreme Court's jurisdiction is the only one specifically defined in Article III of the Constitution. It cannot be increased or decreased by Congress.

A.   **Original Jurisdiction**   The Supreme Court has original jurisdiction in the following types of cases:

•Disputes between two or more states (*exclusive*)

•Actions in which ambassadors, public ministers, or foreign consuls are parties

•Disputes between the United States and a state

•Actions by a state against citizens of another state or against aliens.

Of these, only the first (disputes between states) is exclusive; all others are concurrent, original jurisdiction, which means that lower federal courts also have original jurisdiction in these areas. As a practical matter, then, the only original action that must be heard by the Supreme Court is one involving a dispute between two or more states.

B.   **Appellate Jurisdiction**   The Supreme Court has appellate jurisdiction of all appeals from (1) the United States Court of Appeals and from (2) the highest appellate court of each state—but only if the state appeal presents an issue concerning federal law.

Beginning in 1988, appellate cases have reached the Supreme Court almost exclusively by ***writ of certiorari***. To obtain the writ, an appellant from the court of appeals must file a petition for writ of *certiorari* with the Supreme Court, asking the Court to hear the appeal. Granting the writ is discretionary. The Court generally grants a writ only when the justices believe that the case has sufficient national importance to warrant the Court's attention.

The writ of *certiorari* also is used to resolve issues within the federal court of appeals when there is serious conflict among the circuits.

U.S. Court of Appeals   The U.S. Court of Appeals is the intermediate appellate court in the federal court system. It is divided into 13 circuits: 11 circuits numbered according to their respective regions of the country, the Court of Appeals for the District of Columbia, and the Court of Appeals for the Federal Circuit.

The Court of Appeals for the Federal Circuit has exclusive appellate jurisdiction over all cases involving copyright, patent, trademark, and plant variety protection. It also has exclusive appellate jurisdiction over decisions of the U.S. Claims Court, U.S. Court of International Trade, and the U.S. Court of Veterans Appeals.

The Court of Appeals has appellate jurisdiction over all appeals taken from final decisions of the U.S. District Court except those involving cases within the exclusive appellate jurisdiction of the Court of Appeals for the Federal Circuit (*see above*). It also has appellate jurisdiction of some (but not all) final decisions appealed from federal administrative agencies.

U.S. District Court   The U.S. District Court is the trial court in the federal court system. There are more than 90 districts across the United States. Each state and territory has at least one district. The U.S. District Court has original jurisdiction in a number of areas, the most prominent of which are (1) federal question cases and (2) diversity of citizenship cases.

A *federal question* case is an action arising under the Constitution, laws, or treaties of the United States.

A *diversity of citizenship* case is a civil action between the citizens of different states where the matter in controversy exceeds $75,000, exclusive of interest and costs.

The U.S. District Court has original jurisdiction in these additional areas:

•Admiralty, maritime, and prize cases *(exclusive)*

•Suits brought by the United States, its agencies, or officers *(exclusive)*

•Suits against the United States or its officers (concurrent with U.S. Claims Court up to $10,000)

• Suits to compel officers of the United States to perform their duty (plaintiff seeks a writ of **mandamus**)

• Removal of suits against federal officers in state courts

• Suits in bankruptcy *(exclusive)*

• Suits in copyright, patent, trademark, and plant variety protection *(exclusive)*

• Suits involving improper collection of Internal Revenue and customs duties

• Suits involving civil rights

• Suits affecting ambassadors and other public ministers and consuls (*exclusive* as a practical matter, even though it is concurrent with U.S. Supreme Court).

A defendant may remove a case from state court to the federal court in the same district as the state court if (1) the defendant is not a resident of that state; (2) if the case could have been filed in federal court originally; (3) if the state court from which the case is removed has jurisdiction; and (4) in diversity cases only, if there was complete diversity between plaintiffs and defendants both at the time the case was filed in state court and at the time it is removed to federal court. When the U.S. District Court exercises its jurisdiction in diversity of citizenship cases, it applies state substantive law to decide the case. *Refer to section on judicial decision-making later in this chapter and to the chapter on Litigation (Chapter 10) for more details.*

The U.S. District Court has appellate jurisdiction of some (but not all) final decisions taken on appeal from federal administrative agencies.

Federal Specialty Courts Congress has established a number of courts under Article I of the Constitution. These are legislative courts, sometimes called federal specialty courts. Judges of federal specialty courts have specified terms, typically 15 years. Unlike the judges of constitutional courts, their salaries are not protected from congressional decreases. The most prominent federal specialty courts are listed here.

• *United States Court of International Trade.* Hears disputes between citizens and the government based upon import and export matters.

• *United States Claims Court.* Hears claims of citizens against the government based upon federal law or contracts; concurrent jurisdiction with U.S. District Court for taxpayer claims against IRS for improperly collected taxes.

• *United States Tax Court.* Hears taxpayer challenges to tax deficiency determinations issued by the IRS.

• *United States Court of Military Appeals.* Hears appeals from the Courts of Military Review.

• *United States Court of Veterans Appeals.* Reviews decisions of the Board of Veterans Appeals.

In addition, two Article I courts have been created and annexed to the U.S. District Court (an Article III court). They are the following:

• *Federal Magistrate Court.* Assists the U.S. District Court in areas such as hearing minor cases if the parties consent, conducting preliminary hearings in federal criminal cases, and conducting pretrial conferences in federal civil cases.

• *Bankruptcy Court.* Original jurisdiction (by referral from U.S. District Court) in all bankruptcy matters and in some civil or criminal matters related to debtors.

State Court Systems

State court systems vary from state to state; however, most of them follow an organizational structure that is similar to the federal court system. In the typical state court system, there is a supreme court; one or more intermediate appellate courts; a court of general jurisdiction; a county court; a small claims court; and a variety of specialty courts. Specialty courts may include a probate court, a family court, a juvenile court, a traffic court, and other courts as the state legislature may authorize.

State courts have concurrent jurisdiction with federal courts in all matters except those which are exclusively within federal jurisdiction, such as bankruptcy.

If a state case involves a federal question or issue, the case may be appealed to the U.S. Supreme Court following an unfavorable ruling by the state's highest court. The federal issue must be raised at the trial stage or it is waived. Matters that are purely of state interest (probate, divorce, adoption, and the like) cannot be appealed into the federal court system unless they also involve a federal issue (estate tax, due process, or equal protection, for example).

Judicial Decision Making

The decision makers in the trial process are the judge and the jury. The jury decides the facts of the case; the judge decides the law. When a case is tried without a jury (a bench trial), the judge fulfills a dual role by deciding both the facts and the law to be applied to those facts. At the appeal stage, the appellate judge reviews the accuracy of trial judge's decisions on the law. This section of the *Review Manual* reviews only the judge's role in deciding the law.

Law carries different weight in the decision-making process, depending on whether it is primary law or secondary law. ***Primary law*** carries the greatest weight in the decision-making process. In a state case, primary law includes the constitution, statutes, administrative rules and regulations, and case law of the state as well as the federal Constitution and any federal statutes (if there is a direct conflict between the two jurisdictions). Primary law is ***mandatory law***; to the extent that it relates to the facts and issues of the pending case, it must be followed in the pending case. Procedural rules are primary law as well.

Secondary law includes the constitution, statutes, and case law of other states. The jurisdictions of other states are of equal level, unlike the federal jurisdiction (*see above*). Also included as secondary law are legal encyclopedias, annotations, restatements, and treatises. Secondary law is ***persuasive law***; it may assist a court in reaching a decision in the pending case, but it need not be followed if the court does not wish to do so.

The judge has many substantive and procedural rules to consider at every stage of the trial. Much of the judicial decision-making process relates to proper interpretation and application of substantive law in the form of constitutional provisions, statutes, and common law. Common law is applied only in state cases (other than Louisiana, which is the only state that follows the civil law system from its French heritage) and in federal diversity cases.

<u>**Constitutions and Statutes**</u>   When a constitutional provision or a statute of the jurisdiction applies in a case, it takes precedence over all other legal rules. In this situation, it is mandatory law and must be followed to reach the decision.

Unless a particular statute violates some constitutional provision (constitutions carry more weight than statutes), the court's job is to determine the meaning of the statute and then to apply it to the facts of the case to determine the result. A judge cannot ignore the statute just because she does not like it; neither can she interpret it to mean something other than what the legislature says. If the statute passes constitutional requirements, the court must apply it as it stands.

Courts generally read (construe) statutes in criminal cases more narrowly or strictly to give every advantage to the defendant, while still complying with what the statute says. If a statute says that "a motorist *may* come to a complete stop at any intersection," a court is unlikely to allow anyone to be convicted under the statute. The word *may* indicates that stopping is optional.

The words used in statutes are given their ordinary meaning. If the words of a statute are ambiguous, a court is permitted to consider the statute's legislative history in determining what purpose the statute was intended to accomplish.

<u>Common Law</u>   If no constitutional or statutory provision applies or if its application leaves gaps in the final decision, state courts—and federal courts hearing diversity cases—supply the appropriate legal rules through common law principles.

Once an issue is decided by a court, the holding (rule of law) stated in that case is followed by that court and by lower courts of the same jurisdiction in all future cases involving similar facts and issues. The holding is precedent for all such future cases. The process of reviewing past cases is called ***stare decisis*** (*discussed above*). When a past case that has similar facts and similar issues is found, the holding of that case may be a ***precedent*** for the current case. If a precedent, it is ***mandatory law*** and must be followed in deciding the current case.

The holding of a past case is precedent only if:

> •it is found in a case decided by the present court or by a higher court;

> •the prior case was recorded (published); and

> •it is contained in the majority opinion of that court.

If all of these requirements are met, the holding of the case is precedent; and it is followed. If the facts or issues of the past case and the current case are sufficiently different or if one of the above requirements is missing, the holding is not precedent.

Recall that even if the prior case is precedent in the current case, a court is free to consider the surrounding circumstances and the societal changes since the prior case was decided to determine if the rule still fits. If it does not, common law principles are flexible enough to allow those adjustments that may be necessary to fit the rules to the current case.

If there are no applicable statutes and no precedents in the case law of the jurisdiction, the court is presented with a ***case of first impression***. In a civil law system (one based substantially on codified statutes) or in the federal system (based only on the Constitution and federal statutes), the court's hands would be tied. Without a statute covering the subject, such a court could do little. In a common law system, a case of first impression is handled by looking to other jurisdictions for a similar case to provide guidance. If none are found or if they are unsatisfactory, a common law court can draw analogies from existing case law and statutes.

For instance, if a company manufactures a new product called a skymobile and if no statutes yet exist to regulate its use, a common law court can decide whether the skymobile is more like an airplane or is more like an automobile. Depending on the outcome of that analysis, the court can apply common law rules applicable either to airplanes or to automobiles. If the legislature does not agree with the court's decision concerning the skymobile— or does not agree with the court's decision in any other area—the legislature is free to enact statutes to deal with the matter.

Federal courts sitting in diversity must apply the same state substantive law (including common law) that a state court of that district would apply. This is the only situation in which federal courts use common law principles. Even when a state's common law applies as the substantive law in a federal diversity case, the federal court applies its own rules of procedure (Federal Rules of Civil Procedure), not the rules of procedure of the state court.

Conflicts of Law   Because the substantive laws of one state can vary widely from the substantive laws of another state, a conflict of law can arise (1) when the facts of a case occur in a state other than the forum state; or (2) when the facts of a case occur in more than one state. Conflicts of law questions sometimes are referred to as ***choice of law*** questions.

When either of these situations occurs, the forum court may be uncertain about whether to apply the substantive law of its own state or whether to apply the substantive law of the foreign state. A federal court sitting in diversity can encounter the same situation. To alleviate this problem, each state has developed a set of conflicts-of-law rules to help courts decide if and when to apply the substantive law of a foreign state. The forum court always follows its own procedural rules, no matter which state's substantive law is followed.

Issues involving conflicts of law can become highly complex. The material in this section provides only an overview of basic terminology and concepts. More detailed information is outside the intended scope of this *Review Manual*.

In tort cases, the traditional approach to a conflict of law is to apply the law of the state where the wrong was committed (*lex loci delicti commissi*). The current trend of cases, however, is to replace the traditional rule with the significant relationship rule. Using the *significant relationship rule*, the court applies the substantive law of the place having the most significant contacts with the occurrence or event. As a practical matter, this frequently is the state where the wrong was committed.

In contract cases, the rules are different than in tort cases. Courts traditionally have used several different approaches:

- *lex fori:* the law of the state where the suit is filed;

- *lex loci solutionis:* the law of the state where the contract was to have been performed;

- *lex loci contractus:* the law of the state where the last act occurred, which was required to create a binding contract;

- the law of the state agreed to by the parties as part of their contract; or

- the law of the state having the most significant contacts with the events and the parties (*significant relationship* rule).

The Uniform Commercial Code (UCC), which applies to the sale of goods, uses a rule similar to the significant relationship rule when parties fail to specify a choice of law. The UCC provides no assistance, however, when the subject of the contract is employment, services, construction, or real estate.

Full Faith and Credit   Article IV of the U.S. Constitution requires that "full faith and credit shall be given in each state to the public acts, records, and judicial proceedings of every other state."

This provision requires each state to enforce the final judgments of all other states, without regard to the differences in substantive law and public policy from state to state. The only basis for refusing to enforce a final judgment of another state is when the issuing state did not follow constitutional requirements in obtaining the judgment, such as notice and an opportunity to be heard. If the defendant had the requisite minimum contacts with the issuing state and if the state properly exercised its long-arm statute, procedural due process requirements likely were met; and the resulting final judgment must be honored.

Thus, if loan sharking is legal in State A but not in State B, and if State A obtains a valid final judgment against a defendant, State B must enforce the judgment—even when the source of the underlying debt is repugnant to the public policy of State B. Article IV does not make judgments self-executing, however. The party who seeks enforcement still must initiate action in State B according to State B's judgment enforcement procedures.

Article IV applies only to states. Federal courts are held to the same requirement, however, by federal statute.

Comity   Comity relates to the recognition of the public acts (legislative, executive, or judicial) of one nation by another nation. Comity is a matter of courtesy; no international law requires it.

U.S. courts ordinarily honor the judgments of foreign countries unless it would be repugnant to public policy or prejudicial to citizens' interests in general to do so. A Canadian judgment on a defaulted promissory note, for example, likely would be honored by U.S. courts under the doctrine of comity.

Limitations in Judicial Decision Making

Not every case can be decided by a court, even if jurisdictional requirements are met. Other factors may preclude parties from bringing their dispute before the court. Non-jurisdictional obstacles are reviewed in this section.

Case or Controversy   Article III, § 2 of the U.S. Constitution requires that there be a case or controversy before parties can maintain legal action. In general, this means that *no advisory opinions* will be issued by the federal courts. An advisory opinion is one rendered on the basis of hypothetical facts. Some states allow their courts to issue advisory opinions; others do not.

Because of the case or controversy requirement, **no collusive suits** are permitted. A collusive suit is one based on a friendly agreement to litigate an issue, just to see how it comes out or—even worse—to influence the result in a certain direction by agreeing that one party will not put up a genuine struggle. A genuine case or controversy requires true adversaries to litigate the issues fully.

Parties to the suit must have **standing**, which means that their rights must be personally and immediately affected by the issues in the suit. One who is denied a medical treatment because of a state statute, for instance, has standing to challenge the statute. His physician does not.

The issue in the case must be **ripe** for judicial decision. It cannot be based upon something that might happen in the future. There must be an actual, full-blown dispute. For example, if a college official tells a student that the student's admission application will be denied if it is submitted, a lawsuit by the student probably would be dismissed if it were filed. The dispute is not ripe for decision, because the student's application has not been denied. It may very well be that the application will be accepted, notwithstanding what the official says now.

A very narrow distinction from the ripeness doctrine is the declaratory judgment action, which may be an appropriate remedy when a case is on the verge of becoming a full-blown dispute (*see below*).

The issue in the case cannot be moot. **Moot** is the opposite of ripe. An issue is moot if it has become irrelevant or academic at any stage of the proceeding, including the appeal. Courts will not decide moot cases, because the decision will not affect the litigants one way or the other. For example, if the student in the above example applies to college and is refused admission for discriminatory reasons, she could file suit and receive an injunction ordering her admission for the duration of the case. If she graduates before the case is concluded, the case is moot; and it will be dismissed. No matter what the court decides at that point, it will not affect the student.

Bar   Litigation may be barred (prohibited) from being litigated for several reasons, the two most common of which are (1) statute of limitations and (2) the doctrine of *res judicata*.

A **statute of limitations** is set by the legislature and requires that a civil action in a certain type of case must be filed within a fixed time after the cause of action first arises. The time limit varies from state to state; it also varies according to the type of case. For example, a state may set a four-year limitation on oral contracts; a five-year limitation on written contracts; and a two-year limitation on malpractice claims. If the complaint or petition is not filed within that time period, it is barred. The plaintiff loses the right to sue after the time limit expires.

Most statutes of limitation are *tolled* (put on hold) by infancy (being a minor), insanity, imprisonment, court order, fraudulent concealment by a fiduciary, and so forth. Every state is slightly different. If the statute is tolled because of infancy, for example, the minor usually has a reasonable time after becoming an adult in which to file the action. Whether a particular amount of time is reasonable usually depends on the circumstances.

If final judgment has been rendered in a case, the doctrine of *res judicata* prevents the same facts from being litigated again between the same parties. *Res judicata* literally means "the thing decided." The doctrine applies to a final judgment on the merits, to a motion for summary judgment, and to a dismissal with prejudice to future action. For *res judicata* to apply, (1) the parties must be the same or must be in privity with the original parties; and (2) the factual basis must be the same as the first suit. For example, if a plaintiff loses a case in a small claims court, she cannot file another case against the same defendant under a different legal theory if the underlying facts are the same. Neither can she file part of her claim, wait to see if she wins, and then file another claim if both claims are against the same defendant and are based on the same facts.

Immunity   Certain defendants are immune from civil prosecution for tort liability. For varying reasons, they are protected from potential liability.

Sovereign immunity insulates a government from tort liability on the premise that the "king can do no wrong." Sovereign immunity applies to any governmental unit (federal, state, or local). A military hospital, a prison, and a public school are immune from tort actions because of sovereign immunity.

A government may waive its sovereign immunity in whole or in part. The federal government, for example, waived a portion of its sovereign immunity when it enacted the Federal Tort Claims Act in 1946. Tort actions now may be brought against the federal government except for discretionary acts of government employees or for acts of the military in time of war.

Sovereign immunity does not apply when government assumes a non-governmental role, such as sponsoring rock concerts for profit, owning a horse racing track, or engaging in other commercial enterprises.

Sovereign immunity extends to government officials so long as the official acts within the scope of her authority and in the discharge of her official duties. Immunity is very strong for high-ranking government officials who exercise many discretionary powers, such as judges. The immunity does not apply, however, when the official steps outside the powers of her office and invades the constitutional rights of others. For example, if a judge discharges a female deputy sheriff because the judge thinks a male deputy presents a better image in the courtroom, there is no immunity for the judge's decision.

Nonprofit organizations traditionally have been provided with a *charitable immunity* from tort actions. Many states have restricted this type of immunity, simply because many charitable organizations have become huge business operations and can afford to purchase insurance protection, the same as any other business.

Most states allow a limited *parental immunity* from suit by unemancipated children in the areas of child-rearing and discipline. The immunity does not apply when a parent is abusive to a child.

Many states recognize a limited *contractual immunity* by allowing enforcement of an *exculpatory clause* on a case-by-case basis. The court looks at the subject matter of the contract, the clause itself, the relation of the parties, and the relative bargaining power of the parties. Such a clause may not be enforceable by a slum landlord against a poor tenant who does not read or write English. On the other hand, such a clause may be enforceable by a ski resort against a college student who rents a pair of skis for the day but does not take the time to read the rental agreement.

Judicial Remedies

In addition to its function of applying applicable law to cases, a court also must decide the type of relief that the winning party is entitled to receive in a civil case. A basic maxim of law is, *"For every right, there is a remedy."* To some extent, selection of a proper remedy depends on what the litigant requests. If the remedy is damages, deciding the amount is within the province of the jury up to a certain point. The judge ensures that the remedy is one which is permitted by the substantive laws of the state.

The court's goal is to put the injured party in the same position where she would have been if the injury had not occurred. To the extent that a statute addresses the issue of remedies, the statute must be followed. In the absence of a statute, however, the court applies common law principles to establish the type and amount of relief that a party may receive. Those decisions initially are based upon whether the case is (1) at law or (2) in equity.

Law and Equity   The concept of law courts and equity courts in America has existed since the first English colonists settled in this country. Historically, if a case involved both legal issues and equity issues, the litigant had to file two actions in two separate courts—and have two separate trials. Physical separation of the two courts continued until the early 1900s, when they were merged. Although the merger streamlined many of the procedures connected with dual law-and-equity cases, the distinctions between the two forms of action (and the relief that can be obtained) continue to be significant.

1. Identification of the parties often is different. In law actions, parties are identified as the plaintiff and the defendant. In equity actions, they typically are identified as the petitioner and the respondent.

2. Parties in law actions generally are entitled to a jury trial. No juries are allowed in equity actions.

3. The final order in a law action is a judgment; the final order in an equity action is a decree.

4. In the usual case, a judgment in a law action simply declares that Party A owes money to Party B. If Party A does not pay, there is no special penalty. No matter what happens, Party A cannot go to jail for simple nonpayment of a debt.

    However, a decree is a personal order of the court to do (or to refrain from doing) some specific act. If Party A does not obey, she is in contempt of court and may be penalized accordingly. The punishment for civil contempt in most states can be as severe as incarceration for a period of months or until the party obeys.

When legal and equitable issues exist in a single case, the jury determines the facts concerning the legal issues; the judge decides everything concerning the equity issues. If it is necessary to try legal issues separately (at a different time) from equitable issues, the process is called a ***bifurcated trial***.

Remedies at Law   Only a few legal remedies remain as carryovers from the early common law writ system:

> •*Replevin*, which requires return of specific personal property in the defendant's possession; and

> •*Ejectment*, which requires return of specific real property in the defendant's possession.

With these exceptions, remedies at law take the form of money (called damages). *Damages* always result in the payment of money. However, the basis or purpose for awarding damages determines how much money is awarded. The purpose of damages always is to make the plaintiff whole, but making the plaintiff whole means different things in different situations.

Damages must have been *foreseeable* at the time a contract is made or at the time the tort occurs. Damages that are too far removed from the contract (or the tort) are not foreseeable and cannot be awarded. In addition, the plaintiff has a duty to *mitigate* his damages. In other words, he must take reasonable steps to minimize his losses. If he fails to mitigate, his damage award is reduced by the amount of loss that could have been prevented through mitigation. Damages must be proved with a "reasonable degree of certainty" at the time of trial. This means the plaintiff must provide evidence of his losses when he seeks compensatory damages.

   A.   Compensatory Damages   Compensatory damages focus on the plaintiff's losses. Compensatory damages are further classified as either general damages or special damages. Special damages may be called consequential damages in some jurisdictions. By black-letter definition, *general damages* are those losses that anyone in the plaintiff's situation would incur. *Special damages* are those losses that are special (unique) to this particular plaintiff.

The goals of general damages and special damages are the same in both contract and tort cases; however, because the basis for the losses are different, the damages may seem to be different. They are not.

> Bill agreed to build a house for Dan for $100,000 on an existing foundation. Bill broke his arm and could not do the job. Dan had to pay $200 for plastic sheeting to re-cover the foundation while he found another contractor. He had to pay the second contractor $115,000 to build the house.

In this contract case, Dan lost the benefit of his bargain when he had to pay the second contractor $15,000 more than he originally had agreed to pay Bill. The benefit of his bargain ($15,000 in this case) is Dan's general damage. He also incurred $200 in special damages.

Had Bill started to work on the house before he broke his arm, he might be able to receive payment or credit for the value of his work. This is called **quantum meruit,** which is awarded on a quasi-contract theory.

> Judy was injured in an automobile accident. She was driving a car that was a gift from her parents when she graduated from high school. Both of her parents since have died, and the car means a great deal to her (although it is worth only $4,000). The accident was the fault of Betty, who was the driver of the other car. Judy was in the hospital three weeks and could not return to work for two months.

Judy's general damages are her pain and suffering as a result of her physical injuries and $4,000 for the value of her car. The jury decides the dollar value of Judy's physical pain and suffering. Her special damages are her medical bills and lost wages. The law does not compensate for the sentimental value of her car.

B.   Punitive Damages   Sometimes called exemplary damages, the purpose of punitive damages is to punish the defendant for outrageous conduct, such as causing injury while driving under the influence of alcohol or a controlled substance. An employer who fails to pay earned wages may be required to pay punitive damages in addition to compensatory damages (the wages).

Punitive damages are not allowed in some states. Where they are allowed, they serve the purpose of teaching a lesson to the defendant. They also deter others from engaging in the same conduct by making an example of the defendant.

C.   Nominal Damages   The purpose of nominal damages is to vindicate a right that has been violated when no monetary loss has occurred. A court typically awards a trivial amount plus court costs in that situation.

> Karen grows prize roses for a hobby. She owns a corner lot, which neighborhood children use as a shortcut on their way to and from school.

> Same facts, except that one little girl tramples a new rosebush, which is valued at $10.

In the first example, Karen is entitled to be vindicated for the trespass. A judge might award $1 and court costs, $10 and court costs, or some other trivial amount as nominal damages. In the second example, Karen is entitled to compensatory damages of $10. Even though the amount is small, it represents compensation for an actual loss. It cannot be termed nominal damages when an actual loss has occurred.

Nominal damages may be awarded in either contract or tort cases.

D. Liquidated Damages Liquidated damages arise in contract cases only. They are damages agreed to by the parties at the time the contract is made, and they represent the parties' reasonable estimate of losses in the event of breach. A liquidated damages provision is appropriate when damages are difficult to determine, such as lost profits for a new business.

Unless a liquidated damages provision is excessive or unless the parties occupy grossly disproportionate bargaining positions, courts are inclined to enforce a provision for liquidated damages.

Equitable Remedies Equitable remedies are fashioned by courts to achieve fairness when legal remedies are inadequate for that purpose. Therefore, a plaintiff's threshold objective is to demonstrate to the court that he has ***no adequate remedy at law***. That is, he must show that money cannot compensate for his injury.

In addition, a petitioner who seeks equitable relief must be blameless in the matter; otherwise, equity will not intervene. Thus, the maxim: *He who comes into equity must come with clean hands.*

A. Restitution Restitution focuses on the defendant's gains rather than on the plaintiff's losses. Restitution serves a different purpose than compensatory damages; it prevents defendants from profiting by their wrongful conduct.

> Mary steals stock certificates valued at $40,000 from Joe. She cashes in the certificates and spends the money on trips and clothes.
>
> Same facts, except that Mary sells the stock at a premium price of $50,000 to a person who wants them for a special purpose.

In both examples, Joe's losses are the value of the stock certificates: $40,000. If compensatory damages were his only option, Mary would have to repay that amount; and she would keep $10,000 profit. Restitution prevents Mary from being unjustly enriched by allowing Joe to reach Mary's ill-gotten gains. The court uses the legal fiction that Mary has created a ***constructive trust*** for Joe's benefit, with Mary as the trustee. By using the doctrine of ***tracing***, the court is able to "trace" the stock certificates to the cash. Mary, then, would be required to make an ***accounting*** for the profits she received.

If Mary had made a down payment on real estate with the proceeds, tracing could have been used to protect Joe's interest by placing an ***equitable lien*** of $50,000 on the real estate. The equitable lien then can be foreclosed in the same way that any other lien on real estate is foreclosed.

Yet another form of restitution is ***subrogation***. Subrogation applies when a person (other than an intermeddler) pays the debt of another. An insurance contract typically contains a subrogation clause.

> Wayne is injured through the negligence of George. Wayne's insurance carrier pays the medical bills. In a suit against George, Wayne subrogates his claim for medical bills to the insurance carrier. If Wayne wins, the carrier is reimbursed for the medical bills; and Wayne receives the balance of the judgment.

Restitution may be awarded in either contract or tort cases.

B.   Injunction   An injunction is a personal order to a respondent to do (or to refrain from doing) a specific act. An injunction, therefore, may be *mandatory* or *preventive*. The rules to obtain an injunction vary slightly from state to state, but they generally are similar to the format described here.

The petitioner who seeks injunctive relief often needs interim intervention to keep matters at a *status quo* pending trial. For example, if the petitioner claims ownership of trees on a boundary line and wants to prevent the respondent from chopping them down, the trees likely will be gone by the time a full hearing can be scheduled; and injunctive relief will have become moot.

At the beginning of her suit (or at any later time), the petitioner may seek a ***temporary restraining order*** (TRO). The initial TRO hearing often is ***ex parte***, which means that only one party (the petitioner) is heard on the matter. She must, by motion and sworn affidavit, demonstrate that she has no adequate remedy at law and that she will suffer irreparable harm if the TRO is not granted, compared with little or no harm to the respondent if it is granted. In addition, the judge must be convinced that the petitioner has a reasonable chance to win on the ultimate issues of the case.

If the judge grants the TRO, the petitioner ordinarily must post a bond to cover the respondent's damages in case the petitioner ultimately loses; and a copy of the TRO must be served on the respondent personally before it has any effect. If the judge does not grant the TRO (the trees are cut down), the lawsuit often becomes moot.

A temporary hearing is scheduled within a very short time, perhaps within seven or ten days. At the temporary hearing, both parties are present and have an opportunity to present their sides in a setting that is substantially less formal than a trial. After hearing the evidence, the judge issues a ***temporary injunction*** if it still appears that the petitioner may win ultimately and that the *status quo* should be maintained until trial. On the other hand, the judge dissolves the TRO if it appears to have been granted improvidently. In this circumstance, petitioners frequently do not pursue the case further.

At the trial of the case, a ***permanent injunction*** is issued if the petitioner wins. Unlike other litigation, the trial of an injunction case often is anti-climactic. One who is successful in obtaining a TRO and is also successful in obtaining a temporary injunction seldom will lose at the trial.

NOTE: *Libel or slander cannot be enjoined or restrained because of First Amendment speech protections. After the fact, the injured plaintiff can seek damages, however.*

C.   Declaratory Judgment   A declaratory judgment action is a suit that asks the court to declare the rights of parties in an impending dispute. The dispute must be imminent (ready to happen) and not merely a probability. In addition, one or both of the parties must be in danger of facing personal peril (prosecution under a criminal statute) or a great financial burden (tearing down a whole building) if the dispute actually occurs.

> The State of Utopia recently enacted a statute that makes it unlawful to operate a commercial bingo hall after dusk but which permits nonprofit bingo halls to operate after dusk. William operates commercial bingo halls all around the state, and most of his business is after dusk. William believes the statute is unconstitutional. The statute goes into effect on January 1.

In the example, if William operates his bingo halls after January 1, he will be subject to criminal prosecution. If he stops operating the bingo halls while he sues to challenge the statute, he will face financial ruin; and his case likely will become moot. A declaratory judgment may resolve the dilemma.

If William can obtain a declaratory judgment after the statute is passed but before it takes effect, his rights may be determined before he takes irreversible action one way or the other. Similarly, if the statute becomes effective right away, William may be able to combine the declaratory judgment action with a request for injunctive relief, pending the outcome of the case.

A declaratory judgment can be obtained in nearly every type of case (contract, tort, civil rights, and so forth).

D.   Rescission   Rescission is an equitable remedy available only in contract cases (one cannot rescind a tort). When rescission is granted, the underlying contract is cancelled and made void—as if it never had existed. When money has already changed hands in furtherance of the contract, rescission and restitution frequently are granted at the same time.

A contract may be rescinded as a remedy for fraud, misrepresentation, unconscionability, duress, or certain types of mistakes.

E.   Reformation   Like rescission, reformation is an equitable remedy available only in contract cases (one cannot reform a tort). Reformation typically is sought to correct errors in the document evidencing a contract or in a deed of conveyance when the document (or the deed) does not reflect the parties' agreement accurately.

Recall that the contract is the parties' underlying agreement. The document labeled "Contract" is merely evidence of that contract. Reformation can change (correct) only the document evidencing the contract; it cannot change the contract terms themselves.

> Pam agrees to purchase a pasture from Carla at $100 an acre; both parties believe the pasture contains ten acres of land. They execute a purchase agreement to satisfy the Statute of Frauds. At the closing, Carla provides a warranty deed to Pam for ten acres at $100 an acre; and Pam pays $1,000. Pam then discovers that the pasture contains 9.4 acres.

In this example, reformation may be used to correct the deed so that it reflects the parties' true agreement, which was to purchase and sell a 9.4-acre pasture.

Although not connected directly to the remedy of reformation, Pam also may be entitled to abate (reduce) the purchase price if the parties' agreement was to buy pasture at $100 an acre. At $100 an acre, Pam received only $940 in value; $60 should be returned to her. If, however, the parties' agreement was to purchase this particular pasture for $1,000 and if the language "10 acres at $100 an acre" was merely a convenient way to describe the pasture, Pam received the benefit of her bargain (the pasture she wanted). Abatement would not be appropriate in the latter situation.

F. Specific Performance Specific performance, too, is an equitable remedy available only in contract cases (one would not demand specific performance of a tort). This remedy may be available when the subject matter of the contract is unique, such as an original Renoir painting. The only way to make the disappointed buyer whole is to award her the Renoir. Money frequently is inadequate when unique property is in dispute.

Alternative Dispute Resolution
Alternative dispute resolution (ADR) is precisely what the name implies. It provides a way to settle parties' claims without the expense and delay of a full-blown trial through (1) a pretrial procedure designed to evaluate the parties' claims and to effect settlement, (2) arbitration, or (3) mediation. The Rules of Professional Conduct of some states require attorneys to advise their clients of ADR options.

A. Court-Annexed ADR Court-annexed arbitration programs have been initiated in a number of federal district courts with substantial success. In addition, approximately half of the states have some form of court-annexed ADR, whether authorized by state statute or by local court rule.

In a court-annexed program, parties are required to submit to a type of pretrial arbitration or pretrial conference before their cases are docketed for trial. A court-appointed arbitrator, hearing officer, or magistrate conducts the proceeding. This individual may be a lawyer (such as the magistrate), but the programs of many state courts permit nonlawyers (including legal assistants) to serve as the arbitrator or hearing officer for certain types of cases.

The presiding officer assists the parties in laying all the issues on the table, with the goals of disposing of non-issues and of bringing the parties to a compromise position. In some situations, the presiding officer may inform the parties of results of recent cases similar to theirs and may assist them in predicting the probable outcome of their case. Court-annexed programs may take the form of an arbitration proceeding or may take the form of a mediation conference.

Parties who are unable to resolve their disputes through a court-annexed program are entitled to proceed to trial, although they frequently find that the results at trial are strikingly similar to the results predicted during the ADR proceeding.

B.   Arbitration   Arbitration has existed for many years in the business world as a voluntary method of resolving disputes without litigation. An impartial arbitrator, usually a person with expertise in the area of the parties' dispute, listens to evidence presented by both sides and renders a decision. As part of the agreement to arbitrate, the parties agree that the arbitrator's decision will be binding.

If either party is dissatisfied with the decision (believes that errors were made by the arbitrator), the decision can be appealed into the court system.

Panels of impartial arbitrators can be identified through the American Arbitration Association, the Center for Public Resources, or the Federal Conciliation and Mediation Service. The Better Business Bureau, which operates in most major cities, can supply contact information for these organizations.

C.   Mediation   Mediation is also a voluntary method of dispute resolution. The primary distinction between arbitration and mediation is that mediation is not binding on the parties.

In a mediation conference, an impartial third party presides over the conference and attempts to help the parties reach an agreement. This may be done in a variety of ways; but the objective is to identify areas of common ground and to present viable options to resolve those areas of genuine dispute. A mediation conference is much less structured than an arbitration proceeding. Labor union negotiators traditionally have turned to mediation when they were unable to reach a compromise. Mediation is a particularly useful alternative in family law cases as well.

A mediator sometimes makes recommendations but never makes decisions. Therefore, unsuccessful mediation participants are free to proceed through the judicial processes if they choose to do so.

This chapter, together with the remaining chapters on substantive law and with the accompanying self-tests, should provide a basic review of the principles and procedures that may be encountered on the certifying examination. If the applicant is unfamiliar with any of the material covered, he or she is advised to consider close study of a relevant textbook or other study aid as well as the applicable Rules and statutes. *See the bibliography for additional study references.*

General Law Self-Test

Allow an uninterrupted 30-minute period to answer all questions. At the end of 30 minutes, check your answers against those in the Answer Key Section of this Review Manual. Deduct two points for each incorrect answer (100 total possible points). Unanswered questions are counted as incorrect answers. Follow directions carefully and observe the time limit precisely to provide an accurate self-assessment.

Choose the most correct answer to the following questions unless a specific question instructs you to do otherwise.

1.   Today's equity court descends from the:

    a.   king's court.
    b.   queen's court.
    c.   court of champerty.
    d.   court of chancery.
    e.   none of the above.

2.   The U.S. Supreme Court consists of how many justices?

    a.   three
    b.   seven
    c.   nine
    d.   eleven

3.   The Bill of Rights is found:

    a.   in the first fourteen amendments to the U.S. Constitution.
    b.   in the first ten amendments to the U.S. Constitution.
    c.   in the First and Fourteenth Amendments to the U.S. Constitution.
    d.   in all of the amendments to the U.S. Constitution.

4.   Two sources of primary law are:

    a.   legal references and judges.
    b.   decisions of courts and enactments of legislative bodies.
    c.   U.S. Supreme Court and case law.
    d.   legislation and statutory law.

5. True or False. *Stare decisis* is a guiding principle whereby a court is bound by prior cases.

6. True or False. According to the Seventh Amendment, persons are entitled to a jury trial in civil cases where the amount in controversy exceeds $20.

7. True or False. When rights of citizens conflict with each other, the courts choose the rights that are more important and uphold those, which means that the less important rights are no longer recognized.

8. True or False. Congress could expand the jurisdiction of the U.S. District Courts by vesting in them jurisdiction of all cases including local and state matters.

9. True or False. Personal jurisdiction of federal courts generally is determined under the principle of maximum contacts.

10. True or False. Article II of the Constitution grants the President the exclusive right to declare war on behalf of the United States.

11. A single court can be authorized to exercise:

    a. only original jurisdiction.
    b. only appellate jurisdiction.
    c. both original and appellate jurisdiction.
    d. none of the above.

12. Which of the following courts is authorized to exercise original jurisdiction in certain types of cases?

    a. U.S. Supreme Court.
    b. U.S. District Court.
    c. State District (or Superior) Court.
    d. All of the above.
    e. None of the above.

13. Neither a court nor the parties ever can waive:

    a. concurrent jurisdiction.
    b. personal jurisdiction.
    c. subject matter jurisdiction.
    d. none of the above.

14.　　True or False.　　　The U.S. Supreme Court is known as the supreme law of the land.

15.　　True of False.　　　The federal Constitution grants exclusive power to Congress to establish and to operate a post office.

16.　　True or False.　　　When both a criminal charge and a civil action arise from the same set of facts, a guilty verdict for the criminal charge means the defendant will be found liable in the civil action as well.

17.　　True or False.　　　*Stare decisis* and precedent mean the same thing.

18.　　True or False.　　　As it relates to court systems, concurrent jurisdiction means more than one court has the power to hear a case.

19.　　True or False.　　　The power of all federal judges derives from Article III of the Constitution.

20.　　True or False.　　　Laws relating to contracts are examples of private laws.

21.　　True or False.　　　Article I of the Constitution grants Congress the exclusive right to control intrastate commerce.

22.　　The federal government has preempted several areas of regulation, including:

    a.　　interstate commerce
    b.　　the postal service
    c.　　Both a and b
    d.　　Neither a nor b

23.　　The prohibition against mandatory self-incrimination in criminal cases is guaranteed by the:

    a.　　First Amendment.
    b.　　Fifth Amendment.
    c.　　Sixth Amendment.
    d.　　Eighth Amendment.
    e.　　None of the above.

24.   The federal intermediate courts of appeals are established by:

    a.   federal statute.
    b.   U.S. Constitution.
    c.   U.S. Supreme Court.
    d.   None of the above.

25.   Disputes between two or more states may be heard either by:

    a.   only the U.S. District Court.
    b.   only the U.S. Supreme Court.
    c.   either the U.S. District Court or the U.S. Supreme Court.
    d.   none of the above.

26.   The United States Court of International Trade formerly was known as:

    a.   U.S. Court of Customs.
    b.   U.S. Court of Claims.
    c.   U.S. Court of Customs and Patent Appeals.
    d.   none of the above.

For each of the following definitions, supply the correct legal term or phrase.

27.   _____   party defending an appeal

28.   _____   now for then

29.   _____   order commanding a public official to do that which the law requires her to do

30.   _____   an article of personal property

31.   _____   clause of pleading that asks for damages

32.   _____   constitutions, statutes, and case law

33.   _____   geographic location of trial

34.   _____   sworn declaration that the execution of an instrument is voluntary

35. _____ law making conduct illegal after the fact

36. _____ one with personal knowledge of a fact

37. True or False.   Because there is no federal common law, federal courts do not have jurisdiction to decide contract cases.

38. True or False.   Those who participate in mediation proceedings are bound by the decision of the mediator.

39. True or False.   The U.S. Supreme Court decides questions based upon stipulated facts that have been certified to it by lower courts.

40. True or False.   Federal courts of appeals properly may be referred to as circuit courts of appeals.

41. True or False.   Generally speaking, a case is appealed to the U.S. Supreme Court by filing a petition for writ of *certiorari*.

42. True or False.   The power of a state's legislative body to enact laws in areas relating to the health, safety, and welfare of its citizens is known as its welfare power.

43. True or False.   A uniform law is one adopted by Congress as a proposal to states, which each state is free to adopt in its entirety, adopt with modifications, or not adopt at all.

44. True or False.   The Model Penal Code was drafted by the American Law Institute.

45. True or False.   When federal constitutional issues are involved, the U.S. Supreme Court is required to hear the case.

46. If a case were filed by 50 women, none of whom is pregnant, to challenge a state's abortion statute, the case most likely would be:

    a.   dismissed for lack of standing.
    b.   dismissed under the standards doctrine.
    c.   dismissed under the mootness doctrine.
    d.   dismissed under the overbreadth doctrine.

47.   The doctrine under which powers are divided between the federal government and the states is known as:

    a.   constitutionalism
    b.   federalism
    c.   feudalism
    d.   none of the above

48.   Laws relating to rules of evidence are examples of _____ laws.

    a.   procedural
    b.   private
    c.   case
    d.   secondary

49.   A law providing that no legal assistants may serve on boards of directors of national banks would be a(n):

    a.   *ex post facto* law.
    b.   bill of attainder.
    c.   *ipso facto* law.
    d.   none of these is correct.

50.   A law that describes how a defendant must be served with summons in a case is an example of:

    a.   substantive law.
    b.   secondary law.
    c.   adjective law.
    d.   none of the above.

Chapter

8

BUSINESS ORGANIZATIONS

Go as far as you can see; and when you get there, you will be able to see farther.

—Anonymous

The law of business organizations covers the creation, operation, merger, and liquidation of various business enterprises. It includes sole proprietorships, general partnerships, limited partnerships, joint ventures, joint stock companies, and corporations. Of these, the sole proprietorship, the partnership, and the corporation are the three most common forms of business organization used in the United States. The legal assistant who works with the commercial clients of a law firm must have a thorough understanding of the concepts, rules, and procedures that govern the existence and activities of commercial entities.

In addition to the summary of general principles provided in this *Review Manual* and an up-to-date textbook or treatise covering business organizations, the applicant may find it helpful to review the complete texts of the Uniform Partnership Act (UPA), the Revised Uniform Limited Partnership Act (RULPA), and the Revised Model Business Corporation Act (RMBCA) in preparation for the CLA/CP® examination. The materials in this chapter are based upon selected sections of these Acts as well as upon general principles of jurisdiction, agency law, and contract law.

Sole Proprietorship

The most common form of business organization is the sole proprietorship. A sole proprietorship exists when one person owns a business operation plus its assets and carries on the business enterprise as the sole owner. Unlike a corporation, the sole proprietorship requires no charter from the state to exist.

Advantages   The greatest advantage of the sole proprietorship is its flexibility. As the only owner, a sole proprietor operates the business as he or she chooses within the bounds of the law. The owner may hire employees to assist with the business operation, but the owner retains ultimate responsibility for all decisions concerning the business.

If the business will sell goods, the owner must obtain a sales tax license (services are also taxed in some states); and if the business will have employees, state and federal tax identification numbers must be obtained. Certain types of businesses require special licensing (taxi service, physician services, child care); these licenses must be obtained where necessary. Otherwise, there are no special formalities required to begin a sole proprietorship.

The sole proprietorship is treated as an extension of its owner for income tax purposes, which allows the owner to apply business losses against other personal income in computing tax liability. Moreover, individual tax rates generally are less than corporate tax rates.

Disadvantages   The disadvantages of the sole proprietorship stem from its complete identity with its owner. As a practical matter, the business and the owner are one. Capitalization of the business comes from the owner, either through direct contributions or through financing, which generally is dependent—at least in part—upon the credit worthiness of the individual owner.

Likewise, liabilities of the sole proprietorship are the unlimited personal liabilities of its owner, which means that trade creditors look to the owner's personal assets to satisfy trade debts when business assets are insufficient. Unlimited personal liability exists for business contracts and business torts of the sole proprietorship, making it possible for the owner to lose all personal assets as well as all business assets if an unfavorable judgment is entered against the business. This is very different from the corporate business structure, in which an owner's personal liability typically is much more limited *(see below)*. A sole proprietor may negotiate to limit her contract liability to business assets only; however, her tort liability for business activities generally cannot be limited by agreement.

The duration of a sole proprietorship is limited by the life of its owner. In the usual situation, this means that the sole proprietorship is liquidated upon the owner's death. The liquidation process can be difficult unless proper authority has been given to a trustee or to the personal representative of the owner's estate to operate the business, to sell its assets, and to distribute the sale proceeds. If the business is inherited or is purchased by another person, a new sole proprietorship is created in the new owner.

General Partnership

General partnerships are governed by the Uniform Partnership Act (UPA), which has been adopted in whole or in part in all states except Louisiana. A general partnership is an "association of two or more persons to carry on as co-owners a business for profit." R.U.P.A. § 6(1). The traditional law firm, for example, is organized as a general partnership.

By definition, a partnership requires at least two persons who intend to affiliate for the purpose of operating a business. The term *person* can include an individual, a partnership, a corporation, or other entity. The intent to associate as partners may be based upon a formal, written partnership agreement (always the preferred method); upon an oral agreement; or upon conduct of the partners. The concept of co-ownership implies that contributions, ownership of assets, rights to profits, obligations for losses, and management of the partnership are shared equally by the partners. Although a different arrangement is permissible, it must be stated specifically and clearly in a written partnership agreement to avoid application of the general rule.

Standing alone, however, mere co-ownership of property does not indicate that a partnership exists, even if the property produces income that is divided among the property owners.

Finally, the definition of a partnership excludes charitable, fraternal, religious, trade association, or labor union purposes, for example, because it requires the partnership to carry on a business "for profit." This means that the partnership must be operated with the intent to generate a profit, whether or not a profit actually is generated. Like other business organizations, partnerships can and do experience financial losses.

A partnership is a "pass-through" entity for taxation purposes, which means that each partner is taxed on his, her, or its proportionate share of deductions, credits, profits, and losses at the personal income tax rate applicable to that partner. The partnership is not taxed separately.

Formation and Existence The requirements to form a partnership are similar to the requirements to establish a sole proprietorship (sales tax license and other licenses, if applicable; state and federal tax identification numbers if there will be employees). The prudent business person will insist upon a written partnership agreement, sometimes called articles of partnership, to govern the partners' rights and obligations; however, where there is no agreement or where the agreement fails to address a specific issue, terms will be supplied by the Uniform Partnership Act (UPA).

A partnership may exist for any length of time to which the partners agree. If the partnership is intended to exist for one year or more, there must be a written agreement to comply with the Statute of Frauds. If no term is stated, it will be presumed that the partnership is one "at will," which may be terminated by any partner upon notice to the other partners.

If the names of all partners are part of the partnership name, registration of the partnership's business name generally is not required. If fewer than all of the partners names are used or if an entirely different name is used, most states require registration of the business name. Sanctions for noncompliance vary from state to state, but typically deny the partnership the right to use that state's court systems until the partnership complies with the assumed business name statute by registering the partnership name.

A frequent question in partnership law is whether the partnership is an aggregate of its partners or whether it is a separate legal entity. Under common law rules, a partnership was viewed as an aggregate. This meant, for example, that all partners had to be named as defendants if a partnership were sued. If an entity theory were used, the partnership could be named as the defendant without the need to name each of the partners.

The UPA incorporates both theories in its provisions, treating the partnership as an aggregate for some purposes and as a separate entity for other purposes. For example, all partners are personally liable for partnership debts (aggregate theory). However, the partnership may acquire, hold, and convey property; and partnership assets, liabilities, and transactions are separate from those of individual partners (entity theory).

Many statutes follow the same hybrid approach, treating the partnership as an aggregate for some purposes and as an entity for others. Both the Uniform Commercial Code and federal bankruptcy law, for instance, define the term *person* to include a partnership. Most states allow a partnership to sue and to be sued in the partnership name. Tax laws, however, treat the partnership as an aggregate by attributing income and expenses to individual partners *(see above)*.

A.   Partnership Property   Each partner generally contributes to the partnership's capital account when the partnership is formed. A partner's capital contribution may be in the form of real property (land and/or buildings), personal property (typically vehicles, machinery, or equipment), cash, or personal services. Although there is no legal requirement to do so, it is important to state the value of each partner's capital contribution if contributions vary from partner to partner. If no amount is stated, it will be presumed that each partner's capital contribution is equal to the capital contributions of all other partners. Each subsequent advance by any partner should be recorded, along with its value, for the same reason.

Property of the partnership may be held in the partnership's name or may be held in the name of any partner as an agent of the partnership. Property purchased with partnership funds is presumed to be partnership property, owned by all partners as tenants in common. No partner may sell partnership property without the consent of all other partners; neither can a partner, for instance, sell her fractional interest in specific partnership property. A partner's personal creditors cannot reach partnership property to satisfy the partner's individual debt. If a partner dies, partnership property belongs to the surviving partners and not to the heirs of the deceased partner.

Financial Structure   Initial capitalization of the partnership comes from contributions made by its partners. Contributions may or may not be equal in value. If no value is stated, it will be presumed that contributions were equal; and profits will be divided equally. Even if capital contributions are unequal, profits will be divided equally among all partners unless the partnership agreement provides for a different ratio of distribution.

> Anderson, Baker, and Cunningham form a partnership to operate a catering business. Anderson contributes a delivery van valued at $20,000; Baker contributes $40,000 in cash; and Cunningham will operate the business on a daily basis without salary for the first year, valued at $20,000. The business operates at a loss of $15,000 during the first year and generates a profit of $60,000 during the second year.

Absent a contrary provision in the partnership agreement, both the first year's loss and the second year's profit will be allocated equally among Anderson, Baker, and Cunningham.

At the beginning of the partnership described in the example, Anderson's partnership interest is $20,000; Baker's, $40,000; and Cunningham's, $0. At the end of the first year of operation, Anderson's partnership interest is $15,000 (the $20,000 van minus $5,000 loss); Baker's is $35,000 ($40,000 cash minus $5,000 loss); and Cunningham's is $15,000 ($20,000 salary minus $5,000 loss).

Although no partner may sell or assign specific partnership property to a third party without consent of the other partners, she may sell or assign her partnership interest. Her partnership interest (but not specific partnership property) also may be reached by her individual creditors or may be inherited by her heirs. The new owner of the partnership interest is entitled to payment of its value as well as to payment of profits to which his assignor would have been entitled, but the new owner does not become a partner and has no management authority *(see below)*. Partnerships often purchase insurance policies on the lives of individual partners to provide a method of paying the value of a deceased partner's partnership interest to his or her heirs.

The value of a partnership interest typically is calculated by a formula that includes the partner's initial contribution and subsequent advances, increased by surplus profits, and decreased by undistributed losses and withdrawals from the partnership. The precise valuation formula should be stated in the partnership agreement.

If a partner uses individual assets to pay undisputed debts to firm creditors, that partner is entitled to proportionate reimbursement from the other partners.

Management   The law presumes that all partners will devote their full time and attention to operating the partnership business without compensation and that each partner will have equal management authority concerning the business. If the partners desire a different management structure, they must provide for it in the partnership agreement.

In the example given above, for instance, Anderson, Baker, and Cunningham agreed that Cunningham should be compensated for his daily services to the business (implying that Anderson and Baker would not be involved in daily operations); and what would have been paid to him as salary should be applied, instead, as his capital contribution during the first year. Unless Cunningham is named as the managing partner, however, all three partners have an equal voice in management decisions. Without regard to the variance in their capital contributions, they each have one vote; and the partnership is authorized to engage in various activities by majority vote of its partners. The partnership agreement may alter this structure in any way that is satisfactory to the partners.

A *silent partner* is one who assumes all benefits and burdens of her partner status except in the area of management decisions.

Complete books and records must be maintained, and any partner is entitled to inspect the books or to receive an accounting at any time.

Liability of Partners   Like sole proprietors, members of a general partnership have unlimited personal liability to partnership creditors if the assets of the partnership are insufficient to satisfy partnership debts.

If any partner incurs liability or expenses in the ordinary course of the partnership business, she is entitled to reimbursement from the partnership or from the remaining partners. A partner who leaves the firm remains personally liable for debts incurred while she was a partner in the firm unless an indemnification provision is included in the original partnership agreement. New partners are personally liable for firm debts existing when they join the firm only if they agree to such liability. If a new partner does not assume existing debts, she is personally liable for only those obligations incurred after she becomes a partner.

Dissolution and Termination   When any partner is no longer associated with the partnership business, for whatever reason, the partnership is dissolved. However, the remaining partners (assuming there are two or more remaining) may elect to continue the business. Under strict interpretation of partnership law, a new partnership is created by the remaining partners and continues to operate under the terms of the original partnership agreement. In other situations, the dissolution may require termination of the partnership and "winding up" of the business operation.

Because a partnership is formed by agreement of the parties, it may be terminated by agreement of the parties. The original partnership agreement may provide for termination upon the occurrence of a specific event, such as the death or disability of a partner or a stated period of consecutive operating losses. Dissolution may be necessary if the partnership business becomes unlawful (for example, a statute adopted to outlaw all movie theaters after January 1 of next year) or when partners simply cannot agree about important matters related to the business. Whenever possible, a written dissolution agreement should be put into effect; the better practice is to include dissolution provisions in the original partnership agreement.

If the remaining partners cannot or do not wish to continue the business, dissolution requires that the partnership be terminated and "wound up." Notice of dissolution must be provided to all persons who may have a claim against the partnership. All partnership assets are gathered and liquidated, paying creditors (other than partners) first. All valid debts must be paid in full before anything can be distributed to partners.

Limited Partnership

A limited partnership is a partnership of two or more persons formed in compliance with a state's limited partnership statute with one or more general partners and one or more limited partners as members of the firm. General partners have unlimited personal liability for partnership debts, while limited partners have no liability for debts or losses beyond their investment in the partnership. If a person is both a general partner and a limited partner in the same partnership, she has the liabilities of a general partner in relation to creditors. It is also possible for a corporation to be a general partner in most states, which may diminish the concept of unlimited personal liability of the general partner in some circumstances.

The National Conference of Commissioners on Uniform State Laws adopted the Uniform Limited Partnership Act (ULPA) in 1916, which was adopted by all states except Louisiana. ULPA was updated and revised in 1976, with further amendments in 1985, by the Revised Uniform Limited Partnership Act (RULPA). RULPA and its amendments have been adopted by a substantial majority of states, although some states still operate under the former ULPA. (Louisiana has adopted neither version of the Act.)

Limited partnerships differ from general partnerships in two important ways:

1.   A limited partnership can be formed only by complying with specific statutory requirements, which include filing a certificate to provide notice to creditors that some partners have limited liability for partnership debts. A general partnership can be formed by private agreement without any formal filing requirements.

2.   Limited partners, unlike general partners, may not participate in the management or control of the business.

Formation and Existence   RULPA requires members of a limited partnership to sign and file a certificate with the secretary of state showing the name and address of the limited partnership, the name and address of each partner, and identification of an agent for service of process. Amendments to the certificate must be filed to show important changes in the limited partnership structure or capitalization. In addition to the certificate, members of a limited partnership typically execute a private limited partnership agreement to govern the affairs of the business.

The term limited partnership must be included as part of the firm name. In addition, the surname of a limited partner cannot be used as part of the firm name unless it is also the name of a general partner or unless the firm had used the name before admitting the limited partner. If this rule is violated, the limited partner may be liable to creditors to the same extent as a general partner.

RULPA requires a limited partnership to maintain an office in the state of incorporation, which need not be its place of business, where the following records must be maintained for inspection:

- a current list of names and addresses of all partners;

- a copy of the certificate of limited partnership and all amendments;

- a copy of all financial statements and tax returns for three years; and

- a copy of any written partnership agreement that exists.

In addition, the limited partnership must maintain an agent for service of process within the state of incorporation.

Financial Structure   A limited partner's contribution may take the form of cash, property, or a promise to contribute future cash or property. RULPA permits contribution of services; the former ULPA does not. A limited partner must make the contribution represented in the certificate of limited partnership; and if she fails to do so, the contribution may be enforced against her or against her estate.

The profits, losses, and distributions are allocated among partners according to the limited partnership agreement. ULPA does not provide a basis for making these distributions if the partnership agreement fails to do so. RULPA, however, provides that if the limited partnership agreement is silent on the topic, profits, losses, and distributions are allocated on the basis of the value of contributions made by each partner as shown in the limited partnership records retained by the partnership. This is different from the rule applied to general partnerships by UPA, which provides that partners share profits and losses equally if the subject is not covered by the partnership agreement.

A limited partner may lend money to the partnership; however, ULPA restricts loans made by limited partners if the loans are secured by firm assets. RULPA contains no specific prohibition but, rather, defers to each state's fraudulent conveyance statute.

Management   The general partners manage the business of the limited partnership and incur personal liability to creditors if partnership assets are insufficient. Limited partners are investors only and generally have no voice in management. They may be granted voting rights by the limited partnership agreement; without such a provision, however, RULPA provides no voting rights other than the unanimous consent required to admit a new general partner.

If a limited partner participates actively in the management of the partnership business, she loses her limited liability insulation and is treated as a general partner. ULPA reaches this result in all cases; RULPA, however, grants unlimited liability only as to those persons who transact business with the partnership with knowledge of the limited partner's participation—unless the limited partner exercises powers similar to those reserved for general partners.

RULPA attempts to clarify types of conduct by a limited partner which do not result in the loss of her limited liability status. Permissible conduct includes

> • serving as a contractor, agent, or employee of the limited partnership or of a general partner;
>
> • consulting or advising a general partner concerning the limited partnership's business;
>
> • acting as surety for the limited partnership;
>
> • attending a meeting of partners or requesting such a meeting; and
>
> • voting on vital partnership matters such as dissolution, changing the nature of the business, or the admission or removal of a general partner.

Liability   The liabilities of the general partners in a limited partnership are similar to those in a general partnership. Limited partners are liable only to the extent of their investments in the limited partnership unless

> •the limited partner's name appears in the name of the limited partnership;
>
> •the limited partner participates in the management of the partnership business in an unlawful way; or
>
> •false statements are made in the certificate of limited partnership, and the limited partner takes no action to correct the defect.

If any of these prohibitions occur, the limited partner involved loses the insulation of limited liability and is treated as a general partner.

Dissolution and Termination   Limited partnerships, like general partnerships, may be dissolved by agreement of the partners. The partnership is dissolved upon the withdrawal of a general partner unless the right to continue the business is stated in the limited partnership agreement or unless all partners consent to the continuation. Withdrawal of a general partner occurs upon the retirement or other voluntary withdrawal of a general partner, upon the death of a general partner, upon the dissolution of a corporate general partner, upon the removal of a general partner according to the terms of the limited partnership agreement, or upon the bankruptcy of a general partner.

Unless the business is continued, firm assets are collected and distributed according to statute. Outside creditors are paid first. After creditors are paid, ULPA gives preference to certain distributions to limited partners over general partners; RULPA, however, does not. Under the RULPA distribution scheme, limited and general partners are treated substantially the same.

Limited Liability Company

The limited liability company (LLC) is a hybrid form of business ownership. Although statutes differ from state to state, an LLC offers the best of both worlds: the limited liability of a corporation and the income pass-through of a partnership for tax purposes.

One or more persons may create an LLC by filing a certificate of organization with the state, usually with the secretary of state. Instead of shareholders or partners, an LLC has members. The members may manage the affairs of the LLC or may assign this task to a manager, who can be (but does not have to be) a member. The liability of each member is limited to his or her investment unless the specific liability results from his or her personal conduct (i.e., malpractice).

In addition to the certificate of organization, every limited liability company should include in its operating agreement the LLC's purpose; the type and amount of member investment; allocation of income; transferability of a member's interest in the LLC; and the procedure to be followed in the event of dissolution. Unlike a partnership, the LLC does not cease to exist upon the death of a partner. Rather, an LLC may exist for a specific period of time or its existence may be perpetual, as prescribed within the certificate of organization.

Similar to corporations, it is possible in most states to pierce the limited liability company veil to reach individual members who use the company to defraud creditors or investors. There is little case law in most states to provide a picture of how this works with the LLCs of that state. However, some states simply have held that the circumstances permitting the corporate veil to be pierced should apply to limited liability companies as well.

The Uniform Limited Liability Company Act was drafted by the Commission on Uniform State Laws, but only a small minority of states have adopted it as of this writing. Although nearly every state has enacted LLC statutes, there is little uniformity among them beyond the topics mentioned here.

Joint Venture

A joint venture involves the combining of efforts by two or more persons for one transaction or for one event only. It resembles a partnership in many respects and may be evidenced by a written agreement. A joint venture is different from a partnership, however, since it does not contemplate a continuing relationship between or among the parties. Once the transaction or event occurs, the joint venture is concluded.

A joint venture may exist between an entertainer and a promoter, for example, for a specific concert or show.

Joint Stock Company

The term *joint stock company* or *joint stock association* derives its name from the fact that its members pool their capital into a common fund (joint stock) rather than each member owning his or her own stock separately. This business form is not prevalent today; when it exists, it typically is an unincorporated business enterprise with ownership interests evidenced by shares of stock. It may have articles of association and may be subject to regulation by a particular state's statutes; however, it is not regarded or treated the same as a corporation.

Shareholders are personally liable for association obligations; and the association's affairs generally are managed by a board of directors and by officers who serve as agents or employees of the shareholders.

Corporation

A corporation is an artificial person created by or under authority of state statute to carry on a business or activity separately from its creators, owners, or investors. A corporation has unlimited liability for corporate obligations; however, its owners' liability is limited to the amount of their investment. A corporation may have perpetual existence, which means that it is unaffected by changes in ownership. Like a natural person, a corporation may own property, may sue and be sued, may enter into contracts, and may be subject to criminal liability. As artificial persons, corporations are entitled to many of the protections of natural persons under the federal and state constitutions.

For purposes of establishing personal jurisdiction, a corporation is a citizen of the state where it is incorporated as well as of any state where it does sufficient business to establish minimum contacts with that state. A California corporation that sells insurance policies to Kansas residents from its office in California, for instance, is a citizen of California and a citizen of Kansas for purposes of personal jurisdiction and federal venue statutes.

Corporations are classified by type and may fit more than one classification. A ***public corporation*** is created by a government entity to administer government purposes. A local government may create a municipal corporation, for example, to administer the affairs of a city. The federal government has created public corporations, such as the Federal Home Mortgage Association, to administer special federal programs. A ***private corporation*** is created by private persons for private (as opposed to public) purposes. Private corporations generally are either nonprofit corporations or for-profit corporations.

A ***nonprofit corporation***, sometimes called an eleemosynary corporation, is one organized typically for educational, religious, or charitable purposes. The income earned by a nonprofit corporation is devoted to its nonprofit purpose (such as providing educational programs or scholarships) and may not be used to enrich those who operate or manage it. By contract, a for-profit corporation, more typically called a ***business corporation***, is one organized to operate a business enterprise, with profits from the business being distributed to its owners. The balance of this chapter is devoted almost exclusively to the business corporation.

A ***publicly held corporation*** is one owned by many shareholders and whose stock is publicly traded (bought and sold on the open market). Large corporations, such as General Foods or General Motors, are publicly held corporations. A ***closely held corporation***, sometimes called a close corporation, is one owned by one shareholder or by a small, closely connected group of shareholders. Unlike shareholders of publicly held corporations, shareholders of close corporations often serve as directors and officers of the corporation as well.

The ***professional corporation*** is a type of close corporation formed by a small group of professionals (lawyers, accountants, doctors) to carry on the practice for which they are licensed. Unlike shareholders of other types of corporations, shareholders of a professional corporation remain personally liable for their professional activities affecting third parties. Professionals traditionally incorporated to take advantage of retirement plans and tax benefits available to corporate employees that were not available to self-employed persons. (Federal tax laws now have been changed to provide similar retirement benefits to self-employed persons as well as to corporate employees.)

A ***domestic corporation*** is one which operates in the same state in which it was organized or created. A ***foreign corporation*** is one operating in a state that is different from the one in which the corporation was organized or created. For example, a corporation organized in Tennessee and operating in Texas is a domestic corporation in Tennessee—but is a foreign corporation in Texas.

A ***subsidiary corporation*** is one whose stock is owned entirely or in substantial part by another corporation. The corporation owning the majority of shares in a subsidiary corporation is called a ***parent corporation***.

A ***Chapter S corporation*** is a small business corporation which, under certain situations, may elect to have its undistributed taxable income taxed to its shareholders under federal tax laws as if it were a partnership. The Chapter S status generally avoids corporate income tax on profits, and corporate losses may be claimed by shareholders (*see below*).

A *limited liability corporation* is a corporate form authorized by a growing number of states, intended as a hybrid of the most attractive characteristics of the partnership and corporate forms of organization. Until more states enact statutes authorizing existence of the limited liability corporation, typical provisions and characteristics cannot be stated with reasonable accuracy.

The Decision to Incorporate   Distinctive attributes of the corporation, including centralization of management, free transferability of ownership interests, perpetual existence, and limited liability of owners (shareholders) make the corporate form advantageous for large businesses. For small businesses, however, the advantages often are illusory. Centralized management, transferability of ownership interest, and continuity of existence can be provided by specific provisions in a partnership agreement. The limited liability of the corporation loses much of its value when creditors require shareholders to guarantee corporate obligations personally, which happens fairly often in small, closely held corporations.

Creating and operating a corporation involves expense, complexity, and formalities not present in a partnership. For these reasons, the corporation is not always the most desirable form for a small business. Incorporation is most commonly indicated if limited liability is an important consideration and if federal income tax treatment is favorable.

Preincorporation   If the corporate form is desirable to operate a particular business, someone must take charge of bringing the corporation into existence. It is possible to create the corporation and then to organize it; however, the organization often is done before the statutory requirements to incorporate are met. The person or persons who plan and organize the business affairs of the intended corporation are called *promoters*. A promoter's activities typically include discovery and development of the idea for the business, arranging for needed capital, securing property and personnel to operate the business, and ultimately complying with the statutory formalities to create the corporation.

A promoter who contracts on behalf of a proposed corporation is liable on the contract unless she discloses that the corporation has not yet been formed. If a preincorporation disclosure is made, the promoter may characterize the transaction as an offer to the corporation, to be accepted or rejected after its formation. The preincorporation agreement between the promoter and the third party may provide that the promoter is liable, but will be released if the corporation is formed subsequently and assumes liability on the contract.

Once the corporation is formed, it may accept the preincorporation offer, or may adopt or assume the preincorporation contract. Corporate liability for the promoter's actions requires some affirmative act by the corporation after its formation to show its consent to the preincorporation transaction. After a corporation is formed, the promoter has a fiduciary duty to the board of directors and to the shareholders to act in good faith, to deal fairly, and to make full disclosure. A promoter may not take secret profits in violation of her fiduciary obligations.

Incorporation   Incorporation is governed by state statute. At one time, the corporation laws of Delaware were the least restrictive in the country; and, as a result, many corporations were incorporated there. The American Bar Association adopted a Model Business Corporation Act (MBCA) and, later, the Revised Model Business Corporation Act (RMBCA), which has been enacted in whole or in part by many states. As a result of this and other more liberal laws affecting corporations, more states have become strong competitors of Delaware in attracting corporate citizens.

Specific incorporation procedures vary from state to state; however, they follow the same general pattern. In the usual situation, one or more persons, called ***incorporators***, draft and execute a document called ***articles of incorporation***. (Because a corporation is a person, a corporation may be the incorporator for another corporation.) The articles of incorporation and the required fee are filed typically with the secretary of state, who issues a ***certificate of incorporation*** if the articles meet all statutory requirements. Corporate existence generally begins when the certificate of incorporation is issued. Some states have additional requirements, such as recording the articles of incorporation in a local office (for example, the county clerk) or publishing a notice of incorporation in a newspaper of general circulation.

Required contents of the articles of incorporation vary according to the laws of the incorporating state; however, these requirements generally include

- the name of the corporation;

- its duration (whether perpetual or for a specific, limited time);

- the purpose(s) for which the corporation is organized (many statutes allow a very broad statement of purposes, such as "to transact any and all lawful business for which corporations may be incorporated in this state");

•a statement of the authorized classes of stock, the authorized number of shares, the par value of shares, and the rights and preferences of shares or shareholders;

•the address of the corporation's registered office and the name and address of the registered agent (for service of process and notices);

•the names and addresses of the original directors comprising the board of directors; and

•the name and address of each incorporator.

Other information may be included as the incorporators believe appropriate. The articles of incorporation is the controlling document of the corporation. Amendment of the articles must follow specific statutory rules, which usually include a requirement that all amendments be filed with the secretary of state.

After the certificate of incorporation is issued, the organizational meeting is held by the directors named in the articles of incorporation. If no directors are required to be named in the articles, the organizational meeting is held by the incorporator(s). The overseer of this meeting generally is the attorney retained to complete the incorporation process. At the organizational meeting, subscriptions received from potential shareholders for the purchase of stock may be accepted or rejected; the form of stock certificate is adopted; the form of corporate seal is adopted (if a corporate seal is required by state law); preincorporation contracts may be accepted or rejected; a corporate bank account is authorized, together with a designation of those persons who will be authorized to sign checks and to borrow money on behalf of the corporation; and bylaws are adopted. If a particular state's statutes require it, first meetings of shareholders and directors may follow the organizational meeting to accept or reject the actions taken at the organizational meeting.

Bylaws are the written rules that supplement the articles of incorporation in governing the corporation's internal affairs. Bylaws may contain any terms or provisions desired by corporate shareholders, which are consistent with the laws of the state and also are consistent with the controlling articles of incorporation. Bylaws usually are adopted during the corporation's organizational meetings of shareholders and directors and may be amended by the corporation's board of directors, although amendment can be reserved to shareholders only. A set of bylaws may cover things such as procedures required to sell and to value shares (in closely held corporations); the method of filling vacancies for directors or officers that occur between elections; the duties and

Personal liability of shareholders may be sought in either contract or tort cases. A person who is injured in an automobile accident in which an employee of the corporation was the negligent driver may seek damages from the corporation under a theory of *respondeat superior*, for instance.

Courts are more reluctant to pierce the corporate veil in contract cases than in tort cases. A contract claimant deals with the corporation voluntarily and generally has the opportunity to secure the personal guaranty of one or more shareholders if she wishes to do so. If corporate credit is unacceptable and if the shareholders refuse to incur personal liability, the third party can refuse to enter into the contract. Tort claimants, on the other hand, are involuntary creditors. Their claims easily may be frustrated by undercapitalized, underinsured corporations; and courts are more willing to impose liability in these situations.

Corporate Financial Structure

A corporation must have a source of funds with which to acquire assets and to operate. Most funds of ongoing corporations are generated by reinvesting earnings back into the business. An additional method, and usually the initial method, of raising corporate funds is the issuance of corporate securities in exchange for cash, property, or services transferred to the corporation.

A *security* is a share or other interest in the property of the corporation (an equity security) or an obligation of the issuer (a debt security). Equity securities, such as stock shares, are those that create an ownership interest in the business. The owners of equity securities are called shareholders or stockholders. In contrast, debt securities are obligations of the corporation that must be repaid. A debt security creates a debtor-creditor relationship between the corporation and the holder of the debt security. Typical debt securities include notes, debentures, and bonds.

Corporations often use both equity securities and debt securities to finance the business. The combination of debt securities and equity securities of a particular corporation is known as the corporation's *capital structure*.

Equity Securities   The equity securities of a corporation (shares of stock) are the units into which the ownership of the corporation is divided. They represent the underlying ownership interests and confer three basic rights upon the shareholders:

1.   The right to share in distributions of corporate profits (dividends) when declared by the board of directors

2.   The right to vote on important corporate matters and thereby to participate in control

3.   The right to a proportionate share of net assets upon liquidation of the corporation.

Not all ownership interests (shares of stock) are created equal. The articles of incorporation may divide shares into classes. If classes are created, the articles of incorporation must describe the designations, preferences, limitations, and rights of each class in relation to other classes. The voting rights of any class of shares may be limited or denied entirely, or special voting rights may be provided. In addition, a corporation may issue stock in preferred or special classes that have preference over other classes in (1) the payment of dividends, or (2) the distribution of assets of the corporation upon liquidation. Classes of shares that have these types of preferential rights are called **preferred shares**. Preferred shares generally are nonvoting shares.

By contrast, **common shares** are the residual ownership interest in the corporation. Common shares are entitled to payment of dividends only after shares with a dividend preference are paid. They are entitled to distribution of assets upon liquidation only after creditors (including holders of debt securities) and preferred shareholders receive distributions. If a corporation has only one class of shares, it is, in effect, common stock regardless of what it may be called.

Most states permit a corporation to have more than one class of common stock, each possessing different rights and privileges.

The articles of incorporation may make certain classes of stock subject to reacquisition (redemption) by the corporation at a fixed price. These are **redeemable shares**. Although redemption or "call" provisions typically apply only to preferred shares, some states permit redeemable common shares as long as there is at least one class of voting common shares which is not subject to redemption. Redemption of a class of shares may be mandatory or optional and may be total or partial, as determined by the articles of incorporation.

The articles of incorporation also may provide that shares of a given class can be converted into shares of another class on some predetermined ratio. These are **convertible shares**. The ratio generally takes stock dividends and stock splits into account to protect the conversion privilege against dilution. The MBCA and some state statutes prohibit conversion of one class of stock into a class (1) having prior or superior rights to dividends or (2) having prior or superior rights to corporate assets upon liquidation. Under these types of provisions, for example, preferred stock may be converted to common stock; however, common stock may not be converted to preferred stock.

A given class of shares often possesses both redemption and conversion privileges. If so, after the call for redemption, the shareholder generally has a limited time within which to exercise the conversion right. Redemption and conversion privileges often are found in debt securities as well *(see below)*.

A corporation may create and issue *stock options* that entitle the option holders to purchase a stated number of shares of a given class from the corporation at a specific price and usually within a limited period of time. Options may be purchased either in connection with or independently of the corporation's issuance of other securities. They may be issued as incentives to corporate directors, officers, or employees.

Stock options generally are evidenced by certificates called *stock warrants*, which characteristically are long term. By contrast, short-term share options are called *stock rights* and often are issued in connection with the issuance of debt securities or preferred stock. Both warrants and rights of publicly held corporations are freely transferable and are publicly traded. Their value depends on the difference between the stock's market price and the option price.

A shareholder has *preemptive rights* when she has the right to purchase a proportionate share of a new issue of common stock (or of securities that are convertible to common stock) before it is offered for sale to others. Whether preemptive rights are granted by the articles of incorporation or by statute, they provide a method of protecting a shareholder's proportionate interest in the corporation. Preemptive rights are more common in closely held corporations than in publicly held corporations *(see below)*.

A.   Issuance of Stock   A corporation has the power to create and to issue the number of shares stated or authorized in its articles of incorporation. The law generally places no limit on the number of shares of various classes that can be authorized; neither does it require that all authorized shares be issued. Some states, however, impose a tax according to the number of authorized shares, which creates a practical ceiling on the shares which are authorized.

Shares of issued stock are represented by stock certificates. The *stock certificate* merely is evidence of the holder's undivided ownership interest; it is not the stock itself. Because the ownership interest is undivided (cannot be separated from the corporate assets), a stock certificate is the method used to show the owner's stock interest.

Some or all of the authorized shares are issued to shareholders for consideration; these are known as ***outstanding shares***. Shares are outstanding until they are later reacquired by the corporation through redemption, conversion, or repurchase. Shares reacquired by the corporation are known as treasury shares or ***treasury stock***.

Shares may be issued with a par value or may be "no par" shares. ***Par value*** is the dollar amount stated as the value of the share in the articles of incorporation. Historically, par value was the selling price of the shares. Today, however, par value often has little connection with the selling price of the stock. Both par and no par shares are issued for the amount is determined by the board of directors (unless the right to determine value is reserved to shareholders).

Stock may not be sold for less than par value. Consequently, par stock often shows a nominal par value (such as $1.00). Absent fraud, the judgment of the board of directors about the consideration to be paid for stock is conclusive. Treasury stock may be sold for any price set by the board of directors without regard to the par value stated on the stock.

B.   Payment for Stock   Before a corporation is formed, stock subscriptions are one method to acquire investment capital or the assurance of investment capital. A preincorporation ***stock subscription*** is an offer by a would-be shareholder to purchase a specified number of previously unissued shares of the corporation. Stock subscriptions can be made either before or after the corporation is formed. When stock subscriptions are made after the corporation is formed, they constitute bilateral contracts between the subscriber and the corporation. When stock subscriptions are made before the corporation is formed, they constitute irrevocable offers under both MBCA and RMBCA provisions.

Payment terms for stock subscriptions generally are set by the board of directors; payment must be uniform for all shares of the same class. In general, the stock certificate is not issued until the subscription price is paid in full. If a subscriber defaults in the agreed payments, the board of directors may collect the debt in the same way as all other debts of the corporation are collected.

Securities registration requirements generally prevent the use of stock subscriptions for equity securities issued by publicly held corporations.

C.   Watered Stock   As consideration for issuance of stock, shareholders and subscribers must pay the value of the stock as determined by the board of directors. Although consideration usually is expressed in dollars, money is not the only consideration permitted. Some states permit the consideration to be paid in property or in services as well as in cash. Using this approach, a promissory note cannot constitute payment for the stock. However, the RMBCA permits stock to be issued either in exchange for a promissory note or in exchange for a contract for future services to the corporation.

Stock issued and paid for at the full value established by the board of directors are *fully paid and nonassessable* shares. Stock issued for something less than the full value established by the board of directors is ***watered stock***. Issuance of watered stock can occur when a shareholder pays nothing for the shares (*bonus stock*) or when a shareholder pays less than full value for the shares (*discount stock*).

Watered stock dilutes the value of stock held by all other shareholders, because it dilutes their equity interests in corporate assets. When this occurs, the remedy is cancellation of the offending shares. Watered stock also inflates the corporation's capitalization, which may mislead creditors (securities regulations prevent many of the previous abuses in relation to creditors of publicly traded corporations). If creditors are involved, the offending shareholder(s) can be required to pay the additional amount necessary to reach the value of the stock set by the board of directors.

A subsequent good faith purchaser of the stock incurs no liability to the corporation or to its creditors for consideration that was not paid by the original shareholder. Likewise, a creditor to whom the stock is transferred as collateral is not liable. In both situations, the transferor (the original shareholder) remains liable for the watered amount of the stock: actual value less value paid.

Debt Securities   Debt securities are issued in exchange for loans made to the corporation. As is true of any other loan, debt securities typically require periodic interest payments and ultimate repayment of principal. The holder of a debt security is a creditor of the corporation and, as a creditor, has a claim on corporate assets that is prior to the claims of any shareholders.

Publicly held corporations frequently issue debt securities in the form of either bonds or debentures. A ***bond*** is an obligation secured by a lien or a mortgage on specific corporate property; the holder of a bond is a secured creditor of the corporation. By contrast, a ***debenture*** is an unsecured corporate obligation; a holder of a corporate debenture is an unsecured creditor of the corporation.

Corporate bonds and debentures generally are long-term obligations, issued in fixed denominations (perhaps $1,000) with a fixed interest rate, which is called the coupon rate. Bonds and debentures most often are handled by a financial institution which serves as the trustee under a trust agreement—sometimes called a ***trust indenture***—between the corporation and the trustee for the benefit of the security holders.

In addition to bonds and debentures, corporations frequently obtain either short-term or long-term loans from commercial banks and similar lenders in exchange for promissory ***notes*** from the corporation, either secured or unsecured. Suppliers of goods or services (trade creditors) also may extend credit or corporations on a secured or unsecured basis.

If money can be borrowed from outside creditors, one possible advantage of debt financing is ***leverage***, sometimes called *trading on equity*. Leverage occurs when the total investment in the business (debt + equity) yields a higher rate of return than the cost of borrowing money (interest rate).

> Ajax Corporation has a total investment of $1,000,000 and generates $150,000 a year in earnings, which yields a 15 percent rate of return. As long as the interest rate stays below 15 percent, Ajax should borrow as much of the $1,000,000 investment as possible. The difference between the rate of return and the interest rate is additional profit. If, however, earnings are so poor that they fall below the interest rate, the difference is an additional loss.

Shareholders frequently lend a portion of their investment to the corporation, rather than use all of it to purchase stock. Since interest payments on the debt are deductible and dividend payments on the stock are not, shareholder debt often reduces the problem of "double taxation" associated with corporations (corporation is taxed on its profit, declares dividends, and shareholder is taxed on dividend income).

Because of the tax advantages of corporate debt that is payable to shareholders, the Internal Revenue Service (IRS) has been able to reclassify some corporate debt as shareholder stock interest, particularly in those corporations with excessive debt capitalization. A corporation with a high debt-to-equity ratio (four to one or higher) commonly is known as a *thin corporation* and may be subject to debt reclassification under IRS regulations.

Dividends and Redemption

When a corporation transfers corporate money or property to its shareholders, the transfer is a *distribution*. When the distribution comes from the corporation's current or past earnings, it is a ***dividend***. A dividend may or may not be proportionate to share ownership. Preferred shares, for example, may have preferential rights to dividends over other shares. In addition, a corporation's redemption or repurchase of its shares may produce a disproportionate distribution.

Any distribution (whether by dividend or by corporate liquidation) may affect the rights of creditors and of various classes of shareholders. As a result, limitations are placed upon the distributions that a corporation lawfully can make.

Dividends   Dividends typically take the form of cash, property (such as shares of stock of a subsidiary), or stock. A stock dividend means stock of the corporation declaring the dividend. (Stock of a subsidiary corporation is property—it is not stock—of the corporation declaring the dividend.) A corporation pays dividends only by declaration of its board of directors. Once declared, a dividend is a legally enforceable obligation of the corporation and cannot be repealed or retracted by the board of directors. Whether or not to declare dividends is influenced by such factors as corporate earnings, future capital needs of the business, and shareholder expectations. Federal income tax consequences to major shareholders can affect dividend and retention policies in closely held corporations.

Shareholders usually participate in dividends in proportion to their ownership interests, as determined by the classes of shares identified in the articles of incorporation. Preferred stock, for example, typically receives dividends before common stock receives dividends.

The articles of incorporation may provide that preferred stock be cumulative, cumulative-to-the-extent-earned, or noncumulative. *Cumulative preferred* stock receives a prescribed dividend for the current year as well as for all prior years in which a preferred dividend was not paid by the corporation—before any dividend may be paid for common stock. *Cumulative-to-the-extent-earned preferred* stock carries forward and accumulates any unpaid dividends to the extent that the corporation had earnings to pay the dividend but did not pay it.

> Ajax Corporation had earnings in 2007, no earnings in 2008, and substantial earnings in 2009. If the preferred stock is cumulative-to-the-extent-earned and if dividends are to be paid in 2009, the dividends for 2007, 2008, and 2009 must be paid for the preferred stock before any dividend is paid for common stock.

Noncumulative preferred stock receives only the prescribed dividend for the current year (prior years need not be paid) before dividends are paid for common stock.

Regardless of the cumulative or noncumulative status of preferred stock, the articles of incorporation may provide that preferred stock be either participating or nonparticipating. ***Participating preferred*** stock receives the preferred dividend fixed by the articles and also participates in dividends paid to other classes of stock. ***Nonparticipating preferred*** stock receives only the preferred dividend stated in the articles of incorporation; it does not participate in any other dividend payments made to other classes of stock.

A.   Stock Dividends   Unlike cash or property dividends *(see above)*, stock dividends do not distribute corporate assets to the shareholder. Instead, a stock dividend distributes additional shares of stock (or fractional shares) for each share owned. A stock dividend increases the number of shares comprising the corporation's equity and, at the same time, proportionately reduces the percentage of ownership of each share. The additional shares generally—but not always—are of the same class as the original shares.

The MBCA permits—but does not require—a corporation to issue either (1) *fractional shares* of stock or (2) *scrip* in lieu of fractional shares. A particular state may follow the MBCA or may authorize corporations to issue only fractional shares or only scrip.

> Ajax Corporation declares a one percent stock dividend entitling shareholders to receive one additional share of stock for every 100 shares owned. John owns 150 shares of Ajax stock.

If the corporation issues fractional shares, John will receive 1.5 shares of stock as his dividend. The holder of a ***fractional share*** is entitled to a fractional voting right, a fractional dividend, and a fractional distribution if the corporation is liquidated. By contrast, ***scrip*** is a certificate representing a percentage of a full share. When the holder accumulates enough scrip certificates (scrip may be bought and sold), she may surrender them for one full share of stock. Unless the board of directors provides otherwise, scrip certificates do not entitle the holder to the same voting, dividend, or liquidation rights as fractional shares. In addition, the board of directors may provide that scrip becomes void if it is not exchanged for full shares within a certain time period.

B.   Stock Split   A stock split is similar to a stock dividend, since each increases the total number of outstanding shares without distributing corporate assets. They are different, however, in the way they affect corporate capital accounts. When a stock dividend is declared, the value of the stock is capitalized (transferred from the earnings surplus account to the capital

account—either as additional stated capital or as additional capital surplus). There is no transfer of earnings to capital in a stock split.

A stock split simply creates more shares of stock (two-for-one, three-for-one), with each share valued at a proportionately lesser amount. In a two-for-one split, for example, shares valued at $100.00 each would be valued at $50.00 each after the split. Stock splits sometimes are used to reduce the per-share value of stock, making it more attractive to a larger group of investors. Stock splits typically require approval of the board of directors and may require amendment of the articles of incorporation to authorize the issuance of additional shares of stock or to change the par value of authorized stock.

Stock splits typically do not create tax consequences.

Funds Available to Pay Dividends   To protect corporate creditors and, to a lesser degree, to protect preferred shareholders, state law limits the distribution of corporate assets to shareholders. Although there is some variation, all states essentially follow the insolvency test found in both the MBCA and the RMBCA. Under the *insolvency test*, dividend payments are prohibited if the corporation is insolvent or would be rendered insolvent by the distribution. Insolvency may be either equity insolvency or bankruptcy insolvency.

Equity insolvency is the inability to pay debts as they become due in the ordinary course of business.

Bankruptcy insolvency is the excess of total liabilities over total assets.

If a corporation is insolvent under *either* insolvency test, the Model Acts prohibit payment of a dividend to shareholders.

When a corporation is solvent, all states permit dividends to be paid to the extent of the corporation's unrestricted and unreserved earned surplus. Earned surplus means retained earnings and typically includes all accumulated profits of the corporation since its formation, reduced primarily by prior dividend distributions.

When a corporation is solvent, some states permit dividends to be paid from either surplus capital or earned surplus. These states typically permit dividends to be paid unless the dividend would cause an impairment of the stated capital (total par value); however, dividends from surplus capital may be limited if there is no earned surplus.
</body>

Only a handful of states permit what are known as *nimble* dividends, where dividends can be paid from current profits even if a deficit exists in the earned surplus accounts from losses in prior years.

State statutes generally impose liability upon directors for unlawful dividends or for other unlawful distributions. Under both Model Acts, a director is liable to the corporation for the amount by which the declared distribution exceeds the legally permissible amount if she votes for or assents to the declaration of a dividend or other distribution in violation of statutory limits or in violation of the articles of incorporation. Such a director may have a defense to liability if she exercised *due care* in declaring the dividend by relying upon financial statements or upon the opinions provided by corporate officers, accountants, attorneys, or employees.

Repurchase and Redemption   Under both the MBCA and the RMBCA, a corporation has the power to acquire its own shares of stock through repurchase. It also has the power to issue stock (usually preferred stock), which can be redeemed by the corporation at a later time. These types of shares are called treasury stock after they are repurchased or redeemed, and are the functional equivalent of authorized but unissued shares. After the repurchase or redemption, each outstanding remaining share represents a proportionately larger interest in a smaller group of corporate assets.

A repurchase or a redemption is similar to a cash or property dividend, because the corporation distributes corporate assets to shareholders without consideration. Unlike a dividend, however, a repurchase or redemption involves an element of exchange: shares of stock in exchange for corporate assets. When the repurchase or redemption is partial, it causes a disproportionate distribution of corporate assets to the selling shareholders; dividends, on the other hand, generally are paid to all shareholders in proportion to their ownership interests.

A corporation may repurchase its own shares for one of several reasons. In a closely held corporation, the repurchase may be necessary to buy out one or more shareholders. In a publicly held corporation, the repurchased shares may be used to fund employee compensation plans or to acquire other corporations. Moreover, significant repurchases may drive up the price of the remaining shares as a defensive measure against a hostile takeover bid.

Repurchases and redemptions are classified as corporate distributions and are subject to the same legal restrictions as dividends, including the insolvency test (*see above*).

Corporate Taxation

Like individuals (and consistent with its identity as a separate legal entity), a corporation is subject to taxes levied by federal, state, and local governments based on the amount of income earned each year.

Double taxation occurs when corporate profits are taxed at the corporate rate, the after-tax balance is distributed to shareholders as dividends, and the dividend income is taxed again (to the shareholder) at the individual income tax rate. With parent-subsidiary corporations, this can become triple taxation. For example, when the subsidiary pays its tax and distributes remaining profits to its parent corporation (the sole shareholder) as dividends, those dividends become part of the parent's income; and the parent pays tax on it before distributing the balance to the individual shareholders as dividends, which are included in the shareholder's individual income tax.

Large corporations simply accept this disadvantage, because the corporate form offers many advantages that are critical to operating a large business. Small corporations, however, may have options available to minimize the double taxation effect. For example, when shareholders also are officers or employees of the corporation, as is frequently the case, they may be paid salaries by the corporation, which are deductible as a corporate expense and therefore not included in the net taxable income of the corporation. Another option is to use a portion of the shareholder's investment to lend money to the corporation rather than to buy shares of stock. In this way, the interest on the loan is an expense to the corporation. This works well, as long as the corporation's debt-to-equity ratio is not excessive (*see above*). In addition, shareholders may purchase equipment and lease it to the corporation (rather than buying stock); the shareholder then receives rental payments on the equipment, which is an expense to the corporation.

Another approach is to leave profits in the corporation as retained earnings; since no dividends are distributed, only the corporate tax is paid. This option has only limited advantages, because retained earnings increase the value of the remaining, outstanding stock, which means a capital gains tax for the shareholder if the stock is sold. Even more limiting is the fact that a separate accumulated earnings tax is levied against the corporation when it retains excessive earnings.

Chapter S Election   A small business corporation may elect not to be taxed at the corporate rate. Instead, its income (whether distributed as dividends or retained by the corporation) is passed through in proportion to shareholders' ownership interests and is taxed at each shareholder's respective individual income tax rate. The corporation thus receives the same tax treatment as a sole proprietorship or partnership. This provides two advantages over corporate tax treatment: (1) profits are not subject to double taxation and (2) if the shareholder actively participates in the business, corporate losses may be taken as ordinary losses against the shareholder's personal income which, in turn, reduces the shareholder's personal income tax liability. The qualifications for a Chapter S election are as follows:

- No more than 100 shareholders (spouses are treated as a single shareholder, no matter how the stock is held by them).

- Shareholders must be natural persons (no corporations or partnerships).

- There can be only one class of stock (different classes are permitted if their only difference is voting rights).

- No nonresident aliens as shareholders.

Making the election to be taxed as a Chapter S corporation for a given fiscal year must be done within certain time limits (any time during the preceding fiscal year or no later than three months into the current fiscal year). Once made, the election continues until it is terminated by a majority of the shareholders; until the corporation receives more than 25 percent of its income from passive sources (rents, dividends, interest) for three consecutive years; or until the corporation acquires its 101st shareholder.

Chapter S status may be desirable during the first few years of operation, when the corporation is most likely to incur losses.

Section 1244 Stock   Section 1244 of the Internal Revenue Code provides a separate method for shareholders of small business corporations to receive favorable tax treatment if they sell Section 1244 stock or if the stock becomes worthless. Rather than take a capital loss, which is what ordinarily would occur with losses on stocks, the shareholder can treat the loss as ordinary loss—which means she can credit it against ordinary income to reduce her personal income tax liability.

The definition of a small business corporation is different for Section 1244 stock than it is for a Chapter S election. To qualify as Section 1244 stock, the amount of money to be raised by selling Section 1244 stock plus the corporation's equity capital cannot exceed one million dollars total.

Another major difference is that a Chapter S election applies to all income and all shareholders of the corporation. By contrast, Section 1244 applies only to a specific group of stock shares to which Section 1244 benefits will attach when they are offered for sale to prospective shareholders. The number of persons to whom the stock is offered is quite limited and usually involves existing shareholders. A single shareholder, then, may own some shares that are from the Section 1244 group and some shares that are not. If losses are incurred, the Section 1244 shares receive a different, more favorable tax treatment (ordinary loss) than the regular shares (capital loss).

Other Tax Advantages   Corporations traditionally have been allowed to deduct certain types of expenses incurred in providing fringe benefits to employees to encourage their long and faithful performance. In addition, there are some tax advantages to employees under qualified incentive plans without regard to whether the employee is also a shareholder or not. These include stock options; qualified pension and profit-sharing plans; medical and dental reimbursement plans; and life, health, and accident insurance programs.

For example, a qualified profit-sharing plan allows the corporation to deduct profits accumulated for employees under the plan. At the same time, the employee is not taxed on those amounts until payment is made, which often is not until the employee reaches retirement age and a more favorable income tax bracket. Premiums for health and life insurance plans are expenses to the corporation but are not treated as taxable income to the employee.

Favorable tax treatment of these types of fringe benefit packages once was unique to the corporation. In recent years, however, many of the same tax incentives are available to self-employed persons.

Corporate Management

Once a corporation is formed, it is managed by individuals whose functions, rights, authority, and duties are governed by statutes, case law, administrative regulations, and internal sources such as the corporation's articles of incorporation, bylaws, resolutions, and private contracts. Corporate management responsibilities are divided among shareholders, the board of directors, and corporate officers. As owners of the corporation, shareholders elect a board of directors, which has ultimate responsibility to manage the corporation. The directors, in turn, elect or appoint corporate officers and give them authority to operate the corporation consistent with the management policy set by the board of directors. The officers frequently appoint executive officers, who hire employees to undertake the day-to-day activities of the business. Collectively, the officers and directors comprise the management of the corporation.

In a small, closely held corporation, the same individuals frequently are shareholders, directors, and officers simultaneously.

Shareholders   Shareholders (stockholders) are the owners of the corporation; however, their management involvement generally is limited to election of directors and extraordinary corporate matters such as amendments to the articles of incorporation, sale of corporate assets other than in the ordinary course of business, merger or consolidation, and dissolution. The power to adopt, amend, or repeal bylaws frequently is reserved to the shareholders by the articles of incorporation.

A.   Shareholder Meetings   Shareholder voting generally is done at either annual or special meetings. Corporations typically hold an annual shareholders' meeting at a time specified in the corporation's bylaws. The primary purpose of the annual meeting is to elect a board of directors; however, other business also may be conducted at the annual meeting. In addition, annual management reports may be given; bylaws may be amended or repealed; and management resolutions may be considered and adopted (or rejected) by vote of the shareholders.

In addition to the annual meeting, special meetings may be called by the board of directors, by the holders of a specified number of shares, or by other persons named in the bylaws or in the articles of incorporation. Special meetings are called to consider important matters that cannot wait until the next annual meeting.

Advance, written notice of the date, time, and place of both annual and special meetings must be given to each shareholder who is entitled to vote. In addition, notice of special meetings must include the purpose for the meeting, and only business related to that purpose may be conducted at the meeting.

Shareholders may cast their votes in person at either annual or special meetings or may authorize others to vote their shares by proxy. A quorum of shareholders must be present to conduct business, either in person or by proxy. A majority of the shares entitled to vote generally constitutes a quorum. Although the articles of incorporation may specify a different percentage, most state statutes provide that a quorum may not be less than one-third of those shares entitled to vote. Unless stated otherwise in the bylaws or articles of incorporation, a majority vote of the quorum is needed to deal with any matter brought before the meeting.

The MBCA and many state statutes allow shareholders to take action without a meeting if written ***consent*** to the action is signed by all shareholders entitled to vote on the issue. The consent-in-lieu-of-meeting avoids unnecessary formal meetings and can be especially useful in closely held corporations, where many decisions are unanimous.

To determine which shareholders are entitled to notice of a meeting, to demand a special meeting, to vote at meetings, or to take other shareholder action, the bylaws or the board of directors may set a ***record date***. Persons listed in the corporate records as registered owners of voting shares on the record date are entitled to vote. Statutes generally require the record date to be set within a specified period before the meeting, such as "not more than 70 days before the meeting." Once the record date is established, the officer or agent in charge of the stock transfer books prepares a complete voter list or ***voting record*** of shareholders entitled to vote. The list must be made available to shareholders for inspection and copying at the time of the meeting and, in some states, in advance of the meeting.

B.   Shareholder Voting   Unless a different provision is made in the articles of incorporation, each outstanding share (regardless of its class) is entitled to one vote on each item presented at the meeting. The articles may permit more than one vote to any class of stock, but all shares within the class must have the same rights.

Treasury stock and stock held by other corporations which are controlled by the issuing corporation (subsidiaries) are not entitled to vote and are not counted in fixing the number of outstanding shares. Redeemable shares are entitled to vote—unless a notice of redemption has been mailed and there is sufficient money on deposit with a financial institution to redeem the shares.

The voting rights of any class of stock may be limited or denied by the articles of incorporation. However, if an amendment to the articles of incorporation that would alter the rights of the shares of that class (changing the number of authorized shares, preemptive rights, and so forth), shareholders are entitled to vote as a class, even though they have no voting rights otherwise. In addition, a nonvoting class of shares is entitled to vote when the question relates to merger or voluntary dissolution of the corporation.

C.   Election of Directors   Shareholders may elect directors either by straight voting or by cumulative voting. ***Straight voting*** is the method by which each share is entitled to one vote on each matter, including one vote for each director position to be filled. Since directors generally are elected by a plurality of votes, the shareholder with the largest number of shares effectively elects all of the directors. State laws concerning shareholder voting generally follow this method; however, shareholders always may select a different method through bylaws or by shareholder agreement (*see below*).

To ensure representation of minority shareholders on the board of directors, many states require ***cumulative voting***, which applies to election of directors only. Under a cumulative voting method, each shareholder is allowed to aggregate her votes by multiplying the number of her total shares × the number of director vacancies to be filled. Her aggregate votes then may be cast in favor of one director or may be allocated in any way desired by the shareholder.

> Casey owns 800 shares of Ajax Corporation. At the annual meeting of shareholders, nine directors will be elected to the board. Casey has 7200 votes, which he may cast for one director or may allocate among director vacancies as he sees fit. If he casts all votes for a single director, he cannot vote in the election of any other directors.

As the number of directors on the board increases, the number of minority shares needed to elect a single director increases; thus, the impact of cumulative voting of decreases.

D.   Proxy Voting   A ***proxy*** is the grant of authority to another to vote a stockholder's shares. Many states require the proxy to be in writing and signed by the shareholder. The proxy holder need not be a shareholder but must be competent to serve as an agent. A general proxy allows the proxy holder to vote on all issues presented at the meeting. Unless the proxy itself provides otherwise, both the MBCA and the RMBCA provide that a proxy is valid for 11 months.

Like other agency relationships, appointment of a proxy is revocable by the shareholder at any time; revocation also may occur upon the death or incapacity of the shareholder (the proxy holder must have notice under the RMBCA before the proxy is revoked). A proxy may be irrevocable if it is "coupled with an interest" or is "given as security." For example, when a shareholder pledges her shares as collateral for a loan, the lender may require her to provide an irrevocable proxy to vote the shares as well. When the debt is fully paid, however, the irrevocable proxy is extinguished.

E.   Voting Trusts and Agreements   A person who accumulates enough shareholder proxies can obtain control of a corporation or, at least, can ensure representation on the board of directors. Voting trusts and voting agreements can accomplish a similar result by controlling large blocks of stock. A ***voting trust*** is created when a group of stockholders transfers legal title to their shares to a trustee in exchange for voting trust certificates. The trustee has the power to vote the shares, subject to any limitations in the trust agreement. Corporate dividends and other distributions generally are passed through the trust to the equitable owners of the shares (the owners of the trust certificates).

Early cases refused to enforce voting trusts on the basis that separating the right to vote from other rights of ownership was against public policy; however, modern corporation statutes uniformly authorize voting trusts, subject to certain restrictions. For instance, the RMBCA requires a voting trust to be in writing and signed by all participating shareholders. In addition, it is valid only for 10 years unless the parties extend it.

The voting trust may concentrate control of a large block of shares in one individual or in a small group of individuals, who can elect directors and thus control the corporation. Voting trusts frequently are used in corporate reorganizations to give control to former creditors whose debts are reclassified as stock as part of the reorganization plan.

A shareholder ***voting agreement***, sometimes called a ***pooling agreement***, is a less formal method of control. Unlike the voting trust, which transfers legal title of the shares to a third party, a voting agreement is a contract between two or more shareholders concerning the way in which their shares will be voted on certain issues, including election of directors. Shareholder voting agreements are enforceable under general contract principles and usually are authorized by statute. Shareholder agreements typically are used to allocate and to maintain control in closely held corporations.

F.   Shareholder Right to Information   The law requires every corporation to keep appropriate accounting books and records, minutes of its shareholders' and board of directors meetings, and detailed records of its shareholders. Shareholders have the common law and statutory right to be kept informed of corporate affairs and, therefore, have the right to inspect corporate records for "proper purposes." The articles of incorporation may grant an absolute right of inspection for some types of records, such as the articles of incorporation, bylaws, and so forth.

The statutory right of inspection generally is limited to those who own a minimum number of shares or who have been shareholders for a minimum time or both. For example, a state statute may provide inspection rights only to those shareholders who own at least five percent of the outstanding stock of the corporation or who have been shareholders for at least six months. The shareholder exercises the right by a written demand upon the corporation, which states the purpose of the demand.

A "proper purpose" is one gauged to protect the shareholder's interest in the corporation, such as determining the corporation's financial condition, the value of shares, the propriety of dividend payments, discovering the existence of dishonesty or mismanagement by corporate officers or directors, or communicating with other shareholders to solicit proxies or to publicize mismanagement. Improper purposes include harassment or extortion, acquiring trade secrets for personal benefit or for the benefit of a competitor, and obtaining the stockholder list to sell for profit.

G.   **Preemptive Rights**   An existing corporation may issue additional shares of stock to finance corporate operations or expansion. Existing shareholders may have a preemptive right in new shares of stock issued by an existing corporation. A ***preemptive right*** allows an existing shareholder to purchase a new issue of shares in proportion to her present interest in the corporation before any shares are sold to others. A preemptive right is more valuable in a closely held corporation than it is in a publicly held corporation. If it is exercised, a preemptive right prevents dilution of a shareholder's financial or voting interest in the corporation. Preemptive rights generally are governed by statutes that allow them to be limited or denied by appropriate provisions in the articles of incorporation.

Even when preemptive rights exist, they can be exercised only for new issues of stock—not for shares previously authorized but unissued. In addition, preemptive rights generally *do not apply* to

- shares issued for property or services rather than for cash;

- shares issued in connection with merger, consolidation, or reorganization;

- shares issued to satisfy conversion or option rights;

- treasury shares; or

- shares issued to directors, officers, or employees under compensation or incentive plans.

Directors   All corporate power is exercised by or under the authority of the board of directors, which manages the business and affairs of the corporation. As part of its basic management function, the board of directors

- *makes basic policy decisions (products, services, prices, labor relations, and so forth);*

- *appoints, supervises, and removes corporate officers and other executive personnel and delegates authority to them to act on behalf of the corporation;*

- *determines executive compensation, including pension and retirement plans;*

- *determines if, when, in what form, and in what amount dividends will be paid;*

- *determines financing and capital structure;*

- *adopts, amends, and repeals bylaws (unless that power is reserved to the shareholders in the articles of incorporation);*

- *participates with shareholders in major changes such as merger, consolidation, or dissolution; and*

- *supervises the overall operation of the business.*

Directors may be *insiders*—individuals who are also officers or employees of the corporation or its affiliates. They also may be outside directors—individuals who are not affiliated with management. Boards of large publicly held corporations include a mixture of both inside and outside directors.

A.   Board of Directors   Older corporate statutes required a board of directors to consist of at least three persons; however, modern statutes typically permit one- or two-person boards of directors. The number and qualification of directors are specified in the articles of incorporation or in the bylaws.

The initial board of directors, named in the articles of incorporation or appointed by the incorporators, serves until the first meeting of shareholders. This meeting generally is held shortly after incorporation. Permanent directors are elected by the shareholders at that meeting and at each annual meeting thereafter. Both the MBCA and the RMBCA provide that if a corporation has nine or more directors, the articles of incorporation may provide for two or three classes of directors. If two classes are authorized, each class serves a two-year term and is elected every other year, which results in staggered terms. If classes of directors are not specified in the articles, all directors are elected annually.

After incorporation, the number of directors may be increased or decreased by amendment of the articles of incorporation or bylaws. A reduction in the number of directors does not shorten any incumbent director's term. A director whose term has expired continues to serve until a successor is elected and qualified. Because directors continue in office until their successors are elected and qualified, the corporation's power to transact business is unaffected by delay or failure to hold an annual meeting of shareholders.

Vacancies on the board are filled according to statutory provisions or according to the bylaws. Typical statutes provide that remaining board members elect or appoint director vacancies caused by death or resignation. Vacancies caused by an increase in the number of directors may be filled by the directors as well, although some states require shareholder action. A director elected to fill a vacancy generally serves until the next meeting of shareholders at which directors are elected.

During her term of office, a director may be removed by the shareholders for cause (fraud, breach of duty, and so forth), usually by a majority vote. Both the MBCA and RMBCA allow a shareholder vote to remove a director without cause unless the articles of incorporation provide otherwise.

B.   Actions of Board of Directors   Management authority is vested in the board of directors as a group—not in its individual members. As a result, directors generally must act in properly called meetings that provide an opportunity to discuss, deliberate, and reach a collective judgment. The timing and details of board meetings typically are governed by detailed bylaw provisions. They may be either regular or special meetings and may be held either within or outside the state of incorporation. All types of business may be conducted at both regular and special meetings; however, directors are entitled to advance written notice of special meetings.

In general, a majority of the number of directors fixed by the articles or bylaws constitutes a quorum for the transaction of business. The articles or bylaws may require a greater number to reach a quorum, and some states allow less than a majority (one-third, for example) of the members to constitute a quorum. Many states also permit board meetings to take place by telephone.

If a quorum is present, a majority vote of those directors present constitutes the act of the board unless the articles or bylaws require a greater number. Each director is entitled to one vote and generally cannot vote by proxy. Both Model Acts permit directors to act without a meeting if a written **consent** stating the action taken is signed by all directors. A consent-in-lieu-of-meeting has the effect of a unanimous vote.

A director who objects to an action authorized by a majority of the board must either request that her dissent be recorded in the minutes of the meeting or must give written notice of **dissent** within a short time after the meeting. Either action eliminates the dissenting director's potential personal liability for the action taken.

C.   **Committee Action**   The board of directors of a large corporation often delegates much of its management authority to corporate officers, to executive committees, or to other committees appointed by the board. If permitted by the articles of incorporation or bylaws, the board of directors may establish one or more committees and may appoint one or more members of the board to serve on them. A committee exercises the board's authority to the extent specified by the board or provided in the articles or bylaws. The most common is the executive committee, which performs board functions between meetings of the full board. Other committees might include an audit, a nomination, a compensation, and a finance committee. To prevent excessive delegation of board authority, committee powers are limited by statute. The Model Acts state that a *committee may not*

- authorize distributions;
- approve a merger (even when shareholder vote is not required);
- fill vacancies on the board of directors;
- adopt, amend, or repeal bylaws; or
- authorize or approve reacquisition or sale of shares.

These important matters must be undertaken by a vote of the full board of directors.

Officers   Corporate officers conduct the day-to-day affairs of the business and are appointed (or removed) by the board of directors. Officers are agents of the corporation to whom the board delegates authority to administer policy decisions of the board of directors. Corporate officers typically include a president, one or more vice presidents, a secretary, and a treasurer. In addition, various junior officers may be appointed (assistant treasurer, assistant secretary, assistant vice president, comptroller). The duties of the corporate officers are outlined in the bylaws.

Officers generally serve at the pleasure of the board of directors and are subject to removal at any time. However, if a valid employment contract exists between the officer and the corporation, premature termination may constitute a breach of that contract.

A.   Authority of Officers   Unlike directors, officers are agents of the corporation; and their conduct is governed by general principles of agency law. Like all other agents, a corporate officer's authority to act for the corporation (the principal of the agent) derives from:

(1)   Actual authority, whether express or implied;
(2)   Apparent authority; or
(3)   Corporate ratification of a previously unauthorized act.

An officer's express authority derives from one of four sources: (1) state corporation statutes; (2) the articles of incorporation; (3) the bylaws; or (4) resolutions of the board of directors. The most typical and most reliable of these is a resolution of the board of directors that authorizes the transaction in question.

Like other agents, a corporate officer may possess a degree of implied authority to act which flows from her express authority. Although some courts have upheld an implied authority of a corporate president to bind the corporation in certain situations, prudent third parties always will require a resolution of the board of directors to ensure corporate liability on important transactions negotiated by officers.

Even if the officer possesses no actual authority (express or implied), the corporation may be bound by the officer's apparent authority or may be bound on the grounds of ratification. **Apparent authority** arises when a person (here, the corporation) leads third parties to believe that another (here, the corporate officer) has authority to act on that person's behalf. Third parties who reasonably rely on the officer's apparent authority may be able to bind the corporation despite the officer's lack of actual authority.

Notwithstanding actual or apparent authority, the corporation may be bound by an officer's conduct if it ratifies the previously unauthorized act of the officer.

Duties of Management   Corporate management (directors, officers, and sometimes controlling shareholders) has legal duties to the corporation and, in some situations, to its shareholders and creditors. The most important legal duties are based upon common law rules, which have been codified by statute in most states:

- ■*the duty to exercise reasonable care in managing the corporation;* and
- ■*the fiduciary duty of loyalty to the corporation.*

In addition to the duties of care and loyalty, state statutes typically impose liability upon officers and directors for commencing business before the required minimum capital has been contributed; for improper dividends or repurchase of corporate stock; for improper distribution of assets upon liquidation; and for unlawful loans to corporate directors, officers, or shareholders.

A.   Duty of Care   The MBCA and RMBCA require directors and officers to discharge their duties in good faith, in a manner that they reasonably believe to be in the best interests of the corporation, and *with the care that an ordinarily prudent person in a like position would exercise under similar circumstances.* Simply stated, officers and directors are liable to the corporation for negligence in the performance of their responsibilities. The duty of care does not, however, make management liable for mistakes or errors in judgment. Under the ***business judgment rule***, officers and directors are not liable for honest, unbiased transactions undertaken with reasonable care, even if it later turns out that the act was ill-advised or was mistaken.

Negligent mismanagement may involve negligent selection or supervision of employees, inadequate consideration or research of major decisions, or authorizing unnecessarily risky or unusual transactions. Directors and officers also are required to keep themselves reasonably informed of corporate affairs. Most state statutes allow officers and directors who act in good faith to rely upon information prepared by other corporate officers or employees, attorneys, public accountants, or a committee of the board of directors.

The business judgment rule insulates most management decisions from attack; however, recent court decisions have eroded its protection when, in the court's view, an officer or director fails to "act in an informed and deliberate manner" in reaching management decisions. In the wake of these decisions and faced with rising liability insurance costs, many outside directors resigned from the boards of publicly held corporations; declined to sit for re-election; or refused nominations. In response, most states have enacted statutes to limit the personal liability of corporate directors when money damages are involved. They fall into two categories: (1) ***charter option*** statutes, which permit the articles of incorporation to limit or eliminate a director's liability for damages or (2) ***self-executing*** statutes, which automatically limit a director's liability, subject to stated exceptions. The RMBCA uses a charter option provision, which permits the articles of incorporation to limit a director's liability for *money damages* (not for equitable relief) *to the corporation or to shareholders* (not to third parties) for any act or omission except

- •the amount of any financial benefit received by the director to which she is not entitled (such as money received as a result of breach of her duty of loyalty);

- •intentional infliction of harm on the corporation or its shareholders;

- •improper corporate distributions (dividends or repurchase of shares); or

- •intentional violation of criminal law.

B.   Duty of Loyalty   Like other fiduciaries, corporate directors and officers have a strict duty to act honestly, in good faith, and solely in the interest of the corporation regarding matters that are within the scope of the fiduciary relationship.

The duty of loyalty may be breached when a director or officer has a ***conflict of interest*** (whether actual or potential) with the interest of the corporation (1) which she *fails to disclose* and (2) which *results in unfairness* to the corporation. In this context, fairness is judged by whether an independent corporate fiduciary dealing at arm's length would have entered into the transaction. The officer or director asserting the validity of the transaction has the burden of proving fairness.

Conflicts of interest may arise in transactions between the fiduciary (officer or director) and the corporation involving sale of corporate property to a director, purchase of property from a director, or contracts between a director and the corporation. Conflicts can arise in transactions (1) between the corporation and the fiduciary personally or (2) between the corporation and another entity in which the fiduciary is an officer, director, partner, or otherwise is financially interested.

In addition to the prohibition against conflict of interest, officers and directors cannot compete with the corporation in business transactions. This means that a fiduciary cannot use corporate assets or personnel to conduct personal business; cannot use customer lists or trade secrets for personal benefit or use them for sale to others; cannot solicit corporate customers for personal ventures; and cannot receive secret profits, kickbacks, or commissions on corporate transactions.

Many wrongful competition cases involve the ***corporate opportunity doctrine***, which prevents corporate officers and directors from diverting business opportunities in which the corporation may have some expectancy, property interest or right, or that in fairness should belong to the corporation. Corporate opportunity issues are tied closely to business ethics and are decided on a case-by-case basis. It is possible that a fiduciary may be permitted to divert opportunities which the corporation is unwilling or unable to pursue; however, recognizing that corporate inability is a defense to diversion may reduce management's incentive to use its best efforts to resolve the corporation's inability to pursue the opportunity. The more prudent approach for fiduciaries is to steer clear of these types of opportunities without regard to whether the corporation can undertake them or not.

C.   Duties to Minority Stockholders   Directors are under a statutory duty to manage in the best interests of the corporation as a whole. They have fiduciary responsibilities when they take actions involving issuance or redemption of shares and similar activities, which prevent them from attempting to favor one shareholder group at the expense of another. For example, directors who authorize issuance of additional shares in an attempt to dilute the voting power of minority shareholders unfairly (freeze them out) violate their fiduciary duties.

The typical shareholder has no fiduciary duty to the corporation and is entitled to vote her shares for directors or on other corporate matters in any way she chooses. However, a shareholder with controlling interest in a block of stock may have fiduciary duties to minority shareholders. For example, controlling shareholders may not use their ability to elect directors or to approve extraordinary corporate matters in order to take actions that unfairly affect the rights of minority shareholders.

Extraordinary Matters   Matters that are outside the scope of ordinary management transactions typically require participation by both the board of directors and shareholders. The most notable of these transactions include amendment of the articles of incorporation, merger, sale of substantially all corporate assets, and voluntary dissolution. *Dissolution is discussed at the end of this chapter*.

Extraordinary changes usually require notice and vote of the shareholders as well as filing with the secretary of state of the incorporating state. To protect minority shareholders who dissent from major corporate changes, statutes generally provide an ***appraisal remedy***, which allows dissenting shareholders to be paid in cash for their shares.

A.   Amendment of Articles of Incorporation   A corporation may amend its articles of incorporation to include any provision permitted by law at the time the amendment is filed. Amendments typically involve changes in capital structure. If the change adversely affects the rights of one or more classes of shareholders, specific approval of the adversely affected class (usually be a majority or two-thirds vote) may be required in addition to the approval of the directors and shareholders. Dissenting members of the class generally are bound by the vote but may be able to assert statutory appraisal remedies (*see below*).

If the amendment is approved, documents reflecting the change are filed with the secretary of state.

B.   Merger and Consolidation   Any two or more corporations may be merged into one of them (called the surviving corporation) or may consolidate to form a new corporation. In a merger, one corporation survives and the other corporation dissolves. By contrast, in a consolidation, both corporations dissolve upon the creation of the new corporation. The corporation remaining after the merger or consolidation succeeds to the rights and liabilities of the prior corporation(s). Thus, creditors' rights are not affected by merger or consolidation.

To accomplish the combination, a plan of merger or a plan of consolidation is approved by resolution of the respective boards of directors and is submitted for approval by the stockholders of both corporations. An appraisal remedy is available to dissenting stockholders of either corporation.

A short-form merger is available for parent-subsidiary combinations, which allows the boards of directors to adopt a resolution to effect the merger (no shareholder vote by either corporation) when the subsidiary corporation is wholly owned or substantially wholly owned (90% or more) by the parent corporation. Short-form merger statutes create no appraisal rights in the minority stockholders of the parent corporation; however, dissenting stockholders of the subsidiary generally are provided with appraisal rights.

C.   Asset or Stock Purchase   When one corporation purchases all, or substantially all, of the assets of another, the corporate existence of both corporations is unaffected. Instead, the form of corporate assets changes. The selling corporation, for example, sells inventory, equipment, and real estate in exchange for cash or securities of equal value. After the sale is concluded, the selling corporation may liquidate and distribute the assets to shareholders or may remain in existence as a holding company or as an investment company.

The sale or lease of all or substantially all corporate assets outside the ordinary course of business is an extraordinary transaction and requires both board resolution and shareholder approval by the selling corporation. Dissenting shareholders are entitled to appraisal remedies. In addition, an asset sale may invoke the bulk sale provisions of a particular state's version of the Uniform Commercial Code.

Shareholder vote of the corporation purchasing the assets is not required (board resolution is required, however), and shareholders of that corporation who object are not entitled to appraisal remedies.

A similar result is achieved when one corporation purchases all, or a controlling block, of another corporation's stock. The stock purchase can be accomplished by a negotiated sale with one or more major stockholders, by purchase on the open market, or by ***tender offer*** to existing shareholders. Overall shareholder approval is not required; instead, individual shareholders of the target company decide whether or not to sell their shares. This is the method used to accomplish a hostile takeover. If the buyer accumulates enough shares to control the corporation, it may be operated as a subsidiary (if the buyer also is a corporation); it may be merged into the corporation that makes the purchase; or it may be liquidated. Because the sale involves no action by the acquired company's board and requires no shareholder approval, appraisal remedies are not available. Securities regulations may affect a tender offer (*see below*).

D.   Appraisal Remedy   State statutes afford shareholders a right to dissent from certain extraordinary corporate transactions and to obtain "fair value" payment for their shares. Fair value is the value of the shares immediately before the action was taken to which the dissenter objects. Fair value is determined by judicial proceeding only if the dissenting shareholder and the corporation cannot agree on a fair price for the shares.

The appraisal remedy typically is available to shareholders who dissent from major corporate action that requires shareholder approval (*see above*). Where the appraisal remedy is available, the statutory procedure must be followed strictly or the remedy may be lost. Generally speaking, if the action is one that creates dissenter rights, the notice of the meeting at which the vote will be taken must inform the shareholders of their right to dissent. Before the vote, an objecting shareholder must file a written notice of intent to demand fair compensation for her shares and must refrain from voting her shares in approval of the action. If the corporation and the shareholder do not agree on the fair value of the shares, a judicial proceeding is filed to appraise the shares. The corporation, then, is required to pay the fair value determined through the judicial appraisal.

Because dissenting shareholders must be paid in cash, a number of dissents may block the corporation's proposed action.

Special Problems of Closely Held Corporations

State corporation statutes apply to all corporations but are designed with publicly held corporations in mind, having freely transferable stock and a tri-level management structure. Most corporations, however, do not fit this model. Most are closely held corporations, with few stockholders (who generally play significant roles in all levels of management) and no public market for the stock. In fact, the stock of closely held corporations frequently is subject to transfer restrictions that limit the purchasers. As a practical matter, this often means that only other shareholders may purchase stock.

Because shareholders often serve as directors and officers as well, management is conducted on a much more informal basis than in a publicly held corporation. The business may operate by unanimous or majority shareholder consent, much like a partnership. As a result, it is easy to ignore or to forget corporate formalities; and management functions can become blurred. Disregard of corporate formalities may allow outsiders to pierce the corporate veil and to impose personal liability on the shareholders.

Shareholder agreements are extremely common in closely held corporations; and their effect sometimes extends to agreements concerning director functions, such as paying dividends or employing a particular shareholder as an officer. The trend in the RMBCA and in a growing number of states is to permit agreements of this type. Some states allow closely held corporations to dispense with the board of directors entirely. RMBCA § 7.32(a)(1).

Whether or not shareholder agreements are used, operating a closely held business as a corporation often leads to disputes. If any person or group within the corporation controls the power to elect a majority of the directors, this faction can out-vote the minority on a consistent basis and can effectively exclude them from management functions. In addition, the faction can "freeze out" the minority by refusing to pay dividends, while simultaneously draining corporate earnings in the form of salaries, bonuses, or rental payments to majority shareholders. Because there is no outside market for the stock, a disenchanted minority shareholder may be locked into the corporation.

If they are negotiated during the incorporation stage, various methods may be available to alleviate some of the problems. One method is to provide for greater than majority voting requirements, usually unanimous. This gives the minority a veto power over unfair management actions. Another method is to create separate classes of stock for majority and minority shareholders, with greater dividend rights to the majority but with both classes entitled to elect an equal number of directors. Still another is a mandatory agreement requiring the majority shareholders or the corporation to buy out the minority at a price fixed by a predetermined formula.

The drawback to most of these methods is deadlock, which may be overcome by a provision requiring the parties to submit disputes to an arbitrator for a binding decision when they cannot agree. In addition, a provision can be included to require one faction to buy out the other. If all else fails, the shareholders (usually the minority) may petition the court for involuntary dissolution, which is available in both deadlock and oppression cases. The RMBCA allows the corporation or any shareholder to avoid dissolution by electing to purchase the shares owned by the complaining shareholder at fair market value.

Special Problems of Publicly Held Corporations

Publicly held corporations face entirely different sets of problems than those faced by closely held corporations. Their stock is freely transferable, usually on the open market through stock brokerage houses; but it is subject to strict and highly complex securities regulation. In addition, their larger size frequently subjects them to more rigorous scrutiny by various administrative agencies in the areas of antitrust, environmental protection, equal employment opportunity, and labor law.

Securities Regulation   The inherent characteristic of a publicly held corporation is publicly traded securities (stocks and bonds). Industrial growth at the turn of the century was aided by the sale of corporate securities to the general public to provide money for expansion. Most of the sales were legitimate, but many were not. To prevent citizens from being swindled by worthless stock schemes, many states adopted legislation in the early 1900s to regulate the distribution and sale of securities. The purpose of the statutes was to prevent fraud upon unsuspecting investors by selling them securities that were worth no more than "so many feet of blue sky." To this day, state securities statutes are known as *blue sky laws*.

State blue sky laws generally require registration of the securities brokers and dealers as well as registration of all securities offered or traded in the state. They also require disclosure of pertinent information concerning the security and its issuer. The state securities commissioner evaluates the merits of the investment before securities can be offered for sale in that state.

After the stock market crash in 1929, it became obvious that state blue sky laws were inadequate to police securities fraud. Congress used its (interstate) commerce clause powers to enact federal legislation for the purpose, beginning with the Securities Act of 1933 and the Securities Exchange Act of 1934, which created the ***Securities and Exchange Commission*** (SEC). The SEC continues as the primary securities regulator in the nation.

Securities laws and regulations strive for full disclosure of accurate information to investors concerning securities traded on the open market. They also prohibit insider trading. Certain types of small offerings (limited dollar value and limited number of investors) are exempt from SEC regulations, as are intrastate offerings; securities exchanged in corporate reorganizations and bankruptcy proceedings; offerings by banks and other regulated entities; insurance policies; and short-term commercial paper.

Securities regulation is a law practice specialty area of its own, and detailed discussions concerning it are beyond the scope of this *Review Manual*.

Antitrust Regulation   Also as a result of turn-of-the-century abuses, Congress used its interstate commerce power to enact the Sherman Antitrust Act, the Clayton Act, and the Federal Trade Commission Act to curtail the establishment of monopolies and the price fixing problems that came with them. During that time period, stockholders of large corporations had formed stock trusts which controlled virtually all commercial activity in specific areas (railroads, oil, sugar, cotton, whiskey). Federal legislation, together with administrative regulations and enforcement from the Federal Trade Commission (FTC), focused on "busting" the trusts and continue to police interstate commerce activities that resemble the older business trusts.

Today, the reach of the FTC extends not only to interstate monopoly activity (corporate consolidations and mergers) but also to price fixing, restraint of free competition, and unfair trade practices addressed by consumer protection laws. The break-up of AT&T in recent times was based on antitrust laws, for example; and today's franchises and chain stores must comply with antitrust laws.

Antitrust laws have resulted in the prohibition against corporate directors sitting on the boards of competing corporations, so that it is not permissible for a person to be a corporate director for both Standard Oil and

Mobil Oil, for example. Antitrust laws also prevent tying one product to another in such a way as to require purchasers to pay a higher price than they otherwise would have paid. For example, a corporation cannot offer seminars requiring participants to purchase study tapes at a higher price than the study tapes cost when purchased alone.

Other Government Regulation   Small corporations are not immune to government regulation; however, their small size exempts them from some regulatory requirements. Large corporations tend to operate across interstate lines more frequently, tend to have more employees, and tend to become involved in more complex transactions. As a result, government regulation is more pervasive in relation to large corporations. Only a few of those areas are mentioned here.

The *Environmental Protection Agency* (EPA) controls toxic waste emitted by businesses into the environment. This includes land pollution, water pollution, and air pollution. A business can be fined for violating EPA regulations in addition to being required to pay the cost of rectifying the pollution problems. The EPA regulations extend not only to businesses who create waste but also to their lenders in some situations. Businesses are required to perform environmental impact studies for many of their business activities and to report to the EPA.

The *Equal Employment Opportunity Commission* (EEOC) controls discriminatory practices of businesses in the areas of hiring, promotion, and firing of employees who fall within the protected classes of race, color, gender, religion, and national origin. The EEOC enforces Title VII of the Civil Rights Act of 1964 and related statutes. Companies with more than 15 full-time employees are subject to its regulation; larger companies are expected to adopt affirmative action plans and to keep detailed records of all employees hired, promoted, and fired. (Age discrimination is covered by separate statute.)

The *Occupational Safety and Health Administration* (OSHA) controls safety of the workplace. Businesses must provide safety devices for workers (masks, safety glasses) in certain types of industrial fields and, in general, strive to avoid a dangerous working environment.

In addition, businesses that employ workers who are members of a collective bargaining unit (labor union) must negotiate satisfactory contracts with the union and must follow certain procedures established by the Wagner Act. A business that violates any of those provisions may be subjected to administrative processes before the *National Labor Relations Board* (NLRB).

The agencies mentioned here represent only a few of the regulatory bodies that control the activities of large corporations. A corporation's cost of compliance with the various regulations of so many governmental agencies is extremely high, but the cost of noncompliance is even higher.

Corporate Litigation

A corporation is an artificial person created by state statute. It has the capacity to sue and be sued in civil actions and can be prosecuted for violation of a criminal statute, such as the federal Racketeer Influenced Corrupt Organizations Act (RICO). Upon dissolution, the corporation's capacity to sue and be sued generally continues for a limited time.

Corporate litigation can involve claims by or against the corporation. Some claims can be asserted either by the corporation or by someone standing in its shoes, such as a trustee in bankruptcy or a shareholder in a derivative action.

Before any suit involving a corporation can be initiated, however, litigants must meet the threshold procedural requirements involving subject matter jurisdiction, personal jurisdiction, and venue. A state's subject matter jurisdiction and personal jurisdiction over domestic corporations is extremely broad, as is its *in rem* and *quasi in rem* jurisdiction over corporate property located within its boundaries. Many states require a foreign corporation operating within its borders to name an agent for service of process before the foreign corporation lawfully can conduct business in the state.

State and federal courts may exercise concurrent personal jurisdiction over corporations in diversity of citizenship actions, including shareholder derivative actions. *(See the American Legal System (General Law) chapter for a more detailed discussion of jurisdiction and venue.)*

<u>Shareholder Derivative Actions</u>   When a corporation is injured by the negligence or wrongdoing of its officers or directors, it is unlikely that the wrongdoers will initiate a suit in the name of the corporation that names themselves as defendants. In this situation, one or more shareholders may bring a derivative suit in the name of the corporation against the insider-wrongdoer. The shareholder does not sue in her individual capacity but, rather, as a representative of the corporation. Any judgment resulting from the suit is paid to the corporation, not to the shareholders. The shareholder receives an indirect benefit, however, in the protection of her investment in the corporation. A successful plaintiff-shareholder is entitled to reimbursement from the corporation for her reasonable expenses, including attorney fees.

Most shareholder derivative actions are filed in federal court under federal securities laws or on diversity of citizenship grounds. To ensure that shareholders do not abuse the derivative action by filing *strike suits* (suits filed merely to secure a favorable private settlement rather than to redress a corporate wrong), derivative actions are subject to a number of restrictions.

A.   Exhaustion of Corporate Remedies   Before filing a derivative action, the shareholder must either (1) make demand upon the board of directors to enforce the claim or (2) prove that such a demand would be futile, such as where the wrongdoers control the corporation. Typically, the suit cannot be filed until 90 days after the demand unless the 90-day waiting period would cause irreparable injury to the corporation.

B.   Contemporaneous Share Ownership   The plaintiff-shareholder in a derivative action must have been a shareholder at the time the alleged wrong took place. Persons acquiring shares after that time by operation of law (for example, by inheritance) also are eligible plaintiffs. In addition, the plaintiff must own shares both when the action is filed and continuing to the entry of final judgment. This requirement ensures that the plaintiff has a financial stake in the suit throughout the pendency of the action; prevents an outsider from "buying into a lawsuit" to harass corporate management; and, in federal cases, prevents collusion in establishing jurisdiction for diversity of citizenship.

C.   Security for Costs   A few states require plaintiffs owning less than a stated percentage of the outstanding shares of the corporation to provide security (usually by posting a bond) to cover the reasonable costs of litigation, including attorney fees, that may be incurred by the corporation or others in defending the suit. Courts often permit the plaintiff to bring additional shareholders into the suit to satisfy the minimum percentage, which eliminates the need to provide security.

D.   Settlement and Dismissal   To discourage strike suits and unfair settlements, the Federal Rules of Civil Procedure (Rule 23[1]) and the RMBCA require court approval for dismissal or compromise of derivative suits, as well as notice to other shareholders of the terms of the compromise. The RMBCA and a number of state statutes specifically require the dismissal of a derivative suit if an independent group of directors determines in good faith and after reasonable inquiry that maintaining the derivative action is not in the best interests of the corporation. To protect the corporation, however, the court must assess the good faith and independence of the directors and the reasonableness of their inquiry.

Indemnification for Litigation Expenses   When directors, officers, and other corporate personnel must defend lawsuits filed against them based upon execution of their corporate responsibilities, the statutes of all states allow some type of indemnification by the corporation. The MBCA permits indemnification if the defendant acted in good faith and in a manner reasonably believed to be in the best interests of the corporation in carrying out his or her duties. If the suit relates to criminal conduct, the defendant also must have had no reasonable cause to believe that the conduct was unlawful.

Statutory provisions concerning indemnification generally are not exclusive. Therefore, many corporations include detailed provisions concerning indemnification in their articles of incorporation or in their bylaws.

Corporate Dissolution

Unless its existence is limited in the articles of incorporation, a corporation's existence or duration is perpetual. Once created, therefore, some formal action must be taken by the corporation or by others to terminate the corporation's existence. Termination of a corporation's existence is done by dissolution, either voluntary or involuntary.

Voluntary Dissolution   The procedure for voluntary dissolution is similar to the procedure for other major corporate changes. The board of directors adopts a resolution, which must be approved by the shareholders. As an alternative, the MBCA permits dissolution without board action by unanimous written consent of all shareholders. The document reflecting the decision to dissolve (articles of dissolution, for example) then is filed with the secretary of state. Upon dissolution, corporate assets are liquidated, creditors are paid, and any remaining proceeds are distributed to shareholders according to their respective ownership preferences and interests.

To protect creditors in the dissolution process, notice of dissolution is given to creditors directly and by publication (usually in a newspaper of general circulation in the place where the corporation's principal office is located).

The corporate existence continues for a stated time (for example, two years) after dissolution to "wind up" the corporation's affairs. During this time, the corporation may continue to sue and be sued on predissolution claims.

Involuntary Dissolution   State corporation statutes also provide for involuntary dissolution of a corporation, sometimes by judicial proceedings and decree. Proceedings may be initiated by the state attorney general, the secretary of state, shareholders, or creditors. The MBCA permits dissolution of a corporation in an action filed by the state attorney general if the corporation has (1) failed to file its annual report or to pay its franchise tax timely; (2) procured its articles of incorporation through fraud; (3) exceeded or abused its legal authority; or (4) failed to maintain or to appoint a registered agent or failed to notify the state of a change in registered agent.

In an action by shareholders, the court may order liquidation of the corporation if it is proved that

- the directors are deadlocked over management of the corporation, the shareholders are unable to break the deadlock, and irreparable injury to the corporation is imminent;

- the acts of directors or those controlling the corporation are illegal, oppressive, or fraudulent;

- corporate assets are being misapplied or wasted; or

- the shareholders are deadlocked in voting power and have failed for at least two consecutive annual meetings to elect successor directors for terms that have expired (or would have expired if new directors had been elected).

A creditor may obtain judicial dissolution by proving (1) that it obtained a judgment against the corporation, the judgment is unsatisfied, and the corporation is insolvent or (2) that the corporation has admitted in writing that the creditor's claim is due and owing and that the corporation is insolvent.

In addition, a corporation's assets may be liquidated in bankruptcy proceedings and the proceeds used to pay creditors. The bankruptcy court does not dissolve the corporation, *per se*; however, the effect is virtually the same. When all of a corporation's assets are liquidated, the corporation is nothing more than an empty shell.

The formation, operation, and dissolution of business organizations is a complex area of legal practice. The material in this chapter and the self-test provide a summary of its principles that a corporate legal assistant should know. Further references and study aids are listed in the bibliography.

Business Organizations Self-Test

Allow an uninterrupted 30-minute period to answer all questions. At the end of 30 minutes, check your answers against those in the Answer Key Section of this Review Manual. Deduct two points for each incorrect answer (100 total possible points). Unanswered questions are counted as incorrect answers. Follow directions carefully and observe the time limit precisely to provide an accurate self-assessment.

Choose the most correct answer to each of the following questions unless a specific question instructs you to do otherwise.

1.   Shareholders can be held liable for:

    a.   illegal acts of the corporation.
    b.   *ultra vires* acts of the corporation.
    c.   full payment for watered stock received.
    d.   fraud committed by the board of directors.

2.   Brittany, a Certified Public Accountant, sits on the board of directors of three corporations. Brittany:

    a.   has violated her duty of loyalty to each of the corporations.
    b.   has violated the Sherman Act.
    c.   has not violated her duty of loyalty if she refrains from voting on issues that concern more than one of the corporations.
    d.   has not violated her duty of loyalty if the corporations do not compete directly with each other.

3.   A corporation is created:

    a.   by agreement of the parties.
    b.   by franchise.
    c.   by expanding business interests.
    d.   by statutory authorization.

4.   Stock warrants are used to implement:

    a.   cumulative voting.
    b.   the preemptive right.
    c.   access to corporate stock records.
    d.   dissolution of the corporation.

5. The "business judgment rule":

    a. applies to actions of the directors.
    b. protects directors from all liability.
    c. makes directors liable for errors in business judgment.
    d. makes officers liable for errors in business judgment.

6. Tim owns 100 shares of ABC Corporation. The corporation makes a new issue of 10,000 shares. According to his share certificate, Tim is entitled to purchase an additional 100 shares at the time of the new issue. This is an example of:

    a. right of first refusal.
    b. shareholder restrictions on transfer and ownership.
    c. preemptive rights.
    d. participation rights.

7. True or False. A share of stock with a stated par value of $10, which is sold and issued initially for $8, is an example of watered stock.

8. True or False. Partnerships must be formed by written agreement and in strict compliance with the partnership statutes of a particular state.

9. True or False. A corporation cannot be a domestic corporation and a foreign corporation at the same time.

10. True or False. A debenture is a corporate obligation secured by a lien or by a mortgage on specific corporate property.

11. True or False. A corporation may be incorporated in more than one state.

12. A *de facto* corporation is one that:

    a. has complied with statutory rules and exists in fact.
    b. is used by its shareholders as a conduit for personal activities.
    c. has not complied with statutory rules but operates as a corporation.
    d. is used by its shareholders to defraud creditors.

13. If a limited partner were to participate in the operation of the partnership in any way,

    a. the limited partnership would be treated as a general partnership except for taxing purposes.
    b. the limited partner would become jointly and severally liable, along with the general partner, for all partnership debt.
    c. the partnership would be dissolved.
    d. None of the above.

14. Each of the partners in a general partnership:

    a. has no personal tax liability for partnership income; it is the liability of the partnership.
    b. bears equal personal liability for tax on partnership income.
    c. bears personal tax liability in proportion to the partnership income received by him or her.
    d. None of the above.

15. The Uniform Partnership Act was formulated by the:

    a. American Law Institute.
    b. National Conference of Commissioners on Uniform State Laws.
    c. National Association of Partnerships.
    d. American Bar Association.

16. True or False.   Stock splits and stock dividends achieve the same result in relation to the transfer of earnings to capital.

17. True or False.   For purposes of federal litigation, a corporation is deemed to be a citizen of the state where it has its principal place of business as well as of the state where it is incorporated.

18. True or False.   Each partner in a general partnership is an agent of the partnership for purposes of conducting partnership business.

19. True or False.   Corporations cannot be found guilty of criminal acts, because corporations cannot be sentenced to prison terms.

20. True or False.   A corporation must transact all or most of its business in a state where it is incorporated.

21.   True or False.   A partnership generally is treated as an aggregate for purposes of taxation and as a separate entity for purposes of litigation.

22.   A domestic corporation is:

    a.   a corporation whose officers reside in the state where the corporation transacts business.

    b.   a corporation whose principal place of business is in the forum state.

    c.   a corporation whose principal activities relate to family services.

    d.   a corporation chartered in the forum state.

23.   A foreign corporation:

    a.   is chartered in a foreign country, such as Canada.

    b.   is a synonym for the term "alien corporation."

    c.   may require a certificate of authority to do business in states where it is not chartered.

    d.   may transact business only in foreign states.

24.   If the organizers of a small corporation anticipate losses during the first two to three years of operation, which of the following options will provide the best tax treatment for shareholders in the usual situation?

    a.   Chapter S election

    b.   Section 1244 stock

    c.   Nonprofit status

    d.   Leverage financing

25.   Rachel and Cori form a partnership. Rachel contributes $75,000 to the partnership, and Cori contributes $25,000. At the end of the first year, the business realizes a profit of $10,000. Since no agreement concerning distribution of profits was made, how much will each receive?

    a.   Rachel will receive $7,500; Cori, $2,500.

    b.   Each will receive $5,000.

    c.   Rachel will receive $3,750; Cori, $1,750.

    d.   None is correct.

26.   Which of the following is *not* among the duties of a director?

    a.   Declare dividends

    b.   Elect officers

    c.   Issue stock

    d.   Sign contracts on behalf of the corporation

27.   An advantage of incorporation is:

    a.   perpetual existence.

    b.   limited liability.

    c.   corporations are separate taxing entities.

    d.   All of the above.

    e.   None of the above.

28.   Under the Revised Uniform Limited Partnership Act, a limited partner may not:

    a.   vote on partnership matters such as dissolution.

    b.   serve as an employee of the limited partnership.

    c.   act as a surety for the limited partnership.

    d.   supervise employees of the limited partnership.

29.   A public corporation is:

    a.   one whose stock is traded publicly.

    b.   one created by government to administer government purposes.

    c.   one whose activities are subject to public scrutiny.

    d.   one which has one or more subsidiary entities.

30.   For which of the following acts is a director most likely to be found personally liable?

    a.   Investment of corporate funds in a venture that loses money.

    b.   Failure to supervise the president's actions.

    c.   Creation of a new product line that is unsuccessful.

    d.   Breach of warranty for a faulty product made by the corporation.

31.   Cumulative voting is a term that applies in which of the following situations?

    a.   Voluntary dissolution of a corporation

    b.   Election of shareholders

    c.   Election of directors

    d.   Election of officers

32.   The "business judgment rule":

    a.   applies to actions of the directors.
    b.   protects directors from all liability.
    c.   makes directors liable for errors in business judgment.
    d.   makes officers liable for errors in business judgment.

33.   Which of the following business entities typically provides the most flexibility in terms of management policy?

    a.   Sole proprietorship
    b.   Partnership
    c.   Limited partnership
    d.   Corporation

34.   True or False.   Holders of fractional shares of stock and holders of scrip certificates generally enjoy the same voting rights within the corporate structure.

35.   True or False.   A partnership may be a shareholder in an "S" corporation.

36.   True or False.   A director is always an agent of the corporation.

37.   True or False.   Corporate directors and officers generally owe no direct duty to individual shareholders of the corporation.

38.   Which of the following classes of stock is *never* granted voting rights?

    a.   Common stock
    b.   Preferred stock
    c.   Treasury stock
    d.   Watered stock

39.   The right of a shareholder to force the corporation to buy his or her stock following a merger is called:

    a.   repurchase rights.
    b.   appraisal rights.
    c.   preemptive rights.
    d.   preferred rights.

40.   The duration of a corporation may be:

    a.   dissolved upon death of the parties.
    b.   perpetual.
    c.   subject to liability.
    d.   terminated by a lawsuit.

41.   A shareholder derivative action may be initiated in response to:

    a.   negligence by management that injures a shareholder.
    b.   management's election to dissolve the corporation.
    c.   a strike suit filed by management.
    d.   negligence by management that injures the corporation.

42.   True or False.   A corporation sometimes is treated as a person within the meaning of the federal Constitution.

43.   True or False.   A corporation may be subjected to criminal charges.

44.   True or False.   A close corporation may restrict the rights of shareholders to transfer stock by means of shareholder agreements.

45.   True or False.   Maria and Lilly form a partnership. If Maria sells her partnership interest to Allen, Allen will receive all of the benefits and burdens of partnership status when the sale is consummated.

46.   Which of the following actions by shareholders requires more than a majority vote?

    a.   Election of directors
    b.   Election of directors by cumulative voting
    c.   Resolution to merge with another corporation
    d.   Resolution to amend the date of the annual meeting

47.   Each of the partners in a general partnership:

    a.   has joint liability for all partnership debt.
    b.   has joint and several liability for all partnership debt.
    c.   is liable for partnership debt in proportion to his or her capital contribution.
    d.   None of the above.

48.   If the members of a limited partnership fail to provide a basis for making distributions of profit to partners, the Revised Uniform Limited Partnership Act:

      a.   provides for equal distributions to partners.
      b.   provides for distributions to limited partners only.
      c.   provides for distributions according to each partner's capital contribution.
      d.   makes no provision for distributions.

49.   A four-lawyer firm incorporated. They did not elect to be a Chapter S corporation. At the end of the first year, they show a taxable income of $64,000. They have decided that they each will remove $5,000 from the corporation. They should:

      a.   declare bonuses of $5,000 each.
      b.   declare dividends of $5,000 each.
      c.   receive loans of $5,000 each.
      d.   None of the options is better than any other.

50.   Joe, Brian, and Nolan form a partnership to operate a movie theater franchise. The partnership realizes a profit in the first year of operation. Under general partnership rules and assuming that all profit is distributed to the partners, what amount will each partner receive?

      a.   An amount equal to his or her percentage of the total capital contribution.
      b.   An amount equal to his or her percentage of the total capital contribution after taxes.
      c.   The same amount as all other partners.
      d.   The same amount as all other partners minus his or her capital contribution.

Chapter
9

CONTRACT LAW

A verbal contract isn't worth the paper it's written on.
—Samuel Goldwyn

A contract is a single promise or a set of mutual promises, the performance of which is recognized as a legal duty and the breach of which will result in a remedy granted to the nonbreaching party. A contract may be categorized by its type (whether unilateral or bilateral), by its method of formation (whether express, implied, or quasi), by its validity (whether void, voidable, or unenforceable), and by its status (whether executory or executed).

Unilateral or Bilateral

The *traditional **unilateral contract*** consists of a single promise made by the offeror to the offeree, which seeks performance from the offeree rather than a promise of performance.

> Max promises to pay Sam $100 if Sam paints Max's house.
> If (and only if) Sam paints the house, Max will be obligated
> to pay him $100.

The *traditional **bilateral contract*** consists of a promise given in exchange for a promise (mutual promises). Under both the Uniform Commercial

Code (U.C.C.) and the Restatement (Second) of Contracts, however, a bilateral contract may be created either by mutual promises *or* by the start of performance.

> Max promises to pay Arnold $100 if Arnold will promise to paint Max's house, and Arnold promises to paint Max's house for $100.   *(bilateral contract)*

> Max promises to pay Arnold $100 if he will promise to paint Max's house, and Arnold begins painting the house. *(bilateral contract)*

Under the modern view, most contracts are classified as bilateral, with traditional unilateral contracts occurring only in two situations:

1.   Where the offeror clearly indicates that performance is the only manner of acceptance, in which case no contract is formed until the act is done; and

2.   Where there is an offer to the public that clearly contemplates acceptance only by performance, such as an offer of a reward for the return of a lost item.

Express, Implied, or Quasi-Contract

The classifications express, implied, and quasi-contract refer only to the way in which the contract was formed; they have no bearing on the enforceability of a contract.

An **express contract** is one formed *by specific words*, either *oral or written*.

An ***implied contract*** is one formed by an indication of assent other than specific words, such as *by conduct*. This is sometimes called a contract "implied in fact." Turning on the bathroom light and running the water every morning indicates acceptance of utility service and brings the concomitant obligation to pay for the utilities used.

A ***quasi-contract*** is not a contract in any technical sense. It is a legal fiction created by courts *to prevent unjust enrichment* of a defendant by allowing the plaintiff to seek restitution of a benefit conferred upon the defendant. This is sometimes called a contract "implied in law." For instance, a physician who treats an unconscious accident victim found in the middle of a street may be able to recover under quasi-contract, even though her services were not requested by the victim or by anyone else.

Void, Voidable, or Unenforceable

The term *void contract*, although a misnomer, is used to refer to a purported contract—an agreement that had *no legal effect* and was invalid from the start, such as an agreement to commit murder. It would be more precise to say that such an agreement is simply not a contract at all. No contract ever was created because of a defect in its formation (illegality of purpose). Nevertheless, the term "void contract" continues in popular use.

A *voidable contract* is one that one or both parties may *choose to avoid* or may ratify. Most contracts of minors are avoidable, for instance, at the option of the minor upon reaching the age of majority. An exception to this general rule is a contract made for the necessities of life, such as room and board, medical treatment, and the like.

An *unenforceable contract* is one that cannot be enforced because of *defenses to the contract*, none of which relate to its formation. Examples of such defenses include Statute of Frauds, statute of limitations, unconscionability, and so forth.

Executory or Executed

An **executory contract** is one in which *some obligation or duty remains to be done* by one or more of the parties.

An *executed contract* is one in which all parties have *fully performed* their obligations and duties under the contract terms.

Formation of a Valid, Enforceable Contract

Regardless of how they are presented, all issues concerning contract formation boil down to these three: (1) existence of **mutual assent**, (2) existence of **consideration**, and (3) absence of **defenses** that would prevent enforcement of the contract terms.

Mutual Assent

Mutual assent is often called the ***meeting of the minds*** or intent to contract. Whether a meeting of the minds has occurred is determined objectively, based upon the words and conduct of the parties. Each party is bound by the apparent intention manifested (shown or demonstrated) to the other. Mutual assent requires both *offer and acceptance.*

The Offer   To create a power of acceptance in the offeree, the offer must be an objective expression of a *promise, undertaking,* or *commitment* to enter into a contract; the terms of the offer must be ***definite and certain***; and the offer must be ***communicated*** to the offeree.

It is important to distinguish between a promise or an undertaking that can form the basis of an offer and other types of communication or conduct:

Statements obviously made *in jest or in anger* are not offers and cannot create a contract, even if they are purportedly "accepted."

Generally, an **advertisement** is viewed as an *invitation to make an offer*, not as an offer to sell. The classic exception is where a defendant store, for instance, lists a specific item (rather than a group) for a specific price on a "first come, first served" basis.

An **auction** is considered a *solicitation for offers* (bids). The exception is where the auction is conducted without reserve, in which case the auctioneer cannot withdraw the goods once the bidding starts.

An **invitation to bid** is ***not an offer*** unless it contains language to indicate otherwise, such as, "I will sell my law library for the highest cash bid received by me within the next 30 days." This is an offer. Each bid received within the 30-day period is an acceptance, which will be effective unless a higher bid is received. The situation would be different, however, if this statement were made: "I will consider selling my law library for the highest cash bid received by me within the next 30 days." This is not an offer but is merely an invitation to bid or a statement of preliminary negotiations.

The **terms of the offer must be definite and certain**. This means that there must be enough of the essential terms stated so that a contract based upon those terms could be enforced. Generally, essential terms include ***identity of the offeree*** and ***subject matter***; the ***price*** to be paid; the ***time*** of payment, delivery, or performance; the **quantity** involved; and the **nature** of the work or performance required.

A.   Identity of Offeree   There must be some statement that identifies the offeree or the class to which the offeree belongs in order to substantiate that the offeror intended to create a power of acceptance.

> Alice offers a $100.00 reward to the person who finds and returns her lost cat. Here, the offeree cannot be identified specifically when the offer is made. Performance by returning the lost cat constitutes both an identification of the offeree and an acceptance of the offer.

B.   Definite Subject Matter   The subject matter of the offer must be certain. A court cannot enforce a promise if it cannot tell what the promise is. It is not necessary that every material term be spelled out, as long as there is some objective standard by which to supply missing terms.

In real estate transactions, for example, the offer must identify the land and the price. Courts will not imply terms to identify the property, the price to be paid, or the terms by which the price is to be paid (mortgage terms, for instance).

In sale of goods, the quantity offered must be definite or must be capable of being determined. If a seller offers to sell all of her outputs or if a buyer offers to buy all of his requirements, the quantity can be determined by extrinsic, objective facts (the history of outputs or the history of requirements). If there is no history of outputs or of requirements, which may be true of new businesses, the quantity cannot be implied.

The duration of an employment contract must be stated; otherwise, the offer will be construed as one contemplating a contract that can be terminated at will by either party. If the contract states a rate of pay, such as $2,000.00 a month, some courts will infer that the offer is for the minimum period stated (one month in the example).

Unless the parties have shown that they do not want a contract until they agree on price, a reasonable price will be implied for goods under U.C.C. § 2-305. Likewise, unless the parties have specified that time is of the essence, U.C.C. § 2-309 provides for performance within a reasonable time.

When terms are missing, the U.C.C. and modern cases presume that the parties' intent is to include reasonable terms. This presumption cannot be made, however, if the parties have included a term that is too vague to be enforceable.

> An agreement to divide profits "fairly" is too vague.
>
> An agreement to purchase a ring for "$100.00 or less" is too vague.

If the uncertainty stems from the offeror having given a choice of acceptances to the offeree, the offer becomes definite when the offeree makes her selection.

> Bill offers to sell Jean any ring in the display case for $100.00. Once Jean selects a ring, the offer will have become definite.

If an offer specifically states that the price, quantity, or other material term will be agreed upon at a future date, the offer is too uncertain. This situation is different from having omitted a material term. Instead, the offeror has specifically reserved the right to name the term; there is no basis for a court to imply a reasonable term.

C.   Communication to Offeree   The offer must be communicated to the offeree before the power of acceptance can be created.

> Bill finds Jean's wallet containing her driver's license and all of her credit cards. He returns it to her, unaware that she had advertised a $50.00 reward. Because Bill did not know about the offer, there can be no mutual assent and, without mutual assent, no contract.

Termination of Offer   When the power of acceptance created by a valid offer is terminated before acceptance, acceptance can no longer be made. Termination of the offer can occur in a number of different ways.

A.   Revocation   The offeror may terminate an offer by communicating revocation to the offeree before acceptance has occurred. The revocation may be communicated directly to the offeree by the offeror or may be communicated indirectly, where acts of the offeror, made known to the offeree by a reliable source, would indicate to a reasonable person that the offer has been revoked.

> Mrs. O'Leary offers to buy home-grown, white potatoes for her restaurant from Bill, a potato wholesaler, if he can find any for her. In his travels, Bill is told by one of his best customers that Mrs. O'Leary just signed a contract with the customer's neighbor to buy all of the white potatoes that he can produce. This information should indicate to Bill that Mrs. O'Leary's offer to him has been revoked.

Offers made by publication may be revoked by comparable means.

An offer published in the *Portland Post* may be revoked by publication of the revocation in the Portland Post but not by publication in *People* magazine or in the *Wall Street Journal*.

A revocation becomes effective when it is received by the offeree. If the revocation is made by publication, however, it becomes effective when it is published.

B.   Limitations on Revocation Powers   In general, an offeror may revoke an offer at any time. This power may be limited in the circumstances shown below.

1.   Option   An option is an independent contract in which the offeror receives separate consideration from the offeree to keep an offer open for a stated period of time, such as an option to buy real estate. The consideration paid for the option is separate from any consideration that will be paid if the option is exercised. If the offeree does not exercise the option by purchasing the real estate, there is generally no refund to the offeree of the consideration paid for the option.

2.   U.C.C. Firm Offer   A firm offer by a merchant to buy or to sell goods, represented by a signed writing that promises to hold the offer open for a stated time, cannot be revoked for lack of consideration during that time. If no time is stated, a reasonable time is inferred, not to exceed three months. U.C.C. § 2-205.

3.   Detrimental Reliance   Detrimental reliance prevents revocation of an offer for a reasonable time when the offeror should expect that the offeree would rely on the offer to his or her detriment. At the very least, the offeree would be entitled to damages measured by the extent of detrimental reliance. Restatement 2d § 90.

4.   Part Performance of a Unilateral Contract   Unilateral contracts generally contemplate acceptance by full performance, rather than by a promise to perform. Where performance has been started but is not complete, it would be unfair to allow the offeror to revoke the offer.

The Uniform Commercial Code, as well as the First and Second Restatements, provide that such an offer becomes irrevocable once performance has begun; and the offeree is given a reasonable time within which to complete the performance.

The majority view is contained in § 45 of the First Restatement, which reasons that a contract is formed at the moment when performance begins, with the offeror's duty to perform conditioned upon completion of the act within a reasonable time or within the time stated in the offer. Under the Second Restatement, an option contract is formed upon the start of performance by the offeree, making the offer irrevocable for a reasonable time. It is as if the offeree's part performance is consideration to keep the offer open for a reasonable time.

C.   Rejection   The offer may be terminated by a simple rejection from the offeree, which is effective at the time the rejection is received by the offeror. It also may be terminated by a counteroffer from the offeree. Use care to differentiate between a counteroffer (which constitutes a rejection) and a mere inquiry (which does not terminate the offer when the inquiry is consistent with the offeree's continued consideration of the original offer).

> Adam offers to sell his farm to Bill for $100,000. Bill replies, "I am not willing to pay that much." When he sees that Adam is unwilling to lower the price, Bill says, "All right, I will pay $100,000." Because Bill's rejection terminated his power of acceptance, there is no contract.

> Adam offers to sell his farm to Bill for $100,000. Bill replies, "Let me think about it; but if you want to close the deal right now, I will give you $80,000." Adam does not respond, and Bill accepts the $100,000 price the next day. There is a contract.

D.   Lapse of Time   Lapse of time may terminate an offer, whether the lapse of the time specified for acceptance by the offeror or the lapse of a reasonable time when no time is specified. When the offeror's terms are unclear as to time, such as "by return mail," a reasonable time for return mail is implied.

E.   Termination by Operation of Law   If either party dies or is adjudged insane or incompetent prior to acceptance, the offer is terminated without the need to communicate the death, insanity, or incompetence to the other party. Restatement 2d § 48. The offer will not terminate, however, if any of the rules limiting the offeror's power to terminate apply (such as an option contract, where the offer is irrevocable because of the consideration given to keep it open).

If the subject matter of the proposed contract becomes illegal, the offer will terminate by operation of law.

The Gilded Lily Partnership offered to lease a building from Benny Bigtime to operate a bingo parlor. Before Benny accepted the offer, the city council outlawed bingo games within city limits. The offer automatically is terminated by operation of the new law.

The Acceptance   Acceptance is a manifestation of assent to the terms of an offer, given in the manner prescribed or permitted by the offer. By manifesting assent, the offeree exercises the power given by the offeror to create a contract.

Generally, only the person to whom an offer is addressed has the power of acceptance. One may also have a power of acceptance if he or she is a member of a class to which an offer has been directed. If the offer is made to the general public, anyone may qualify as an offeree. Performance by anyone knowing of the offer will cut off the power of every other person to accept, provided that the offeror desires only one performance (reward for return of lost property).

Unlike rights under an existing contract, the offeree's power of acceptance cannot be assigned. An exception exists for option contracts, since the power to accept is itself a contract right in a contract of this type.

A.   Common Law Rule   Under common law rules, different or additional terms in the acceptance make the response a rejection and a counteroffer, unless it is clear that the original offer is still being considered (*see above*). The distinction is illustrated in the following situations:

> 1.   Statements by the offeree that make implicit terms explicit do not prevent acceptance, such as, "I accept provided that you can provide marketable title." This is a valid acceptance because the obligation to convey marketable title is implicit in the offer to sell.

> 2.   A grumbling acceptance is nonetheless valid, as long as it stops short of dissent, such as, "This is highway robbery, but I must have this briefcase. Wrap it up."

> 3.   A request for clarification does not necessarily indicate a rejection and counteroffer. For instance, "Would you be willing to come down another $10.00 on the price?" seeks clarification or further negotiation; it is not a rejection.

B.   U.C.C. (Battle of the Forms)   When the offer is for the purchase or sale of goods between merchants, the common law rules for acceptance have been altered substantially by U.C.C. § 2-207. Unlike common law rules, the proposal of additional terms by the offeree does not constitute a rejection and counteroffer if the acceptance is otherwise definite and timely. Under the U.C.C., a contract is formed nevertheless, subject to the limitations shown below. The only question is whether the additional terms will be included or excluded.

     1.   Consistent Terms   The additional terms proposed in the offeree's acceptance become terms of the resulting contract if they are consistent with (do not materially alter) the allocation of economic risks and benefits or impair a remedy that would be available otherwise, and the offeror does not exclude them by objecting specifically to their inclusion within a reasonable time.

     2.   Inconsistent Terms   If the additional terms proposed are inconsistent (materially alter the contract), a contract is formed; but its terms include only those contained in the offer. The inconsistent, additional terms become part of the contract only if the offeror expressly assents to their inclusion.

     3.   Either Party Can Avoid Effects of § 2-207 If an offeror wishes to avoid the addition of consistent terms proposed by an offeree under § 2-207, he may do so by expressly limiting acceptance to the terms of the offer. Similarly, an offeree who does not wish to form a contract unless the offeror consents to additional terms can respond with a clear rejection and a counteroffer.

C.   Acceptance Must Be Communicated   Subject to a few exceptions, the general rule is that the acceptance must be communicated to the offeror. Like the offer, the acceptance is judged by an objective standard. The offeree's subjective state of mind is irrelevant.

     1.   Common Law   Whether an acceptance became effective upon dispatch or upon receipt depended upon whether the offeree used an authorized method of communication under common law rules. Unless a specific method of communication was required by the offeror, the method used by the offeror to transmit the offer was impliedly authorized for transmittal of the acceptance.

2.   U.C.C. and Second Restatement   Most courts today ignore the technical common law rules concerning acceptance. Under the U.C.C., an offer may be accepted by any "medium reasonable in the circumstances." U.C.C. § 2-206. The offeror still may limit acceptance to a particular method but must do so clearly, since any ambiguity will be construed to allow the offeree to use any reasonable means.

3.   The Mailbox Rule   Acceptance by mail or by a similar medium creates a contract at the moment of posting, properly addressed and stamped, unless

(a)   the offer stipulates that acceptance is not effective until received; or

(b)   an option contract is involved (acceptance under an option contract is effective only upon receipt). Restatement 2d § 63.

In most states, a revocation is effective only upon receipt (*see prior discussion*). Under the mailbox rule, a contract is formed if the acceptance is sent before the revocation is received. This is true even though the acceptance is sent (by offeree) after the revocation is sent and is received after the revocation is received.

> Kathy made an offer to Dale on July 23 to purchase his 1955 classic Cadillac, specifying that acceptance must be made by United States mail. Dale received the offer on July 25 and mailed his acceptance on July 26. In the meantime, Kathy located a better vehicle and sent her revocation of the offer to Dale on July 25, which he did not receive until July 27. Kathy received Dale's acceptance on July 28. A contract is formed, and Kathy is obligated either to purchase Dale's auto or to pay damages.

4.   Acceptance by Unauthorized Method   If an acceptance is sent by an unauthorized method (or improperly sent by an authorized method), it still may be effective if it is actually received by the offeror while the offer remains open.

> Betty made an offer to Joe, specifying that acceptance should be by facsimile; but Joe's fax machine is broken, so he mails the acceptance. The acceptance will not be effective until it is received by Betty, assuming that the offer is still open at that time.

Same as above, except that Betty specified that acceptance should be by letter. Joe incorrectly addressed the envelope when he sent the acceptance. His acceptance will not be effective until Betty receives it, assuming that the offer is still open.

5. **Crossing Offers** If offers containing exactly the same terms cross in the mail, they do not create a contract despite the apparent mutual assent. An offer cannot be accepted until there is knowledge that it has been made.

D. **Acceptance without Communication** An executory bilateral contract may be formed without communication of acceptance in limited situations:

1. **Express Waiver** An offer, by its terms, may waive any communication of acceptance. For instance, an application for insurance may state: "Your application is an offer only, pending acceptance by our home office." This is similar to the concept of solicitation of offers discussed previously.

2. **Silence as Acceptance** An offeree who silently receives the benefits of services (not goods) will be held to have accepted a contract for them if the offeree (1) had a reasonable opportunity to reject them and (2) knew or should have known that the offeror expected to be compensated. Restatement 2d § 72(1)(a).

Alice, a local golf pro, gave a free golf lesson to Ben. She told him that a series of 10 lessons would cost $100.00. Ben did not ask for the lessons and remained silent when he learned of the cost. Ben finally stopped the lessons after five had been given. By his silence, Ben accepted Alice's offer of a 10-lesson course and must pay the contract price, not just the value of the five lessons given.

When the offeree receives goods, he or she may be held to have accepted a contract for the goods, even though the offeror did not intend to do so. The unintentional acceptance may be made by exercising dominion over the goods in a way that is consistent with ownership of the goods. Restatement 2d § 72(2), U.C.C. § 2-606(1). If this occurs, the offeror has a choice among a contract action, a tort action for conversion, and a quasi-contract action for the fair value of the goods.

Ann receives a mailer from Discriminating Book Club, soliciting her membership and asking her to complete a card and send it back to the Book Club. Although Ann did not complete or mail the card, the Discriminating Book Club began sending books to her. Ann gave the books away as gifts. Since giving the books away is inconsistent with the Book Club's ownership of them, Ann will be held to have accepted the Book Club's offer, even though she did not intend this result. (This contract will be effective, however, only if Discriminating Book Club elects to sue "on the contract," rather than in tort or in quasi-contract.) Had Ann simply kept the books and waited for the Book Club to ask for them back, there would be no contract since Ann would not have exercised dominion over them. Restatement 2d § 72, Illustr. 7, 8, and 9.

Note: Many states have adopted statutes that change this result when unsolicited goods are sent by mail. They allow the recipient to treat the goods as "unconditional gifts." These are sometimes referred to as "Book of the Month Club" statutes.

Consideration

Most legally enforceable contracts contain a bargained-for exchange (change in position) between the parties, which is called consideration. Although substitute doctrines may permit enforcement of an agreement without consideration (discussed *infra*), look for consideration first. It is only when consideration is not present that substitutes for consideration should be considered.

There are two requirements for consideration: (1) there must be a bargained-for exchange between the parties and (2) the bargained-for exchange must provide some benefit to the promisor or must provide some detriment to the promisee (legal value).

Mary promises to sell her used car to John for $100.00 in exchange for John's promise to pay $100.00 to Mary.

Both requirements of consideration are present. The promise of Mary induced a detriment in the promisee, John. John's detriment induced Mary to make the promise. Therefore, Mary's promise was bargained for. Secondly, both parties suffered a detriment: the detriment to Mary was the transfer of her ownership of the car to John, and the detriment to John was the payment of $100.00 to Mary.

Although this definition may sound complicated, the gist of it is that a promise is supported by consideration if

1.   the promisee gives up something of value or restricts his liberty in some way (suffers a legal detriment); and

2.   the promisor makes the promise as part of a bargaining process, that is, he makes the promise in exchange for the promisee's giving of value or restriction of liberty (the promisee's legal detriment).

These two components of consideration generate two very different groups of cases in which consideration problems arise. The "bargain" element appears most often in cases that do not involve business dealings, such as a promise to make a gift. The "legal value" or "legal detriment" element appears most often in business-related contracts where it is unclear whether one of the parties has given up anything.

<u>Bargained-For Exchange</u>   For a promise to be supported by consideration, the promisee's "detriment" must have been bargained for by the promisor. One of the primary reasons to require a bargained-for exchange is to prevent the enforcement of a promise that is intended as a promise to make a gift.

A.   Gift   In the usual promise to make a gift, the promise is not enforceable in a court of law because it lacks consideration. Such a promise is not a bargained-for exchange; neither is legal detriment suffered by the promisee.

> George says to Henry, "I promise to give you $5,000.00 when
> I die."

George's promise is not supported by consideration and is unenforceable for two reasons. First, George did not make the promise as part of a bargain, that is, he was not trying to obtain anything from Henry. Second, Henry suffered no legal detriment; he didn't do anything, spend anything, or give up anything to obtain the promise from George.

A promise may be present even though the promisor does not receive economic benefit from agreement.

> Uncle Ed promises his niece, Karen, $10,000 if she does not
> marry before the age of 25. Karen waits until she is 25 to
> marry.

This promise is enforceable. Even though Uncle Ed received no economic benefit from Karen's restraint, he did obtain something that he wanted (his niece's forbearance); and he bargained for it. In addition, Karen sustained a legal detriment by not marrying until she reached age 25, which she had a legal right to do from the age of majority. The mere fact that the promisee incurs a legal detriment, however, does not always mean that the promisor obtains a corresponding benefit.

> "Come over to our house, and I will give you our old refrigerator."

> "If you take care of me in my old age, I will leave my entire estate to you."

The promise in the first example is unenforceable. Although the promisee incurs a detriment by going to the promisor's house (which she is not otherwise required to do), the promisor receives no benefit. Rather, coming to the house is the condition to receive the gift. If the promisee comes to the house to find that the promisor has changed her mind about giving away the refrigerator, the promisee has no cause of action. In the second example, however, the promisor receives a benefit that she has bargained for specifically: care in her old age. At the same time, the promisee incurs a detriment in caring for the promisor. Consideration is present and the promise is enforceable.

B.   Past Consideration or Moral Obligation

If the detriment had already been given or performed before the promise was made, most courts would reason that it was not given or done in exchange for the promise and, therefore, does not satisfy the "bargained-for" requirement.

> After working for 50 years at Bilkum & Billum, Lee retired. At her retirement party, Henry Billum promised Lee a pension of $500.00 a month for life because of her many years of loyal service to the firm.

This promise is unenforceable under the general rule, because there is no "bargained-for" exchange for the promise of a pension. Note the exceptions below, however.

1.   Technical Defense

If the past obligation would be enforceable except that a technical defense stands in the way—such as a *statute of limitations, discharge in bankruptcy*, and so forth—many courts will enforce the new promise if it is *in writing* or if it has been *partially performed*.

2.   Promise to Pay for Past Requested Act

Under the modern trend, if acts previously performed were

requested by the promisor, the new promise is enforceable (*see pension example above*). Many of states have extended this rule to cover *unrequested* acts as well if they were rendered during an emergency.

<u>Legal Value</u>   As a general rule, courts of law will not inquire into the adequacy of consideration. In other words, they will not intervene if one party contracts to sell an item of high market value for a low price. However, a court of equity may inquire into the relative values exchanged by the parties and may deny an equitable remedy where it finds a contract price to be unconscionable.

When the consideration is *token* only (entirely without value), the consideration generally will be held insufficient. Courts reason that this indicates a gift rather than bargained-for consideration.

Parties to written agreements sometimes recite that the consideration is $1.00 or some other *nominal* sum. Frequently, the recited amount has not been paid; and it was never intended that it be paid. Most courts hold that evidence may be introduced to show that no consideration was paid. This situation should not be confused, however, with the recitation of "$1.00 and other valuable consideration" that is often shown on deeds. The phrase "other valuable consideration" is used merely to avoid showing the precise purchase price in the deed records.

A.   Preexisting Legal Duty   The traditional rule has been that the promise to perform (or the performance of) a preexisting legal duty is not sufficient consideration to create a contract.

> Andrew offered a $100.00 reward for the return of his Rolex watch, which had been stolen while he was lunching at Benny's Burger Barn. Tom, one of the police detectives assigned to the case, recovered the watch. Tom's performance of his official police duty is not sufficient consideration to enforce payment of the reward.

Because the traditional rule is disfavored by so many courts, a number of exceptions have evolved.

1.   New or Different Consideration   If the promisee gives something new in return for the promise she now seeks to enforce or agrees to vary her preexisting duty in some way, there is consideration. It generally is immaterial how slight the change is, since courts are anxious to avoid the results of the preexisting legal duty rule.

2.   Honest Dispute as to Duty   If the scope of the legal duty owed is the subject of honest dispute, then a modifying agreement relating to it ordinarily will be given effect.

3.   U.C.C. Exception   Under U.C.C. § 2-209(1), an agreement modifying an existing contract that is subject to the Uniform Commercial Code is binding without consideration, as long as the parties act in good faith.

B.   Existing Debts   Existing debts present a recurring problem, which is only a variation of the preexisting legal duty rule. For instance, partial payment of a debt is not sufficient consideration to support a promise by the creditor to discharge the entire debt. However, courts generally will attempt to avoid this result by applying one of the exceptions.

C.   Forbearance to Sue   The promise not to sue or not to file a claim constitutes consideration if the claim is valid or if the claimant reasonably and in good faith believes the claim is valid. Forbearance of the right to have a claim decided by a court is a detriment recognized as consideration.

Mutuality of Consideration   Consideration must exist on both sides of the contract, that is, the promises must create mutual obligations.

> John promises to buy "all of the widgets that we may order"
> from Worldwide Widget Co.

John's promise is illusory, since he is still free to buy widgets anywhere else that he chooses or to buy no widgets at all.

A.   Requirements and Output Contracts   Requirements contracts (a promise to buy all that I require) and output contracts (a promise to sell all that I produce) are enforceable. Consideration is present, because the promisor suffers a legal detriment when she gives up the right to purchase the goods that she may need from (or the right to sell the goods that she produces to) another source. U.C.C. § 2-306.

Requirements and output contracts may not be unreasonably disproportionate to a stated estimate. Absent a stated estimate, they may not be unreasonably disproportionate to any normal or otherwise comparable prior requirements or output. In this way, the promisee is protected if the promisor attempts to alter quantities in an unforeseeable way. This is so, even though the attempted alteration is made in good faith.

The fact that one of the parties to a requirements or output contract may go out of business does not make the promises illusory. Some courts have refused to enforce such agreements where the promisor did not have an established business history, because there was no basis for estimating quantity. The Uniform Commercial Code avoids this problem by reading "good faith" into the agreement. That is, the promisor must operate the plant (or conduct the business) in good faith and according to commercial standards of fair dealing in the trade so that the output or the requirements will approximate a reasonably foreseeable amount.

B.   Conditional Promises   Conditional promises are enforceable (no matter how remote the contingency may be) unless the "condition" is entirely within the promisor's control.

> Kathleen promises to send her niece, Olivia, to law school if Olivia has stopped seeing her current boyfriend by the time she graduates from college.
>
> Kathleen promises to send her niece to law school if it snows on August 15.
>
> Kathleen promises to send her niece to law school if Kathleen loses ten pounds by the end of June.

The first two promises are enforceable; the third is not. Whether Kathleen does or does not lose 10 pounds is entirely within her control—the arguments of lifelong dieters notwithstanding.

A promise to buy if satisfied with the goods is not illusory since one cannot reject the goods unless dissatisfied. The courts have assumed that the party will exercise his or her right to reject in good faith. The Uniform Commercial Code is in accord. U.C.C. § 1-203.

C.   Right to Cancel or Withdraw   Although reservation of an unqualified right to cancel or withdraw may be an illusory promise, the consideration is valid if this right is restricted in any way, for example, the right to cancel upon 30 days' notice.

D.   Best Efforts Implied   The promise furnishing mutuality may be implied by a court in appropriate circumstances. Courts have increasingly tended to supply such promises in order to sustain agreements that might otherwise appear to be illusory.

Acme Corporation is granted the right to sell Worldwide widgets exclusively in return for one-third of the profits. The agreement is silent about the obligations of Acme Corporation. Courts will imply a promise by Acme to use its best efforts to sell the widgets.

E.   Voidable Promises   Voidable promises are not objectionable on mutuality grounds. Restatement 2d § 80.

Frank entered into a contract with 17-year-old William. William's power to disaffirm his contractual obligations will not prevent his promise from serving as consideration.

F.   Unilateral or Option Contracts   Unilateral contracts (enforceable once performance has started) or option contracts (enforceable because one has purchased the time to decide whether to accept the offer or not) are not objectionable on mutuality grounds.

G.   Choice of Alternative Courses   A promise to choose one of several alternative means of performance is illusory unless each alternative involves some legal detriment to the promisor. However, if the power to choose rests with some third party not under the control of the promisor, this is itself a legal detriment and supplies valuable consideration even if one or more of the other alternatives carries no legal detriment.

Smith, who is Jack's English professor, tells Jack that in return for Jack's promise to pay $250, Smith will (1) give Jack swimming lessons, (2) paint Jack's portrait, or (3) teach Jack's English class on a regular basis during the balance of the term, with the choice of performances to be Smith's. Since alternative (3) represents a preexisting duty owed by Smith to the university, it involves no legal detriment; and Smith's promise does not constitute legal detriment for Jack's promise to pay $250.

Same as above, except that Smith allows Jack to select the performance. Legal detriment is present, even if Jack chooses alternative (3).

Same as first example, except that Smith selects either alternative (1) or (2). Either selection cures the problem of legal detriment.

Substitutes for Consideration   Although consideration is necessary to make an executory bilateral agreement enforceable, certain substitutes for consideration can make an agreement at least partially enforceable.

A.   Promises Under Seal   Common law recognized the seal (a wax impression or notary's mark) as a substitute for consideration. A sealed promise was enforceable without anything more. However, the statutes in many states have abolished all distinctions between sealed and unsealed documents. In still other states, the seal raises only a rebuttable presumption of consideration. The Uniform Commercial Code has eliminated the seal entirely as consideration for sales contracts.

B.   Promises in Writing   A promise in writing may be enforced despite the absence of consideration in a few states simply because it is in writing. Except to the extent that it has been adopted by the Uniform Commercial Code for transactions between merchants, most states do not follow this rule.

Under the Uniform Commercial Code, any claim arising out of an alleged breach of a sales contract can be discharged in whole or in part by a written document signed by the claimant. U.C.C. § 1-107. Neither is consideration required to modify a written contract in good faith. Likewise, oral modifications are valid, unless the contract specifically prohibits such modification. Modifications of contracts covered by the Statute of Frauds (goods valued at $500 or more) must be in writing.

Merchants may bind themselves to keep an offer open for a period of no longer than three months if the offer so states and if it is a signed writing. If the offer form is supplied by the offeree, the clause promising to make the offer irrevocable must be separately signed by the offeror. U.C.C. § 2-205.

C.   Promises to Pay Obligations Barred by Law   A promise to pay a legal obligation barred by law is enforceable if the promise is in writing or if there has been partial performance, such as a partial payment. The new promise will be enforceable according to its terms, not according to the terms of the original obligation.

> Bill owes Mary $1,500, the collection of which is barred by the statute of limitations. Bill promises in writing to pay Mary $1,000 of the original debt. Mary can enforce the new promise without further consideration on her part but only to the extent of $1,000.

Similarly, a contract made by a person who lacks capacity is not enforceable. However, if that person affirms the contract upon attaining or regaining capacity, the new promise is binding against him or her.

D.   Promissory Estoppel   Consideration is not necessary where the facts indicate that the promisee relied to his or her detriment upon the promise of the promisor. In that instance, the promisor will be estopped to deny liability to the promisee to prevent injustice, although the liability may be limited by the losses incurred by the promisee. To enforce a claim of promissory estoppel, the promisee must be able to show: (1) The promisor reasonably should have expected to induce action or forbearance on the part of the promisee; (2) of definite and substantial character; and (3) the action or forbearance occurs.

> Ann orally promises to sell her chicken farm to Betty. Betty, in reliance upon Ann's promise, buys 500 chickens for the farm. If Ann refuses to go through with the deal, Betty cannot enforce the sale because of the Statute of Frauds; however, she may be able to recover her losses related to purchase of the chickens because of promissory estoppel (her detrimental reliance).

Contract Defenses

To be enforceable, a contract must be free of legally recognized defenses. A contract defense is a defect that prevents enforcement of a promise or agreement of the parties. The defect may be based upon lack of capacity of one of the parties to the contract or it may be based upon certain types of errors, misrepresentations, or public policy concerning the subject matter or terms of the contract.

Lack of Capacity   Contract defenses based upon lack of capacity generally involve one of three types of incapacity: minority, mental incapacity, and intoxication. Contracts made with persons who lack the capacity to contract are voidable, at the election of the incapacitated person.

A minor, sometimes called an infant, is a person who has not yet reached the statutory age of adulthood (majority). Many states, however, have adopted legislation that terminates minority if the minor marries, enters military service, or is otherwise fully emancipated from his or her parents. Since the contract of a minor is voidable, the minor may ratify the contract upon reaching the age of majority. The minor may ratify the contract by expressly affirming it or by failing to disaffirm it within a reasonable time after reaching majority. Even though minors are not generally bound by contracts made during legal minority, adults who contract with minors are bound.

> Joe Adult entered into an installment sale contract with Gary Teen for a car when Gary was 17 years old, requiring

payments to be made once a month for three years. The age of majority in Gary's state of residence is 18. Joe then changed his mind and wanted out of the deal.

Hot Hits Recording Co. entered into a contract with Gary while he was 17 years old, the terms of which required Gary to purchase one musical selection a month for the next 10 years.

In the first example, Joe Adult may not avoid the contract with Gary. Gary, however, may avoid the contract within a reasonable time after reaching his 18th birthday. In that event, Gary will be required to return the car and may be required to pay for its rental value while it was possessed and used by him.

In the second example, Gary may disaffirm the contract within a reasonable time after reaching his 18th birthday. If he continues to purchase musical selections every month until he is 19, however, his right to disaffirm may have been lost through the passage of time.

There are certain situations where the minor may not avoid contracts made during minority. If the minor misrepresents his or her age or if the contract provides the minor with necessities of life, the minor usually cannot avoid the contract. Necessities of life generally include such things as food, shelter, and so forth; what constitutes a necessity depends on the particular minor's station in life. The statute that carves out the necessity of life exception generally encompasses such things as student loans, insurance contracts, and the like.

A person whose mental capacity is so deficient that he or she is incapable of understanding the nature and significance of a contract may disaffirm it, either personally (in a lucid moment) or through his or her legal representative. One who has been adjudged insane or mentally incompetent by a court of law lacks the capacity to contract. As with minors, mental incompetents are liable for necessities of life furnished to them, not under the contract but, rather, under a quasi-contract theory.

A person who is so intoxicated as not to understand the nature and significance of a particular contract may either avoid or affirm the contract when he or she is sober. Again, there may be quasi-contractual liability for necessities furnished during the period of intoxication.

Lack of Consent   Even when a person has the legal capacity to contract, offensive pressure exerted by one party against the other may make any consent to the bargain ineffective. Lack of genuine consent may fall into one of four general categories: duress, undue influence, misrepresentation, and fraud.

A finding of **duress** requires a ***coercive threat*** of sufficient gravity that it induces the other party to manifest assent to an agreement to which he or she would not have assented otherwise. Advice, suggestion, or persuasion is not coercive standing alone. Likewise, fear of embarrassment or annoyance does not generally constitute duress. For coercion to exist, there must be threatened injury; and the victim must give assent while under the influence of this threat.

The coercion may be a gun held to the head of the victim or threatened harm to a family member or to property of the victim. Threat of criminal prosecution constitutes duress when fear of the prosecution overcomes judgment and deprives the victim of the exercise of free will. Threat of civil prosecution, however, is not duress. In extreme situations, economic distress or business compulsion may be grounds for duress (*see also unconscionability, infra*).

> ABC Parts Co. contracted with Weisenheimer Industries to supply super-widgets for Weisenheimer's federal contract. The super-widgets were specially manufactured according to unique specifications. After supplying a portion of the super-widgets, ABC found that it was losing money and submitted a price increase for Weisenheimer's approval. Because there was no other source for the super-widgets on such short notice, Weisenheimer had no choice but to pay the higher price. Weisenheimer then sued to have the price increase refunded and won based upon the business compulsion (duress) defense.

Undue influence results when the will of the dominant person is substituted for the will of the victim. Undue influence exists when a ***confidential relationship*** is used to create an ***unfair bargain*** for the victim. Family relationships, such as husband-wife or parent-child, often give rise to confidential relationships. Likewise, fiduciary relationships fit into this category, such as attorney-client, guardian-ward, or trustee-beneficiary.

A contract is not voidable simply because a confidential relationship exists. It is voidable because the dominant party uses the relationship to his or her own advantage in obtaining the assent of the weaker party. A legitimate suggestion or persuasion may influence the weaker party; but when methods go beyond persuasion and prevent the victim from acting freely, undue influence is present. Whether independent advice was provided to the weaker party is an important factor in determining fairness of the contractual arrangement.

Misrepresentation is the ***innocent or negligent misstatement*** of a material fact made by one party and relied upon by the other party as a basis for entering into an agreement to his or her damage. Distinguish actionable misrepresentation from the puffing that sometimes occurs when a salesperson touts his or her product as "the best on the market." Puffing is not misrepresentation. Likewise, giving an opinion is not misrepresentation.

Fraud is defined in the same way as misrepresentation, with the additional element of *scienter* required. If a defendant knows that what she says is false or if she recklessly disregards the truth or falsity of what she says, scienter is present. The burden then shifts to the plaintiff (victim) to show that he relied upon the intentional misstatement and that his reliance was reasonable or justifiable.

> Slick Sam says to a prospective buyer, "You won't find a better buy than this little beauty." *(Puffing)*

> Slick Sam says to a prospective buyer, "You won't find a better buy than this little beauty. It was driven only to church on Sundays." *(Unless it is true, the latter statement may be the basis for fraud.)*

> Slick Sam says to a prospective buyer, "I bought the Brooklyn Bridge last month and am prepared to let you have it for a reasonable price." *(No fraud—reliance on this statement is not justified.)*

> Slick Sam, repeating what he was told by the former owner, says to a prospective buyer, "Mary Todd Lincoln stayed in this house when she visited New York." *(Unless it is true, the statement is a misrepresentation; because scienter is absent, however, it cannot form the basis for fraud.)*

Mistake   A mistake is an assumption that is different from the facts. Although textbooks often classify mistakes as either unilateral or mutual, these classifications are practically useless in determining when a mistake will constitute a defense to contract formation and when it will not. At the heart of the mistake defense is the concept that mutual assent is lacking. In other words, there is no agreement because of some confusion by one (unilateral mistake) or both (mutual mistake) of the parties about a material fact. Either way, the contract is voidable, using the remedies of rescission and restitution.

There are some underlying philosophies that affect the mistake defense when it is raised:

1.   Although contract law usually looks at the objective intent of the parties (shown by words and actions), the parties' subjective understanding of the facts is the focus in determining whether a mistake exists.

2.   Mistake as a contract defense means mistake of past or present (but not future) material fact, not mistake of law. That a party is mistaken about the legal results of a particular fact or conduct is not included among the bases of the mistake defense. The law does not relieve parties who have merely made a bad bargain.

3.   Negligence in failing to read the terms of a contract before signing it is not the kind of mistake contemplated by the mistake defense.

A.   **Mutual Mistake**   A mutual mistake occurs when both parties are mistaken about a past or present material fact relating to the agreement. A mutual mistake goes to the heart of the bargain and prevents the formation of a contract. This kind of mistake is sometimes referred to as a latent ambiguity.

> Slick Sam contracts with Frank Farmer to sell Frank a prize cow. Unknown to either Sam or Frank, the prize cow died during the night. No contract is formed.

> Ann agrees to sell goods to Betty and to ship them from Bombay on a freighter known as the Peerless. Betty agrees to the terms. Neither knows that there are two freighters known as Peerless, one scheduled to depart in September and one scheduled to depart in December. Ann believes she has sold goods to be shipped on the Peerless leaving in December. Betty believes she has purchased goods to be shipped on the Peerless leaving in September. No contract is formed.

B.   **Unilateral Mistake**   A unilateral mistake is one made by only one of the parties to the agreement.

> Burt agrees to buy an expensive ring from Ernie, believing Ernie to be a wealthy person with a similar name. Ernie is unaware of Burt's mistake concerning identity and has done nothing to cause the mistake to be made. Burt may not avoid the contract, even though Burt would not have agreed to buy the ring if he had known Ernie was not the wealthy person whom Burt supposed him to be.

> George advertises a computer system for sale. Sally's employee inspects the equipment and offers $2,000 for it. Afterward, Sally discovers that the equipment will not handle a particular software program. Sally may not avoid

the contract based upon mistake, because George did not know of the mistake nor should he have known of it.

Where ambiguity exists and is known to one party (but not to the other), a contract will be enforced according to the intention of that party who was unaware of the ambiguity.

> Kathy agrees to purchase Dale's classic Cadillac. Unknown to Kathy, Dale has two classic Cadillac vehicles. Kathy intended to purchase one of them, and Dale intended to sell the other. The contract will be enforced so that Kathy will purchase the one that she intended to purchase, because Dale knew of the ambiguity. Kathy did not.

C.   Mistake in Transmission   When a mistake is made by an intermediary in the transmission of an offer or in the acceptance, the party who chose the intermediary generally bears the risk of the mistake. However, if the party receiving the message should have been aware of the mistake, no contract is formed.

> ABC Company solicited bids for building a parking lot. Better Parking, Inc. sent its $10,500 bid by telegram. The telegraph company made a mistake, transmitting the bid at $1050. All of the other bids received by ABC were in the $10,000 range. ABC may not accept the $1050 bid, because it is apparent that a mistake has been made.

D.   Mistake in Value   When parties make assumptions concerning the value of the subject matter of the contract, those assumptions will be upheld by courts. This is particularly true when the subject matter is subject to fluctuations of value, such as publicly traded stock. However, when both parties are mistaken about the value, the rules concerning mutual mistake will prevail.

> Arnold agrees to sell his prize cow to George for a minimal price, both parties believing that the cow is no longer fertile. After the purchase, George discovers that the cow is carrying a calf. This mutual mistake will support a rescission of the contract.

Illegality   If either the subject matter or the consideration of a contract is illegal at the time of the offer, there is no valid offer; and no contract is formed. Contracts may be illegal because they violate a constitution, a statute, or public policy as defined by courts. Illegality problems arise most often in these areas: agreements made in restraint of trade; gambling contracts; usurious contracts; agreements obstructing justice; and agreements concerning torts or crimes.

If the illegality occurs after the contract is formed, the supervening illegality discharges the contract because its performance has become impossible.

Unconscionability   Unconscionability is an equitable theory applied to contracts that are so unreasonable that they offend the conscience of all reasonable people. Under U.C.C. § 2-302, a court may refuse to enforce the entire contract, may refuse to enforce only the unconscionable portion, or may limit the unconscionable provision to avoid an unconscionable result. Unconscionability is used as a defense when the bargain is one-sided and one of the parties has substantially superior bargaining power over the other party.

Whether unconscionability exists is a question of law to be decided by a judge rather than by a jury. There is no precise definition for unconscionability, but courts use these criteria to determine its existence:

A.   Hidden, Risk-Shifting Provisions   Standard, preprinted forms sometimes contain provisions that seek to shift a risk normally borne by the stronger party to the weaker party. Typically, these provisions are in fine print, are inconspicuous, and are incomprehensible to the average person even when brought to his or her attention. They generally include: (1) "add-on" clauses that subject all property of the buyer to repossession if the buyer fails to pay for a newly-purchased item; (2) unreasonable liquidated damage provisions; (3) disclaimers of warranty provisions; and (4) confession of judgment clauses, which are illegal in most states on constitutional grounds.

B.   Adhesion Contracts   Adhesion contracts are those that contain unconscionable provisions concerning procurement of necessary goods, such as a refrigerator or an automobile, when the buyer is unable to purchase similar items from any seller without agreeing to a similar provision. In other words, the buyer has no choice. These contracts generally involve illiterate or non-English-speaking consumers, who unwittingly agree to pay three or four times the normal price of the item.

Statute of Frauds   The Statute of Frauds is a statute enacted in most states that requires certain types of contracts to be in writing to be enforceable, even though all other elements of contract may be present. Agreements included among Statute of Frauds provisions are as follows:

A.   Executor or Administrator   An agreement by an executor, administrator, or personal representative to pay the debts of the estate out of his or her own funds must be in writing.

B.   Debts of Another   A promise to answer for the debt of another must be in writing, such as a guaranty for a loan. A promise to be primarily liable for the debt need not be in writing, even though the benefits of payment are conferred upon another.

C.   In Consideration of Marriage   A promise made in consideration of marriage, as an inducement to marry, must be in writing (other than a return promise to marry).

D.   Interest in Land   A promise creating an interest in land must be in writing. Interests in land include such things as the sale or purchase of real estate; a mortgage or other security interest or lien in real estate; a lease for more than one year; timber or minerals to be severed by the buyer; or an easement. There may be others. A contract to construct a building does not create an interest in land and does not need to be in writing for purposes of the Statute of Frauds.

Where part performance has occurred, equity may take the contract out of the Statute of Frauds. For instance, if a seller conveys real estate under an oral contract to sell and if the buyer then refuses to pay the purchase price, a court of equity may intervene. Similarly, where the purchaser under a land contract has paid all of the payments and the seller refuses to convey title, a court of equity may intervene to take the contract out of the Statute of Frauds and to require specific performance.

E.   Performance within One Year   A contract that, by its terms, cannot be performed within one year must be in writing. The date of the agreement (not the date when performance is to begin) is used to calculate the one-year period. If it is possible to complete the contract within one year, the contract need not be in writing, even though its actual performance is concluded beyond the one-year period.

F.   Goods Priced at $500 or More   U.C.C. § 2-201(1) requires that contracts for the sale of goods of $500 or more be in writing. Under common law, this type of contract was taken out of the Statute of Frauds if a partial payment on the goods were made. The Uniform Commercial Code modifies this result by making such oral contracts enforceable only to the extent of the payments made and accepted or to the extent of goods received and accepted.

The Uniform Commercial Code permits enforcement of oral contracts for goods of $500 or more in some situations:

    1.   If goods are being specially manufactured for a particular buyer and are not suitable for sale to others, an oral contract may be enforced.

2.   If the party against whom enforcement is sought admits in pleadings, discovery, or testimony that the contract was made, the oral contract may be enforced to the extent that its existence is admitted.

3.   A written confirmation between merchants is sufficient against the sender of the confirmation and is sufficient against the recipient unless he or she sends written objection within ten days of its receipt.

G.   Satisfaction of the Writing Requirement   To satisfy the requirement of a writing, there must be a note or memorandum that contains the essential terms of the agreement, including (1) identity of the parties; (2) identity of the subject matter; (3) the essential terms; (4) recital of the consideration; and (5) signature of the party (or agent of the party) to be charged.

Under the Uniform Commercial Code, the following elements satisfy the requirement of a writing: (1) quantity; (2) signature of the party to be charged; and (3) a writing "sufficient to indicate" that a contract was formed. U.C.C. § 2-201.

H.   Effect of Noncompliance   Noncompliance with the Statute of Frauds may render the contract unenforceable. In almost all cases of noncompliance, however, the noncomplying party still can recover the reasonable value of his or her performance or restitution of a benefit conferred under a quasi-contract theory.

Rights and Duties of Nonparties

Once it is determined that a valid, enforceable contract has been formed, the next question is whether any nonparty to the contract has rights or duties in connection with it.

The general rule is that a contract confers benefits and imposes duties only on the parties to the contract. Two important exceptions to this general rule include third-party beneficiaries and those to whom contractual rights or duties are transferred. The rights and duties conferred upon third-party beneficiaries stem from the original contract. In the latter situation, the rights and duties do not stem from the original contract but, rather, are transferred subsequently when one of the original parties transfers rights (assignment) or duties (delegation) to a third party.

Third-Party Beneficiary Contracts   A third-party beneficiary is one who is intended to receive the benefits of a contract created by someone else. The first distinction to be made is whether the third party is an intended beneficiary (who can recover) or is an incidental beneficiary (who cannot recover).

> Bill lends money to Jack in exchange for Jack's promise to buy Bill's mother a Cadillac when Jack graduates from law school. Bill's mother is an intended beneficiary. The local Cadillac dealership is an incidental beneficiary and cannot sue to enforce Jack's promise.

Under traditional common law rules, there are two categories of intended beneficiaries: creditor beneficiaries and donee beneficiaries. A creditor beneficiary is one to whom the promisee owes a debt (or to whom a debt is claimed). A donee beneficiary is one to whom the promisee intends to make a gift of the benefit being conferred. Bill's mother is a donee beneficiary in the example shown above. The Second Restatement has dispensed with these distinctions; it uses only the term "intended" beneficiary, without any distinction between creditor beneficiaries and donee beneficiaries.

A.   Third-Party Beneficiary v. Promisor   The third-party beneficiary (Bill's mother in the above example) may sue the promisor (Jack in the above example) on the contract. The promisor may assert any defense arising from the formation of the contract. Defenses arising after the contract is formed (supervening illegality, impossibility, failure of a condition, and the like) may defeat a suit brought by the beneficiary.

B.   Third-Party Beneficiary v. Promisee   A third-party creditor beneficiary may sue the promisee on the existing obligation between them. Any contract between the promisor and the promisee does not discharge the promisee's obligation to the third party. The rights of the third-party beneficiary are cumulative. She need not elect between the third party promisor and her own debtor (the promisee). She may sue both but can obtain only one satisfaction.

A third-party donee beneficiary (Bill's mother) may not sue the promisee (Bill) because the promisee's act is gratuitous. This is true even when the third-party beneficiary has relied on the contract to her detriment (perhaps by building a garage for the Cadillac).

C.   Promisee v. Promisor   When the contract involves a creditor beneficiary and a promisee has been required to pay the beneficiary on the original debt, the promisee then may recover against the promisor.

If the debt has not yet been paid to the third-party beneficiary by the promisee, the promisee can compel the promisor to pay as agreed by filing suit for specific performance.

Where a donee beneficiary is involved, the majority rule now is that the promisee has a cause of action against the promisor. Since the promisee rarely ever suffers any actual damage, however, the promisee usually will receive only nominal damages. For this reason, many courts have resolved the problem by allowing specific performance in this situation as well.

Assignment of Rights   When a contract already has been created and when one of the parties subsequently seeks to transfer rights under the original contract to a third party, this transfer is accomplished by assignment.

> Oscar agrees to provide cleaning service to the Super Shopper Store for a fee of $1500 a month. After the contract is underway, Oscar agrees to transfer his right of payment to the Second National Bank, with the payment to be applied to Oscar's equipment loan at the bank. The transfer is an assignment.

In the above example, Oscar is the assignor; Second National Bank is the assignee; and Super Shopper Store is the obligor.

Although nearly all contractual rights may be assigned, there are some exceptions:

A.   Obligor's Duty Changed   If assignment of rights would alter the obligor's duty substantially, assignment will be prohibited. One example is a personal service contract where the obligor would have to perform a service substantially different for the assignee than would have been performed for the assignor. Another example might be a requirements and output contract, where the requirements of the assignee may be substantially different than the requirements of the assignor.

B.   Obligor's Risk Changed   When the assignment would alter the obligor's risk substantially, assignment will be prohibited without the obligor's consent.

> Bill's auto is insured by Best Insurance Co. Bill sells the auto to Susan, who intends to use it as a taxi. Bill cannot assign his rights under the insurance contract to Susan without Best's consent, since the assignment would alter Best's risk substantially.

C.   Assignment Prohibited by Law   A right cannot be assigned if the assignment is prohibited by law. For instance, many states have statutes that prohibit, or at least limit, wage assignments.

D.   Assignment Prohibited by Contractual Provision   The power to assign cannot be limited by contract; however, the right to assign can be. Where parties seek to bar assignment by contract provision, the provision must be clear and unequivocal that any purported assignment is void. A contractual provision barring assignment is ineffective against assignments by operation of law (bankruptcy, death, and so forth).

Assignment Requirements   Assignments are not required to be in writing as a general rule; however, some assignments must be in writing to be effective:

1.   Assignments of wages;
2.   Assignments of interests in land;
3.   Assignments relating to sale of goods of $500 or more; and
4.   Assignments of security interests under U.C.C.'s Article 9.

A.   Partial Assignments   Contract rights may be transferred to one assignee or they may be divided and transferred to more than one assignee. Likewise, the assignee may transfer some of the rights under a contract and retain others.

B.   Revocability   If an assignment is given in exchange for consideration, it is irrevocable. An assignment given gratuitously (no consideration exchanged) is revocable unless the obligor has already performed or unless the assignee has changed his or her position in reliance upon the assignment (detrimental reliance). In the latter situation, the assignor is estopped from revoking the assignment.

C.   Effect of Assignment   The effect of assignment is to establish privity of contract between the obligor and the assignee. The assignee replaces the assignor as the real party in interest; and the assignee is entitled to performance under the contract, subject to any defenses that the obligor may have against the assignor.

D.   Successive Assignments   When the first assignment is revocable (gratuitous), a subsequent assignment will revoke the first one. Generally, when the first assignment is irrevocable, the first assignee has priority over any subsequent assignees.

The Uniform Commercial Code has resolved this problem by imposing filing requirements. U.C.C. § 9-302. If the filing provisions apply to a particular transaction, the assignee who is the first to file will prevail.

Delegation of Duties   Duties or obligations under a contract are not assigned. Rather, they are delegated when a party to the original contract wishes to have another person perform his or her duties under the contract.

> Oscar agrees to provide cleaning service to the Super Shopper Store for a fee of $1500 a month. After the contract is created, Oscar authorizes Mostly Maids, Inc. to perform the cleaning service for him at a fee of $1000 a month. This authorization is a delegation.

In this example, Super Shopper Store is the obligee; Oscar is the delegator; and Mostly Maids, Inc. is the delegate (sometimes called the "delegatee").

A.   Duties Subject to Delegation   In general, all duties are capable of delegation to third parties except duties requiring personal judgment or skill (artistic performance); duties involving a trust relationship (attorney-client); duties which, if delegated, would change the expectancy of the obligee (output contract); and duties which are covered by a contract provision that restricts or prohibits their delegation.

B.   Requirements for Delegation   No special rules or formalities are required to delegate duties under a contract. The delegation may be either oral or written. There is no requirement that the word "delegate" be used; the delegator need only manifest a present intention to transfer or to delegate the duty.

C.   Rights and Liabilities of Parties   The rights and liabilities of parties in relation to delegated duties are shown below.

1.   Obligee   Other than those duties that cannot be delegated (*see above*), the obligee must accept performance from the delegate.

2.   Delegator   The delegator remains liable on the contract even if the delegate expressly assumes the contract duties. If the obligee expressly consents to the delegation, however, this situation may create a novation (see subsequent discussion under Discharge).

3.   Delegate   When the delegate promises to perform the contractual duties and when that promise is supported by consideration, a third-party beneficiary contract is created by the delegator and delegate, with the obligee as the third-party beneficiary. In that event, either the obligee or the delegator can compel performance or can bring suit for nonperformance.

Construction and Interpretation of Contracts

Courts use specific rules of construction when they interpret contracts. In general, contracts are construed as a whole, with specific clauses subordinated to the contract's overall intent. Words are construed according to their ordinary meaning, unless it is clear that they are intended to be used in a technical sense (term of art). When parties intend words to be used in a technical sense, it is prudent to provide the technical definition as part of the contract document.

When provisions appear to be inconsistent with each other, courts look to see whether some of the provisions are printed (a form contract), while others are written or typed. If both are present, written or typed provisions will be given more weight than printed provisions.

Courts look at the custom and usage of a particular business or industry in construing contract terms. Where possible, courts prefer to validate contracts rather than to invalidate them. Because of this inclination, courts try to construe provisions to make them operative unless this practice clearly would contradict the overall intention of the parties.

Parol Evidence

When parties express their contract in writing with the intent that it embody the full and complete expression of their agreement, any other expressions— whether oral or written—made prior to or contemporaneous with the writing are inadmissible to vary the terms of the writing. This is known as the parol evidence rule. In other words, the written terms expressed in the contract may not be changed by parol evidence of what the parties actually intended.

Notwithstanding its name, the parol evidence rule is regarded as a rule of substantive contract law rather than as a rule of evidence. It is designed to put the apparent intention of the parties (expressed by the writing) into effect and to assist in judicial interpretation by having a single source of proof (the writing) concerning the terms of the contract.

When the parol evidence rule is raised concerning a particular contract, the judge—not the jury—must decide (1) whether the written document was intended as a final expression of the parties' agreement and (2) whether the written document is a complete integration or is only a partial integration of the parties' agreement.

The more complete that a document appears on its face, the more likely that it was intended as a final expression. Where the document contains a merger clause, reciting that it is complete on its face, this clause strengthens the presumption that all negotiations were merged into the written document. If the judge determines that the written document is the final integration of the parties' agreement, no extrinsic evidence will be admitted to vary any of the terms contained in the document.

There are a number of situations where the parol evidence rule does not apply to exclude evidence. These are discussed below.

Attack on Validity   Any party to a written contract may attack the contract's validity. In this circumstance, the party concedes that the written document reflects the agreement but asserts that the agreement never came into existence because of formation defects (duress, mistake, illegality, misrepresentation, and so forth) or because a condition precedent never occurred.

> Jill signs a real estate contract, agreeing to sell her house to Jack, but Jill and Jack agree orally that the contract will not become effective until Jill finds another house to buy for herself.

The parol evidence rule does not come into play until a fully binding contract exists; therefore, Jill ordinarily will be allowed to introduce evidence that the stipulated event (the condition precedent) has not yet occurred.

To Clarify Ambiguity   If there is ambiguity concerning the terms of a written agreement or if there is a dispute concerning the meaning of those terms, parol evidence can assist the fact-finder in correctly interpreting the agreement. If the meaning of the agreement and its terms are plain, parol evidence is inadmissible.

To Refute Consideration   The parol evidence rule will not exclude extrinsic evidence to show the consideration actually paid. For instance, if a written contract recites that $100 has been given, parol evidence may be admitted from the defendant to show that $100 was never paid.

Subsequent Modification   Since the parol evidence rule applies only to prior or contemporaneous negotiations related to the agreement, parol evidence can be admitted to show subsequent modification of the written contract. In other words, parties may show that the written contract was changed in some way after it was originally made.

U.C.C. Rule   Under the Uniform Commercial Code, a party may not contradict the written document but may add consistent, additional terms unless (1) there is a merger clause or (2) the court finds that the writing was intended as a complete and exclusive statement of the terms of the agreement. U.C.C. § 2-202. Under this Code section, the terms of a written contract may be explained or supplemented by showing custom and usage in the trade or by showing the course of performance to date.

Enforcement of Contracts

The area of contract enforcement deals with discharge of contract duties, breach of contract, and remedies for breach. Before any of these things can be considered, however, there must be an initial determination that a party has a present duty to perform and has not done so. To make this determination, one must be able to distinguish between a promise to perform and a condition, sometimes called a condition precedent.

Promise v. Condition   A promise is a commitment to do or to refrain from doing an act. A promise in a contract may be unconditional or conditional. An unconditional promise is absolute; a conditional promise may become absolute by the occurrence of the condition. When the promise is unconditional, the failure to perform will constitute a breach of the contract.

A condition is an event, other than the passage of time, the occurrence of which will create an absolute duty to perform and the nonoccurrence of which will extinguish any duty to perform. There can be no breach if the condition has failed to occur. Instead, failure of the condition discharges the liability of the promisor, whose obligations never mature.

> Frank Farmer agrees to sell his prize cow to Jane for $500, with possession of the cow to be given on October 31. On October 15, the cow dies.

In the above example, is delivery of a specific cow a condition? If so, the death of the cow will discharge Jane's duty to pay; however, Jane will have no cause of action against Frank if the condition does not occur. Or, has Frank promised to sell his prize cow (whether the cow that died or another prize cow), giving Jane the right to sue for breach of contract?

As the example shows, it is important to know whether a provision will be interpreted as a promise or as a condition. The basic test is the "intent of the parties." In making this determination, courts look at the specific words used and the context of the entire agreement; the prior practices of the parties; and the customs within that business or industry. Recall that in doubtful situations, courts prefer to validate the contract rather than to invalidate it. However, if occurrence of the stipulation goes to the heart of the contract's consideration, it is probably a condition rather than a promise. In the above example, it is likely that a court would find that delivery was a condition to Jane's duty to pay. Alternately, the court may find that there was a mutual mistake, in that the subject matter of the contract (the prize cow) was destroyed.

Both Condition and Promise   A particular contract term may be a promise for one party and a condition for the other. These are often called constructive conditions.

> Ben promises to repair Adam's car by December 1 if Adam will promise to pay Ben $200 for the repairs on that date. Adam agrees.

In this example, Ben's promise to repair the car by December 1 is an absolute promise, and his performance is a condition of Adam's duty to pay $200.00 on December 1.

A contract term may be both a promise and a condition for the same party.

> Alice agrees to buy Jim's house if she can secure the necessary financing. Alice attempts to secure financing but is unable to do so.

Alice is subject to both a promise and a condition. The condition is that she be able to secure financing; the promise is that she will make reasonable attempts to secure it. If Alice makes reasonable attempts but is unsuccessful, the failure discharges any further duty on the part of either party.

Excuse of Condition   As a general rule, if a party's duty to perform is conditional, there is no duty to perform until the condition occurs. However, situations may exist that require performance even though the condition has not occurred. In these situations, the condition is excused.

A.   Hindrance   If a party's duty is conditioned on the occurrence of an event and that same party wrongfully prevents the event from occurring, the occurrence of the event (condition) may be excused; and the party must perform despite the non-occurrence. In determining whether a party has contributed to the non-occurrence of a condition to his or her own duty, the test is one of good faith. If the party acts in bad faith, the condition will almost always be excused; and that party will be required to perform.

> Alice agrees to buy Jim's house if she can secure the necessary financing. Alice later decides that she does not want the house and does not attempt to secure financing.

B.   Breach   A material breach of the contract when performance is due will excuse the non-breaching party's duty to perform. A minor breach, on the other hand, may suspend the non-breaching party's duty to perform but will not excuse it.

C.   Anticipatory Repudiation   Anticipatory repudiation occurs when a party, prior to the time required for performance, indicates unequivocally that he or she will not perform when performance is due. Under common law rules and under the Uniform Commercial Code, anticipatory repudiation occurs only when there is an executory bilateral contract (duties remaining on both sides).

When the nonrepudiating party has no duty remaining to be performed by him or her, the doctrine of anticipatory repudiation does not apply. The nonrepudiator must wait until the time originally agreed for performance before a cause of action arises. Until then, the repudiator may withdraw the repudiation and perform as required by the original contract.

> Bill agrees to pay $50.00 on December 1 for Frank's used aquarium, with the aquarium to be delivered on November 15. On November 1, Bill unequivocally informs Frank that he no longer wishes to buy the aquarium and will not pay $50.00 for it. (*Anticipatory repudiation applies.*)

> Bill agrees to pay $50.00 on December 1 for Frank's used aquarium, with the aquarium to be delivered on November 15. The aquarium is delivered as agreed; and on November 25, Bill announces that he will not pay $50.00 for it. (*Anticipatory repudiation does not apply, since Frank's performance is complete. Frank must wait until December 1 passes to initiate suit.*)

When anticipatory repudiation occurs, the nonrepudiating party may select one of four options:

1.   Treat the anticipatory repudiation as total repudiation and sue immediately;

2.   Suspend performance and wait until the performance date to sue;

3.   Treat the anticipatory repudiation as an offer to rescind, resulting in discharge of the contract; or

4.   Ignore the anticipatory repudiation and urge the promisor to perform as originally agreed.

D.   Substantial Performance   The condition of full performance often may be excused if a party gives substantial performance. In other words, if a party has committed a minor (insubstantial) breach but has performed in all other respects, she has substantially performed. In this situation, the other party's duty of performance becomes absolute. The rule of substantial performance does not apply to an express condition, however, if it would contradict the stated intent of the parties.

> Dick agrees to build a new house for Jane, using plans that, among other things, call for Newton locks on all doors and windows. Dick uses Newton locks on the doors but cannot obtain Newton window locks for another eight weeks. He uses Benning window locks instead, which are of similar quality.

Although Dick breached the contract by not using Newton window locks, the deviation is minor. Accordingly, Dick has substantially performed; and Jane now has a duty to perform her duty by paying for the house. Because of the doctrine of substantial performance, Dick is able to enforce the contract rather than sue in quasi-contract. Jane will be able to deduct or to sue for damages (if any) that she suffers as a result of Dick's incomplete performance.

The substantial performance doctrine was developed primarily to prevent forfeiture for minor defects in construction contracts. When the sale of goods is involved, U.C.C. § 2-601 gives the buyer the right to reject goods (perfect tender rule) subject to six exceptions:

1.   The parties may agree otherwise.

2.   Rejection of goods under an installment contract is permitted only if the installment is nonconforming and if the nonconformity substantially impairs the value of the installment.

3.   The seller's failure to provide for reasonable shipment or promptly to notify the buyer of shipment gives the buyer the right to reject only if material delay or loss occurs.

4.   If the buyer has accepted the goods, she no longer has the right to reject.

5.   Bad faith rejection by the buyer for an immaterial defect may preclude her right of rejection.

6.   Although the buyer has the right to reject for any defect in general, the seller has the right to cure if there is any time remaining for performance under the contract.

E.   Divisible Contracts   Like the doctrine of substantial performance, divisibility of a contract into units prevents the harsh result of forfeiture. Where a party performs one of the units of a divisible contract, she is entitled to the agreed equivalent for that unit, even if she fails to perform the other units. The other party, however, may have a cause of action for the remaining units and, at the same time, may withhold his counter-performance for those units.

The divisibility rule can be applied only when the contract can be divided into units in a reasonable way. The test is one of fairness. When contract terms expressly state that the contract is *entire* or is otherwise indivisible, courts will honor the parties' intent.

Under the Uniform Commercial Code, goods covered by a single contract must be tendered in a single delivery unless it is clear that the parties intended otherwise. When a contract for sale of goods authorizes or requires deliveries in separate lots, it is an installment contract. U.C.C. § 2-612 covers installment contracts:

1.   If the price may be apportioned, it may be demanded for each lot unless a contrary intent is shown.

2.   The buyer may reject an installment if the defect materially impairs the value of that installment and cannot be cured. If adequate assurance is provided by the seller, the buyer must accept the installment.

3.   The buyer may declare a total breach only if the defects materially impair the value of the entire contract. Even a material breach can be waived and the duties reinstated if the buyer demands further performance or if the buyer sues only for past installments.

F.   Waiver or Estoppel   One who is to receive the benefit of a condition may manifest words or conduct to waive the condition. If the condition is waived and if the other party changes her position in reliance upon the waiver, the waiver will be binding (estoppel). The waiver may be retracted, however, at any time before the other party has changed her position to her detriment in reliance upon the waiver.

> Frank agrees to buy a computer "in perfect working order" from Richard. When delivered, the computer has minor defects; but Frank elects to take delivery anyway.

By taking delivery, Frank waives the "perfect working order" condition. However, he may nonetheless be entitled to damages for the defects in the computer. Waiver relates only to waiver of the right to treat the failure of condition as a total breach for purposes of excusing counter-performance.

Discharge of Contract Duties

Duties under a particular contract may be discharged (released or extinguished) in a number of different ways. When a contract duty is discharged, that duty is no longer enforceable.

Performance   One way to discharge contract duties is by performance, and the vast majority of contracts are discharged in this way. A good faith ***tender of performance***, made according to contract terms, likewise will discharge a party's duty to perform when the tendering party has the present ability to perform and when the other party refuses to accept performance.

> Joe pays $20.00 to Fred for a tennis lesson to be given on the following Tuesday. When Tuesday arrives, Joe fails to appear for the lesson, although Fred is present and ready to provide it.

Illegality   If the subject matter of the contract becomes illegal after the contract is formed, this supervening illegality will discharge the contract.

Impossibility   Contractual duties are discharged when it becomes impossible to perform them. The impossibility must be objective (could not be performed by anyone) and must occur after the contract is formed. If the impossibility exists when the contract is formed, the issue is one of formation—not one of discharge.

When a contract is discharged because of impossibility, each party is excused from duties yet to be performed under the contract. Either party may receive restitution under a quasi-contract theory for performance given before the impossibility occurred. If the performance to be given becomes impossible in part, the duty is discharged only to that extent. The remainder of the performance may be required, even if the remainder may involve additional expense or difficulty.

Temporary impossibility suspends contract duties but does not discharge them. When performance becomes possible, the duty of performance springs back into existence unless the burden on either party is substantially more than or is substantially different from the burden originally contemplated.

Death or physical incapacity of a party necessary to perform contract duties (personal services contract) discharges the contract. If the subject matter of the contract is destroyed through no fault of the promisor after the contract is formed, the contract is discharged unless the risk of loss has already passed to the buyer (such as certain sales of goods under the Uniform Commercial Code).

Impracticability   A number of courts will discharge contractual duties when performance becomes impracticable. To qualify for discharge by impracticability, the party required to perform must encounter extreme and unreasonable difficulty or expense that could not have been reasonably anticipated. It is not enough that performance has become more difficult or more expensive than anticipated; it must be extreme and unreasonable. Typical examples of commercial impracticability under the Uniform Commercial Code include war, labor strikes, or similar, unforeseen events that dramatically affect performance.

Frustration   If the purpose of the contract has become frustrated (without value or virtually without value) by a supervening event that could not have been foreseen reasonably when the contract was formed, performance may be discharged.

> Beth agrees to rent Mary's summer home at Myrtle Beach for her family's vacation during the last two weeks in August. On August 10, a hurricane causes extensive damage to the entire South Carolina coastline. Although the vacation home receives only minor damage, Myrtle Beach is declared part of a disaster area. The purpose of the contract is frustrated, since no one would want to vacation in a disaster area.

Rescission   A contract may be rescinded by agreement between the parties (mutual rescission). The agreement to rescind is itself a binding contract supported by the consideration of each party's giving up the right to performance by the other.

To be effectively discharged by rescission, there must be executory duties on both sides. The U.C.C. provides that the rescission of a contract for the sale of goods must be in writing when the original contract so requires. For contracts not governed by the U.C.C., many courts will permit oral rescission even though the original contract requires a rescission to be in writing.

When one party wants to rescind and the other party does not (unilateral rescission), the party seeking rescission must have adequate legal grounds to force the rescission. Adequate legal grounds may include mistake, misrepresentation, duress, undue influence, or failure of consideration.

Modification   If a contract is modified, the modification discharges those terms of the original contract that are the subject of the modification. The modification does not discharge the entire contract, however.

Ordinarily, the modification must be by mutual agreement. Under the doctrine of reformation, however, either party may bring an equity action to have written terms modified when the writing, through mistake or misrepresentation, does not state accurately the terms upon which the parties agreed.

No consideration is necessary when the effect of the modification is to correct an error in the original contract. Contracts for the sale of goods may be modified without new consideration. U.C.C. § 2-209(1).

Substituted Contract   A contract may be discharged by substituting a new contract in its place. The new contract may expressly revoke the original contract; but if the terms of the new contract are inconsistent with the terms of the original contract, the original contract is impliedly revoked and discharged.

Novation   Novation occurs when a new contract substitutes a different (new) party to receive benefits and to assume duties under the terms of the original contract. Novation requires agreement among all parties, including the new party; and when that agreement is reached, the contractual duties of original parties are extinguished (discharged).

Release   A release or an agreement not to sue will discharge contractual duties when the release is in writing and is supported by new consideration. When a contract for the sale of goods is involved, the release or agreement not to sue must be in writing but need not be supported by new consideration. U.C.C. § 1-107.

Accord and Satisfaction   An accord is an executory promise by one party to give a substituted performance and by the other party to accept the substituted performance as discharge of an existing duty.

> Eve owes Adam $1,000 under an existing contract. Eve offers Adam a new widget worth $750 in lieu of the existing debt. Adam accepts. The new consideration is sufficient to support a valid accord.

Where a genuine dispute exists concerning the amount due under an existing obligation, an agreement to pay a portion of the amount claimed will be treated as a valid accord by most courts.

Standing alone, an accord does not discharge the prior contract. Rather, it suspends the right to enforce the original contract in deference to the terms of the executory accord agreement. When performance under the accord agreement is complete, satisfaction occurs; and the combined accord and satisfaction will discharge the original contract.

Account Stated   An account stated is an agreement between parties concerning a final balance due from one party and payable to the other. The final balance covers a number of transactions and merges the transactions by discharging claims related to the individual transactions. To qualify as an account stated, there must have been more than one prior transaction between the parties.

An account stated need not be in writing unless one or more of the original transactions was subject to the Statute of Frauds. An account stated need not be express; it may be implied.

> After a number of individual sales between Betty and Ruth, Betty presents Ruth with a bill for $500.00 covering all previous transactions. Unless Ruth objects within a reasonable time, the bill will become an account stated. Betty then may sue for the account stated rather than for the combination of previous transactions.

Lapse   When the duty of each party is a condition to the duty of the other party, contractual obligations may lapse if neither party performs when his or her performance is due.

Wally contracts with Sam to sell Sam 500 shoe horns on January 20 for $750.00. On January 20, Wally fails to tender the shoe horns and Sam fails to tender $750.00. Six months later, Wally tenders the shoe horns but Sam refuses to accept them. The contractual obligations of both parties have been discharged by lapse.

Operation of Law   When a party to a contract obtains judgment against the other for breach of contract, the contractual duty of performance is merged in the judgment, which discharges the contract. Instead, the judgment debtor is obligated for whatever performance is required by the judgment, usually the payment of damages. An arbitration award works essentially the same way.

A discharge in bankruptcy likewise bars any right of action on the contract.

Breach of Contract

A breach of contract occurs when (1) a promisor is under an absolute duty to perform and when (2) the duty of performance has not been discharged. Implicit in the determination of whether the duty of performance has been discharged is an assessment of whether the nonperformance (breach) is material or minor.

Material Breach   A breach is material if the promisee does not receive the substantial benefit of her bargain as a result of the promisor's failure to perform or as a result of the promisor's defective performance. If the breach is material, the nonbreaching party may treat the contract as terminated, in which event her duty of counter-performance is discharged. In addition, she will have a right to one or more remedies for breach of the contract.

Minor Breach   A breach is minor if the promisee receives the substantial benefit of her bargain despite the promisor's defective performance. A minor breach may include small delays in completing the performance when time is not critical or small deficiencies in the quality of performance when precision is not critical. The effect of a minor breach is to provide a remedy to the nonbreaching party for the breach, but it does not relieve the nonbreaching party of the duty to perform under the contract.

When a minor breach is accompanied by anticipatory repudiation, however, the nonbreaching party may treat it as a material breach. In this situation, she is relieved of any further duty to perform under the contract; and she is permitted to sue immediately for damages.

Timely Performance   When the defaulting party has a duty to perform immediately, her failure to perform is a breach. Unless the nature of the contract makes performance at a specific time essential or unless the contract's terms provide that time is of the essence, the failure to perform on time ordinarily is a minor breach. Where merchant contracts are concerned, however, timely performance as agreed is important; and an unjustified delay is a material breach.

The nonbreaching party who sues for breach of contract must show both the ability and the willingness to perform but for the breaching party's failure to perform.

Contract Remedies

Once a plaintiff shows both (1) material breach by the defendant and (2) no material breach by the plaintiff, a remedy is available to redress the breach. Depending upon the facts of the case and the legal issues that they raise, there may be more than one remedy available to the plaintiff. In that event, the plaintiff must select the most advantageous remedy among them.

The purpose of a contract remedy is to put the plaintiff where he or she would have been if the contract had not been breached. In other words, a contract remedy attempts to give the plaintiff the benefit of his or her bargain. This is sometimes referred to as the plaintiff's expectation interest or expectancy and can take the form of damages or specific performance.

If a plaintiff wants to rescind the contract (does not want to buy the house if the defendant misrepresented that Mary Todd Lincoln slept there), she cannot obtain contract damages. Instead, the court will restore the plaintiff to her original position (before the contract was formed) by restoring to her any benefits that the defendant may have received, perhaps an earnest deposit or a down payment.

Similarly, when one party has conferred benefits on the other under an agreement that cannot be enforced, equity may intervene to disgorge the benefits from the defendant under a quasi-contract (restitution) theory.

Damages   The remedy awarded most often for breach of contract is contract damages. With some limited exceptions, damages must be proved to a reasonable degree of certainty; they cannot be speculative. Damages may be classified as compensatory (general), consequential (special), punitive, nominal, or liquidated.

A.   Compensatory (General) Damages   Compensatory damages are awarded to a plaintiff to put her where she would have been if the contract had been performed by the other party. Compensatory damages are designed to give the plaintiff the benefit of her bargain. This may be the contract price, the profits to have been realized from the contract, or the amount that she must pay to buy substitute performance.

> Andrew agrees to buy Ben's farm for $70,000.00. On the scheduled date of closing, the farm is valued at $73,000.00. If Ben refuses to sell, Andrew's general damages loss as a result of Ben's breach will be $3,000.00.

B.   Consequential (Special) Damages   In addition to compensatory damages, a plaintiff may be able to recover other losses incurred as a consequence of the breach, provided that they were reasonably foreseeable at the time the contract was made; that there is a causal ("but for") relationship between the damages and the breach; and that they can be proved with a reasonable degree of certainty.

> In the above example, Ben knows that Andrew intends to operate a chicken farm on the land. After signing the purchase agreement, Andrew contracts with ABC Poultry to purchase 900 chickens and makes a deposit of $500.00. Since Ben knew of Andrew's intention, it was reasonably foreseeable that Andrew would contract for chickens. If Andrew must forfeit the $500.00 deposit as a result of the breach, Ben may be liable for that amount as consequential damages.

C.   Punitive Damages   Punitive damages are designed to punish or to penalize the defendant for bad conduct above and beyond a simple breach of contract. In states where punitive damages are permitted, for instance, an employer who refuses to pay wages to an employee may be liable for punitive damages over and above the amount of the wages.

Punitive damages ordinarily are not allowed in commercial contract cases and are awarded in other contract cases only in very limited circumstances.

D.   Nominal Damages   Nominal damages may be awarded when the defendant has breached the contract but no monetary loss is proved. Nominal damages are awarded more frequently in tort cases than in contract cases, simply because breach of a contract usually results in a measurable monetary loss.

E.   Liquidated Damages   Liquidated damages are those damages agreed upon by the parties at the time the contract is formed.

Liquidated damage provisions are used most often where the parties recognize that damages will be difficult to prove in the event of breach (such as lost profits of a new business, violation of a literary license agreement, and so forth). As long as a liquidated damages provision is reasonable (does not amount to a penalty), a court will enforce it without requiring that it be substantiated.

Measure of Damages   Damages may be measured (calculated) in a number of different ways, depending upon the type of contract involved and the facts surrounding its breach. Implicit in all measures is the concept that a plaintiff is required to mitigate (minimize) his or her losses.

   A.   Sale of Goods   When a contract involves the sale of goods, the Uniform Commercial Code prescribes the remedies available to both the seller and the buyer. U.C.C. § 2-703 describes the remedies of a seller when the buyer breaches, and U.C.C. § 2-711 describes the remedies of a buyer when the seller breaches.

   Seller's Remedies   When the buyer wrongfully rejects goods, wrongfully revokes acceptance of goods, or fails to make a payment, the seller may

   1.   withhold delivery of the goods;

   2.   stop delivery of the goods in the hands of a carrier;

   3.   resell the goods and recover the difference from the defaulting buyer, measured as the difference between the resale price and the contract price;

   4.   cancel the contract;

   5.   recover the contract price from the defaulting buyer if (a) the goods have been accepted or, if conforming goods have been lost or damaged, within a reasonable time after the risk of loss passes to the buyer; or (b) the goods have been identified to the contract and the seller is unable to find another buyer; or

   6.   recover ordinary contract damages for nonacceptance, measured as the difference between

the market price at the time and place for tender and the contract price, together with any consequential damages.

Buyer's Remedies   When the seller fails to deliver goods or when the buyer properly rejects goods or properly revokes acceptance of goods, the buyer may:

1.   cancel;

2.   "cover" by purchasing substitute goods on the open market and recover from seller the difference between the price of the substituted goods and the contract price;

3.   recover specific goods identified to the contract if the buyer has paid all or a portion of the purchase price;

4.   recover damages for nondelivery, measured as the difference between the market price at the time when buyer learned of the breach and the contract price, together with any consequential damages; or

5.   obtain specific performance in limited circumstances (see U.C.C. § 2-716).

B.   Contracts for Sale of Land   The standard measure of damages for breach of contracts for the sale of land is the difference between the contract price and the fair market value of the land at the time when the land was to have been conveyed.

C.   Construction Contracts   The measure of damages in construction contracts depends upon the identity of the breaching party (whether the contractor or the owner) and the point at which the breach occurs.

Owner Breaches:

Before Construction Begins: Builder receives the profit she would have made on the contract.

During Construction: Builder receives the profit she would have made on the contract plus any costs that she has incurred to date.

After Construction Completed: Builder receives the full contract price plus interest.

Contractor Breaches:

Before Construction Begins: Owner receives the cost of completion (the amount over the contract price that it will cost to complete the construction).

During Construction: Owner receives the cost of completion unless completion would entail economic waste. In that event, owner receives the difference in the value of the land at the time of breach and the value of the land as it should have been if the contract had been performed.

If the contractor's breach is unintentional (negligent), she may be able to recover the reasonable value of her services and costs under a quasi-contract theory. She cannot recover under the contract, of course, if she is the breaching party. If the contractor's breach is intentional, she may be denied recovery of any kind—even in quasi-contract.

By Late Completion: Owner receives damages for loss of use (rental value) until construction is completed. If loss of use cannot be calculated readily or was not foreseeable at the time the contract was made, the owner may be limited to the interest on the value of the building as a capital asset.

Specific Performance   Specific performance is an equitable remedy by which a party is ordered by a court to fulfill his or her contractual obligations. Because it is an equitable remedy, the plaintiff must demonstrate to the court that there is no adequate remedy at law before specific performance can be granted. In other words, if the plaintiff can be compensated with money, she cannot obtain an order of specific performance.

As a general rule, specific performance in contract cases is limited to those situations where the subject matter of the contract is unique, because money will compensate for most contract losses. Notice the examples below, however.

> Mark agrees to sell an original painting to Ellen. Before delivery is to occur, however, Mark receives a higher offer for the painting. He informs Ellen that he will not honor their contract. Ellen may be able to obtain an order of specific performance because the painting is an original and is therefore unique.

> Alice agrees in writing to sell her house to Betty for $85,000. This is Betty's dream house. It is located one block from the school and six blocks from her place of employment. It is perfect in every way, right down to the red and green ceramic tiles in the kitchen. Alice subsequently changes her mind about selling the house. Because the house is unique (no other house is exactly like this one), Betty may be granted the remedy of specific performance.

> Same situation, except that Betty (rather than Alice) changes her mind about buying the house. Specific performance is not appropriate on these facts, because Alice does not care whether she sells to Betty or to some other buyer, as long as she receives the $85,000 purchase price. If Alice is forced to sell the house for $82,000, she can obtain damages from Betty of $3,000; but she cannot force Betty to buy the house.

Rescission and Restitution   When a breach occurs, the nonbreaching party may elect to rescind the contract (treat it as if it had never existed). In that event, each party would be required to return any benefit or partial performance to the party by whom it was given. This is done either by returning tangible property or by returning the dollar value of the benefit or of the service. The purpose is to restore each party to the same position as before the contract was made.

Restitution damages focus on the gains of the defendant; compensatory damages focus on the losses of the plaintiff.

Reformation   Reformation is used in equity to correct errors in the document that contains the written terms of the parties' agreement. When an error is made in a written contract provision, the error can be "reformed" to reflect the correct provision. For example, if parties agree to sponsor an auto show on May 16 and if the written contract indicates a May 26 date, reformation is available to reflect the agreed date.

Reformation cannot be used to change the terms to which the parties agreed, however. When parties want to change an agreed term, a modification of the contract is used (*see above*). Modification discharges the old contract provision in favor of the new provision.

Quasi-Contract   Quasi-contract is not a contract at all. Rather, it is a legal fiction created by equity courts to prevent unjust enrichment of a defendant at the expense of a plaintiff. Quasi-contract is used as a remedy to obtain the reasonable value of services or other performance when no contract exists. It is also used by a breaching party to recover the reasonable value of her performance or services prior to the breach, such as the breaching contractor who builds part of the house but does not finish it (*see prior discussion*).

> Jack is hired by the Springfield Chamber of Commerce for $7,000 to organize a summer arts festival, payable upon conclusion of the festival. Two weeks before the festival, Jack becomes involved in a dispute with the Chamber's executive director and quits. As a general rule, Jack cannot bring an action on the contract if he is the breaching party. However, he can recover the value of his services under a quasi-contract theory, even if the value of his services proves to be more than the contract price.

Tort Actions   Courts have become increasingly receptive to imposition of a tort duty, as well as a contract duty, when there is a reasonably foreseeable risk of harm in connection with the performance of the contract duty. Therefore, improper performance of a contract may result in tort liability to the injured party as well. A few examples of this include the areas of products liability, professional liability, and infliction of emotional distress. The injured party may elect to waive the contract and sue in tort in this type of situation. In any event, she must choose one or the other; she cannot receive both contract damages and tort damages.

> Bill contracted with Morbid Mortuary to provide funeral services for his deceased wife. Everything proceeded routinely until the funeral procession was on its way to the cemetery. During the trip, the back door of the hearse flew open and the casket dropped onto the street; it was struck by the mortuary's limousine in which Bill was a passenger; and it broke apart, hurling the corpse into the oncoming lane of traffic.

On these facts, Bill may elect to bring a tort action against the mortuary for emotional distress, assuming the tort damages would be greater than the contract damages that he could recover.

The material in this chapter and the following self-test provide a basic review of the major issues and principles involved in contract law. The applicant who is unfamiliar with any of the issues or principles covered or who wants a more thorough review than can be provided in a text of this type should consult the bibliography for additional study references.

Contract Law Self-Test

Allow an uninterrupted 30-minute period to answer all questions. At the end of 30 minutes, check your answers against those in the Answer Key Section of this Review Manual. Deduct two points for each incorrect answer (100 total possible points). Unanswered questions are counted as incorrect answers. Follow directions carefully and observe the time limit precisely to provide an accurate self-assessment.

Choose the most correct answer to each of the following questions unless a specific question instructs you to do otherwise.

1.   An assumption of mortgage clause in an agreement for the sale of land is most advantageous to the:

   a.   seller.
   b.   buyer.
   c.   mortgagee.
   d.   broker.

2.   Duress probably exists when:

   a.   a man sells his house to pay for his wife's funeral.
   b.   a school withholds a student's diploma until his tuition is paid.
   c.   a gas station requires payment before putting gas in customers' cars.
   d.   an employee is told by a supervisor to buy company stock or be fired.
   e.   All of the above.

3.   The law that requires contracts for the sale of real estate to be in writing is known as the:

  a.   Statute of Frauds.
  b.   statute of limitations.
  c.   adverse possession law.
  d.   parol evidence rule.

4.   True or False.   A court is unlikely to set aside the exchange of an airplane for a car for lack of consideration.

5.   True or False.   A contract with an emancipated minor is voidable because the minor lacks capacity.

6.   True or False.   Conditional contracts for the sale of land cannot be assigned.

7.   True or False.   An oral contract for the sale of goods valued at $2,000 may be voidable because of noncompliance with the Statute of Frauds.

8.   True or False.   To prevail in an action based upon undue influence, the victim must prove, among other things, that he was subjected to an unfair bargain in which he lost money.

9.   True or False.   Under the parol evidence rule, agreements made subsequent to the agreement in dispute are inadmissible to show the intended terms of the original agreement.

10.   True or False.   Steve agrees to pay $100 on June 1 for Bob's used lawn mower, with the lawn mower to be delivered on May 15. The mower is delivered as agreed, and on May 25, Steve announces that he will not pay the $100. Anticipatory repudiation does not apply on these facts, since Bob's performance is complete. Bob must wait until June 1 to file suit.

11.   An option cannot be sold or assigned legally if the original consideration for the option was:

  a.   cash.
  b.   a promissory note.
  c.   love and affection.
  d.   a personal check.

12.   Builder contracts with Owner to construct a garage on Owner's property for a price of $10,000. Assume that Owner commits a total breach of the contract at a point when Builder already has incurred costs of part performance of $3,000, and Builder would have to spend another $6,000 to finish the job. Builder is entitled to a recovery of:

    a. $1,000.
    b. $3,000.
    c. $4,000.
    d. $5,000.

13.   The primary difference between fraud and misrepresentation is:

    a.   scienter.
    b.   the amount of damages that can be obtained.
    c.   the type of damages that can be obtained.
    d.   Two of the above.
    e.   None of the above.

14.   Legal grounds to rescind a contract may include:

    a.   mistake.
    b.   misrepresentation.
    c.   duress.
    d.   undue influence.
    e.   All of the above.
    f.   None of the above.

15.   True or False.   Mitch rents a car to Pablo for $50 a day. The car has a broken headlight, which Pablo repairs. When the car is returned three days later, Mitch says, "In consideration of your repair of the headlight, I will not charge you for renting the car." Mitch cannot change his mind later and enforce the original rental agreement.

16.   Contractual intent generally is present:

    a.   in an agreement to meet for lunch made between two friends.
    b.   when a person signs a pledge for a charitable donation.
    c.   when an actor agrees to give an agent 15% of her earnings.
    d.   in two of the above selections.
    e.   in none of the above selections.

17.   Pat and Jackson contract for 1,000 pounds of lapoderm, an ingredient used by Pat to produce an expensive wax for wood, at $5.00 a pound. The lapoderm is to be delivered in four equal installments over a four-month period. After 250 pounds of lapoderm are delivered and paid for, Jackson's lapoderm plant closes, and no further shipments are made. The market price of lapoderm at the time of the breach is $2.50 a pound. In a suit against Jackson, what amount will Pat recover?

     a. $7,500
     b. $5,000
     c. $1,875
     d. $0

18.   True or False.   Ryan offers a $10,000 reward for the return of his kidnapped child. Bart, the kidnapper, returns the child. Bart can collect the reward.

19.   True or False.   Ryan offers a $10,000 reward for the return of his kidnapped child. Martin, an FBI agent assigned to the case, recovers the child. Martin can collect the reward.

20.   True or False.   Allison promises to buy goods only from Nick but reserves an option to cancel by giving written notice to Nick. Allison has given sufficient consideration to support a contract.

21.   True or False.   An assignment generally cannot be made without the express consent of all parties.

22.   True or False.   A counteroffer serves as a rejection of the original offer.

23.   Jay and Scott contract for the construction of Jay's new home by Scott for $225,000. After the home is approximately 75 percent completed, Jay and Scott disagree about installation of the entry way doors. Jay becomes obnoxious, and Scott leaves the job site in complete frustration. Scott later calls Jay and tells him that he can't work on the house any longer and wants his money for the work already completed. Jay refuses, saying that unless Scott completes the house, he will be paid nothing. Which of the following statements is true?

     a.   Scott can receive contract damages of $225,000 because the house is substantially completed.

b.   Scott can receive contract damages equal to 75 percent of the contract price because the house is 75 percent completed.

c.   Scott can receive contract damages equal to 75 percent of the contract price because Jay's conduct amounts to frustration of the contract's purpose.

d.   Scott cannot receive contract damages but can receive quasi-contract damages.

e.   None of the above is true.

24.   True or False.   An offer creates a power of acceptance in the offeree and a corresponding liability on the part of the offeror.

25.   True or False.   Jordan and Adrian enter into a written agreement that provides, "Adrian will purchase a parcel of land for $8,000 or less from Jordan." The agreement is enforceable.

26.   True or False.   A woman, who is going to Europe for two years, contracts for the care of her car while she is gone. She agrees in writing to pay a man $500 to wax the car once every four months during her absence. This is a binding contract.

27.   True or False.   An unenforceable contract is one which one or both parties may elect either to avoid or to ratify.

Questions 28–30 are based on the following facts: Braden purchased 100 bolts of standard blue wool, No. 1 quality from Hadley. The sales contract provided that Braden would make payment prior to inspection. The bolts of fabric were shipped, and Braden paid the purchase price. Upon inspection, however, Braden discovered that the fabric was No. 2 quality. Braden tendered the fabric back to Hadley and demanded return of the purchase price. Hadley refused on the ground that there was no difference between No. 1 quality and No. 2 quality.

28.   Which of the following statements regarding the contract provision for pre-inspection payment is most correct?

a.   It constitutes an acceptance of the goods.

b.   It constitutes a waiver of the buyer's right to reject nonconforming goods.

c.   It does not impair the buyer's right of inspection or his remedies.

d.   It is invalid.

29.   What is Braden's remedy, assuming that the goods were nonconforming?

   a.   Specific performance.
   b.   Damages for the difference between the value of the goods delivered and the value of conforming goods.
   c.   Damages for the price paid plus the difference between the contract price and the cost of buying substitute goods.
   d.   None, since he waived his remedies by agreeing to pay prior to inspection.

30.   Can Braden resell the wool fabric?

   a.   Yes, in a private sale.
   b.   Yes, in a private sale but only after giving Hadley reasonable notice of his intention to resell.
   c.   Yes, but only at a public sale.
   d.   No.

31.   When anticipatory repudiation occurs, the nonrepudiating party may:

   a.   treat the anticipatory repudiation as a total repudiation and sue immediately.
   b.   suspend performance and wait until the performance date to sue.
   c.   treat the anticipatory repudiation as an offer to rescind, resulting in discharge of the contract.
   d.   Any one of the above.
   e.   None of the above.

32.   Kay orally agrees to sell a building to Wanda for use as a gymnasium. In reliance upon Kay's promise, Wanda contracts for 100 pieces of exercise equipment. If Kay refuses to go through with the deal, Wanda may be entitled to receive:

   a.   contract damages.
   b.   collateral estoppel damages.
   c.   promissory estoppel damages.
   d.   restitution damages.

33. Larry and Margo enter an agreement whereby Larry agrees to purchase Margo's home subject to the sale of Larry's current residence. This is an example of a:

    a. promise.
    b. condition precedent.
    c. condition concurrent.
    d. condition subsequent.
    e. None of the above.

34. Andrew leaves his automobile, a 1951 Chevrolet, with the Metro Garage for minor repairs. The car was a gift to Andrew from his parents when he graduated from college. Andrew has taken excellent care of the car, it has very low mileage, and it means a great deal to him now that both of his parents have died. The car is destroyed in an accidental fire at the Metro Garage. In a suit against the Metro Garage, what will Andrew be able to recover?

    a. The market value of the car.
    b. The market value of the car plus mental anguish.
    c. The market value of the car plus punitive damages.
    d. Nothing, since a bailment contract existed between Andrew and Metro Garage.

35. True or False.   An offer made to B can be accepted by C.

36. True or False.   An offer to purchase real estate is a contract.

37. True or False.   An option contract must be supported by consideration.

38. True or False.   Express contracts are formed by manifestations of assent other than oral or written language.

39. True or False.   Manor Corporation is granted the right to sell Worldwide Widgets exclusively in return for one-third of the profits. The agreement is silent about the good faith obligations of Manor Corporation; consequently, courts will not enforce this contract.

40.   True or False.   Cora promises to buy certain goods from Rick "only if I (Cora) take my son into the business." Valid consideration exists.

41.   True or False.   Carol promises to deliver goods to Rich "only if her son comes into the business." Valid consideration exists.

42.   The difference between compensatory damages and restitution damages is:

    a.   Compensatory damages seek to compensate; restitution damages seek to restore.
    b.   Compensatory damages focus on what the defendant gained from the plaintiff; restitution damages focus on what the plaintiff lost.
    c.   Compensatory damages focus on what the plaintiff lost; restitution damages focus on what the defendant gained from the plaintiff.
    d.   None of the above statements is accurate.

43.   True or False.   Ray has an option until June 10 to buy Eddie's automobile. Ray sends an acceptance by mail on June 9. It arrives on June 11. A valid contract exists.

44.   True or False.   The difference between a bilateral contract and a unilateral contract is the number of promises involved.

45.   True or False.   Under the parol evidence rule, prior oral agreements are merged into the written agreement; however, prior written agreements are not.

46.   True or False.   Under U.C.C. § 2-201, the requirements of a writing are satisfied if there is some memorandum that shows the quantity of goods ordered; no signature of the buyer or seller is needed.

Questions 47–50 are based on the following facts: Bev's Typewriter Service advertises used ICM typewriters for sale at $100 each at its store. Laura Sheldon, who lives 250 miles away, mails Bev a check for $500, with a note stating, "Send me five of the used ICM typewriters that you have advertised."

    Bev checks his inventory and finds that she has only two of the used ICM typewriters left, but she has plenty of Ogilvie typewriters. She sends Laura two ICMs and three Ogilvies by common carrier. En route, the two ICMs are stolen. The carrier delivers only the three Ogilvie units.

Laura is short of equipment, so she uses the machines that were delivered. One week later, however, the secretaries complain about the Ogilvie typewriters. Laura then writes to Bev, "I reject the three machines you sent me. Return my $500." Bev refuses to do so.

47.   Concerning the theft of the two ICM typewriters during shipment:

a.   Bev must bear the loss because she selected the carrier and made the arrangements for shipment.

b.   Bev bears the loss because she is a merchant and, in the absence of a contrary agreement, bears the risk of loss until the goods are delivered to the buyer.

c.   Laura bears the loss because the typewriters were advertised for sale at Bev's store; therefore, the risk of loss passed there.

d.   Laura bears the loss because title to the goods passed to her upon shipment.

48.   The legal effect of Laura's retention and use of the Ogilvie typewriters for one week before notifying Bev of her rejection was:

a.   An acceptance of the three machines if Laura knew they were not ICMs.

b.   An acceptance only if Laura's use was more than was reasonably necessary to determine whether the Ogilvies were acceptable substitutes.

c.   Not an acceptance because the goods were nonconforming.

d.   A waiver of any damage claim against Bev based upon nondelivery of the ICM machines.

49.   Assume that Laura's retention and use of the typewriters did not constitute an acceptance. Which of the following remedies is available to her?

a.   Damages measured by the difference between the contract price and the cover price.

b.   Restitution of the $500 advance payment.

c.   Resale of the Ogilvies, with Laura retaining the profit from the sale proceeds.

d.   Both a and b but not c.

50.   Assume that Laura's retention and use of the typewriters did constitute an acceptance, which she subsequently and justifiably revoked. Which of the following remedies is available to her?

    a.   Damages measured by the difference between the contract price and the cover price.
    b.   Restitution of the $500 advance payment.
    c.   Resale of the Ogilvies, with Laura retaining the profit from the sale proceeds.
    d.   Both a and b but not c.

LITIGATION

If you find a path with no obstacles, it probably doesn't lead anywhere.

—Anonymous

Litigation is at the heart of the American legal system. Everything that lawyers do is gauged either to avoid litigation or to prepare for litigation. Therefore, every paralegal, regardless of his or her practice area, must know litigation fundamentals. Litigation paralegals must know substantially more than the fundamentals, however, to succeed on this portion of the CLA/CP® certification exam.

Applicants who select litigation as one of their substantive law subsections will be familiar with state laws and rules concerning litigation, of course. However, a national examination can test applicants' knowledge of state rules only in a very general way. Applicants will be well served by focusing on general litigation principles as well as by intensive study of the Federal Rules of Civil Procedure. Review the Federal Rules of Evidence, the Federal Rules of Appellate Procedure, and federal statutes related to jurisdiction and venue as well. *(Specific statutes are referred to throughout this chapter.)* In addition to these materials, refer to the American Legal System (General Law) Chapter 7 of this *Review Manual* for summaries related to court systems, subject matter jurisdiction, standing, and venue. The materials related to segregation of relevant facts, which are found in the Judgment chapter (Chapter 4) of this *Review Manual*, likewise will be helpful.

Unless stated otherwise, when the term *Rule* is used throughout this chapter, it refers to a rule of the Federal Rules of Civil Procedure.

One of the most effective ways to study any technical area is to create a timeline or a flow chart. Use this tool in addition to—not in place of—other study methods. A sample form for a flow chart for the Federal Rules of Civil Procedure is included on the following page.

The sample form is not complete. It represents an initial draft or outline of the flow chart, with only the most basic procedural elements of a federal litigation. Re-create and increase the flow chart's physical size by transferring it to several sheets of paper (tape them together lengthwise to see the continuum). Imagine a hypothetical case and plot it from beginning to end on the flow chart, adding to and expanding each of the basic elements to show the significant features about each element (how, when, and why it is used), timing, requirements, and exceptions stated in the Rules or in related statutes.

Once the basic flow chart is completed, it can be expanded to include step-by-step procedures for various hypothetical contingencies (methods of serving summons on multiple defendants in varying situations, obtaining a deposition of an out-of-state witness, and so forth).

Working with a flow chart similar to this one helps to clarify the system that controls the litigation process. Flow charts are helpful to learn or to review any area of substantive or procedural law, because each area has its own system. Familiarity with the system makes it easier to recall details in a testing situation or on the job.

FEDERAL CIVIL LITIGATION FLOW CHART

PLEADINGS

Complaint
Rule 3
Rule 8(a)
Rule 9

Summons
Rule 4

Answer
Rule 8
Rule 12(a)

Reply to Counterclaim
Rule 7(a)

Preliminary Motions
Rule 12(b)

Motion for Judgment on the Pleadings (after pleadings closed)
Rule 12(c)

DISCOVERY

Interrogatories
Rule 33

Request to Produce
Rule 34

Request for Physical or Mental Examination
Rule 35

Depositions
Rules 30, 31

Requests for Admission
Rule 36

Motion to Compel
Rule 37

Motion for Summary Judgment (during/after discovery)
Rule 56

TRIAL

Voir Dire

Opening Statements

Pretrial Conference
Rule 16

Pretrial Order or Scheduling Order
Rule 16

Plaintiff's Case

Direct Testimony & Exhibits
Cross-Examination
Rebuttal

Motion for Judgment as a Matter of Law (jury trials only)
Rule 50

Motion for Judgment on Partial Findings (nonjury trials only)
Rule 52(c)

Defendant's Case

Direct Testimony & Exhibits
Cross-Examination
Rebuttal

Motion for Judgment as a Matter of Law (both jury and nonjury trials)
Rule 50

Closing Arguments

Jury Instructions

Jury Deliberation

Verdict

Judgment

POST-TRIAL

Motion for Judgment as a Matter of Law
Rule 50

Motion to Amend Judgment
Rule 59(e)

Motion for New Trial
Rule 59(a)

APPEAL

Notice of Appeal

Appellate Briefs Filed

Oral Arguments

Decision (Affirm, Reverse, or Remand)

Selecting the Proper Court

Selecting the proper court involves three separate and distinct issues, considered in this order: (1) subject matter jurisdiction, (2) personal jurisdiction, and (3) venue. ***Subject matter jurisdiction*** is the power or authority of a particular court to decide a specific type of case. ***Personal jurisdiction*** is the power or authority of a particular court over specific litigants. ***Venue*** refers to the geographical location(s) within a jurisdiction where the case should be tried. *(Refer to the American Legal System (General Law) Chapter 7 for a discussion of other types of jurisdiction.)*

<u>Subject Matter Jurisdiction</u>   The U.S. District Court (federal trial court) is a court of limited jurisdiction, which means that it does not have authority to decide all types of cases. Rather, its subject matter jurisdiction is conferred by statute. Of all of the areas for which subject matter jurisdiction is granted to the U.S. District Court, the three invoked most frequently are (1) cases in which the United States, its agencies, or its officers are parties; (2) cases involving federal questions; and (3) cases involving diversity of citizenship.

1.   The United States, its agencies, or its officers are parties if named either as a plaintiff or as a defendant in the lawsuit. 28 U.S.C. §§ 1345, 1346.

2.   A case involves a federal question if it is a "civil action arising under the Constitution, laws, or treaties of the United States." 28 U.S.C. § 1331.

3.   A case involves diversity of citizenship if it is a civil action "where the matter in controversy exceeds the sum or value of $75,000, exclusive of interest and costs, and is between . . . citizens of different states." 28 U.S.C. § 1332. Special rules apply in determining whether both parts of diversity jurisdiction requirements are met.

The amount in controversy, exclusive of interest and costs, must exceed $75,000 in diversity cases, which means that it must be at least $75,000.*01*. A claim valued at $75,000 or less does not meet the jurisdictional requirement. If a suit involves a statute which awards attorney fees, the attorney fees may be included to reach the jurisdictional minimum. A plaintiff with more than one claim against a defendant may combine her claims to reach the required amount. If there are multiple plaintiffs, however, each plaintiff's claim(s) must exceed $75,000; the claims of different plaintiffs cannot be combined to reach the required amount. If multiple plaintiffs are common owners of property and if the property is the subject of the dispute, the total value of the property is used to determine whether the minimum amount is met—not the value of each plaintiff's undivided interest in the property.

The diversity of litigants in diversity cases must be complete diversity, based upon each litigant's state of citizenship (domicile). **Domicile** is the permanent home of the litigant. In determining domicile, a court may consider where the litigant is registered to vote, where automobiles are registered, or other factors that indicate a permanent home. For example, a retiree domiciled in New York may reside in Florida during the winter months, returning to New York in the spring. Even though the retiree maintains a residence in Florida, her domicile continues in New York.

A person may have several residences but can have only one domicile. By contrast, a corporation may be domiciled both in its state of incorporation and in the state where its principal place of business is located for purposes of federal diversity claims. If a corporation is incorporated separately in several different states, it may be domiciled in each of those states at the same time for purposes of determining diversity. If the corporation issues insurance policies, it is domiciled in the state of its incorporation, in the state where its principal offices are located, and in the state of the insured. 28 U.S.C. § 1332(c).

Complete diversity means that no plaintiff can be a citizen of the same state as any defendant. If there is a common state of domicile between any plaintiff and any defendant, diversity jurisdiction is destroyed even if the claims exceed $75,000. For purposes of establishing diversity, the District of Columbia is treated as a separate state.

> Alice and Bob are citizens of Colorado. They want to join in a suit against the Charter Corporation, which is incorporated in Delaware and maintains its headquarters office in New Jersey.

> Daniel is a citizen of New Jersey. Eugene is a citizen of New York. They want to join in a suit against the Charter Corporation, which is incorporated in Delaware and maintains its headquarters office in New Jersey.

Assuming the jurisdictional minimum amount is met, complete diversity exists in the first example; and the case may be filed in the U.S. District Court. No plaintiff is a citizen of the same state as any defendant; it makes no difference that both plaintiffs are citizens of the same state. In the second example, however, diversity is not complete. Daniel is a citizen of New Jersey, and the corporation's headquarters office also is in New Jersey. If Daniel were dropped as a plaintiff in the suit, complete diversity would exist for purposes of federal jurisdiction; and Eugene could proceed in the federal trial court. If Daniel and Eugene want to sue as joint plaintiffs, however, they must do so in state court.

Diversity of citizenship must exist (1) when the complaint is filed in federal court or (2) both when the action is filed in state court and when the action is removed to federal court (*discussed below*). Once established, diversity remains in effect for the duration of the lawsuit even if a litigant changes her domicile (permanently moves to a new state) during that time.

When a federal court sits in diversity, it applies state (not federal) substantive law, using conflicts of law principles. (*Conflicts of law are discussed in the chapter on American Legal System [General Law], Chapter 7.*) Diversity jurisdiction cannot be exercised in probate or domestic relations cases, because these are within the exclusive jurisdiction of state courts.

Supplemental Jurisdiction   Supplemental jurisdiction was a new term for old concepts when it first was codified as 28 U.S.C. § 1367. Supplemental jurisdiction allows additional claims and additional parties to be added to an existing federal case without independently satisfying the requirements of federal subject matter jurisdiction. Before this statute was enacted, additional claims and additional parties were added through the judicially created doctrines of pendent jurisdiction and ancillary jurisdiction.

Under the ***pendent jurisdiction*** doctrine, a state-created claim between parties sometimes could be added to a *similar federal question claim* pending in federal court between the same parties, even though the federal court would not have had jurisdiction if the state-created claim were filed separately.

> Alice is a citizen of California and is employed by the Baker Corporation, which is incorporated and has its principal place of business in California. Alice is next in line for promotion to a supervisor's position, but the position is given to a younger male because he is the sole support of his family. Alice ultimately files suit in federal court based upon equal employment opportunity provisions of Title VII. Alice believes that her employer also has violated the California statute concerning equal employment opportunity.

There is no independent federal subject matter jurisdiction for Alice's state claim against her employer (no federal question and no diversity of citizenship). However, under the doctrine of pendent jurisdiction, Alice could have added the claim for violation of state law to her federal claim, because both would have been similar and would have arisen from a *common nucleus of operative fact*. She now may achieve the same result through the supplemental jurisdiction provisions of 28 U.S.C. § 1367. The same statute makes it clear that supplemental jurisdiction may be used to require additional parties to defend a state-created claim in federal court, even though they are not named as defendants in the federal question claim.

Before statutory supplemental jurisdiction was enacted, the ***ancillary jurisdiction*** doctrine was created by judges for use in cases where diversity existed for at least one claim between one plaintiff and one defendant and where additional claims or additional parties were sought to be added to that core claim. Ancillary jurisdiction generally was used to provide federal jurisdiction over claims made by parties other than the plaintiff when there was no independent federal subject matter jurisdiction for the claim (counterclaim, crossclaim, or third-party complaint).

> Bob, a citizen of Missouri, took his van to Charlie's Garage, also located in Missouri, for brake work. After the van was picked up, the brakes failed within three blocks of the garage, striking a car driven by Alice, a citizen of Illinois. Alice filed a diversity action against Bob in federal court, alleging negligence.

In this example, Bob likely will want to file a third-party complaint against Charlie's Garage because of the failed brakes. However, because Bob and Charlie's Garage are citizens of the same state, there is no diversity between them; and Bob's third-party complaint could not meet the federal requirement for subject matter jurisdiction if it were filed independently. Under the former judicial doctrine of ancillary jurisdiction (now statutory supplemental jurisdiction), this problem would be resolved in favor of allowing Bob to file the third-party complaint.

To avoid situations in which parties may contrive to circumvent the federal diversity jurisdiction statute, 28 U.S.C. § 1367 prevents supplemental jurisdiction from being invoked in some situations where the core claim is based upon diversity only. Supplemental jurisdiction in diversity cases does not apply to:

- claims by a plaintiff against a third-party defendant;

- claims by or against one who was made a party to the action under Rule 19's compulsory joinder provisions;

- claims by a plaintiff against a defendant who was made a party to the action under Rule 20's permissive joinder provisions. (The exclusion does not apply to claims by a plaintiff against a co-plaintiff who was made a party to the action by permissive joinder.); and

- claims by a prospective plaintiff who attempts to intervene under Rule 24.

Although the federal court has authority to exercise supplemental jurisdiction in relation to compulsory counterclaims, crossclaims, or claims of third-party defendants, it may decline to exercise supplemental jurisdiction if the claim presents a novel or complex question of state law, if the claim predominates over those claims for which the court has original jurisdiction, or if the court has dismissed all claims for which it had original jurisdiction.

Supplemental jurisdiction is designed to facilitate subject matter jurisdiction only. It does not remove the requirements for exercise of personal jurisdiction or for service of process.

Removal Jurisdiction   Removal jurisdiction evolved in an era when defendants from other states were viewed with suspicion and may have been prejudiced in favor of local plaintiffs in state court actions. Allowing the out-of-state defendant to remove the case to federal court was designed to minimize the "home town" advantage enjoyed by the plaintiff. Although state boundary lines no longer present the barriers that they once did, removal jurisdiction continues as a way for defendants to avoid favoritism to the plaintiff, whether real or perceived.

As a general rule, any case filed in a state court may be removed by the defendant to federal court if the federal court could have exercised original jurisdiction over the case when it was filed initially. 28 U.S.C. § 1441. *A plaintiff never can seek removal.* In diversity cases, removal can occur only if no defendant is a citizen of the state in which the state court action was filed. Moreover, the defendant is subject to the additional requirement that complete diversity of citizenship must exist both at the time the original state action was filed and at the time when removal is sought.

A federal court may exercise removal jurisdiction only if the state court in which the action was pending originally had jurisdiction.

> Alice files suit against Bob in state court for relief on a patent held by Bob. The federal court has exclusive jurisdiction of patent matters. Realizing the error, Bob attempts to remove the case to federal court.

This example highlights what can be a ridiculous result: The federal court cannot exercise removal jurisdiction because the state court did not have jurisdiction to hear the case in the first place. Bob's best option is to raise the issue of lack of subject matter jurisdiction in the state court proceeding. If Alice's claim is dismissed by the state court on that basis (which it should be), Alice will be forced to file a new action in federal court.

Removal generally is determined from the facial allegations of the plaintiff's claim. Assume that a plaintiff has a federal claim that could be raised but elects not to raise it. With neither diversity jurisdiction nor a federal claim, the defendant has no basis for removal.

28 U.S.C. § 1441(c) provides that when a federal question claim is joined with a "separate and independent" claim that could not be removed if it were filed alone, the entire case may be removed to federal court; and the federal court may decide all issues or, in its discretion, may decide the federal question issue and remand all issues in which state law predominates. The same is not true of federal diversity claims. If a diversity claim is joined with a "separate and independent" claim that could not be removed if it were filed alone, no part of the case may be removed to federal court.

If a defendant has taken extensive action in the state court proceeding, she may not be able to remove the case at all. When removal is possible, notice of removal generally must be filed in the federal court within 30 days after the defendant receives service of the state court claim. All but nominal defendants must join in the notice of removal. The notice must contain those facts which entitle the defendant to remove the case to federal court. Once the notice has been filed, the state court may take no further action in the case unless the federal court determines that removal jurisdiction does not exist and remands the case to state court. 28 U.S.C. § 1446 *et seq.*

Personal Jurisdiction   Personal jurisdiction, also called *in personam* jurisdiction, is the court's authority to reach a decision affecting a particular person or entity. Personal jurisdiction involves the due process requirement that a party must be given notice and an opportunity to be heard. Intertwined with the due process requirement is a particular court's authority to give notice; its power to require a party to appear before it; and, if the party fails to appear, its power to impose sanctions.

Personal jurisdiction over plaintiffs is not a problem, because plaintiffs voluntarily submit themselves to the court's jurisdiction when they file their complaints. Therefore, personal jurisdiction issues generally relate to a court's authority over defendants.

Personal jurisdiction historically has been limited by state boundary lines. Although state lines continue as an important limitation for personal jurisdiction, enactment of long-arm statutes and conduct of the defendant make it much easier to acquire authority over out-of-state defendants than it once was. A ***long-arm statute*** typically allows courts to "reach out with a long arm" and pull defendants back to the forum state to defend themselves when they engage in conduct which causes injury in the forum state. Where a long-arm statute exists, both the state and the federal courts of that state may use it to acquire personal jurisdiction over out-of-state defendants.

Notwithstanding any other rules, jurisdiction over a defendant cannot be exercised unless the defendant has at least **_minimum contacts_** with the state in which the forum court sits. This means that the defendant must have engaged in some voluntary, affirmative act directed at the forum state (selling products, goods, or services in the state; telephone solicitations into the state; visiting the state; incorporating in the state). Once personal jurisdiction is established, it continues throughout the litigation.

In general, personal jurisdiction over an individual may be exercised when the individual

- is domiciled within the forum state;
- is present within the forum state;
- consents to suit within the forum state;
- commits tortious acts which cause injury within the forum state; or
- does business within the forum state.

A state may exercise personal jurisdiction over a domestic corporation (one incorporated in the forum state). A state also may exercise personal jurisdiction over a foreign corporation by requiring the corporation to appoint an agent to receive in-state process when it is registered or licensed as a foreign corporation in that state. In federal diversity cases, a corporation is a citizen both of the state where it is incorporated and the state where it has its principal place of business.

Service of Process   As a general rule, service of process in federal court cases can be made only within the territorial limits of the state in which the federal court sits. However, Congress has enacted laws to increase the territory of possible service in certain types of cases. For example, Rule 14 third-party defendants and Rule 19 indispensable parties may be served anywhere outside the state so long as it is within a 100-mile radius of the place (courthouse) where the case is filed. Nationwide service of process is permitted in interpleader cases (_discussed below_) and in cases filed against federal officials or federal agencies. In addition, services of process in federal cases can be made according to the forum state's long-arm statute. A defendant who is not within the forum state cannot be served with process if she cannot be served under one of these provisions, even if she more than meets the minimum contacts requirement.

Other than the summons, complaint, or a subpoena, all federal service must be made by the U.S. Marshal, a deputy U.S. Marshal, or a person specially appointed. A summons, complaint, or subpoena may be served by the Marshal if a party first obtains a court order. Absent a properly signed waiver of service of summons *(discussed below)* from the defendant, the summons and complaint may be served by anyone 18 or older who is not a party by delivering the summons and complaint to the party personally (personal service) or by leaving them at his dwelling with a person of suitable age and discretion who resides there (substitute service). A subpoena likewise may be served personally by anyone 18 or older who is not a party to the action. An attorney, for instance, can serve a summons, complaint, or subpoena.

Process can be served upon corporations by serving an officer or a general/resident agent of the corporation. In addition, service of process can be made in any way permitted by state law, including certified mail.

Venue   Venue refers to the place (the geographic location) within a jurisdiction where trial should occur. Venue does not become an issue until personal jurisdiction has been established. In state court actions, venue typically lies where the cause of action arose, where the defendant resides, or where the defendant has either a place of business or an agent. The venue statute of a particular state may provide for other places as well.

Under 28 U.S.C. § 1391 (2003), there are three basic methods to determine whether venue exists in a particular federal judicial district (some states have more than one federal judicial district):

1.   If any defendant resides in the district and all defendants reside in the state in which the district is located (applies both to federal question cases and to diversity cases);

2.   If a substantial part of the events or omissions giving rise to the claim occurred in the district or if a substantial part of the property that is the subject of the action is located in the district (applies both to federal question cases and to diversity cases); or

3.   If all defendants are subject to personal jurisdiction in the district (applies to diversity cases only) or if any defendant "may be found" in the district and there is no other district in which the action may be brought (applies to federal question cases only).

Alice, a citizen of Minnesota, files suit in federal court against Bob, a resident of the Eastern District of Michigan, and against Charles, a resident of the Western District of Michigan.

> Allen, a citizen of Maine, files suit in federal court against Barbara, a resident of the Southern District of New York, and Charlotte, a resident of Massachusetts.

In the first example, venue is proper either in the Eastern District of Michigan or in the Western District of Michigan, because either district is the residence of at least one defendant; and each is located in a state in which all defendants reside. Since there is no state in which all defendants reside in the second example, venue must be based either upon the "place of events or property" or upon the catch-all provisions (see #3 above). Recall that personal jurisdiction must be satisfied before venue is considered.

The older "where the claim arose" language was replaced in 1990 with the language found in #2 above.

When a case is filed in a particular federal judicial district, the court may decline to hear the case if it determines that the district is a ***forum non conveniens***. In other words, if more than one federal court meets jurisdictional and venue requirements and if trial of the case in the forum court would pose substantial inconvenience to the defendant and to witnesses, the court may decline to hear the case in favor of a court that would provide a more convenient forum. Although federal courts occasionally do apply the doctrine of forum *non conveniens* to move a case to another judicial district, the majority of cases indicate that if a defendant meets the requirements for personal jurisdiction, including minimum contacts, it generally is difficult for her to convince a judge that the forum is not convenient.

Parties

Within the context of litigation, a party is a principal in the lawsuit (either a plaintiff or a defendant). Rule 17(a) requires parties to be real parties in interest. A ***real party in interest*** is either one who was damaged or one who caused damage (directly or indirectly) in a specific transaction or occurrence. In other words, a manufacturer which produces a defective product may be a real party in interest. The manufacturer's lender, however, is not a real party in interest even though it has a definite interest in the outcome of the suit. An entertainer who loses her vision permanently from using the defective product is a real party in interest. Her spouse also may be a real party in interest if the spouse is denied love and affection of the entertainer as a result of the injury. The entertainer's manager, however, is not a real party in interest.

A real party in interest is one who has standing in the suit; she often is a necessary or indispensable party *(discussed below)*.

Rule 17(b) requires that a party must have the capacity to sue or to be sued. Minors or incompetent persons, for example, do not have this capacity. As a result, they must sue or be sued through a legal representative. If a guardian does not already exist (a parent may be a natural guardian of a minor child), a **guardian ad litem** may be appointed by a court for purposes of the litigation. A corporation has the capacity to sue or to be sued, since it is an artificial person created by the state of its incorporation.

Joinder of Parties   More than one plaintiff or more than one defendant may be joined in a single suit (1) if their claims arise from the same transaction or occurrence (or same series of transactions or occurrences); and (2) if their claims present a common question of law or of fact that will apply to all of them. This is a **permissive joinder**. Rule 20. The common question must be a substantial one in relation to all claims. The existence of other questions that are not shared by all parties does not bar joinder, however. An airplane crash, for example, may produce multiple plaintiffs who qualify for permissive joinder. If any plaintiff does not want to join in the action of the other plaintiffs, she may file her own, separate action if she wishes to do so.

When multiple plaintiffs are joined in a diversity case under Rule 20, the claims of each plaintiff must meet the jurisdictional minimum amount. A plaintiff is allowed to aggregate her claims to reach the jurisdictional amount. However, multiple plaintiffs are not allowed to combine their claims.

> Eugene has a claim against Bob of $80,000 based upon an auto accident. Alice has a claim against Bob of $70,000 for negligence based upon the same auto accident. She also has a claim against Bob of $50,000 for breach of contract. Connie and David have claims against Bob of $50,000 each for negligence arising out the same auto accident in which Eugene and Alice were involved.

Assuming that all other requirements of diversity are met in the above example, Eugene and Alice may join as plaintiffs in the same action against Bob under Rule 20. Eugene's claim meets the jurisdictional amount, and Alice's aggregate claims meet the jurisdictional amount. Neither Connie nor David, however, may join in the action; neither meets the jurisdictional minimum, and they cannot combine their claims for that purpose.

When multiple defendants are joined under Rule 20, the requirements of personal jurisdiction, including minimum contacts, must be met for each defendant. Federal courts in diversity cases follow the long-arm statutes of the state in which they are located. Venue requirements also must be met. When codefendants reside in different states, it still may be possible to satisfy venue requirements in diversity and federal question cases by filing suit in that district where a substantial portion of the events occurred.

Rule 19 covers situations in which additional parties must be joined once the jurisdictional requirements are met. Joinder under Rule 19 is a ***compulsory joinder.*** Two types of parties are addressed in Rule 19:

(1)   **Necessary Parties**   A ***necessary party*** is one who has an interest in the controversy and who should be joined if possible for the sake of justice; however, if the party's joinder is impossible because of jurisdiction or venue problems, the suit could continue without him. A junior lienholder in a foreclosure action might be a necessary party, for example.

(2)   **Indispensable Parties**   An ***indispensable party*** is one whose interest is so essential that litigation without him would be unjust. If an indispensable party cannot be joined because of jurisdiction or venue problems, the suit must be dismissed. For example, if only two of six endorsers of a promissory note can be joined, the remaining four endorsers likely will be indispensable parties. *Shields v. Barrow*, 58 U.S. 130 (1855).

Dismissal resulted in the *Shields* case because some of the defendants were residents of the same state as the plaintiff, which destroyed diversity. In this type of situation, dismissal by a federal court does not prevent the plaintiff from pursuing a remedy in state court. Today's long-arm statutes avoid many of the personal jurisdiction problems that the *Shields* plaintiff faced.

Intervention   Rule 24 allows a person who was not an original party to the suit to enter the suit upon her own initiative. This process is called intervention, and the person who intervenes is the *intervenor*. The intervention may be either ***of right*** (Rule 24[a]) or ***permissive*** (Rule 24[b]).

A stranger to the lawsuit has an automatic right to intervene (permission is not required) if she has an interest in the property or transaction which is the subject of the lawsuit, if disposition of the suit may impair that interest, *and* if her interest is not adequately represented by the existing parties.

> The Small Business Administration (SBA) sues the principals of a leasing company for loan default and seeks, among other things, repossession of certain equipment. A lessee of the equipment sought to be repossessed may be able to intervene as a matter of right.

In addition to the intervention provided under the Federal Rules of Civil Procedure, federal statutes sometimes give outsiders the right to intervene. For example, the United States has a statutory right to intervene when the constitutionality of an act of Congress is in issue.

Even if the lessee in the above example cannot intervene as a matter of right, it is possible that permissive intervention may be allowed by the court under Rule 24(b) if there is a common question of law or fact. For example, if a restrictive easement on land leased by the federal government is in dispute and if Bill's land (also leased by the government) contains the same type of restrictive easement, for instance, Bill may be able to obtain permissive intervention even if he cannot intervene as a matter of right.

Interpleader   Interpleader is allowed in federal courts and in most state courts to protect a party from having to pay the same claim twice in situations where he is uncertain who the proper claimant is.

> Gibraltar Insurance Company issued an insurance policy on the life of Sam Finkel. The named beneficiary is "Susan Finkel, spouse of the insured." Sam was married to Susan when the policy was issued in 1990. They divorced last year, and Sam married Bunny two months before his death. Both Susan and Bunny claim the policy proceeds.

If Gibraltar pays the policy proceeds to Susan and if it evolves that the proceeds should have been paid to Bunny, Gibraltar will have to pay the proceeds again. Faced with this situation, Gibraltar can protect itself by filing an interpleader action in which both Susan and Bunny are named as defendants and can require the claimants to litigate the beneficiary issue. In this way, Gibraltar avoids exposure to double liability.

In federal practice, interpleader actions may arise under Rule 22 or under the statutory interpleader provisions of 28 U.S.C. § 1335. The differences between the two types of interpleader actions relate to subject matter and personal jurisdiction.

Without a federal question, a Rule 22 stakeholder (Gibraltar in the above example) cannot be a citizen of the same state as any claimant; and the amount in controversy must exceed $75,000. Service of process is made according to the general rules for federal civil suits. The stakeholder is not required to deposit the disputed property with the court, however.

Without a federal question, statutory interpleader requires only that some pair of claimants must be citizens of different states. What this means is that the stakeholder and one or more claimants can be from the same state, as long as there is diversity between at least two of the claimants. For example, if Gibraltar and Susan were citizens of the same state in the example above, jurisdiction still would be possible so long as Susan and Bunny were from different states. The amount in controversy must be in excess of $500 under statutory interpleader, which is substantially less than in Rule 22 interpleader actions. Service of process may be made anywhere in the United States. However, unlike Rule 22 interpleader actions, the stakeholder must deposit the disputed property with the court.

Impleader   If a defendant claims that a third person is liable to the defendant for all or part of the plaintiff's claim (generally due to indemnity, subrogation, contribution, or breach of warranty), the defendant may ***implead*** that person by filing a third-party complaint. In the third-party complaint, the original defendant is identified as the *defendant and third-party plaintiff*; the third person is identified as the *third-party defendant*.

Both subject matter and personal jurisdiction requirements are relaxed somewhat for third-party claims. Third-party claims fall within the court's supplemental jurisdiction, and third-party complaints may be served anywhere within 100 miles of the federal courthouse—even if the place of service is outside the state and is beyond the scope of the state's long-arm statute (the ***100-mile bulge*** provision).

Class Actions   When there are large numbers of people with similar claims against the same party, which could lead to many lawsuits and potentially inconsistent results, Rule 23 allows a class action to be filed if certain requirements are met:

- *The class must be so large that joinder of all of its members is not feasible;*

- *There must be questions of law or fact which are common to the class;*

- *The claims or defenses of the representatives of the class must be typical of class members; and*

- *The representatives must represent the interests of the class fairly and adequately.*

A class action may be warranted, for example, when a national mortgage company appears to have overcharged the escrow accounts of many thousands of mortgagors located all over the country. Such a case likely would qualify as a class action under Rule 23(b)(3). Of the three types of class actions permitted, the most common type by far is the one provided by Rule 23(b)(3). Its requirements are (1) that the questions of law or fact which are common to the class predominate over any questions which affect individual members only; and (2) that a class action is superior to other, available methods to adjudicate the controversy fairly and efficiently. Members of a Rule 23(b)(3) class action may "opt out" of the class if they wish to do so, which is not true of other types of class actions.

Within 90 days after a complaint in a class action suit is filed, the plaintiff must file a motion with the court to determine whether the case can be maintained as a class action. Rule 23(c)(1). This is called "certifying the class."

Consolidation   Even though claims are made by filing separate complaints, a court nevertheless may order multiple suits to be consolidated for trial and judgment if the suits involve the same parties and contain common issues of law or fact. For example:

> A bankruptcy trustee for a national trucking company files 1000 separate lawsuits in the same court against 1000 separate freight customers to collect under-charges billed by the bankrupt trucking company over the preceding seven years. The court could order all cases consolidated for trial at the same time in this situation.

Pleading

Pleading in state and federal courts historically has taken three different forms: (1) *common law pleading* (different form required for each type of action, highly technical, significant for historical reference more than anything else); (2) *code pleading* (designed to disclose the facts upon which the claim is based); and *notice pleading* (designed only to give sufficient notice of the claim or defense).

Many states still follow the rules of code pleading, which emphasize the statement of facts—not conclusions of law—in the pleadings filed with the court. The federal courts use notice pleading exclusively, with facts to be determined through discovery procedures and with issues to be determined at the mandatory pre-trial conference.

Under the Federal Rules of Civil Procedure, only three pleadings are allowed: a complaint, an answer, and a reply to a counterclaim (if a counterclaim has been filed). Rule 7. Unlike the procedure in many states, a federal plaintiff need not respond to new issues raised by the answer; it is presumed that the new issues are denied under federal procedure. Counterclaims, crossclaims, and third-party complaints are the procedural equivalents of a complaint. The proper responsive pleading to a crossclaim or to a third-party complaint is an answer. The proper responsive pleading to a counterclaim is a answer to counterclaim *(see Rule 7)*.

The form of pleadings in federal court is governed by Rule 10 and may be supplemented by local court rules.

Complaint   All civil actions in federal court are commenced by filing a complaint. Rule 3. The federal complaint is equivalent to the petition used to initiate civil actions in many state courts.

As a general rule, the complaint should contain:

- the caption of the case, which identifies the court, the parties, and the name of the pleading (complaint, in this case);

- a jurisdictional allegation (statement of the statute or other basis for invoking the jurisdiction of the federal court);

- a short, concise statement of the claim(s) or defense(s) showing that the pleader is entitled to relief. Rule 8. This statement is the heart of the complaint and may be presented in several, separate paragraphs (refer to Form 9 of the Federal Rules for an example);

- a statement of the relief or remedy sought by the pleader (whether general and special damages, punitive damages, an injunction, or other relief);

- the demand for judgment (sometimes called the *ad damnum* clause, the prayer, or the "wherefore" clause) against the opposing party;

- signature of the pleader's attorney. Under Rule 11, the attorney's signature indicates that the attorney has made reasonable inquiry and believes the allegations are well grounded in fact. If it evolves that the pleading was made frivolously, the attorney may be subjected to personal sanctions by the court; and

•verification, if required. Very few types of claims require verification in federal court. The subscription of the attorney (*see above*) generally is sufficient. When verification is required, it takes the form of an affidavit of the party, swearing that she has read the pleading and that the statements contained in it are true to the best of her knowledge, information, and belief. The party signs the affidavit, typically before a notary public.

If the complaint refers to documents, such as a promissory note, a copy of that document should be attached to the complaint as an exhibit. Rule 10. Pleading special matters (such as fraud, conditions precedent, or special damage) must comply with Rule 9. The complaint is filed with the clerk of the U.S. District Court for the appropriate district, together with a Civil Cover Sheet; a request for jury trial (if a jury trial is desired and if the request is not stated in the complaint); a request *(praecipe)* for issuance of summons upon each of the named defendants; and the appropriate filing fee. The federal courts (and some state courts) require electronic filing of pleadings, motions, and the like; and local court rules generally contain detailed procedures for filing a complaint within a particular federal judicial district.

The court clerk issues a summons (sometimes called process) for each named defendant. The summons provides (1) notice of the suit and (2) an opportunity to be heard by filing a timely answer or other timely response. As a general rule, the plaintiff's attorney must send to each defendant a summons, a copy of the complaint, a form for waiver of service, and a notice of the consequences for failure to waive service. *See Official Forms 1A and 1B of the Federal Rules.* Rule 4(d). If the waiver of service is signed and returned to the plaintiff's attorney within 30 days after it was sent (60 days if the defendant is located in a foreign country), the defendant is given additional time (60 days after the request for waiver was sent or 90 days after the request for waiver was sent if the defendant is located in a foreign country) in which to answer or to otherwise respond to the complaint. If any defendant fails to sign and return the waiver within the prescribed time, service may be made by anyone who is 18 years old or more and who is not a party in the case *(see additional discussion of service of process under personal jurisdiction, above)*; and that defendant will pay the costs of service, no matter who ultimately wins at trial. Either a signed waiver of service of summons (or service of the summons) must be obtained within 120 days after the complaint is filed; otherwise, the action is subject to dismissal without prejudice.

The signed waiver of service is filed with the court for each defendant. If particular defendant fails to sign and return the waiver timely, however, a proof of service of summons is filed with the court after the summons has been served.

After the action has been commenced, all pleadings, motions, notices, and so on are served upon all adverse parties or, if adverse parties are represented by counsel, upon their attorneys by U.S. mail. Rule 5.

Challenges to the Complaint   If any defendant wants to challenge the sufficiency of the complaint or matters connected with it, the proper procedure is to file a motion for that purpose within the statutory 21-day period. If a motion is filed, the answer need not be filed until the motion matters have been resolved.

A motion is not a pleading; it is a request to the court for an order granting relief to the moving party. Motions may be made before, during, and after trial. However, this section deals specifically with preliminary motions—those which seek relief based upon some defect in the complaint, improper joinder of parties, improper court, or similar deficiency in filing the complaint.

Some types of defects, if not objected to at the beginning of the suit, are waived and cannot be raised at a later time. Lack of personal jurisdiction is one such issue. In addition, the challenges under subsections (2)–(5) of Rule 12 must be joined in the same motion; otherwise, the omitted challenges are waived. By contrast, lack of subject matter jurisdiction can be raised for the first time at any stage of the lawsuit, including the appeal.

The bases for preliminary challenges to a complaint in federal court are found substantially in Rule 12. Of these, the most common are:

- *Lack of subject matter jurisdiction.* Rule 12(b)(1).

- *Lack of personal jurisdiction.* Rule 12(b)(2). In state court, this may be called a *special appearance.*

- *Improper venue.* Rule 12(b)(3).

- *Insufficiency of process.* Rule 12(b)(4).

- *Insufficiency of service of process.* Rule 12(b)(5).

- *Failure to state a claim upon which relief can be granted.* Rule 12(b)(6). In state court, this may be called a *demurrer*.

- *Failure to join a Rule 19 indispensable party.* Rule 12(b)(7).

•*Motion to make more definite and certain,* when the complaint is so lacking in facts or is so vague that it is difficult to tell whether a claim has been stated or not. Rule 12(e).

•*Motion to strike* "from any pleading any insufficient defense or any redundant, immaterial, impertinent, or scandalous matter." Rule 12(f).

The form of motions in federal court is governed by Rule 7(b). Unless it is made during trial or during a hearing, a motion must be in writing; must set forth the specific grounds for the motion as well as the relief sought; and must be signed by the attorney. Local court rules frequently require motions to be accompanied by a notice of hearing and a short memorandum of law which contains arguments and legal authorities in support of the requested relief. A copy of the motion and related documents must be served upon all adverse parties or their attorneys.

At least 14 days' notice must be given under Rule 6(d) for hearings in federal court. That time frame may be enlarged or reduced in state court.

The Answer   By signing a waiver of service, the defendant has 60 days after the waiver was sent to her (90 days if in a foreign country) to file an answer. Rule 12(a). Without a signed waiver, the answer is due 21 days after service of summons. Time is calculated by omitting the day of service and by including the last day of the period unless the last day is a Saturday, a Sunday, a holiday, or a day when the clerk's office is inaccessible. Rule 6. In that event, the last day for filing becomes the next day that the office is open.

If, instead, preliminary motions are filed to attack the complaint, the defendant has 14 days in which to file her answer after the ruling on the motion is made. If a defendant has filed Rule 12(b) motions that are overruled, she may elect to restate them as part of her answer.

The answer in federal court must respond to each of the allegations stated in the complaint in one of the following ways:

•Admit it;
•Deny it;
•Admit part of it and deny the rest of it; or
•Neither admit nor deny based upon lack of personal knowledge.

Any allegation in the complaint that is not addressed in the answer is deemed admitted. The defendant may file an answer in the form of a ***general denial***, in which the defendant "denies each and every allegation of the complaint except those allegations which are against the interests of the plaintiff." Even if an answer denies each allegation separately, it merely prevents default judgment from being entered and holds the plaintiff to strict proof of the allegations made. It does not raise affirmative defenses.

More typical—and more desirable—is an answer which responds to each of the allegations of the complaint and, continuing in the same numbered paragraph format, asserts any and all affirmative defenses that the defendant may have to those allegations. An *affirmative defense* is an assertion which—if it can be proved at trial—will negate the plaintiff's claim. Payment of a claimed debt, expiration of a statute of limitations, or noncompliance with the Statute of Frauds are three examples of affirmative defenses that might be pleaded in the defendant's answer. There are many others, the most common of which are listed in Rule 8(c).

In addition to (or instead of) affirmative defenses, the defendant's answer may claim a setoff against the plaintiff's claim. A *setoff* is an assertion which—if it can be proved—will reduce the plaintiff's claim but will not cancel it entirely.

Counterclaim and Crossclaim

A counterclaim is the pleading used by a defendant to state a claim against a plaintiff, which typically is filed with the defendant's answer in a combined pleading labeled *Answer and Counterclaim*. A counterclaim is either compulsory or permissive. Rule 13.

A *compulsory counterclaim* arises from the same transaction or occurrence upon which the plaintiff's complaint is based. It is compulsory because the defendant is required to raise it in the same litigation; and if she fails to do so, it will be barred and never can be raised again. Because the defendant is required to raise all compulsory counterclaims, the Federal Rules waive the $75,000 jurisdictional requirement for compulsory counterclaims in diversity cases. The counterclaim's value does not matter in federal question cases *(discussed above)*.

A *permissive counterclaim* arises from a different transaction or occurrence than the one upon which the plaintiff's claim is based. The defendant is not required to raise a permissive counterclaim; therefore, a permissive counterclaim in a diversity case must meet the same jurisdictional requirements as the plaintiff's original complaint.

Benjamin was a driver and tour guide with Jolly Trolley Co. His salary was $1200 a month. Benjamin took his friends on a tour during off-duty hours last July. During the tour, Benjamin

> lost control of the trolley, and it smashed into a building.
> The trolley was destroyed, and Benjamin was injured. Jolly
> Trolley fired him and then sued Benjamin for destruction of
> the trolley. Benjamin believes the trolley malfunctioned and
> wants to sue Jolly Trolley for his injuries as well as for his last
> four months' wages, which were not paid.

In the example, Benjamin's claim for injuries arises from the same transaction or occurrence as the destruction of the trolley; therefore, it is a compulsory counterclaim. If he does not raise it, he will have waived the right to do so. His claim for wages, however, arises from the employment relationship between Benjamin and Jolly Trolley and is a permissive counterclaim. He may raise it in the existing litigation or may file a separate suit. If the existing suit were filed in federal court, the wage claim would not meet the $75,000 requirement and could not be filed. It could, however, be filed separately in a state court.

A crossclaim is one filed against a coparty, either plaintiff v. plaintiff or defendant v. defendant (usually defendant v. defendant). It must involve the same subject matter (transaction, occurrence, or property) as the original complaint or a counterclaim. A crossclaim generally is filed at the same time as the answer to the complaint or at the same time as the reply to a counterclaim.

The proper responsive pleading is an **_answer to counterclaim_** (or **_answer to crossclaim_**), which must be filed within 21 days after service (60 days for the United States). The answer addresses itself only to the allegations of the counterclaim (or crossclaim) and is the procedural equivalent of an answer to the complaint.

Amendment of Pleadings   If the pleading is one to which the opponent must respond (such as a complaint), Rule 15 allows the pleading to be amended without court permission at any time before the responsive pleading is served. If the pleading is one to which no response is required (such as an answer to a complaint that is not accompanied by a counterclaim or crossclaim), the pleading may be amended without court permission within 21 days after it is served.

> Plaintiff files her complaint in federal court and serves it upon
> the defendant. On the 9th day after service, the defendant
> files a Rule 12(b)(6) motion. Because the motion is not a
> pleading, the plaintiff may amend her complaint as of right
> during the remaining twelve days of the 21-day period unless
> the defendant files an answer before the amendment is filed.

If the responsive pleading already has been served or if more than 21 days have passed, the pleading may be amended by permission of the court or by consent of the opponent. The federal courts, like most state courts, are very liberal in granting leave to amend pleadings—even during trial if it can be done in such a way that the opponent is not subjected to unfair surprise.

Default Judgment   If no responsive pleading or motion is filed in connection with a complaint, counterclaim, crossclaim, or third-party complaint within the 21-day time limit (60 days for the United States), the nonresponding party is in default; and judgment may be entered against her without a trial.

If the claim is for a ***sum certain*** (an amount not subject to reasonable dispute), the clerk of the federal court may enter default judgment upon submission of an affidavit concerning the amount due. Rule 55(a). If the claim is not for a sum certain, the request for default judgment is submitted to the court with affidavits. The court may require a hearing to prove damages before the default judgment is entered. Rule 55(b)(2). In either situation, the plaintiff is limited to the amount of damages claimed in the complaint.

If multiple defendants are involved and if only one defendant defaults, entry of a default judgment may preclude the plaintiff from proceeding against the remaining defendants. This rule varies from jurisdiction to jurisdiction.

Once a default judgment has been entered, it can be enforced in the same way as any other judgment.

Even though a default judgment is entered, the defendant can move to have it ***set aside*** Rule 55(c) ***for good cause*** under Rule 60(b). Good cause may include, among other things: mistake, inadvertence, surprise, excusable neglect, fraud, or misrepresentation by the opposing party.

Discovery

Subject to certain limitations, discovery is a formal, pretrial process designed to give all parties access to the same evidence that will be available to all other parties at the time of trial. If each party knows what all other parties know about the case, a more accurate assessment of the case is possible; and pretrial settlement is more probable. Discovery is available in both federal and state courts, and many state discovery rules mirror the federal rules very closely.

The purposes of discovery are to obtain evidence that might not be available at trial because of a witness's age, poor health, or absence from the jurisdiction; to narrow the issues for trial; to avoid unfair surprise during trial; and to encourage settlement before trial. When discovery procedures are used improperly (purely to harass, to delay, or to increase costs), the discovering attorney may be subject to court sanction. Rule 26(g). In addition to the Federal Rules, the Model Rules of Professional Conduct provide disciplinary sanctions against attorneys who make frivolous discovery requests.

Discovery is **self-executing**, that is, the parties implement discovery procedures on their own, with little court intervention. In general, counsel for parties must meet to establish an overall discovery plan (Rule 26[f]) and, within 14 days afterward, must make certain disclosures (Rule 26[a]) before any formal discovery occurs *(see below)*. Under Rule 29, for example, they may agree to increase the number or depositions or interrogatories or to extend the time to answer discovery requests under Rules 33, 34, and 36 if it does not conflict with other rules. Prior court approval is required for mental or physical examinations under Rule 35. Otherwise, the court becomes involved in the discovery process only when problems arise that the parties cannot resolve themselves.

The Federal Rules of Civil Procedure allow local courts to decide whether to require filing of all discovery requests or responses with the court in a particular jurisdiction. Most local jurisdictions allow requests and responses to be *served* upon the appropriate party or parties, with copies to all other parties and with only a notice of service *filed* with the court.

Discovery Devices   Several types of discovery devices are permitted by the Federal Rules, including interrogatories, requests to produce documents or things for inspection, requests for physical and mental examination of persons, requests for admission of facts, and depositions upon either oral or written questions. Discovery devices may be served upon *parties only* (except depositions, which may be taken of parties and nonparties alike and except a Rule 45 subpoena *duces tecum* as described below). The permitted discovery devices can be used in any sequence desired and can be used in combination with other discovery devices once the Rule 26(f) meeting has occurred and once the required disclosures have been made.

Rule 26(a) requires the parties to disclose either at their discovery meeting or within 14 days thereafter: (1) name, address, telephone number, and subject matter of information for anyone "likely to have discoverable information" to support the claims or defenses; (2) a copy or description of all relevant documents, electronically stored information, and tangible things to support its claims or defenses; (3) computation of damages and supporting documents; and (4) liability policies, if any, related to the dispute.

At least 90 days before trial, parties must disclose expert witnesses, including their opinions, data, exhibits, qualifications, amount received for testifying, and so forth. At least 30 days before trial, parties must disclose all witnesses who will or may be called at trial and must provide a list of exhibits that will or may be used. Within 14 days thereafter, parties may file objections regarding depositions to be used, objections regarding admissibility of materials identified in support of a claim or defense. Disclosures are designed to avoid many of the routine topics of discovery in which parties historically engaged, although traditional discovery devices still play an important role.

A.   **Interrogatories**   Interrogatories are a series of written questions served by one party upon another party, which must be answered under oath. Rule 33. Interrogatories provide a very inexpensive method to obtain background material such as personal data, employment or medical history, or prior involvement in lawsuits. As a result, interrogatories often are among the initial discovery devices used.

No party may serve more than 25 interrogatories, including subparts, without (1) a stipulation to serve more or (2) permission of the court. State courts often limit the number of interrogatories as well. When multiple sets are used, many courts require that the interrogatories be *numbered sequentially* from one set to the next. For example, if the first set of interrogatories to a party ends with Interrogatory No. 7, a second set to the same party must begin with Interrogatory No. 8. Some courts require ***engrossment*** of interrogatories, which means that the propounding (discovering) party must provide enough space between interrogatories to insert answers. Even if engrossment is not required by court rule, the job of the litigation team is much simpler if interrogatory questions and answers—including any supplemental answers—are engrossed (combined) in one document.

The responding party must answer interrogatories in good faith and must supply the requested information unless a privilege or other basis for objection exists. However, the responding party is not required to provide information which is not in her custody or control or which is in the public domain. Neither is she required to compile reports or summaries, for example, that are not required by the Federal Rules and that do not exist already if the cost and degree of difficulty required to search the records will be about the same for either party. Instead, the responding party is allowed to specify in her answers to interrogatories those business records which contain the information so that the propounding party can examine the records himself to obtain the information he seeks.

Rule 33 requires the responding party to answer interrogatories within 30 days of their service. Answers to interrogatories are signed under oath by the party upon whom they were served, but objections to any particular question(s) are signed by the responding party's attorney. Objections are made to those interrogatories which are outside the scope of discovery (*discussed below*), too burdensome, too vague, too broad, or which request information that is privileged or that is classified as attorney work product.

When the attorney for the propounding party receives objections (or receives incomplete or unresponsive answers) to interrogatories, she may elect to compel answers under Rule 37 (*discussed below*), to redraft and resubmit the offending interrogatories, or to do nothing. ***Note:*** For a detailed review of helpful techniques in drafting interrogatories and answers to interrogatories, refer to the chapter on Litigation Skills found in the *NALA Manual for Paralegals and Legal Assistants*, Fifth Edition (Cengage).

B.   Request for Production of Documents, Things, and Land for Inspection   Rule 34 provides that any party may request any other party to produce designated documents, electronically stored information, tangible things, or to allow inspection of land which is under the control of the responding party. The request can be served any time after compliance with the Rule 26(f) meet-and-confer requirement, provided that the initial disclosures required by Rule 26(a) have been made (*see above*).

The responding party must either comply with the request or file appropriate objections within 30 days of service. If the request is for production of documents and if the number of documents is small, the responding party may elect to forward copies of the documents to the propounding party's attorneys.

However, when large numbers of documents are involved, the responding party may find it easier to make them available for inspection by opposing counsel. In that event, the responding party must identify all documents which may be responsive to the request, often grouping them by categories named in the request. This means that a document control system must be devised and implemented. Paralegals typically participate actively in this and most other discovery procedures. Opposing counsel, then, visits the document production site—often with one or more paralegals—to inspect, select, and copy those documents which she believes are relevant. ***Note:*** A detailed discussion of document control systems and procedures is contained in the *NALA Manual for Paralegals and Legal Assistants*, Fifth Edition (Cengage).

Nonparties cannot be subjected to a direct Rule 34 request to produce; however, Rule 34(c) provides that nonparties can be required to produce documents and things under Rule 45 subpoena procedures. Under Rule 45, a nonparty can be served with a ***subpoena duces tecum***, which is an order "to appear and to bring with you" those items listed on the subpoena. This change creates the functional equivalent of a Rule 34 request to produce served on a party.

Unless the nonparty's attendance is required for deposition, hearing, or trial, he does not need to appear personally if the requested documents or items are produced for inspection. Objections to a subpoena *duces tecum* must be served on the party who initiated the subpoena within 14 days after the subpoena is served. If the time for compliance is less than 14 days, objections must be served before the time for compliance.

C.   Request for Physical or Mental Examination   Unlike other discovery devices, a Rule 35 examination is not self-executing. The requesting party must file a motion to request it. An order for examination will be entered if the requesting party can show existence of both of the following conditions:

1. *The physical or mental condition of a party (or a person in the custody or control of a party) is an issue in the case;* **and**

2. *Good cause.*

The constitutional right of privacy makes the scope of discovery under Rule 35 more narrow than it is under the other discovery rules. It is not enough that a party's physical or mental condition is relevant; it must be part of the actual controversy in the case. For example, one who claims permanent disability resulting from an accident may be subjected to a Rule 35 physical examination. However, mental examination of a plaintiff is not warranted simply because the defendants believe he filed suit as a result of mental delusions—not even if their belief is true.

D.   Requests for Admission   After the discovery meeting and initial disclosures, any party may serve upon any other party written requests for admission under Rule 36, seeking admission of the truth of:

- *statements of fact;*
- *opinions of fact;*
- *application of law to fact;* or
- *the genuineness of any document.*

The purpose of a request for admission is to narrow the facts and issues to be proved at trial—not to obtain information (Rule 33 interrogatories) and not to inspect documents (Rule 34 request to produce). Answers or objections to requests for admission are due in 30 days or the requests are deemed admitted.

A party cannot be compelled to answer requests for admission under Rule 37; however, if a party fails to admit the truth of any request and if the requesting party proves conclusively the subject matter of the request at trial, the court may require the non-answering party to pay reasonable expenses connected with proving the matter.

E.   Deposition   A deposition is a discovery device used to record the sworn testimony of a witness prior to trial. No witness may be deposed more than once except by stipulation or court order, and depositions are limited to a maximum of 10 per side except by stipulation or court order. Depositions may be oral (Rule 30) or upon written questions (Rule 31). They may be taken of any party or of any nonparty who is believed to have information related to the case. A Rule 30 deposition may be videotaped or may be taken by telephone if the parties agree or if the court orders it. If a deposition is taken either before the complaint is filed or before the Rule 26 discovery meeting, court permission must be obtained.

After the discovery meeting, depositions of parties may be taken simply by providing notice to the party-deponent and to all other parties; court permission is not required. If the party-deponent fails to appear, her attendance can be compelled under Rule 37. Because a nonparty witness is not subject to the sanctions of Rule 37, caution dictates that a subpoena be used to ensure attendance even though the Federal Rules do not require it. Failure to obey a subpoena subjects the nonparty to contempt of court.

A *subpoena* is a document typically issued by the court clerk (an attorney also can issue a subpoena as an officer of the court under the Federal Rules) commanding a person to appear personally at a specified time and place to give testimony. Rule 45. A *subpoena duces tecum* requires a person to appear to testify and to bring documents, books, records, papers, or other tangible things.

A subpoena must be served personally and may be served by anyone who is 18 or more years old. The server might be a deputy from the U.S. Marshal's office, a professional process server, or a paralegal. A subpoena must be accompanied by the current witness fee and round-trip mileage (no witness fee or mileage accompanies a subpoena issued by a United States agency or official). Proof of service is filed with the court issuing the subpoena.

When a corporation is subpoenaed, the corporation—not the deposing party—selects the person who will testify on its behalf. Neither a nonparty nor an agent of a nonparty can be commanded to travel to a deposition which is more than 100 miles from her home, place of employment, or place where she regularly transacts business. If the subpoena contemplates testimony at a trial, however, a nonparty witness can be commanded to travel to the trial, without regard to distance, from anywhere in the same state where the action is pending.

Ann lives in California. Her deposition testimony is sought in a federal court action pending in New York; Ann is not a party in the case. Attorneys for the parties may take Ann's deposition in California by traveling to California and having a subpoena issued by the appropriate California federal court to take Ann's deposition in California. Her attendance at the New York trial cannot be compelled, however, because she is outside the subpoena range of the New York federal court and does not live, work, or regularly transact business in New York.

Before a deposition occurs, the deponent's attorney usually reviews the deposition procedure as well as questions likely to be asked with the deponent. Lawyers often provide a written checklist to the deponent, which contains suggestions such as (1) listen to the entire question before attempting to answer it; (2) if you don't understand a question, ask to have it repeated or explained; (3) if you do not know the answer to a question, say that you do not know; do not guess or make assumptions; and (4) tell the truth. Caution is exercised in allowing review of data before the deposition because once any portion of any document is used to refresh the deponent's recollection, the entire document must be made available to opposing counsel.

In the typical situation, the deposition is conducted in a lawyer's office, with the attorneys for the deponent and for each party present. The deponent is sworn by the court reporter or other person authorized to administer oaths, is questioned by the discovering party's attorney, and usually is cross-examined by one or more of the attorneys for the other parties. The deposition proceeds roughly in the same way as examination and cross-examination of witnesses at trial, except that attorneys often agree to reserve certain types of objections for trial (other than form of the question, form of the answer, or similar irregularity—which cannot be reserved until trial). Rule 32(d)(3)(B). Reserving as many objections as possible allows the deposition to flow more smoothly, which saves time and expense for all parties.

The deposition questions and responses are recorded, usually by a court reporter or stenographer, who then transcribes the deposition and presents it to the deponent for signature. The deponent reviews the deposition and signs it, noting transcription errors contained in the deposition, if any. A transcription error occurs when the court reporter transcribes something different from what the deponent actually said. An erroneous statement, which actually was made by the deponent, is not a transcription error.

Many attorneys prefer oral depositions for discovery, because they allow spontaneous exchanges between the attorney and the deponent. Response to a particular question may suggest additional questions that could not have been foreseen or asked if discovery were limited to interrogatories, for example. Equally important is the opportunity to see the witness in person and to evaluate his demeanor, style of presentation, and familiarity with the facts prior to trial.

A Rule 31 deposition upon written questions is similar to an oral deposition, except that the questions to be asked are provided by the discovering party's attorney in advance of the deposition. Written cross-examination questions likewise are provided in advance by attorneys for the other parties. The presiding officer asks the questions, which are answered by the deponent, followed by cross-examination questions. The questions and answers are recorded and transcribed. The lack of flexibility and the absence of spontaneity makes a deposition upon written questions much less attractive to most attorneys than is an oral deposition. As a result, Rule 31 depositions are used infrequently.

Whether the deposition is oral or is upon written questions, the deponent's attorney may object to a particular question if it is outside the scope of discovery and may instruct the deponent not to answer. The deposing attorney has several options in this situation:

1.   Rephrase the question;

2.   Announce a continuance of the deposition until a judicial ruling is obtained concerning the question and whether the deponent is required to answer it; or

3.   Have the court reporter note both the question and the objection in the transcript and proceed with other questioning. Near the close of the deposition, announce a continuance of the deposition until a judicial ruling is obtained concerning this and any other questions to which objections have been made.

Scope of Discovery   Rule 26 generally provides that parties may discover anything (not privileged) which is relevant to the subject matter of the action or which is reasonably calculated to lead to admissible evidence. Even before formal discovery begins, the Federal Rules require parties to disclose the identity of persons likely to have knowledge of any discoverable matter, to calculate their damages, to describe or to provide relevant documents, and to disclose the existence and content of any related liability insurance policies. Identity of expert witnesses and their opinions must be disclosed before trial. Privileged information, however, need not be disclosed and cannot be discovered.

A *privilege* is a protection against compulsory disclosure which is given to certain types of information, such as a trade secret or a communication between certain categories of people (attorney-client, physician-patient, clergy-parishioner, or husband-wife, for example). A person cannot be required to disclose privileged matters either at a deposition (Rule 26) or at trial (Federal Rule of Evidence 501 in federal question cases or state privilege rules in diversity cases).

In addition, a **_work product immunity_** applies to a lawyer's preparations for trial. This immunity may be absolute or qualified, depending on the circumstances. **_Absolute immunity_** is given to documents containing the subjective thoughts of a party's lawyer or other representative, including legal theories, conclusions, opinions, or mental impressions and is nearly impossible to overcome. (Although an opposing party cannot obtain documents of this type, her attorney can ask by interrogatory what a party's legal theories are as they apply to the facts in the case.) A **_qualified immunity_** is given to other documents prepared for trial, which can be overcome only with a strong showing that the opposing party has a substantial need for the materials and that their equivalent cannot be obtained by other means. If a lawyer or representative took notes during an interview with a potential witness who later died without giving any other statements or interviews, for example, the notes may be discoverable because of the qualified immunity.

Both parties and nonparties always can obtain copies of their own prior statements concerning the subject matter of the action.

A matter is **_relevant_** to the subject matter of the action if it makes the existence of a material fact more or less probable than it would be otherwise. However, a matter may be relevant without being admissible at trial. Even if information is not relevant, it still can be discovered if it is _reasonably calculated to lead to admissible evidence_.

> Bill is sued in federal court for negligence in connection with an automobile accident. He receives interrogatories which contain these questions: (1) "How fast were you driving at the time of the accident?" and (2) "How old is your wife?"

Bill's answer to the first question is both relevant and admissible in a negligence action. If he was speeding at the time of the accident, that fact may have substantial probative value in determining negligence. Bill's answer to the second question, no matter what it is, is not relevant to any of the issues in a negligence case; and it is not reasonably calculated to lead to admissible evidence. The question is objectionable, at the very least.

Resisting Discovery   Anyone (whether a party or a nonparty) from whom discovery is sought may resist the discovery attempt either

(1) by obtaining a ***protective order*** or (2) by raising a timely ***objection*** to the question or request.

If the person wants to resist the time, place, or method of discovery or wants to resist an entire area or line of questioning, a Rule 26(c) protective order may provide the better solution. For example, a protective order can prevent discovery of a trade secret; can order a deposition sealed after it is taken (to be opened only by court order); or can order that discovery not be made in certain topic areas. A judge can fashion the scope of a protective order to fit the situation presented.

A protective order always can be issued by the court in which the main case is pending. If a deposition is involved, the protective order can be issued either (1) by the court in which the action is pending or (2) by the court in the district where the deposition is scheduled to be taken.

By contrast, if the person wants to resist a specific question or a few specific questions, making timely objection may be the better course of action. Objections are made to discovery requests in the same way that objections are made at trial. The most commonly raised objections are that the request is outside the scope of discovery under Rule 26 or that it seeks privileged information. In addition to these, objections to interrogatories may arise if the interrogatories are unnecessarily burdensome.

<u>Compelling Discovery</u>   If a person makes a timely objection, fails to comply, or refuses to answer a discovery request or a deposition question, the burden falls upon the party making the request (or asking the deposition question) to seek a court order compelling discovery if he or she wishes to pursue the matter. An evasive or incomplete answer is treated as a failure to answer.

If a person then refuses to obey an order compelling discovery, the court may impose sanctions. Initial sanctions typically include requiring the person to pay the extra expenses (costs and attorney fees) incurred because of his noncompliance. If the person is a party and persists in disobeying the order, a court may prevent the disobedient party from making certain claims or from raising certain defenses. It can strike any portion of the pleadings, or it can go as far as dismissing a disobedient plaintiff's complaint or entering default judgment against a disobedient defendant. The court's contempt powers may be used in connection with either parties or nonparties except when the disobedience relates to a Rule 35 physical or mental examination.

Like protective orders, an order compelling discovery may be entered by the court where the action is pending or, in the case of a deposition, the order may be entered either by the court where the action is pending or by the court where the deposition is to be taken.

Orders compelling discovery generally are ***interlocutory*** (not final) orders and, therefore, are not subject to immediate appeal. There are exceptions:

1.   *When a party is subject to criminal contempt for failing to comply with the order.* This is because criminal contempt carries criminal sanctions, including imprisonment. Incarceration arising from civil contempt, however, is imposed for coercive reasons: when the person complies with the court order, incarceration ends.

2.   *When the discovery order is directed to a nonparty, it may be appealed immediately.* This type of order is interlocutory for the main action and parties, but it is final for the nonparty witness. If the nonparty were to wait until the end of the case, she could not appeal because she would not be a party to the final decision.

3.   *A discovery order may be appealed under the Interlocutory Appeals Act* if it presents a "controlling question of law" in the case, if immediate appeal will expedite the litigation, and if the appellate court agrees to accept the appeal. 29 U.S.C. § 1292. Parties seldom are able to meet all three of these criteria.

A party can appeal a discovery order once a final judgment is entered in the case, either alone or with other claimed errors; however, the discovery issue generally will have become moot by that time.

Use of Discovery at Trial   Whether information obtained through discovery is admissible at trial depends on the discovery device and, in some situations, depends on the way in which a party seeks to use the discovery.

Rule 33 answers to interrogatories can be used by an adverse party for any purpose, including impeachment and as evidence of the truth of the answer. If the party who answered the interrogatory wishes to contradict the answer in her trial testimony, she may do so; and the trier of fact must weigh the credibility of the conflicting information.

Documents and records produced under Rule 34 are subject to the same admissibility rules as any other document and record offered in evidence. There are no additional requirements or limitations imposed because of the discovery device.

Rule 35 physical and mental examinations nearly always are admissible at trial, because this type of examination could not have been conducted in the first place unless a court previously had determined that the party's physical or mental condition was in controversy in the case. There may be a question of doctor-patient privilege, but that privilege is waived if the examined party requests and obtains a report of the examining physician. Rule 35(b)(2).

Rule 32 governs the use of depositions taken under Rule 30 or Rule 31. The first question to be answered is whether the deposition statement would be admissible if the deponent were testifying at trial. For instance, if a deponent makes a hearsay statement (one to which none of the hearsay exceptions apply) during a deposition, the statement remains hearsay for trial purposes; and it cannot be admitted as evidence at the trial. The issue of admissibility is raised by objection at trial, made at the time the statement is offered into evidence at trial. (Recall that certain objections, including admissibility, are reserved when depositions are taken.)

Even if the deposition statement would be admissible if it were made in person by the deponent at trial, it will be allowed in its deposition form only if it falls within one of these categories:

1.   Subject to its admissibility, the deposition statement of any trial witness may be used to impeach that witness's credibility. Rule 32(a)(1).

2.   Subject to its admissibility, the deposition statement of an adverse party—including depositions of officers or directors if the adverse party is a corporation—may be used for any purpose at trial. Rule 32(a)(2).

3.   Subject to its admissibility, the deposition statement of any party or nonparty may be used for any purpose if

    a.   the witness is dead;

    b.   the witness is more than 100 miles from the place of trial;

    c.   the witness is too ill to testify;

    d.   the witness is outside the subpoena range of the court; or

    e.   exceptional circumstances exist to justify use of the deposition rather than live testimony. Rule 32(a)(3).

If only part of a deposition is offered into evidence at trial, an opposing party may offer any other parts of that deposition which should be considered in fairness with the first part. Rule 32(a)(4). This prevents a statement from being taken out of context.

Termination without Trial

Not every complaint results in a full trial on the merits. For example, if Rule 12(b) defects in the complaint are not or cannot be cured, the complaint is dismissed; and no trial occurs. A dismissal can be either with or without prejudice to future action. A ***dismissal without prejudice*** means that the claim may be filed again if the party elects to do so. A ***dismissal with prejudice*** means that the claim cannot be filed again, which invokes the *res judicata* doctrine (*discussed later in this chapter*).

This section reviews the ways in which a case may be ended without a full trial. Although termination generally is discussed in terms of the complaint, keep in mind that counterclaims, crossclaims, and third-party complaints are subject to termination on any of the same grounds as a complaint.

Voluntary Dismissal   A plaintiff in federal court may dismiss her own complaint *once* without prejudice if she does so before the defendant serves his answer or moves for summary judgment. After the answer or motion for summary judgment is filed, the plaintiff must obtain court permission to dismiss her complaint.

The first dismissal is without prejudice; but if the plaintiff re-files the complaint and then voluntarily dismisses a second time, the second dismissal is with prejudice. Rule 41(a)(1). Many state court systems have adopted a similar rule.

Involuntary Dismissal   A complaint in federal court can be dismissed involuntarily under Rule 12(b). In addition, it can be dismissed involuntarily under Rule 41(b) either for failure to prosecute the claim or for disobedience of a court order. If the involuntary dismissal results from lack of jurisdiction, insufficient service of process, improper venue, or failure to join an indispensable party, the dismissal generally is without prejudice.

After the pleadings are closed (both the claim and its responsive pleading are filed), a party may move for ***judgment on the pleadings*** under Rule 12(c). The moving party must show that she is entitled to judgment based solely upon the contents of the pleadings. If a complaint claims nonpayment of a promissory note and if the answer admits the note but claims the defendant did not pay because he was studying in Brazil, for example, a Rule 12(c) motion is appropriate.

A slightly different variation is the procedure to obtain a ***summary judgment*** available under Rule 56. To prevail on a motion for summary judgment, a party must show that there is *no genuine issue of material fact* and that she is *entitled to judgment as a matter of law*. Unlike Rule 12(c), however, Rule 56 permits the judge to go beyond the pleadings to the facts established by discovery or by sworn affidavits filed with the motion. Affidavits must include only those facts about which the affiant has personal knowledge and which would be admissible at trial. A summary judgment motion can be made until 30 days after the close of discovery.

The party opposing a motion for summary judgment must be given at least 21 days' notice of the hearing and is permitted to file a resistance to the motion, together with opposing affidavits. Movant then has 14 days to file a reply if a reply is warranted. In deciding whether to enter summary judgment, the judge must consider all of the facts in the light most favorable to the nonmoving party (resolving any doubt in favor of the nonmoving party). Using that standard, if the evidence (affidavits and discovery results) establishes that there is no genuine dispute for a trier of fact to decide, the judge enters judgment according to the substantive legal rules which govern the issues in the case.

The judge may enter either a summary judgment or a partial summary judgment. A ***partial summary judgment*** is one which resolves one or more issues in the case but which leaves others for the trier of fact to decide. For example, affidavits and discovery results may show conclusively that liability of a party exists; but if there is a genuine factual dispute concerning damages, a partial summary judgment is entered on the issue of liability only.

If the case proceeds to trial and if the plaintiff fails to prove facts supporting her claim for relief, the judge can dismiss the complaint before the defendant begins his case. The procedure in a *nonjury* trial is for the defendant to make a motion for ***judgment on partial findings*** under Rule 52(c) when the plaintiff rests. In a *jury* trial, the defendant makes a motion for ***judgment as a matter of law*** under Rule 50 when the plaintiff rests, which is the functional equivalent of a directed verdict in state court actions. The directed verdict no longer exists in federal courts. Instead, either party may move for judgment as a matter of law when the defendant rests. The judge grants judgment as a matter of law if there is *no legally sufficient evidentiary basis for a reasonable jury to have found for that party with respect to that issue*. Rule 50(a)(1).

When a Rule 50 motion for judgment as a matter of law is made by either party at the close of the defendant's case in a jury trial, the judge may reserve her decision until after the case has been submitted to the jury—even if she believes that judgment should be granted to the moving party as a matter of law. By waiting, she avoids a judicial catch-22. If the jury decides in favor of the moving party, the motion is moot. If the jury decides against the moving party, the judge still may enter judgment as a matter of law on the basis that no reasonable jury could have found against the moving party. This effectively overturns the jury verdict in much the same way as a judgment notwithstanding the verdict (judgment NOV) under prior federal rules. (Judgment NOV no longer exists under the Federal Rules; however, it continues in many state courts.)

Pretrial Conference

Rule 16 of the Federal Rules (and similar provisions in state court systems) give the judge authority to conduct a pretrial conference, which is used to identify uncontested issues, to define and simplify contested issues, to identify witnesses and exhibits for trial, and to set case progression deadlines for motions, discovery, and related matters. The theory of a pretrial conference is that if parties are required to define their legal and factual issues clearly, they will be more willing to settle the case.

Even if the judge in federal court does not conduct a pretrial conference, she must issue a scheduling order *within 120 days* after the complaint is filed. Rule 16(b). A ***scheduling order*** sets a time limit for joinder of additional parties, amendment of pleadings, filing motions, and completion of discovery.

If a party anticipates that an opposing party may attempt to introduce evidence at trial which is both irrelevant and unfairly prejudicial, it may be that a simple objection will be inadequate to remove the information from the jurors' minds. For example, if a party's counsel anticipates that her adversary may ask the question, "Isn't it true that you have been married 17 times?" during cross-examination of her client in a negligence case, an objection to the question most certainly would be sustained. However, simply hearing the question might prejudice many of the jurors. In this sort of situation, the attorney may file a ***motion in limine*** to preclude all lines of questioning concerning the client's prior marriages. This type of motion generally is considered at the pretrial conference, if there is one; if not, then it is considered at some point shortly before trial begins. If the order is granted to preclude the topic and if opposing counsel disregards the order during trial, his disregard could result in a mistrial.

If a pretrial conference is held, it is followed by a ***pretrial order*** issued by the judge, which summarizes the results of the pretrial conference in terms of contested and uncontested issues as well as identification of witnesses and exhibits. (Witnesses and exhibits to be used only for impeachment purposes need not be identified.) Case progression deadlines are included. A final pretrial order is binding on all parties and effectively replaces the pleadings in establishing the basic outline for the trial.

Any party (or the lawyer for any party) may be subject to sanctions if he or she fails to participate in the pretrial conference, participates in bad faith, or fails to comply with progression deadlines or with any other requirement established by the pretrial order. Rule 16(f).

Trial Procedure

As the time for trial draws near, the litigation team stays in touch with individuals on its witness list and organizes the evidence amassed during discovery for use at trial. Paralegals have become increasingly important in this process. The trial notebook is prepared, which contains final pleadings, the outlines for the opening statement and closing argument, witness lists, exhibit lists, and short briefs on evidentiary issues which are expected to arise during the trial (called pocket briefs). When the trial date is set, witnesses are contacted once again, their testimony is reviewed with them, and subpoenas are issued for all nonparty witnesses. *(Issuance of Rule 45 subpoenas was discussed earlier in this chapter.)*

The purpose of trial is to present all admissible facts to an impartial fact finder, who then decides which party should win (reaches a verdict) based only upon (1) those facts which the fact finder believes are true and (2) the trial judge's instructions concerning the legal results of those facts. In the traditional trial setting, the jury decides the facts; and the judge decides the law.

The federal civil trial process is governed substantially by the Federal Rules of Civil Procedure and by the Federal Rules of Evidence. State courts are governed by similar rules adopted in their states. The material in this section reviews the basic procedural rules governing trials. Evidentiary rules are addressed only in a peripheral way.

Trial by Jury   The Seventh Amendment to the U.S. Constitution guarantees the right to a jury trial in all cases "at common law" in which the amount in controversy exceeds $20.00. This amendment applies to federal trials, but not to state trials.

The Seventh Amendment does not state how many individuals must serve on a jury. The 12-person jury is a product of history and tradition. The Federal Rules require a jury of "not fewer than six members. . ." Rule 48. If the jury shrinks to fewer than six members during the trial, a mistrial is declared unless the parties agree to continue. To avoid this situation (the Federal Rules do not permit alternate jurors), the local court rules of many federal courts provide for more than six jurors to be selected. If one or more jurors must be excused for illness or for some other reason before the trial is finished, there still are "not fewer than six" to render the verdict.

Although trial by jury is the hallmark of the American judicial system, not every case is tried to a jury. Juries are not permitted in equity cases, for instance, or in tax court. Even if parties are entitled to a trial by jury, they may waive that right if they prefer to have the case tried to a judge. In these situations, the judge sits as both the fact finder and the trial judge; and her final judgment generally includes both findings of fact and conclusions of law. In federal court, parties who are entitled to a jury trial must request it specifically when their complaints are filed; otherwise, jury trial is waived.

When a trial by jury is permitted and is not waived, the jury's verdict in federal civil cases must be unanimous unless the parties in the case agree otherwise. Many states permit jury verdicts which are less than unanimous in civil cases.

Jury Selection   The pool of potential jurors must be drawn from a representative cross-section of the community. The jury pool may be taken from lists of persons holding a valid driver's license, from voter registration lists, or from other sources likely to produce the required cross-section.

Potential federal jurors (the precise number varies from district to district) are selected to serve as jurors through a process called *voir dire*. During ***voir dire***, potential jurors are examined first by the trial judge and then by the attorneys to determine whether they are able to reach a fair and impartial verdict. If a potential juror answers questions in a way which shows that she cannot reach an impartial verdict, she is ***challenged for cause*** by an attorney for one of the parties and is excused.

Cause exists if the potential juror knows any of the parties, their attorneys, or any prospective witnesses in the case or if the potential juror demonstrates bias or prejudice which would influence a verdict for or against either party. If a potential juror states that she might be influenced, for example, by pretrial publicity about the case, she may be challenged for cause. Because there is no limit to the number of challenges for cause that can be made, jury selection for cases involving controversial issues or controversial parties may extend over a period of days or weeks.

In addition to challenges for cause, each party in a federal civil trial receives three peremptory challenges. A ***peremptory challenge*** allows a party to dismiss a potential juror without demonstrating cause for dismissal. Peremptory challenges are useful when a potential juror provides information to indicate bias, but insists upon questioning that he is able to render a fair and impartial verdict. For example, a potential juror in an auto negligence case may be the husband of an insurance adjuster; yet, the juror may insist that he could be fair to both parties in reaching his verdict. Most plaintiffs claiming damages for injuries likely would use one of their peremptory challenges to dismiss this potential juror.

Opening Statements   Once the jury is selected, the trial begins with opening statements. Because production of witnesses and evidence at trial rarely follow the precise chronology of the transaction or occurrence being litigated, opening statements allow each party to explain to the jury how the evidence will be presented and what it will prove. Attorneys cannot argue the merits of the case or comment on the credibility of witnesses during opening statements; these are reserved for closing arguments. The plaintiff's attorney generally makes the first opening statement, followed by the defendant's attorney.

Opening statements typically are limited to 10 or 15 minutes for each party. Experienced trial attorneys agree, however, that these few minutes are critical to the rest of the trial. Although the attorney cannot argue her client's case during her opening statement, she certainly can capitalize on this opportunity to present her client's case in its best light without using argumentative language or demeanor. If she knows, for example, that her opponent intends to offer damaging evidence, she can talk about the evidence that minimizes its impact when the jurors hear it during trial. If her client is a large corporation, she can use the opening statement to provide it with human qualities through those officers or directors who will testify at trial. A well-organized, thoughtfully prepared opening statement can be a major factor in winning or losing a very close case.

Sequence of Trial   After opening statements are concluded, the plaintiff presents her case by offering evidence in the form of witness *testimony* (testimonial evidence offered through fact witnesses and expert witnesses), *exhibits* (documentary evidence or tangible evidence), and *audiovisual aids* (demonstrative evidence in the form of photographs, charts, diagrams, or models). The Federal Rules of Evidence govern the required foundation for and admissibility of specific evidence forms. Attorneys must object to the admissibility of evidence immediately as it is presented during trial, or the objection is waived. When an objection is made, all questions stop until the trial judge rules on the objection by sustaining it or by overruling it.

The plaintiff's goal is to prove facts to support each of the contested legal issues stated in the complaint (in the pretrial order, if one was entered). To achieve that goal, the plaintiff's case proceeds from witness to witness, with the plaintiff's attorney conducting a *direct examination* of each witness and with the defendant's attorney conducting a *cross-examination* of each witness if desired. If cross-examination produces facts which were not covered by direct examination, the plaintiff's attorney generally may conduct a *redirect examination* concerning those new facts only. She cannot re-hash facts disclosed during the direct examination. If redirect examination occurs, the defendant's attorney likely will be permitted to *recross-examine* the witness. In addition to testifying about the facts of the case (or offering opinions, if the witness is an expert), witnesses are used to lay foundation for the introduction of exhibits into evidence unless the parties' attorneys previously have stipulated to their foundation. When all evidence has been presented, the plaintiff rests.

At the close of the plaintiff's case, the defendant may make a motion for judgment on partial findings under Rule 52(c) or a motion for judgment as a matter of law under Rule 50(a) if the defendant believes that the plaintiff failed to prove (offer evidence on) any element which is necessary for an ultimate verdict in favor of the plaintiff. As a cautionary procedural measure, the defendant's attorney may make this motion without regard to his assessment of the outcome. By making the motion, even if he thinks that it may be overruled, he preserves his client's right to raise the issue on appeal. (*Both motions were discussed earlier in this chapter.*)

If the defendant's motion for judgment on partial findings is overruled, the defendant begins his case in chief. The defendant's goal is to refute the evidence produced by the plaintiff or to prove the required elements of the affirmative defenses stated in his answer (or stated in the pretrial order, if there is one), or both. The defendant's case proceeds from witness to witness in the same way as did the plaintiff's case. When all evidence has been presented, the defendant rests.

If new issues are raised by the defendant's case, the plaintiff may be permitted to present further evidence in *rebuttal*. In that circumstance, she must confine her evidence to the new issues only; she cannot re-hash her case in chief.

At the close of all evidence, either or both the plaintiff and the defendant may make a motion for judgment as a matter of law under Rule 50(a), which replaces the motion for directed verdict under previous federal rules. The trial judge may rule on the motion(s) when they are made but is more likely to reserve the ruling until after the jury's verdict is returned. (*Judgment as a matter of law was discussed earlier in this chapter.*)

Closing Arguments   After each party rests (and if motions for judgment as a matter of law are either overruled or reserved for decision), closing arguments are made to the jury. The plaintiff's attorney is allowed to address the jury first, but she may choose to be last if she believes there is a tactical benefit in doing so.

Generally speaking, more time is allotted for closing arguments than for opening statements. This is the attorney's opportunity to persuade the jury to the justness of his or her client's position. The attorney may point out any gaps between what the opposing counsel said in his opening statement that he would prove and what he did prove; may comment on the credibility of witnesses, using care not to alienate the jury; and may argue the sufficiency or weight of evidence. Although there are some limitations on what can be said or done during closing argument, the attorney is given fairly wide latitude in attempting to persuade a jury.

Jury Instructions   At the close of all evidence, any party may file written request(s) with the trial judge that a specific jury instruction be given to the jury. Rule 51. The requests typically include supporting legal authority for the judge to consider. (Many states have compiled a reference book of standard jury instructions, which are grouped according to subject matter.) The judge considers all such requests and, when appropriate, incorporates them with the full set of jury instructions that ultimately will be given.

After closing arguments are concluded, the trial judge instructs the jury concerning those rules of law which apply to the jury's findings of fact, generally by reading the jury instructions aloud to the jury and then by providing them in writing. They typically include instructions on the evidence, burden of proof (*discussed below*), pertinent law, and application of the law to the facts as the jury determines the facts to be. In federal courts, and in some state courts, the trial judge has the right to comment on the quality and weight of evidence if she chooses to do so.

Objections to jury instructions must be made before the jury retires for deliberation.

Burden of Proof   The term *burden of proof* may have one of several meanings when it is used in connection with civil trials. Its most general meaning is the standard of proof which is assigned to a claimant as the ***burden of persuasion*** in the case. For example, the standard of proof assigned to the government in a criminal trial is "beyond a reasonable doubt." The standard of proof (burden of persuasion) assigned to a claimant in a civil trial is "by a preponderance of the evidence." A matter is proved by a ***preponderance*** if the jury believes it is *more likely than not* that the matter is true.

The preponderance standard frequently is explained to juries by using the example of tipped scales. In the example, the plaintiff and the defendant begin the case with evenly balanced scales. If the weight of the plaintiff's evidence tips the scales in her favor, however slightly, she wins by a preponderance of the evidence. If the combined weights of evidence on the plaintiff's side and the defendant's side tip the scales in favor of the defendant or if the combined weights tip the scales back and forth but end evenly weighted at the end of the case as to each party, the plaintiff (the claimant) cannot win by a preponderance of the evidence.

In addition, the jury's belief (sometimes called a finding) must be actual— not one based on statistics or on mathematical probabilities. For example, the statistical fact that more teenage males drive carelessly than do teenage females does not justify a jury's finding that an unidentified teenager, who was seen driving carelessly, was a male.

The Verdict   Once the jury has been charged (provided with jury instructions), members of the jury retire to a private jury room where they select a foreman and deliberate their verdict. If a unanimous verdict is required, a jury that cannot reach a unanimous decision is called a ***hung jury***, which generally provides the basis to declare a mistrial. If a mistrial is declared for this or for any other reason, a new trial is conducted with a new jury.

The jury may return a general verdict, a general verdict with interrogatories, or a special verdict, depending on the jury instructions. A ***general verdict*** simply declares which party is the winner.

A ***general verdict with interrogatories*** declares which party is the winner and, in addition, requires the jury to answer questions about specific findings of fact. Rule 49(b). If the findings of fact are consistent with the general verdict, the verdict is entered. If the findings of fact are inconsistent with the general verdict, the judge may either (1) enter judgment according to the findings of fact or (2) order a new trial. If the findings of fact are inconsistent with each other, the judge must send the case back to the jury for further deliberation.

A ***special verdict*** requires a special, written finding for each fact in the case. Rule 49(a). Special verdicts have been frowned upon by several U.S. Supreme Court Justices on the basis that they allow a trial judge to exercise too much control in deciding the ultimate outcome of a case. Whether for that reason or for some other reason, special verdicts are used infrequently by federal courts.

Procedures and Motions after Verdict or Judgment

After the jury returns its verdict in the case, an order of judgment (sometimes simply called a judgment) is prepared and entered as part of the official court file. Absent an appeal, the entry of judgment generally is the final action taken in the trial process. This is how most cases end. However, if procedural matters are pending or are raised when the verdict is returned, those matters must be resolved before the judgment can be entered.

A.   Motion for Judgment as a Matter of Law   If any party moved for a judgment as a matter of law under Rule 50(a)(1) at the close of evidence and if a ruling on the motion was reserved by the trial judge (which often will be the case), the judge must rule on the motion before any judgment is entered. If the verdict is in favor of the moving party, the motion becomes moot. If the verdict is against the moving party, however, and if the judge determines there was no legally sufficient evidence upon which a reasonable jury could have found as it did, the judge may enter judgment as a matter of law in favor of the moving party. This effectively overturns the jury verdict in much the same way as did a judgment notwithstanding the verdict (judgment NOV) under prior federal rules. Judgments NOV and directed verdicts no longer exist after the 1991 amendments to the Federal Rules; instead, they are combined under Rule 50(a)(1) in the (new) judgment as a matter of law.

B.   Motion for New Trial   A motion for new trial must be filed *within 10 days of the entry of judgment* (Rule 59) and may be accompanied by supporting affidavits, giving the adverse party 10 days after the motion for new trial to file opposing affidavits. Filing a motion for new trial is a prerequisite for appeal in many state courts, but this is not true in federal court.

The goal of a motion for new trial is to allow the trial judge to correct prejudicial errors which occurred during the trial. A ***prejudicial error*** is one which both (1) affects a substantial right of the moving party in the trial process and (2) was objected to by the moving party at the time of its occurrence. By contrast, if a mistake was made which did not affect a substantial right of the moving party, it is a ***harmless error***. Prejudicial errors require a new trial to be conducted; harmless errors do not. If a motion for new trial is denied, the moving party either may accept the judgment as it stands or may appeal if the party believes that prejudicial errors occurred during trial.

Prejudicial error which justifies the grant of a new trial can include any one or more of the following:

1. *Judicial error*, such as the improper admission or exclusion of evidence or an improper jury instruction.

2. *Improper conduct of a party, witness, or attorney* during the trial if there is substantial risk that the conduct influenced the verdict.

3. *Improper conduct of a juror*, such as allowing himself to be exposed to outside influence or concealing bias during *voir dire*.

4. *A verdict which is against the weight of the evidence.* In federal courts, the verdict must be against the clear weight of the evidence, must be based upon evidence which is false, or must be one which will result in a miscarriage of justice. It is not enough that the judge disagrees with the verdict.

5. *Newly discovered evidence* which is material and which was not, and could not have been, known at the time of trial.

6. *The verdict is excessive or is inadequate.* When damages are fixed by law or are liquidated as part of a contract and when a verdict is returned in excess of that amount, the verdict may be set aside as a matter of law and a new trial ordered. Similarly, when damages are fixed by law or are liquidated as part of a contract and when a verdict is returned for less than that amount, the verdict may be set aside as a matter of law. When the amount of damages is within the discretion of the jury, but the verdict clearly is out of line with the evidence, the verdict may be set aside.

When a trial judge determines that the excessiveness of a verdict is caused by the jury's miscalculation (mathematical error) of the damages, she may be able to correct the error through ***remittitur***, under which the winning party agrees to reduce the damages to a specific amount. If the winning party does not agree, the judge may order a new trial. Conversely, when the damages awarded by a verdict are grossly inadequate because of jury miscalculation, the trial judge may correct the error by ordering a new trial unless the losing party agrees to increase the damages to a specific amount (***additur***). *Remittitur* is well-established both in federal and state courts. However, the U.S. Supreme Court has ruled that *additur* cannot be used in federal courts because it violates the Seventh Amendment. The Seventh Amendment does not apply to state courts, however, which continue to use *additur* to correct inadequate damage awards.

As an alternative to *remittitur* or *additur*, a trial judge may grant a partial new trial on the issue of damages only.

C.   Motion for Order *Nunc Pro Tunc*   A motion for an order *nunc pro tunc* in state courts generally seeks to correct clerical types of errors when there is no question about what the order of judgment should have contained. For example, if the order of judgment states that judgment is entered in favor of the "plaintiff, Joe Brown" when the plaintiff's name is Joe Bowen, an order *nunc pro tunc* is used to correct the error in the order of judgment. In federal court, the same result is accomplished by filing a ***motion to alter or amend judgment*** within *10 days* after the judgment is entered. Rule 59(e).

Appellate Review

The losing party in the trial court may have a higher court review the trial court proceedings for prejudicial error by filing an appeal. Similarly, the winning party may assume the procedural posture of a losing party for purposes of appeal if she does not win as much as she thinks she should have won. In general, the party who appeals to a higher court is the ***appellant***. The party who defends an appeal is the ***appellee***. In some state courts and under some federal statutes, the parties are identified as the petitioner and the respondent.

Appellate Procedure   Appeal of a federal trial court's decision is governed by the Federal Rules of Appellate Procedure (Fed. R. App. P.). An appeal of right (one which does not require permission from the appellate court) is initiated by filing a ***notice of appeal*** with the clerk of the federal trial court, which must be done either (1) within 30 days after entry of the final judgment or order in the case or (2) within 30 days after motions under Rules 50, 52, or 59 are denied (including denial of a motion for new trial under Rule 59). Fed. R. App. P. 4(a)(4). This period is enlarged to 60 days if the United States or any of its officials or agencies is a party. In addition, if a party can show excusable neglect, the period can be extended for an additional 30 days after the expiration date or for an additional ten days after the order of extension, whichever is later. Once a notice of appeal is filed, any other party also may file a notice of appeal (called a ***cross-appeal***) within 14 days after the first notice of appeal is filed or within any time period set by Fed. R. App. P. 4, whichever is later. If a notice of appeal is filed prematurely (before a final judgment is entered), it has no effect and must be re-filed at the proper time to perfect the appeal.

Recall that some federal appeals, such as an appeal under the Interlocutory Appeal Act (28 U.S.C. § 1292), require the permission of the appellate court before they can be filed. This type of appeal is not an appeal of right. Instead, a petition for permission to appeal is filed. The specific procedure is outlined in Fed. R. App. 5.

When the notice of appeal is filed, the appellant also must pay a ***docket fee*** under Fed. R. App. P. 3(e) and may be required to a ***bond for costs***, which is called an appeal bond. Fed. R. App. P. 7. A transcript of the record must be ordered by the appellant within 10 days after filing the notice of appeal (Fed. R. App. P. 10), which must be prepared by the court reporter of the federal trial court and filed in the court of appeals court within 30 days after the transcript of the record is ordered. Fed. R. App. P. 11. The ***record*** consists of the pleadings, the transcript of testimony, the exhibits received in evidence in the trial court, and the docket entries of orders and other matters which are certified by the clerk of the trial court.

Appeals in state courts generally require a notice of appeal within a specified time, typically 30 days from the entry of the final judgment or from the order denying a new trial (when a motion for new trial is required before the appeal can be filed). Unlike federal court, however, there is no provision for enlargement or extension of the appeal time in many state courts.

Once the appeal is docketed in the appellate court (the court of appeals in the federal system), the appellate court assumes jurisdiction of the case. In both state and federal courts, the appellant and the appellee file ***appellate briefs***, which must conform to the rules of procedure and local court rules of the appropriate appellate court. Fed. R. App. P. 31 requires the appellant's brief to be filed and served within 40 days after the date on which the record is filed in the court of appeals. The appellee then has 30 days to file her brief, running from the date of service of the appellant's brief. If the appellant files a reply brief to the appellee's brief, the reply brief must be filed and served within 14 days after the appellee's brief.

After all briefs are filed, ***oral arguments*** are scheduled. In some situations, the appellate court may waive oral argument on its own motion. When oral argument occurs in a federal court of appeals, it generally is conducted before a three-judge panel and usually is limited to no more than

30 minutes for each side. Once oral arguments are concluded (or waived, if that is the situation), the appellate judges hold conferences to determine how they will rule. One judge usually is selected to write the opinion. The **decision and opinion** may take several months, depending on the court's case load and the complexity of the issues in the case.

If the losing party on appeal disagrees with the federal court of appeals decision, she may request a **rehearing** under Fed. R. App. P. 40; and, if she still loses, she may file **petition for writ of certiorari** with the U.S. Supreme Court. *(See chapter on General Law for further discussion.)*

Stay Pending Appeal   To prevent enforcement of the judgment entered by the trial court while the appeal is pending, the appellant (or the losing party) files a motion for an **order of stay**. If the order is granted, the moving party typically must file a **supersedeas bond** in connection with the order. The purpose of the bond is to assure the winning party that the judgment will be paid if the appellant ultimately loses the appeal. If the motion for order of stay is denied for any reason, the trial court winner is free to enforce the judgment without waiting for the appeal process to be concluded.

Scope of Appellate Review   Appellate review in state court actions may be either *de novo*, *de novo* on the record, or on the record. An appeal *de novo* usually arises when an appeal is taken from a court or agency where no record is made, such as a small claims court or a property tax board, to a court of record. An **appeal de novo** means that the appellate court is allowed to try the case anew, as if no prior proceedings had occurred. Witnesses are allowed to testify, and evidence is received; the appellate court is not bound by the findings of fact or by the conclusions of law of the lower court or agency.

More typical in state court actions is an **appeal de novo on the record**, which means that the appellate court's review is limited to the record made in the trial court. The appellate court generally does not re-evaluate the evidence or the findings of fact (whether by the judge or by a jury) unless they are clearly erroneous, but the appellate court is not bound by the conclusions of law reached by the trial court.

An **appeal on the record** is one in which the findings of fact reached by the trial court are given the greatest deference by the appellate court. However, the appellate court gives no greater deference to the trial court's conclusions of law for this type of review than for any other. Appeals from administrative agency decisions frequently are on the record.

The scope of appellate review generally operates in federal courts in much the same way as an appeal *de novo* on the record in state courts. Findings of fact are set aside only if they are "clearly erroneous." Rule 52(a). The federal Court of Appeals is not bound by the conclusions of law reached by the federal trial court, however (*see above*).

Disposition by Appellate Court   If a case is filed improperly (untimely notice of appeal, no record filed with the appellate court, or other material defect), the appellate court may dispose of the appeal by dismissing it without decision. Absent dismissal, the appellate court may dispose of the appeal by a decision which invokes one of the following actions:

1.   ***Affirm*** the lower court decision if, upon review of the record, the appellate court determines that findings of fact were not clearly erroneous and that no prejudicial errors were made. Most appellate cases are disposed of in this way.

2.   ***Reverse*** (change) the lower court decision (1) if, upon review of the record, the appellate court determines either that findings of fact were clearly erroneous or that prejudicial errors were made and (2) if the facts in the record are sufficient for the appellate court to render a fully informed judgment on the merits.

3.   ***Reverse and remand*** with instructions for further proceedings (1) if, upon review of the record, the appellate court determines either that findings of fact were clearly erroneous or that prejudicial errors were made but (2) the facts in the record are *insufficient* for the appellate court to render a fully informed judgment on the merits. For example, if the appellate court reverses the trial court's summary judgment, the record will not contain sufficient facts to render a fully informed judgment on the merits. In that situation, the case will be remanded to the trial court for further proceedings (in this case, a trial).

Res Judicata

Res judicata literally means *the thing adjudged*. A basic premise of the American legal system is that every person is entitled to her day in court—but she is entitled only to one. She cannot re-litigate the same case over and over again. The doctrine of *res judicata* limits a party's litigation right to one time only when the parties, issues, or claims are the same. If a final judgment on the merits is entered in a case, that judgment is *res judicata* as to all future suits involving the same parties and the same issues (claims). Recall that a dismissal with prejudice to future operates as a judgment on the merits and invokes the ***res judicata*** doctrine *(discussed above)*.

Res judicata may be asserted either in a preliminary motion as a defect of a complaint or in an answer as an affirmative defense.

Although the term ***res judicata*** frequently is used in the generic sense defined above, it technically encompasses two subsidiary doctrines which are slightly different from each other: (1) merger and bar and (2) collateral estoppel.

Under the doctrine of ***merger and bar*** (sometimes called ***claim preclusion***), the claims of the parties are merged into the judgment. The claims no longer exist, and any future action between the same parties on the same claims is barred because of the merger. Merger and bar applies to claims that actually were litigated as well as to claims that could have been litigated but were not.

> Adam sues Bill for a claim of negligence of $1000. Judgment ultimately is entered in favor of Adam for $500 on his claim. Adam's $1000 claim is merged into the $500 judgment. By operation of law (merger and bar), Adam cannot sue Bill for $1000 again. Neither can he sue Bill for the remaining $500 of his claim. The entire claim is merged into the judgment.

By contrast, the doctrine of ***collateral estoppel*** (sometimes called ***issue preclusion***) prevents the same issues from being litigated by the same parties in different actions. Determination of the issue in the first case disposes of the same issue in the second case. Collateral estoppel applies only to those issues litigated; it does not apply to issues which could have been litigated but were not.

> Patty sues Elizabeth for negligence resulting in property damage to Patty's automobile. Judgment is entered in favor of Elizabeth. Then Patty files a second complaint, this time claiming personal injuries caused by Elizabeth's negligence in the same accident. Because the issue of Elizabeth's negligence was decided in the first case, that issue must be decided in the same way in the same case involving the same parties—even though the claims are different (property damage v. personal injury).

> Patty sues Elizabeth for an installment payment on a rental agreement and wins. Patty sues Elizabeth again for a different installment payment due on the same rental

> agreement; but this time, Elizabeth defends that the rental agreement never was signed. Collateral estoppel does not apply to the second suit if the validity of the rental agreement was not raised and actually litigated in the first suit.

Many intricacies exist in applying the rules for merger and bar and for collateral estoppel; however, they are beyond the intended scope of this *Review Manual*.

Parties Bound   If an issue or a claim is litigated in one action and appears again in a subsequent action, only certain parties in the subsequent action are bound by the first judgment on the merits. Clearly, the parties to the first litigation are bound by a final judgment on the issues and claims. In addition, persons **in privity** with those parties also are bound, including:

- successors in interest, such as a subsequent owner of property;
- beneficiaries of a trust in which the trustee was a party to the action;
- principal or agent of a party to the action; or
- bailor or bailee in relation to a party to the action.

One who is a stranger to the first action (neither a party nor in privity with a party) is not bound either by the claims or by the issues litigated in the first action.

Enforcement of Judgments

In the usual situation, a judgment (unlike a decree) simply is an order or declaration by a law court that one party owes money to another party. The party who owes the money is the ***judgment debtor***; the party to whom the money is owed is the ***judgment creditor***.

A judgment does not include a requirement that the money owed must be paid by a certain time or that it must be paid at all. Unless a judgment debtor voluntarily pays the judgment, the judgment creditor must initiate proceedings to enforce (execute) the judgment. These proceedings are ancillary to the main litigation in which the judgment was entered.

Rule 64 provides that the procedure for execution of judgments is the same procedure used in the state where the federal district court is located. If a federal statute is involved, the federal statute governs to the extent that it applies; however, most federal judgment executions follow state rules.

Although procedures for judgment execution vary from state to state, the execution devices are similar. For example, nearly all states provide some type of ***writ of execution***, which is used to ***levy*** against personal property assets of the judgment debtor which are in the possession of the judgment debtor (vehicle, boat, art collection). The property is seized, usually by a local law enforcement official, and is sold. After expenses of levy and sale (and satisfaction of any lienholders of the property), the proceeds are applied against the judgment. If the proceeds are insufficient to satisfy the entire judgment, additional personal property can be seized and sold. Any other enforcement remedy available can be used either in place of or in addition to execution and levy.

Garnishment is used to obtain personal property assets of the judgment debtor which are deposited with or are in the possession of a third person (someone other than the judgment debtor). The most common garnishees are banks holding deposits for the judgment debtor and employers holding earned wages for the judgment debtor. The specific amount of money subject to garnishment is the amount held by the garnishee at the moment when the garnishment notice is received. For example, if a checking account has a balance of $40.00 when the bank receives the garnishment notice, only $40.00 can be subjected to the garnishment proceeding—even if the judgment debtor deposits $10,000.00 into the account one hour later.

Some types of payments cannot be garnished. For instance, Social Security benefits are not subject to garnishment. However, once the benefits are deposited into a recipient's bank account, they lose their character as Social Security benefits and are subject to general garnishment statutes.

Most states provide statutory exemptions of certain property amounts from levy or garnishment. For example, many states provide a wage exemption to a judgment debtor which is equal to the minimum hourly wage then in force. Garnishment of a debtor's wages, then, would be subject to the minimum wage limitation *if the debtor claims the exemption*. If the exemption is not claimed, it is not given. If the exemption is claimed, however, the judgment creditor can receive only that portion of the judgment debtor's earned wages which exceed the hourly minimum wage amount.

Most states allow a judgment to be enforced as a lien against real property owned by the judgment debtor through the process of judicial *foreclosure and sale*. Foreclosure and sale of real property operates much the same as levy of personal property, but it generally involves a more detailed and time-consuming procedure to arrive at the point of sale. When real property ultimately is sold to satisfy the judgment lien, the judgment creditor receives the proceeds after expenses, prior lienholders' claims, and the interests of other owners of the property (such as a spouse) are paid. Unless the judgment debtor has a substantial equity interest in the real estate, foreclosure and sale may not be cost effective.

If the judgment creditor believes that the judgment debtor may have concealed assets or may have transferred assets for less than their fair market value (a fraudulent conveyance), Rule 69 allows the judgment creditor to conduct ***post-trial discovery*** (usually interrogatories or depositions) to obtain details concerning the judgment debtor's assets. State courts provide a similar device, sometimes called a debtor's examination.

A judgment debtor who has no assets, who owns assets with liens that equal or exceed the value of the assets, or whose assets consist entirely of exempt property is ***judgment proof.*** Because this situation arises often, the wise plaintiff and her litigation team should check the prospective defendant's financial situation carefully and quietly before suit is commenced.

This chapter, together with the chapter on the American Legal System (Chapter 7), found earlier in this *Review Manual* and with the self-tests provided for both chapters, should provide a basic review of the principles and procedures that may be encountered on the certifying examination. If the applicant is unfamiliar with any of the material covered, he or she is advised to consider close study of a relevant textbook or other study aid as well as the applicable Rules and statutes. *See the bibliography for additional study references.*

Litigation Self-Test

Allow an uninterrupted 30-minute period to answer all questions. At the end of 30 minutes, check your answers against those in the Answer Key Section of this Review Manual. Deduct two points for each incorrect answer (100 total possible points). Unanswered questions are counted as incorrect answers. Follow directions carefully and observe the time limit precisely to provide an accurate self-assessment.

Choose the most correct answer to each of the following questions unless a specific question instructs you to do otherwise.

1.   The U.S. District Court is a court of _____ jurisdiction.

    a.   general
    b.   personal
    c.   limited
    d.   None of the above

2. Redirect examination of a witness during trial may occur:

    a. only during the plaintiff's case in chief.
    b. only during the defendant's case in chief.
    c. only during the plaintiff's rebuttal.
    d. None of the above.

3. All post-trial motions are calculated:

    a. from the time the verdict is entered.
    b. from the time the parties rest.
    c. from the time the judgment is entered.
    d. from the time the jury is sequestered.

4. When a nonparty witness is subpoenaed for a deposition in a particular case, which of the following sanctions may be imposed if she refuses to appear and to testify?

    a. Criminal contempt sanctions.
    b. Civil contempt sanctions.
    c. Entry of judgment against her.
    d. Dismissal of her complaint.

5. Proceedings to enforce a judgment are called:

    a. execution proceedings.
    b. garnishment proceedings.
    c. ancillary proceedings.
    d. judgment proceedings.

6. In a civil bench trial in federal court, which of the following motions properly may be filed by the defendant's attorney at the close of the plaintiff's case?

    a. Motion for judgment on partial findings.
    b. Motion for judgment as a matter of law.
    c. Motion for directed verdict.
    d. Motion for dismissal.

7.   The proper method for objection to the issuance of a subpoena in a civil case is:

   a.   motion to suppress.
   b.   motion to quash.
   c.   motion *in limine*.
   d.   motion to dismiss.

8.   In a civil trial in federal court, which of the following motions properly may be filed at the close of the defendant's case?

   a.   Motion for judgment on partial findings.
   b.   Motion for judgment as a matter of law.
   c.   Motion for directed verdict.
   d.   Motion for dismissal.

9.   True or False.   Neither the court nor any of the parties ever can waive personal jurisdiction.

10.   True or False.   A state court of general jurisdiction may hear a case based upon a federal civil rights statute.

11.   True or False.   The term "engrossment" is used to indicate that interrogatory questions and their answers related to a particular party are numbered sequentially from one set of interrogatories to the next.

12.   True or False.   Answers to interrogatories must be verified by the party to whom they are addressed.

13.   True or False.   All of the discovery methods provided in the Federal Rules of Civil Procedure are self-executing.

14.   True or False.   The Federal Rules of Civil Procedure govern procedural matters such as the use of privileged communications in federal civil trials.

15.   True or False.   The time limitation for responding to a counterclaim is 20 days after the date of its service.

16.   True or False.   A plaintiff may aggregate her claims against a single defendant to reach the minimum dollar amount required to establish federal diversity jurisdiction.

17. True or False.   In a federal diversity action, the plaintiff may be able to invoke the federal court's supplemental jurisdiction to file a claim against a third-party defendant.

18. Fiona (a citizen of Colorado) sues Lupe (a citizen of California) in California state court for an auto accident that occurred in Nevada. Fiona claims $100,000 in damages arising from Lupe's negligence related to the auto accident. If Lupe wants to remove the case to federal court under diversity of citizenship jurisdiction,

    a. she cannot remove the case to any federal court.
    b. she can remove the case to a Colorado federal court.
    c. she can remove the case to a Nevada federal court.
    d. she can remove the case to a California federal court.

19. Mary holds a second mortgage on property which is the subject of a foreclosure action filed by the Small Business Administration (the first lienholder) in federal court. If Mary cannot be served with summons under any applicable statute or federal rule, which of the following statements is most accurate?

    a. The suit must be dismissed because Mary is an indispensable party.
    b. The suit must be dismissed because Mary has no minimum contacts with the forum state.
    c. The suit must be dismissed because Mary is a necessary party.
    d. The suit may continue because Mary is a necessary party.

20. Which of the following forms of pleading operate under the Federal Rules of Civil Procedure?

    a. Fact pleading.
    b. Notice pleading.
    c. Code pleading.
    d. Claim pleading.

21. Which of the following issues is waived if it is not raised immediately by the defendant in a federal civil action?

    a. Personal jurisdiction.
    b. Subject matter jurisdiction.
    c. Ancillary jurisdiction.
    d. Removal jurisdiction.

22.   Ruth is sued in federal court for nonpayment of a $95,000 promissory note in a diversity case. The complaint alleges that Ruth has made no payments on the note, but Ruth has cancelled checks showing that she has paid more than $20,000 to the lender. Which of the following terms most accurately states the way in which Ruth's payments should be characterized in her answer?

    a.   A denial of the plaintiff's claim.
    b.   An affirmative defense to the plaintiff's claim.
    c.   A setoff against the plaintiff's claim.
    d.   A reduction of the plaintiff's claim.

23.   Sam Smith sues Bill Barnes and Mary Mitchell in federal court for negligent operation of an amusement park. Mary claims she should be indemnified by Bill for any negligence that may have occurred, because she is a limited partner in the business that operates the park. Mary should file:

    a.   a counterclaim.
    b.   an answer and counterclaim.
    c.   acrossclaim.
    d.   an answer and crossclaim

24.   Walter Oz has been sued in federal court and timely filed his answer to the complaint. Shortly after the answer was filed, Walter wanted to add an additional defense. Which of the following statements is most correct?

    a.   Without the court's permission, Walter has 10 days from filing to amend his answer.
    b.   Without the court's permission, Walter has 14 days from filing to amend his answer.
    c.   Without the court's permission, Walter has 21 days from filing to amend his answer.
    d.   Without the court's permission, Walter cannot amend his answer.

25.   True or False.   The usual method of serving process on a corporation is to serve its president.

26.   True or False.   Interpleader is initiated by one who already is a party to an existing lawsuit.

27.   True or False.   Depositions cannot be conducted before a civil complaint is filed.

28.   True or False.   Juries may decide issues related to both law and fact in simple cases.

29.   True or False.   The pleadings allowed in a federal civil case include complaint, answer, counterclaim, crossclaim, and (sometimes) reply.

30.   True or False.   A permissive counterclaim is one which requires the court's permission before it can be filed in a civil case.

31.   True or False.   If a criminal charge is pending, the defendant may not be sued in a related civil case until the criminal case is concluded.

32.   True or False.   It is unethical for a lawyer knowingly to offer evidence during litigation which he or she knows is perjured.

33.   True or False.   Interrogatories under Rule 33 may be served on any person who may have personal knowledge of the facts involved in a particular litigation.

34.   When a case is appealed, the appellate court will base its decision on:

        a.   the credibility of the witnesses.
        b.   the record of the lower court.
        c.   reevaluation of the facts presented to the jury.
        d.   None of the above.

35.   If a paralegal is instructed to ensure that a particular witness personally appears and brings specific documents with him, which of the following should be issued?

        a.   Summons.
        b.   Subpoena.
        c.   Subpoena *duces tecum*.
        d.   Subpoena *capias*.

36.   If a person fails to answer interrogatories within the time specified, which rule of the Federal Rules of Civil Procedure provides the remedy for this failure?

        a.   Rule 33.
        b.   Rule 34.
        c.   Rule 36.
        d.   Rule 37.

37. The purpose of a summons is to:

    a. notify the defendant to appear at the stated place and time.
    b. notify the defendant that suit has been filed and the time limit in which to respond.
    c. notify the defendant that depositions have been scheduled.
    d. notify the defendant that trial has been scheduled at a stated place and time.

38. True or False. Because answers to interrogatories are given under oath, the answering party may use his or her own answers to prove the truth of their contents.

39. True or False. A civil action is commenced in federal court when the complaint is filed.

40. True or False. The answer day for interrogatories can be extended without court approval if all parties agree to the extension and if the extension does not interfere with the time for completing discovery, for hearing a motion, or for trial.

41. True or False. Objections to interrogatories must be filed within 10 days after the interrogatories are served.

42. When computing the deadline for response:

    a. include the day of service.
    b. count only ordinary working days.
    c. exclude the day of service.
    d. schedule it for Friday if the last day falls on Saturday.

43. If a plaintiff denies the allegations of a counterclaim, she must respond:

    a. 10 days from date of service.
    b. 14 days from date of service.
    c. 21 days from date of service.
    d. 30 days from date of service.

44. General discovery provisions are contained in:

    a. Rule 16.
    b. Rule 26.
    c. Rule 27.
    d. Rule 28.

45.   True or False.   If subject matter jurisdiction is defective, the parties may agree among themselves to waive this requirement.

46.   True or False.   An interlocutory appeal is the method used to obtain appellate review of a discovery order prior to the time of trial.

47.   True or False.   Summary judgment exists in most state court litigations but no longer exists in federal court litigations.

48.   True or False.   Scheduling orders are mandatory in federal civil litigation.

49.   A local court rule is an example of:

    a.   substantive law.
    b.   procedural law.
    c.   adjective law.
    d.   a and c.
    e.   b and c.

50.   Jackson (a citizen of South Carolina) and Einstein (a citizen of Oklahoma) want to sue Cassidy (a citizen of Iowa) and Chang (a citizen of Iowa) in connection with violation of a federal statute. The incident occurred in Iowa. Which of the following courts has subject matter jurisdiction of the case?

    a.   South Carolina federal court.
    b.   Oklahoma federal court.
    c.   Iowa federal court.
    d.   All of the above.
    e.   None of the above.

Chapter 1
Communications

1. lend
2. its
3. was
4. averse
5. bad
6. born
7. is
8. were
9. nauseated
10. Regardless
11. his
12. fewer
13. comprises
14. I—together
15. C
16. I—We
17. I—whom
18. I—were
19. I—among
20. C
21. I—*omit*
22. I—hyperbole
23. I— "didactic,"
24. d
25. c
26. a
27. a
28. c
29. b
30. d
31. c
32. d
33. c
34. b
35. c
36. c
37. d
38. a
39. c
40. b
41. d
42. d
43. b
44. a
45. a
46. h
47. f
48. b
49. d
50. c

Chapter 2
Human Relations and Interviewing Techniques

1. True
2. False
3. False
4. False
5. True
6. b
7. a
8. c
9. b
10. a
11. True
12. False
13. True
14. False
15. False
16. d
17. c
18. c
19. b
20. c
21. True
22. False
23. True
24. True
25. False
26. d
27. c
28. a
29. c
30. d
31. False
32. True
33. False
34. False
35. True
36. a
37. a
38. b
39. b
40. True
41. False
42. True
43. False
44. True
45. False
46. True
47. a
48. a
49. True
50. False

Chapter 3
Ethics

1. False
2. True
3. False
4. False
5. False
6. False
7. True
8. False
9. False
10. True
11. False
12. f
13. a
14. d
15. b
16. e
17. a
18. c
19. d
20. c
21. a
22. True
23. True
24. False
25. True
26. False
27. True
28. False
29. d
30. c
31. b
32. d
33. d
34. c
35. b
36. f
37. c
38. False
39. b
40. True
41. False
42. True
43. False
44. False
45. False
46. False
47. True
48. a
49. d
50. d

Chapter 4
Judgment and Analytical Ability

1. False
2. True
3. False
4. False
5. True
6. d
7. c
8. c
9. d
10. c
11. c
12. e
13. b
14. c
15. a
16. b
17. d
18. b
19. c
20. c
21. a
22. b
23. b
24. c
25. a
26. d
27. b
28. e
29. c

See sample essay answer at page 582

Chapter 5
Legal Research

1. b
2. b
3. c
4. d
5. c
6. b
7. a
8. b
9. True
10. False
11. False
12. False
13. False
14. True
15. False
16. d
17. d
18. a
19. a
20. b
21. d
22. False
23. True
24. False
25. True

26. True
27. False
28. False
29. False
30. True
31. False
32. d
33. c
34. d
35. a
36. b
37. True
38. True
39. False
40. d
41. b
42. c
43. c
44. c
45. True
46. False
47. False
48. False
49. a
50. c

Chapter 6
Legal Terminology

1. True
2. True
3. False
4. True
5. e
6. a
7. h
8. j
9. f
10. b

11. d
12. g
13. k
14. l
15. c
16. b
17. c
18. d
19. a
20. False
21. False
22. False
23. False
24. b
25. c
26. b
27. d
28. b
29. a
30. False
31. False
32. False
33. True
34. a
35. d
36. c
37. e
38. g
39. b
40. b
41. debenture
42. pro bono
43. relevant
44. supersedeas
45. devise
46. code
47. assignment
48. bylaws
49. allegation
50. recidivist

Chapter 7
American Legal System

1. d
2. c
3. b
4. b
5. True
6. True
7. False
8. False
9. False
10. False
11. c
12. d
13. c
14. False
15. True
16. False
17. False
18. True
19. False
20. False
21. False
22. c
23. b
24. a
25. b
26. a
27. appellee
28. nunc pro tunc
29. writ of mandamus
30. chattel
31. ad damnum
32. primary law or mandatory law
33. venue
34. acknowledgment

35.	ex post facto	20.	False	6.	False
36.	witness	21.	True	7.	True
37.	False	22.	d	8.	True
38.	False	23.	c	9.	False
39.	False	24.	a	10.	Truc
40.	False	25.	b	11.	c
41.	True	26.	d	12.	c
42.	False	27.	d	13.	d
43.	False	28.	d	14.	e
44.	True	29.	b	15.	False
45.	False	30.	b	16.	d
46.	a	31.	c	17.	d
47.	b	32.	a	18.	False
48.	a	33.	a	19.	False
49.	b	34.	False	20.	True
50.	c	35.	False	21.	False
		36.	False	22.	True
		37.	True	23.	d
		38.	c	24.	True
		39.	b	25.	False
		40.	b	26.	True
		41.	d	27.	False

Chapter 8

Business Organizations

		42.	True	28.	c
		43.	True	29.	b
1.	c	44.	True	30.	b
2.	d	45.	False	31.	d
3.	d	46.	c	32.	c
4.	b	47.	b	33.	b
5.	a	48.	c	34.	a
6.	c	49.	a	35.	False
7.	True	50.	c	36.	False
8.	False			37.	True
9.	False			38.	False
10.	False			39.	False
11.	True	**Chapter 9**		40.	False
12.	c			41.	True
13.	b	**Contract Law**		42.	c
14.	c			43.	False
15.	b	1.	b	44.	True
16.	False	2.	d	45.	False
17.	True	3.	a	46.	False
18.	True	4.	True		
19.	False	5.	False		

47. b
48. b
49. d
50. c

Chapter 10
Litigation

1. c
2. d
3. c
4. b
5. c
6. a
7. b
8. b
9. False
10. True
11. False

12. True
13. False
14. False
15. False
16. True
17. False
18. a
19. d
20. b
21. a
22. d
23. d
24. c
25. False
26. False
27. False
28. False
29. True
30. False
31. False

32. True
33. False
34. b
35. c
36. d
37. b
38. False
39. True
40. True
41. False
42. c
43. c
44. b
45. False
46. True
47. False
48. True
49. e
50. d

Judgment and Analytical Ability

SAMPLE ESSAY ANSWER:

MEMORANDUM

TO: Michael Parkins, Paralegal
FROM: Virginia Koerselman Newman, Staff Attorney
DATE:
RE: Landon Gray Employment Termination

Our client Landon Gray has been employed by the District Attorney's Office for the State of Anywhere for the last 22 years. He recently was fired for the unlawful sale of junk food at his workplace, and he visited with me this morning about his termination.

Mr. Gray is married and has three children, two of them in college. His wife is the nutritionist for Pinefield Public Schools. His youngest daughter, Chloe, is in middle school; Chloe sold nearly 400 boxes of Girl Scout cookies this year, some of them to people in Landon's office. To help his daughter, Landon delivered boxes of Girl Scout cookies to coworkers from the trunk of his car over the lunch hour. His car was parked in the employee parking lot.

When James Oliver, Chief Deputy District Attorney, heard about the delivery of contraband cookies, he called Landon to his office immediately. Following a heated discussion, James fired Landon and ordered him to leave that very day. Mary Littleton helped Landon put his personal belongings into a small file box, and he left.

Earlier this year and in response to a World Health Organization study showing that one in every five Utopian workers is obese, the federal congress passed a number of statutes designed to limit workers' access to junk food while at work. The rationale was that obese people are less productive at work; miss work more often; and place a greater burden on the health care system. The congress then declared the workplace a "Sugar-and-Fat-Free Zone" and encouraged employers to establish zero tolerance policies for noncompliance.

Landon Gray is a very physically fit man who works out three or four times a week. None of the coworkers involved in this incident is obese, although several may be close to it.

Attached are the statutes that I want you to consider in reviewing this matter. Using these statutes, prepare a memorandum to me that evaluates the probable result of a legal proceeding on behalf of Mr. Gray. The memorandum should include facts, issues, discussion, and conclusion sections.

Selected Statutes

---

§ 15-245. The government of the United Utopian States is granted the power to assemble a military to protect its borders and its citizens; to coin money; to operate a post office system; to protect interstate commerce; to ensure the right of citizens to pass freely from one state to another; and to enact legislation in furtherance of these enumerated powers. All other powers are reserved specifically to the states and to the people.

§ 24-109 Classification of Crimes. The range of punishment that may be set for particular classification of crimes is:

Class I felony	10–50 years	or	$20,000–$100,000 fine	or both;
Class II felony	5–20 years	or	$5,000–$50,000 fine	or both;
Class III felony	1–20 years	or	$1,000–$25,000 fine	or both;
Class IV felony	1–10 years	or	$100–$10,000 fine	or both;
Class I misdemeanor	6–12 months	or	$100–$5,000 fine	or both;
Class II misdemeanor	3–9 months	or	$50–$2,000 fine	or both;
Class III misdemeanor	60–180 days	or	$50–$1,500 fine	or both;
Class IV misdemeanor	30–90 days	or	$25–$1,000 fine	or both.

§ 52-115. A food product, food ingredient, or food additive exceeds statutory limitation (1) if its sugar content is greater than 10 grams or (2) if its fat content is greater than three (3) grams. Any food item described herein or any food item generally known for its high sugar content or for its high fat content shall be known as junk food and thereby prohibited under the provisions of this Act.

§ 52-714. It shall be a Class IV felony to sell, purchase, exchange, ingest, or consume any high-sugar or high-fat food or food ingredient to, with, or by any employee within the jurisdictional boundaries of the United Utopian States or its territories.

Such foods likewise are banned from cafeterias, lunch rooms, meeting rooms, kitchens, vending machines, or stores located in or within 150 feet of any building that contains businesses with employees.

§ 52-723. It shall be a Class III misdemeanor to accept, possess, procure, or solicit any high-sugar or high-fat food or food ingredient to, with, or by any employee within the jurisdictional boundaries of the United Utopian States or its territories.

§ 67-4224. No federal statute or regulation shall impinge unnecessarily or limit unreasonably the personal liberty or freedom of any citizen unless the government can show a compelling state interest that cannot be accomplished by any other means and the statute or regulation is narrowly tailored to satisfy the compelling state interest.

SAMPLE ANSWER:

MEMORANDUM

TO: Virginia Koerselman Newman, Staff Attorney
FROM: Michael Parkins, Paralegal
DATE:
RE: Landon Gray Employment Termination

You have asked me to evaluate selected statutes as they relate to your client Landon Gray and his recent termination from employment.

<u>Facts:</u>   Landon Gray had been employed for 22 years by the District Attorney's Office for the State of Anywhere when his youngest daughter sold Girl Scout cookies to an unknown number of Mr. Gray's coworkers. From the trunk of his car in an employee parking lot, Mr. Gray delivered an unknown number of boxes of Girl Scout cookies to these coworkers over his lunch hour.

When James Oliver, the Chief Deputy District Attorney, learned about the delivery, he fired Mr. Gray immediately for sale of contraband cookies.

<u>Issues:</u>   1.   Do Girl Scout cookies qualify as the type of foods that are banned by the statutes?

           2.   Has Landon Gray violated the statute prohibiting sale of high-sugar, high-fat foods?

           3.   Has Landon Gray violated the statute prohibiting possession of high-sugar, high-fat foods?

4.   Does the government of United Utopian States have authority to enact a junk food ban covering every workplace in the nation and to impose criminal sanctions?

<u>Discussion</u>:   The reason Girl Scout cookies are popular is that they taste good: and they taste good because they contain both sugar and fat. As such, Girl Scout cookies likely fit within the definition of junk food under § 52-115. Among other things, § 52-714 forbids any employee from selling high-sugar or high-fat foods. The facts state that Landon Gray's daughter sold the cookies to some of Gray's coworkers. Gray did not sell cookies to anyone. His daughter, who attends middle school, was the seller; and she is not an employee.

Because our client was an employee and because he distributed the cookies to his daughter's customers from the trunk of his car, it appears that he may have possessed them within the meaning of § 72-723. Using the analogy of possession of drugs by having them in one's car, a court very well may conclude that Mr. Gray possessed the contraband cookies. If so, he can be found guilty of a Class III misdemeanor, which carries a sentence of 60 to 180 days or a fine of $50.00 to $1,500.00 or both.

§ 15-245 recites the powers held by the United Utopian States and says it can legislate only in the areas of the enumerated powers: to assemble a military, to coin money, to operate a post office, to protect interstate commerce, and to ensure citizens' freedom of movement among the states of the nation. Nowhere in these enumerated powers does one find anything from which to extrapolate the criminalizing of the sale or possession of Girl Scout cookies. Accordingly, this power—if it exists at all—is reserved to the states and to the people by the statute's own words. It is not a power of the federal government except to the extent that the federal government has pulled it out of thin air.

If the power to enact such a statute is found to exist, that power necessarily is limited by the provisions of § 67-4224. This statute requires the federal congress to demonstrate a compelling state interest and a narrowly tailored regulation to resolve it when such statute impinges or limits the liberty or freedom of any citizen. Assuming that Landon Gray is a citizen, he and every other employee in the nation are entitled to the protections of this statute. It limits the government's power to act even if it can show a compelling state interest. The power to restrict possession of cookies and similar foods (which we should not concede), a crime resulting from possession of a Girl Scout cookie seems far beyond a narrowly tailored solution.

<u>Conclusion</u>:   1.   Girl Scout cookies appear to qualify as junk food under the statute.

2.   Landon Gray did not sell anything to anyone; all he did was to deliver the cookies that his daughter had sold previously.

3.   Mr. Gray may have possessed the Girl Scout cookies in the trunk of his car when he was delivering them to his daughter's customers.

4.   The statutes stating the powers of the government and its limitations seems to create no legitimate connection to Girl Scout cookies or anything else that affects the general welfare of citizens; this power is reserved to the states and to the people. Even if such a connection can be found, making it a crime to possess a Girl Scout cookie does not seem to conform to the requirement for narrow tailoring imposed on the federal government by these statutes.

BIBLIOGRAPHY

General References

NOTE: *Black's Law Dictionary* is the authority for all law definitions.

Garner, Bryan A., ed. *Black's Law Dictionary*, 9th Ed. St. Paul, MN: West, 2009.

Meinzinger, Miller, Roger LeRoy, and Mary Meinzinger, *Paralegal Today: The Essentials*, 6th Ed. Clifton Park, NY: Delmar Cengage Learning, 2014a.

Meinzinger, Miller, Roger LeRoy, and Mary Meinzinger, *Paralegal Today: The Legal Team at Work*, 6th Ed. Clifton Park, NY: Delmar Cengage Learning, 2014b.

National Association of Legal Assistants, *NALA Manual for Legal Assistants: A General Skills and Litigation Guide for Today's Professionals*, 5th Ed. Clifton Park, NY: Delmar Cengage Learning, 2010.

Oran, Daniel, and Mark Tosti, *Oran's Dictionary of the Law*, 4th Ed. Clifton Park, NY: Delmar Cengage Learning, 2008.

Philo, Harry M., Linda Miller Atkinson, and Harry M. Philo, Jr., *Lawyers Desk Reference*, 9th Ed. St. Paul, MN: West, 2009.

Statsky, William P., *Legal Thesaurus/legal Dictionary: A Resource for the Writer and Computer Researcher*, Clifton Park, NY: Delmar Cengage Learning, 1985.

Statsky, William P., *Introduction to Paralegalism: Perspectives, Problems, and Skills*, 7th Ed. Clifton Park, NY: Delmar Cengage Learning, 2009.

Communications References

NOTE: Strunk & White's *The Elements of Style* is the authority adopted by the NALA Certifying Board.

Fowler, H. Ramsey, and Jane E. Aaron, *The Little, Brown Handbook*, 12th Ed. New York: Pearson Longman, 2012.

Freeman, Harrop Arthur, *Clinical Law Training: Interviewing and Counseling*, St. Paul, MN: West, 1972.

Hurd, Hollis T., *Writing for Lawyers*, Pittsburgh, PA: BookSurge, 2009.

Strunk, William, and E. B. White, *The Elements of Style*, 4th Ed. Needham Heights, MA: Allyn & Bacon, 2000.

Vernolia, Jan, *Write Right! A Desk Drawer Digest of Punctuation, Grammar, and Style*. Berkeley, CA: Ten Speed, 1996.

Wydick, Richard C., *Plain English for Lawyers*, 5th Ed. Durham, NC: Carolina Academic Press, 2005.

Ethics References

American Bar Association, *Model Rules of Professional Conduct*. Chicago, IL: American Bar Association, 2012.

Lynton, Jonathon, and Terri Lyndall, *Legal Ethics and Professional Responsibility*. Clifton Park, NY: Delmar Cengage Learning, 1994.

Morrison, Laura, and Gina DeCiani, *Legal Ethics for Paralegals and the Law Office*, Clifton Park, NY: Delmar Cengage Learning, 1995.

National Association of Legal Assistants. "Code of Ethics and Professional Responsibility." National Association of Legal Assistants. http://www.nala.org/code.aspx (accessed August 28, 2013).

National Association of Legal Assistants. "Model Standards and Guidelines for Utilization of Legal Assistants." National Association of Legal Assistants. http://www.nala.org/model.aspx (accessed August 28, 2013).

Statsky, William P., *Introduction to Paralegalism, Perspectives, Problems and Skills*, 7th Ed. Clifton Park, NY: Delmar Cengage Learning, 2009.

Judgment and Analytical Ability References

Edwards, Linda L., *Practical Case Analysis*, Clifton Park, NY: Delmar Cengage Learning, 1996.

Rombauer, Marjorie Dick, *Legal Problem Solving: Analysis, Research, and Writing*, 5th Ed. St. Paul, MN: West, 1991.

Statsky, William P., *Introduction to Paralegalism, Perspectives, Problems and Skills*, 7th Ed. Clifton Park, NY: Delmar Cengage Learning, 2009.

Statsky, William P., and R. J. Wernet, *Case Analysis and Fundamentals of Legal Writing*, 4th Ed. Clifton Park, NY: Delmar Cengage Learning, 1994.

Legal Research References

NOTE: *The Bluebook: A Uniform System of Citation* is the authority for this section.

Barkan, Steven M., Roy M. Mersky, and Donald J. Dunn, *Fundamentals of Legal Research*, 9th Ed. New York: Foundation Press, 2009.

Cohen, Morris, Robert C. Berring, and Kent C. Olson, *How to Find the Law*, 9th Ed. St. Paul, MN: West, 1989.

Columbia Law Review, Harvard Law Review, University of Pennsylvania Law Review, and The Yale Law Journal, *The Bluebook: A Uniform System of Citation*, 19th Ed. Cambridge, MA: Harvard Law Review Association, 2011.

Hein, Edward H., *Legal Research for Paralegals*, Clifton Park, NY: Delmar Cengage Learning, 1996.

Rombauer, Marjorie Dick, *Legal Problem Solving: Analysis, Research, and Writing*, 5th Ed. St. Paul, MN: West, 1991.

Shepard's, *How to Use Shepardizing*. McGraw-Hill, 1984.

Statsky, William P., and R. John Wernet, Jr., *Case Analysis and Fundamentals of Legal Writing*, 4th Ed. Clifton Park, NY: Delmar Cengage Learning, 1994.

Walston-Dunham, Beth, *Practical Legal Research: Skills and Strategies for the Legal Assistant*, Clifton Park, NY: Delmar Cengage Learning, 1994.

West Law Finder: A Legal Research Manual. St. Paul, MN: West, 1993.

Wren, Christopher G., and Jill Robinson Wren, *The Legal Research Manual: A Game Plan for Legal Research and Analysis*, 3rd Ed. Legal Education Pub, 2002.

American Legal System (General Law) References

Carper, Donald L., John A. McKinsy, and Bill W. West, *Understanding the Law*, 6th Ed. Mason, OH: South-Western Cengage Learning, 2012.

Currier, Katherine A., and Thomas E. Eimermann, *Introduction to Law for Paralegals: A Critical Thinking Approach*, 5th Ed. Aspen Publishers, 2012.

Walston-Dunham, Beth, *Introduction to Law*, 6th Ed. Clifton Park, NY: Delmar Cengage Learning, 2012.

Business Organizations (Corporations) References

Hamilton, Robert W., *The Law of Corporations: In a Nutshell*, 6th Ed. St. Paul, MN: West, 2011.

Moye, John E., *The Law of Business Organizations*, 6th Ed. Clifton Park, NY: Delmar Cengage Learning, 2005.

Schneeman, Angela, *The Law of Corporations and Other Business Organizations*, 6th Ed. Clifton Park, NY: Delmar Cengage Learning, 2013.

Contract Law References

Farnsworth, E. Allan, *Contracts*, 4th Ed. Aspen Publishers, 2004.

Frey, Martin A., *Introduction to the Law of Contracts*, 4th Ed. Clifton Park, NY: Delmar Cengage Learning, 2008.

Thomas, Melinda, *Contract Law for Paralegals*, Clifton Park, NY: Delmar Cengage Learning, 1997.

Weaver, Jefferson Hane, *The Compact Guide to Contract Law: A Civilized Approach to the Law*, St. Paul, MN: West, 1990.

Litigation References

NOTE: Because procedural rules differ from state to state, all procedural questions are based on the Federal Rules of Civil Procedure and on generally accepted practice and procedure.

Bruno, Carole A., *Paralegal's Litigation Handbook*, 2nd Ed. Clifton Park, NY: Delmar Cengage Learning, 1993.

Hart, William, and Roderick D. Blanchard, *Litigation and Trial Practice*, 6th Ed. Clifton Park, NY: Delmar Cengage Learning, 2007.

Kane, Mary Kay, *Civil Procedure: In a Nutshell*, 6th Ed. St. Paul, MN: West, 2007.

McCord, James W. H., *The Litigation Paralegal: A Systems Approach*, 5th Ed. Clifton Park, NY: Delmar Cengage Learning, 2008.

Weinstein, Mark, *Introduction to Civil Litigation*, 3rd Ed. Clifton Park, NY: Delmar Cengage Learning, 1993.

INDEX